W9-BRJ-691

THE ★ ULTIMATE ★ BASEBALL ★ ROAD ★ TRIP

Josh Pahigian & Kevin O'Connell

THE ★ ULTIMATE ★
BASEBALL ★ ROAD ★ TRIP

A Fan's Guide to Major League Stadiums

THE LYONS PRESS
Guilford, Connecticut
An imprint of The Globe Pequot Press

Copyright © 2004 by Joshua Pahigian and
Kevin O'Connell

ALL RIGHTS RESERVED. No part of this book may be
reproduced or transmitted in any form by any means,
electronic or mechanical, including photocopying and
recording, or by any information storage and retrieval
system, except as may be expressly permitted in
writing from the publisher. Requests for permission
should be addressed to The Lyons Press, Attn: Rights
and Permissions Department, P.O. Box 480, Guilford,
CT 06437.

The Lyons Press is an imprint of
The Globe Pequot Press.

10   9   8   7   6   5   4   3   2   1

Printed in the United States of America

Book design by Diane Gleba Hall

ISBN 1-59228-159-1

Library of Congress Cataloging-in-Publication Data
is available on file.

CONTENTS

INTRODUCTION

BEFORE YOU READ about our journey through the Major Leagues and before you begin to plan your own baseball odyssey, we thought it worthwhile to give you a quick synopsis of what our goals were in taking our trip, writing our book, and offering it to you. If you find yourself in the sports section of your local bookstore thinking, "Nice looking book, but is it worth the coin?" these first few pages are intended to give you a better idea of what exactly you hold in your hands. If you're sitting in your study with a warm cup of Sunday morning cocoa or in your game room with a frosty pint of Friday night lager, then this introduction is meant to set the tone for what will be an entertaining, informative, and motivational reading experience. Or, if you find yourself trying to explain to your spouse, parents, employer, or psychologist that spending two months on the road in pursuit of baseball nirvana is a perfectly rational thing for a person to do, the pages that follow will help you refine your winning argument.

The Ultimate Baseball Road-Trip is part travel manual, part ballpark atlas, part baseball history book, part epic narrative, and part restaurant and city guide, all rolled into one handy volume. As baseball fans, we all know that no two ballparks are the same. And thank goodness for it. Each ballpark in this great land of ours possesses its own unique history, attractions, flavors, and rituals. Ordinarily it requires many visits to fully appreciate the quirks and nuances of each ballpark and city. But unfortunately this isn't always a viable option. As vacationing fans we usually have just one or two precious games to spend enjoying the ballparks we visit in faraway cities. And often that leaves us feeling shortchanged, thinking that if only we had known about *this restaurant* or *that bit of history* ahead of time we would have spent our time and money differently or made our trip that much more worthwhile. Sometimes the issue at

Kevin and Josh at Wrigley Field

Photo by Paul Schmitz

stake is ticketing. There's nothing in the world quite so aggravating as ordering the most expensive tickets available only to find out upon entering the ballpark that you could have had better seats for the same price—or for even less money. Other times, ballpark food is the issue. How often have you spent a fortune on a mediocre ballpark meal, only to later hear about some rare ballpark delicacy inside or outside the stadium you weren't aware of? Other *can't-miss* attractions that many of us so often do miss when we visit new parks include eccentric fans, player rituals, autograph and ball opportunities, and unusual hometown traditions. This book will arm you with as much foreknowledge as possible, so that you can maximize the scant few days you have to enjoy each new ballpark you experience and its surrounding city. We'll lead you to the very heart of each big league town's hardball culture ensuring that you'll experience a feeling of accomplishment as you speed away, the skyline of the city just "done" in the rearview mirror, and visions of the next ballpark already dancing in your thoughts.

We freely admit to having undertaken this project with one single overriding objective in mind: to spend one glorious summer on the road visiting every Major League Baseball park on our publisher's dime. Mission accomplished. Conducting the necessary research for this book meant traveling around this great land of ours, going to game after game, eating scores of hot dogs and brats, and talking to interesting fans, players, and ballpark employees along the way. You know, living the proverbial "life of Riley." And boy did we. We had a blast. And you should too.

We're guessing that you bought this book because you are considering embarking on your own journey into the mythical American baseball pastoral. Or maybe some special holiday season gift giver saw *The Ultimate Baseball Road-Trip* and thought of you. If so, more the better because that means it's probably winter as you're reading this. It's brutally cold outside. The snow is mixing with freezing rain and sleet. You can't find live baseball on TV anywhere. Even the Caribbean World Series on Univision has finished, and now you're relegated to at least another month before pitchers and catchers report for spring training. So how do you endure the cabin-fever blues and rise above the horrors of Arena Football and the National Boring Association? The wheels in your head start turning. You dream of Opening Day and its promise of a new season for the sport you love. So you plan a few trips to your local ballpark to see the home team play. But you've been there before, right? Like a few hundred times, and as great a place as it is, you wonder what it would be like to watch a game or two at one of the other parks. Why not plan a road trip, you think? Maybe you could follow your home team to see a game in a faraway city. You could make a little vacation of it. But why stop there? Your mind continues, greedy for more. You plan another trip. And another. Your summer starts to take shape. You envision a string of warm summer days spent in the bleachers of big league ballparks—the ghosts of the old-time greats floating ethereally across their fields of glory, the heroes of today showcasing their many talents. It's a beautiful dream. Sunshine, high blue skies, the green grass of the infield, red puffs of dirt exploding in the catcher's mitt. Wow. You feel better already, don't you? We know we do.

You hold in your hands the best guide on the market for the kind of road trip you're envisioning. You have not selected one of those travel guides that offers the same old generic information culled off the Internet: microscopic road maps, floor plans of the local five-star hotels, and in-depth analyses of the local antiquing scenes. You are the owner of a first-edition copy of *The Ultimate Baseball Road-trip*. This is the most thorough book of its kind available to baseball fans. You won't find driving directions to zoos, amusement parks, or art museums in these pages. This is a *baseball* travelers' guidebook. And we don't just give you the easy stuff. We've worked for it. We've tasted all thirty big league weenies, checked out the sight line from every seat in every section of every ballpark in the Majors, scoured graveyards for famous players' tombstones, haggled with scalpers, and done whatever else was necessary, excruciating and demanding though it may have been. And we've written down all of our experiences, mixed with equal helpings of humor and history for your baseball appetite, along with dribbles of trivia, ketchup, mustard, and peanut shells.

The way we see it, baseball is the ultimate spectator sport. Unlike other live sporting experiences that tend to fall flat when a par-ticular game happens to be a tad on the dry side, baseball has the tendency to enchant us even more than usual on its supposed off days. Think about what you've done during a lopsided game that hasn't kept your busy and continuously curious mind occupied. You've taken in the atmosphere of the ballpark, checked out the fans around you—paying particular attention to those belonging to whichever gender your imagination finds most intriguing, and you've eaten, by God. You've stuffed your gullet with the delicacies that only the ball yard can offer. You've swatted beach balls and reluctantly done the wave. You've tried to snag foul balls, begged outfielders for warm-up balls, sung "Take Me Out to the Ball Game," and harassed the nearest visiting players. You've made friends with some nearby fans and enemies of others. You've recited statistics and ballpark lore and relived your favorite moments from your own history at the park and from the home team's. You've always gotten your money's worth.

What better way to see this great land of ours than through a tour of the historic and modern ballparks of the National Pastime? It still is the National Pastime by the way—don't let those NASCAR or bass fishing enthusiasts feed you any of that tripe that their sport has overtaken baseball in popularity. Other sports seem to come and go, passing in and out of favor, experiencing radical changes in the face of new technology. But baseball has always been America's game. Baseball has remained pure and constant and reassuring between those two familiar white lines. And it always will. How do we know? Take the tour, and we think you'll understand. This is a *pilgrimage* we're advocating, make no mistake about it.

The two weary travelers who lead you on your journey are Kevin, a footloose Northwesterner who may run out of gas for lack of preparation, but can improvise and knows how to have fun in virtually any situation, and Josh, a New Englander who always likes to have his next few steps clearly mapped out and may be a tad on the uptight side, but is rarely left without tickets or tollbooth change. Learning from the pitfalls we suffer and triumphs we celebrate in faraway cities and ballparks, you will better prepare yourself for your own baseball road trip.

Finally, we'd like to say that we respect the intelligence of you, our reader. After all, it's already been established that you are a baseball fan and that you had the good taste to pick up our book. So what does this mean? It means we are going to treat you like the intelligent fan you are. You appreciate the nuances of the game, the history surrounding it, and the aesthetic charm it holds. So we're not going to start at square one. This isn't "baseball for dummies." We're going to assume you have a general knowledge of the game and its history and we're going to skip over the basic stuff. We're going to give you *new* stories, *new* stats, and *new* information that will astound you. Unlike other books of its kind, *The Ultimate Baseball Road-Trip* provides more than phone numbers for ticket offices, maps of ballparks, driving directions, and all of that other stuff you can find on the Internet for free. This book dishes out the inside scoop pertaining to the parks, teams, and players and gives you a slew of tips that you'll be able to really use when planning and conducting your own ballpark tour. For example, we fill you in on the scalper etiquette surrounding each park, the best seating sight lines, the best spots to snag batting practice balls and autographs, the best ballpark treats, the places to find free parking outside the parks, the places to encounter the players hanging out after the games, parking their cars, dropping off their dry cleaning, and so on. We also make sure you're aware of the "must-dos" and "better-don'ts" of each base-

flat tire

Photo by Josh Pahigian

ball park and city. No one likes to look like a tourist, right?

This book provides a certain range of knowledge and the beginnings of a baseball sophistication that money can't buy and that only experience can truly confer. It is designed to delve into the soul of each ballpark, its team, city, and fandom and to render the good, the bad, and the ugly concerning all of these factions in its quest for the ultimate American baseball experience. Every thing you need to plan your own road trip is right here at your fingertips. So order those plane or train tickets. Or get that tune-up you've been putting off. Plot your itinerary and get ready to hit the road. *The Ultimate Baseball Road-Trip* will lead you.

Touch the Green Monster at Fenway. Catch a long ball in the shadows of the Warehouse in Baltimore. Sample the garlic fries at PacBell, the barbecued eel at Safeco, the toasted ravioli at Busch. Chant "Let's Go Mets!" alongside Cow-Bell-Man at Shea, and have a water ice with Rita in Philly. Experience it all, as you enjoy the most magical summer of your life. The summer you'll tell your grandkids about one day—the summer you visited every ballpark in the big leagues.

Have fun, drive safely, and eat well.

Your friends,
Josh and Kevin

THE ★ ULTIMATE ★ BASEBALL ★ ROAD ★ TRIP

BOSTON RED SOX, FENWAY PARK

A Little Green Diamond in the Heart of Historic Beantown

BOSTON, MASSACHUSETTS

215 miles to New York City
315 miles to Montreal
320 miles to Philadelphia
420 miles to Baltimore

SIMPLY STATED, there is no experience comparable to a day game at Fenway Park. Inside Boston's hardball cathedral, the grass seems greener, the crack of the bat crisper, and the excitement in the air more palpable than anywhere else. All of the new ballparks built in recent years have been designed with Fenway's magic in mind, as ballpark architects have made pilgrimages to Boston in much the same way that church builders once flocked to Rome to visit the Sistine Chapel. "Retro" is the name of the game now, and Fenway is the inspiration. Baltimore's Oriole Park at Camden Yards mimics Fenway's quirky field dimensions, cozy confines, and bull pens. Cleveland's Jacobs Field replicates Fenway's famous left field wall with a miniature Green Monster of its own. Texas's Ballpark at Arlington and Florida's Pro Player Stadium mirror Fenway's manually operated scoreboard.

Fenway is a time machine. You leave the twenty-first century and enter the 1920s when you walk through the turnstiles and behold the narrow rows of wooden seats, the famous nooks and crannies, the slate scoreboard, trademark deep green paint, and old-time pipe organ. This dead-ball-era dinosaur has been home to such baseball immortals as Cy Young, Babe Ruth, Jimmie Foxx, Tris Speaker, Carl Yastrzemski, and many more. It has placidly admired the play of its stars and endured, generation after generation, while the city and world surrounding it have changed beyond recognition. Once you experience a game at Fenway—gaze up at the mighty Green Monster, touch Pesky's Pole in right field, sit for a moment in Ted Williams's red seat in the right field bleachers—you will forever be a convert to the park, if not the team that plays there. You'll feel like baseball was invented specifically for the purpose of being played at Fenway. So turn off your cell phone, buy a cup of suds and a hot dog, and squeeze into your seat.

While Fenway brings fans closer to the players than any other park in the Majors and immerses them in the tempest-tossed sea of maniacal masochists who make up "Red Sox Nation," the park really does "squeeze" fans into their seats. The New England writer John Updike aptly described Fenway Park as a "lyrical little bandbox," calling attention to the park's intimate atmosphere and snug (if not cramped) seats. Sure it's old and clunky. That's what gives it charm. Its quirks and age are precisely what make it lovable.

So where'd they come up with the name Fenway Park? No, it wasn't on account of some generous beneficiary, some John Q. Fenway. Boston's fens were a backwater of the Charles River. The Fen Way was the name of the road that ran alongside them. Thus, the name "Fenway Park." That's correct, this park is built on former swampland. The Fens were declared inhabitable in 1777 after a decade-long effort by Boston to level the city's Tri-Mountain and dump the landfill in the 450-acre marsh that became the Fenway District. When Fenway Park was constructed in 1912 it was designed to fit into the actual confines of a city block. That's why it has so many seemingly illogical angles, twists, and turns.

After christening Fenway with a 2–0 exhibition win over Harvard University on April 10, 1912, the Sox defeated the New York Highlanders (a precursor of the Yankees), 7–6, on April 20 in the first real game. The opener was overshadowed, however, by the sinking of the Titanic in the icy North Atlantic. So much for celebrations.

The Red Sox won five World Championships between 1903 and 1918, but haven't won another one since. After winning the 1918 Series, the team sold the young ace of its pitching staff, Babe Ruth, to the New York Yankees for $100,000. Some New Englanders believe that while the Babe was swatting home runs in the Big Apple, he placed a curse on his former team that has prevented the Sox from winning another World Series. Since the Bambino left town, Boston has taken the World Series the full seven games in 1946, 1967, 1975, and 1986, only to lose in heartbreaking fashion each time.

There are no "Red Sox fans." Rather, there are "*long-suffering* Red Sox fans," and there are plenty of them.

Fenway Park itself has seen some dark days, too. On May 8, 1926, a fire destroyed the left field bleachers (now boxes and grandstands). For seven years ownership cried poverty while third-basemen, shortstops, and left fielders tiptoed into the charred ruins in pursuit of foul pop-ups. These were indeed dark days for the Red Sox . . . dark and sooty. Finally, in 1934 the team repaired the fire damage and reinstalled seats along Fenway's left field line.

The thirty-seven-foot high Green Monster that looms over the field in left was erected during the 1934 renovations. The Wall as it is also known to locals, consists of concrete coated with wood, plated with tin, and painted trademark Fenway green. Prior to its construction, Duffy's Cliff, a ten-foot steep embankment named after Sox left fielder Duffy Lewis, kept most drives to left field in play, but not quite enough—so they built the Wall. The oddity and intimidating height of this massive structure gives visiting left fielders the creeps, and the home team a decided advantage. But more on the Wall later.

At the time of Fenway's construction, Major League relief pitchers ordinarily warmed up on the field of play behind the outfielders in fair territory. But in 1940 the Red Sox brought in the right field fences, and added twenty-three-foot-deep bull pens between Fenway's playing field and bleachers. It was no coincidence that a sweet-swinging rookie named Ted Williams had burst onto the scene the year before.

Teddy Ballgame, aka the Kid, aka the Splendid Splinter, responded by regularly depositing long balls into "Williamsburg," as the bull pens came to be known.

In a good decision, the Red Sox brought back the National League scoreboard to the Wall in 2003 after a twenty-seven-year absence. The NL board now resides in its old location beside the American League board. It had been in storage in a South Dakota warehouse since 1976 when the Red Sox padded the lower eight feet of the Wall to make it safer for outfielders.

Lansdowne Street

Photo by Josh Pahigian

Unfortunately Red Sox management has made a few ill-conceived attempts to modernize Fenway in recent decades, perhaps most notably by building The 406 Club, a premium seating area, high above home plate. After the glassed-in structure was completed in 1989, Sox third-baseman Wade Boggs claimed that it blocked wind currents that had previously pushed his looping fly balls to left field onto the Wall for easy doubles. As purists, we're not particularly enthralled with the massive Jumbotron in center field either, or the electronic display board above the Monster that registers the speed of each pitch, but usually if we ignore these concessions to modernity they don't take too much away from our Fenway experience.

One of Fenway's crowning moments came in 1999 when the Red Sox hosted the All-Star Game. In a ceremony on the field prior to the game, the diamond kings of today's game—Mike Piazza, Nomar Garciaparra, Sammy Sosa, and countless others—flocked to Ted Williams and surrounded him, looking more like wide-eyed kids than professional athletes. The baseball fan in all of us never really dies. Later, during the game, Red Sox hurler Pedro Martinez treated the hometown crowd by striking out five of the six batters he faced en route to capturing the game's MVP honors.

On Opening Day 2002, the Red Sox celebrated the advent of the John Henry ownership era in Boston by unfurling an enormous American flag that spanned the full length of the Green Monster as native son Steven Tyler (of Aerosmith fame) belted out the National Anthem. After the "Star Spangled Banner," a large contingent of New England Patriots emerged from behind the flag, toting the Super Bowl trophy they had won the previous winter. As the Red Sox and Blue Jays looked on from the baselines, the Pats threw out the ceremonial first pitches en masse. "It looked like a giant snowball fight out there," said Josh, who haggled with the scalpers and landed in Section 17, only to see the Sox lose in a slugfest.

The good news for purists is that Henry—after paying $700 million for the team—doesn't have the money to build a new ballpark in

The Green Monster

Photo by Josh Pahigian

Boston anytime soon. Instead, he is committed to increasing Fenway's seating capacity to whatever extent that is structurally possible. First, he added two rows of premium seats right on the field between the dugouts and the screen behind the plate in 2002. Then he opened up the gate beneath the right field stands that had long confined bleacher fans to the bleachers and kept them from wandering into the rest of the ballpark. He built a food court beneath the stands in right center. Next, he received permission from the city of Boston to block off Yawkey Way on game days and put turnstiles at either end of the street, making it a festive part of the ballpark, similar to Eutaw Street in Baltimore. This has gone a long way toward easing the usually congested concourses inside the ballpark proper, but has come at the expense of many of the private sausage vendors who previously set up shop on Yawkey, and are now relegated to Lansdowne Street behind the Wall.

The biggest change Henry has made, however, involved the construction of 294 new seats above the Green Monster to start the 2003 season. At least the Sox didn't skimp when it came

to hiring an architect. Ballpark design expert Janet Marie Smith joined the Sox in 2002 as the team's vice president for planning and development and oversaw the entire operation. While we love the view from these now-coveted seats, we miss the image of home run balls nestling into the screen above the Monster. Also in 2003, Henry and co. added eighty-seven new field-level seats behind home plate and 133 dugout seats down the lines. The home plate seats debuted at $275 a piece, and the seats down the line at $225 each. Wow! This is a baseball game you know, not a prizefight.

We understand what Henry is trying to do. He paid a king's ransom to buy the team and ballpark and now he's trying to bleed Fenway for every cent he can like any good businessman would. And for that, we can't blame him. We just hope he doesn't lose sight of Fenway's many unique traditions and distort its old-time feel and eccentricities in the process. So far, so good, but we'll be keeping an eye on him in the years ahead.

TRIVIA TIMEOUT

Undergrad: Why is there one red seat in Fenway's right field bleachers while the rest are green?

Masters: What does the Morse code message on Fenway's left field scoreboard say?

PhD: What are the three prerequisites for a Red Sox player to be eligible to have his number retired? (Hint: here's a list of Sox legends whose numbers *aren't* retired: Babe Ruth, Cy Young, Jimmie Foxx, Jim Rice, Roger Clemens, Wade Boggs.)

Look for the answers in the text.

Getting a Choice Seat

Combine the Majors' tiniest ballpark with one of the most loyal fan bases and it all adds up to one hot ticket. Fenway has the highest average ticket price in the Majors. If planning ahead is your thing, buy your tickets when they go on sale in mid-January like Josh does. You might even be able to capitalize on one of the early season "family" nights, for which the team offers discounted bleacher and Grandstand tickets. On the other hand, if you adhere to Kevin's school of road-trip preparation and opt not to plan ahead at all, you'll likely find yourself buying standing-room tickets at the box office or paying a last-minute visit to Scalper Haven on game day.

Home Plate and Dugout Seats

One of the first things new ownership did when it took over in early 2002 was add 160 seats right on the field between the dugouts and the home plate screen. Then in 2003, the Sox added another 220 seats, some behind the plate and some down the baselines. You can't get any closer to the action in the big leagues. But for $275—well, let's just say they'll never be an option for us no matter how many copies of this book we sell.

Monster Seats (Sections 1–10)

These barstool-style seats are primarily sold to groups, with leftover tickets sold on a single-game basis. Just remember, once you buy that single seat, you may be sitting in the midst of the Afraid of Heights Anonymous Club of Greater Boston or some other group that has purchased most of the other 294 tickets above the Wall. No matter, be sure to bring your glove.

Section 1 is right above the left field foul pole while Section 10 is located high above the field in right center field. We like the seats in Sections 1–4 the best, since they're closest to the plate.

Field Boxes (Boxes 9–84)

These infield box seats provide the best view of the action. Season ticket holders sit here and also folks who spend $200 a pop on eBay. But don't be discouraged; Fenway offers plenty of great seats within your means and power of procurement.

Loge Boxes (Boxes 99–166)

These seats are owned by season ticket holders. If you have the chance to score Loge seats on the black market, go for it. They're all great.

Right Field Boxes (Boxes 1–7, 87–97)

Some of these are decent, especially the first few rows (A–F) of boxes 86 and 87 in home run territory. But as a rule, we don't recommend the Right Field Boxes. For less money, the lower bleachers in right and center field provide a better view.

Roof Boxes (Roof 1–43)

While these provide a bird's-eye overview of the field, they also seem to sell short the Fenway Experience. If you're like us, you want to be down in the crowd where the real fans are. You want to look up at the Wall, want the players to hear you when you yell, and feel the mist when you spit. Don't you? We know we do, although we admit we've toned down our act a bit since an unfortunate incident involving Jose Canseco during one of our Fenway visits a few years ago.

Canseco was visiting Boston with his Tampa Bay Devil Rays for an early April game. It was raining cats and dogs, and most of the season ticket holders had headed for cover. So

Sellout Index: 95% of games sell out
Seating Capacity: 34,892
Ticket Office: 617-267-1700
www.redsox.com

naturally, we departed our dry Grandstand seats, which were under the roof, and headed down to the boxes to seat hop. Real fans aren't afraid of rain—not even April-cold rain. We settled into a pair of seats five rows behind the Tampa Bay on-deck circle and congratulated ourselves for braving the elements. But when a Rays rally shortly thereafter made it clear to Josh that his beloved Red Sox were headed for a loss, things got a little bit out of hand.

"Look at him," Josh said.

"Who? Jose Canseco?" Kevin asked, following Josh's icy stare to the behemoth swinging a doughnut-weighted practice bat in the on-deck circle. "You were his biggest fan when he played for the Sox, no?"

"Yeah, as if. Where's your Madonna now, Jose?" Josh scoffed under his breath, remembering Canseco's tabloid romance with Madonna. "Where's your Madonna, now?"

"Why don't you ask him?" Kevin suggested.

"What?"

"Yell it out. You'll never be this close to him again. If you want to send him a message, this is your chance. What's he gonna do, come up into the stands and beat you up? Go for it."

Kevin had a point. But Josh, whose picture might as well appear next to the term "passive-aggressive" in *Webster's* dictionary, held his tongue, even as Jose stepped to the plate and lined a double off the Wall.

Two more soggy innings passed. As the Sox continued to flounder at the plate and in the field, Josh's frustration grew. Meanwhile Kevin, for the sake of livening up what was turning out to be a somewhat lackluster ball game, fed his friend Fenway brew after Fenway brew. Josh didn't disappoint, but neither did Canseco.

When Canseco finally stepped back into the on-deck circle prior to his next at-bat, Josh was ready for him. "Hey Jose, where's your Material Girl now?" he called out boldly. Then he

howled the backing vocals, "Ma-terial . . . Ma-terial . . . Ma-terial," surprisingly on key.

Canseco continued swinging his weighted bat like an automaton.

Josh bellowed out, "Like a viriiirriiirgin, touched for the very first time . . . like a viriiir-riiirgin . . ."

Several choruses of this drew a series of angry looks from nearby fans, until finally Canseco turned and squinted into the box seats, offering not quite a smirk, but not quite a smile either. The battle had been joined. Josh shut his mouth and looked accusingly at Kevin, as if he were the heckler, but it was a tough sell. Most of the remaining fans in the section were pointing at Josh.

Canseco proceeded to step to the plate and blast the next pitch over the Wall. And it was a *blast*. As he trotted around the bases, halfway between third and home the surly slugger slowed down, located Josh in the stands, and pointed right at him. True story. April 16, 1999. Ever since Josh has had a recurring nightmare involving Canseco, Madonna, and inexplicably the artist formerly known as "Prince." Go figure.

Grandstands (Sections 1–33)

Compared to other parks, Fenway's Grandstands are close to the field and offer excellent views of the action. But beware, there are large metal support columns—approximately two feet wide—that rise up in each section. And trust us, they ain't see-through. The team sells tickets marked "obstructed view" at regular price. Do not buy these under any circumstance! A restricted view seat means you will be straddling one of these columns for nine innings, staring all the while at its peeling paint and seeing very little of the game. If tickets are tight and you find yourself debating the merits of an obstructed view seat, consider standing room instead.

Aside from the obstructed view seats, there are no bad Grandstand seats on the left field side at Fenway, which means you'll be happy with any ticket in Sections 23–33. Behind the plate, Sections 19–22 provide a great view of the mound and batter's box, but as the row numbers increase, fly balls tend to disappear from sight due to the overhang of the second deck. So if you want to sit in the Grandstands behind the plate, score tickets in rows 1–10 so the overhang won't be a factor. On the first-base side, the Grandstands offer a clear view of the field, the Wall, and the famous neon CITGO sign that hovers high above Kenmore Square, but once you start working your way toward deep right field (especially Sections 4–9) the seats aim toward the center field bleachers, rather than the infield. The result: a bevy of support columns interrupting your sight lines and a stiff neck the next morning from looking over your left shoulder to see the plate. Also, you'll have a sore rump from sitting on a wooden seat all night. But just about any Grandstand seat at Fenway will give you a sore rump. Except for those in Section 33 (comfortable plastic!), all Grandstand seats at Fenway are made of oak and are exceptionally narrow. These original seats were designed for the turn-of-the-century New Englander who was apparently five feet, four inches tall and had an ass of granite. Don't fret though, it's all part of the Fenway experience.

Bleachers (Sections 34–43)

We prefer bleacher seats to Grandstand Sections 1–9. And in truth, quite a few bleacher seats offer a better view of the action than the Right Field Boxes do. Bleacher seats are made of comfortable plastic, there are no support columns interfering with sight lines, and all of the seats face home plate. So why are the right field Grandstands more expensive than the bleachers? A good question.

Our favorite bleacher seats are in Sections 34 and 35, located in straight away center field. This is a great place to call balls and strikes or to catch a long ball. It's also a prime location to heckle the center fielder. Just be sure to call him by his uniform number and not his name. Even when superstars like Bernie Williams and Ken Griffey, Jr. visit Boston, they find themselves relegated to mere number status by the unrelenting Fenway Faithful. "Hey 24, you ain't squat!"

Section 40 is another bleacher favorite of ours, as it places fans directly behind the Sox bull pen, beside the center field Green Triangle. This is a great place to scope out the Red Sox relief corps and check out the bleacher groupies as they flock down to ogle the pitchers. As you're probably aware, chicks dig middle relievers.

Speaking of ballpark hanky-panky, if you're a college kid looking for a good time, the bleachers are the way to go. Plenty of people your own age, plenty of beer flowing, and plenty of fun. If you're willing to put forth the effort, you should have a better than even chance of "making friends" in the bleachers.

On the other hand, if little Timmy or Grandpa Harold are accompanying you on your baseball road trip, you might prefer Grandstand seats, as sometimes the bleachers cross the line between a "PG-13" and "R" rating. While management prohibits blow-up dolls or "offensive inflatable objects," as the PA announcer calls them prior to the start of the first inning, there's still enough "going on" out there to make a choirboy blush.

Prior to the advent of the John Henry era in 2002, an iron gate beneath the stands kept the "Bleacher Creatures" from mingling with the rest of Fenway's patrons. But the gate is open now, so if you're not content with your upper bleacher seats and want to see if you like the view in standing room better, feel free to roam.

Standing Room

If you're like Kevin and show up on game day without a ticket, we recommend that you buy a standing-room ticket in lieu of throwing yourself to the mercy of scalpers. About eight hundred day-of-game standing room tickets go on sale at 9:00 A.M. at the Red Sox ticket office on Yawkey Way. These often sell out during summer months, so get to the window as early as possible. You know a team's doing well when it can charge fans $18 and not even provide them with a seat, eh?

A standing room ticket is your pass to any of the designated standing areas behind the Grandstands. As a rule, if you look behind the last row of Grandstands and do not see "No Standing" written in faded yellow paint on the ground, you are in one of the standing areas. Pretty simple, right? These spots provide a better view of the action than many bleacher seats do, and certainly a better look than from the overpriced right field Grandstands. The spot to stand for a great view of the game is behind Section 26, between third-base and home plate. But here's a tip: during the hot 'n' sticky dog days of July, stand behind Section 22 to bask in the cool breeze that wafts in off Yawkey Way through an upper opening in the park. It's at least fifteen degrees cooler here, which can mean a lot when it's the difference between one hundred degrees and eighty-five. But beware: this same cool breeze often makes standing or sitting behind home plate (Sections 19–22) a chilly affair in early April and late September. So plan accordingly: dungarees, mittens, hooded sweatshirt, flask of happy juice— whatever it takes.

Monster Top standing-room tickets are sold separately and are much more difficult to procure. A scant twenty-four of these precious tickets are put on sale at 9:00 A.M. each day and usually the folks who get them have been waiting in line outside the ticket office since about 5:00 A.M. It's time to ask yourself the question: "Just how big of a fanatic am I?"

SEATING TIP

THE FIRST FOUR ROWS of Section 33 are situated right up against the Monster. Touch the Wall, taunt the left fielder, catch a foul ball, and enjoy a great view of the game. But there's a catch. Sections 32 and 33 are "family" sections, meaning you can't drink beer in these seats. But trust us, if you can do your drinking before or after the game, these seats are a steal at outfield Grandstand prices because unlike all other Grandstand seats at Fenway these don't have Box and Loge seats between them and the field.

The Black Market

It is illegal to sell a ticket for more than 10 percent above face value in Massachusetts unless you have paid the state a fee, which gives you a license to sell tickets at any price you choose, no matter how obscene, outlandish, or ridiculous. It is also illegal for liquor stores to sell alcohol on Sundays in Massachusetts, except during the winter holiday season, which runs from December 1 through December 31. During deer season, Massachusetts hunters are prohibited from using "electricity" as a killing aid, yet they are allowed and even encouraged to use exploding bullets. Don't ask us to explain the arbitrary rules of this quirky commonwealth. We're just as baffled by them as you. Massachusetts calls them "blue laws." We call them arcane and provincial. But never fear, your prospects of scoring sweet black market tickets aren't so grim. The bottom line is that you can always get a case of Sam Adams from a liquor store's backdoor if you're willing to pay a few extra bucks for it, the state's deer population is waning daily, and ticket scalping is thriving in the Bay State.

You will find a herd of shady individuals congregating in Kenmore Square prior to each Red Sox game. Ask anyone who happens to be loitering in the Fenway district for directions to **Pizzeria Uno** and chances are the loiterer will be a scalper himself and will offer you a deal. If not, follow his directions to the Uno, and you'll soon find yourself in the heart of Scalper Haven. The Haven is located directly across from the Uno on Brookline Avenue, just before the bridge that crosses over the Massachusetts Turnpike (I-90). When you come upon an assortment of grubby, beer-bellied men with wads of tickets and cash in their hands, you'll know you're there. You may also note the scent of BO and cigarette smoke on the breeze. But again, don't despair. As you get closer to the park, the aroma of sweet sizzling sausages, onions, and peppers will overpower this stench.

"WHERE IS ROGER?"

FROM THE "WOW" department: four infield box seats to the Pedro Martinez / Roger Clemens matchup in the 1999 AL Championship Series went for $12,000 on eBay. The Red Sox won the game, 13–1, and Roger's wife, Debbie, burst into tears as Sox fans rhythmically chanted, "Where is Roger?" then rejoined "In the shower!" during innings four through nine. We love this rivalry.

For ordinary sellouts, expect to pay double face value for seats in the bleachers, and 50 percent above face for Grandstands and Boxes. Double those figures if it's a Yankee game and double them again if it's a playoff game. When dealing with scalpers, remember that Grandstand Sections 10–33 are all good, as are all lower Bleacher Sections. Just watch out for that red "obstructed view" stamp.

Before/After the Game

Boston's Fenway district has traditionally provided much of the housing for the city's college population. You will find Boston University, Northeastern University, and Emerson College particularly well represented in this section of town. And you'll find that the neighborhood is exponentially more crowded between September and May than it is during the summer months. You'll also find that there are plenty of bars and clubs nearby, and that the area is a bit on the dirty side. Despite the trash lining the sidewalks, the Fenway is a safe place to walk between the hours of 6:00 A.M. and 2:00 A.M., and a safe enough place to leave your car unattended at curbside, unless you're driving a Jag or Beemer on your ballpark tour. But really, is there a city sidewalk left in America where you can leave your Beemer and feel good about it? Does Toronto count?

Getting to Fenway

Fenway Park was built into the footprint of an actual city block: thus its highly irregular dimensions and only a small parking lot, which is reserved for select season ticket holders only. There are a number of private lots—which charge approximately $25 per car—located in the blocks surrounding the park at which you will usually be able to find a spot, excepting the rare weekday afternoon game when the lots are chock-full of commuter cars.

Because driving to Fenway means fighting heavy traffic on the way into town, getting lost in Boston's maze of winding, narrow, one-way streets, and fighting brutal car and pedestrian traffic after the game, we recommend taking advantage of the MBTA. The oldest subway in the country is safe, clean, and affordable, and you'll have no problem following the crowd to the ballpark from the Green Line's Kenmore

Square stop. Take the "T." Tell 'em Kevin and Josh sent you and they'll only charge $1.25.

Outside Attractions

PLAYER PARKING

If you're arriving four hours prior to the first pitch, stake out a spot on the corner of Yawkey Way and Van Ness Street, where you'll find the Red Sox players' parking lot. Curious what Nomar drives? We're not. We get to Fenway early for parking. Yeah, we know it sounds like stalking and your wife might call it "borderline scary behavior," but you'll be surprised to find dozens of other reasonably stable adults there alongside you. And who knows, you might even get an autograph. If you're waiting for the visiting team's bus to arrive, keep an eye on nearby Gate D. It just isn't this easy to stalk . . . um . . . we mean *rub elbows with* the players in other cities.

BYE-BYE, BASEBALL . . . HELLO SOUVENIR

Though Fenway's gates don't open until two hours before game time, plenty of batting practice (BP) homers find their way over the Green Monster and onto Lansdowne Street during the late afternoon. Grab a spot next to the Sausage Guy (see **Sausages Galore**), keep your eyes on the sky and keep your glove hand ready. The Sox usually begin taking their hacks three hours prior to the first pitch. The visitors begin their session when the gates open. The best action on the street is during visiting BP since every visitor swings from his heels so he can one day tell his grandkids he smacked one over the Wall.

When Fenway hosted the 1999 All-Star game, more than 10,000 people jammed Lansdowne for the home run hitting contest, looking to snag a McGwire or Sosa long ball.

THE BIG SHOW

Sports Radio WEEI, 850 AM, broadcasts its pregame show from the Diamond Club's fishbowl studio on Lansdowne. For those who remember the days of "old bastard baseball," check out former Sox reliever, Dick "the Monster" Raditz in the broadcast booth. He usually signs autographs during commercial breaks when he steps outside to have a smoke or wolf down a sausage.

GETTIN' JIGGY WIT' IT

If you're a baseball fan by day and a super-funky dance machine between the hours of 7:00 P.M. and dawn, check out **Axis**, **Avalon**, or **Jillian's** on Lansdowne Street. We don't recommend it. We don't consider clubbing cool. We're just letting you know why those half-dressed, super-fly chicks are speeding past you while you stand staring at the sky with a Little League glove on one hand and a fistful of sausage in the other as you wait for batting practice homers.

BOWLING ANYONE?

And just to let you know why so many guys are shuffling down Lansdowne Street in bowling shoes: check out the bowling alley entrance located next to Fenway's Gate E. It's not clearly marked, but if you look carefully you'll find it. Where else can you bowl underground, below a Major League ballpark—or any ballpark for that matter? The joint also has pool tables and a small video arcade.

For those interested in rolling a few, consider yourself forewarned that there are no "big balls" at the Ryan Family Amusement Center. Candlepin only. For pin-monkeys not up on the New England bowling scene, candlepin balls are the size of grapefruits, the pins are long and thin like Christmas candles, and it takes three balls to strike out, just like in baseball.

CURSE OF THE BUCKMINO

There's more to the Pizzeria Uno across from Scalper Haven than meets the eye. Look above the street-level restaurant and you'll find the

Hotel Buckminster. In Eliot Asinof's *Eight Men Out*, the definitive account of the 1919 Black Sox scandal, the author identifies this as the place where the conspiracy to fix the 1919 World Series took form. Wiseguy Joseph "Sport" Sullivan reputedly met Chicago White Sox first-baseman Chick Gandil at "the Buck," where the two men agreed upon the figure of $80,000 to put the Series in the proverbial bag. Our survey of less-than-amused Buckminster bellhops and valets revealed that the hotel's staff is widely ignorant of its organization's sordid past.

We wonder, though. What if, after so much hype and press, it isn't the "Curse of the Bambino" that plagues the Red Sox, but rather the "Curse of the Buckmino?" Maybe the baseball gods aren't punishing New Englanders for selling Babe Ruth to the Yankees, but for allowing the most heinous scandal in the game's history to unfold in the shadows of Fenway Park. As evidence to support this transcendental conspiracy theory, we submit Yankee second baseman BUCKy Dent's unlikely home run to win the one game playoff between the Sox and Yankees in 1978. Next, we submit Bill BUCKner's infamous error against the Mets in Game Six of the 1986 World Series. Seems like an awfully big coincidence that two guys nicknamed "Buck" would play starring roles in arguably the two most heartbreaking games in Red Sox history. Doesn't it?

TWINS SOUVENIR SHOP (Yawkey Way)

Located across from Fenway's Gate A, this shop is full of interesting stuff, including a life-sized Larry Bird growth chart and the baseball-shaped golf cart that once chauffeured Sox relievers from the bull pen to the mound.

Watering Holes and Outside Eats

CASK & FLAGON (BROOKLINE AVENUE)

The Cask features plenty of old ballpark and Boston pictures. This is probably your best bet if you want the Red Sox experience. There's usually a line to get in, but it moves fast and you can pick up a quick beer on ice in the foyer once inside the door without having to fight your way to the bar.

BOSTON BEERWORKS (Brookline Avenue)

Beerworks is a bit more upscale than the Cask, and the food's much better. The catch is that you have to drink their microbrew, which isn't the best, but isn't the worst either. Try the Bambino Ale and see if you can break the Curse. Somebody has to! At the very least, we're betting you'll "break the seal."

WHO'S ON FIRST (Yawkey Way)

Located underground below Twins Souvenir Shop, Who's on First doesn't offer much in the way of atmosphere, food, or service, but if you're just grabbing a quickie, it will do. Plus, it's inside the Yawkey Way gates once the team closes off the street.

COPPERFIELDS (Brookline Avenue)

A hot spot after the game for fans and local lasses. Loud music and cold beer.

BB WOLF'S (Brookline Avenue)

Directly across the street from Copperfields, this barbecue joint makes up for being a bit pricey by being more than just a bit spicy. This is the best sit-down lunch spot in the Fenway district. The pulled chicken and pulled pork are both winners. There can never be too much pulled meat on a dinner table as far as we're concerned.

PIZZERIA UNO (Kenmore Square)

If you're in the mood for a casual sit-down place where you'll also stand a shot at picking up some black market tickets, we recommend Pizzeria Uno. (Have we mentioned this place enough?) It's also a solid choice for families, offering a full menu of pasta and ribs, as well as a wide variety of Chicago-style pizzas.

THE RACK (Fanueil Hall)

After the game, hop on the Green Line at Kenmore and take it inbound to Government Center where this upscale bar offers plenty of pool tables, food, and spirits. It's a popular hangout for Red Sox and Bruins players, including Sox shortstop Nomar Garciaparra and Bruins forward Joe Thornton.

YAWKEY WAY

On game days, Yawkey Way is closed to traffic and fans need to pass through the turnstiles to enter it and the ballpark, similar to the setup on Eutaw Street in Baltimore. A festive, pregame locale, Yawkey Way provides plenty of eats, drinks, and entertainment as game time approaches. Watch out for the clowns on stilts and you should be okay.

Team-sponsored food stands operate here, as opposed to the independent vendors outside the gates and on Lansdowne Street. None of the options inside the gates are as good as the sausage sandwiches sold outside, but here's a quick review of the menu.

El Tiante's Cuban Stand offers a grilled Cuban sandwich. We tried it and thought it was good, but not as good as the Cuban sandwiches at Tropicana Field in Tampa Bay and Turner Field in Atlanta. El Tiante's Cuban features grilled deli ham and cheese, topped with mustard and pickle slices. Bottles of El Presidente Cerveza beer are also available.

Former Sox hurler Luis Tiante poses with fans for pictures and signs autographs before every game. Arrive on Yawkey right after the gates open and you'll recognize El Tiante as the distinguished elder gentleman in the white apron.

As personable a guy as they come, El Tiante won twenty or more games for the Sox three times (1973, 1974, 1976) and finished with 229 wins in a nineteen-year career—eight spent with the Sox. He was 3–0 for the Sox in the 1975 postseason, including a win against the A's in the ALCS, and two wins against the Reds in the World Series.

Boston Barbecue offers a barbecue chopped pork sandwich that doesn't hold a candle to the fresh smoked pork in St. Louis and Baltimore. The steak tip sandwich is more expensive and not as tender as the steak sandwiches sold at the Hill Top Steak House stand located beneath the stands in right field.

The Fenway Grill sells sausages that aren't nearly as tasty as those sold by the private vendors behind the Monster; plus the peppers and onions are all soggy rather than fried correctly. However, the Fenway Grill also sells Monster Dogs, which are colossal grilled hot dogs that must weigh close to a pound each. These are perhaps the item most worth ordering on Yawkey Way.

SAUSAGES GALORE (Trademark Food)

No trip to Fenway would be complete without paying a visit to the sausage carts outside the park. You won't find sandwiches this fresh and juicy inside the stadium. Get a hot sausage, sweet sausage, kielbasa, barbecue chicken, or steak tip sandwich. Just make sure you get one. We recommend ordering your sandwich "loaded." That's the local slang for slathered with sautéed peppers and onions. If you forgot the Tums at home, ask for a "naked" sausage instead.

There are a dozen of these carts located on Lansdowne Street and a couple on Yawkey Way, just outside the turnstiles. These folks sell steaming hot meat to baseball fans eighty-one games a year and make a living doing it. God bless 'em! Our favorite is **The Sausage Guy**, as much for the succulence of the Italian sausages he peddles as for the airbrushed picture on his van of a half-naked babe in a space helmet straddling a sausage/rocket ship/use your imagination. **The Sausage King** and **Chi-Chi's** also rate high on our pork-o-meter.

Inside the Park

Have you ever seen anything like it? Three hundred and two feet down the right field line. Three hundred and eighty to straightaway right. Four hundred and twenty to the right-center field power alley. Three hundred and seventy-nine to dead center. Three hundred and ten down the line in left. Wait a minute, perhaps you remember it being 315 to left? It *was* 315 until the Red Sox remeasured under pressure from local sportswriters and adjusted the sign accordingly in the early 1990s. A lot of veteran baseball people still swear it's no more than three hundred feet. The bottom line is that most Sunday hackers could clear the Wall with a pitching wedge and range ball, and that Fenway offers a multitude of nooks and crannies that make a game in Boston unique.

Ballpark Features

THE RED SEAT

Can you find the one red bleacher seat among the sea of green seats in right field? Hint: look toward Section 42, Row 37, Seat 21. If you still can't find it, you probably shouldn't be sitting in the bleachers because you're not going to be able to see squat with such poor eyesight.

The seat marks the landing spot of the longest home run in Fenway history. A fan named Joseph Boucher was sitting in the seat on a sunny Sunday in 1946 when Ted Williams's 502-foot dinger punched a hole in his straw hat and left a bump on his head. A picture of Boucher and his battered hat appeared in the *Boston Globe* the next day with a caption that read simply, "Hole in One."

As a way of saying "sorry to have maimed you," the team awarded Boucher season tickets for life that day and, after walking into the ballpark a lifelong Yankee fan, he switched allegiances and joined Red Sox Nation. For the rest of his life, he suffered along with the rest of New England while his former team won one World Series title after another.

Manny Ramirez hit the *second* longest home run in Fenway Park history—a 501-foot bomb off the light tower in left field against Toronto in June of 2001—and some pundits wondered if Fenway's official tale-of-the-tape tallier fudged the numbers in deference to the Splendid Splinter. We say, it's an imprecise science to begin with, no matter what the fine folks at MCI would have us believe.

THE PESKY POLE

Johnny Pesky—Sox player, manager, major and minor league instructor, and all around good guy—will forever be immortalized by "the Pesky Pole" in right field. Pesky hit seventeen lifetime home runs in a career that spanned eleven seasons. A fair number of those were of the 305-foot variety that just barely sneaked around the foul pole that will forever bear his name.

THE RETIRED NUMBERS

Boston's retired numbers hang above the Grandstands in right field. Until Carlton Fisk's number 27 was retired in September of 2000, the four retired numbers were 1, 4, 8, 9: Bobby Doerr, Joe Cronin, Carl Yastrzemski, and Ted Williams. The numbers used to be arranged 9, 4, 1, 8 and clever Boston fatalists cited this as additional evidence that the hardball gods were mocking the Red Sox for their decades of futility. They pointed out that when read as a date these numbers read: 9/4/18. September 4, 1918, represents the eve of the last World Series won by the Sox.

In order to have his number retired by the team, a Red Sox player must (a) play at least ten years with the Sox, (b) finish his career with the team, and (c) wear a Red Sox hat on his Hall of Fame plaque in Cooperstown. So now you're probably wondering: didn't Carlton Fisk play the last thirteen years of his career with the Chicago White Sox? You're right, but shortly before his number was retired, Fisk joined the Red Sox as a "special consultant to the general manager." Apparently the "rules" don't define a career as a *playing* career.

Even if Babe Ruth and Cy Young had met the team's criteria, you wouldn't see their numbers hanging in the Fens. The Sox didn't issue uniform numbers until 1931.

THE SCOREBOARD

The manually operated scoreboard in left field was installed in 1934. In 1976 it was moved eighteen feet to the right. The team replaced the front facing of the board in 2001, some skeptics said for the sole purpose of preventing "Save Fenway Park" lobbyists from attaining National Historic Landmark status for the Wall to block the old ownership regime from building a new ballpark. At least the Sox were kind enough to replicate former owner Tom Yawkey's hidden message, which still appears in Morse code on the scoreboard. In two vertical stripes, the dashes and dots signify the initials "TAY" and "JRY." Thomas A. Yawkey and Jeanne R. Yawkey, his wife.

INSIDE THE MONSTER

For the past several years, the scoreboard operators inside the Wall have been Christian Elias and Richard Maloney. Over the years, visiting players have made a practice of stopping in to visit Chris and Rich during batting practice. Actually, they couldn't care less about Chris and Rich; they stop in to see the Wall's innards. Countless players' autographs adorn the concrete walls inside the scoreboard.

While visiting town with the Yankees in 1998, David Wells added fuel to the New York/Boston rivalry, penning the message, "Fenway Sucks." Classy, David.

1918

SPEAKING OF the 1918 World Series, Boston beat the Cubs that year, with Babe Ruth winning two games on the pitcher's mound and posting an ERA of 1.06 in seventeen innings.

Here's a tidbit from the "the more things change, the more they stay the same" department. While most other Major Leaguers headed overseas to serve in World War I, players on both teams were granted an extended exemption from military service so the Series could be played in 1918. Unbelievably, players on both teams then threatened to strike unless the owners guaranteed the winning players $2,500 a piece, and the losers $1,000. The owners finally convinced the players that they would appear greedy and self-centered if they squabbled over money while their baseball brethren were risking their lives at war. After the Sox won their fifth Series in five tries, the still-bitter owners refused to issue the traditional World Series rings that players on both teams ordinarily receive. It was out of these ill feelings that the 1919 Black Sox scandal was born.

OFF THE WALL

Fenway is the only park in the Majors that features a fully extended, upright ladder in fair territory. Look carefully at the Wall and you'll find it suspended fifteen feet above the warning track in left field. Before seats were added above the Wall, a member of the grounds crew would line up an extension ladder with the Wall ladder after batting practice. Then he would scale the Monster, tiptoe along the catwalk at the top, and collect the batting practice homers that didn't clear the net. Occasionally, he'd toss a ball into Section 33 on his way down.

The ladder may have company on the Wall soon. According to our sources, John Henry intends to eventually put advertising on the Monster, turning it into a billboard. Traditionalists will cry foul at the bastardization of the hallowed Wall, but they shouldn't be so hasty.

Though it's been simply green for the past several decades, this wouldn't be the first time the Wall has been used for marketing purposes. Gem razor blade and Lifebuoy soap ads adorned it in the 1940s and prior to that, a precursor to the current left field wall contained ads for Arrow collars, Stetson shoes, and Murad cigarettes in the late 1910s.

THE GREEN TRIANGLE

If Bermuda's infamous triangle has contributed to an alarming number of nautical disasters, Fenway's triangle in right-center field has contributed to more than its share of hardball mishaps. Balls hit to this part of the park often wind up going into the score book as triples and occasionally as inside-the-park home runs.

Sox left fielder Mike Greenwell once recorded an inside-the-park grand slam against the Yankees when his shot hit high off the center field wall and then took a crazy bounce into right field. Speaking of Greenie, we wonder: what are the odds that a guy named Green*well* would spend his entire career playing left field directly in front of the most famous green *wall* in all of sports?

THE MONSTER

Upon entering Fenway Park you will feel drawn to the Green Monster. If you're in the main seating area, head out to Section 33, or if you're in the bleachers, head for Section 34. Then lean out and touch the Wall. Don't be shy. Go ahead. Touch it. Lots of people do. Take a picture too. Then check out all of the dents and dings left by seventy years of batted balls. Look closely and you'll see the red marks left by baseball seams.

THE CITGO SIGN

You've seen the famous neon glow of the CITGO sign on TV, hovering above the Wall. And you'll see its beacon of red, white, and blue live if your seats are on the first-base side.

But did you know that in the early 1980s CITGO tried to dismantle and remove the sign, which had been perched above Kenmore Square since 1965?

In 1979, at the suggestion of Massachusetts Governor Edward King, CITGO turned off the sign as a symbol of energy conservation, even though it used only $60 of electricity per week. The sign remained dim for four years and then the company decided to remove it. But a contingent of Fenway residents emerged claiming that the sign was an example of urban neon art and shouldn't be demolished. They asked the Boston Landmarks Commission to grant the sign landmark status. Surprised by the uproar, CITGO reconsidered and refurbished the sign in 1983. It's been glowing ever since.

THE DOWN EAST MONSTER

TODAY, another member of New England's professional baseball community plays in the shadows of a great green wall of its own. In 2003, the Eastern League Portland Seadogs constructed a thirty-seven-foot high replica of Fenway's Green Monster at Hadlock Field in Portland, Maine, after becoming the Red Sox AA affiliate. Maine's Monster comes complete with a scoreboard like the one in Boston, a replica of the CITGO sign, and even a gargantuan Coke bottle at the top, like the one in Boston. The color of the Portland Wall is a bit darker than Fenway Green, however.

THE "PRU"

One of the most prominent features on the Boston skyline, the Prudential Building rises high into the sky over the bleachers in right field. You'll be able to see it if your seats are on the third-base side. During the 1986 World Series, Boston's corporate types displayed their yankee (with a small "y") ingenuity when they turned the "Pru" into a giant billboard. A coordinated effort signaled "# 1" in lights on the building's face, as select office workers left their lights on for the night. During the 1999 playoffs, the building read, "Go Sox."

Fenway Food (Trademark Food)

In an unusual move, we bequeath our Trademark Food designation to the sausage sandwiches outside of Fenway. This is not meant to disparage the inside offerings; the meat on the street is just *that* good. Inside the park, the team has made major strides to upgrade the fare in recent years, most notably by offering selections from a number of local eateries.

FENWAY FRANK (Dog Rating)
The Second Best Hot Dog in the Majors.
It's hard to beat a Fenway Frank topped with ketchup (Josh) or mustard (Kevin), and in fact only one dog in the big leagues rates higher than this Boston beauty. The Fenway Frank has a firm yet still supple texture, while the taste is mild and meaty at once.

Just be sure to purchase your Fenway Frank from one of the vendors patrolling the stands and *not* from one of the concession lines beneath the stands. The vendors are delivering *steamed* dogs while the concession stands cook their dogs on the same metal rollers used to heat weenies at your local Texaco station. If it ain't steamed, it just doesn't "cut the mustard."

If you fall in love with this dog, visit a Boston area supermarket before hitting the road and load up your cooler. Fenway Franks are sold in grocery stores across New England.

BEST OF THE REST
The Hilltop Steakhouse located beneath the stands on the first-base side serves up a tasty array of marinated sirloin steak tips. Mmmm . . . steak!

The Kow Loon, beneath the stands on the left field side, offers a taste of the Orient. The lo mein and chicken fingers received particularly high marks.

Legal Sea Foods, beneath the stands behind home plate, makes a mean bowl of New England Clam Chow*da*!

SAY, "NO, THANKS," AND WALK AWAY
While the spicy-fries available throughout Fenway Park are decent, the specialty "hand-cut" fries found at select concession stands are most decidedly subpar. They never seem fully cooked and always seem lacking in the "flavor" department—a losing combination.

BREW HOO HOO
Fenway does not offer bottled beer or microbrew on tap. Fenway offers expensive watered-down macrobrew. Compounding the problem, the park doesn't offer roaming foam vendors to hand deliver cold frosties as is the case at most other parks. Maybe it's those pesky blue laws at work again. We couldn't get a straight answer on this one. In any case, fans have to retreat beneath the stands to wait in line whenever they're thirsty. If you're sitting in the bleachers, plan on missing a full half inning in line, and if you don't have a Massachusetts ID there is a high probability you will not be served. Your best bet, if you're looking for a buzz: either hit the bars before the game or get to the park early and throw down a few during batting practice. Or better yet, embrace the alcohol-free high of watching a game in baseball's grandest theater.

DIAMOND CLUB
A new option, introduced at the start of the 2002 season is the Diamond Club, located on the Lansdowne Street side of the park. Opening at the start of the seventh inning at which time alcohol becomes no longer available

inside the ballpark, this is a decent place for fans to keep their buzz going.

The Fenway Experience

HAVE A BALL

You'll notice that Fenway Park contains less foul territory than any other big league park. This gives you a better-than-normal chance of snagging an official Bud Selig autographed baseball to take home as a souvenir. So wear a glove if you're on the left field side or in the first few rows of the bleachers, or if you just like wearing a glove.

Sox center fielders traditionally toss a warm-up ball into Section 34 prior to the top of the ninth inning. You'll see a crowd of souvenir-hungry kids flock to the railing as the center fielder trots out to play catch with the left fielder. Take this as your cue to stake out some territory.

If you're sitting in Sections 40 or 41, chances are you'll have a shot at one of the balls Sox

SPORTS IN THE CITY

FOR A PEEK at the site of the old Huntington Avenue Fairgrounds where the American League Boston Nine played prior to Fenway's 1912 opening, hop on an inbound Green Line train to Copley, then take the E-line outbound to the Northeastern University stop.

On campus, you'll find a bronze statue of Cy Young marking the site of the first World Series, which took place in 1903. Young's Boston Pilgrims, an early incarnation of the Red Sox, defeated the Pittsburgh Pirates, five games to three. On May 4 of the next season, Young pitched the first perfect game of the modern era against the Philadelphia A's on this site.

Northeastern's Godfrey Lowell Cabot Physical Education Center features a World Series Exhibit Room, displaying memorabilia from the 1901-to-1911 era.

relievers occasionally toss into the crowd throughout the game. As always, your best bet is to position yourself near a cute kid or pretty lass, then wait for a rebound.

HAVE A BEACH BALL

Whether your trip to Fenway occurs beneath the freezing drizzle of April, the blistering sun of July, or the harvest moon of late September, if you're sitting in the bleachers you will invariably find a number of colorful beach balls flying. Ambitious fans try to launch these over the gap between the bleachers and right field Grandstands, but usually they end up on the field, destined to be destroyed by a member of the grounds crew stationed in the Red Sox bull pen.

In the 1980s Red Sox reliever Bob Stanley made a ritual of theatrically hacking wayward beach balls to death with a rake in the pen. "The Steamer" enjoyed a love-hate relationship with Boston fans. We always liked "the Steamer" though. He had a certain quirky, gooney quality about him that we appreciated.

LADY PINK PANTS (Superfan)

Fenway has a plethora of superfans to its credit, but the one we liked best is a little old lady who sits in the last row of Section 40. You'll recognize her as a superfan when you see her flaming pants. She's been sitting in Section 40 with her radio in her lap and a bag of ice on her head (on hot days) since the dead-ball era. And she never leaves her seat until the final out is recorded.

"YANKEES SUCK"

If the Olde Towne Team has the lead, chances are that at some point the crowd will begin a chant of "Yankees Suck . . . Yankees Suck . . . Yankees Suck . . ." This will occur even if the Sox are playing, say . . . Baltimore. This is a relatively new phenomenon. Yes, it is illogical and pathetic, but it is a Fenway reality. This is

THE BOSTON BRAVES played at Braves Field on Commonwealth Avenue from 1915 until they jumped town for Milwaukee in 1952. The club formed under the name "Boston Red Stockings" as a member of the National Association in 1871, then became a charter member of the National League in 1876. Later, the team was briefly known as the "Beaneaters" before management settled on "Braves" as the team moniker.

Because Braves Field could accommodate more fans than Fenway, on numerous occasions the crosstown Red Sox played important "home" games in the city's National League park, including games during the 1915 and 1916 World Series.

In keeping with Boston tradition, the Braves brought an early World Series title to Boston (1914), then spent the next four decades in the NL's second division. Iron-ically, just five years after leaving town, the Milwaukee Braves beat the Yankees, of all teams, to win the 1957 Fall Classic.

After the Braves left town, Boston University bought the field and converted it to a football field. BU's Nickerson Field isn't worth visiting on your baseball roadtrip, but we think it's an interesting coincidence that the former homes of both the Red Sox and Braves now reside on college campuses. Then again, it seems like you can't take ten steps in this town without landing on one college campus or another.

One final bit of Bambino balderdash: in 1935, Ruth left the Yankees to play for the Boston Braves at age forty. He batted just .181 with six dingers before retiring at the end of May. The next year, he became a charter member of the Hall of Fame.

---

the product of a deep-seeded fixation with New York's baseball prowess.

For those in need of a quick history lesson, here's how it all went down: after winning five World Series in their first fifteen years, the Sox have gone more than eighty years without winning another. The downward spiral began when Sox owner Harry Frazee (a New Yorker at heart) sold Babe Ruth to the Yankees in 1919 to finance the Broadway musical *No, No, Nanette*. The play bombed and the financially strapped Frazee was forced to sell or trade away a number of Boston's other stars in the ensuing years. Meanwhile, the Yankees' reign as the game's most illustrious team began with Ruth's arrival. The "Bronx Bombers" have won twenty-six championships during Boston's drought.

Today, this juvenile, nonsensical, ritualistic chanting is how New Englanders vent their frustration. You have a choice: either frown dourly on the chanters to either side of you, or join them in spite of yourself. We hope you'll do the right thing.

DIRTY WATER

When the Sox win, fans are usually serenaded by the Standels singing "love that dirty water, Boston you're my home," through the PA system after the game. Great tune. The "dirty water" to which the song refers was located in the Charles River, which had a serious pollution problem for years. It's supposedly better now.

Josh was dismayed to hear "Celebration" by Kool and the Gang played after a Sox win in 2003, and hopes the new Red Sox ownership doesn't have something against dirty water.

When Boston loses, run-of-the-mill organ music plays as fans file down the exit ramps. Josh and Kevin say, "Root for a Red Sox win."

NEW YORK METS, SHEA STADIUM

Mother of All "Cookie Cutters"

FLUSHING,
NEW YORK

90 miles to Philadelphia
215 miles to Boston
190 miles to Baltimore
365 miles to Pittsburgh

SHEA STADIUM is indeed a *stadium*. It is not, nor will it ever be mistaken for, a baseball park. While crosstown Yankee Stadium feels like a jumbo-sized ballpark, Shea offers very little of the intimacy and character that can make the ballpark a magical place to spend a summer afternoon. With its steep upper levels, concrete facades, and bright blue motif, Shea is a decent place to *watch* a baseball game, but a below average place to *experience* one. And the environs offer very little to enhance the game-day activities. On one side of the stadium lies a wasteland of muffler huts and chop shops. And on the other side, beyond a sea of parking lots, sits a Latino neighborhood too many blocks away to contribute much to the game-day experience.

Despite its less-than-inspired design and glum surroundings, Shea Stadium has been home to some of the game's brightest stars. And the Mets' loyal and enthusiastic fans ensure a game at Shea is always lively. The Mets, who perennially finish near the top of the National League in home attendance, have won two World Championships in their history—a tradition that many teams would kill for.

If you approach Shea with lowered expectations, like say, when you're going to a Jim Carrey movie, you might have a surprisingly good time. If you head to Queens for the first time after a game in the Bronx, you might be setting yourself up for a letdown. So plot your itinerary accordingly.

The stadium was named after New York attorney William Shea, who helped bring National League baseball back to Gotham after the departure of the Giants and Dodgers in 1958. In 1959, Shea announced his intention to form a third Major League, to be called the Continental League, and to place one of the charter teams in New York. A year later, the league disbanded before it ever played a game, but not until the National League had consented to accept two of its prospective franchises—Houston and

exterior

Photo by Kevin O'Connell

New York—as expansion teams. The expansion of 1962 made the NL a ten-team circuit.

The Mets logo is centered around a baseball that fuses Dodger blue and Giant orange, which also happen to be New York's state colors. The bridge in the foreground represents the Mets bringing National League ball back to New York by "bridging the gap" that existed after the Dodgers and Giants departed. The skyline in the background depicts specific buildings from all five boroughs of New York City, including the Williamsburgh Savings Building, the Woolworth Building, the Empire State Building, the United Nations Building, and a church spire symbolic of Brooklyn.

After playing their first two seasons at the Polo Grounds, on April 17, 1964, the Mets christened Shea with two bottles of water, one from the Harlem River that flows near the Polo Grounds, and the other from the Gowanus Canal, which ran beside Ebbets Field. The Mets lost that first game to the Pirates. And then they kept on losing. For the third straight year the Mets finished last in the NL, posting 53 wins and 109 losses. Nonetheless, Mets fans filled the ballpark to watch their lovable losers. The Mets outdrew the Yankees (who won the AL pennant in 1964) selling 1.7 million tickets to the Yanks' 1.3 million. A full house was on hand to witness Phillies ace Jim Bunning's perfect game against the Mets on Father's Day, and then again when Shea hosted the 1964 All-Star Game.

The team's first .500 season came when the "Miracle Mets" of 1969 surpassed the previous franchise record of seventy-three wins, then proceeded to win twenty-seven more en route to a 100–62 mark. After sweeping the Braves to win the first National League Championship Series ever played, the Mets beat heavily favored Baltimore four games to one, to win the World Series.

As the first of the so-called cookie-cutter stadiums, Shea utilized motorized underground tracks to convert its stands from baseball to football and vice versa. The horseshoe-shaped facility housed the Jets for two decades and was originally designed to be expandable up to ninety thousand seats, should management ever decide to complete the bowl by adding outfield seating on all levels.

In the years after Shea's construction, cities like Philadelphia, Pittsburgh, St. Louis, and Cincinnati followed New York's lead and built multipurpose stadiums of their own. While these highly functional and eerily similar-to-one-another facilities efficiently served two professional teams in each city—baseball and football—they left fans longing for the days when each ballpark was a world unto itself. Today, Mets fans understand that longing perhaps better than the fans in any other city.

The Jets set an American Football League attendance record at Shea in 1967, selling out all seven of their games and drawing 437,036 fans. But in 1973 the Jets had to play their first six games on the road because the Mets needed Shea for the NLCS and World Series (which they lost to Oakland in seven games). The Jets left for the Meadowlands in 1984.

Shea was home to the hated Yankees during the 1974 and 1975 seasons as the Bronx ball yard underwent a massive remodeling. When the New York football Giants played their home games at Shea in 1975, it represented the first time two MLB teams and two NFL teams called the same venue home during the same year.

Renovations made between 1985 and 1987 created fifty luxury suites on Shea's press level and added huge neon doodles of baseball players on the exterior windscreens. We like the windscreens, honestly we do, but couldn't they have done a little bit more to spruce up the outside of the joint? Like, break up the parking lot with a few healthy trees? Or erect statues honoring famous Mets? Or how about painting the exterior concrete some color other than bright blue?

In any case, Shea has played a starring role in three of the most unusual doubleheaders in baseball history:

➤ During the inaugural 1964 season, the Mets and Giants played a nine-hour and fifty-minute doubleheader, the longest in baseball history. The first game must have seemed like a cakewalk after the second went twenty-three innings, spanning seven hours and twenty-two minutes. The Giants swept the twin bill.

➤ On April 15, 1998, another unconventional double dipper took place when the Yankees were forced to play a 12:05 P.M. game against Anaheim at Shea after a beam fell from Yankee Stadium's upper deck. That evening, the Mets hosted the Cubs. Both New York clubs won.

➤ On July 8, 2000, the Mets hosted the Yankees for an afternoon game before the two teams traveled across town to play a night game in the Bronx. The odd twin bill came about when a game between the teams scheduled for Yankee Stadium was rained out in June. The Yankees won both games by identical 4–2 scores. Later that season, the Mets and Yanks met in the World Series for the first time ever, and the Yanks again were victorious.

Two of the most riveting postseason games in recent memory took place at Shea, both extra-inning affairs won by the home team. In 1986, the Mets shocked the baseball world and ruined Josh's winter, coming back from a

interior

Photo by Kevin O'Connell

two-out, two-strike, no-one-on-base, 5–3, tenth-inning deficit to win Game 6 of the World Series. Car horns honked jubilantly throughout New York as Ray Knight streaked toward the plate with the winning run and Bill Buckner slowly turned his back on the infield. Two days later, the Mets won their second championship.

In 1999, Robin Ventura hit a "grand slam single" to win Game 5 of the NLCS against the Braves. The hit ended the longest postseason game ever, a five-hour, forty-six-minute affair. What is it with the Mets and these epic games? Anyway, with a steady rain falling and the bases soaked in the bottom of the fifteenth inning, Ventura smacked a ball over the right field fence. He made it only so far as first-base however, before being swarmed by ecstatic teammates. Because he never circled the bases, he was credited with a single and only one RBI. Had Ventura touched all four, the hit would have been the first walk-off "grannie" in postseason history. Now that's what we call "taking one for the team."

A number of major musical acts played Shea during the stadium's early days, including the Rolling Stones, the Who, the Police, Simon & Garfunkel, Elton John, Eric Clapton, and Jimi Hendrix. And oh, yeah, the Beatles played their first major outdoor American stadium show at Shea on August 15, 1965. If you've never listened to the Beatles, Josh recommends you buy a few of their CDs. Kevin thinks the albums sound better.

Shea was used as a main staging area to get relief supplies to rescue workers at Ground Zero after the September 11, 2001, terrorist attack on the World Trade Center. Then Mets manager Bobby Valentine played an integral role in the operation directing traffic as food and blankets came in and went out. Valentine didn't leave Shea for nearly a week, taking only

Sellout Index: 5% of games sell out
Seating Capacity: 55,775
Ticket Office: (718) 507-TIXX
www.mets.mlb.com

TRIVIA TIMEOUT

Jumbo: How many no-hitters have Mets pitchers recorded since the team's inception?
Concord: Name the only Mets player to have his uniform number retired by the team.

Look for the answers in the text.

---

brief catnaps in his office between working. In the months ahead, he frequently entertained New York City firemen and police officers and their families at Shea and at his nearby restaurant. For his efforts, Bobby V. was named baseball's 2002 Branch Rickey Award winner, which is given annually to a leading humanitarian in the MLB community.

Getting a Choice Seat

Unless the Mets are playing an intracity tilt against the Yankees, you should have no trouble scoring tickets from the box office on game day. Although Shea is located in the geographic and population center of New York City, it rarely sells out because of its expansive upper level. That didn't stop the Mets from raising ticket prices in 2003 under the guise of adopting a new system under which all home dates are classified either Gold, Silver, Bronze, or Value games. For most seating sections, the cheapest of dates—the Value—match the price for all games prior to the advent of the system. So unless you're heading to New York for a matchup against Pittsburgh, plan on paying more. And the people hit the hardest by the increase? The poor folks sitting in the upper level who pay double the price for Gold games verses Value games. In comparison, the season ticket holders down in the box seats pay only a 40 percent premium. Where's the equity in that?

After you wrestle with the Mets schedule and try to identify the best game for your buck, here's one other thing to keep in mind. The odd-numbered sections are on the right field side of home plate, the even sections on the left field side. So if your buddy has tickets in Section 26 and you're trying to find a seat near him, don't make the mistake of buying a seat in Section 27 or 29. Shoot instead for Section 24 or 28.

Inner Field Box/Outer Field Box

The Inner Field Boxes are located below the lower concourse on field level. They are owned exclusively by corporate and season ticket holders as you'll see by the plaques affixed to each box listing their names. The seats are marked to ensure you won't get away with sitting there. Josh says he had a dog that once found the need to mark all of his territory too, but we won't go into that now.

Only a smattering of Outer Field Boxes are available for purchase by the general public as many of these, too, are marked by plaques belonging to the hoity-toity. The few open seats we saw were located near the foul poles on either side of the field.

In general, the field level seats all offer unobstructed views of the action, although the circular shape of the seating bowl places Outer Box ticket holders at a significant distance from the field.

As soon as batting practice ends you need to show your Field Box ticket to an usher in order to access the field level concourse. The staff guards these gates rather tightly.

Loge Box/Reserved

Many of the Loge Box seats belong to season ticket holders as well, which means the best seats the average fan is likely to purchase directly from the Mets are outfield Loge Boxes or Loge Reserved seats. In general, stay away from Rows A and B of the Loge Reserved

because they are obstructed by pedestrian traffic on the walkway.

Given the fact that the corporate raiders have devoured all of the best field level tickets, and considering how steep and high above the field the upper levels are, we recommend buying Loge Box seats in Boxes 474–484 in left field home run territory. Since there are no orange (field level) seats in front of them, these Loge seats are right on the field, and they are elevated a bit which allows a clear view of the

SEATING TIP

DURING BATTING PRACTICE anyone can access the field level even if he has an upper level ticket. So if you're hoping to seat-hop down to the good seats, show up early and don't leave the first level. Gate C opens two and a half hours before game time for fans wishing to watch the Mets' batting practice session. All other gates open two hours before first pitch.

If you're feeling lucky, after BP have a seat. If you can pull it off with confidence, and if no one comes to hassle you, you can stay. We like to call this little game "ballpark roulette," and when we tried it, Kevin's tie-dyed T-shirt gave us away.

infield. We prefer these to Loge Reserved seats near third or first-base for the same price and consider it a toss-up between them and the Loge Reserved seats behind the plate (Sections 1–6) where the field level is not as deep, placing the Loge closer to the field. An added benefit to sitting in the left field Loge Boxes is the chance to chat with Frank Garcia, an affable stadium security guard who whistles a pleasant tune all game long. Give him a few minutes to tuck his shirt in and comb his hair and he's sure to let you take a picture with him.

Reserved sections 1–24 offer good views, but in any section higher than 24 your ability to see the warning track and field on your side of the field will be limited because of the *under-hang*. This gets worse the farther you sit from home plate.

The overhang is also a factor when considering Loge seats. We felt like caged subway rats sitting in many of the Loge Reserved seats. The back two rows are offered at a 60 percent discount because of the awful sight lines in

security guard

Photo by Kevin O'Connell

which fly balls disappear shortly after leaving the bat, not to reappear until they're a few feet above the outfielder's gloves. This overhang effect was worse in the sections behind the plate. Despite the discount, we don't recommend seats higher than Row F.

We should mention that the Loge Boxes behind the plate are not protected by the backstop screen that extends only so high as the first level. Here you'll have plenty of chances to snag a "foul back." Just be sure to wear a glove—or a hockey mask.

Mezzanine Box/Reserved

This is the third level of the stadium. Unlike the Loge, the first row of the Mezzanine Reserved is elevated several feet higher than the boxes, so there's no walkway obstruction.

Again, the under-hang of the deck below is a factor in Sections 24 and higher. In Row L and back, the overhang blocks the view of high fly balls, but not nearly as badly as in the Loge, since these seats are that much higher. In most of the Mezzanine, only the last two rows, O and P, are to be avoided. But beware of seats in Sections 1–11 behind the plate where the overhang is more of a factor and any row higher than H obstructs the view of fly balls.

Upper Box/Reserved

We bought walk-up tickets at the window and landed in Row B of the Upper Reserved in Section 2, right behind the plate. For a cheap ticket, the view wasn't bad at all, though we found it difficult to feel like part of the game perched so high above the playing surface.

Even Major League pop-ups don't make it up as high as Shea's upper deck. The Upper Reserved is very steep, perhaps as much so as Yankee Stadium's upper deck and the rows seem to keep going and going forever, all the way back to Row V.

If you're not terribly afraid of heights, visit Section 2, Row V, and look out the back of the stadium to watch the sun set over Manhattan during the early innings of a night game. It's a shame Shea couldn't have faced Manhattan so all fans could have seen this breathtaking view. Of course, then the setting sun would have been in the batters' eyes. As it is situated, however, Shea offers possibly the worst view in the big leagues beyond the ballpark walls. It's all planes, trains, and automobiles. The expansive parking lot. The 7 Train rolling in and out of the station. And airplanes coming in and taking off from La Guardia. Queens, from this angle, looking postindustrial and forlorn, doesn't make for much of a backdrop for a baseball game. A glowing U-Haul sign typified this on the night we visited. It just read "Haul" as the "U" had burned out. The one saving grace is Riker's Island Bridge, which lights up neon green as darkness blankets the city.

Other than the lousy view, the Upper level isn't so bad. Shoot for tickets in Rows A–K of the Upper Reserved and you won't be disappointed. There's no real sense in spending twice the money for Upper Box tickets. Up so high, what difference does another twenty feet make? Very little, we say.

The Black Market

Shortly after parking in the stadium lot, chances are you'll be accosted, or at least approached, by a scalper. Because there are almost always seats available at the box office, it's usually a buyer's market. If the Mets are having a down year or if a lackluster opponent is in town, you should be able to find field level seats at or near face value. Don't overpay. These guys will make their money ripping off neophytes at Madison Square Garden and the Meadowlands.

Before/After the Game

Unfortunately for Mets fans, Shea was built decades before ballparks like Camden Yards and Jacobs Field popularized the concept of building ballparks in the midst of revitalized urban areas that offer convenient access to restaurants and pubs. Built on the site of the 1964 World's Fair, Shea is surrounded on all sides by expansive parking lots. The Flushing Meadows tennis facility is across the street, but not much else.

If you have time to kill, we mildly recommend exploring the Corona neighborhood, a

fifteen-minute walk away, past the tennis center and through Corona Park. Check out the death star—the big metallic globe of the world that looks like the half-completed *Star Wars* battle star, which was left behind by the World's Fair.

There are Mexican, Dominican, Chinese, and pizza joints near the corner of 111th Street and Roosevelt Avenue, two subway stops before Shea. If you're on foot, just follow the elevated tracks.

If you ride into town in a junker that needs tires, body work, a muffler, struts or brakes, you may be in luck. Visit the north side of the stadium parking lot where you'll find plenty of auto shops.

Getting to Shea

Shea is located at 123 Roosevelt Avenue in Flushing. Take I-95 to the Whitestone Bridge to the Whitestone Expressway to the Northern Boulevard/Shea Stadium Exit. The stadium lot is expansive but not terribly expensive, checking in at $8. Fans sometimes tailgate before games, but it's not technically permitted—though it should be—so wrap those beer cans in tinfoil and leave the hibachi at home. We recommend looking for a free spot on 114th Street. Follow Roosevelt Avenue west, past the stadium, then take a right onto 114th and you'll see a number of legal spots in front of the Ramada Plaza hotel. But get there early.

If you're staying in town and planning to hit the bars in Manhattan after the game, we suggest taking the subway to the ballpark. Hop on the Number 7 Flushing Line, which from midtown takes about thirty-five minutes to arrive at the Willets Point/Shea Stadium station. Bring a copy of the *New York Daily News* for the ride, or just sit back and reflect upon what a moron John Rocker is.

Another option is the New York Waterways ferry, which drops fans off at the

World's Fair Marina, a five-minute walk from Shea. The ferry, which services only Friday, Saturday, and Sunday games, costs $14 round-trip for adults and $10 for children. For a schedule and list of departure points, call 800-533-3779.

Outside Attractions

AN ARRESTING IMAGE

Arriving on the 7 Train for a night game against the Marlins in late September, we excitedly peeked inside the park as we exited the Willets Point railway ramp. Descending the platform stairs, we lowered our eyes to see a large sign on the side of the stadium that read "Baseball is for Kids." True enough, we thought. It's for the kid in all of us. We took a few more steps and bammo, we were confronted with the unwelcome specter of a police bus sitting in the Shea Stadium parking lot bearing the words "Mobile Arrest Center." Yeah, and Turkish Prisons are for kids, too.

Maybe, we thought, the arrest center was stationed here because the U.S. Open was in town next door at Arthur Ashe Stadium, but then we remembered that tennis fans don't commit crimes. The bus was surely here to intimidate Mets fans. It made a lousy first impression, but it made us think twice about tossing our beer and Walkman batteries onto the field later.

AUTOGRAPH HOUNDS

For easy access to arriving/departing players, stake out the Press Gate between stadium Gates B and C. The players' lot is merely a fenced-off partition of the general lot, and if you time it right you can catch players walking from the lot to the entrance of the clubhouse. Just look for the television trucks and there you are. Funny that the Mets have some of the highest profile players in the game, but offer easy access to them outside of Shea.

FIELD OF SCREAMS

Similar to Yankee Stadium, on 114th Street there is a very shabby baseball field that presumably hosts youth and rec league games in the shadows of the Major League facility. The field is actually two fields in one. Two infield diamonds face each other, so that the center fielder of one stands right behind the second base bag of the other with his back to the action of the second diamond, and vice versa. Nonetheless, this might be a decent place to play if the city of Mets put just a few bucks into its upkeep. The kids deserve better.

Watering Holes and Outside Eats

BOBBY VALENTINE'S SPORTS BAR & RESTAURANT (37th and 114th Streets)

Inside the Ramada Plaza hotel a short walk from the stadium is one of the three restaurants owned by former Mets manager Bobby Valentine. This edition, which opened in 2001, represents the only decent sports bar we could find within a twenty-minute walk of Shea.

We were impressed by the collage of trading cards and other sports memorabilia beneath the shellacked bar top. Our seats were near a Harold Baines 1984 Topps, a Princeton versus Harvard ticket stub from a 1953 football game, and cards of Jame Silas, Bill Lee, Rod Carew, and Roberto Clemente. The walls and windows are adorned with a multitude of old-style jerseys, *Sports Illustrated* covers, and photos, many of which are autographed.

Menu items, named after Mets players, past and present (Mookie's fried mozzarella, Wally Backman's chicken fingers, Ojeda's fajitas, etc.), topped out with the Seaver steak at $24.99, but also included pasta dishes in the $13 range, and sandwiches for less than $10. Kevin tried the Gil Hodges's fish wrap for $7.99, and Josh ordered a Single burger for the same price. Both were tasty.

From the "only in New York" department: When Kevin told our waitress that we were writing a book and politely asked her to pose with us for a picture. She said, "no, thanks." When Kevin persisted, saying, "If we use the picture, it could make you famous," she replied, "Yeah, it could make me divorced, too." This left us wondering just what type of photograph she thought we were proposing.

Bobby V's other locations are in Arlington, Texas, where Valentine once managed the Texas Rangers, and in Stamford, Connecticut, where it has been reported he invented the sandwich wrap in 1980. According to Stamford lore, a customer ordered a sandwich, but the kitchen was perilously low on bread, so Bobby improvised with a half piece of pita bread. And now the whole world is doing it, even people in Greece. So step aside lavash and tortilla makers of the world. Bobby V has beaten you all to the lunch . . . err, we mean, punch, with the first-ever wrap.

We wonder where Bobby's next restaurant/managing gig will land him.

LEMON ICE KING (5202 108th Street)
On a hot day, this Corona shop becomes a virtual "must visit." The King offers nearly one hundred flavors of Italian ice. It was a New York City scorcher when we were in town. Kevin tried the grape, which had deliciously refreshing whole frozen grapes in it. Josh's lime was streaked with frozen lime peels. Yum! Other interesting flavors included chocolate, almond, pear, and apple. Maybe the King will open up a stand nearer to the stadium? Please?

RUSTY STAUB'S ON FIFTH (575 Fifth Avenue)
Unlike Mickey Mantle's restaurant, which bore the Mick's name only and little else, this upscale steak house is owned and operated by the former Mets star. Staub, who spent nine of his twenty-three big league seasons wearing the blue and orange, is often on the premises, so if you were a fan, stop in for a visit. As for the food: expensive but good.

MAMA LEO'S (104th Street)
A favorite stop for Queens firefighters and police officers, this Italian bodega serves an array of exceptional Italian sandwiches, hot and cold. We also highly recommend the Mama's location inside Shea Stadium, but more on that later.

Inside the Stadium

Ah, the ballpark. That magical place that seems to exist in a universe all its own. That timeless fantasy land to which we escape when our mundane lives become too much to bear.

In the darkest days of January, sometimes Josh will boil a dozen hot dogs, crack open some peanuts, water down a beer, and pop into his VCR a tape of the Red Sox 1999 Game Five American League Division Series victory over the Indians to simulate that authentic ballpark experience. He closes his eyes and meditates, ensconced by the sounds, smells, and tastes of the game. He listens for the crack of the bat, the old-fashioned pipe organ, the beer man yelling, "beeya heya," the crowd rising to cheer or groan in unison, the laughter of the happy children, the heckling of the happy drunks, the roaring jet engines high overhead. Wait a minute. Jet engines?

Welcome to Shea. The Mets play directly beneath one of La Guardia Airport's main runway paths. Not good.

Hailing from the cookie-cutter era, Shea also provides a rather generic playing environment. We looked for character and eccentricities, and while we found many of each in the loyal Mets fans, we found very little to distinguish the stadium itself.

Despite these drawbacks, Shea is far from the worst place in the league to watch a game. Most of the seats are between the foul poles and the steep incline of each level places fans relatively close to the air space over the field.

Ballpark Features

JESSE DON'T LOSE THAT POSE

Every time Josh enters Shea Stadium, he cringes at the sight of the massive banner that portrays Jesse Orosco's World Series clinching pose after nailing down the 1986 title. The concourse also displays banners of Mike Piazza, John Franco, Lenny Dykstra, Casey Stengel, Keith Hernandez, and other favorite Mets.

TOMATO TIME

At the very least Shea offers a real grass playing field, but the 18-by-20-foot vegetable garden in the Mets bull pen is one of the Stadium's most unique hometown touches. For the past sixteen years, groundskeeper Chris Murphy has tended the garden, growing watermelon, cantaloupes, corn, carrots, pumpkins, tomatoes, sunflowers, zucchini, radishes, and string beans.

The garden began during the Miracle Mets' 1969 season when bull pen coach Joe Pignatano nurtured a lone tomato plant. After the Mets won the World Series, Pignatano planted a more elaborate garden the next spring. The garden has been a Shea staple ever since.

If you order a burger with the works at Shea, the tomato, lettuce, and onion will all be homegrown. Just kidding. But here's a true story. The garden was at the center of controversy in 2000 when by midseason towering sunflower and corn stalks had risen above the right field fence obscuring the visiting dugout's view of the Mets bull pen. When the Phillies complained that this gave the home team an unfair advantage because they couldn't see which players the Mets had warming up in the pen, several stalks were ripped out of the ground.

For a good view, peer into the bull pen from Section 33 of the right field Mezzanine. We spied pumpkins and country-fair-caliber sunflowers during our most recent visit.

Several teams, including the Braves and Tigers, have followed the Mets' lead and now plant veggies in their bull pens.

LUCKY NUMBER: 1966

WHILE 1969 has gone down in baseball lore as the most important year in Mets history, it is unlikely the Miracle season would have occurred if not for a fortuitous turn of events in 1966.

On April 2, 1966, the Mets acquired the rights to University of Southern California pitcher Tom Seaver, thanks to a special lottery that was conducted per orders of Commissioner William D. Eckert.

"Tom Terrific" originally signed with the Atlanta Braves in February 1966, but his contract was later voided when Eckert ruled that the USC season had already begun, signifying the end of the Braves' exclusive bargaining period. The Commish said any team willing to match the Braves' offer should submit a bid. When the Mets, Phillies, and Indians submitted matching offers, their names were thrown into a hat to determine Tom's future home. Champagne bottles popped in Queens when it was announced the Mets entry had come out of the hat—the Magic Hat.

As a rookie in 1967, Seaver won sixteen games. He won another sixteen in 1968. Then, in 1969, he won a "miraculous" twenty-seven games, including a game apiece in the NLCS and October Classic. On April 22, 1970, Seaver set a record that still stands, striking out ten consecutive Padres as the Shea faithful cheered him on. Despite that great performance, Seaver never threw a no-hitter for the Mets, nor has anyone else for that matter.

MAGIC? INDEED!

Every time a Mets player homers, a big red apple emerges triumphantly from the upside-down top hat beyond the fence in center field.

Mets star Mike Piazza went deep during our trip to Shea Stadium, sending into a frenzy the pair of teen-aged girls in the row in front of us. As the ball sailed over the left field wall, they jumped out of their seats and hugged each other, then they started shrieking and pointing down at the field as Piazza trotted around the bases.

"Get ready," one cried. "Get ready. This is going to be good."

The other girl whipped a camera out of her handbag, preparing, we assumed, to snap a shot of the rugged Mets slugger rounding third.

"Chicks dig the sideburns," Kevin said, referring to Piazza's 90210-style facial hair.

"I guess so," Josh said.

But as Piazza trotted past, the gals hardly gave him a look. Then, just as he reached home plate they erupted and began madly snapping pictures of the apple slowly rising out of the Magic Hat. And they weren't alone. Flashbulbs sparkled throughout the stadium, and a warm glow spread over the faces of Mets fans. Then as soon as the apple receded back into the Hat, the trance seemed to pass.

"Bizarre," Kevin said, "simply bizarre."

"I can't grow sideburns," Josh said longingly.

"Bizarre," Kevin said again.

"Not really," Josh said. "I'm Armenian."

THE RETIRED NUMBERS

Notice the four retired numbers hanging behind the visitor's bull pen in left field. What makes these interesting is the fact that only one belonged to a Mets player—41 for Tom Seaver. Of course, 42 is universally retired in honor of Jackie Robinson. And numbers 14 and 37 were worn by Mets managers Gil Hodges and Casey Stengel.

AMAT, AMGN, AMZN . . .

Ah, New York City—the place to make a buck even while relaxing at the ballpark. The message boards that display the pitch type and speed on both the right and left field faces of the Loge deck run stock ticker symbols between every half inning.

Kevin: "Can't we just enjoy the baseball game?"

Josh: "Hey, GE gained fifty-five cents. Peanuts on me!"

Kevin: "Really?"

Josh: "Nah."

Kevin: "There's a surprise."

SAY WHAT?

The batter's eye in center field, which is black during play, lights up with advertising in between innings. We definitely didn't encounter that anywhere else in baseball. And thankfully so.

Stadium Eats

Perhaps because there are so few eating and drinking establishments in the neighborhood surrounding Shea, the Mets have done an excellent job of providing an eclectic concession menu as well as a couple of watering holes inside the stadium. This is one area where Shea handily trumps its Bronx counterpart. So dig in!

AARON'S HOT DOG (Dog Rating)
The sixth Best Hot Dog in the Majors

You have two options: put a little effort into finding a **Glatt's Kosher** stand and get an Aaron's Hot Dog or take the easy route and get a Kahns jumbo dog at just about any Shea Stadium concession location. The choice is yours, but we highly recommend the Aaron's dog, which is not only bigger than the Kahns but firmer. It has a nice tasty finish too.

We give this juicy dog the slight nod over the crosstown Nathan's hot dog at Yankee Stadium.

MAMA'S (Trademark Food)

On the first level concourse behind home plate, you'll find **Mama's Italian Specialties of Corona**. We know $9 seems like a lot for a sandwich, but we took the recommendation of Frank Garcia, the stadium security guard we befriended, and ordered a hot roasted turkey and mozzarella sandwich. The sandwich consisted of approximately ten inches of freshly baked Italian bread stuffed with thin slices of fresh turkey, gooey mozzarella, brown gravy, and roasted red peppers. It was steaming hot and delish. We offer our most hearty endorsement. If you visit Shea Stadium and don't stop by Mama's you'll be doing yourself a disservice. This is one of the best ballpark foods in the Majors.

Other offerings at Mama's included a fresh mozzarella and grilled vegetables sandwich, Mama's Boar's Head Special, which features Genoa salami, mozzarella, mushrooms, and peppers, and assorted salads.

Beware, if you have an Upper Level ticket, once batting practice ends you won't be able to access the first level where Mama's is located. If you don't hit Mama's inside the park, we recommend venturing into Corona where you'll find Mama's original location on 104th Street.

BEST OF THE REST

The **Food Court** in right field on the lower level is accessible from all stadium seating levels but the path to the field level seats is guarded by an usher, so don't get any ideas about sneaking into first level seats from here. If you're in the upper deck, this is a good spot to stand and watch an inning or two at field level, however you will be watching through a net. But hey, it's an upgrade. Plus there are seats and tables where you can chow down and still keep an eye on the action.

At the **Glatt Kosher Stand,** Kevin encountered the best **knish** he'd ever tasted. It was also the first knish he'd ever tasted. It was good though, and baked, not fried like the knish at the Grill Works stands. In case you've never tried knish (like Josh), Kevin said it was best described as "some sort of breaded potato pocket."

Kid Sessions specializes in Italian ice, slush, and churros, which are akin to cinnamon-sprinkled fried dough sticks. Kevin asked another fan what a churro was and she handed him one to try. How nice is that? And it was pretty tasty.

A number of **Sky Scraper Grill** locations are scattered throughout the stadium. We tried the Italian Sausage sandwich, which was nice and spicy—just the way we like 'em.

SAY "NO, THANKS," AND WALK AWAY

Avoid **Caliente Mex Express** and its $7 burrito, especially when the Mexican district on Roosevelt Avenue offers the real stuff and at much cheaper prices. Mexican food, no matter how delicious, should not be expensive.

Kevin, however, had a mighty hankerin' and refused to heed Josh's general warning about stadium burritos. And he paid the price—all night long.

STADIUM SUDS

Located on the first level behind home plate as the name suggests, the **Backstop Bar** offers hard liquor, but not much ambiance. But, hey—hard liquor at the ballpark, and not just for the club level folks! Now we understand the need for the Mobile Arrest Center. Another plus, the Backstop is right next to Mama's.

Casey's Bar and Grill, Stengel's namesake, at least tries to look like a sports bar. Cool pictures of Casey and other memorabilia adorn the walls. The grill features deli sandwiches and pizza. A good place to stand up (there aren't any seats) and drink a quick brew or eat a pastrami sandwich as game time approaches. But calling it a "bar and grill" might be a stretch of the truth. Of course, Casey was known to stretch the truth a bit himself.

Only at Shea

PLANE RACES

Yankee Stadium has its trademark subway races, Miller Park its sausage races, the Metrodome its fishing races. And Shea has Jumbotron jet races.

Each level of the stadium is represented with a different colored jet that corresponds with the color of the seats: orange for field level, blue for the loge, green for the mezzanine, and red for the upper deck. We observed fans cheering halfheartedly for their level's jet to finish first.

The upper-deck plane came through for us with flying colors when we were in town, but we had to wonder what Abner Doubleday would have thought of this ballpark phenomenon, or Orville and Wilbur Wright for that matter?

COW-BELL MAN (Superfan)

Wearing a Mets jersey that bears the name "Cow-Bell Man" across the back, this burly fanatic roams the upper levels of the stadium with his trusty cowbell. Trust us, you'll hear him coming.

Josh: "I didn't know there were cattle farms in the city."

Cow-Bell Man: "Ding, ding, ding."

Josh: "Do you herd dairy cows or steak cows?"

Cow-Bell Man: "Ding, ding, ding."

Josh: "Because I really like steak."

Kevin: "We'll hook you up with some rib eyes in Texas, Josh. Let the poor man be."

The National Baseball Hall of Fame and Museum, Cooperstown, New York

A "must-visit" during your road trip, the Hall of Fame is a convenient stopover on your drive from New York to Toronto. Allow yourself at least a day at the hall to soak up all the history.

From New York City, take I-87 north to I-90 west. From Boston, simply jump on I-90, then get off at Exit 25A which will put you on I-88 west. Continue to Exit 24 at Duanesburg. Take Route 20 west to Route 80 south to Cooperstown.

From the day after Labor Day through the Thursday before Memorial Day weekend, hall hours are 9:00 A.M. to 5:00 P.M. During the summer months, it stays open until 9:00 P.M. Just be sure to plan well in advance with regard to hotel accommodations if planning your visit to coincide with the annual induction-weekend festivities. We recommend staying at one of the many bed-and-breakfasts in New York's Finger Lakes region.

For more information call (888) HALL-OF-FAME or check out www.baseballhalloffame.org.

**THE BRONX,
NEW YORK**

8 miles to Shea Stadium
90 miles to Philadelphia
190 miles to Baltimore
215 miles to Boston

NEW YORK YANKEES,
YANKEE STADIUM

The House That Ruth Built

ALL YOU'VE READ, all the footage you've seen on TV, and all the hype you've heard is true. Yankee Stadium possesses an aura that even Yankee haters must appreciate and respect. Short of stepping out of a time machine and into the Roman Coliseum, fans seeking the pinnacle of sports proving grounds, can do no better than a visit to Yankee Stadium.

Home to twenty-six world champions and forty-one division winners—both records in American professional sports—the stadium does its best to shine by bringing every one of those championship teams to the forefront, as well as the many great players who played on them. Film strips of a storied past flicker on the Jumbotron prior to the game, playing like a choppy home movie before your wondering eyes. The slashing swing of Joe DiMaggio during his fifty-six-game hitting streak; the booming reverberation of Lou Gehrig's inspirational farewell speech; the Babe swatting a big fly; Mickey Mantle gliding back to make a game-saving catch. Memories flash before your eyes and swell in your ears the moment you step out of the dark tunnel and into the bright lights of Yankee Stadium. Maybe there's a hockey rink somewhere in Scandinavia or a soccer pitch in Ireland, or a remote jai alai court in some third-world country that inspires the same degree of awe, mystique, and nostalgia in its own right. But we doubt it. Yankee Stadium has been the unchallenged center of the baseball world for more than eighty years, and shows no signs of surrendering its place of prominence any time soon.

On top of all history, nostalgia, and communal baseball memories that lie within, Yankee Stadium is a beautiful old park. Classy and cavernous, for the past eight decades it has presented visiting players the most imposing environment in the Majors. Upon entering this mystique-laden behemoth, we found ourselves overwhelmed as we surveyed the towering upper decks, the decorative white arches or "filigree" mounted high above the outfield, and the baseball diamond that has played host to so many of the game's great moments. The Yankees' remarkable history of success makes it virtually impossible to recount all of the team's great moments in a book of this format but we will try to hit on a few of the highlights.

It all began inauspiciously enough for the team that would become the Bronx Bombers, with the fledgling American League franchise failing to win a pennant in its first twenty seasons. But once the Yankees got rolling, they dominated the Major Leagues like no other team before them or since appearing in twenty-nine World Series between 1921 and 1962 and claiming twenty World Championships.

The Yankees began as the American League Baltimore Orioles in 1901 then moved to the northern end of Manhattan in 1903. The New York Highlanders took to the field at New York American League Ballpark—aka Hilltop Park—despite protests from the New York Giants camp. Giants management was afraid the Yankees would eat into their fan base and threaten their sustainability. For a long time New York was a big enough town for both teams—as well as the Brooklyn Dodgers— but in the end these fears proved justifiable.

Hilltop Park was located on the west side of Broadway between 165th Street and 168th Street in Manhattan's Washington Heights district, at the highest point of Manhattan Island. The ballpark offered bird's-eye views of the Hudson River and the Palisades in New Jersey. The center field fence measured 502 feet from home plate.

In their second season, the Highlanders, or Hilltoppers as some fans and sports writers dubbed them, challenged the Boston Pilgrims (who would later become the Red Sox) for the AL crown. In the end New York finished a game and a half behind their neighbors to the north in the standings. And thus, a great rivalry was born. Who knew then that decades later the Red Sox and Yankees would still perennially jostle for AL bragging rights? That a Bambino would curse the Red Sox and bless the Yankees? That the two teams would stage an epic battle in 1949, punctuated by a Yankees win over the Sox on the last day of the season to clinch the pennant by a single game? That the two teams would finish tied for first in 1978, setting the stage for Bucky Dent's dramatic home run in a one-game playoff in Boston? That two of Boston's greatest stars—Wade Boggs and Roger Clemens—would win World Series titles in New York after failing to do so in Boston?

Baseball certainly was a different game when the Boston/New York rivalry began. Consider this: Highlanders pitcher Jack Chesbro won forty-one games in 1904, pitching

exterior

Photo by Kevin O'Connell

forty-eight complete games and 454 innings. Today, most premiere pitchers don't win that many games or throw that many innings over two seasons.

After regularly finishing in the AL's second division while the Red Sox racked up World Championships in the 1900s and 1910s, the Yankees seized control of their own destiny in 1919, purchasing Babe Ruth's contract from Boston for $125,000 and a $300,000 loan. The Yankees have been a dynasty ever since. And

interior

Photo by Sean O'Connell

the Red Sox have yet to win another World Series. Playing regularly in the outfield for the first time in his career after pitching for the Red Sox, Ruth hit fifty-four home runs in 1920, shattering the record of twenty-nine he had set the year before. While today we speculate that players are on "the juice" when they exhibit such stunning power surges, Ruth's breakout had more to do with the advent of the juiced or "lively" ball that was introduced in 1920. A year later, the Yankees made it to their first World Series—losing to the Giants in an all–Polo Grounds affair in 1921. The same two teams met again the next year, with the Giants prevailing again.

During the thirteen years prior to Yankee Stadium's opening in 1923, the Yankees had shared the Polo Grounds with the National League's New York Giants. When the Yanks and their slugging Bambino began outdrawing the Giants by one hundred thousand fans per season, they received what amounted to an eviction notice from the Giants. After moving into their new digs across the Harlem River, the Yankees gained a measure of immediate revenge, by besting their former landlords in the 1923 World Series.

The first triple-decked baseball facility to be built and first to be termed a "stadium," Yankee Stadium opened on April 18, 1923, with the home team defeating Boston 4–1, behind a Ruth three-run homer. Constructed in just 284 days, the stadium accommodated more than seventy-four thousand fans on the day of its opening, more than twice the capacity of most other parks in existence at the time. Prior to the replacement of the original wooden bleachers with seats in the 1930s and the enforcement of new fire laws, the stadium often housed crowds approaching seventy-five thousand people.

In the post-Ruth era, new stars like Gehrig, Bill Dickey, DiMaggio, Mantle, Phil Rizzuto, and Yogi Berra continued to win championships for the Yankees. From 1936 to 1939, New York won four straight World Series. The Yanks put together another string of five championships in a row from 1949 to 1953, and combined with the New York Giants and Brooklyn Dodgers to bring the title home to New York nine times in a ten-year span (1949–58) with only Milwaukee's victory over the Yankees in 1957 bucking the trend. Prior to the departure of the Dodgers and Giants, New York was truly the baseball hub of the universe.

Suddenly New York's lone team, the Yankees reached the October Classic four years running, 1960–1964, including a win over the San Francisco Giants in 1962 and a loss to the Los Angeles Dodgers in 1963.

In the 1970s, fiery manager Billy Martin led the Yanks into battle, bolstered by a roster that included larger-than-life stars like Reggie Jackson, Thurman Munson, Ron Guidry, Catfish Hunter, and Goose Gossage. The Yankees may not have been a lovable team in the dying days of disco, but there's no denying they had an aura about them that was second to none. The "Bronx Zoo" became the term that typified the team, as owner George Steinbrenner feuded with Martin—whom he hired and fired five times. Martin and Jackson once came to blows in the dugout. Munson and Red Sox catcher Carlton Fisk squared off in a brawl at home plate. But through it all the Yankees kept winning, bringing home the World Series trophy in 1977 and 1978.

The 1970s was also an important decade for Yankee Stadium. In 1974 and 1975 the Yanks played their home games in crosstown Shea Stadium while the House That Ruth Built was nearly completely demolished and then rebuilt. During these renovations the outfield wall was brought closer to the plate, removing the center field monuments from the field of play. Even so, the field's most distinctive feature remains the deep gap in left center field, known as Death Valley—the place where long fly balls go to die. The fence originally measured 500 feet from home plate before the plate was moved in 1924 to eliminate the "Bloody Angle" in right field, changing the distance to 490 feet. Subsequent renovations brought the fence steadily closer to the plate: in 1937 to 457 feet, in 1976 to 430, in 1985 to 411, and in 1988 to its current 399.

Dave Winfield, Rickey Henderson, and Don Mattingly led the Yankees of the 1980s but to no avail as New York failed to capture a World Championship in the Decade of Decadence, marking the Yankees' first ten-year drought since they started winning titles in the 1920s. By 1990, New York had fallen to the basement of the AL East. Adding insult to injury, Steinbrenner was forced by the commissioner's office to temporarily relinquish control of the team when it was revealed that he had attempted to gain incriminating evidence from a reputed gambler about Winfield. The Big Stein had often derided Winfield for not putting up big enough numbers to justify his lofty contract and Winfield had shot more than a few barbs back at the Boss in the *Daily News*, precipitating the incident.

With Steinbrenner back in the picture, but meddling less, the dynasty righted itself under the management of Joe Torre in the 1990s, beginning with a return to the playoffs in 1995 and a World Series victory over the Braves in 1996.

Gone were the days of the Bronx Zoo's tough and nasty image. Led by likable figures like Bernie Williams, Derek Jeter, Andy Pettitte, and David Cone, the 1998 Yanks set new records with 114 regular season wins and 125 total wins, counting their 3 against the Rangers in the Division Series, 4 against the Indians in the ALCS, and 4 against the Padres, whom they swept in the World Series.

The next season the Yankees and Red Sox met in the postseason for the first time ever, with the AL East champs downing the Wild Card Sox in the ALCS en route to another World Championship.

The Yankees made it three in a row, beating the Mets in the 2000 Series. With the win, fifth-year Yankee shortstop Derek Jeter collected his fourth World Series ring.

Kevin: "Do you think he wears two on each hand? Or all four on one hand like in his famous *Sports Illustrated* cover shot? Or do you think he gets his toes involved?"

Josh: "Sorry, I'm a Red Sox fan. I don't know the first thing about ring etiquette."

TRIVIA TIMEOUT

Granny Smith: The Yankees have honored fifteen players by retiring their numbers, but only fourteen different numbers are retired. Which number is retired twice and which two players wore it? (Hint: they played the same position.)

Look for the answers in the text.

With the Yankees' remarkable success over the years, it is easy to forget that Yankee Stadium has provided the stage for a number of memorable nonbaseball moments as well. So let us remember a few.

In 1923 Boxer Benny Leonard out-slugged Lou Tendler to win the lightweight title at Yankee Stadium. Since then, more than thirty title fights have taken place in the Bronx, including Joe Louis's first-round knockout of Max Schmeling in 1938 and Muhammad Ali's defeat of Ken Norton in 1976.

The stadium has also hosted its share of football games beginning with the 1923 Army-Navy game. In 1928, Knute Rockne issued his famous "Win One for the Gipper" speech in the visitors' locker room, inspiring Notre Dame to beat Army, 12–6. The New York football Giants called the stadium "home" from 1956 to 1973. They played the first sudden-death overtime game in NFL history at Yankee Stadium, falling to the Baltimore Colts, 23–17, in the 1958 NFL championship game that is still widely regarded as one of the best football games ever played.

During their visits to the United States, Popes Paul VI (1965) and John Paul II (1982) celebrated Masses in Yankee Stadium.

Josh: "Those Popes. What front-runners."

Kevin: "They never visited Fenway, eh?"

Sellout Index: 15% of games sell out
Seating Capacity: 57,545
Ticket Office: (718) 293-6000
www.yankees.com

Josh: "No."

Kevin: "Well, you can't blame them. There are churches in Boston that seat more than Fenway."

Getting a Choice Seat

Unless the Yankees are involved in a late-season pennant race or are playing the Mets or Red Sox, it isn't difficult to score tickets on game day. Great tickets may not be available, but you'll at least be able to get into the park. Tier Reserved seats and bleacher seats are available at the box office, and fans who don't mind hitting the ATM will find plenty of scalpers trolling the streets.

Field Championship (Boxes 1–80)

These infield boxes are available only to corporate season ticket holders and VIPs (Paul McCarthy, Rudy Giuliani, Woody Allen—you've seen 'em on the tube). The ushers won't even allow "regular" folks into them during batting practice or after the game. We were, however, able to sneak into Yankee Stadium's exclusive Stadium Club, but more on that later. As for the Field Championship seats, we were able to ascertain that they are the widest seats in the Stadium, are cushioned, and come with their own cup holders. But don't feel bad to be missing out on such great amenities. The slope of the lower boxes is so gradual that the highfalutin folks who sit here inevitably have a sea of heads and hats blocking their view.

Main Box MVP (Boxes 201–221, 247–285, 202–238, 270–288)

Let's clear something up that applies to all Yankee Stadium seating sections with the exception of the bleachers: the odd-numbered boxes and sections are on the right field side and the even ones are on the left field side. Easy enough to remember, right?

Now to the Main Box MVP seats: a limited number of these are made available to the general public. They're great seats, with only the Field Championship boxes between them and the infield grass. We recommend Boxes 201–238 behind the plate.

Field Boxes (Boxes 81–103, 82–138)

Odd-numbered boxes 81–103 are located between the first-base bag and right field foul pole. We don't like these because the seats are angled parallel with the foul line, pointing toward left-center field rather than the infield. If you're bent on heckling the right fielder, you'll be happier with Main Box seats in 327–339, which face the plate and are cheaper.

The Field Boxes along the line in left field (even-numbered 82–138) are positioned at a better angle. We recommend Boxes 114–136, which face the plate in fair territory behind the left field wall. Just watch out for Boxes 110 and 112, where the views from certain seats are obstructed by the foul pole.

Main Boxes (Boxes 290–350, 287–339)

Due to the limited number of Field Boxes on the right field side, these boxes place fans closer to the playing field than those in left field do. Odd-numbered Boxes 327–339 in right field's home run territory are outstanding, whereas even-numbered 326–350 in left field aren't as good because they have a dozen rows of Field Box seats between them and the field. Just watch out for Boxes 323 and 325 in right field, which are screened by the foul pole.

Main Reserved (Sections 1–36)

While the overhanging Loge deck doesn't affect the overhead view in the first few rows of the Main Reserved, fans in these rows con-tend with brutal aisle traffic between the Main Boxes and Main Reserved. And in the rows far back enough to look over the traffic, fans lose sight of fly balls because of the overhang. It's a lose-lose situation. We do not recommend the Main Reserved. The Yankee Stadium experience just isn't the same when you're under a roof, unable to see the steep blue upper deck and the regal flags and white facade atop the stadium in the outfield—not to mention the flight of routine fly balls and the Jumbotron. Sections 31, 33, and 35 are especially laughable since the bleachers, just a few feet to their right, sell for a quarter of the price and provide a better view.

Blame It on the Big Stein

Big Men Beware: Aside from providing the worst view of the skyline in the stadium, the last row of Main Reserved sections provides less leg room than the kiddie-sized bumper cars at Coney Island. Either the architect screwed up on this one, or Yankees owner George Steinbrenner got greedy. Our bet's on the Big Stein. In any case, if you're taller than five foot, seven inches, Row H will cause you serious lap issues, as it has four inches less leg room than any other row in the stadium.

Loge/Loge MVP (Boxes 419–545, 440–548)

The MVP Loge seats on the infield provide a great view of the field, and because they're well above ground level the overhang of the Tier level above doesn't pose a problem, except on the highest of infield pop-ups. The outfield Loge seats aren't bad either.

Tier Box/Tier Reserved (Sections 1–36)

The view from the upper deck or "Tier" level is impressive. High above the field, these seats offer a vantage point from which fans can really appreciate the enormity of Yankee Stadium. In many Tier sections, however, the under-hang of the Tier limits the view of the playing field. So you need to be selective when purchasing Tier seats. Sections 1–10 behind home plate provide a clear view of the entire field. But once you start making your way down the baselines, the view of the foul line and several feet of fair territory on your side of the field become obscured. Up until the foul poles, the Tier sections on the first-base side (11–25) are better than those on the third-base side (12–26). However, once beyond the foul poles, the left field sections (28–36) are much better than those in right (27–35) because fans can see the entire field from the Tier in left, while in right, the under-hang obscures the right field fence and twenty-five feet of field in front of it.

We didn't see much reason to pay twice as much for Tier Boxes, which situate fans just a few feet closer to the airspace over the field than the Tier Reserved does. We also issue this vertigo warning: the Tier is exceptionally steep. If you are afraid of heights or are accident prone, you'd be wise to stay away.

Yuck! The Nastiest Seats in the Big Leagues

Dodger Stadium this ain't. Rows H through M of the Tier Reserved give the term "Bronx Bombers" new meaning. Pigeons roost in the light banks directly above these seats and smear them with—you guessed it—bird poop. Excepting the sections directly behind home plate (1–8) which are not in the drop zone, the "Poop Seats" show up all the way around the Tier level. And if the *seats* are this disgusting—and trust us they are—what do you think the *people* who sit in them look like after a game? We didn't stick around to find out.

Bleachers (Sections 37–43, 49–59)

Yes, they're actual bleachers and provide no seat back; yes, they're alcohol free; and yes, they don't offer access to the rest of the stadium or Monument Park. But you can't beat the price or atmosphere. The right field bleachers (37–43) are significantly better than those in left (49–59) because they're much closer to the action. To begin with, left field is deeper than right field. Add the 80-foot-deep Monument Park that sits between the outfield fence and the first row of the left field bleachers, and you're looking at a 100- to 150-foot disparity (depending on exactly where you're sitting) between the right and left field bleachers' proximity to the plate.

"And the Sign Says, 'You Gotta Have a Membership Card to Get Inside'"

Normally we don't critique VIP seating or dining or rest room areas because we know they're usually off-limits to our readers and because they're usually off-limits to us. Plus these exclusive areas usually provide about as much authentic ballpark experience as watching a game on TV while lounging in the swimming pool. While we weren't able to infiltrate the aforementioned Field Championship Boxes, we did gain access to Yankee Stadium's exclusive Stadium Club located on the lower level beneath Section 14. This highly exclusive bar and restaurant is supposed to be available only to Field Championship season ticket holders. A line of bouncers at the door make sure it stays exclusive, and there's a special pass that season ticket holders get—one for each game—to ensure exclusivity.

We realize you may never see the inside of "the Club," so we'll give you a taste of what it was like. Man, was it exclusive! The hardwood floors were shiny and not the least bit grimy like most ballpark floors. There was a full bar. The game appeared on multiple TVs. Our waitress was shapely and attentive and she even laughed at a few of Kevin's jokes until she realized we weren't going to order anything.

The Stadium Club dress code was obviously designed to promote exclusivity. Among the prohibitions listed on a sign at the door were "muscle-shirts, sleeveless T-shirts, tank tops, shorts above mid-thigh, abbreviated attire, and rubber thongs." The term "rubber thongs" slowed our minds down for a moment, and not necessarily in a bad way. We let some mental images form as we wondered aloud if this were really a problem—ladies showing up in skimpy little rubber thongs—so we asked our waitress if the thong rule was indicative of a thriving S&M scene in NYC. Sadly, she informed us that the term "rubber thongs" was supposed to mean flip-flops, worn on people's feet, and not to the type of thong worn to conceal—but just barely—a woman's bum on the beach. Incidentally we were told that *that* type of thong—rubber or otherwise—would be prohibited by the "abbreviated attire" clause. Pretty exclusive, huh?

Kidding aside, the only feature of the Stadium Club actually worth noting was the series of stained glass windows along the back wall of the sitting area. These windows depicted the Yankee logo, the classic overlaid "NY" found on Yankee caps, and the faces of famous Yankees like Babe Ruth, Mickey Mantle, and Roger Maris. The images of the players cut in glass seemed almost holy.

How did we get into the Stadium Club? A season ticket holder Kevin met in the sausage line volunteered his passes after Kev talked up our book and corresponding magical mystery tour of the Majors. And you thought New Yorkers were unfriendly?

The Black Market

Being the intrepid baseball reporters that we are, and upholding our vow to test everything hands on, Josh left it up to Kevin to get the lowdown on the River Avenue scalper scene, even though we already had tickets to the game.

"What about that guy?" Josh pestered. "What's wrong with him?"

"Let me pick my moment," Kevin said.

"But that guy looked good. Are you sure you can handle this?"

"Do you want to do it?" Kevin asked, more than just a little bit annoyed.

"It's starting to look like I might have to," Josh said.

"Be my guest," said Kevin.

"Well . . . I . . ." Josh stammered.

"I'll tell you what, go test some pork kebobs and leave this to me."

If Kevin was dragging his feet, it was understandable. He considered approaching one of the Bronx's rugged young scalpers and saying, "Excuse me, my good man. We're writing a book and were wondering if you could spare some time to teach us the ins and outs of the local scalper scene, in order that we might help our readers gain the upper hand when haggling with you." This didn't seem like a wise move. He

---

SEATING TIP

WE KNOW YOU'RE PLANNING to hit Shea Stadium during your NYC visit, and we hope you're thinking about catching a minor league Brooklyn Cyclone or Staten Island Yankee game too, but if you can find the time we highly recommend attending two games at Yankee Stadium. Spend the first one in the Tier or right field Main Boxes from which you'll be able to access Monument Park before the game and check out all of the angles and views the stadium has to offer. Then spend your second game with the hard-core fans in the right field bleachers. Just don't let on if you're a Red Sox or Mets fan.

---

decided, rather, to pose as a ticketless pigeon, then shy away from a deal at the last minute.

He looked around, found a "businessman" in a leather jacket, and gave him a "Let's do business," nod.

"What you want?" the scalper asked.

"Something in the boxes."

The man flashed a $55 Main Championship seat.

"How much?" Kevin asked.

"Hundred."

"Too much for me," Kevin said sheepishly.

The man made a motion as if to walk away, then said, "What d'you wanna pay, hombre?" He was willing to deal, but Kevin was faced with his initial fear. If he named a price and the scalper agreed to it, then presto-bango, he'd be expected to purchase a ticket he didn't need.

"How about thirty?" Kevin said, low-balling to the point of being ridiculous.

The man looked as though he'd been stabbed.

Kevin shrugged an "oh, well," and began to slink away. Hopefully, he had gotten enough information to satisfy Josh, who was watching from a safe distance while working on his fifth pork kebob in two days.

But the consummate professional wasn't finished with Kevin. "It's a sellout," he called out. "You ain't gonna find seats like this for less than $80." He was putting on the hard sell, and something about his desperation made Kevin feel all the more guilty for wasting his time. When he finally broke free of the man, Kevin was suddenly set upon on all sides by a feeding frenzy of other scalpers.

"No, no, I already have a ticket," he tried to explain.

"What? You playing games, wise guy?" a voice called out.

"No. He's looking to trade up!" another voice announced.

"No," Kevin protested. "I don't need a ticket."

"Sure you do, buddy," a rough face said.

"Listen, half price right over here. Best deal in Yankee Town."

Kevin was in the midst of slightly antagonized hucksters while Josh was sucking down a skewer of tasty pork. That seemed about right. The moral of this tale: scalpers are professionals who are out to make a profit, but that doesn't mean you can't get good tickets near face value in Yankee Town. These tough guys make their living factoring in variables like the chance of showers, the star power on the opposing team, and the volume of people filing down the subway steps. And like stockbrokers watching the price of an IPO plummet, scalpers know when it's better to get something rather than nothing. The longer Kevin demurred, the lower the prices fell. Of course, he did have the fact that he wasn't really interested in buying on his side.

Before/After the Game

Most folks think of the Bronx as the seedy core of the Big Apple—an unsavory place where crime and delinquency run wild. While the "scenery" on the Cross-Bronx Expressway hasn't done much to help the Bronx's image, the borough's "Rotten Apple Rap" has also been promulgated by the Big Stein himself. As a negotiating ploy while struggling to iron out a new stadium lease agreement with the city, King George blasphemed the Bronx and threatened to move his team out of the borough. He portrayed the streets around the stadium as a veritable war zone. Then when attendance predictably dropped in the wake of his smear campaign, he cited this as additional evidence against the Bronx. Not surprisingly, he changed his tune as soon as a new lease agreement was struck. But the damage had been done.

All of that said, the Bronx ain't Disneyland. But if you don't stray far from the stadium and make a point to come in with the ball game crowd and go out with it, you shouldn't encounter problems. We were in town for Friday and Saturday night games and while we elected to keep our wallets in our front pants pockets to play it safe, at no point did we feel threatened. And Josh tends to feel threatened in the mall, in the woods, alone in a phone booth, just about anywhere—so that's saying something.

Getting to Yankee Stadium

Driving into the Bronx means contending with brutal traffic. On the plus side, the parking situation is pretty convenient: a well-lit multilevel garage sits right next to the stadium on the corner of River Avenue and 157th Street, and there are a number of other lots nearby. Signs for these appear almost immediately after exiting I-87 (the Major Deegan Expressway) at Exit 4 coming from the northbound lane or Exit 6 from the southbound lane. However, because of the traffic we recommend taking the subway to Yankee Stadium if possible. The 161st Street Stop is located right in front of the stadium on River Avenue. It is serviced by the number 4 Lexington Line, the B Train (weekdays only), and the D Train. A trip from midtown Manhattan takes thirty minutes on a number 4 local train, or twenty minutes on an express. At $2.00 per ride, it's a bargain.

Another alternative is New York Waterway's Yankee Clipper Ferry that docks on the Harlem River and is a short walk from the ballpark. The ferry costs $10 per round-trip for adults and $7.50 for children. It stops at piers in both Manhattan and New Jersey, and arrives at the stadium half an hour before game time. It departs half an hour after the last out. For more information call (800) 53-FERRY.

Outside Attractions

THE BABE RUTH TOUR

Well worth the $10 price for adults and $5 for children, the stadium tour offered by the Yankees is available every day at noon, except when there's a day game. The tour brings fans down to the dugouts, into the Yankee clubhouse, up to the press box, and out to Monument Park. You don't need a reservation so long as you show up at the Press Gate by 11:30 A.M. But just to be sure, call the Babe Ruth Tour hotline at (718) 579-4531.

DIAMONDS IN THE ROUGH

You'll notice youth softball and soccer fields located on River Avenue just a block from the stadium. It is *really* cool that grade school kids have the chance to play ball in the shadows of Yankee Stadium. However, it is *really* shameful that these fields are in such poor condition. Someone (King George or New York City) should put a few dollars into upgrading these.

WATERING HOLES AND OUTSIDE EATS

There are a number of bars and eateries on River Avenue that are all more or less identical—overpriced, barely on the clean side of condemned, and filled with just enough memorabilia to make them worth a quick look-see. For those who don't mind venturing a bit deeper into the South Bronx, we suggest checking out the food and spirits on nearby Gerard Street. Follow 161st Street just one block away from the stadium, take a right, and you'll be there. If time allows before or after the game, we also recommend checking out a couple of sports bars in Manhattan.

BILLY'S SPORTS BAR AND RESTAURANT (River Avenue)

Here, you'll find mural busts of Billy Martin, Babe Ruth, Mickey Mantle, Joe DiMaggio, and Marilyn Monroe. We weren't brave enough to try anything off the menu, but the beers were cold and frosty.

STAN'S SPORTS BAR (River Avenue)

This is the place to be if you're twenty-two, single, and looking to "bump uglies" with a stranger or two. But on the George Costanza scale, Kevin gives the men's room just one star out of ten—and that ain't good.

THE BALLPARK BAR AND GRILL (River Avenue)

Features bottled beer on ice, fifty bowling lanes, air-hockey, retro video games (including Miss Pac Man), and a quickie fast-food menu. What more do you need?

YANKEE PIZZA AND BURGERS (River Avenue)

The line of folks waiting at this order-at-the-window fast-food shack alerted us to the fact that it was a fan favorite. We recommend picking up a skewer of spicy pork kebobs as you walk past. This is the most satisfying meat on River Avenue. It's tender, tasty, and hot, hot, hot!

U.S. CHICKEN (Gerard Street)

This little joint is the culinary highlight of Yankee Town offering great eats at great prices. It costs more to get a single regular hot dog ($4.75) inside Yankee Stadium than it does to get four pieces of fried chicken, a jumbo order of french fries, and a soda ($4.50) at USC. And this isn't any old chicken platter we're talking about. The bird is tender, plump, and moist. The fries are plentiful. The soda pop is ice cold and sparkling with carbonation. Aside from the scrumptious chicken, we recommend the jumbo shrimp meal, which features seven large shrimp, fries, and a soda for $4.25. Other deals include forty chicken wings for $10, a burger meal for $4, a double burger meal for $5, and twenty-one fried shrimp for $3.25. The menu also includes barbecued ribs, pizza, gyros, corn on the cob, and mashed potatoes. The only drawback is there's no seating area—just a counter to stand at while you chow. But don't let that scare you off. U.S. Chicken rules!

THE NEWSROOM SPORTS BAR
AND JAZZ CLUB (Gerard Street)

Before or after stuffing yourself with chicken, consider stopping into this quirky little bar right next door. The Newsroom features live Jazz from 10:00 P.M. until 3:00 A.M. after ball games and $3 beers. The decor combines sports and jazz, which in our book go together almost as well as farming and Nintendo. Still, it's a friendly place with cheap drinks.

THE YANKEE TAVERN (Gerard Street)

Located across the street from the Newsroom, the Yankee Tavern is the cleanest and most upscale of establishments in the South Bronx—not that that's saying a heck of a lot. Catering to a slightly older crowd than the drink-'em-quick bars on River Avenue, the Tavern features a separate dining room and pub menu that offers such eclectic delights as a shrimp parmesan sub. Kevin tried the chicken parmesan dinner and gave it two red thumbs up.

THE ESPN ZONE (Times Square)

Perhaps you've visited one of the other ESPN Zones across the country and figure you've already seen the zillion-TV-screen theme, the monitors over the urinals, the interactive games, the ESPN set in the dining room, and the unspectacular $12 hamburger plate.

But there's still a reason to duck into the Times Square ESPN Zone. Don't even order anything. Just say you're going upstairs to the bar and on your way up check out the 10-by-12-foot Babe Ruth photo mosaic on the wall. Composed entirely of baseball cards of Yankee players, up close it looks like nothing more than an impressive display of cards. But as you step away from the wall, the image of the Bambino's face comes clearly into focus. Artist Robert Silvers used two thousand cards to create the image in 1999. Among the cards we spotted on the wall were those of Yankee greats and not-so-greats like Bob Shirley, Al Downing, Jose Rijo, Billy Martin, Wade Boggs, Chris Chambliss, Walt Williams, and 1,993 others.

MICKEY MANTLE'S RESTAURANT
(42 Central Park South)

The mural renderings of Yankee Stadium and Fenway Park are impressive, as are the game jerseys (Mantle, Ted Williams, Jackie Robinson), magazine covers, and autographs adorning the walls of this upscale pub. The in-house souvenir shop offers a diverse selection of memorabilia, too. Just bring your wallet. A burger goes for $13, and most entrées check in somewhere between $18 and $30. We were informed that steak and seafood were the house specialties, but since we had already coughed up $7 apiece for a draft beer, we were "priced out" when it came time for dinner, and can't vouch for the food's quality. It *looked* and *smelled* good, though.

In case you're wondering, the owners purchased the naming rights from the Mick in 1989. Beyond that, he never had much to do with the place.

THE SOUVENIR SCENE (River Avenue)

Notice anything peculiar about the five or six food/souvenir/drinking establishments directly across the street from Yankee Stadium? How about the fact that they all bear the "Stan" name? From **Stan's Sports World** to **Stan the Man's Baseball Land**, to **Stan's Sports Bar**, half the block is monopolized by an elusive mystery man known only as "Stan," or sometimes "Stan the Man." This entrepreneur has obviously done well by the Yankees, and maybe that's why his stores feature 99 percent Yankee garb, instead of the usual 70 percent (or so) hometown bias. Even the non-Stan-affiliated shops in Yankee Town sell almost exclusively Yankee merchandise. We searched hat, shirt, and baseball card racks for anything without an NY emblem on it, and found only a single autographed picture of Pete Rose to represent the other twenty-nine teams and the National Baseball Hall of Fame (sarcasm intended).

So if you're looking for a Kansas City Royals cap, you're out of luck. If you're in the market for any and all things Yankee, this may very well be the epicenter of your universe. But shop around. Kevin price-checked the cost of a fitted Yankee cap and found that inside the stadium and on the Plaza it cost $30; at Stan's shops it cost $27–$30 and at **Ballpark Souvenir** on River Avenue, it cost $24.

THE PLAZA

In between the stadium entrance gates and the parking garage, sits a large brick plaza called "the Plaza," which is similar to the plaza at Camden Yards, except unlike the one in Baltimore which is inside the park and accessible only to ticket holders, this plaza is outside the gates and accessible to all. This proves a surprisingly good place to haggle with scalpers, but it doesn't impress in the way of food, souvenirs, and goings-on. All of the souvenir, hot dog, and pretzel stands are owned by the same company, instead of by the mom-and-pop operations found outside other stadiums. As a result, the food is all the same and the vendors are college kids making $7 an hour; there's no diversity of tastes, and no diversity of characters. Further detracting from the atmosphere, credit card companies and other promoters—given permission by the team to set up shop here—accost fans at every step, offering to trade bobble-head dolls or free Yankees shirts for social security numbers and mothers' maiden names. And all the while, the 1914 Circus Calliope boxcar emits an incessant stream of carousel music that seems designed to drive fans from the Plaza. Perhaps the music is meant to evoke an old-time "Take me out to the ball game" feel, but Josh nearly bought a souvenir bat to smash the thing.

One "new" Yankee Stadium landmark pointed out to us by our pal Mark Alberti was born on the plaza shortly after the renovation of the mid-1970s. While on the Plaza, check out the large baseball bat that rises up right near the stadium. This was actually a working chimney for years before Joe Garagiola looked at it one day and thought that if you added a knob to the chimney's top, it would look like a bat. Days later, he pitched this idea to Louisville Slugger and the bat manufacturing company bit. With some cosmetic changes, the chimney was transformed into a replica of a Babe Ruth model baseball bat. For the new generation of Yankees fans, "the Bat" has become a meeting ground for friends before and after games.

The Plaza hot dogs are Hebrew National foot-longs that sell for a dollar less than the foot-longs inside the stadium. Why Plaza dogs are served on tiny regular-sized buns is anyone's guess. Who wants to eat a dog that's hanging out two inches on either side? Likewise, we were astonished that the vendors don't let fans apply their own condiments (kraut, ketchup, mustard), but insist on doing it themselves. Such is the cost-cutting arrogance of a corporate weenie machine that knows it has a market cornered. That said, the Hebrew dog is tasty despite being largely naked and imprecisely topped.

Inside the Stadium

Take a moment to breathe in the history as you look at the field for the first time. Sure, the stadium has been renovated extensively over the years, and sure the outfield fences have been moved around a bit—but think about it. This is where Babe Ruth swatted homer upon homer to usher in the lively ball era in the early 1920s. This is where Lou Gehrig delivered perhaps the most moving speech in American sports history in 1939, telling 61,808 fans that he considered himself "the luckiest man on the face of the earth," for having the chance to play for them, although he'd just been diagnosed with a terminal illness. This is where Maris and Mantle staged their epic battle in 1961. This is where Chris Chambliss connected on a walk-off homer to win the final game of the 1976 ALCS,

and was mobbed by fans who accompanied him around the bases. This is where "Mr. October," Reggie Jackson, went deep on three consecutive pitches to ice the Los Angeles Dodgers in the 1977 World Series. This is where George Brett of the Royals went ballistic in 1983 after his home run against Rich Gossage was ruled an out because he had too much pine tar on his bat. This is where Don Larsen achieved perfection against the Brooklyn Dodgers in the 1956 Series and where David Wells and David Cone pitched the fifteenth and sixteenth perfect games in MLB history in the 1990s. This is where all the great Yankees earned their stripes. You stand in the presence of greatness, a sports dynasty like none other.

This process of reflection will make you feel either tingly with nostalgia or nauseated with disgust, depending upon whether or not you subscribe to the motto "Peace, love, and Yankee baseball." But even if you're the second most ardent Yankee hater (with Josh, of course, being numero uno), here's betting you'll find yourself admitting that Yankee Stadium is an impressive monument to the game you love.

Ballpark Features

THE ESSENCE OF "CLASS"

One of Yankee Stadium's most striking features is the regal white filigree that runs the length of the outfield high above the bleachers. With a flag adorning each buttress, these charming arches lend an air of dignity to the field below that seems more befitting a theater or cathedral. Well done!

The steel on this facade is one of the few remaining ornaments left over from the old Yankee Stadium. It was removed from the old roof and placed in its current location during the most recent renovation. It also changed color, from green to white at this time to better match the new blue and white stadium interior. Mantle once dented it with a homer—the longest in stadium history—that hit the old facade at the leftmost edge of the right field grandstands and bounced back onto the field.

DEATH TO FLIES

Your eyes will also be drawn to Death Valley in left center. Try to picture the pasture as it was prior to the remodeling efforts that brought the fence in by more than one hundred feet. Even if you're a person with the dullest of imaginations—say, the architect of New Comiskey Park in Chicago—you'll have little trouble envisioning this. That's because the original retaining wall that separated the playing field from the left field bleachers still stands. You'll see it separating the bleachers from Monument Park, behind the new wall.

MONUMENTALLY COOL

Get to Yankee Stadium early and take a stroll through Monument Park. The gate is located at field level in front of Section 36 and is open from the time the ballpark gates open until forty-five minutes before the first pitch. Over the years, television has shown you glimpses of the retired numbers, plaques, and monuments beyond the left field fence, but Monument Park needs to be experienced firsthand. With fourteen retired numbers, celebrating the careers of fifteen players, the Yankees honor more players than any other team in MLB. The retirees are: number 1 for Billy Martin, number 3 for Babe Ruth, number 4 for Lou Gehrig, number 5 for Joe DiMaggio, number 7 for Mickey Mantle, number 8 for Yogi Berra, number 8 for Bill Dickey, number 9 for Roger Maris, number 10 for Phil Rizzuto, number 15 for Thurman Munson, number 16 for Whitey Ford, number 23 for Don Mattingly, number 32 for Elston Howard, number 37 for Casey Stengel, and number 44 for Reggie Jackson.

Notice the two number 8s. Berra inherited fellow catcher Dickey's number 8 in 1947. Between them, the Hall of Fame backstops hit 560 home runs and played in twenty-five of twenty-eight All-Star Games between 1933 and 1062. They both later coached and managed the Yankees. In 1972 their numbers 8 were simultaneously retired during a ceremony at the stadium.

The Yankees made Gehrig's number 4 the first uniform number ever retired in baseball when they paid the "Iron Horse" the ultimate compliment in 1939.

Munson is also honored in the Yankees locker room where his old locker remains empty to this day, with the number 15 posted at its top. The thirty-two-year-old catcher died tragically on August 2, 1979, when the plane he was piloting crashed in Canton, Ohio. More than fifty-one thousand fans turned out at Yankee Stadium for a memorial service the next day.

The original three monuments—honoring manager Miller Huggins, Ruth, and Gehrig—stand in their original location where they were in fair play until the 1974–75 renovations brought the fence in by twenty-seven feet. Back in the day, these obstructions, along with the flagpole, which was also in play, gave opposing outfielders fits, while DiMaggio and Mantle learned to play around them flawlessly.

The Mantle monument was added in 1996. We're not sure why there isn't one honoring Joltin' Joe. There should be.

Mounted on the original outfield wall are bronze plaques honoring the Yankee players whose numbers have been retired as well as a number of other famous Yankees, including Lefty Gomez, Allie Reynolds, Joe McCarthy, and Ed Barrow. Barrow was the former Red Sox manager who converted Babe Ruth from pitcher to outfielder. After switching sides (noticing a pattern here?), Barrow became the first Yankee general manager to bring the team a pennant in 1921. Colonel Jacob Ruppert, the owner who bought Babe Ruth, is also honored with a plaque, as are Popes John Paul II and Paul VI.

Enjoy your time in Monument Park. Just be sure to keep off the grass that lines the slate walkway and keep an eye out for incoming batting practice homers. When Josh sat down on the low wall to pose alongside Babe Ruth's number 3 for a picture, he was quickly and sternly reprimanded by a stadium employee. No hard feelings. Then two seconds later, an Alfonso Soriano BP homer caught Josh in the chest. The stadium employee picked up the ball and kept it. The bastard.

BULL PEN HANKY-PANKY

While tooling around Monument Park, you'll have the chance to peek into both bull pens. On days when he was pitching, Yankee right-hander Roger Clemens adopted a disturbing ritual. Departing the bull pen after warming up, he would stop at the Babe Ruth monument and say a silent prayer to the Bambino. Then he would kiss the monument.

It was therefore fitting that on the fifty-fifth anniversary of Babe Ruth Day on June 13, 2003, at the stadium, Clemens seized the stage against the Cardinals and achieved two remarkable milestones in the same game. Early in the contest "the Rocket" recorded strikeout number four thousand of his career, boosting him into the company of Nolan Ryan and Steve Carlton who were the only other hurlers to crest the 4K plateau. By the end of the night, Clemens had also sealed up his three hundredth career win, with a little bit of help from the New York bull pen. With the W, Clemens became the twenty-first big league pitcher to bag three hundred games.

Josh: "Given the prevalence of the four-man rotation, and the short hook afforded pitchers by managers and their specialized bull pens these days, Roger may be the last pitcher to win three hundred games."

Kevin: "Make that *next to last*. Mr. Maddux will soon be joining him."

THE "CRAZY SCREEN"

Yankee Stadium contains more foul territory behind home plate than any other park in the big leagues. Maybe that's why fans keep trying to get closer to the action. On numerous occasions, fans have fallen or jumped from the upper levels onto the screen suspended behind the plate to keep foul balls from maiming fans in the lower boxes. Perhaps the most bizarre such occurrence was during an early season Red Sox game in 2000 when a fan leapt from the upper level, settled on the screen, and then remained there—playing dead while the teams took more than ten minutes to complete the inning. After the third out was recorded, he suddenly began climbing up the screen, only to be apprehended by security personnel when he reached the top. Now we've done some crazy things in our day, but this is one phenomenon we have a hard time understanding. We're also intrigued, as well as annoyed, by those moronic souls who jump out of the stands to run around on the field. What are they thinking? The Bronx drunk tank doesn't sound like any place to spend five minutes, let alone an entire evening.

THE ZIM SCREEN

From the team that revolutionized the baseball bat by adding a knob to the bottom of the handle in the early 1920s, introduced uniform numbers to the game in 1929, and unveiled the first electronic message board in 1959, comes another brilliant innovation. In 2000 the Yankees added a four-foot-high screen in front of both dugouts amid fears that another foul ball off Don Zimmer's misshapen noggin would do permanent damage to their affable bench coach. The impetus came when Zim took a liner off his bean during the 1999 American League Division Series versus Texas. A number of other teams have since followed suit.

Incidentally, the Yankee dugout was on the third-base side until 1946 when it moved across the diamond to its current location.

THE VOICE . . . [PAUSE] . . . FROM THE . . . [PAUSE] . . . SKY

Usually public address announcers, like umpires, are doing a good job if you can sit in the park for a full nine innings without noticing them. They're complementary parts, meant to keep things moving along so that the main attractions—the players—can wow us with their many talents. But every once in a while someone comes along that you do notice, and in a good way. Bob Sheppard, Yankee Stadium's PA announcer, came along fifty-one years ago, and he's still at it. To put that in perspective, the octogenarian with the distinctive speech pattern predates Mickey Mantle. We love how he lets each syllable hang in the air in his super-cool, low-key style.

THE JEFFREY MAIER SEATS

Remember the little kid who reached over the right field wall and snatched Derek Jeter's fly ball from the grasp of Oriole right fielder Tony Tarasco during the 1996 ALCS? Remember how umpire Richie Garcia called it a home run instead of a fan-interference out? Remember twelve-year-old Jeffrey Maier flashing his smile on *Good Morning America* and *The Letterman Show* the next day? Remember the check Steinbrenner sent him two days later, for "embodying the Yankee Spirit?" Okay, we made that last one up. But if you answered "yes" to any of the preceding questions, you might as well take a pregame stroll out to Box 331 to relive the moment from the meddling kid's point of view.

Stadium Eats

Considering that New York City is renowned for its exquisite culinary delights, the food selection at Yankee Stadium is a major disappointment. The ballpark basics are here—dogs, fries, nachos, chicken fingers, bagged peanuts, Cracker Jack, ice cream—but fans interested in taking a bite out of the Big Apple aren't offered too much else.

PASTRAMI ON RYE (Trademark Food)

The food court on the lower level features a **Kosher Deli** stand. We thought the hot pastrami on rye was excellent. Our sandwich (yes, we split one) was fresh, warm, and thick with tender, lean meat. For $8.50 it would have been nice if it had come with a *full* kosher dill pickle, rather than a half, but where else in the Majors can you eat pastrami in your seat? The Deli also sells corned beef sandwiches (with half pickles).

NATHAN'S HOT DOG (Dog Rating)

The Third Best Hot Dog in the Majors

The Yankee Stadium foot-longs cost a dollar more than the franks on the Plaza, but they're worth it. The Nathan dog resonates on the tongue almost like a slice of kielbasa—salty, sweet, and bursting with juice—and the bun is large enough to accommodate a full foot of frankfurter. Signs promoting Nathan's flash the trademark slogan, "Nathan's: More than Just the Best Hot Dog!" As much as we like this salty dog, we wonder what the whiz kids in Nate's marketing department are thinking? Are they saying that the Nathan dog transcends being a hot dog? If so, what the hell do they think it is? We'll chalk this up as another example of that New York City bravado.

BEST OF THE REST

The **Yankee Bake Shop** on the second level offers an assortment of freshly baked cookies. We split a black and white cookie because it reminded us of a stand-up routine Jerry Seinfeld did on his television show, *Seinfeld,* about how society should try to emulate the black and white cookie. Other offerings include the

Yankee logo cookie and the pinstripe cookie. They all tasted about the same to us.

The **Sidewalk Café** is located between Gates 4 and 6 on the first level. A large iron fence separates Café-goers from fans on the Plaza outside. The Café offers a patio with picnic tables for fans who don't like eating in their seats as well as a slightly more expansive menu than inside the stadium proper. Such items as steak, grilled chicken, and barbecued pork sandwiches are popular sellers as well as a forty-four-ounce soda. Now, that's what we call a "bladder-buster."

Sweet Nuts is next to the Red Hook stand on the first level and sells hot roasted nuts. Josh tried the honey and cinnamon roasted cashews, which were tasty at first, but sickeningly sweet by the time the bottom of the bag came into view.

SAY "NO, THANKS," AND WALK AWAY

The Italian sausages we tried were undercooked and bland. What a travesty!

STADIUM SUDS

Yankee Stadium features plenty of brew stands and roaming vendors peddling a diverse selection of plastic-bottled beer. The best selection is at the **Beers of the World** stand beneath Section 3 on the first level, which has Corona, Becks, Heineken, Amstel Light, Miller Lite, and Bud. Despite the giveaway price of $6.50 per twelve-ounce plastic bottle (that's $156 per case) there's hardly ever a line!

Red Hook, located on tap on the first level, is the only microbrew available in Yankee Stadium. Kevin rates it "okay," but just okay.

STICK IT TO "THE MAN"

Because beer and soda are outlandishly overpriced at Yankee Stadium, we offer a happy alternative to blowing $20 on three ballpark frosties. The **Designated Driver Booth**, located on the field level beneath Section 4, is open for the first five innings of every game. If you're twenty-one or older, you can cash in here. In return for promising to drive your drinking friends home safely after the game you can get coupons redeemable for three *free* sodas.

The Yankee Stadium Experience

THE BRONX ZOO

It is impossible to walk into Yankee Stadium without a preconceived notion of what the place is all about. We've all heard it referred to as the Bronx Zoo. We remember the four-inch buck knife tossed from the upper deck that hit California's Wally Joyner in the arm; Boston's Jim Rice going into the stands to retrieve his cap after it was swiped by the fans in the left field corner; and opposing players being doused with beer, stung by tossed batteries, and tormented by cruel epithets in the outfield. We remember countless incidents of fans running onto the field or jumping onto the screen behind home plate. Taking all of that into account, our visit was relatively uneventful.

Yankee fans are intense and universally decked out in special edition World Series hats and jackets. Unlike fans in other cities who root for their team to win, these folks *expect* the Yankees to win. To their credit, Yankee fans live and die by their team, and anything less than victory and total domination is unacceptable to them. New Yorkers are accustomed to being number one, in baseball as in theater, entertainment, business, fashion, and a zillion other things. Hell, New York is even the home to "more than just the best hot dog." These folks are brash and unapologetic. They're number one, and they're happy to remind you if you wear anything other than a Yankee cap.

ROLE CALL

One of the stadium's coolest traditions is carried on by the fans in the right field bleachers. When the Yankees take the field in the top of the first inning, these diehards stand in unison and greet each Yankee starter by chanting his name or nickname until he turns and acknowledges them with a wave or tip of the cap. "De-rek Je-Ter," clap-clap—clap-clap-clap, "De-rek Je-Ter," clap-clap—clap-clap-clap, "SO-ri-Ah-NO," clap-clap—clap-clap-clap, "SO-ri-Ah-NO." And so on.

CRAZY POT WHACKER (Superfan)

Decked out from head to toe in pinstripes and buttons saying things like "Conserve Water: Shower with a Friend," Crazy Pot Whacker is a superfan in the best sense of the word. By day, he is seventy-eight-year-old Freddy Schuman; by night, he is a Yankee fanatic who walks around all during the game, visiting all levels and sections of the stadium with a huge kitchen pot strapped to his chest. Freddy writes a new message on the pot every day. "Four-peat is a treat," was the one we saw. As he tours the park with his pot, he hands his stick to fans who pound out their Yankee pride on his chest. Give him a "Thwack! Thwack! Thwack!" for us when you see him.

PUT YOUR MONEY ON THE 4

Check out the late-inning Subway Race on the Jumbotron and root for your favorite train—the 4, B, or C—to arrive at Yankee Stadium first. It's almost the same as the daily airplane race at crosstown Shea Stadium—only different. If you're in the bathroom or waiting in line for food and miss the action on the screen, don't despair. Keep your eyes on the gap between the right field bleachers and the main section of the stadium and you'll see the real subway rumble onto the River Avenue platform every few minutes. Before the scoreboard was put up in the outfield, folks on the platform (and on rooftops) would assemble to watch the game for free.

TRASH DAY

All right. Here's one thing the folks running Yankee Stadium could work on: keeping nap- kins, hot dog wrappers, and other miscellaneous debris off the field.

While there have been plenty of incidents over the years of Yankee fans universally tossing trash on the field to express their displeasure with a bad call or unfortunate turn of events, that's not what we're talking about. We're talking about any old regular season game in May or June when the Yanks are winning and the crowd is content. Why is it that by the seventh inning the field will invariably be littered with windblown trash? You've surely noticed this on TV, and it's even more noticeable in person. Perhaps the wind gusts off the Harlem River and the overhanging upper deck contribute to this. Or are we making excuses to mask the ugly truth? Are New Yorkers cavalier when it comes to disposing of their ballpark dog wrappers? You make the call.

YMCA

We find this craze almost as annoying as the wave, but since it has ingrained its presence in our beloved game, we must give props where props are due. New York's Village People brought the world the song, "YMCA," then they showed us all how to spell the chorus with our bodies. And now their local team has put an interesting twist on the league-wide seventh inning ritual that is YMCA-mania. Check out the grounds crew as they dance and drag the infield before the seventh inning. We're not experts, but is that what Paula Abdul would call "super-spank" choreography?

OLD BLUE EYES IS BACK

A lot of teams have a special local song they play over the PA system after the home team wins. It should come as no surprise that at Yankee Stadium, Frank Sinatra (who was actually from Hoboken, New Jersey) belts out "New York, New York." The tune resonates throughout the stadium at near eardrum-shattering

HEADSTONE HUNTING

FOR HARD-CORE FANS, or those who simply enjoy an occasional graveyard jaunt, the Cemetery of the Gate of Heaven in Hawthorne, New York, makes for an interesting excursion. Just half an hour's drive from the Bronx, this massive and very scenic cemetery is the burial site of Babe Ruth (Section 25, Plot 1115, Grave 3), Billy Martin (Section 25, Plot 21, Grave 3), and MLB umpire John McSherry (Section 44, Plot 480, Grave 3), who died on the field in Cincinnati on opening day of the 1996 season. To find the Gates of Heaven, take Route 287 north to Route 100 A north, to Route 100 north.

Photo by Kevin O'Connell

Babe Ruth grave

Ruth's headstone reads, "May the divine spirit that animated Babe Ruth to win the crucial game of life inspire the youth of America." When we visited in September 2002, it was adorned by two half-empty bottles of Bud Ice, a pint of Old Slugger Beer, pictures of the Bambino, pennies, flowers, an American flag, the book cover of *Babe: The Legend Comes to Life*, Yankee hats, baseballs, golf balls, a wiffle bat, a wooden bat, Yankee Stadium ticket stubs, and a lipstick kiss on the cherublike face on the tombstone.

Martin's stone contains a quote from the four-time Yankee skipper: "I may not have been the greatest Yankee to put on the uniform, but I was the proudest." A black-and-white picture of Billy with Mickey Mantle leaned against the stone, along with a few of the same half-empty Bud Ice bottles and a tennis ball.

---

decibels as fans depart. Then, after Old Blue Eyes finishes the last chorus, there is a brief lull—spanning maybe half a second—before the song starts over again. And you'll hear it starting up a third time as you walk up the hill to U.S. Chicken. It's a big anthem by a big singer. What we find interesting—from an anthropological perspective—is that they also play "New York, New York," after Yankee losses, though not quite as loudly.

THE YOGI BERRA MUSEUM AND LEARNING CENTER (Little Falls, New Jersey)

In 1996 Yankee great and longtime Montclair, New Jersey, resident Yogi Berra received an honorary doctorate from Montclair State University. Two years later, the school opened a baseball park on campus named after Yogi, and two years after that the Yogi Berra Museum and Learning Center opened. The museum features plenty of Yankees memorabilia as well as exhibits from the Negro Leagues and interactive exhibits for children.

From the New Jersey Turnpike take Exit 16W to Route 46 west. Take the Valley Road exit (immediately after the Six Brothers Diner). At the end of the exit ramp, turn right onto Valley Road. Go about a quarter of a mile and turn right into the university entrance. The museum is atop the hill on the right. Hours are Wednesday through Sunday, noon until 5:00 P.M. and admission is $6.

TORONTO BLUE JAYS, SKYDOME

A Dome with a View

TORONTO,
ONTARIO, CANADA

260 miles to Detroit
300 miles to Cleveland
330 miles to Cooperstown
340 miles to Montreal

MIDWAY THROUGH the 1989 season Toronto unveiled a revolutionary new sports facility that many Canadians believed would forever change the course of ballpark construction in North America. And for a while it looked like they might have been right. Opting to call this new behemoth simply "SkyDome," Toronto proclaimed its new stadium capable of hosting professional baseball, football, and basketball games. Not only was this the biggest, baddest dome Major League Baseball had yet seen, but it came complete with a retractable roof. On nice days, fans would be treated to outdoor baseball. And on those crisp Canadian April nights they'd enjoy indoor baseball. The future had arrived and for once Canada was leading the way. It must have been a pretty good feeling. Especially when road trippers from all over the continent made SkyDome one of the hottest new tourist destinations of the early 1990s.

With a successful team on the field, fans flocked to SkyDome and the Blue Jays set new American League attendance records four years running. For the first time in a long time, perhaps ever, Torontonians could say their local nine played on the best ball field in the country. Some even said in the world.

Baseball, forever relegated to second fiddle in the Great White North, where hockey and bigger-field football rule the icy tundra, had finally established itself in Toronto with SkyDome as its megalithic cement foothold. Torontonians loved their team and perhaps loved SkyDome a little bit more. What the good folks in Ontario didn't realize, however, was that meanwhile back in the good old U.S. of A. the fickle winds of change were again blowing, and blowing in the opposite direction. The ballpark designers in Baltimore had a new vision, or rather, a retro-y-new vision. A vision that was to send dome lovers everywhere on their ear: Oriole

Park at Camden Yards. Soon cities across the land were building smaller, more intimate ballparks like those of baseball's glory years. Nosebleed seats, plastic grass, concrete construction, and symmetrical field dimensions fell out of favor as real grass, steel and brick construction, ivy, and quirky outfield nooks and crannies returned to take their rightful places in ballparks from Seattle to Philadelphia.

"But we still have a retractable roof!" Canadians cried. "Let's see you top that." And top it, the crafty Americans did. In the lower forty-eight, new ballparks sprang up that offered the same safeguard against inclement weather as SkyDome, while also featuring open air and natural grass; in other words, these parks offered "real" outdoor baseball, even when their lids were on. The good-hearted Canadians had been foiled by their North American allies yet again. But wait, it got worse. After Toronto won back-to-back World Championships in 1992 and 1993, the labor disagreement of 1994 wiped out the second half of the season and the entire postseason. In most cities, the game has rebounded. In Toronto, it still hasn't.

The weak Canadian dollar has rendered the Blue Jays incapable of competing with U.S. teams for free agents. And the refusal of Rick Moranis to star in a second *Strange Brew* movie, combined with his eagerness to play the lead in any and all *Honey, I Shrunk the Kids* sequels the American drivel writers can churn out, has soured many Canadians on the American National Pastime. They say, "We've got hockey and curling. And Canadian football— real football! The Blue Jays, well they can just can take off, eh?" And so, sadly the Jays now play before a half-empty SkyDome. And the tourists that came to visit in the 1990s? They're spending their greenbacks at smaller, more intimate ballparks in the States.

Upon entering SkyDome for a late-season tilt between the Jays and Tigers, we were both impressed by the sheer size of the building compared to the other domes we had visited on our trip. And we both had fun trying to figure out how much the concession items cost in U.S. dollars. But once the baseball game began, we realized how far removed we were from the idyllic American ballpark experience. It only seemed fitting when, later, the team kicked off the seventh inning stretch with a song other than "Take Me Out to the Ball Game."

But we should not forget the contribution SkyDome made to the evolution of ballpark design. Prior to its existence, the only retractable roof stadium in Major League history was Montreal's Stade Olympique, which eventually became a fixed dome after years of mechanical failure, and then still later, became an open-air ballpark when the roof was removed. Fans in cities like Seattle, Phoenix, and Milwaukee who are thankful for their respective roofs should remember SkyDome. And they should pay it a visit. In fact, every fan should. In archaeology, they may still be searching for the missing link between man and beast. In ballpark evolution, we know right where it is: north of the border in downtown Toronto, which we might add, is one hip city.

From the outside, SkyDome is too big to photograph—unless your lens is as wide as Peter Gammons's forehead. By the time you back far enough away, another building is inevitably blocking your view. Best to buy a postcard. And aren't domes usually round or at least oval-shaped by nature? SkyDome looks like a concrete block from the outside. Leave it to the Canadians to make a square dome. We don't really mean to disparage our fair neighbors to the north. Canada is a wonderful and peaceful nation with whom we are proud to share a border. It's just that the Jays entered the American League the same year as Kevin's beloved Seattle Mariners, and while Toronto was winning back-to-back World Series Championships, the M's were still in search of back-to-back winning seasons. It's pure jealousy. As for Josh, he really is angry that there hasn't been a *Strange Brew II*.

Aside from the shape and size of the dome, another complaint of ours is that there really isn't much of a ballpark feel outside the place. One lone concrete pillar near the ticket window celebrates the 1992 and 1993 World Series Champion Jays. The outdoor speaker system plays vacuous Canadian rock. Extremely weird golden figurines hang mounted to the dome's exterior, pointing skyward and praying (for a real ballpark perhaps?).

Inside, SkyDome resembles the Metrodome or Kingdome, only larger. The Astrodome was eighteen stories high. SkyDome is thirty-one. Those extra stories leave room for five levels of seating, plenty of luxury boxes, three restaurants facing the field, a 348-room hotel, and the roof's hardware. The roof doesn't open all the way, but does leave 91 percent of the seats exposed to the sky when retracted. Only the seats in center field remain under the hard top, which consists of four panels, three movable and one stationary, that stack on top of one another. Together these weigh twenty-two million pounds! When closed, the roof seals up tight 282 feet above the playing field. The process takes about twenty minutes at a cost of $500 CAN. This may sound expensive but at the recent exchange rate we figured it was only about $7.50 American.

In 1995, two thirty-pound roof tiles fell during a game, injuring seven fans, but for the most part the roof has functioned well and left few injured fans in its wake.

If you're in town on a nice day and you want to see the phenomenon that is SkyRoof, arrive a couple hours before the game and wait for it to retract. Or better yet, time your visit to the CN Tower next door so you can look down on the roof as it slowly uncovers the field. It really is something to see.

exterior

Photo by Kevin O'Connell

SkyDome opened June 5, 1989, with Milwaukee downing Toronto 5–3. Exhibition Stadium had served as home to the Blue Jays from the time they joined the American League as an expansion team in 1977. A longtime football facility, Exhibition Stadium was modified to accommodate 43,737 baseball fans. It had artificial turf and was famous for its damp and chilly nights thanks to its proximity to Lake Ontario.

On September 15, 1977, the shoddiness of Exhibition Stadium came into play as the Blue Jays won by forfeit when Baltimore manager Earl Weaver pulled his team off the field in the fifth inning, saying that the tarps covering the outfield bull pens created a hazard for his players.

In 1983 the Major League players, or at least one of them, struck back against Exhibition Stadium and its lakeside playing environment when Yankees right fielder Dave Winfield beaned a seagull with a warm-up toss between innings. Winfield's throw toward the Yankee dugout picked the bird clean out of the air, sending it spiraling to its death. Canadians and environmentalists were furious but Winfield escaped the country without facing criminal charges.

The Ex was demolished at age fifty in 1998, shortly after the Blue Jays threatened to return to it if a new lease agreement couldn't be worked out with SkyDome ownership. Ironically, the Belgian brewery, Interbrew SA, that owns the Blue Jays also owned a 49 percent stake in the dome at that time. The problem,

interior

Photo by Kevin O'Connell

apparently, was with the dome's other partners. Sportsco International, L.P, has since purchased the controlling interest in SkyDome.

The 1991 All-Star Game was played at Sky-Dome and fittingly, for the first time ever, two Canadian pitchers went home with decisions. Toronto's Jimmy Key got the win and Montreal's Dennis Martinez took the loss, as the American League prevailed 4–2. Of course the two hurlers weren't really Canadians, but then again, don't we think of Neil Young as an American? Sure, we do.

The very next year the dome hosted the first World Series games played outside of the United States and the Jays claimed their first title, beating Atlanta four games to two. Key and reliever Duane Ward earned two wins apiece in the Series.

In 1993 Toronto made it back-to-back championships, beating Philadelphia in six games. Joe Carter ended the Series with a go-ahead three-run homer against Phillies closer Mitch Williams in the bottom of the ninth.

The Canadian Football League's Argonauts have won three Grey Cups since moving to SkyDome (1991, 1996, 1997). To facilitate an easy conversion from baseball to football, Sky-Dome's field level seats are on tracks, allowing them to be rolled away to expand the field. And there are never any of those unsightly football lines lingering on the baseball field that artificial turf often brings. The baseball turf is unzipped and replaced with the football turf when conversion takes place, a process involving more than eight miles of zippers. Kevin notes that's more unzipping for one game than he did all through college.

The National Basketball Association's Toronto Raptors played their home games at SkyDome from 1995 to 1998, before moving to the Air Canada Centre.

Canadian track and field star Donovan Bailey won a highly publicized 150-meter race

TRIVIA TIMEOUT

Baby Blue: Name the first player to hit a home run into SkyDome's fifth level.

True Blue: Which future NBA All-Star once played for the Blue Jays? (Hint: he played in the second most postseason games in NBA history.)

Blue Jay Blue: On September 14, 1987, the Blue Jays set a record by hitting ten home runs in one game. Name the six homer hitters.

Look for the answers in the text.

against American Michael Johnson at Sky-Dome in 1997. Chalk one up for the Great White North.

Many musical groups have played Sky-Dome, ranging from Kevin's beloved Three Tenors to Josh's hometown favorites, New Kids on the Block. Word to your Tenor, Donnie.

Getting a Choice Seat

SkyDome is a big place (is this an understatement, or what?) that hasn't come close to selling out since the strike of 1994 dampened the city's hardball enthusiasm. The drop in value of Canadian currency has also hurt. So use these factors to your advantage and get up to see a game on the cheap, scoring good tickets at a 40 percent discount given the exchange rate.

Visiting a game now, it's hard to believe the Jays once set new attendance records four years in a row, drawing: 3,885,284 fans in 1990; 4,001,058 in 1991; 4,028,318 in 1992; and 4,057,947 in 1993. The Jays barely attract 1.5 million these days, which works out to about 18,000 per game, so there's really no need to order tickets ahead of time unless you want primo seats, and even then, we recommend haggling with the scalpers rather than paying the team's top-dollar prices.

Sellout Index: 0% of games sell out
Seating Capacity: 50,516
Ticket Office: (888) OK-GO-JAY
www.bluejays.mlb.com

100 Level

The first level offers SkyDome's only open concourse from which fans can see the action while waiting in line for food and drinks. And with the slow-moving lines at SkyDome, that's worth something.

Rows number 1 to 42 in the lower bowl, with ushers checking tickets frequently to thwart seat-hoppers.

The first level is divided into six different price ranges, starting at $24 for outfield seats and increasing to $180 for "In the Action" seats behind home plate.

We recommend Field Level Baseline seats on the left field side, which offer a striking view of the roof and CN Tower overhead, which Kevin characterizes as a concrete space needle.

Avoid the last several rows of Sections 119—121 on the first-base side where the overhang of the second deck becomes a major problem. Stay in Rows 1–30 if you can.

The Outfield seats are quite a bit higher than the Infield seats and are plagued by a significant overhang problem of their own. Avoid Rows 7–13 of Sections 101–108 and Sections 135–142. The good news is that the foul poles don't restrict sight lines since they're made of see-through yellow mesh.

200 Level

If you thought the overhang was bad on the first level, wait until you get to the second. Here, the third deck creates a grievous overhang, while the deck below your feet creates an equally unpalatable obstruction. It's like watching the game on TV. Hey, at least it's wide-screen.

From the Outfield seats we couldn't see the warning track on our side of the field. And from many of the seats in the back rows we couldn't see much of anything because of the concrete support structures at the back of the level. In Sections 204–206 and 242–246 especially, stay in Rows 1–6 to avoid these lousy seats.

Around the infield, the 200 Level is club seating. We sneaked in long enough to check out the bar and restaurant. We didn't try any of the food but we did stick our noses in a couple of people's plates and were very impressed, especially when we compared the fare to what the plebs were eating in the rest of SkyDome. The corned beef sandwich, boneless buffalo wings, quesadillas, and "sacrifice" bunt cakes all looked tempting.

Beware, if you're not in the club, the concession stands on the 200 Level are very crowded since there is only one main concession stand for common folk on either side of the club. The level was half empty on the day we visited, yet people were still waiting ten deep in line for food and drink.

500 Level (SkyDeck)

Because the 300 and 400 Levels consist of private boxes around the infield and the hotels and restaurants in the outfield, the 500 Level or SkyDeck is exceptionally high above the field.

Separate entranceways for each SkyDeck section create many obstructed views. But take heart, these sections are so rarely full that should you wind up with a stinker you'll be able to move over a seat or two for a better sight line.

Every row on the SkyDeck level has its own railing in front of it. This minimizes slightly the lingering feeling that you may at any moment stand up—say, to go get a hot dog—then suddenly lose your balance and plummet to your death from this exceptionally high and steep deck. The personalized railing also allows the Blue Jays to take the concept of "stadium seating" to the extreme. Once seated, your feet will be down around the shoulders of the fan in the row in front of you. The steep incline keeps the SkyDeck relatively close to the airspace directly over the field.

The only SkyDeck seats that allow a full view of the field are in Sections 518–533. The first several rows of these seats provide the best view available on the SkyDeck.

Avoid Sections 504–508 in right field due to the significant under-hang that blocks much of right field. In left, avoid all sections on the outfield side of Section 538.

All the way around the upper bowl, beware of seats behind Row 22 because they may be obstructed by the light-support structures.

Because there were so few fans in the upper level when we visited, we found very few open concession stands on the concourse. Those that were open for business only offered the basics. Making matters worse, a 500 Level ticket will not allow you to access the field level concourse with its grilled dogs, Canadian bacon sandwich, and other specialty items. You must buy at least a $24 200 Level ticket to access field level.

Take Off, Eh?

Oakland's Jose Canseco became the first player to hit a fair ball into the 500 Level with a 540-foot blast in Game Four of the 1989 American League Championship Series. We suggest taking a pregame stroll out to Section 542 to appreciate just how far Canseco's bomb traveled. Whether he was on the "roids" or not, we were impressed.

The Black Market

Scalpers selling tickets below face value currently present a major problem for the Blue Jays. A sign hanging at the main ticket window encourages fans to purchase tickets from the team, not scalpers. As much as we initially wanted to give our George Washingtons to the

Jays, we had a change of heart when the ticket teller told us we wouldn't be able to access field level if we bought 500 Level seats.

"Even if it's the last day of the season and the last day of our road trip and we're low on cash?" Josh asked.

"No," the man said. "If you buy the cheap seats, then you better sit in 'em, eh?"

"Even if we're soon-to-be prolific American authors and need to scope things out for our readers?" Kevin tried.

"Especially if you're authors," the ticket teller said. "In this country the rules are the same for everybody. No privilege situations, not for you, not for the Queen Mum."

"Is she the one on all the money?" Josh asked.

"But our book is about SkyDome. It could lead to bigger profits for you and—"

"We don't care what your book is aboot."

Aboot? What a hosehead.

Welcome to communist Canada. Taking a cue from the sign practically pleading with us to avoid the scalper scene, we told the ticket teller to "take off," and set out to find a scalper. And sure enough we located one between Gates 11 and 12 operating in plain view of the Canadian Mounted Police.

With just a small amount of haggling, we scored two 200 Level Outfield tickets ($24 face value each) for a total of $30 CAN. That's less than $10 U.S. each. Not bad, eh?

Before/After the Game

Toronto is a large cosmopolitan city with much going on and many cultural influences that buck the stereotypes. Despite the tongue-in-cheek humor we may poke at Canada and its citizens, the truth is we found Toronto exceptionally clean and remarkably affordable. The people we encountered were friendly and spoke a dialect of English similar enough to our own.

SkyDome is located on the border of Toronto's Theatre District in a neighborhood that offers plenty of places to eat and drink. So do partake. The city is also home to a lively club and music scene. On a street corner outside the Dome, we picked up a copy of a free weekly entertainment guide called *Eye*, that listed everything from alternative concerts to jazz clubs to independent films playing in the city to phone numbers for perverts in search of phone sex. There were even a number of provocative pictures next to the phone numbers. It was quite the little publication.

Getting to SkyDome

From the south, take the QEW/Gardiner Expressway to the Spadina Avenue Exit. SkyDome is visible well in advance of the exit. Follow Spadina north for one block, then turn right onto Bremner Boulevard, which leads to plenty of privately owned parking lots. If you

gargoyles

Photo by Kevin O'Connell

get disoriented, look for the CN Tower (easily visible from just about anywhere in Ontario) and drive toward it.

The parking lots in the immediate vicinity of SkyDome charge between $10 and $20 CAN on game days. We found a lot for $5 CAN on Front Street and saw another for the same price on Blue Jay Way (wasn't that a Beatle tune?) between Front and Wellington.

The subway is also a viable alternative for those staying in the city. Union Station on the Yonge/University line is only a few blocks from SkyDome.

Outside Attractions

THE CN TOWER

Beside SkyDome stands the world's tallest building, the CN Tower, which measures 553.33 meters, or 1,815 feet, for those not terribly familiar with the metric system. The tower, which was classified as one of the Seven Wonders of the World by the American Society of Civil Engineers in 1995, serves as both an important telecommunications center and a tourist attraction. Each year more than two million people visit the tower to take in the stunning view from its observation deck.

The tower was designed in the early 1970s to remedy the atrocious television reception city residents were experiencing as a result of a construction boom that had rendered Toronto's preexisting TV towers too short to contend with the city's many skyscrapers. The tower was completed in 1976. Much to their chagrin, Torontonians soon discovered that there was nothing good on Canadian TV anyway. Just hockey and lame comedy acts and occasional late-night skin flicks. Thankfully, cable TV was just around the corner.

Today the CN Tower serves several television stations and FM radio stations. It also houses several restaurants, an arcade, a movie theater, and tourist shops.

A trip to the top costs $22 CAN, well worth it if you have time to kill in Toronto. For more information, call (416) 601-3796.

HIPPO TOURS

If you'd like to see the city by land and sea, take a Hippo Tour on one of the amphibious busses that float and drive around Toronto. For information, call (416) 703-HIPO. We thought about it, before opting to sit this one out. There were just too many kids barking (or whatever noise a hippopotamus makes) on the Hippo for our tastes.

LEGENDS OF THE GAME
(King Street and John Street)

Just a block from SkyDome sits Canada's largest sports collectibles store. With everything from trading cards and autographs, to jerseys and gear, this is a great shop. We were impressed by the rich collection of hockey memorabilia (duh) and the surprising amount of Muhammad Ali collectibles (did he have a Toronto connection we don't know about?).

SIGN ON THE DOTTED LINE (or Sweet Spot!)

After games, visiting players exit SkyDome through Gate 5 and either wait there for taxis or walk to the nearby visiting teams' hotel. On getaway days however, the players take a bus from inside the dome straight to the airport, so don't bother waiting after the last game of a series.

Many Blue Jays players live in long-term apartments inside SkyDome, so keep your eyes open when you're out and "aboot" town.

DOME TOUR

We took the reasonably priced SkyDome tour and found it average as far as ballpark tours go. Our lukewarm feelings may stem from the fact that we were unable to walk on the field because the visiting team was taking extra batting practice on the day we visited. We did get to see and even touch a small piece of the turf though. It's number 8 grade Astroturf, one and one-fourth inches thick. We also enjoyed seeing the extensive collections of Exhibition Stadium and Argonauts memorabilia on display in the luxury boxes.

The tour began with a mildly interesting video about the construction of the dome. We wish we could provide details on this, but as soon as the tape started rolling, Josh fell asleep and Kevin struck up a conversation with a nice man named Warren from Buffalo who was visiting Toronto for a cement expo.

Watering Holes and Outside Eats

Not surprisingly, the streets surrounding Sky-Dome have been developed with American tourists in mind. Familiar chain restaurants abound. But with just a little bit of effort, the road-tripping fan can do better. Plenty of saloons and eateries—many with patio or rooftop seating—reside on and around King Street, between the dome and the Theatre District. Don't be scared off by those seemingly high prices. You're playing with Canadian money, remember? This is your chance to enjoy an upscale meal for cheap bucks. Our recommendation is to sample a pregame hot dog from one of the Shopsy vendors outside Sky-Dome, then don't waste your appetite or money inside the dome, but go out for dinner after the game. A $22 steak is only really setting you back about $12, so eat up!

Just remember, it's Canadian money, not Monopoly money, so don't go overboard. Josh ordered two entrées for himself, then tried to convince Kevin to split the bill. A typical Josh scam, that Kevin might have fallen for if he had had just one more beer.

GRETZKY'S (99 Blue Jays Way)
Wayne Gretzky's restaurant is appropriately located at 99 Blue Jay Way. "The Great One," you surely remember—unless you were born in

Texas—wore uniform number 99 during his illustrious NHL career.

A sign on the front of this trendy sports pub says, "Eat your face off." Clever. Very clever. Gretzky's was jam-packed when we visited after the game. With table hockey for the kids, and a souvenir shop and memorabilia chronicling Wayne's rise to greatness adorning all the walls, this is a solid pick for a pre- or postgame meal and a must-visit for any serious sports fan. After all, he is "the Great One."

PEEL PUB (276 King Street)
Massive television screens, massive pitchers of beer, and massive portions of pub grub. This is actually a satellite operation of a famous Montreal restaurant that aspires to keep it simple, keep it cheap, and keep it Canadian—at least that's what our waitress told us. She was talking about the restaurant, right?

MONTANA, THE LAST BEST PLACE (145 John Street)
For a classier meal, visit this upscale steak house. The expansive menu features plenty of red meat as well as chicken wings, ribs, seafood, and handmade flat bread.

R.D.'S BARBECUE AND BLUES (14 Pearl Street)
Appealing to Josh's love of Southern barbecue and Kevin's appreciation of the blues, R.D.'s is our pick of Pearl Street establishments. Try the long-bone ribs. We give 'em four messy thumbs up.

CROCODILE ROCK (240 Adelaide Street)
Here's your chance to play a little air guitar and stomp around in your sneakers while chubby chicks with smoker's cough angle for drinks. When you tire of the '80s rock, pay a visit to the beer garden outside.

On Friday and Saturday nights expect to find a line outside after 10:00 P.M. The menu features Creole dishes like jambalaya (Kevin's pick) and New Orleans Steak (Josh's pick).

CORA PIZZA (656 Spadina Avenue)

How 'bout some cheap late-night pizza after working up an appetite at the bars?

SHOPSY HOT DOGS
(Front, University, and King Streets)

On game days, Shopsy carts abound in the streets around SkyDome. Each offers beef dogs and Polish and Italian sausages, topped to your liking. Shopsy provides every imaginable topping, ranging from different kinds of relishes and mustards to pickles, onions, peppers, corn, hot sauce, barbecue sauce—you know, the works—and then some.

These big juicy hot dogs are slit multiple times, then grilled. They come served on enriched yellow buns. Load one up! For $2 CAN, they're a steal. Josh ate four, and still put away two rib platters at R.D.'s afterward. Man, we've said it before: the kid is small, but he sure can eat.

CHUNKY FRIES (Front Street)

Several vans park on Front Street selling hand-cut french fries, a Toronto favorite. We tried **Bozo's Roadhouse**. Bozo's salty skin-on fries tasted about as good as French fries can get. Kevin doused his with vinegar as all good Anglophilic Canadians do (though he argued that the Irish did it first), while Josh stuck to good old American ketchup.

Inside the Dome

Upon entering SkyDome, we were immediately struck by the sheer size of the place. A marvel of modern technology as they say, it is impressive. The ball field, on the other hand, is rather drab. First off, the outfield is perfectly symmetrical at 400 feet to center, 328 feet down the lines, and 375 feet to the alleys. And worse, the ten-foot high outfield wall has a gutter behind it—a gap of fifteen to twenty feet that doesn't allow outfielders to contend with fans for home run balls. Unless they're exceptionally well struck, most dingers simply fade into oblivion between the outfield wall and the outfield seats. How thoroughly unromantic.

We didn't care for the Astroturf either. SkyDome has a roof, so how about growing some real grass, or at the very least laying some of the Devil Rays' faux shag-turf? Maybe the Jays could introduce a real dirt infield then, as well. After all there have to be some advantages to allowing the sun in. But we know what the turf proponents will say: "then what will we do for football, eh?" We don't have the answer. But as it stands now, when the roof is closed the game feels artificial, and when it's open sunlight shimmers on the Astroturf, which seems wrong in a whole other way. We agree with Jeremy Giambi: nothing beats grass.

Ballpark Features
HOMETOWN HEROES

Before the game, check out the display cases on the concourse behind Section 102. These celebrate great Canadian baseball players such as Larry Walker . . . Larry Walker . . . and, you guessed it, Larry Walker. Rob Ducey and Fergie Jenkins get their share of props too. We looked for Eric Gagne and Corey Koskie exhibits but couldn't find them. Maybe they'll have some set up by the time you visit.

We did find a display case containing all three bases from the first interleague game pitting Montreal against Toronto on June 30, 1997. Members of both teams signed the bases, which have red maple leaves stenciled onto them.

We also found a display of balls from the Blue Jays ten-homer game against the Orioles on September 14, 1987. Toronto established a new single game long ball record, en route to an 18–3 triumph at Exhibition Stadium. Signing their names in the Blue Jays dinger-diary were

Ernie Witt (3), Rance Mulliniks (2), George Bell (2), Lloyd Moseby, Fred McGriff, and Rob Ducey. Another interesting item was the pitching rubber from 1993 World Series signed by Juan Guzman.

NONRETIRED

While the Blue Jays have not retired the numbers of any of their former players, they do display the names of some former stars on the outfield face of the SkyDeck. This self-styled "Level of Excellence" honors players like Tony Fernandez, Joe Carter, George Bell, and Dave Steib, former manager Cito Gaston, and former general manager Pat Gillick.

One former Blue Jay whose name and number don't appear here is Danny Ainge. The light-hitting second-sacker played for Toronto from 1979 to 1981 while also playing college hoops at Brigham Young University. He quit baseball after being drafted in the first round by the Boston Celtics in 1981 and went on to play in more NBA playoff games than any player in history with the exception of Kareem Abdul-Jabbar. Did Danny make the right choice? We think so. He hit just .220 in 211 Major League games before trading in his spikes for high-tops.

DISNEY WOULD BE PROUD

Similar to the outfield fences in Anaheim, Sky-Dome's outfield fence pays tribute to great players and magical moments in Blue Jays history. Massive newspaper headlines overlaid on the walls recall Dave Steib's no-hitter, Pat Borders's postseason heroics, Alfredo Griffin's 1979 Rookie of the Year campaign, and Billy Koch's rookie saves record (thirty-one saves in 1999). We found it odd that Koch, who was playing with the A's when we visited, would still be featured at SkyDome, especially since his Blue Jays career lasted only three years. Maybe the team will replace his headline with one for Kelvim Escobar by the time you visit.

DIGITIZED PENS

The bull pens are hidden behind the outfield walls in right and left field. From the 200 Level outfield seats, fans can look down to see television cameras pointed at the practice mounds. The cameras provide a feed to dugout monitors that allow both managers to see who is warming up.

Josh: "Janet Marie Smith would not be pleased."

"Kevin: "Can it, Irv."

BASEBALL IN THE GREAT WHITE NORTH

ONE OF THE Hometown Heroes displays contains a bench seat from old Maple Leaf Stadium in Toronto. Also on exhibit are articles of Toronto Maple Leaf and Montreal Royal memorabilia. We found a picture of Sparky Anderson, who played for and later managed the Leafs, and another of Royal player, Tommy Lasorda.

No, we're not talking hockey; the Maple Leafs and Royals were minor league baseball teams that played in Canada.

Originating in 1887, the Maple Leafs were a longtime member of the International League (called the Eastern League prior to 1912), until the expansion Blue Jays arrived.

The Eastern League Royals began play in Montreal in 1890 but struggled to establish a fan base before being acquired by Charlie Trudeau—father of the future Canadian prime minister, Pierre Elliot Trudeau. In 1940, the Brooklyn Dodgers purchased the Royals, and six years later Jackie Robinson broke organized baseball's color barrier, playing second base and batting .349 for Montreal. A year later, he would break the Major League color barrier.

JUMBO FUN

SkyDome makes full use of its center field Jumbotron, which is billed as "the largest video screen in North America." We couldn't decide if there was a bigger screen at some soccer stadium in Brazil, or if that was simply the politically correct (read Canadian) way of saying, "Our TV is bigger than any in the United States." In any case, a constant program of music, trivia, and commercials plays on the board during the game and between innings, starting with a pregame show. This seemed like something we'd expect to find in New York or Anaheim, but hey, who are we to pass judgment? Wait a minute, that's our job. Well then, we feel the Jumbotron is fitting for SkyDome—overblown and thoroughly un-Canadian.

VIDEO GAMES

Sponsored by PlayStation, free portals at numerous locales on the 100 Level offer fans the chance to try their hand at new video games. Josh, who still owns an Atari 2000, opted not to partake, while Kevin showed some twelve-year-olds a thing or two, joy-sticking his way through Time Splitters and Test Drive. First he beat them, then he took their lunch money. Then he bought a hot dog.

MOBILE CARD SHOPS

Baseball, hockey, basketball, and football trading cards can be purchased from vending machines throughout the dome. Packs cost anywhere from thirty-five cents to $1 CAN. Fleer and Upper Deck packs seemed most prominent, though the results of Josh's survey should be considered unofficial.

Stadium Eats

Up until 1999, Ronald McDonald had the concession deal here. Eewww! Now Sports Service, the new concessionaire, is trying to upgrade the quality of SkyDome's food and offer more points-of-service to remedy the long lines and cluttered concourses that frustrated fans during Mickey D's ten-year reign of fast-food mediocrity.

Unfortunately, the concession stands still looked like McDonald's restaurants. You'll see what we mean when you step up to the counter to order a hot dog and Coke. We almost expected the counter woman to ask us if we wanted to super-size our order. The selection was nearly as bad—just the usual ballpark basics like dogs, fries, nachos, and chicken fingers. And we found the lines surprisingly long and slow moving.

Fresh grilled offerings and specialty items like stuffed pretzels and sushi are available only to fans with first and second level tickets on the first level concourse. What's that all "aboot?"

BACK BACON SANDWICH (Trademark Food)

Available only on the first level concourse, this sandwich represents one of the few tastes of local flavor available at SkyDome. It consists of salty Canadian bacon stacked with white cheddar cheese, served on a kaiser roll. All in all, a pretty good sandwich.

GRILLED BLUE JAY DOG (Dog Rating)
The Eighth Best Hot Dog in the Majors

While the regular stadium dog is unremarkable, we really enjoyed the grilled jumbo dog we purchased from one of the first-level kiosks. This specialty frank is on a par with the Shopsy dogs available outside the dome—same size and same great taste, though it costs nearly twice as much.

Slit several times and served on a poppy seed roll, this all-beef frank scores high in the areas of taste and texture. Beware, however, we found the grilled onions that accompanied our dogs just plain awful. Usually we love onions, but these wound up on the ground below our seats. They had obviously been on the grill way too long. Smarten up, Canada. There's a right way and there's a wrong way to sauté onions.

BEST OF THE REST

Kevin ordered a **Mr. Twisty** gourmet pretzel filler, a pretzel stuffed with pizza sauce and cheese. It was interesting, but not great. Twisty also offers a jalapeño-stuffed pretzel, which we plan on trying next time we visit SkyDome.

Only two company spokesmen remain in today's food and beverage industry whom Josh feels he can trust. The Colonel and old Uncle Orville. No, SkyDome doesn't offer KFC. But its **Orville Redenbacher** popcorn is second to none. Keep on popping, old boy. Keep on popping!

SAY "NO, THANKS," AND WALK AWAY

While **Pizza, Pizza** may have an uninspired name and make an equally uninspired pie, it sure hosted an exciting pregame promotion when we were in town.

Before the game, they trotted a fan named Adam out to left field and put a glove on his hand, announcing that if he could successfully catch three balls shot into the air by a pitching machine, every fan in the ballpark would win a free slice of cheese pizza.

Adam caught the first two, then missed the third. But kindly, the Pizza, Pizza officials, after a brief huddle, decided to give him another chance.

Josh cheered wildly as Adam adjusted his Blue Jays cap, pounded his mitt, and gave the crowd an enthusiastic thumbs up. Then the Pizza, Pizza kingpins dropped the ball into the machine and it shot high into the air. Adam trekked back, staggered for a moment, and then, at the very end, made a little leap to snare the ball in the webbing of his glove. A snow cone catch!

Always anxious to beat the crowd, Josh didn't wait around to watch Adam celebrate.

Instead, he sprinted to the nearest Pizza, Pizza stand to pick up his free slice, only to be informed that the offer was invalid at all Sky-Dome Pizza, Pizza locations. The pizza-faced hoser behind the counter said Josh would have to take his ticket stub to a non-SkyDome, Toronto-area Pizza, Pizza to redeem his prize. Thanks for nothing, Adam.

The lesson learned: always read the fine print on the Jumbotron.

SKYDOME RESTAURANTS

Another option is to eat at **Windows**, **Sight Lines**, or **The Hard Rock Café**, all of which offer table views of the field year-round.

The best of these is Windows, which has three hundred feet of frontage in center field. It offers five levels of tiered seating, comfortable chairs, and open windows that allow the sounds of the game to penetrate. A pregame table costs $24 CAN. Once the game starts, the cost is $45 for the table for the entire game. Entrées are reasonably priced. Fresh carved turkey or beef on a fresh roll, for example, goes for $13.95. More expensive entrées include prime rib, roasted New Zealand lamb, fresh seafood, and gourmet salads. If you just want to check it out, visit on a nongame day and avoid the table charge.

The only downside to Windows and the other restaurants is that patrons cannot access the rest of SkyDome from them. But if you're in town for a couple of games, give it a try.

STADIUM SUDS

LaBatt Blue is served in a twenty-eight-ounce container, which is just big enough for the hardy fans of the northland. It's understandable that Jays fans like their LaBatts. On March 26, 1976, the preexisting Major League Baseball owners approved LaBatts Brewing Company as owner of the Blue Jays, making it official that the Junior Circuit would field a team in Toronto the next season.

If you're looking for a choice of American beers, visit **Fanatics Sports Bar**, located on the first level concourse. The "bar," and we used this word somewhat skeptically, was still a work-in-progress when we visited. However, we were told that eventually it will offer patio seating that will allow fans to get a breath of fresh air on the sidewalk outside while still being technically "inside" SkyDome.

The SkyDome Experience

SkyDome must be a rocking good time when full, but it feels rather cavernous and sterile these days on account of the many empty seats. The game has a very postmodern flavor to it with the PA system and Jumbotron playing especially prominent roles in the festivities.

BLUE JAY CHEERLEADERS (Superfans)

One thing these crazy Canucks have done right is incorporate cheerleaders into the American National Pastime. Actually, we can't give Canada all the credit; cheerleaders have been an important part of the Caribbean World Series for years. But the Blue Jays fly girls are impressive. Wearing red spandex pants and skimpy belly shirts, they dance on both dugouts (Yet another reason to sit down the baselines!). But if you can't nab dugout seats, don't fret. The girls travel from section to section during the game leading fans in cheers of "Let's go, Blue Jays."

They're Canadian, eh, and they're busting a move for your viewing pleasure, so kick back and enjoy the show.

FEELING LUCKY

No, we don't have a sordid tale to report regarding our interaction with the Blue Jays cheerleaders. We're talking fifty-fifty raffle. For $2 fans can buy a ticket. Half the proceeds support the Blue Jays Charitable Foundation. The other half goes into the pot. The winner took home $1,250 on the day we visited.

POST-GAME FIREWORKS

No, we still don't have a sordid cheerleader tale. But after a Jays win the team sets off fireworks whether the roof is open or closed. Indoor fireworks! And you thought Neil Young was the best thing Canada had going for it!

FEDEX IT TO ME

Catch a home run ball at SkyDome and you'll become a member of the FedEx Home Run Club. An attendant will come to your seat and take the ball from you. Then, the very next day, FedEx will deliver the ball to your house signed by the player who hit it.

FedEx also delivers the ceremonial first pitch and a bag of game balls to the ball attendant via a company van that rumbles out of left field and drives to the infield just before the national anthems.

Josh says, "Where's Leslie Nielsen when you need him?" Remember the outfielder who got run over by a car on the field in *Naked Gun*? Or was that a tiger that hit him? Or was it O. J. Simpson? Yeah, it was the Juice.

THE FASTEST GROUNDS CREW ON EARTH

In the middle of the fifth inning, cheer for the self-proclaimed "Fastest Grounds Crew on Earth," as crew members rapidly rake the tiny plots of dirt around the bases to the tune of the "William Tell Overture." Yes, it's meant to be tongue-in-cheek since they only have four little rectangles of dirt to level. We couldn't help but think, though, that even the Blue Jays organization was poking fun at the ballpark.

"OK BLUE JAYS"

Before singing "Take Me Out to the Ball Game" during the seventh-inning stretch, Torontonians sing "OK Blue Jays," the official team song. Written by a local group called The Bat Boys, this is a kicking Canadian rock song.

SPORTS IN THE CITY

EXHIBITION STADIUM

DON'T WASTE YOUR TIME visiting Exhibition Place, the site of old Exhibition Stadium beside Lake Ontario. The ballpark is now a parking lot. Funny thing is, former players say it's a better place for a game now that it's been paved.

It was still a sad day when we visited hoping to find some remnant of the old park. Instead, we were informed by a guy waving two orange flags that we would have to pay $5 if we wanted to enter the lot. People were parking where we presumed the infield used to be, as they arrived for an indoor truck show called "truck world."

"AAARRR-GOES . . . AAARRR-GOES . . ."

Another way to fit in with the locals is by joining in this familiar "Aaarrr-goes" chant whenever there's a lull in the baseball game. They love their football in these parts.

Also, pronounce the city's name "Tronno." If you enunciate the second "t" as Americans are wont to, everyone will know you're one of "Them" and start sniffing for greenbacks. And you don't want people sniffing around you when you're trying to enjoy a baseball game.

The Canadian Baseball Hall of Fame and Museum

If you enjoy looking at the Canadian baseball exhibits on SkyDome's first level, consider visiting the Canadian Baseball Hall of Fame and Museum in St. Mary's, Ontario. For visitor info, check out www.baseballhalloffame.ca.

Fergie Jenkins and Jackie Robinson are the only members of the United States National Baseball Hall of Fame and Canada's hall. Here's betting Larry Walker joins the exclusive club some day.

The Hockey Hall of Fame

You're in Canada. So check out the hockey hall of fame, you hoser! It's located just a few blocks from SkyDome at 161 Bay Street.

A self-proclaimed "stick-handler," Kevin enjoyed putting a few shots on goal in the interactive area, while Josh stared longingly for several minutes at Lord Stanley's Cup.

"Pretty cool, eh?" Kevin said, trying to snap Josh out of his trance.

"Yeah," Josh said. "If I had a cup that big, I'd eat baked beans out of it."

"I'll catch up with you later," Kevin said.

And we went our separate ways, but we both found plenty to keep us occupied and fascinated at the hall.

For information, visit www.hhof.com.

On Our Way to Toronto

Kevin Refused to Take Part in Role-playing of Any Kind

Toronto represented the last stop on the 2002 edition of our road trip. After catching a game in Cleveland the day before, we headed to Canada for a Sunday afternoon game that would bid the 2002 season farewell.

Josh was driving our rented Dodge Sebring, and since he'd never left the United States before, he was a bit antsy.

"What if they don't let me in?" he asked.

"I'll leave you at the border and come back for you after the game," Kevin said.

"Really, you'd do that?"

"Of course not. Don't worry. They'll let you in. It's Canada. They let everyone in," Kevin said. Quite paradoxically, Kevin then launched into a lengthy story about one of his Seattle friends, Dana, who had been turned away at the border on her way to Vancouver.

"I don't have my social security card," a post-9-11 Josh said, riffling through his wallet as he nearly veered off the road.

"Stop worrying," Kevin said. "They'll let you in."

"Maybe we could do some role-playing," Josh suggested. "You be the border guard, and I'll be me."

"Huh?"

"Ask me some of the questions like he will, just for practice."

"I don't think that will be necessary," Kevin said. "They'll ask for our names and destination and that will be it. It's not like we're trying to smuggle heroin."

"Heroin! I didn't shave this morning. What if they think I look seedy?"

"You don't look seedy."

"I just have a feeling it's going to be an ordeal," Josh said.

And sure enough it was, no thanks to the two Wrigley Field chairs Josh had purchased in Chicago that currently resided in the Sebring's backseat.

"What are those rusty old things?" the border guard asked, pointing to the chairs.

"Wrigley Field Stadium chairs, sir," Josh stammered. "I have a certificate of authenticity for each of them if you'd like to see."

"Why do you have chairs from Wrigley Field in the backseat if you're just going to Tronno for a game?" the guard asked, suspiciously.

Josh rifled through a folder of papers, looking for the two certificates of authenticity the Cubs had made for the chairs using Microsoft Word. He handed the crumpled-up pieces of paper to the man and tried his best not to stutter. "B-b-b-because we're on our baseball road trip, sir, collecting all sorts of stuff from ballparks and stadiums, taking pictures. You know . . . living the American, er . . . North American . . . dream."

"Yeah," the guard said mildly perturbed, after inspecting the documents. "Go on then. Just don't get any ideas aboot the chairs at SkyDome."

"I won't, sir," Josh said sincerely. "Honest, I won't."

"Go on!"

"For a while I didn't think they were going to let me in with those chairs," Josh said afterward.

"They let everyone in," Kevin said.

"Except your friend?"

"Right, except for my friend, my friend Dana Hackett."

MONTREAL EXPOS, OLYMPIC STADIUM

Stade Olympique

MONTREAL,
QUEBEC, CANADA

330 miles to Boston
340 miles to Toronto
380 miles to New York City
480 miles to Philadelphia

OUR BASEBALL ADVENTURE took place during Major League Baseball's dying days in Montreal. Although a decision on the ultimate destination of the Expos had yet to be reached by MLB at the time of our visit to Quebec in 2003, we had to double-check the schedule to make sure the Expos weren't on a home trip to San Juan, Puerto Rico, before we packed up the road-trip car and headed north. Anyway, by the time we arrived in town there didn't seem to be much point in going through the motions in Montreal anymore. Not with the city, its team, and its fans hamstrung by MLB. Not after an underhanded deal made behind closed doors had allowed the other twenty-nine Major League teams and their owners to assume control of the Expos in 2002. And not after those other twenty-nine owners had ordered Expos general manager Omar Minaya to slash the team's payroll prior to the 2003 season, forcing him to deal staff ace Bartolo Colon. Not after the Expos had gotten off to a great start in 2003, only to lose their momentum in early June when an extended road and home trip took them away from Montreal for twenty-five straight days. During the odyssey the team logged a grueling 11,310 miles in air travel and recorded just eight wins in twenty-two games.

Are we being too hard on MLB, you may ask, blaming the commissioner and his cronies for the anemic state of the game in Montreal? Well, let's consider the facts, starting all the way back at the beginning. Then we'll let you decide for yourself.

Believe it or not, upon entering the National League as an expansion team in 1969, Montreal outdrew the three other teams who joined the league that year—the Los Angeles Angels, San Diego Padres, and Seattle Mariners. The Expos were the only franchise among the group to eclipse the one-million mark in attendance, drawing 1.2 million fans to Jarry Park.

A thirty-five-thousand-seat temporary stadium, Jarry was widely considered the worst ballpark in the Majors, yet Montreal fans often filled the place. Jarry's clubhouses were down the left field line, requiring players to walk behind the stands to get to their dugouts. And the ballpark was oriented so that the setting sun blinded first-basemen as they awaited throws from the left side of the infield. What's more, none of the seats in the one-level stadium were covered by a roof, so on rainy nights fans had nowhere to hide. But Jarry had at least one thing going for it. On sunny days, fans could abandon the game and make use of a public swimming pool located just outside the gates beyond the right field fence. But most fans stayed until the last out before taking a dip.

The Expos fans brought a hockey-crowd mentality to games. Sometimes a raucous cheer would rise up in the stands at a time when nothing special was happening on the field, cuing players and fans alike that a girl in a skimpy skirt or tight top was making her way down an aisle. One fan bought a season ticket for his dog and brought the pup to every home game, where the dog would actually sit in his seat and howl.

In each of their first six seasons, the Expos attracted more than a million fans to Jarry Park. Mind you, this was at a time when the average National League team was drawing 1.3 million per season. Montreal consistently placed in the middle of the pack in attendance. At the same time, the city was awaiting completion of Olympic Stadium, which would not only host the 1976 Summer Games, but then provide the Expos with a revolutionary new playing field. Eventually, you see, the intention was to make "the Big O" a retractable-roof dome. Talk about being ahead of its time, eh? The facility was also to be the Major League's first fully bilingual ballpark, providing all public address announcements in both English and French. Decades later, the Expos would unveil the second bilingual park—Hiram Bithorn Stadium in San Juan—under much less optimistic circumstances for the franchise.

The City of Montreal finished constructing Olympic Stadium just in time for the 1976 Olympics. The following year, the dome became the Expos' new home. Unlike Turner Field in Atlanta, however, which was remodeled to accommodate baseball after hosting the 1996 Summer Games, Montreal did little more than throw down artificial turf and paint baselines on the plastic in preparation for the Expos' arrival. Nonetheless, the team was soon drawing more than two million fans per season to its new digs. So far, so good. The team had a strong following in its community and a brand new stadium.

Outside Olympic Stadium a 623-foot-high inclined tower hung—and still hangs—above the center of the playing field like a loon's neck. A

exterior

Photo by Josh Pahigian

65-ton Kevlar roof, suspended by cables, hangs from the tower. The roof was originally meant to open and close in forty-five minutes. But it never worked properly, so the Big O eventually became a fixed dome when management gave up on the retractable roof idea in 1989. In 1998, however, the Expos removed the umbrella at midseason, making Olympic an open-air facility. But the big top was eventually put back in place.

Although the Expos never won a National League pennant in Montreal, their fans hung with them for more than two and a half decades. Montreal was never the best baseball town going, but it was never the worst either. Then things all started to unravel in 1994. After watching the Toronto Blue Jays celebrate World Championships in 1992 and 1993, the Expos were poised to go deep into the playoffs in 1994. They had the best record in baseball (74–40) and had drawn 1.3 million fans to fifty-five home dates when the season ended on August 12 because of the players' strike. In their final home game, played on August 4, against the Cardinals, the Expos drew a crowd of 39,044 fans. Not too shabby, eh?

As Tom Glavine led the Players Association into battle, his Atlanta Braves sat six full games behind the Expos in the NL East standings. But the season never resumed, and the next year the Expos sank to last place in their division having lost key players like Ken Hill, Marquis Grissom, Larry Walker, and John Wetteland to the clutches of baseball's new economic realities. The fans eventually returned to the ballparks in many big league cities, but in Montreal, they never did. With gate revenue on the decline and the Canadian dollar sinking steadily against the U.S. greenback, Montreal was unable to retain its emerging stars in the years ahead. In addition to the players mentioned above, other key losses included Pedro Martinez, Cliff Floyd, Moises

Alou, Delino DeShields, David Segui, Rondell White, and Jeff Fassero, all of whom departed via free agency or lopsided trades designed to reduce payroll. Feeling betrayed by the game, the Montreal fans now really stopped turning out at the ballpark.

By 1999 home attendance had sagged to less than ten thousand fans per game. Late that year, a group of fourteen Canadian investors and one American—New Yorker Jeffrey Loria—purchased the team. Plans were drawn up for a new open-air ballpark in downtown Montreal and local residents began talking baseball again. For a while it looked like Montreal might make a comeback. Then disagreements among different factions of the ownership group—disagreements about whether the new ballpark should have a retractable roof—doomed the Expos' chances of staying in Montreal. The ballpark plan fell through. And without so much as a local TV deal, by 2001 the Expos were drawing only seven thousand fans per game, less than eleven minor league teams that season.

The final death knoll for the Expos came in February of 2002 when Loria sold his controlling interest in the team to Major League Baseball's other twenty-nine owners for $120 million. In turn, Loria bought the Florida Marlins from John Henry, who turned around and bought the Boston Red Sox from the Yawkey Trust. Loria brought with him to Florida his front office staff from Montreal, leaving the Expos without personnel and without even so much as scouting reports on the other NL teams. Under the ownership of MLB, the Expos finally replaced Olympic Stadium's aged green carpet. Tellingly, however, the new artificial turf was leased, not bought, by the league, with a club option for a second year, signifying quite clearly that MLB had no intention of laying down roots—even artificial ones—in Montreal.

As for the three-way franchise swap: many fans saw Bud Selig's fingerprints all over it. How could the other twenty-nine owners run their own teams and the Expos franchise without violating some sort of conflict of interests rule? By all appearances, the commish hoped to contract the Expos altogether and in doing so to gain an upper hand with the players heading into the 2002 labor negotiations. When he couldn't find grounds to legally eliminate another team (necessary to maintain an even number of teams in the league) the only recourse left was to move the Expos.

On July 15, 2002, Loria's fourteen Canadian limited partners sued him and Major League Baseball under the RICO ACT, accusing the defendants of conspiring to eliminate baseball in Montreal. A U.S. federal judge later ordered the partners to settle with Loria in arbitration and stayed the case against MLB. What a cruel lesson in American "justice" for these Canadians who had their hearts in the right place!

Prior to the 2003 season, it was decided that Montreal would play a portion of its home schedule in Puerto Rico in an effort to continue baseball's globalization. And so, ironically, Baseball sought to expand its presence near the equator while it sought to extricate itself from the Great White North. From a business perspective, this actually made good sense. Latin America had long been a market of growing interest for MLB. Of the 849 players on Major League rosters to start the 2002 season, 222 were born outside the continental United States. Of that total, sixty-five players hailed from the Dominican Republic, followed by thirty-eight from Puerto Rico, and eighteen from Venezuela.

With a forty-year old winter league stadium already in place, San Juan was chosen to host twenty-two of the Expos' eighty-one home games in 2003. What difference would it make to the Expos and their fans, MLB reasoned, not stopping to take into account that the Expos players had gone 49–32 at home in 2002. All that the twenty-nine owners of the Expos focused on was that Montreal had placed last in baseball in 2002 with an attendance of 812,545 fans for eighty-one home games. Even if the twenty-two San Juan games drew 15,000 fans apiece, the powers that be figured those games would bring in more revenue than twenty-two games in Montreal. Never mind that the Expos players would have to be on the road for weeks on end and that the schedule would make it virtually impossible for the team to have a championship season. It should be noted however that the Players Association had a say in the proceedings, voting to allow the San Juan experiment to take place so long as the league paid to fly the players' families to Puerto Rico and to house them on the island when the Expos were away.

San Juan's Hiram Bithorn Stadium—or Hi Bithorn for short—was named after the first player from Puerto Rico to make the Major Leagues. A right-handed pitcher, Hi Bithorn posted a 9–14 mark for the Chicago Cubs as a rookie in 1942, then went 18–12 with a 2.60 ERA the next season. But Bithorn missed the 1944 and 1945 seasons when he spent two years in the U.S. Marine Corps during World War II. He came back to win six games for the Cubs in 1946 and one for the crosstown White Sox in 1947 before retiring. He attempted to make a comeback a few years later in the Mexican winter league but on New Year's Day 1952 he was shot to death by a policeman in El Mante, Mexico. Details of the incident were very sketchy. Bithorn was just thirty-five years old at the time of his death.

While Bithorn's name may not be a familiar one in most American households, he has long been considered a hero in the Latin American community. Not only did he pave the way for today's Puerto Rican stars like Roberto and

Sandy Alomar, Carlos Beltran, Javy Lopez, Ivan Rodriguez, Carlos Delgado, Bernie Williams, and Juan Gonzalez, but he also preceded other Latino stars like Roberto Clemente, Juan Marichal, and Orlando Cepeda who followed him to the big leagues. As for the Expos, they began the 2003 season with six Latino players on their roster, including pitcher Javier Vasquez, a native of Puerto Rico. Further strengthening the team's Latin American connection, general manager Omar Minaya grew up in the Dominican Republic.

Before the Expos' first game at Hi Bithorn, Cepeda threw out the first pitch. Then pop star Marc Anthony sang the U.S. and Puerto Rican National Anthems, which were followed by the Canadian anthem. Four flags flew at the stadium, those of the United States, Puerto Rico, Canada, and San Juan. When it finally came time to play ball, the Expos trounced the Mets 10–0 before 17,906 screaming fans.

Booming salsa music and gyrating cheerleaders (as are customary in the Caribbean World Series) contributed to a festive game-day atmosphere during the Expos' island adventure. And the piña coladas sold in the stands were made from fresh pineapple and coconut juice and plenty of rum. But most observers agreed that Hi Bithorn was not fit for Major League competition. At just 315 feet down the lines and 360 to the power alleys, the park quickly distinguished itself as a hitter's paradise. In the first sixteen games at Hi Bithorn, the Expos and their opponents combined to hit sixty-three home runs. If players "went yard" at that rate during the course of a full season, San Juan's ballpark would project to yield 319 long balls in eighty-one games, or 16 more than Coors Field surrendered in 1999 when the Rockies and their opponents established the record for most dingers in a park. Hi Bithorn's other distinguishing feature was its bright green-colored artificial turf, which quickly had

fans all across America scratching their heads during SportsCenter and trying to adjust the tint on their TV sets.

In their first sixteen games at Hi Bithorn, the Expos went 10–6 and drew an average of 14,216 fans, as compared to the 11,330 they averaged through midseason 2003 in Montreal. San Juan has a great baseball history and the natives have a passion for the game, but given the limited prosperity of the city, economically it doesn't seem ready to support a big league team. And as the situation in Montreal has demonstrated, more is needed than a love of the game to keep Major League ball in a town. For the better part of two decades Montreal's citizens showed enthusiasm for hardball and the capacity to support their Expos. And history was on the Expos' side too. Despite its label as a hockey town in a hockey country, Montreal has baseball roots dating as far as Jackie Robinson's first venture onto a professional (non-Negro League) field in Montreal in 1946. Robinson started at second base for the Montreal Royals—a Brooklyn Dodgers minor league affiliate—who played their home games at Delorimier Downs. Robinson batted .349 and scored 113 runs to lead the Triple-A International League in both categories. In the postseason, he led Montreal past the Louisville Colonels of the American Association to win the "Little World Series" for Montreal. Playing before a hostile crowd in Kentucky, Robinson collected game-winning hits in the final two games of the Series.

While Robinson departed Montreal for the Major Leagues the next spring, minor league baseball continued to flourish in Montreal for another two decades. Then Major League Baseball was successful in the city for the better part of three decades. And now MLB has turned its back on the city.

When fans stopped turning out for Brewers games in Milwaukee, the league helped the town gain support for a new ballpark that would bring back fans and enable the team to spend more money on players. When fans stopped turning out in Pittsburgh, the same course of action was followed. But rather than help Montreal devise a plan to replace obsolete Olympic Stadium, and rather than helping to establish a stable ownership group in the city, the league has done everything possible to ensure that baseball does not survive in this great town. Montreal was a convenient partner to pair with the Minnesota Twins when the commissioner threatened the players with contraction leading up to the last labor negotiation. So in order to seize control of the team MLB bailed Loria out of Montreal, rather than leaving him to work with the local community and build a new ballpark in the city. When contraction fell through, MLB was left holding the bag in the form of the Expos. Obviously the team would fetch much more money from a prospective buyer should the buyer be allowed to take the team to a city in the States. So MLB made no effort to revive the Expos in Montreal, letting Olympic Stadium slip into disrepair, ordering Minaya to pare payroll, and offering local fans no hope. Conveniently, the league could then point to the understandably low attendance at Olympic Stadium and say that the town was no longer interested in supporting a team. For the record, Josh and Kevin say Montreal got a raw deal.

Getting a Choice Seat

Olympic Stadium is rarely a quarter full. Odds are, a high school baseball game not far from your home will outdraw an Expos game this spring. So plan on buying your tickets from the team on game day. Hey, the good news is that every fan has an excellent chance of going home with a foul ball, right?

When you arrive at the billeteria (French for "ticket window"), don't be thrown by the French words on the stadium seating map. With only four price categories, ordering tickets has never been easier. And even if you buy a lousy seat, you'll be free to move to just about anywhere you like within the stadium.

Sellout Index: If we could put a negative number here, we would!
Seating Capacity: 46,500
Ticket Office: (800) GO-EXPOS
www.montreal.expos.mlb.com

VIP (Sections 101–118, 119–124: First Rows Only)

Trust us, you don't have to be a very important person to sit in any of these infield VIP sections. All you need is $36 CAN, or roughly $22 U.S. These are the only seats in the joint for which the ushers check tickets, and they were 75 percent empty when we visited. Beginning with Row A and ending with Row V, these are comfortable Major League seats, as compared to the rest of the park, which features awful hard plastic seats.

Section 101 is right behind the plate. Even-numbered sections continue on the third-base side and odd-numbered sections continue on the first-base side. Sections 118 and 117 are even with the corner bags.

A two-foot rise of Plexiglas runs along the wall between the field and the stands to protect fans in the first rows from foul liners. If you'd

---

TRIVIA TIMEOUT

Facile: Name the only player to enter the Hall of Fame with a Montreal Expos cap on his plaque.

Difficile: Number 10 appears twice among the Expos' retired numbers. Which two players wore it?

Look for the answers in the text.

---

like to be able to look over the glass, shoot for a seat in Row C or higher.

Kevin: "Don't they know this is a baseball field and not a hockey rink?"

Josh: "Remember how close you came to getting beaned by that foul ball in Arlington?"

Box Seats (Sections 119–124; Sections 101–118, Behind Midlevel Concourse)

There's really no sense paying $24 CAN to sit in these sections. While ushers do check the tickets of fans heading down into the VIP boxes, they do not check tickets in these Box sections anymore, meaning that they might as well be General Admission. So why pay three times more than you have to?

Sections 119 to 124 beyond the infield down the lines provide decent views of the field, but we prefer the Box Seats behind the midlevel concourse on the infield in Sections 101 to 118. In the latter sections you will be farther from the field, but closer to the infield. Shoot for Sections 101 to 109 between the on-deck circles and you won't be disappointed. Just be sure to steer clear of Rows A through D behind the first (of the two) midlevel concourses. The seats behind this concourse are not elevated, meaning that aisle traffic is a serious concern for anyone in the first four rows.

Terrace (Sections 125–130; 101–118, Back Rows; 119–124, Midlevel of Sections; 201–219, Second Level around Plate)

Ushers were not checking tickets in these sections either, so again we must recommend instead buying a General Admission ticket, and then seat-hopping into any of these sections.

The Terrace seats in the back rows of Sections 101–118 are on the infield and quite good. The next best seats in this price range are those in the first few rows of Sections 201–210 behind the second concourse behind the plate. Here, the seats are elevated above the con-

course so aisle traffic is not a concern, but any Row higher than L should be avoided because of the overhang of the upper deck, which blocks the view of pop-ups.

Sections 125–130 place fans in the outfield corners. These seats are not only far from home plate but angled so that they leave fans looking over their shoulders all day long to get a gander at the infield.

General Admission

All of the seats not encompassed by the three price ranges profiled above fall into the General Admission category. Fans with GA tickets choose their seats when they enter the park and are free to sample as many areas as they like during the game.

Sections 220–224 provide excellent views out near the corner bases. We were disappointed by the quality of the home run seats in left and right field. Usually these are our favorite cheap seats. But not in Montreal. Here again the seats begin without first rising suitably above the walkway, making any seat in Rows A through D undesirable. So much for shooting for that front row seat where you might be able to reach out and catch a homer. Basically the "best" home run territory seat is located about twenty feet behind the outfield fence. To start, there's the lousy first four rows to account for between the field and Row E, then there's the four-foot-wide concourse, then there's the five-feet-worth of scaffolding for the manually operated out-of-town scoreboards.

Sections 133 and 134 should be avoided because of their foul net obstructions but since this is General Admission, this knowledge will have no bearing on the ticket buying process for you; you'll figure it out when you get inside the park, sit down, and realize there's a two-foot-wide red net blocking your view of the action.

The upper deck was closed entirely when we visited, and by all indications it will be used very sparingly for the remainder of the Expos' tenure in Montreal. We'll leave it to you to figure things out for yourself if you spend Opening Day in Montreal (why would you?) and a huge walk-up crowd leaves you unable to find a General Admission seat on the first level. We were able to ascertain from the first level that (1) the Upper Boxes consist of the first ten rows of the upper level, which are located below the midlevel walkway; (2) the seats behind the walkway are elevated enough to take the potential distraction of pedestrian traffic out of play; and (3) the potential obstruction of the deck's under-hang is not a major issue thanks to the fact that the upper deck begins above the back rows of the expansive lower level.

SEATING TIP

➜ IF YOU ARE a college student with a valid college ID, a senior citizen, a kid, or a woman, or if you're traveling with a large group of friends, check at the ticket window to see if you are eligible for a 50 percent discount on your ticket.

In recent seasons, every Monday has been Group Night (half off admission for groups of twenty-five or more), every Tuesday has been Senior Citizen night, Thursday—Ladies Night, Friday—Student Night, and Saturday and Sunday—Kids Days.

Kevin: "What about Wednesday night?"

Before/After the Game

It's a shame that Major League Baseball couldn't stay forever in Montreal—a high energy, European-style city full of fun things for the road tripper to do and tasty things for him to eat. The area immediately around the ballpark isn't the most exciting, but happy times are just a short drive away.

This sports complex of sorts also includes the famous Montréal Biodôme and the Aréna Maurice Richard, a hockey arena. The good news is that there's no sea of parking lots surrounding these facilities, thanks to the underground garage located between the dome and the Pie IX Métro station. A nifty walkway connects the Métro station to the parking garage to the dome—providing a very efficient way to get folks in and out of the park. On the Sherbrooke side of the complex a botanical garden provides plenty of green grass and visually appealing hillsides, while an insectarium provides plenty of bugs.

Getting to Olympic Stadium

Olympic Stadium is located at 4549 Avenue Pierre-de-Coubertin. Now don't freak out because the traffic signs are in French. It's really not that difficult. Just remember: north = *nord*, south = *sud*, east = *est*, and west = *ouest*.

From Toronto, take Highway 401 Est until it becomes Highway 20 in Quebec. Stay on 20 Est until you see Dorval Airport, then exit at Côte-de-Liesse (Highway 520). Stick with Highway 520 Est until it ends at a set of traffic lights and hop onto Highway 40 Est. Remain on 40 Est until the Pie IX Boulevard Exit, then follow the blue signs for Olympic Stadium, which is located at the corner of Pie IX and Sherbrooke.

From New York State, follow I-87 until it becomes Highway 15 in Quebec. Stay on 15 Nord until the Champlain Bridge Exit, which will drop you onto the Decarie Expressway heading north. Take the exit for 40 Est and then exit onto Pie IX Boulevard.

From Vermont, take I-89 until it becomes Highway 35 in Quebec. Stay on 35 Nord until the exit for Highway 10. Take Highway 10 Ouest until the Champlain Bridge. Take the Champlain Bridge exit and get on the Decarie

Expressway. Remain on Decarie until the exit for Highway 40. Take 40 Est to the Pie IX Boulevard Exit.

The team parking garage charges $12 CAN. If you don't mind a ten-minute walk, consider parking in the Biodôme lot at the corner of Viau Street and rue Pierre-Charbonneau, where the cost is only $7 CAN.

Even though the ballpark crowd is rather small, driving in Montreal can be a pain. The city streets get clogged up at rush hour and on weekend nights because of heavy traffic and the many pedestrians and bicyclists weaving in and out between the cars. And just about every street is one way.

For folks staying in town, we highly recommend Montreal's Métro subway, which is clean, smooth, and safe. And it goes everywhere. Walkways connect the Green Line's Pie IX and Viau stations to Stade Olympique. A one-day Métro pass costs just $7 CAN.

Outside Attractions

THE TOWER

The bizarre inclined tower that holds up the parachute that covers the middle of the dome is a real oddity, and one worth spending an extra minute or two checking out. We recommend driving past the park on Sherbrooke, an elevated road that provides a roof-level look at this monstrosity. The Sherbrooke vantage point allowed us to see just how rusty the metal portions of the roof and tower were and just how faded and nasty the concrete portions were. We also observed many missing panels from the tower as well as a ring of cor-

Photo by Josh Pahigian

roded green copper around the roof of the dome.

SPACE-AGE WASTELAND

After parking the car, walk up one of the many ramps that lead to the upper concourse. The entrance gates and ticket windows on this level may all be closed because the upper deck is not often used for seating these days, but fans are still allowed to roam these levels before the game. We tried to picture this vast concrete ghost town as it must have appeared when full of excited baseball fans. It wasn't easy to envision, but we tried.

BREAKING BARRIERS

Located outside the main entrance gate, a statue of Jackie Robinson portrays the man who broke baseball's color barrier. The statue depicts Robinson talking to two children, one presumably Caucasian and one presumably African American. We can only hope that once Major League Baseball leaves town, the city of Montreal will find an appropriate place to display this statue.

Watering Holes and Outside Eats

For the best nightlife in Montreal, stroll along Crescent Street, which offers great restaurants, awesome bars, and—our favorite—European-style dance clubs!

Keep your eyes open for street vendors selling cigars on Sainte-Catherine. In Montreal actual Cubans are available since there's no embargo between Canada and Cuba. Yeah, you may want to stick to your guns and not throw any of your money Castro's way, but try to look at your purchase as an investment in Cuba's national baseball team.

Boulevard Saint-Laurent provides a festive atmosphere during its frequent Friday festivals. Even when folks aren't dancing in the street, this is a great place to sample some smoked meat and/or *poutine* (see Stadium Eats below) along with some local bars.

The Old Port in northeast Montreal on the St. Lawrence River houses shops and restaurants that cater to a slightly more mature crowd than the Crescent Street neighborhood.

MOE'S DELI AND BAR
(3950 Sherbrooke Street Est and Pie IX)

This is the nearest restaurant to the park and it's not a bad option to consider for those breezing into town shortly before the first pitch. With a classy wooden bar and plenty of booths and tables, Moe's offers everything from Asian spring rolls to buffalo wings to quesadillas to pizzas to burgers to smoked meat sandwiches. Entrées include steaks, ribs, chicken, and pasta dishes. Most items are in the $4 to $12 CAN range.

SMOKED MEAT
While the fine dining establishments in Montreal are legendary and relatively cheap given the current exchange rate, not to be overlooked is this town's smoked meat. The locals eat this mouthwatering cured beef brisket piled high on fresh bread, slathered with mustard, and served with a gherkin and some fries. While lots of joints serve the stuff, Josh ranks **Schwartz's Hebrew Delicatessen** (3895 Boulevard Saint-Laurent) at the very top of the list. Schwartz's smokes its meat on the premises, whereas most places in town buy their meat presmoked. It's cheap—at about $6 CAN for a big sandwich and a black cherry cola. We ate our sandwiches sitting at the shiny silver deli counter, which gave us an excellent view of the slabs of meat in various stages of preparation.

Across the street at **The Main** (3864 Boulevard Saint-Laurent) the meat is nearly as tender and juicy, and it's a buck cheaper. The lines are shorter too. The Main also smokes its own meat.

Other popular smoked-meat restaurants that deserve mention are **Ben's** (990 Boulevard de Maisonneuve) and **Lester's Delicatessen** (1057 Bernard Street in Outremont). But neither of these joints smokes its own meat on site. Rather, they buy it presmoked, then warm it up and slice it. This type of smoked meat is sliced thinner (almost as thin as deli meat) than the homemade type served at Schwartz's and the Main, and tastes more like pastrami than corned beef.

One final word of advice that applies to all of these places: ask for your meat "lean" or expect it to come marbleized with juicy and delicious but potentially heart-clogging fat. It's common practice for patrons to ask for a lean cut, so don't be bashful. This isn't like asking for a pizza without the sauce. However, for the record, we did not ask for any of our meat lean. And we ate five smoked-meat sandwiches between us (Josh 3; Kevin 2).

CHINESE TO PLEASE
A real eye-opener for us was the caliber of oriental food in Montreal's Chinatown, which

rates nearly as good as the eats in Boston and New York's Chinese districts. We tried the dim sum at **Kam Fung** (1071 rue Saint-Urban) and the lobster at **Mon Shing** (rue la Gauchetiére and rue Saint-Urban) and both were excellent. After Kevin picked up the dim sum tab, he stuck Josh with paying for the much more expensive lobster.

DUNDEE'S (2010 rue Crescent)

This spacious pub is perhaps the most happening hangout on the most happening street in the most happening area of Canada's most happening town. The beer is cold, the food is decent, and the waitresses are cute.

TROIKA (2171 Crescent)

If you're looking to feast on a platter of wild boar while sipping vodka, this is the place for you. Serving Russian cuisine with a French influence, Troika is definitely one of those places you just don't find in the States.

LES HALLES (1450 Crescent)

With a menu that ranges from lobster to prime rib to quail breasts to venison, Les Halles has been serving fine French cuisine since 1971. Expect to pay a lot but to leave satisfied. Also be sure to call for a reservation; otherwise you'll never get seated. We recommend the chateaubriand followed by the raspberry tart and house coffee.

CASINO DE MONTREAL (Parc Jean-Drapeau)

Located on Notre Dame Island just half an hour outside of downtown, the casino opened in 1993 and has been a tourist jackpot ever since for the city. Open twenty-four hours a day, seven days a week, fifty-two weeks per year, the casino is accessible by car and by public transportation.

By auto, take the Bonaventure Autoroute to Exit 2—the Port of Montréal/Pierre-Dupuy Avenue, and then cross the Concorde Bridge.

By foot, catch the casino shuttle bus (No. 167) that picks players up at the Jean-Drapeau Métro station on the Yellow Line.

Younger readers will be happy to know that the minimum age to play is just eighteen.

Inside the Stadium

Olympic Stadium was the dirtiest ballpark we visited during our trip. Hands down. No, there wasn't trash overflowing in the aisles. At the time of our visit MLB was still cleaning the joint between games. But the facility itself was coated with grime and riddled with decay, making it terrible to look at. We couldn't find an inch of concrete in the seating bowl that wasn't chipped or stained or smeared with some sort of soiling. A particular strain of black mildew (or was it mold?) seemed to be growing and thriving on the cement throughout the park.

As for the seats, they are in even worse shape. While the blue seats down near the infield have obviously been added in recent years, the yellow seats found on the rest of the first level are old, tiny, and practically coated with wads of bubble gum stuck to them over the years. Beneath the gum, the seats are made of hard plastic, with bottoms contoured to fit the average human buttocks—meaning that there is a raised ridge that bisects each seat perpendicularly where the crack of one's butt is supposed to be. This means that if you shift in your seat, or try to cross your legs, the crack ridge uncomfortably presses into your back-side. Not good, especially for a thin guy like Josh who doesn't have a lot of built-in padding back there. Kevin felt no discomfort, however.

The Jumbotron is located beyond the center field fence and together with the black curtain that hangs beneath it, it cuts the dome in half. There are seats located way behind the Jumbotron and curtain that are not used for baseball games (or anything else these days). The visual effect of the Jumbotron bisecting the facility reminded us of Syracuse University's Carrier Dome, which is cut in half by a curtain when basketball (as opposed to football) is on the docket. For basketball this may be okay, but for baseball it makes the facility seem ticky-tacky and temporary.

The bull pens are located beyond the first- and third-base bags in outfield foul territory. Due to the limited foul ground in this part of the park, there is barely room for two mounds and two catcher boxes. Seeing two pitchers warm up simultaneously in the same pen made us think of the time we went to the driving range to hit golf balls in the thin air of Colorado. Of course, we had the benefit of large wooden separators between us to prevent any stray shots from hitting the person in the carrel next to us, a luxury bull pen catchers in Montreal are not given.

The air inside the park was also rather foul. It had been a warm day outside and either the Olympic Stadium AC was on the blink or it had been turned off by cost-conscious MLB. Maybe Selig and co. would have been able to afford AC if we had forked over the $20,000 they were asking for the rights to print the officially

licensed ballpark seating maps in our book. Oh, well. In any case, it was hot and muggy inside. Some fans took off their shirts. Others sat and sweated in their uncomfortable seats.

The oxygen content was further compromised by the many fans smoking cigarettes in the seating area even though smoking at Olympic Stadium was supposedly restricted to the concourses. We changed sections only to find a contingent of smokers puffing away in our new spot. Apparently smoking is as hip in Montreal as it is in Europe and the ushers don't do anything to extinguish the trend.

The only small ray of light in this otherwise dark and sterile environment for a game was in fact a ray of light—courtesy of the setting sun. That's right, during the first few innings of night games enough sunlight shines through the upper level left field walkways to cast a few solar spotlights on the outfield turf—approximately ten feet wide each. Shadow puppets anyone?

Ballpark Features

FOUL NETS

Olympic Stadium's foul poles are, in fact, not poles but rather two-foot-wide red nets adorned all the way up with white maple leaves. These nets span from the top of the outfield fences up to the roof. They are tattered and faded and pretty sad to see. Even when they were new, they must have looked hideously out of place. This is baseball, eh? Foul poles are supposed to be poles, and they're supposed to be school-bus yellow in color. Anything less is unacceptable.

A fluorescent orange line painted on the roof is aligned

Photo by Josh Pahigian

PROUD TO BE AN EXPO

GARY CARTER was one of many superb players to wear the Expos blue, white, and red. But unlike other Montreal stars like Pete Rose, Andre Dawson, and Tim Raines, Carter was enshrined in the Baseball Hall of Fame at Cooperstown wearing an Expos cap on his plaque. The catcher, who played twelve seasons with Montreal, including his first eleven seasons and final one, was inducted to the hall in 2003.

In nineteen total seasons, the popular backstop hit 324 homers and drove in 1,225 runs, while also winning three Gold Glove Awards. Carter's best season was in 1984 when he established personal bests with 175 hits, a league-leading 106 RBI and a .294 batting average, playing in a remarkable 159 games. After the season he was traded to the New York Mets where he would help develop young pitchers like Dwight Gooden, David Cone, Ron Darling, and Sid Fernandez. After winning a World Series with the Mets in 1986 and later playing for the Giants and Dodgers, Carter went "home" to Montreal to finish his career with the Expos in 1992. To put the exclamation point on his fine career, in his final game, played September 27, 1992, against the Cubs, Carter doubled home the only run in a 1–0 Expos victory.

with the foul line down below to help umpires make the right call should a ball ever hit that part of the roof, which to our knowledge one never has.

THE "OPEN AIR" SCOREBOARDS

Behind the outfield fence, fans in the left and right field bleachers are able to look down into the two manually operated out-of-town scoreboards to see teenagers on scaffolding sliding appropriately numbered plywood slabs into the board. This bush-league feature of the ballpark sure demystifies the appeal of the old-style scoreboard that used to keep us waiting and waiting for a score of interest, then magically change when we least expected it.

PIRATES GOLD

A gold seat (whereas the rest are blue) in the right field upper deck marks the landing spot of a 535-foot home run hit by Pittsburgh slugger Willie Stargell on May 20, 1978. A decade earlier at Jarry Park, Stargell had hit a shot that landed in the swimming pool beyond the right field fence on July 16, 1969. To this day the pool is referred to as *la piscine de Willie* by local fans. As for the gold seat, folks still call it *la belle site*.

RETIRED AND RE-RETIRED NUMBERS

The Expos' retired numbers hang in right field: number 8 for Gary Carter, number 10 for Andre Dawson, number 10 for Rusty Staub, number 42 for Jackie Robinson.

Yes, you read that right, both Dawson and Staub wore number 10. In 1993 the number was retired for Staub, who had worn it from 1969 to 1971 and then again in 1979. But in the meantime, Dawson had worn it for the Expos from 1976 to 1986. And so, in 1997, the number was retired again, this time in honor of "the Hawk."

Kevin: "The number 10 retired twice, hilarious. What do you expect from a country that has an eight-team football league and two of the teams have the same name?"

Josh: "Yankee Stadium has two retired number 8s."

Kevin: "Oh, yeah."

THE WALL OF EXCELLENCE

The Wall of Excellence is located on the first-level concourse behind home plate. The Wall features twenty-two plaques that honor former Expos stars like Dawson, Raines, Carter, Staub, Tim Wallach, Hubie Brooks, Woodie Fryman, Steve Rogers, Warren Cromartie, Bill Lee, Enos Valentine, Jeff Reardon, Larry Parish, and Bill Gullickson.

While some of these folks are legitimate players worth remembering and celebrating, most are not. Consider the case of Fryman, who ranks ninth all time in team history with a winning percentage of just .495, or the case of Lee, who had a decent career, but pitched only four seasons for the Expos, earning twenty-five wins and six saves. We have more respect for those teams with so-so histories that are aware of their lack of glory, and therefore don't start honoring any average Major Leaguer to have worn their uniform.

Kevin: "Like the Mariners?"

Josh: "Precisely."

The Wall also displays a plaque for Charles R. Bronfman, the man who founded the Expos. But the biggest plaque of all is the one dedicated to Jack Roosevelt Robinson.

Also nearby are reproductions of every Expos team photo since the club's first season in 1969. The Expos mascot Youppi first appears in the 1990 team photo, then, after being included for the ten following years, he disappears in 2000 and has not made his way into the picture since. We enjoyed the older photos that provided glimpses of Jarry Park.

We found it ironic that not far from these tributes to Montreal's baseball past, kids were playing foosball and air-hockey at coin-operated table games.

Stadium Eats

Olympic Stadium provides an eating experience that is truly unique. While traditional American ballpark fare is available (and not very good), we recommend sampling some of the local flavor. Don't plan on waiting for the traditional roving vendors to come by with treats, as we didn't spot any vendors patrolling the stands when we were in town. We're not sure why. Even minor league teams sell food in the stands. Oh well, at least the concourses and concession stand lines are never crowded.

MONSIEUR SMOKED MEAT (Trademark Food)

The meat at Monsieur's is not quite as tasty as the stuff served at Schwartz's and the Main and it's a few bucks more expensive. The sandwiches are premade and come pretopped with mustard. We got ours before the game started and the freshly baked bread and juicy meat were still in excellent condition. We can't vouch for any sandwich served say, after the third inning, or so, however. The meat is sliced thinner than at the joints on Saint-Laurent, and it's not as fatty. But still, this is a very respectable trademark food for Olympic Stadium.

MONTREAL SUPER DOG (Dog Rating)

The Twenty-eighth Best Hot Dog in the Majors

We were initially optimistic upon being handed our Expos jumbo dog. After all, it was made to order, boiled, and quite large. Plus it was served on a sesame-seed bun, which made it original. We observed many locals ordering these topped with cole slaw, but we ordered ours plain, then immediately ripped it in half. Josh topped his with ketchup and Kevin topped his with mustard. We both took an enthusiastic bite out of our respective half, then looked at each other and frowned. Though the dog was juicy and cooked properly, we didn't care for its extremely mild taste. When it came time to mix the meat, clearly beef was not featured prominently on the list of ingredients, and the dog's taste suffers as the result.

Instead, we recommend spending an extra buck and a quarter to get an all-beef kosher dog. Look for the sign that says "100% Boeuf Kasher."

BEST OF THE REST

Poutine is also a local specialty. Take some crispy french fries, smother them in gravy, and top the whole mess with gooey cheese curds, and you've got the favorite snack food of Québec. You can certainly do better at one of the greasy spoons in town, but the ballpark

OVER THE YEARS the fans of Montreal enjoyed some special moments at Olympic Stadium, even if some of them occurred at the expense of the home team.

The first game at the Big O was played on April 15, 1977. But much to the disappointment of the 57,592 fans in attendance, the Expos lost to the Phillies 7–2.

After the strike-shortened regular season in 1981 the Expos came within one win of reaching the World Series. Boy, did the MLB brain trust ever screw up that postseason. Take the National League for example. After Philadelphia won the first half of the NL East season with a record of 34–21, Montreal won the second half with a record of 30–23. So the two teams met in a first-round playoff series to determine who would play the winner of a similar series between NL West winners Los Angeles and Houston. So while these four split-season winners advanced to the playoffs, St. Louis and Cincinnati, who had posted the best overall records in their respective divisions during the entire season, were left out of the playoffs.

After winning the first two games of the best-of-five playoff series at home by identical scores of 3–1, Montreal dropped two straight games in Philadelphia before winning the Series in Philly behind a 3–0 Steve Rogers shutout over Steve Carlton. With the win, Montreal earned the right to play the Dodgers for the NL pennant. The Championship Series would ultimately account for the most painful moment in Olympic Stadium history. With the best-of-five Series knotted at two games apiece, the Expos scored a run against Fernando Valenzuela in the bottom of the first inning of Game Five to take an early lead. But the Dodgers tied the game in the fourth and took the lead in the top of the ninth on a home run by Rick Monday en route to a 2–1 win and a series victory. "Blue Monday" would become an infamous baseball moment in Montreal.

Josh: "At least the Dodgers went on to beat the Yankees in the World Series."

Kevin: "True enough. But who's to say the Expos wouldn't have done the same?"

The very next season Montreal hosted the All-Star Game. The 1982 National League squad had a decidedly maple flavor as Expos Rogers, Carter, Dawson, and Raines were all in the starting lineup and Al Oliver and Jim Fanning were on the bench. Rogers hurled three innings of one-run ball to earn the decision in a 4–1 National League win.

On April 13, 1984 in the Olympic Stadium home opener, Pete Rose collected hit number 4,000 of his career in his only season with the Expos. In August, Rose was traded back to Cincinnati.

On August 6, 1999, Tony Gwynn wrapped out hit number 3,000 of his career in the first inning of a game in Montreal. We can't help but think that such a great hitter deserved a better stage for his career-topping moment.

---

poutine—served in Styrofoam cups—is freshly made and tasty.

The pizza at **Comptoir à Pizza** rates much higher than normal ballpark pizza. Get this, it actually tastes freshly made. The crust is crunchy and the cheese is not dried out. We recommend the plain cheese slice as opposed to the pepperoni, which we didn't care for since the meat tasted more like salami. We assumed this was a Canadian thing, kind of like Canadian bacon. You know, some things just don't translate well.

The **Kojax Souflaki** stand makes fresh pita wraps to order, which we found refreshing in this age of premade, prewrapped ballpark sandwiches. We suppose it's a lot more feasible to make food fresh when your ballpark only attracts ten thousand fans per night, as opposed to the thirty thousand at most parks.

SAY "NO, THANKS," AND WALK AWAY

We saw the Aramark logo on the Tex-Mex stand and kept on walking. Besides, Texas and Mexico are miles from here.

STADIUM SUDS

Molson Export is the beer of choice among Expos fans, while Molson Dry is also available. Prior to our visit we had heard tell of vendors patrolling the stands selling mixed drinks at Olympic, but we didn't see it.

The Stade Olympique Experience

We visited Montreal for the first Expos home game after a twenty-five-day, twenty-two-game road- and home trip that began in late May and spanned most of June 2003. Of the 11,355 fans who attended the game, many had dressed for the occasion or brought signs with them to the ballpark in support of the home team. Honest, it felt more like a crowd of, say, 14,355 because of the enthusiasm of the fans in the ballpark cheering as if the game might be the last one they'd ever see. We suppose for some folks this was true.

YOUPPI

The much-maligned Youppi has served as mascot of the Expos since 1979. Shaggy, orange, and androgynous, Youppi wears a white Expos uniform with an exclamation point where the numbers should be. When we visited, he spent most of the game groping fans, male and female alike.

This furry fellow's name may mean, "yippee" in French, but Tommy Lasorda wasn't happy to see Youppi dancing atop the Dodgers dugout during a game at Olympic Stadium on August 23, 1989. The mascot was ejected from the game by umpire Bob Davidson after Lasorda took exception to his shenanigans and complained. Adding insult to injury, the Dodgers beat the Expos 1–0 in a twenty-two-inning marathon.

CHAIR CLANGING

At first we weren't sure why the Expos fans were clanging their spring-loaded seats up and

---

SPORTS IN THE CITY

THE CANADIAN BASEBALL LEAGUE

IN DECEMBER OF 2002 at a time when hope of a hardball renaissance in Montreal seemed nearly extinguished, the Canadian Baseball League emerged, announcing its formation and saying that it would begin play the following spring in cities throughout Canada.

The independent minor league announced that among its teams would be the Montreal Royales. Initially the franchise hoped to play its 2003 home games at Olympic Stadium. When the city of Montreal and the Expos prevented this, the new league decided that the Royales would play their home games on the road until the Expos left town in 2004 or 2005.

Also participating in the seventy-two-game inaugural season were the Calgary Outlaws, London Monarchs, Niagara Stars, Kelowna Heather, Saskatoon Legens, Trois-Rivieres Saints, and Victoria Capitals.

A number of former Major Leaguers with Canadian roots took the lead in establishing the league, starting at the top with Commissioner Ferguson Jenkins. Jenkins was born in Chatham, Ontario. Other familiar baseball names like Gary Roenicke, Willie Wilson, Jody Davis, and Andres Thomas also signed on as team managers.

In 2003, the vagabond Royales played their nine home series in various host cities across Canada. The team did, however, practice in Montreal and make promotional appearances in the city with an eye toward connecting with the local community. Several Royales games were also televised on the Score Television Network.

The level of play in 2003 was higher than many observers from the States had expected it to be. The CBL requires that each team maintain at least five native Canadians on its roster. So with a strong contingent of American and International players, the league rates somewhere above rookie-level ball, and somewhere below the independent Northern League. Here's hoping it catches on.

---

down—creating quite a cacophony. Were they trying to punish the ancient yellow chairs for being so darned uncomfortable, we wondered? Then we figured out that this was the Montreal way to "make some noise" and encourage the home team to mount a rally.

Given the fact that there are so many empty seats these days, seat clanging has never been easier. You don't even need to stand up. Odds are that at least one seat next to either side of you will be empty, so just reach on over and start clanging it up and down. If it breaks, then just move over a seat or two and go to work on another one.

AMERICAN MUSIC

We had to chuckle at the selection of tunes played over the PA system between innings. It was funny to hear the *Cops* theme song segue into Madonna's "La Isla Bonita," then into the Beatles' "Come Together," then into AC/DC's "All Night Long," then into the score from *The Good, the Bad and the Ugly*, then into the Rolling Stones' "Under My Thumb," then into Michael Jackson's "Bad."

These French Canadians must make some funky mix tapes.

JARRY PARK

After eating at Schwartz's, we followed Boulevard-Saint-Laurent across Mont Royal and continued heading straight for about two miles before we came upon Jarry Park, formerly the home of the Expos, and currently a major outdoor recreation and sports complex.

The park's main attraction is Stade du Maurier, which is used for pro-tennis events. But there are also plenty of attractions for amateur athletes. We found a playing field or court for just about every sport we could imagine. The park includes several baseball and softball diamonds, soccer fields, a roller-hockey rink, bike trails, jogging trails, a dog-walking area, volleyball courts, a skater's park complete with a half-pipe, a playground, and a kiddie pool. The public swimming pool that used to be beyond the baseball field's outfield fence remains, and nearby there is an attractive duck pond with a fountain in the middle.

This is as good a place as any to stretch your legs after the long ride to Canada. Who knows, maybe you can get in on a pickup game with some Canucks. The park is located at the intersection of rue Jarry and Boulevard-Saint-Laurent and is also accessible from the Jarry Métro station.

BALTIMORE,
MARYLAND

105 miles to Philadelphia
190 miles to New York City
245 miles to Pittsburgh
380 miles to Cleveland

BALTIMORE ORIOLES, ORIOLE PARK AT CAMDEN YARDS

The Ballpark That Changed Everything

WHEN ORIOLE PARK at Camden Yards opened in 1992, it signaled the renaissance of the American ballpark, and provided teams across the country a blueprint for what the future would hold. Oriole Park arrived just in time. A year prior, the White Sox had unveiled the uninspired new Comiskey, and the most recent additions to the Major League landscape before that were Sky-Dome (1989), the Metrodome (1982), the Kingdome (1977), and Olympic Stadium (1977). Notice a trend in the latter four? Arena baseball. The game needed Camden Yards, a throwback to its glory days that reminded owners, fans, and even players that the ballpark can be a magical place.

We shudder to envision how the past ten years would have unfolded for our boys of summer had it not been for Camden. We see baseball languishing in the late 1990s, unable to rebound from the strike-shortened atrocity that was the season of 1994. We see few, if any, baseball-only facilities being constructed in the latter half of the decade. "Just look at the new baseball field in Chicago—it hasn't done anything to improve attendance," owners and city officials say, and "We're better off building a cost-effective four-tiered dome to accommodate all of our pro sports teams, fishing expos, and monster truck rallies." We see fans staying home, unmotivated to embark on hardball odysseys. We see an empty place on the bookshelf where the *Ultimate Baseball Road-Trip* should be.

Imagine the regal brick exterior, cozy atmosphere, and eccentric field dimensions of Fenway Park combined with wide aisles, spacious concourses, and great concession offerings, and bingo—you have Camden Yards. Not only did this fan-friendly facility forever raise the bar for other MLB parks, but it did so smack dab in the middle of downtown Baltimore, paving the way for subsequent "urban renaissance" ballpark projects in cities like Cleveland, Detroit, and Pittsburgh. Prior to Camden Yards, cities built new ballparks when their current digs started falling apart. Post-Camden, owners of structurally sound, functional facilities began building new and improved ballparks to provide a more authentic environment for the game and to draw more fans. Since Oriole Park opened, the cookie-cutter stadium has gone the way of the spitball as teams have sculpted diamonds reflective of their cities' unique personalities and historics.

Ironically, Camden Yards was designed by the same Kansas City architectural firm—Helmuth, Obata, and Kassabaum (HOK)—that drafted the blueprints for the new Comiskey Park. Thanks to the mulligan it took in Chicago and the help it received on the Camden project from an architectural consultant named Janet Marie Smith, HOK has since become a leading authority in the field (pun intended) of ballpark construction.

The Maryland Stadium Authority initially drafted plans for a multitiered stadium similar to the new Comiskey, before Smith said, "No, no, no." She insisted on building a baseball-only facility that mimicked early 1900 parks like Ebbets Field, Shibe Park, and Fenway Park. Old-style features at Camden include an ivy-covered hitter's backdrop in center field; a twenty-five-foot-high "mini-monster" in right; a low, open-air press box; a sunroof atop the upper deck; steel support tresses; attractive brick facades; an elegant main entranceway; and a festive plaza outside the park. These elements combine to make Baltimore's ball yard quite the little time machine. The only

thing missing as far as we could tell is an old-fashioned pipe organ. Instead, the O's play dance club and rock 'n' roll sound bites over the PA system. Why, we don't know.

More than just cosmetic touches, HOK introduced a number of innovations designed to increase fan enjoyment of the game, most notably the two-tiered bull pen model, which has since been copied in many new parks, and a special adjustable seat for handicapped people that now exists at all thirty MLB parks, known as the "Camden Seat."

interior

Photo by Kevin O'Connell

Oriole Park was built in thirty-three months for a cost of $110 million, which seems like a paltry figure compared to later ballpark construction standards. Site acquisition and preparation cost the State of Maryland an additional $100 million. The publicly funded project was financed through a new instant lottery game that was approved by the Maryland legislature in 1987. All of the proceeds from the game went toward the ballpark, which angered some Maryland citizens who pointed out that the park was being funded by the poor, who they said play the lottery more frequently than well-to-do folks. Angering folks still further, Maryland's legislature had rejected previous attempts to use money from a new lottery game to improve education. When it came down to it, Maryland didn't want to lose its baseball team the way it lost its football team when the NFL's Baltimore Colts jumped town in 1984, taking forty years of gridiron memories with them.

Renovations to the trademark B&O Warehouse that looms over right field also took thirty-three months. The circa 1905 building is the longest free-standing structure on the East Coast at 1,016 feet, but it had fallen into a state of disrepair by 1988. Nearly all of its 982 windows were broken, all eight floors were rat infested, and when workers tried to power-wash the brick exterior, the mortar began crumbling, necessitating workers to clean the bricks by hand, one brick at a time.

Once used to support the Baltimore and Ohio Railroad, the nation's first operational rail dating from 1827, today the B&O contains restaurants and shops on its lower levels and Orioles executive offices on the top floors. It also houses a bank of lights for the ballpark on its roof.

For the ballpark's rather lengthy name—Oriole Park at Camden Yards—we can thank two factions of state officials within the Maryland Stadium Authority, which owns the ballpark. One group favored "Oriole Park," the name of the baseball field used by Baltimore's National League team of the 1890s (more on this team later), while the other preferred "Camden Yards," in recognition of the area in which the ballpark is located.

The O's christened Camden with a 2–0 win over Cleveland on April 6, 1992, and went on to win ten of their first eleven games, the best start

TRIVIA TIMEOUT

Egg: After leaving the National League to become a charter member of the American League in 1901, the Baltimore franchise soon departed for another city. Where did the original Orioles go?

Hatchling: Which two famous Oriole home runs are commemorated by two orange seats (amid a sea of green seats) in the Camden outfield?

Big Bird: Which player hit a ball through a window of the B&O Warehouse during a game?

Look for the answers in the text.

in MLB history for a team opening a new ballpark. Consider it redemption for the 1988 season when the O's set the record for most losses to open a season with an incredible 0–23 start.

More than forty-eight thousand fans, including President Bill Clinton and Vice President Al Gore, turned out to see Cal Ripken break Lou Gehrig's Iron Man record, playing in his 2,131st consecutive game on September 6, 1995. As usual, Cal soaked up the spotlight, belting a dramatic home run through a sea of shimmering flashbulbs. Years later, Ripken's record-breaking game was voted the most memorable moment in Major League history by baseball fans in a promotion that concluded during the 2002 World Series.

Kevin: "Hey, wait a minute, wasn't the streak really 2,131 moments?"

Josh: "That's what happens when you let the fans vote."

In Camden's first ever playoff game, Brady Anderson homered to lead off the home half of the first against Cleveland in Game 1 of the 1996 American League Division Series. The Orioles won the game 10–4 but went on to lose the series.

Camden's single-game attendance record was set during the 1997 ALDS when 49,137 fans rubbed elbows to see the O's take on the Mariners.

Prior to Camden's opening, the Orioles played at Memorial Stadium—a converted football field—from 1954 to 1991. Even after substantial renovations, Memorial continued to look a lot like a football stadium. A high oval structure from the outside, Memorial was surrounded by parking lots. Inside, the expansive outfield led to many pitchers' duels and triples.

Frank Robinson hit the only fair ball out of Memorial Stadium in 1966 when his drive cleared the left field bleachers.

In 1969, the first American League Championship Series game was played in Baltimore, as the O's beat the Twins 4–3 in twelve innings.

Ripken began his games-played streak on the Memorial diamond, playing third-base against the Blue Jays on May 30, 1982.

In Memorial's first five seasons no team hit more than three homers in a game, thanks to the 446-foot-deep outfield wall that extended virtually straight across from the right field to left field power alley. Though management gradually brought the fence closer to the plate through the years, the Orioles and their opponents combined to average 125 home runs per season at Memorial.

Since moving into Camden Yards, the O's and their opponents have swatted 169 big flies per season. Oriole Park is universally considered a hitter's park on account of its shallow outfield power alleys and low outfield walls.

The O's are the only American League team guaranteed to begin every season with a home game, thanks to their proximity to the White House and the ceremonial first-pitch opportunity for the president. Of course, when baseball eventually returns to D.C., all that may change.

From 1911 to 1960, the American League Senators played in Washington's Griffith Stadium, a double-decked classic ballpark featuring a center field wall that zigzagged around five houses and a large tree. And yes, the U.S. president traditionally signaled the start of each new season with a toss off the Griffith mound.

The baseball spirit is trying very hard to resurrect itself in the District of Columbia, and Baltimore owner Peter Angelos is endeavoring to prevent it from doing so because he thinks a team in nearby D.C. will hurt attendance in Baltimore. Here's hoping for a hardball renaissance in the capital—and for the continued success of baseball in Baltimore.

Getting a Choice Seat

Word spread quickly when Camden Yards first opened, prompting fans throughout the country to flock like migrating—well—Orioles to Baltimore. But since drawing a franchise-record 3.7 million fans in 1997, tickets have become easier to come by. This can be attributed to the O's struggles on the field and to the fact that more than a dozen other new ballparks now exist to attract road-tripping fans. But weekend games during the summer still sell out, as do most games against the Yankees and Red Sox.

Sellout Index: 20% of games sell out
Seating Capacity: 48,876
Ticket Office: (888) 848-BIRD
www.theorioles.com

Club Box
(Sections 204–270, Sections 272–288)

Located on either side of the press box and extending to the outfield, the Club Boxes cater to those highfalutin types who like to be pampered. The Club Boxes offer access to a special air-conditioned concourse, exclusive bar and lounge areas, and waitress service from the seats. But they don't bring you down close to the action like the field-level seats. We think the choice here is fairly obvious. At least we hope it is. You're here to watch a baseball game, not to wax your ego.

Field Box (Sections 20–54)

Located between first and third-base, these are great seats and they're reasonably priced. The rows elevate quickly allowing you to see over the fans in the rows in front of you, unlike the field-level seats at, say, Yankee Stadium where a sea of heads obstructs your view unless of course you're sitting with Mayor Giuliani in the first row.

Sorry, Seat Hoppers

During batting practice fans are allowed to wander into the field boxes regardless of whether they have a ticket, but once the game begins ballpark staff strictly monitors access to these sections.

Now, we understand the need to keep the high rollers happy, but is it really necessary to guard these seats as strictly as the O's do?

During one of our visits, the Birds were losing by six runs heading to the top of the ninth and fans were flocking out of the park. It was a brutally hot August day and the fair-skinned Irishman, Kevin, was melting into his seat in the right field bleachers.

"How 'bout we upgrade to the shade?" Kevin suggested through parched lips, pointing at the half-empty field boxes on the first-base line.

"No chance," Josh said. "I tried the last time I was here. You need a ticket."

"Not in a six-run game in the ninth," Kevin reasoned, and he was on his way. Josh, as always, skeptically tagged along.

Kevin first tried appealing to common sense in his negotiations with the thirtysomething woman guarding the empty seats behind the first-base bag. "But they're two-thirds empty," he cried. When that didn't work, things got ugly. In an attempt to appeal to her sense of sympathy, Kevin pointed out his sunburn and lifted his shirt to show the woman his tan lines. And that was all it took.

She pulled out her walkie-talkie and called for backup.

Bye-bye Kevin.

After a posse of men and woman in bright yellow shirts escorted Kevin away, one lingering staffer turned to Josh, who had settled quietly into a seat in row C, and said, "This is why we work so hard to keep the riffraff out."

Josh smiled, thanked the man for "taking out the garbage," then sat back in his shady seat to watch the last half inning.

The moral to the story: Not only is this the cleanest ballpark in the Majors, but it's probably the easiest place to get booted. So do behave.

Field Box (Sections 14–18, 56–68)

Yes, Oriole Park features two different seating areas called Field Boxes. These Field Boxes are a few bucks cheaper than the ones listed above. Located beyond the bases and angled somewhat toward the infield, they are still great seats and they're easier to sneak into than the Field Boxes on the infield.

Lower Box (Sections 6–12, 60–64)

We much preferred the sight lines from the lower boxes on the left field side (60–64) because they are angled nicely toward the infield. We were unable to see significant portions of the right field line from the right field boxes, whereas the left field line was not as severely obstructed from the seats in left. The right field seats improve on the infield side of Section 10. But if in doubt, go for seats in left, which also offer a striking view of the Warehouse.

Beware of the first four rows of Section 6 in right field where a series of railings obstruct the view.

Terrace Box (Sections 19–53)

Still the first level, but behind the concourse, Sections 19–53 place fans in the infield behind the field boxes. This is the best spot to watch the game if the forecast is iffy, as the overhanging club level provides shelter. Just don't get caught any farther back than Row H, or you won't be able to see the city skyline beyond the outfield walls because of the overhang. Don't worry about being in Row A as the tier is elevated enough so that you'll be able to see right over the walkway traffic.

Terrace Box (1–17, 55–65)

In the first-base side, Section 17, which is parallel with the first-base bag, provides a much better view than Section 1 out by the right field foul pole. In left field, Sections 55–65 extend from third-base to two-thirds of the way down the left field line. Section 55, near third, is the best bet in this range. In general, we liked the view from the left field Terrace Boxes than those in right field.

Lower Reserve (Sections 19–53; Sections 4, 7–17, and 55–87)

Avoid the lower reserve seats on the infield (19–53, 7–17) because they are located underneath a significant overhang.

We liked the open-air feel of the first few rows of Sections 79–87 in left field.

Left Field Lower Boxes (Sections 66–86)

This is one of the shallowest left fields in baseball so it's easy to stay involved in the game from here. We suggest bringing a glove as home run balls frequently touch down. This is also a primo location to shag during batting practice.

While we weren't crazy about Sections 66–70 in foul territory, we highly recommend Sections 74–86, which face the plate and offer a clear view of the action.

Seats screened by the left field foul pole are sold as obstructed view seats.

Unless you're hell-bent on spilling a beer on the left fielder, you may want to avoid the first

---

SEATING TIP

THE BEST SEAT for your buck is in Lower Reserve Section 4 in right field, the only Lower Reserve section that doesn't have other seats in front of it. We liked Section 4 even better than Section 6 where the seats cost significantly more, because 4 is angled perfectly to look right in at the infield. Great seat. Great price.

---

row of Left Field Lower Boxes, where shorter folk like Josh have to sit on the edge of their seats to see over the outfield wall. Kevin, on the other hand, appreciated the extra leg room.

Eutaw Street Reserve (Sections 90–98)

Baltimore's equivalent of bleachers, the Eutaw Street seats offer actual chair backs. Section 90 is located in center field just before the bull pens, while Section 98 is in right field to the left of the out-of-town scoreboard. Because these seats are at field level, near Boog's Barbecue and reasonably priced, and because the bleacher atmosphere is surprisingly festive, bordering on rowdy, we recommend these seats over even the most expensive upper-level seats. And yes, you can access other parts of the park from these sections.

Upper (Boxes 316–356, 306–312, 358–388); Reserve (Sections 306–312, 360–388)

We've consolidated our review of the entire upper level into one section. Why? Because Oriole Park features eighteen seating price levels and it would take ten pages to review them all separately. Why can't they all be like Montreal? Kidding, of course. While it may seem ridiculous to offer so many different price ranges, we don't mind. This way you know you're not getting stuck in the "worst" section of your price range.

As for the upper-level seats, we recommend the Upper Reserved rather than the Upper

Boxes, considering the Boxes are 50 percent more expensive and only marginally better. It's not frighteningly steep in Camden's upper level like in some parks, and the sunroof will keep you dry on rainy nights and fair skinned on sunny days if you're in row D or higher of the Reserve. We really liked the view from 332 behind the plate.

On the third-base side there's no underhang problem until you reach Section 374 in left field. Walking from 374 out toward Section 388 in left center field, we noted that the view of left field gradually disappears. While the prospect of saving a few bucks may be tempting, we don't recommend sitting in the Left Field Upper Reserve (Sections 368–388).

For fans seated in right field, near first-base or behind home plate, a negligible corner of fair territory in right field is hidden from view.

If you're attending a night game, consider avoiding the upper-level seats on the first-base side unless you want to look directly into the setting sun for the first few innings. Or, if you're looking for a tan, pull off that tank top and have at it. To each his own—that's what we say.

To see St. Mary's Industrial School for Boys—now called Cardinal Gibbons School—where native son Babe Ruth came of age, visit the top row of Section 355 and locate the long white building about a mile from the park. Look to the right of the building where a tall brick steeple breaks the skyline. That's St. Mary's. Worth driving over for a visit after the game? Only if you're a ridiculously avid fan of the baby Babe and feel the experience could bring some sort of great meaning to your life. Josh went.

Standing Room

The team puts six hundred standing-room tickets on sale on game day once all other tickets have sold out. Fans who purchase standing room are allowed to stand behind the bull pens in left-center on the club level or in right field in front of Boog's Barbecue. The left field location is a bit farther from the plate, but offers a better view for shorter fans who will be unable to see the whole field over the wall in right.

The Black Market

Showing up in Baltimore without a ticket? Fear not.

The Orioles deserve major props for providing a "Scalper-free Zone" outside of Gate F where fans arriving at the park with surplus tickets can legally sell their extras to other fans in need of seats. It is illegal to sell tickets above face value and the O's strictly enforce this within the SFZ. A police officer is on hand at all times to make sure that the prices stay at or below the printed price and that no one sells more than four tickets to any one game. This is a ballpark innovation that should, and hopefully *will* be imitated. So do take advantage.

As is the case at many of the new parks, Orioles tickets are bar-coded and never ripped by a ticket taker, so be careful not to mistakenly purchase a ticket for a prior game.

Before/After the Game

The neighborhood surrounding the ballpark offers a small-town, festive atmosphere befitting this intimate old-time ballpark. We highly recommend following Conway Street to the Inner Harbor, which features plenty of places to eat and drink, outdoor music and street performers, and a festive good time right on the docks of Chesapeake Bay.

Getting to Camden Yards

Camden is easily accessible from Route 95. Take Exit 53 onto Martin Luther King Boulevard and follow it half a mile until it turns into a two-way street. Then turn right onto Pratt Street, which will take you to a number of metered spots or to the parking garages on South Eutaw Street. The lots closest to the ballpark charge $10 or more, but there are plenty of garages in the $6 range, if you don't mind walking an extra block. If you're in town on a Sunday, look for a two-hour nonresident parking spot or find an open meter. If arriving early on a weekday, find an open meter and plug it until 6:00 P.M. and stay all night. But while you're out at the bars, remember 8:00 A.M. comes early.

Another alternative is public transportation. The Penn Line of the Maryland Transit Authority's light rail system stops at Camden Yards, and the Charles Center Metro Subway Station is just two blocks from the ballpark. The MTA also operates park-and-ride lots with express bus service on game days. For more information, visit www.mtamaryland.com.

Outside Attractions

THE "JANET MARIE SMITH HONORARY" BALLPARK TOUR

On most days during the season, even when the Orioles are playing at home, the team offers several ballpark tours. Tickets can be purchased at the main ticket window, or in advance at (410) 547-6234, for a reasonable price. The tour takes fans into the luxury boxes, club level and function rooms, into the control room and press box, and down to the home dugout and onto the warning track. As far as ballpark tours go, we thought this was a pretty informative and interesting one.

Our aged guide, Irv, spent most of our time together singing the praises of Janet Marie Smith. Josh counted twenty-three evocations of her name during the hour-long tour. But Irv also served up plenty of facts, with a side order of humor.

THE BALTIMORE BAMBINO

A four-foot-high Babe Ruth statue, located outside of Gate H on Babe Ruth Plaza, depicts a teen-aged Bambino holding a bat over his shoulder and holding a right-handed fielders glove in his left hand. One problem: Ruth was a lefty. Shortly after Camden opened, a number of visiting sports writers pointed out the apparent gaff.

According to Irv, however, the statue makers made no mistake. We'll let you decide for yourself, but we think this story is questionable at best. Irv said a saloon owned by the Babe's father, George Herman Ruth, Sr., once stood where Oriole Park's center field bleachers now reside (confirmed as true). The baby Babe, or Georgie as he was then called, spent his early years in this environment learning to cuss, gamble, smoke, and drink (highly believable). By age seven, Georgie was such a handful that his parents sent him to St. Mary's Industrial School for Boys, a reform school run by Xaverian Brothers on the outskirts of town (also true). The Xaverians taught Georgie to play baseball, but because the school didn't have any lefty gloves, he learned to catch the ball with a righty glove on his left hand, then take the glove off and throw the ball with his left hand, kind of like Jim Abbott did years later. While this may be believable, the statue clearly depicts Ruth as a teenager, by which point he had become a legitimate professional prospect. It seems hard to believe someone wouldn't have found him a left-handed glove by say, age eighteen. We think the statue crafters messed up, then fell back on this obscure bit of lore to cover up. We also think there's a good chance Irv may have made up the story entirely on his own. We did not notice him drinking, though.

In any case, to finish the story, Georgie left St. Mary's in February 1914, when Jack Dunn, owner of the minor league Baltimore Orioles, signed him to a pro contract. Because Georgie was only nineteen, Dunn had to accept legal guardianship of him. When he arrived at spring training, his veteran teammates teased him, calling him Dunn's "Baby." The nickname eventually became "the Babe." Five months later, Dunn sold Ruth's contract to the Boston Red Sox (some guardian, eh?), and just ten months after leaving reform school, the Babe started his first Major League game.

Another Maryland son, Lefty Grove, won 109 games for the International League O's before embarking on his Hall of Fame Major League career. Though he went on to win exactly three hundred Major League games with the Philadelphia A's and Red Sox, there's no statue of Lefty at Camden Yards. We can't help but think though, that if there were, Lefty would probably be wearing a glove on his left hand instead of his right, and that Irv would have a darned good reason for it.

SPORTS ART GALLERY

If you like baseball, or if you like art, or if you like baseball and art, you should consider visiting the largest sports art gallery in the United States, which is located right outside Oriole Park's Gate A.

Kevin has been a water-color-painting fool ever since he visited.

Josh, in Texas: "Did you take notes on the outfield sight lines?"

Kevin: "No, but I painted a beautiful picture of the center field wall. Do you think it's worthy?"

Josh: "For the museum?"
Kevin: "No. For my refrigerator?"
Josh: "I'd leave that up to your wife."

Watering Holes and Outside Eats

If you only have an hour to spare before the game, you'll find plenty of chain-type restaurants at Harbor Place, including Hooters, Capital City Brewing Co., ESPN Zone, Pizzeria Uno, Hard Rock Café, and the Cheesecake Factory.

If you have more time, we suggest avoiding the chains and sampling the local flavor. We paid $5 for a water taxi pass. The taxi departed from Harbor Place and provided us unlimited boat rides for the rest of the day. We visited Little Italy and Fells Point via jitney and give them both high marks. We also heard great things about the late-night bar scene in the Federal Hill district, which is also accessible by sea, but we didn't go there. Honestly, we didn't.

Fells Point features plenty of cobblestone and an aged feel to go with its plethora of pubs. One word of warning, however: if you leave your car in a garage near Camden Yards, settle up at the bar and get back on the bay by 11:00 P.M. Monday–Thursday, midnight on Fridays and Saturdays, and by 9:00 P.M. on Sundays. Otherwise you'll be left with a long and expensive cab ride, or a cold and difficult swim back to Camden once the water taxis dock for the night.

THE BABE RUTH BIRTHPLACE AND MUSEUM

LOCATED AT 216 Emory Street, just two blocks northwest of the ballpark, the BRB&M is a must visit for any baseball fan. Look for the painted baseballs leading away from the ballpark and follow them, and in a few minutes you'll be there. There are sixty of these balls in all. Josh counted. Sixty balls for sixty homers in a single season. Makes good sense.

The Ruth Museum is situated in the old row house once owned by the Babe's maternal grandfather, Pius Schamberg. It's a festive old brownstone decked out with bunting, something the Babe rarely did.

Highlights inside include the 714 Home Run Club exhibit, which chronicles the Babe's blasts, the 500 Home Run Club exhibit honoring the big leaguers who have reached the five hundred-dinger plateau, and a plethora of Johnny Unitas memorabilia.

During the season, the museum is open Monday through Sunday, 10:00 A.M. until 5:00 P.M., and until 7:00 P.M. on game days. A printable coupon for reduced admission can be found at: www.baberuthmuseum.com.

MAX'S ON BROADWAY

(Fells Point, 735 S. Broadway)

Featuring sixty beers on tap and more than two hundred bottled beers, this is our favorite Fells Point pub. Pool tables, a lively atmosphere, a huge nacho platter, and sports on the tube. What else is there? How about a kicking 1980s soundtrack blaring through the speakers? Yup, Max's has that too.

Kevin tried the McHenry Lager, which had a good taste and nice finish. Josh tried the Clipper City Pale Ale, which had a light hoppy flavor. The Yuengling and Oliver Cream Ale are also popular selections.

Max's could have kept us happy all day long if not for the grueling research that lay before us (i.e., sampling as many additional Fells Point pubs as possible before the 7:05 P.M. game between the O's and Angels).

KOOPER'S TAVERN

(Fells Point, 1702 Thames Street)

See, if we had stayed at Max's all afternoon we couldn't have told you to steer clear of Kooper's, which may look intriguing from the outside but is nothing special. The service was slack and the brew selection mediocre.

THE DAILY GRIND

(Fells Point, 1720 Thames Street)

Yeah, it sounds like a dance club, but the Grind is actually a coffeehouse. If you're in Crab City on a Sunday morning, or just in the mood for a different kind of brew, this is the place to be.

EAT BERTHA'S MUSSELS (Fells Point, Broadway)

Kevin's pick for Baltimore seafood. Plenty o' crabs for your sawbuck.

SABATINO'S

(Little Italy, Bond Street and High Street)

Having eaten in both Boston's North End and New York's Little Italy during earlier legs of the road trip, we were not terribly eager when Josh's old college buddy Jay McCarthy, who lives in D.C., offered to take us to Little Italy for lunch. Once you've had the best, it's not easy to settle for the rest. And what could hold a candle to Italian in Boston or New York? Well, Baltimore came pretty darn close. We were pleasantly surprised, and not just because we walked right past the police station where the exterior shots were filmed for the TV show *Homicide: Life on the Streets*.

Sabatino's was excellent. Josh recommends the meatballs and homemade rigatoni, while Kevin highly endorses the gnocchi. The sauce was excellent on both. Kevin also tried a bit of Jay's veal and Jay's calamari (did we mention Jay was paying?) and liked them both. Entrées range from $10 to $20.

Josh, in his best Brando: "Look at how they massacred my boy."

Kevin: "Sonny was short for Santino. Not Sabatino."

Josh: "I will seek no vengeance for my son, for I have reasons that are selfish."

Kevin: "Enough already. I'm trying to eat, here."

Other restaurants in Little Italy recommended to us include **Chiparelli's**, **Rocco's Capricio**, and **Panino's**. All are within a block of Sabatino's.

PICKLES PUB (520 Washington Boulevard)

Located right outside the ballpark, this local tavern is the best bet if you're looking to grab a quick one as game time approaches. Most locals order Polish dills or gherkins on the side.

THE BIRDS NEST GRILLE AT CAMDEN

(Russell Street)

If you're looking for a bite to eat, this might be a better bet than Pickles. The cod cakes and popcorn shrimp are local specialties.

GODDESS (30 S. Eutaw Street)

As far as we're concerned, there's no place for a second-rate topless (but not bottomless) strip club just two blocks from a Major League ballpark. But if you were into that type of thing (like our friend Jay), we suppose Goddess would be the place for you. It's the tops!

CAMDEN STREET AND EUTAW STREET VENDORS

Dozens of mom-and-pop vendors set up outside the ballpark. And the competition keeps the prices low.

When we visited bags of peanuts and all-beef dogs were going for $1 each. One vendor was offering a Polish sausage, bag of chips, and bottle of soda for $3.50. Here's hoping the prices stay this low. Boog makes a mighty fine sandwich inside the gates, but it isn't cheap. So if you're road-tripping on a limited budget, eat up before the game.

Inside the Park

Though it has been labeled a "hitter's park," according to the numbers, Camden gives pitchers more than a fighting chance. In its first ten seasons, 1992–2001, the Orioles and their opponents scored a total of 6,390 runs at Camden, while they scored 6,616 on the road. The teams combined to bat .263 at Camden and .268 on the road. Camden did prove slightly more homer friendly, as the O's and their foes spanked 1,688 long balls at Camden compared to 1,613 on the road, but the small outfield limited the number of doubles (2,307 at Camden, 2,763 on the road).

Management moved home plate seven feet toward the backstop prior to the 2001 season in an attempt to make the park even friendlier to pitchers. Though you wouldn't think seven feet would make that big of a difference, it did. Camden, which had averaged 172 homers per year since 1997, yielded only 137 in 2001. This may have been partly because of the ineptitude of the Orioles lineup that year, but nonetheless the team restored the original

dimensions in time for the 2002 season. Good call. Plus it puts every outfield seat that much closer to the action.

Ballpark Features

EUTAW STREET

Though it may not appear to be, Eutaw Street is technically inside the ballpark since you need a ticket to access it on game days.

Eutaw Street's Gate H opens two hours before game time, and while the ballpark itself doesn't open for another half hour, history buffs, ball hawks, and big eaters will find plenty to keep them occupied here.

THE WALL HALL

The Oriole's Hall of Fame, located on Eutaw, is actually a *Wall* of Fame. Bronze plaques honor former Baltimore stars like Cal Ripken junior and senior, the Robinson boys, knuckleballer Hoyt Wilhelm, Davey Johnson, and jokester Rick Dempsey (who could do a great Babe Ruth impression despite batting only .233 in his twenty-four-year career).

FLYING HIGH

A flag court behind the bleachers in right-center field ranks the teams in each of the American League's three divisions according to their position in the standings in rows of flag poles: five poles each for the Eastern and Central divisions, and four for the West. The banner of the first-place team flies closest to center field and the others follow in order. This is similar to the flag system at Wrigley Field, although in Chicago all of the flags for a division are strung on a single pole, with the top team's flag flying at the top of the pole and the others' below it in order.

BRASS BALLS

Hang around the flag court with a glove on your hand and you might wind up with a souvenir. Balls frequently touch down here during batting practice.

In between the cracks of the bats, check out the brass balls emblazoned on the brickwork below your feet. Each of these commemorates the landing spot of a home run hit onto Eutaw during a regulation game. The hitters' names are engraved on the balls.

Through the 2002 season, twenty-seven balls had landed on Eutaw, though Baltimore fans were still waiting for the first homer to hit the B&O Warehouse on the fly. The B&O is only 444 feet from home plate, and though the prevailing wind blows off the water toward right field, not a single slugger reached the Warehouse during Oriole Park's first decade. This is because the wind bounces off the Warehouse and back into the park, knocking down fly balls to right. The distance is also deceptive since the playing field is sixteen feet below street level.

The Orioles originally envisioned balls bouncing off the Warehouse with regularity, and reinforced the B&O's first three stories with shatterproof windows. Ken Griffey Jr. hit the first floor of the Warehouse on the fly during the 1998 All-Star Game home-run hitting contest, but that, of course, didn't count. And Kevin Bass once bounced a ball through a wide-open second-story window, probably much to the chagrin of the man or woman who ordered all that shatterproof glass.

HIT THE LOTTERY

The "Hit it Here" logo on the fence in right-center field features a hand pointing to an "L," in reference to a the state lottery, which helped finance the stadium. "We say, L for Losers!"

ORANGE SEATS

While most seats inside the park are deep green, single orange seats appear in left and right field. The left field seat commemorates the landing spot of Cal Ripken, Jr.'s 278th home run, which broke Ernie Banks' record for a shortstop. Alex Rodriguez has since surpassed Banks, too, though he still had a way to go to catch Cal in the record books at the time of this printing. The right field seat is where Eddie Murray's five hundredth long ball landed. The homer made Murray one of only three players to collect 500 home runs and 3,000 hits in his career, along with Willie Mays and Hank Aaron, and made one lucky fan very happy. Eddie's five hundredth fetched $500,000 at auction.

Now, you see why Kevin, Josh, and Ronnie Woo Woo were so intent on snagging Sammy Sosa's five hundredth at Wrigley.

THE TEMPLE CUP

THE O'S WON four straight National League pennants, 1894–1897, and claimed the Temple Cup in 1896 and 1897. Prior to the advent of the modern World Series, the Temple Cup pitted the first- and second-place regular season finishers in the NL against one another in a best-of-seven series.

The Baltimore dynasty of the late 1890s boasted six future Hall of Famers: John McGraw, Wilbert Robinson, Hughie Jennings, Dan Brouthers, Joe Kelley, and Wee Willie Keeler. The five-foot four-inch Keeler made famous the quote, "I hit 'em where they ain't," and invented the Baltimore Chop, a batting method that saw him draw the infielders toward the plate with a bunt attempt, then chop down on the pitch to bounce the ball over the fielders' heads.

Baltimore was a charter member of the American League in 1901 before moving in 1903 to New York to become the Highlanders, who would later become the Yankees. Baltimore then went more than half a century without a Major League franchise, before the St. Louis Browns moved to the city in 1954 and became the American League Orioles.

But minor league baseball always thrived in Baltimore. From 1919 through 1925 the International League Orioles won seven straight pennants, a feat unmatched in professional hardball to this day.

AISLE SEATS

Each aisle seat in the ballpark bears an insignia of the original Baltimore Baseball Club Emblem, which, according to legend, Janet Marie Smith found while combing the Oriole archives. The logo dates from 1890.

OLD POLES

If you're feeling exceptionally bored before the game, or just nostalgic, stroll on down to the outfield boxes and check out the foul poles, which were brought over from Memorial Stadium when the O's moved.

ROOST, ROOST, ROOST FOR THE HOME TEAM

Mounted atop the game-progress board in center field are two enormous Orioles, intended to serve as weathervanes. The smoke from Boog's barbecue pit is a much more accurate weather gauge, however. Though they're right next to each other and subject to the same wind currents, the birds were pointing in opposite directions during our visit. According to our sources they weigh seven-hundred-fifty pounds each, which begs the question: what was Janet Marie thinking?

Beneath the birds, notice the sign promoting *The Sun*, Baltimore's leading newspaper. When the official scorer rules a ball a *hit*, the

"H" in "The" lights up. When he rules an error, the "E" lights up. This is reminiscent of the Schaefer beer sign that adorned the top of the Ebbets Field scoreboard and served the same purpose in the 1940s.

TOWERING

If you're sitting on the first-base side or behind the plate, you'll be able to see the distinctive Broma Tower that rises out of downtown Baltimore beyond the fence in right-center. Believe it or not, this clock is larger than Big Ben, with a diameter of twenty-four feet. Built in 1911, the Tower mimics the Palazzo Tower of Florence, Italy. Yeah, like we've been there. Check out our upcoming book, *The Ultimate European Tower Road-Trip,* for more details.

Prior to installation of the clock in 1936, a massive imitation seltzer bottle pierced the Baltimore skyline atop the tower. The bottle was taken down when strong winds threatened the structure's support system.

LEAKY RUBBER

Baltimore takes great pride in its leaky rubber. During our tour, Irv held up a full glass of water and then proceeded to spill it on the rubber warning track. Miraculously, the water seeped right in and the rubber dried in seconds. The rubber track that lines the perimeter of the entire field is porous and guaranteed to never puddle.

While it never needs raking and while it drains wonderfully, Josh and Kevin still endorse real dirt or crushed stone warning tracks. Sorry, Irv. It's a neat parlor trick. But this is an old school park and those bouncy ground-rule doubles are a bummer.

Stadium Eats

While its standard fare is average, Oriole Park offers a few specialty treats that are unique and sure to satisfy.

clock

Photo by Kevin O'Connell

BOOG'S BARBECUE (Trademark Food)

Located on Eutaw Street, Boog's offers pit-smoked beef, pork, and turkey sandwiches, as well as a platter that comes with baked beans and coleslaw. We both agreed that the pork was juicier than the beef, but both were excellent. We plan to try the turkey next time we're in town.

Barbecue-wiz Boog Powell smacked 339 home runs in a career spanning seventeen years, the first fourteen of which were spent in Baltimore (1961–74). We mean no disrespect to Boog or his exploits on the field, but Powell's best contributions to the Oriole organization may very well be those he's been making right now at the barbecue pit. The slugger usually stops by half an hour before game time to inspect the quality of the day's roast, so bring one of his old baseball cards if you're an autograph hound. Just don't be upset if he signs his name using tangy barbecue sauce.

For convenience sake, Boog's sandwiches are also available at the **Third Base Deli** and in the upper level, but we recommend visiting the actual pit beyond the fence in right field where the meat is always fresh and steaming hot.

ESSKAY HOT DOG (Dog Rating)
The Twenty-first Best Hot Dog in the Majors

This is a below average ballpark dog. The best thing it has going for it is that it's nearly 1.5 inches in diameter. A stout weenie if we ever saw one. Unfortunately, it's a short one too. Not even big enough to fill its own bun, which is a major faux pas where we come from. Why pay the markup inside when good dogs abound outside the park? If frankfurters are your thing, or if you just like saying "frankfurter," sample three or four frankfurters before the game for the price of one frankfurter inside the park.

BEST OF THE REST

Right beside Boog's stand on Eutaw Street, **Babe Ruth's Ribs** serves up a tasty barbecue

SUPERFAN

HE'S NOT JUST A FAN, he's also a ballpark employee. But get this, we found a guy who hasn't missed a home game since the 1950s. Octogenarian Ernie Tyler is working on a streak that dwarfs Cal Ripken's by comparison. The head attendant of the umpires' room, first at Memorial Stadium, now at Camden Yards, he has worked more than thirty-four hundred consecutive home games.

Tyler has had the pleasure of meeting such luminaries as Michael Jordan, John Belushi, and Presidents Reagan, Bush (the elder), and Clinton. His job is to "rub up" the game balls prior to each contest. And he rubs up quite a few, since the life span of the average ball is only about three pitches.

At most ballparks the umpires do the rubbing but not in Baltimore, where they defer to the master.

Incidentally, the baseballs are rubbed with mud to allow pitchers a better grip on the rawhide. Delaware River mud is the only mud sanctioned by MLB at a cost of more than $100 for an eighteen-ounce container. And Selig says none of the owners are making any coin!

Josh: "We used to rub our balls with mud back home in Charlton, Mass."

Kevin: "I really don't want to hear any more fishing stories, Josh."

treat of its own. The Bambino Rib Platter isn't cheap, but it is tasty and the meat practically falls off the bone.

Crab cakes are a Baltimore staple, and the ballpark cake sandwich is worth ordering if you don't have time to visit an authentic crab shack before or after the game.

For a sit-down meal, check out **Past Times Restaurant**, located on the first floor of the Warehouse. Menu items include crab cakes, salad, and standard ballpark fare.

STADIUM SUDS

The premium beer on tap is Yuengling. It's a Pennsylvania brew and is featured in the Pittsburgh chapter.

SPORTS IN THE CITY

THE RIPKEN MUSEUM (Route 40 and West Bel Air Ave, Aberdeen, Maryland)

ON THE RIDE from Baltimore to Philadelphia, or vice versa, why not make a pit stop in Aberdeen, Maryland, hometown of the Ripken family?

Located just five minutes from Exit 85 of I-95, **The Ripken Museum** resides in a building that formerly served as Aberdeen City Hall. Since opening in 1996 it has welcomed tens of thousands of baseball fans to its memorabilia-filled rooms. This is a great quickie stop. Spend an hour perusing the memorabilia and gift shop, then right back on the highway.

The main attractions are displays related to the careers of the three Ripkens—Cal Sr., Cal Jr., and Billy—but we also enjoyed the other exhibits featuring old-time bats, balls, helmets, gloves, et cetera.

Just follow the signs from I-95 and you should have no trouble finding the museum. It is open seven days a week from 11 A.M. until 3 P.M. and admission is only a few dollars. For more information visit www.ripkenmuseum.com or call (410) 273-2525.

Black Outs, Train Delays, and Urban Legends

In its short history, Camden has seen more than its share of games delayed or canceled for reasons other than foul weather.

On the second day of the 2001 season, Boston right-hander Hideo Nomo pitched an early season no-hitter that would have gone into the books even earlier, if the start of the game hadn't been delayed by forty-five min-utes because of a power outage inside the ballpark.

On July 18, 2001 a sixty-two-car freight train derailed and burst into flames inside a century-old railroad tunnel beneath Howard Street. The thirty-six-hundred-foot train was carrying hydrochloric acid and other haz-mats that sent billowing clouds of acrid smoke into the air and forced the O's to call off the second game of a doubleheader against Texas.

The most overblown cancellation occurred August 14, 1997, when a game against Seattle was postponed because of electrical problems. Internet rumors soon spread news of a deep and far-reaching conspiracy.

O-NLY IN BALTIMORE

During the traditional singing of the National Anthem, Oriole fans express their hometown pride by bellowing "O" for Orioles, when the singer starts to sing, "*Oh* say does that star-spangled banner yet wave . . ."

Kevin says, "Oh, puh-lease."

CRABBING

Another tradition unique to Oriole Park is the daily game of crab hide-and-seek on the Jumbotron. Three crabs appear, then one hides a ball beneath its shell, making like a Times Square huckster. The crabs frantically scramble about the Jumbotron while fans try to keep track of which one has the ball.

Josh: "It's the one on the right . . . I mean the left . . . I mean the middle."

Kevin: "Wake me when it's over."

PHILADELPHIA PHILLIES, CITIZENS BANK PARK

PHILADELPHIA,
PENNSYLVANIA

105 miles to Baltimore
190 miles to New York
245 miles to Pittsburgh
420 miles to Boston

A New Ballpark in the City of Brotherly Love

I N MOST TOWNS watching politics is about as much fun as watching paint dry. But in Philadelphia the local political scene seems to change its course faster than a Brandon Duckworth two-seamer. The political battle over where, when, at what cost, and even if a new park was to be built was a ferocious contest that dragged on in the newspapers, courthouses, and at city hall for years. And with a number of lawsuits still pending at the time of this publishing, the battle still isn't over yet.

But that doesn't mean the Phillies' new ballpark wasn't greeted with open arms by the majority of baseball fans in the City of Brotherly Love. With a seating capacity around forty-three thousand, the ballpark would fit neatly inside of its predecessor, the sixty-two-thousand-plus-seat Veterans Stadium with room to spare. Clearly, it is an improvement as far as intimacy is concerned. Four main entrance plazas at the corners of the ballpark each have a slightly different character, each focusing on an aspect of Philadelphia's history and culture. Upon first seeing the exterior of the ballpark one is struck by the generous use of brick and stone for the facade, and the red steel of the light towers and beam supports for the seating structure. At night three smaller light towers encased in glass glow brilliantly at locations representing first-base, third-base, and home plate above the stadium.

Classic elements from earlier Phillies ballparks were taken into consideration for the interior design and replicated by the architects. The "bowl style" seating on the lower level has an unusually low grade to it, and was inspired by similar seating at the Baker Bowl and Shibe Park (later known as Connie Mack Stadium). The shape of the outfield fence, with its boxed-out irregular segment in left-center field is also reminiscent of Shibe. Beyond the outfield, beautiful views of the center city skyline offer a wonderful backdrop that was forever lacking at the Vet.

With a family-oriented outfield entertainment area, known as Ashburn Alley in honor of Hall of Famer and former broadcaster Richie "Whitey" Ashburn, there is plenty to do before and after the game. This park offers a complete experience, though not to the same degree that Turner Field in Atlanta does. Like the ballpark scene in Atlanta though, it's a good thing Philadelphia's ballpark was designed to offer the total game-day package because there is still no neighborhood surrounding the Sports Complex of which the park is a part. It's parking lots as far as the eye can see, just as it was at Veterans Stadium, and this is perhaps the main criticism of building the park on this location. *The Philadelphia Inquirer*'s William Becker gave voice to the growing tide of opposition to the new park best in an op-ed piece that read:

The designers of this building faced an impossible challenge: to compensate with architectural amenities for the ballpark's profoundly wrong location. To walk from your car through a parking lot, into a single-purpose building, do your business, walk back through the parking lot and then drive home is a fundamentally suburban experience. . . . One of the important measures of a society is its grand public buildings. They endure long after their sponsors stop telling us what to think about them, and they tell their own story. The story of this ballpark will be timidity in the face of challenge, resulting in a huge opportunity squandered. What a shame.

See, politics can be fun. Well, maybe not fun, but at least interesting. The other locations that had been considered for the ballpark were the Northern Liberties and Chinatown neighborhoods, which would have provided Wrigley Field-like urban settings, and a riverfront downtown location that would have given the new park more of a Pittsburgh Pirates PNC look.

Veterans Stadium

Photo by Kevin O'Connell

But unfortunately in this case, public discourse did not bring about the most desirable result. In 2000 the Phillies and the city of Philadelphia unveiled plans to build their new world-class baseball park just east of Veterans Stadium on the north side of Pattison Avenue, between 11th and Darien Streets. The new location actually expanded the boundaries of the Sports Complex, a goal not necessarily in tune with our vision of the perfect ballpark setting.

Under an agreement ratified by the city council in December 2000, the city of Philadelphia agreed to provide $174 million, with $172 million coming from private financing toward the park's $346 million price tag. Also voted in was a new stadium for the NFL Eagles. The price tag for both new facilities topped $1 billion. That amount of cash seems to border on the ridiculous, even for sports fans like us. But at least the city owns the new ballpark and leases it to the team. Noted retro ballpark designer HOK led an architectural effort that also included the prominent Philadelphia-based firm Ewing, Cole, Cherry, Brott (ECCB), and in November 2001 construction officially began. In June of 2003 Citizens Bank pledged $57.5 million over twenty-five years to secure the new park's naming rights.

The loyal fans of this rabid sports town deserve nothing less than natural grass, a dirt infield, skyline views, and close-to-the-action seats. And they deserve the ballpark quirks that this new park provides. Since opening in 1971, Veterans Stadium had provided none of these ballpark basics. The Vet was the largest baseball stadium in the National League (not including the year that the Colorado Rockies played at Mile High Stadium) with a seating capacity in excess of sixty-two thousand, and was one of the worst places to experience a baseball game. The stadium itself was nondescript and sterile and looked like the air filter of the road-trip car lying alone and dejected in an empty parking lot. The neighborhood surrounding it wasn't a neighborhood at all, but a series of parking lots and the sports complex that includes the Wachovia Center and the new Eagles stadium.

Considering the gimmicks and odd promotions the Phillies featured throughout the Vet years, it seems likely that the team realized from the outset that the stadium was lacking when morphed from football field into baseball diamond. Known for the worst turf in the Majors, the outline of the football gridiron could always be seen across the expanse of the outfield. In this city known for its cheese steaks, the Phillies really trotted out the cheese—as in cheesy—at the start of each season. Before the inaugural baseball game on April 10, 1971, the ceremonial first pitch was dropped out of a helicopter hovering high above the stadium. Phillies catcher Mike Ryan stumbled a bit and bobbled the ball, but ultimately held on for the catch.

The 1972 season began with the first pitch being delivered from famous tightrope walker Karl Wallenda, of the famous Flying Wallendas, from atop a high wire suspended over the field.

In the 1976 bicentennial year, a horseman dressed as Paul Revere trotted out the season's first Rawlings.

Many of the great promotions of this era were brought to Phils phans by the brainstorming of Vice President Bill Giles, and we salute his ingenuity. New ballparks, with all their bells and whistles and corporate-sponsored promotions, pale in comparison to just a little good old-fashioned human ingenuity.

Other interesting Vet quirks—such as a center field water fountain and a home run spectacular on the facade of the fourth level featuring Philadelphia Phil and Phyllis in Colonial garb—were abandoned through the years in efforts to add more seats to the stadium for football. Ugh! At the same time, the city allowed the Vet to slip into disrepair until 1994 when the Phillies took over its management. New blue seats were added, a new out-of-town scoreboard, and in 2001 possibly the worst Astroturf in the big leagues was finally replaced with Nexturf, synthetic grass similar to the kind introduced by the Tampa Bay Devil Rays at Tropicana Field.

Like Fenway Park in Boston, the Vet was built on former marshland in South Philly. With its octorad (an architect's term derived from combining "octagon" and "radius") shape, the facility was completed in 1971, four years after breaking ground. The opening-day crowd of 55,352 represented the largest baseball crowd in the history of Pennsylvania. Philadelphia's Larry Bowa recorded the stadium's first base hit.

Ironically, the Vet years were the golden era of Phillies baseball, with the stadium hosting the MLB All-Star Game in 1976 and 1996, and the World Series in 1980, 1983, and 1993. Playing half his games on the Vet's rug, Mike Schmidt recorded 404 assists in 1974, the most ever by a National League third-basemen. Schmidt won eight Gold Gloves in a row during one stretch, led the NL in homers eight times, and made ten NL All-Star squads. All that from a guy who batted just .196 in 132 games as a rookie in 1973.

Josh: "That's the worst debut performance ever by a Hall of Famer. You could look it up."

Kevin: "What about Tom Glavine? He was just 7–17 in his rookie year."

Josh: "Touché. But Glavine's not a Hall of Famer yet, so technically I'm still right."

Speaking of Hall of Famers, a couple of them enjoyed crowning moments at the Vet. In 1981 Steve Carlton struck out Tim Wallach for his three-thousandth career punch-out. Carlton would finish his career with 4,136 Ks, second on the all-time list. Later in 1981, Pete Rose singled to break Stan Musial's NL record with his 3,631st career hit.

It is truly amazing that the Phillies survived as a franchise for nearly one hundred seasons before winning a world championship. In 1883, the Worcester Ruby Legs (Josh's Great Uncle Vit claimed to have a Worcester friend who played for the team) were disbanded and the franchise moved to Philadelphia. Because the Cincinnati Reds were booted from the National League three years earlier, the Phillies claim the honor of being the oldest franchise in all of professional sports to have remained in the same city under the same name.

On May 1, 1883, Recreation Park, located at the corner of 24th Street and Ridge Avenue and with a seating capacity of sixty-five hundred, was the site for the first Phils game, a 4–3 loss to the Providence Grays. The field, which was occupied by Union Army cavalry during the Civil War, had been used for hardball in the 1860s. In the 1870s, it became part of a horse market, before Phillies owner Al Reach purchased the land and built grandstands. One notable player from this era, pitcher Dan Casey, claimed until his death in 1943 that he was the inspiration for the most famous baseball poem of all time, *Casey at the Bat.*

The Phils then moved into Huntingdon Street Baseball Grounds in 1885. This ballpark was later known as National League Park and Philadelphia Park. It was also nicknamed the "Hump" because the Philadelphia and Reading Railroad tunnel ran beneath the outfield and the ground had been built up in a hump to cover it. In 1894 a fire destroyed the ballpark, and the Phils finished their home season at the University of Pennsylvania. Philadelphia Park was rebuilt on the spot to hold eighteen thousand and featured a cantilevered pavilion, a radical new architectural design.

When the Philadelphia A's came to town as a part of the new American League, they snatched away three of the Phils' best hitters, Nap Lajoie, Ed Delahanty, and Elmer Flick. A cruel joke on the Phillies came as these men were the first five AL batting title champions (though none stuck it out in Philly all that long) and would all eventually be elected to the Baseball Hall of Fame. Bad times were clearly headed the Phillies' way when in 1903 Philadelphia Park collapsed, killing 12 people, and injuring 232. But on the plus side, the Phils and the A's played their first "City Series" exhibition games in 1903. This interleague play predecessor was a tradition that continued for fifty years, and was a fitting event in the City of Brotherly Love.

In 1913 Philadelphia Park was renamed Baker Bowl, by the man himself, William F. Baker, when he bought the team. The right field line was a mere 272 feet to the pole, giving Baker Bowl yet another diminutive moniker, that of the "Cigar Box." A 40-foot wall in right made up of a scoreboard and later, advertisements, held a few balls in, but not many.

The Phils made it to their first World Series shortly thereafter, in 1915. After taking the first game from the Red Sox, the Phillies lost the next four games.

After this crushing defeat, the Phils would enter their darkest period, and for three decades they would rarely rise from the cellar in the standings. They had plenty of great players, but few great teams. Chuck Klein and "Lefty" O'Doul were notable of the era, with Klein winning the Triple Crown for the Phils in 1933, banging out 28 home runs, 129 RBI, and a .368 batting average, and O'Doul batting .398 and recording 254 hits in 1929. But three decades of fan disappointment took their toll and Baker Bowl fell into a state of disrepair that matched the flagging Phillies organization.

Finally in 1938 the Phils left the dilapidated Baker Bowl to share Shibe Park with the crosstown A's. Built in 1909, Shibe was designed by A's owner Ben Shibe and manager Connie Mack. It was the first concrete and steel stadium and originally seated 23,300. In 1925 a double-decked grandstand was built above the entire left field fence, all the way out to dead center field, giving the park its distinctive interior look. Before 1935 folks that lived along 20th Street could view games from their rooftops over the right field fence without paying. Many built bleachers and charged admission to their rooftop views. After Mack lost a lawsuit that attempted to prevent this behavior, thirty-four-foot-high "spite fences" were constructed to block the view. Does this remind anyone of the current situation at Wrigley Field? It didn't make for great public relations then, and it won't now.

But it was the exterior of Shibe Park that set it apart from its peers. Dozens of arches in two tiers made up the brick facades that lined North 21st Street and West Somerset. These two French Renaissance edifices came together and were capped off by a glorious Beaux Arts tower with cupola and dome that formed the main entranceway. From the exterior Shibe looked like a ballpark that belonged in Florence, Italy, next door to Il Duomo, rather than in America.

In 1950 a group of young Phillies players known as the "Whiz Kids," which featured Robin Roberts, Del Ennis, and Willie Jones, made it to the World Series. But they were beaten by the Yankees in four straight games. Though in fairness, three of those contests were one-run games.

Josh: "Perhaps 'Cheez Whiz Kids' would have been a more apt reflection of the city and team?"

Kevin: "Save it for Geno's, will ya?"

In 1952 the Phillies hosted the All-Star Game at Shibe Park; in 1953 the park was renamed Connie Mack Stadium; and in 1955 the A's left Philadelphia for Kansas City, making the Phillies sole owners of a stadium named after the manager of what was once a rival crosstown team. Doesn't quite seem right, does it? It would be a little like the Yankees moving into Shea Stadium and keeping the name. Oh well. Speaking of the Yankees, the old Yankee Stadium scoreboard, all sixty feet of it, was installed in right-center field at Connie Mack Stadium in 1956. Are you reading this George? We call that a primitive form of profit sharing, and your Yanks were leading the way!

The 1964 season may have been the most crushing of all for the Phillies. With only twelve games to play, the Phils held a six-and-a-half-game lead in the NL East over St. Louis. The team then lost ten games in a row before winning its final two to salvage a second-place tie with Cincinnati. The City of Brotherly Love was inconsolable, yet again.

But the 1970s brought a new stadium, the bicentennial All-Star Game, Hall of Famers Mike Schmidt and Steve Carlton, and a cast of great ballplayers and even greater characters that included Greg Luzinski, Bob Boone, and Tug McGraw. But with all the new talent, the Phils' hard luck wasn't over. The team lost three straight NLCS series from 1976 to 1978, one to former Philly second baseman Sparky Anderson's Cincinnati Reds, and two to the LA Dodgers.

The signing of Pete Rose in 1978 seemed to be the missing piece the Phillies had been searching for, and they won their first World Series over the Kansas City Royals in 1980, after nearly a century of middling teams. Mike Schmidt was the MVP of both the season and the Series and Steve Carlton won the Cy Young Award and two games in the October Classic. But the heads-up play of Rose in the final Game 6 proved critical, as Charlie Hustle snagged a pop-up with the bases loaded in the ninth after it had been bobbled by Phillies catcher Bob Boone. Tug McGraw stuck out Willie Wilson for the final out in front of a crazed crowd of more than sixty-five thousand at the Vet. And the first and only World Series had come to Philly

TRIVIA TIMEOUT

Jim's Steaks: A replica of the Liberty Bell hung in center field at the 500 Level of "The Vet." Name the only player to ever ding the bell with a donger of a homerun.

Pat's Steaks: Name the Phillies outfielder who led the NL in outfield chances per game in ten of eleven seasons from 1948 to 1958.

Geno's Steaks: From what island does the Phillies Phanatic purportedly hail?

Look for the answers in the text.

at long last. Cheese steaks for everyone!

The Phils returned to the Series in 1983, but after winning Game 1 in Baltimore, dropped four in a row—the last three at home. The free-wheeling 1993 Phillies squad took Toronto to six games, led by Darren Daulton, Lenny Dykstra, and Mitch Williams, but lost the Series at SkyDome on the first-ever Series-clinching walk-off homer. Game 4 of the Series, played at the Vet, set new Series records for the longest nine-inning game (four hours, fourteen minutes), and the most runs scored (Toronto 15, Philadelphia 14).

Getting a Choice Seat

As is the case at many of the new parks, waiting until game day to buy tickets will land you either up in the third level or out in the parking lot haggling with scalpers. Planning ahead was never necessary at the Vet, but is a wise idea when visiting Philly these days.

Field Level (Sections 101–148)

The Phillies went to great lengths to design a ballpark that provides superb sight lines for fans. For our money, all of the first-level seating "neighborhoods"—namely, clusters of sections pointed toward the plate at their own angle—provide great views.

Most of the Field Level seats on the infield belong to season ticket holders, but if you have the chance to pick up seats on the black market, consider the sections between home plate and first-base (Sections 114–118) or third-base (129–132). On either baseline, you might get lucky enough to score a first- or second-row seat. The sections directly behind the plate (120–128) do not offer the same opportunity, because they are behind the exclusive Diamond Club, which eats up the first several rows. And no, you're not likely to find a scalper with Diamond Club seats.

Sections 101 to 105 in right field and Sections 142 to 148 in left offer excellent chances to score batting practice homers or regulation long balls. Just be sure to steer clear of Section 106 in right field and Section 141 in left as both are screened by the foul poles.

Hall of Fame Club (Sections 212–232)

These are the second-level seats on the infield. You know, the "club" sections. As usual, we appreciate the sight lines, but not the stodgy atmosphere.

Arcade (Sections 233–237)

We don't recommend these second-level seats in foul territory in deep left field. The view is better from the Scoreboard Porch, and for less money to boot.

Pavilion (Sections 201–211)

Located on the Club Level, these right field seats offer a very respectable perch from which to watch the game. The seats don't hang out over the first level like the porch at old Tiger Stadium used to, but they're a heck of a lot closer to the field than the outfield seats at the Vet were. We recommend Sections 201 to 204 in fair territory, which offer a much better view

of the game than do the sections on the foul side of the foul pole.

Scoreboard Porch (Sections 241–245)

These home run territory second-deck seats in left field are a very solid option. And if you're planning to visit the Scoreboard Restaurant, they're even more attractive.

Terrace (Sections 312–333)

These are the upper-deck seats located below the midlevel concourse. In most parks, they're called Upper Boxes. We recommend avoiding distant Sections 330–333 in left field, but otherwise these are good for upper-level seats.

Pavilion Deck (Sections 301–310)

Sections 309 and 310 just beyond first-base provide a decent enough bird's-eye-view of the infield. And Sections 301 to 304 in right field home run territory (as if a ball is ever going to be hit up here) provide a straight-on view of the field. The rest of the sections, we were less than crazy about.

Terrace Deck (Sections 412–434)

Located on the third level, above the midlevel concourse, the Terrace Deck feels right on top of the game compared to the uppermost seats at the Vet. And compared to the rest of the baseball universe, these sections still hold up well. Aim for Sections 414 to 426 to have a quality view of the infield. Don't settle for the cheap seats out in left field (Sections 430 to 434) unless you're really hard up.

Rooftop Bleachers

At Connie Mack Stadium folks on 20th Street enjoyed free views of the game from their own rooftops. The Phillies have attempted to

Sellout Index: 75% of games sell out
Seating Capacity: 43,000 seats
Ticket Office: (215) 463-6000
www.phillies.mlb.com

duplicate the effect with two sections of bleachers atop the outfield entertainment area. Although these seats are miles from the action, they do embrace a feature of the old park that fans found special. Plus, there's something fun about sitting in the peanut gallery every once in a while.

The Black Market

Mill around in the parking lot for a few minutes and the scalpers will come to you. This is the East Coast, so expect to be locking horns with some pretty tough cookies. The town may call itself a City of Brotherly Love but the street-hardened scalpers will rake you over the coals if you let them, so be careful. Check your ticket dates and section numbers, then double-check them, before finalizing any sale.

Before/After the Game

There's a good reason the Phillies have attempted to make the ballpark its own destination, complete with pregame historic attractions and drinking establishments within the stadium walls. There isn't much to do or see in the immediate vicinity of the ballpark. But if you're driving to the ballpark, we recommend arriving at the Sports Complex at least an hour before game time to beat the traffic.

Earlier in the day, we recommend parking in a pay lot in the city and walking along South Street. Plenty of historic sites and unique Philly food can be found here, and when you're ready to head to the stadium, it's just a five-minute drive away.

After the game, we recommend putting your wallet in your front pants pocket and making the daring pilgrimage into south Philly for a late-night cheese steak. As Josh noted upon finishing his third steak sandwich, "If I've placed my life in danger, it was worth every last bite."

Getting to Citizens Bank Park

The best thing about building a ballpark in a sports complex is that it's easy to get to and there's plenty of parking. And thanks to its location at the intersection of two major highways, traffic isn't too bad before or after games. From I-95, take Exit 17 (Broad Street), which leads you right into the stadium lot. From I-76, take Exit 349 (Sports Complex exit).

Either pay the $10 to park at the Sports Complex lots or pass the complex and try to locate a free spot in south Philly. We took a left on Packer Street and followed it a block under the highway overpass, and found a great number of streets on the left that led into a residential neighborhood with plenty of free street parking. The neighborhood looks good and doesn't require a resident sticker. This parking was close to the Vet, but is more than a few blocks from the new park. It is, however, close to the Philadium Tavern (see below) a must-visit on our way to the game.

For fans interested in banging around the city on foot, then heading to the game, the SEPTA Broad Street Subway is accessible from South Philly, North Philly, and Center City subway stations. Take the Broad Street train, southbound, to the last stop (Pattison Avenue).

Staying at the nearby Holiday Inn Stadium seemed like a good idea to us at first, but unless you're just looking for a convenient place to crash after the game, we don't recommend it because there isn't much else to do in the neighborhood—have we stressed that enough now?

Outside Attractions

"BEACONS OF LIGHT" LANTERN TOWERS

The three fifty-foot-tall, glass-encased lanterns are sure to become the signature elements of the new ballpark's exterior. At night they glow and light up like beacons representing the safety of first- and third-bases, as well as home plate.

Kevin: "I have to ask, what happened to second base? Where are the props for the second sack?"

Josh: "Yeah, and they used to put football goal posts on the goal line, too. A light tower right behind second base would be asking for trouble."

VIEW INTO THE NEW PARK—NO CHARGE

While Connie Mack built his "spite fences" to keep folks from seeing in to the park without paying, designers of the new ballpark welcome such peeking at the field that is twenty-three feet below street level. These designers surely realized that allowing people a glimpse of the action will do nothing but make them drool at the excitement occurring inside. These gates, accessible at street level provide a view akin to watching a trailer for a film. They whet people's appetites for more.

THE ITALIAN STALLION

Sure it was only a movie, but the first *Rocky* is still a classic. Rocky Balboa, you'll recall, was the hard-hitting heavyweight from South Philly who dethroned heavyweight champion Apollo Creed in a 1978 rematch rumble, then later KO'd brother-in-law Paulie; the *A-Team*'s "Mr. T," Ivan Drago; and pro fighter "Tommy Gun" Morrison.

First stop: take a quick detour as you walk from your car to the ballpark and check out the Rocky statue on the steps of the nearby Spectrum. Stallone himself commissioned this nine-foot tall bronze piece in 1982 to promote Rocky III. It originally stood at the top of the seventy-two stone steps of the Philadelphia Art Museum at Benjamin Franklin Parkway and 26th Street, then moved to the Spectrum, then moved back to the museum to promote Rocky V. We wish it had stayed at the museum, but it was returned to the Spectrum shortly thereafter, when the movie left the theaters and went to video. Stallone has agreed to make a Rocky VI (who will he fight this time: Osama? Hostile aliens from outer space? Satan?) so maybe the statue will be returning to the museum for a while.

Who can forget the scene in which Rock drinks a blender full of raw eggs then finishes a long run by sprinting up the museum steps and raising his arms in triumph? People still trot up the steps in homage to this day, arms raised and jumping up and down, humming "Eye of the Tiger" and dreaming of Adrian . . . err . . . we mean . . . winning the title.

Watering Holes and Outside Eats

Though there aren't many places near the park, there are some that are worth a walk through the parking lots. But Philadelphia itself is a great food town, and whether you're up for cheese steaks, scrapple, soft pretzels, water ice, or Tastykakes, Philly offers more great places to eat than most cities. Here's hoping the new ballpark helps to develop the area. Exactly where the new places might spring up, we have no idea.

THE PHILADIUM TAVERN
(17th Street and Packer Avenue)

There may not be a great number of joints near the Sports Complex, but this authentic little sports bar makes up for it big-time. Look for the big "T" (as in "Tavern") on Packer Avenue. The Philadium is a great old-school joint, with cold cheap beers and delicious cheap pub food. With nothing on the menu above $8, the food has an Italian bent, but everything is available from burgers to crab legs. This is the place that you want to go to before the game for a slice of what true Phillies sports phanatics are serving up. And the people inside are friendly and knowledgeable sports fans. Josh struck up three conversations, and Kevin struck up zero. That's one for the record books. Two words of warning regarding the Philadium: the bathrooms are most decidedly subpar, and the air quality inside is smoky.

LEGENDS SPORTS BAR
(10th Street and Packer Avenue)

Located inside the nearby Holiday Inn, Legends has always been a passable sports bar, but not a great one, that caters more to Eagles fans rather than Phillies phanatics. You can tell by the garb on the wall, Eagles, 76ers, and Flyers gear far outranks Phillies stuff. This is a place to have some beers and shoot a little pool before the game, and maybe meet some girls or guys staying in the hotel. In the bar you can order food from the adjacent Jaws restaurant, which is a plus, but not a huge plus.

Rumor has it that Jim Fregosi, the former Phillies manager, actually lived out of this Holiday Inn during his tenure with the team. Well, at least his commute to work was short.

JAWS STEAK HOUSE
(10th Street and Packer Avenue)

Named after former Eagle quarterback Ron Jaworski, this steak house is also located inside the Holiday Inn. The menu ranges from steak to salads to seafood, then back to steak again. We both tried the steak and were disappointed that it didn't make our Jaws drop.

THE TURF CLUB (700 Packer Avenue)

Though it may sound like a carpet-makers trade association, this offtrack betting joint is often full on days when the ponies are running. It's close to the park, you can drink and gamble, so how bad can it be? Besides, Kevin likes to hang out with rummies. Josh thinks driving an hour to Atlantic City is a better bet.

ATLANTIC CITY, NEW JERSEY

If you're not just a fan, but a player too, take I-95 South to the AC Expressway after the game. In less than an hour you'll be in Atlantic City. There are twelve casinos to choose from, so if Lady Luck isn't shining on you at the start of the night, just hop on over to a different joint. Our favorites (read the ones where we've actually won a few bucks) are The Sands and Tropicana. We usually try to avoid the three Trump-owned casinos—The Plaza, The Marina, and The Taj Mahal. No need to make that guy any richer than he already is.

RITA'S WATER ICE (239 South Street)

On a hot summer day nothing beats a cool water ice. Delicious strawberry and pineapple are our favorites, but try whatever sounds good to you. Some would call this Italian ice, but in Philly it's water ice. To sound like a local pronounce it "wooder ice."

CHEESE STEAKS APLENTY

Ah, the Philly cheese steak. Boston has its lobster, Chicago its deep-dish pizza, Milwaukee its bratwurst, but during our road trip no regional food titillated our palates quite the way the Philly cheese steak did.

If you've never experienced the Philly cheese steak, here's what you need to know. First off, this is real steak, not the chopped-up grizzle your local pizza and sub shop dishes out. A Philly steak consists of slabs of rib eye—sliced just a bit thicker than deli meat—stacked on top of each other on a freshly baked roll, topped with your choice of either provolone or Cheez Whiz. To indulge in this delicacy, locals and tourists alike shell out $5 a pop.

You can't drive two blocks in this town without seeing a sign for "Steaks" or "Steak Hoagies" or "Cheese Steaks," but here is a list of our favorites.

PAT'S CHEESE STEAKS AND GENO'S STEAKS
(9th Street and 1237 E. Passyunk Avenue)

Operating on opposite corners of the same intersection, Pat's and Geno's are the two most famous steak shops in Philly. And they're less than a mile from the new ballpark. Just follow 9th or 11th Streets away from the park and you'll soon be in steak heaven.

Pat's, which has been doing business since 1930, offers less glitz than Geno's and looks a bit seedier, but it also has more accolades to its credit. Pat's is perennially named "Best Cheese Steak in Philly" by *Philadelphia* magazine's readers' poll.

Geno's, which opened in 1966, features a bright red neon sign and scores of autographed 8-by-10 pictures on its exterior storefront. These include pictures of Tommy Lasorda arguing with National League umpire Eric Greg—both of whom were known to put away a few steaks in their day—Oprah, Bill Cosby, Magic Johnson, Britney Spears, prowrestlers, and strippers.

Both joints stay open until 4:00 A.M. and offer outdoor seating only, twelve months a year. And truthfully, this is not the best neighborhood in Philly. So, on the one hand, we say, "use your head." And on the other, we say that if the bars have just closed and you need a steak fix, you might as well take your chances. What nobler way to die than in pursuit of a good beef-based meal?

So which do we recommend? Pat's or Geno's?

Both. Kevin, who was visiting this magical corner for the first time, liked Geno's a little bit better, citing its crusty roll and tasty meat. Josh, a longtime devotee of Philly steaks, has always maintained that the quality of meat served at Pat's is unparalleled in the city. Make no mistake about it though, both joints are great.

As for your choice of cheeses, true Philadelphians prefer the yellow/orange goo, commonly known as Cheez Whiz, but known locally as simply "Whiz." Whatever you call it, Whiz is always simmering at any good Philly steak joint just a few degrees above the congealing point. But we both prefer the provolone, which seems more like a dairy product and less like a synthetic one.

SPORTS IN THE CITY

OLD PARKS, NO MORE

PREDICTABLY, the old-time Philadelphia ballparks have been demolished. Shibe Park / Connie Mack Stadium would have been the one to preserve, as it was far more architecturally interesting than any of the others. Located at the corner of North 21st Street and West Somerset, the location is now the site of the Deliverance Evangelical Church.

Connie Mack Stadium was being torn down while Veteran's Stadium was hosting the All-Star Game in 1976. Oh, the irony of it all.

Head to North 15th Street, West Lehigh Avenue, and West Huntingdon Street for the location of Baker Bowl. This location also bore the names Huntingdon Street Baseball Grounds, National League Park, and Philadelphia Park. While some of the buildings that surrounded the park still stand, Baker Bowl was demolished, and little remains to tell the tale of its secret baseball history.

Because Pat's and Geno's are often very busy and it is important to the help that you keep the line moving when you order, here is a quick tutorial on Philly vernacular. If you want cheese on your steak, say you want one "wit." If not, say one "wit out." If you just say, you want one "wit," the help will assume you want it "wit whiz." So if you want yours "wit provolone," be sure to ask for one "wit provolone." Whatever you do, don't step up to the window and ask for a "steak sandwich with provolone cheese," because that will scream "tourist" to these provincial Philly cheese heads. We also highly recommend getting your steak "wit" grilled onions.

While visiting this steak haven, you may notice a third restaurant at the same intersection and be tempted—by the long lines at Pat's and Geno's and the promise of indoor seating—to buy a steak at **Sam's Clam Bar**. Do yourself a favor, and resist the temptation.

LORENZO'S PIZZA (9th and Christian Streets)

Located in the heart of Philadelphia's Italian Market, this joint got a nod from local son Will Smith with a mention in his song "Summertime." It has also gotten props from *Philadelphia* magazine, winning best pizza in town in the annual readers' poll. But this section (and city) is about steaks, right? And Lorenzo's delivers a mighty fine steak, too. If you're road-tripping with someone who is trying to watch her cholesterol, this might be the place for you. Not only does Lorenzo's profess to serve the leanest steak in town, but it also offers grilled chicken hoagies.

As the Fresh Prince once rapped:

The weather is hot and girls are dressing less and checking out the fellas to tell 'em who's best riding around in your jeep or your benzos or in your Nissan sitting on Lorenzos

JIM'S STEAKS (400 South Street)

This is where the tourists go to buy their cheese steaks. Located on festive South Street, not far from the Clara Barton House, Liberty Bell, and Rita's Water Ice, Jim's serves a decent steak and offers two levels of indoor seating. You can do better, but you could also do a lot worse. Jim's has been in business for more than sixty years, and some famous visitors have passed through its doors as attested to by the many autographed 8-by-10s on its walls. What is that worth? We have no idea.

Inside the Ballpark

This is the anti-cookie-cutter. The Phillies' new home provides everything that the Vet did not: from natural grass to quirky field dimensions, to striking views of Center City beyond the outfield walls, to baseball-focused sports bars, to monuments and statues that pay tribute to the team's rich history. There is plenty to see and do before the game, so be sure to arrive early.

Ballpark Features

WAVERING WALL

The dimensions and wall configuration of this park might very well be the craziest built in the modern era of retro ballparks. In their attempt to imitate the walls of Shibe Park, the architects made an outfield that will be challenging to play for the outfielders, but equally fair to both pitchers and hitters. A 13-foot-tall wall in right field runs from the foul pole out to the right-center field power alley some 398 feet from the plate. In left, an 8-foot-high wall runs from the pole out to the 385-feet-deep left-center field gap. That's where things get interesting. The left side of a boxed-in area in center field is 12 feet eight inches and comes in from 385 feet to 381 feet. Then the wall runs back to almost straightaway center at 409 feet, but rises from 12 feet, eight inches to 19 feet in the deepest part of the park. Clearly, these dimensions and wall heights will affect play in countless ways. Here's hoping the ball bounces Philadelphia's way, unless of course, the Phillies are playing the Red Sox or Mariners in the World Series. Sorry, we love the steaks but our hometown loyalties run deep.

HISTORIC SIDEBAR HEAD T/C

A REPLICA OF the Liberty Bell originally hung from the center field roof of the Vet. Phillies slugger Greg Luzinski was the only player to ever ring the bell, dinging it with a monster shot on May 16, 1972. That dong was one of seven balls Luzinski launched into the Vet's 500 Level during his career, more than anyone else in stadium history. It seems more than just coincidental to us that a player known as "the Bull" would be the only one to ding the Bell. It's kind of like Mike Greenwell playing in front of the Green Wall for so many years in Boston. Some things are just meant to be.

ASHBURN'S ALLEY

Fans are allowed to enter this festive, history-filled, outdoor entertainment area an hour before the ballpark gates open. Named after Hall of Famer and former Phillies broadcaster Richie Ashburn, the alley extends the entire 625 feet of outfield concourse between the left and right field entrance gates, offering an atmosphere similar to Eutaw Street in Baltimore, only with a better view of the playing field and the bull pens.

Widely regarded as one of the top defensive center fielders of all time, Ashburn made five All-Star teams during his twelve seasons with Philadelphia, and led NL outfielders in chances per game in ten of eleven seasons from 1948 through 1958. He retired after playing the 1962 season with the Mets, having amassed 2,574 hits and batted .308 in fifteen total seasons. He then began a thirty-five-year broadcasting career, which continued until a heart attack claimed his life at age seventy in 1997. Ashburn's number 1 was retired by the Phillies in 1979. He was elected to the Hall of Fame by the Veterans Committee in 1995.

Appropriately, a ten-foot-tall bronze statue of Richie Ashburn running the bases is located behind the batter's eye in center field. Similar statues found here honor the other Phillies greats whose numbers are retired by the team. These include Robin Roberts (36), Steve Carlton (32), Jim Bunning (14), and Mike Schmidt (20).

Not far from the statues, Memory Lane provides an illustrated time line of baseball in Philadelphia, which includes historic moments from the Phillies, Philadelphia A's, and Negro League teams that played in the city.

Stadium Eats

With the opening of the new ballpark, the Phillies made a concerted effort to upgrade the quality of eats available to fans. And for that they should be applauded. We'd still like to see a local cheese steak dealer get a shot operating inside the park (Pat's, Geno's, Jim's) but as of this printing no such deal had been announced.

CHEESE STEAK (Trademark Food)

The cheese steak inside the park is better than the steak sandwich you'll find at 95 percent of the pizza places across America, but it still doesn't do justice to this Philly institution. For a cheaper and much better quality sandwich we recommend saving your appetite for red meat and hitting Pat's and/or Geno's on the way out of town. The two joints are only about a mile from the park.

HATFIELD HOT DOG (Dog Rating)
The 26th Best Dog in the Majors

We were saddened by this dog. Greatly saddened. Soft and watery, this dog had very little bite to it.

Josh: "Why are you getting another one?"

Kevin: "It's dollar dog night. I'm getting another two . . . or maybe three."

Josh: "But you just agreed with me that you didn't like this dog."

Kevin: "Hey, they're only a buck. You keep telling me to be thriftier."

Josh: "You do realize that you can get a pound of ten dogs at the supermarket for two bucks, right?"

Kevin: "The supermarket? What's that? Meg and I always eat out."

BEST OF THE REST

At the left field end of Ashburn Alley **Bull's BBQ** offers picnic tables, pulled pork sandwiches, ribs, and saucy chicken. Luzinski, who hit 307 home runs in a fiteen-year career spent with Philadelphia and the Chicago White Sox mans the grill at just about every game.

On a hot night, nothing beats a water ice . . . or two . . . or three. **Rita's** had a stand inside the

Vet, and here's hoping the new ballpark has left space for this Philly original. We have a feeling it has.

The Scoreboard Restaurant offers a viewing and dining location unlike any other in the big leagues. This two-story restaurant has reached a new height as far as ballpark innovations go. What's next? A restaurant underneath a glassed-in second base? This idea could only have come from the mind of someone who was using the old noodle. What a great new way to experience the game and provide great views of the city out the back windows.

Josh: "I think I can see Geno's and Pat's."

Kevin: "That's great. Did you know there was a game going on out this window?"

Josh: "Yeah, but I can't seem to locate the scoreboard anywhere."

Phanatic

Photo by Kevin O'Connell

STADIUM SUDS

Expect the **Sports Pub Café**, located in the southwest corner of the ballpark, to be bustling with action up until the game begins. Here, you'll find pub food, large-screen TVs, and an assortment of beers on tap.

The Philadelphia Experience

Folks in this town are known for being rabid sports fans. And by rabid, we mean frothing at the mouth. They cheer wildly when their team does well and boo lustily when hometown players don't meet expectations. The fans are every bit as die-hard as the Red Bird fanatics in St. Louis, only much more sardonic and short-tempered. Chalk it up as an East Coast phenomenon, as the fans in Boston and New York are the same way. In any case, with the opening of the new park, expect even more fans to turn out to cheer and boo their Phils, and expect the game-day atmosphere to be festive and electric nearly every night.

THE PHILLIES PHANATIC

Hailing from the Galapagos Islands, this six-phoot six-inch, slightly phat, pheathery green creature with a nose like a megaphone keeps Phills phans entertained all game long. His game-time clowning has inspired the antics perphormed by a generation of other mascots across the nation. He's traveled the world, is a regular on ESPN's *SportsCenter*, and has appeared on many other television shows as well.

A member of the Baseball Hall of Phame, the Phillies Phanatic is the premier mascot in all of sports, rivaled only, perhaps, by the San Diego Chicken. The Phanatic roams the entire ballpark, taunting opposing players and coaches, umpires, and even Philly's own phans. When not spilling popcorn, spit-shining bald heads, dancing with third-base coaches, and riding around on his ATV, the Phanatic phires hot dogs into the crowd with his phour-phoot-long hot dog launcher.

The Phanatic debuted in the early 1970s. Originally Dave Reymond wore the costume but Tom Burgoyne took the mantle in 1998. The costume, which was designed by the same company that designs the *Sesame Street* characters, weighs thirty-five pounds.

THE PIED PIPER OF THE AMERICAN BALLPARK (Superfan)

In the days following the tragedies of September 11, 2001, Jim Minacci took it upon himself to bring an American flag on an eight-foot pole to the Vet for the first game after baseball resumed play. Jim quickly realized that to sit in his seat would mean (a) leaving the flag up to obstruct the view of fans seated behind him, or (b) laying the flag on the ground, which is never done. So he had no choice but to walk around and around the Vet's circular concourses all game long. Along the way people cheered him, offered encouragement, and a posse of followers crept along in his wake, mostly kids. So Jim came back the next night and the next and so on. Walking, walking all game long, stopping only to use the bathroom. He lost ten pounds in September 2001 alone. So he returned the next year for the 2002 season, and then again in 2003, attending several games per year with his flag.

Jim told us, "A lot of people wrote songs or held auctions to raise money for the September 11 victims and to raise the country's spirits. I can't sing. I can't dance. But I can walk. It's just a little something that I can do, and it sets a good example for my son, Dillon."

Though he pays to get into the park, Jim told us he plans to continue the tradition in the new ballpark if the team allows it, and to us it seems fitting. What better place to honor America than in Philadelphia, the birthplace of American independence. And who better to carry our nation's flag than Jim Minacci, a true superfan.

Flag Guy

Photo by Kevin O'Connell

A RECOGNIZABLE VOICE

Bring the portable TV with you to the game if possible. The Ernie Harwell of his generation, Harry Kallas, the Phillies play-by-play man, has been doing games since 1965. For his contributions to the game's airwaves, Kallas was inducted into the Baseball Hall of Fame in 2002. Even though you probably haven't watched too many Phillies games on the local station over the years, here's betting you'll recognize Kallas's distinctive voice. He also narrates many of the videos made by NFL Films. "The battleground—the frozen tundra of Lambeau Field . . ." Yup, that's Harry.

ATLANTA,
GEORGIA

460 miles to Tampa Bay
475 miles to Cincinnati
575 miles to St. Louis
680 miles to Baltimore

ATLANTA BRAVES, TURNER FIELD

The Tomahawk Chopping Grounds

BILLING ITSELF as a "baseball amusement park," Turner Field strives to offer the complete game-day experience. Aside from providing a beautiful lawn for hardball, the ballpark also caters to the interests of hard-core seam-heads and the cartoon-loving kids out there in baseball land, and everyone in between. For students of the game's history, a trip to Turner offers a plaza full of statues and monuments paying tribute to the Braves' great players, a team Hall of Fame, and a still-standing portion of the Fulton County Stadium left field wall over which Hank Aaron's record-breaking 715th home run sailed. For art buffs, Turner features baseball-related sculptures and murals. For armchair managers, Scouts Alley provides scouting reports for fans to review pertaining to current and past players. Sunbathers can lounge at Turner Beach high above right field, while hospitality lifeguards cater to their every whim. Technophiles will find more than five hundred TVs on the ballpark's concourses. Big eaters—and dog-lovers especially—will leave Turner more than merely satisfied. And the kids . . . well, video games, balloon benders, and fuzzy mascots keep them smiling at Tooner Field. Oh, and did we mention the minifield that fans can play on up on the ballpark's third level? Like we said, "the total experience." Does Turner Field try to accomplish too much? Probably. But we enjoyed our visit to Scouts Alley almost as much as the game itself. And we're still talking about the Bison Dogs we ate before the game.

Turner Field came to be when in the mid-1990s the Braves joined forces with Atlanta's Olympic Committee to build a stadium that would be capable of hosting the track-and-field events of the 1996 Summer Games, which could then be remodeled to accommodate baseball. Notice, we said, "remodeled." Unlike Olympic Stadium in Montreal, which underwent few if any baseball-specific modifications before being handed over to Les Expos after the 1976 Games, the Braves did much more than throw down bases and paint white lines on the field. From the start, the architects of Atlanta's Olympic Stadium knew the Braves would be moving in after the Games ended. And so, the facility was designed to allow for an easy conversion to baseball. For example, the huge limestone columns that rise up on the plaza outside the ballpark's main entrance once supported seats for the Olympic field, which was much bigger.

interior

Photo by Kevin O'Connell

After the Games were finished, the Braves paid $35.5 million to demolish and construct where necessary to turn the stadium into a baseball park. Clearly, the team didn't skimp. The remodeling involved reducing the seating capacity from eighty-five thousand to fifty thousand, removing part of the track-and-field complex, and adding the main entrance plaza. All of the work was done between September 1996 and April 1997. Initial construction of the stadium cost the city $207 million, a sum more than recuperated in revenue generated by the Games.

The Braves opened "the Ted," as many locals call the park in honor of Ted Turner, with a 5–4 win against the Cubs on April 4, 1997. Later that year, the team won the first two postseason games played at Turner Field, on the way to a three-game sweep of the Astros in the National League Division Series. The Braves fell in the National League Championship Series, four games to two, however, to the upstart Florida Marlins, who went on to capture the World Series title.

In 1997, the city imploded multipurpose Atlanta Fulton County Stadium where the Braves had played from 1966 to 1996 after moving to Atlanta from Milwaukee. The Braves had shared Fulton with the National Football League's Atlanta Falcons, before the black birds migrated to the Georgia Dome, not far away.

"The Launching Pad" as Fulton was called, was the Coors Field of its era due to its altitude of more than one thousand feet above sea level, which resulted in a bevy of home runs. Now, Turner Field stands right beside the footprint of the old stadium at the very same altitude, but no one makes a big deal of its homer-friendliness in part because of the arrival of Coors Field in Denver, five thousand feet above sea level, and in part because of the many fine pitchers the Braves have trotted out to the mound during the past decade.

Native American features that were interesting—though politically incorrect by today's standards—distinguished Fulton County Stadium from the other multipurpose facilities of its day. Originally "Big Victor," an imposing totem pole stood beyond the outfield fence, his eyes lighting up whenever a Brave homered. Then in 1967 Atlanta fans welcomed Chief Noc-A-Homa's Wigwam to the yard. The tepee stood on a platform behind the outfield fence. The Wigwam was removed in September 1982 as the Braves, expecting to make the playoffs, tried to free up space for extra seats. When the team began slumping, the Wigwam was restored to its rightful place and the Braves rediscovered their winning touch on the way to taking the National League West by a single game over the Dodgers. The Braves were swept in three games in the NLCS by the eventual World Champion St. Louis Cardinals.

Hank Aaron made Fulton County Stadium's 1974 season-opening game memorable, swatting home run number 715 against the Dodgers to break Babe Ruth's long-standing record. After the season, the Braves would trade "Hammering Hank" to Milwaukee and he would finish his career in the same city where it began.

The laughing stock of the National League throughout much of the 1980s, "America's Team," as the Braves were called by TBS, which brought them into households across the nation courtesy of cable TV, rebounded under Ted Turner's ownership. The team posted the best regular season winning percentage in the Majors during the 1990s. The highlight of the Braves' resurgence was a World Series championship, clinched at Fulton County Stadium against the Indians in 1995. Atlanta won the sixth and deciding game 1–0, behind a combined shutout from Tom Glavine and Mark Wohlers. Dave Justice accounted for the lone tally, with a sixth-inning home run.

The last game ever played at Fulton was Game 5 of the 1996 World Series, a 1–0 loss against Andy Pettitte and the Yankees, that left the Braves down three games to one in the Series. No other ballpark, past or since, closed its gates for the last time after a World Series contest. Two days after Fulton's swan song, New York extinguished the Braves' hopes of back-to-back championships with a series-clinching win in Game 6.

Before moving to Atlanta, the Braves had called Milwaukee's County Stadium "home" from 1953 to 1965. To learn about this ballpark, please refer to our chapter on Milwaukee. And prior to their layover in the Land of 10,000 Brats, the Braves had played from 1915 to 1952 in Boston at Braves Field (see our Boston chapter). The franchise's history in Boston actually dates from as far as 1871 when an early incarnation of the Braves played as the Boston Red Stockings in the National Association, which became the National League in 1876. By 1889 the team was more commonly known as the "Beaneaters," and by 1909 the nickname had changed to the "Braves." Always second to the Red Sox in the hearts of New Englanders, the Braves struggled to attract fans to their ultralarge stadium in the 1930s and 1940s. Ironically it was the Red Sox success at capturing World Series titles during the 1900s and 1910s that won over the Boston fans. In the Braves' last season in Boston, only 280,000 fans turned

interior

Photo by Kevin O'Connell

out to see them play. The Red Sox drew 1.12 million that year.

The team moved to Milwaukee in 1952—the first realignment in the National League since 1900. (What is it with Milwaukee and realignment?) The move was a smashing success as the Braves set a National League record, drawing 1.8 million fans. In 1957 Lew Burdette blanked the Yankees in Game 7 of the World Series to bring the Braves their first title since 1914. The next season, the Braves fell to the same Yankees in another seven-game October Classic. Despite the team's success, attendance steadily dropped at County Stadium, reaching its nadir in 1965 when the Braves attracted just 550,000 fans.

So, off to Atlanta the team headed, where in 1966 more than 1.5 million people visited Fulton County Stadium to see Aaron swat home runs and converted-reliever Phil Niekro toss butterflies past opposing batters. The Braves flourished in Atlanta—for a while. But by 1975 they were struggling to draw fans once again. Having dealt Aaron to the Brewers in the off-season, the Braves attracted just 530,000 fans in 1975. Cable television pioneer Ted Turner bought the team that year and added it to his Turner Broadcasting portfolio. And soon fans across the country were "treated" to Braves games on TBS. After investing heavily in talent and winning a World Series championship, Turner shrewdly parlayed Atlanta's 1996 Olympic involvement into a state-of-the-art new ballpark for the Braves. But Turner Broadcasting merged with Time Warner in 2001. And later, the conglomerate merged with AOL. For a while Ted Turner played a leading role in the new company, but when he resigned his post as AOL Time Warner's vice chairman in early 2003, his reign as Braves head honcho officially came to an end. There is some speculation that Turner would like to buy back the Braves, but he has not made a formal offer for the team as of this printing.

We wonder if old Ted got out at just the right time. A few months before his resignation, free agent Tom Glavine had jumped ship and headed to the archrival Mets, and the team had just claimed $24 million in losses for the previous season. And attendance at Turner Field had dropped five years running. Even playoff games weren't selling out in Atlanta anymore. Whether or not he reemerges as head of the Braves, Ted Turner turned the Braves, perennial losers, into the most dominant team in the National League, and brought a premier ballpark to the city. And his contribution to Atlanta Braves baseball should not be forgotten.

The fact that Atlantans had a long love affair with the game of baseball before Ted Turner and even the Braves arrived in town should also not be forgotten. Truly, the game's roots in the city run deep, even if Atlanta has only been a Major League city for four decades. From 1901 to 1965 the Atlanta Crackers were the most successful minor league team in the country. Thanks to their history of winning, the Southern Association Crackers, who spent most of their seasons competing at the Double-A level, came to be known as the Yankees of the minors. The Crackers won seventeen Southern Association titles.

The Crackers originally played at various locations throughout the city before getting their first true home ballpark in 1907 when Ponce de Leon Ballpark opened. But the wooden stadium, which could accommodate nine thousand fans, was destroyed in a fire in 1923, prompting construction of a new stadium called Spiller Field. Spiller could hold nearly fifteen thousand fans, an enormous amount for a minor league park in that era. The Crackers spent their final season playing at an even bigger park. In 1965 they played at Fulton County Stadium, as the city awaited the Braves' arrival from Milwaukee. The Negro

Southern League's Atlanta Black Crackers were nearly as successful as their white counterparts after beginning play in 1919. For more information on both teams, we recommend Tim Darnell's book *The Crackers: Early Days of Atlanta Baseball*.

Compared to the other big league towns south of the Mason-Dixon line, Atlanta is brimming with hardball history. In fact, the city has a baseball past a lot of teams up north would kill for. Winning ball clubs are as much a part of Atlanta culture as peanut butter and Coca-Cola. And after some down years in the 1980s, the Braves have more than done their part to uphold this tradition.

Getting a Choice Seat

As you are probably aware, despite their winning ways the Braves have serious problems filling their ballpark. Well, that may be overstating things a tad. The team does draw close to three million fans per year. But even Braves playoff games usually don't sell out. Have Braves fans been spoiled by the team's success, or is Atlanta's ballpark just too big for the local fan base? Or does the fact that Atlanta is a city filled with people from other parts of the country play a role? The answer: likely all of the above. In any case, we like the cheap tickets—available from scalpers outside the park or from the box office—that result from this fan ennui.

The North Gate opens three hours prior to game time, allowing fans the chance to watch both teams' batting practice sessions from the outfield seats and to visit Scouts Alley and the center field food court.

The concourses at Turner Field are wide, the seats are big and sturdy, and there's ample legroom between rows. Even the outfield and upper-level seats sport

cup holders and every aisle seat bears a swinging Hank Aaron silhouette.

On all levels of the park, odd-numbered sections appear on the first-base side of the diamond, while even-numbered sections are on the third-base side. Section 100 at Field Level is directly behind home plate, as is Section 200 on the Terrace Level, and Section 400 on the Upper Level. There is no Section 300 on the Club Level, because of the press box behind the plate.

TRIVIA TIMEOUT
Arrow Head: Who is the winningest left-handed pitcher of all time?   **Totem Pole:** Which pair of pitching brothers combined to record more career wins than any other brother tandem?   **Wigwam:** Who wrote the song "Take Me Out to the Ball Game"?   *Look for the answers in the text.*

The first row of the upper level begins above the lower-seating bowl's back rows, and thus doesn't cast a sight-blocking overhang on the lower seats, or a sight-blocking under-hang below many upstairs seats. This is a well-put-together ballpark.

Dugout Level (Sections 100–118)

These infield box seats extend from third-base to home plate and then out to first-base. They are sloped at a significant enough pitch to allow shorter fans, like Josh, to see over the heads of fans in front of them. Really, every one of these seats is a winner. Fans without tickets to these sections are welcome to stop by for a peek during the start of batting practice. But an hour before game time an announcement over the PA system asks nonticket-holding fans to vacate the area. This

Sellout Index: 0% of games sell out
Seating Capacity: 49,714
Ticket Office: (404) 522-7630
www.braves.mlb.com

seems fair enough to us. Hey, we figure eventually we'll be able to afford the good seats, and when that day comes, we don't want a bunch of slobs mucking up the view and leaving peanut shells on our seats.

Lexus Level (Sections 307–338)

These club boxes hang down over the first level's Terrace seats. Sure, they're good seats, but are they worth more coin than first-level Field and Terrace seats? We don't think so.

Field Level (Sections 119–129)

Between first-base and the right field foul pole and third-base and the left field pole, are the Field Level seats. A first-row seat in these sections sells for the same price as a back-row seat, so shoot for a low-numbered row. We really liked the sections in this price range closest to the infield. Section 119 just beyond first-base and Section 120 just beyond third are well worth the money. We were less impressed by the sections out near the foul poles (126–130, 125–129) that provide worse sight lines than the Field Pavilion seats that sell for 33 percent less.

Except for in Sections 119 and 120, expect to be unable to see all the way into the outfield corner on your side of the field, but the obstruction is minimal compared to the same effect at many other ballparks.

Terrace (Sections 201–224) and Terrace Reserved (225–230)

Located behind the Dugout Boxes and Field Boxes, the Terrace is elevated slightly above an inner concourse. This is still a first-level view of the game. We liked the view from the Terrace seats behind home plate (Sections 201–208) but weren't crazy about Sections like 220–224 and 219–223 parallel to the outfield foul line. These seats sell for the same price as the ones on the infield and the view is not nearly as

good. As for the Terrace Reserved sections, we do not recommend these seats. Either spend a few bucks more to sit in the Terrace sections behind the plate, or spend a few bucks less and enjoy a straight-on view of the game from the Field Pavilion in home run territory.

The open concourse behind the last row of Terrace seats offers a nice view of the game to folks on the prowl for food or other ballpark necessities.

Field Pavilion (Sections 131–150)

Any seat in this price range will furnish its holder the hope (however remote) of snagging a home run ball. The seats in left field and left-center are especially choice for ball hawks, because the left field power alley is ten feet shallower than the alley in right. Odd-numbered Sections 143–151 in right-center offer the worst chance of getting a ball. Wherever you sit, don't plan on leaning out over the fence to snatch a ball off the top of the wall, as a three-foot dead zone separates the seating area from the outfield fence eliminating the chance of fan interference. If you're looking for a front-row seat, you'll want to remember that in most sections, the Field Pavilion begins with Row 13. We can only assume this lucky number has something to do with the stadium's remodeling after the Olympics.

Sections 131 and 133 are to be avoided because of the right field foul pole, while Section 132 should be avoided on account of the pole in left. You came to watch a baseball game, not to stare at yellow paint.

Terrace Pavilion (Sections 231–248)

These seats are elevated well above the concourse running behind the Field Pavilion, ensuring clear sight lines for fans in the first rows. Because these seats are the same price as Field Pavilion seats, yet significantly farther from the field, try to avoid them if possible.

If for some reason you find yourself relegated to the Terrace Pavilion, aim for the sections in left field (even-numbered Sections 232–248) that have a straight-on view of the plate, rather than those in right that seem to point fans toward the left field foul line instead of the batters' box. Here the overhang will keep you dry on a drizzly night, while it doesn't significantly affect overhead sight lines. Avoid Sections 232 and 233 because of the foul poles.

Upper Box (401–418), Upper Reserved (419–422), Upper Pavilion (423–437), and Skyline (423, 439)

Turner Field's upper deck keeps fans close to the field by extending back at a very steep incline. Sitting in a seat up here, your feet are at the shoulder level of the fan sitting in the row in front of you. Kevin, who gets a little bit dizzy sometimes, almost felt as if he needed his own railing in front of his row similar to those found at SkyDome in Toronto. Truly, these seats are not for the faint of heart. Unsteady older folks, drunks, and vertigo sufferers should do themselves a favor and sit on one of the lower levels. As for the view, it's not bad, especially in the Upper Boxes behind the plate. Tickets cost the same whether they're in Row 1 or Row 27 all the way in back, so shoot for Rows 1–15 of the Upper Boxes around the infield, or Rows 1–10 of the Upper Reserved further down the baselines.

While the Upper Reserved isn't bad, the Upper Pavilion in right field feels far from the plate; it reminded us of the right field upper-deck seats at Jacobs Field in Cleveland.

A sliver of seats in Section 424 in left field and Section 439 in right field sell for $1 as Skyline seats. The left field Skyline is a lot closer to the infield than the Skyline in right. This is the best $1 seat in the Majors, much better than the Uecker Seats in Milwaukee.

Here nothing blocks your view of the field save for the minimal under-hang, which isn't even as bad as the one at Yankee Stadium. These tickets go on sale three hours prior to game time and sell out quickly because they are limited in number. We recommend showing up early and waiting in line for your ticket, then using your spare time to check out the Braves Hall of Fame and all of the other attractions in and around this activity-filled ballpark. And don't worry, you won't have to sit in your Skyline seat if you don't want to. There are usually plenty of empty Upper Box and Upper Reserved seats to accommodate seat hoppers.

Rows 25–27 of the upper deck offer a nice breeze on a hot day.

For the best view of the attractive downtown Atlanta skyline, aim for seats in odd-numbered Sections 403–421 on the first-base side of the field.

Snoozing

While scoping out the upper deck we had to wonder if Ted Turner ever ventured into these upper reaches of the ballpark. Doubtless if he'd sat down to watch a few innings from so high up he would have immediately conked out from lack of oxygen. At least then he would have had an excuse then. You may remember that TV cameras once caught Ted and old-flame Jane Fonda snoozing in the owner's box during a playoff game.

SEATING TIP

IF YOU HOLD an upper-level ticket and want to upgrade your view for a few innings, we recommend standing behind the Field Pavilion seats in Sections 148 and 150 in left-center field. This is also a good perch for keeping an eye on the game while chowing down, after fueling up at the center field food court.

The Black Market

Georgia law allows for buyers on the black market to be prosecuted, as well as sellers. So be very careful in your interactions with scalpers. If you purchase tickets at or below face value, you're legal. If not, you could spend the rest of the night in handcuffs. It's unlikely, but hey, why take chances? Actually, you deserve to wear cuffs if you're waving big bills at the scalpers outside Turner's gates. The ballpark never sells out, so it's a buyer's market. We saw an assortment of ticket merchants in the Blue parking lot.

Before/After the Game

Turner Field is located one mile south of downtown Atlanta. The ballpark exists more or less on an island. No, it's not surrounded by water. It's surrounded by parking lots. But don't despair. Realizing the lack of peripheral activities around their park, and seeking to capitalize on the void, the Braves provide plenty of before-the-game activities inside and outside the park. And for those wishing to truly get down and dirty with Atlanta culture, the city proper isn't that far away.

The area around the park is safe and well maintained. Ralph David Abernathy Boulevard is blocked off before and after the game, creating space for fans to revel in the streets after the home team wins.

Getting to Turner Field

At seemingly all hours of the day traffic in and around Atlanta is horrendous, so if you're staying in town there's no reason not to take advantage of a convenient public transportation option. Take the MARTA Train to Five Points Station, then hop on a free shuttle bus to the ballpark. The shuttles begin three hours prior to the game. In general, however, the MARTA system does not seem to cover much

of the city, so we wouldn't recommend planning to spend the whole day zipping around town on it. Perhaps this lack of a major league subway system is the reason Atlanta traffic is so brutal.

If you drive to the game, Turner Field is located near the intersection of I-75, which bisects the city perpendicularly, and I-20, which bisects Atlanta horizontally. Take I-75 to Exit 246, Fulton Street/Stadium. From the east take I-20 to Exit 58A, Capitol Avenue. From the west, take I-20 to Exit 56B, Windsor Street/Stadium.

As for parking, we hate to say it but the best option is to pay $10 to park in one of the team lots. We saw some street spots in the residential neighborhood on the hillside about a quarter mile south of the ballpark but we weren't compelled to leave our car in this part of the city. Because of the dearth of street spots surrounding the ballpark, and the monopoly that the team has on the lot scene, Atlanta ranks right up there with Kansas City and Arlington as a place where you just have to bite the bullet and pay to park.

We observed a handful of people tailgating in the Green Lot before the game.

Outside Attractions

THE GREEN LOT

The Green parking lot resides on the hallowed ground that once housed Fulton County Stadium. Hallowed for one reason. On April 8, 1974, with 53,775 fans in attendance, Hank Aaron blasted a pitch from Los Angeles's Al Downing deep to left field. The left fielder, a rookie named Bill Buckner, ran to the wall and leapt, but the ball sailed over his outstretched glove and into the record books. With the blast, number 715 of his career, the first player in MLB history alphabetically also stamped his name atop the game's list of prolific swat sultans.

Hammerin' Hank had finished the 1973 season one long ball short of tying Babe Ruth's lifetime mark. During the off-season, Aaron faced intense media hype and suffered threats on his life from racists and other lowlifes who didn't want to see him break the Bambino's record. Once the season began, however, Aaron took care of business with a quiet grace and confidence, the same way he always did. He hit number 714 on his first swing of the 1974 season, taking the Reds' Jack Billingham deep in Cincinnati on April 4. Then a few days later, with the eyes of the nation upon him, he claimed the record as his own.

The video reel of Aaron circling the bases as two fans tag along and spark bulbs flash still gives us goose bumps, even though we've seen the footage about a zillion times and though Kevin remembers watching the event live on TV. And it gave us goose bumps to visit the spot where Aaron's historic homer left the yard, too, even though the "yard" is now a parking lot. The Braves have preserved the moment by leaving part of the left field wall to stand, honoring Hammerin' Hank in perpetuity. A plaque on the wall reads simply "715."

It is easy to visualize the footprint of the old field, because the Braves have outlined the warning track and infield dirt in brick, in lieu of the tar that covers the rest of the lot. Large metal plates lie where the bases once sat. So why not stand at home plate and pretend you're Hammerin' Hank gunning for HR number 715? Then take a trot around the bases, being careful to watch out for cars pulling into the lot.

ON THE PLAZA

Two attractive brick plazas lie adjacent to one another at Turner Field's center field entrance. One plaza is inside the ballpark gates, complete with the biggest food court in the big leagues and a pregame entertainment stage, while the other is outside the gates, housing the ticket windows and interesting attractions that celebrate Braves history and the game of baseball. Build an extra twenty minutes into your pregame itinerary to allow time for perusing this interesting plaza. Considering that there isn't much else going on in the neighborhood around the park, we applaud the Braves for constructing this area. When we visited fans were playing catch, having Taco Bell (located a block away) picnics on the picnic tables provided, and checking out the scenery.

We liked the tiny home plates posted on the plaza's many pillars, telling fans how many feet they stand from home plate (717, 682, etc.) and the pennants hanging down on the stadium wall, one for each of the Braves championship years, spanning the franchise's history in Boston, Milwaukee, and Atlanta.

An arts project accounts for a string of gigantic colorful baseballs—about five feet in diameter each—on the plaza. Each team in the big leagues has a ball of its own that in some way reflects the team's history or character. Kevin's favorite was the Pirates' ball, which depicts a bare-chested Buckaroo holding a baseball in his gold hooked hand. Josh wanted to like the Red Sox ball, but it was a struggle.

Next to the ticket windows resides Monument Grove. Here plaques honor famous Braves like Aaron, Warren Spahn, Phil Niekro, Eddie Mathews, and Dale Murphy. The Braves retired numbers also appear here in three-dimensional red and blue—3 for Murphy, 21 for Spahn, 35 for Niekro, 41 for Mathews, and 44 for Aaron. And there is a bronze bust of Aaron. Here statues also honor four Hall of Famers—Aaron and Niekro, who played for the Atlanta Braves; Spahn who played for the Boston and Milwaukee Braves; and Ty Cobb, a Georgia native who played primarily for the Detroit Tigers. The Aaron, Niekro, and Cobb pieces previously resided across the street at Fulton County Stadium. The Spahn piece—which honors the winningest southpaw of all time—was added in 2003. Spahn won 363 games in twenty-one seasons, and for many years was part of the NL's most lethal one-two punch, combining with Boston Braves teammate Johnny Sain. The Aaron statue appropriately portrays the slugger watching home run number 715 soar off his bat. Cobb is depicted sliding into third-base. A quote on the base of Niekro's statue says, "There's no better Braves fan anywhere than I."

MIGHTY CASEY

One other familiar statue appears on the plaza. With his thick mustache and trademark pose—leaning on a bat—many will recognize the man wearing the Mudville jersey as Mighty Casey from the poem "Casey at the Bat." This seven-foot-tall statue was made by the same sculptor—Mark Lundeen—who made the fourteen-foot bronze "Casey at the Bat" statue outside of the Marlins' Pro Player Stadium and the seven-footers at the Rangers' Legends of the Game Museum and at the Hall of Fame in Cooperstown.

In 1988 Lundeen, who has made eighteen Casey statues in all, was featured in a *Sports Illustrated* article. He told *SI*, "Based on my own frustrating experiences, and those of a lot of other athletes, I decided a few years ago to do a bronze statue of a sports figure who symbolized failing in the clutch, but doing it in style. The poem 'Casey at the Bat' immediately came to mind."

THE BRAVES MUSEUM AND HALL OF FAME

After offering your condolences to the visage of Casey, check out the Braves Hall of Fame. The museum's front door is located beside the ticket windows. This top-notch artifact

---

OH BROTHER!

KNUCKLEBALLER Phil Niekro combined with his younger brother Joe to win more games in a Major League uniform than any other sibling duo. In twenty-four seasons, spanning 1964–1987, Phil posted 318 wins for the Milwaukee and Atlanta Braves, Yankees, Indians, and Blue Jays. Joe, who pitched twenty-two seasons (1967–1988) for the Cubs, Padres, Tigers, Braves, Astros, Yankees, and Twins, won 221 games. Phil pitched until he was forty-eight years old, while Joe finally hung up his spikes at age forty-four. Here's betting that even if El Duque and Livan Hernandez pitch until they're both fifty, they won't come close to matching the Niekros' 539 wins. But who knows? Phil and Joe didn't exactly light the world on fire early in their careers either. If ever someone took an unconventional path to the elusive three-hundred-win plateau, it was Phil Niekro. "Nuxsy" toiled seven long years in the minors before making it to the Show, and even then, spent four years in the Braves bull pen before earning a spot on the rotation. He won a Major League record 121 games after reaching age forty.

Four times Phil pitched more than 300 innings in a season, topping out at 342 in 1979 when he went 21–20 in forty-four starts. Six times he yielded more than one hundred walks in a season, including 1977 when he walked an eye-popping 164 batters. He ranks third all time in bases on balls allowed in a career with 1,809. He once threw six wild pitches in one game and four in one inning, and ranks first on the all-time list with two hundred WP's. He also gave up plenty of gophers—482 home runs to be exact. And despite all this, he posted a very respectable career ERA of 3.35.

Kevin: "So the Niekros won more games than any other pair of brothers. But can you name the brothers who combined to hit the most career home runs?"

Josh: "Hank and Tommie Aaron—768. Tommie hit thirteen in a seven-year career with the Braves. And Hank took care of the rest."

Kevin: "Well done. You know your stats—I'll give you that."

emporium features as its joint centerpieces the Braves' 1995 World Series trophy and Aaron's 715th home run ball. And as bizarre as this may sound, it also displays the knee brace that Sid Bream was wearing when he slid into home plate to beat the Pirates in Game 7 of the National League Championship Series. The cost of admission is $2 and the museum opens three hours prior to game time. On nongame days, the museum is open Monday through Saturday 9:00 A.M. until 3:00 P.M. and Sundays 1:00 P.M. until 3:00 P.M. during the baseball season, and Monday through Saturday from 10:00 A.M. until 2:00 P.M. from October to March.

Josh's favorite exhibit was the old B&O railway car on display, just like the ones the players used to ride in before the days of luxury charters. It's hard to imagine one of today's prima donnas riding in one of these things for twelve hours to get to a game.

Meanwhile Kevin was partial to the display honoring Braves who served in the military like Hank Gowdy (World War I), Bamma Rowell (World War II), and Cold War Reserves like Eddie Haas, Dusty Baker, Joe Torre, and Darrell Evans. The exhibit also includes Spahn's purple heart, which he was awarded after being slightly wounded in the foot while working on the Remagn Bridge in Germany during the World War II.

Watering Holes and Outside Eats

There's not a heck of a lot going on in the immediate vicinity of the ballpark. The only neighborhood bar predates construction of the Ted. For the life of us we can't figure out why other saloons haven't sprung up in the area. If they hadn't by the time of our visit though, we're thinking they won't any time soon. But don't fret, Atlanta is a fun town with plenty of hot nightspots. You'll just have to drive to them after the game.

THE BULLPEN (735 Pollard Avenue)

Right across the street from Turner Field, The Bullpen has a monopoly on the bar and restaurant scene near the park (discounting the presence of a Taco Bell). The Pen features an eclectic menu that offers fried catfish strips, Philly cheese steaks, red hot wings, and more. Games play on TVs mounted above a long bar inside, while a comfortable outdoor porch provides a quality sitting area on cooler-than-normal days.

BUCKHEAD (North of Downtown)

One of Atlanta's most happening nightspots, Buckhead offers a multitude of clubs including our favorites: **BAR Atlanta**, the wildest joint in town (not counting Atlanta's many strip clubs), and **Lulu's Bait Shop**, where drinks come served in gigantic fishbowls. Like Wrigleyville in Chicago, there are just too many bars in Buckhead to do the area justice in this format. Drive to the area, ditch the car, and do some barhopping. You're sure to find a club that suits your fancy.

LITTLE FIVE POINTS

After the game we followed Moreland Avenue into the Little Five Points area, which has a hippy-crunchy feel to it. You know, lots of coffee shops, a few tattoo parlors, and plenty of bars. **The Vortex** and the **Nine Lives Saloon** are popular spots for nightlife, as are the slightly more upscale establishments on Highland Avenue including **The Dark Horse Tavern and Grill**, **The North Highland Pub**, and **Blind Willie's**, a classic blues hangout.

MANUEL'S TAVERN (North Highland Street)

Manuel's has been pouring draughts for Atlantans since 1956. Though we would not define it as a "sports bar" per say, it does feature a fair amount of baseball and football memorabilia on its walls. Old pictures of Atlanta Crackers players are prominently displayed.

But the joint also features a Spuds McKenzie lamp above the bar, and other lame trinkets that drop it down a notch in our book. Or perhaps we're just not appreciating Manuel's fine sense of irony.

That said, Manny's exceptional chicken fingers, which come served with a horseradish dipping sauce, make the bar worth a visit.

While you're at Manuel's look up at the ceiling where numerous playing cards and dollar bills are tacked some twenty-five feet above the barroom. We asked the bartender about this and he told us that a traveling magician who had stopped in many years ago was responsible. The act went something like this. The magician would ask a patron for a dollar bill. Then he would hold out a deck of cards and ask the patron to think of one specific card—any card, any suit. He would shuffle the deck, then throw the entire deck up at the ceiling along with a dollar bill and a thumbtack. The cards would rain down, scattering on the floor. But one card would remain tacked to the ceiling along with the dollar bill. And according to the bartender, the hanging card would invariably be the one the patron had thought of. "It was freaky," the bartender told us. "Really very . . . freaky."

THE VARSITY (61 North Avenue Northwest)

Another Atlanta institution that has a history more interesting than its menu, The Varsity sits on the edge of the Georgia Tech campus. Able to accommodate six hundred cars and more than eight hundred people, this is the world's largest diner. The fast-food dive serves an astounding two miles of hot dogs each day, two thousand pounds of onion rings, twenty-five hundred pounds of french fries, three hundred gallons of chili, and five thousand fried peach pies.

Since its founding in 1928 by W. Frank Gordy—a former Georgia Tech student—The Varsity has developed a vernacular all its own. The men and women working behind the counter call out to customers en masse asking, "What'll ya' have? What'll ya' have?"

Ordering isn't exactly easy because very few menu items are called by names we acknowledged in the rest of the country. For example, a "Glorified Steak" is a hamburger with mayonnaise, lettuce, and tomato; a "Mary Brown" is a hamburger without the bun; a "Bag of Rags" is a bag of potato chips; an order of "Strings" is an order of french fries; a "Heavy Weight" is a hot dog with extra chili; and so on.

While we didn't know exactly what we were ordering, we took solace in the fact that everything was dirt cheap.

Josh ordered a chili steak with a bag of rags, then went back for a hot-pig sandwich. Kevin chose a yellow dog with strings and a fish burger. We thought the food was okay, but nothing special. But that doesn't mean you shouldn't have lunch at the Varsity while you're in Atlanta. It's worth stopping in just to absorb the atmosphere and to say you've been there.

FAT MATT'S RIB SHACK
(1811 Piedmont Road NE)

If you're looking for fine dining, Matt's shack may not be the place for you; in fact, this might not be the book for you either. But if you want good food, good live music, and good times, get in line. After ordering, instead of getting a number, you get a picture postcard of a blues/jazz musician to place on your table so that the wait staff can find you when delivering your order. We highly recommend the baked beans, which are made with a special rum sauce.

ONE STAR RANCH (two locations: 732 N. Main Street and 25 Irby Avenue)

Featuring Texas-style ribs, baked beans, Mexican cornbread, beef brisket, smoked turkey, homemade sausage, and more, the One Star is sure to satisfy. We sat on the outdoor patio next to a stack of split hickory, used to keep the brick ovens smoking.

Josh had the beef brisket with baked beans and French Fries and was very pleased with his choice. However, Kevin . . . poor Kevin . . . ordered wrong. He selected the rib sandwich, which turned out to be three ribs between a bun. The problem was that the bones were still in the ribs, making it impossible to eat the sandwich as a sandwich. He had to eat his bun and ribs separately, which kind of defeated the purpose of calling the order a sandwich. Apparently the One Star does not serve pulled pork. Our friend Mike, however, ordered a smoked turkey sandwich, and the turkey came de-boned. Don't ask us why.

KRISPY KREME FACTORY STORE
(295 Ponce De Leon Avenue NE)

If you like freshly baked doughnuts, drop in for a visit. Krispy Kreme is one of Atlanta's most famous institutions. There are several stores across the city, but this midtown location is hailed as a regional landmark. Look for the neon red "Doughnuts" sign. You haven't tasted a real doughnut until you've tried one of Krispy Kreme's glazed beauties, hot and fresh out of the oven. Krispy Kreme was actually founded in North Carolina in 1937. Now based in Georgia, the company has become a national and even international success.

BALLPARK VENDORS

We encountered a fair number of vendors outside the park, most hocking T-shirts, hats, and Braves gear and a few with hot dogs and other traditional ballpark foods. It isn't the taste orgy that Baltimore and Boston are, but it isn't the black hole that Shea Stadium is either.

On a tip from his friend Tuyet, who graduated from Emory and still lives near Atlanta, Kevin bought a tub of boiled peanuts. That's right, we said, "boiled." Jimmy Carter may like this Atlanta original, but we give the boiled nuts two thumbs down. And if we'd eaten more than a few peanuts each, we might have had to give them two fingers down, too—down our throats, that is. Boiled while still in the shell, these peanuts become soggy and grainy, kind of like mushy lima beans.

"BUY ME SOME PEANUTS AND CRACKER JACK"

Kevin: "Something tells me that when Jack Norworth wrote, 'buy me some peanuts and Cracker Jack,' he did not have boiled nuts in mind."

Josh: "Who?"

Kevin: "You know, Jack Norworth, the vaudeville entertainer who wrote "Take Me Out to the Ball Game" while riding the New York City subway."

As Kevin went on to explain, the irony surrounding baseball's anthem lies in the fact that Norworth had never been to a Major League game when he wrote the song. He was inspired simply by a sign for a new subway stop near the Polo Grounds, when he pulled out a pencil and jotted some words on a piece of scrap-paper in 1908. The lyrics were later set to music by Albert Von Tilzer.

Inside the Stadium

Everything about Turner Field contributes to a pleasant game-day experience for fans. The seating areas and concourses are well maintained, while the ushers are friendly and helpful. A multitude of peripheral attractions keep fans busy before the game. And the concession offerings are excellent. As for the playing field, it's a beautiful patch of lush green grass, accented by the rich red clay for which Georgia is famous. Georgia's clay derives its color from the oxidation of iron-bearing minerals that are common in the state's soil.

The field is several feet below street level so fans entering through the main gates in center field are already on the first-level concourse behind the Field Level seats. We liked this effect. Rather than having to parade with other fans up a winding ramp to get to the ballpark stands, we just walked through the gates and kept heading straight through the festive inner plaza until settling into a pair of "batting practice seats" in the left field Pavilion. Then after BP we headed back up to the plaza where in the shadows of a one-hundred-foot-wide picture of Hank Aaron's 715th home run ball, we sampled food from the diverse food court while keeping an eye on the team's interactive pregame show.

Ballpark Features

SCOUTS ALLEY

Located on the first-level concourse behind the left field seats, Scouts Alley provides an insight into the inner workings of player evaluation and talent development that fans like us will appreciate. Here we found a report on Greg Maddux from 1986. Signed by a scout named Fitzgerald, it read, "This young man could be a good one, with a great change up. He will not be real fast but will improve his curve ball."

Dale Murphy's report, dated 1974, said, "Ideal build for catcher. Team leader. Great arm. Should get better with age and experience. Has good still bat and short stroke. More of a line drive type hitter. Would like to see him be more aggressive. Works hard."

Reports were also posted for current Braves such as Andrew Jones, Mike Hampton, Rafael Furcal, and Paul Byrd. Displays beside these paid tribute to legendary scouts like Connie Ryan and Paul Snyder.

SKY FIELD

Seemingly miles above field level, the third-level Sky Field offers fans seated in the ballpark's upper extremities a place to stretch their legs. A base path with real grass and the same red dirt the players run on down below provides a nice place for a ninety-foot dash.

Josh challenged Kevin to a sprint and handily defeated his overheated partner.

Kevin: "Was the head-first slide really necessary? You were six steps ahead of me."

Josh: "I needed to be sure."

Fans looking to toe the proverbial rubber, can saddle up to the pitcher's mound that also appears on the Sky Field. Just don't unleash a ball from here or it will likely wind up on the field, or in the stands below.

A viewing deck nearby comes complete with mounted telescopes aimed at downtown Atlanta. If you were too lazy to walk over to the Green Lot to check out the Hank Aaron Home Run Wall before the game, this might be your best chance to sneak a peak.

COKE IS IT

While visiting the Sky Field check out the thirty-eight-foot-tall replica Coke bottle made from baseball equipment like gloves, bases, bats, balls, shoes, pitching rubbers, catchers' chest protectors, hats, batting helmets, and Braves jerseys.

Coca-Cola has pledged to hand over $1 million to any fan who catches a home run hit into this area. Never mind that only one-eighth of the area is in fair territory or that a statistician from Yale said there was only a one-in-a-zillion chance it could happen. This area of the Sky Field is an estimated 475 feet from home plate and is 80 feet off the ground.

Kevin: "Are you going to stay up here all game?"

Josh: "I could really use the cash."

Kevin: "I'll meet you at the car after the game."

RETIRED NUMBERS

Retired numbers mounted on the face of the Sky Field in left honor the same players whose retired numbers appear on the plaza outside the park. Each of these numbers is fashioned in a font distinct from the other numbers, making these unique, just like the players who wore them.

Kevin: "Do you think they consulted the players first, like the Hall of Fame does before deciding which team's hat to put on a player's plaque?"

Josh: "Definitely not. If they had consulted the players, Hank Aaron's number 44 would almost certainly be in Book Antiqua print."

Kevin: "Why's that?"

Josh: "I remember hearing that Hank's an avid reader . . . of books . . . and that he has a large collection of antique cars."

Stadium Eats

The plaza in center field houses two food courts that serve a diverse array of treats, while the usual ballpark staples can be found throughout the park. With Turner's many points of sale, the lines in Atlanta rarely grow longer than three people deep. Everything we tasted was fresh and hot and fell into the "good" or "very good" category. This is one of the best eating parks in the Majors.

COCA-COLA (Trademark Food)

What would a trip to the Coca-Cola capital of the hemisphere be without indulging in an overpriced ballpark fountain cola at the Ted? If you're going to shell out five beans for a pop anywhere in the bigs, this is the place to do it. Coke's roots in Atlanta can be traced all the way to 1900 when the company was founded in the same building that still stands at 125 Edgewood Avenue. And remember, Ty Cobb made a fortune investing in the company's stock—much more than he ever made playing baseball. So drink up.

Josh: "You can really taste the molasses in the syrup. And it seems that much more carbonated. Don't you think?"

Kevin: "Umm . . . I wouldn't know. I'm having a beer."

HOT DOG HEAVEN (Dog Rating)
The Tenth Best Hot Dog in the Majors

Billing itself as Hot Dog Heaven, Turner Field offers hungry fans the chance to win two tickets to a future game by eating all twenty-one different dogs served at the ballpark concession stands. No you don't have to eat all twenty-one hot dogs during one game. Hot Dog Heaven punch cards are available at the **Frankly My Dear** stand in the center field food court. After you purchase each dog along the way, the counter-person punches out another dog off your card. We estimated the total cost of all twenty-one dogs would be about $110.

In the interest of accurate reporting, we should mention that some of the "dogs" on the Braves card aren't really hot dogs. For example, number nine is a smoked sausage, number twelve is a bratwurst, number thirteen is an Italian sausage, number 14 is a turkey/chicken sausage with sun-dried tomatoes, and so on. But don't worry, there are plenty of true dog options on the list, including the very tasty standard dog made by Bryan.

The most unique dog we tried at Turner was the Bison Dog, which is also called the "heart-smart" dog, because it is lower in cholesterol than the average frank. Our processed buffalo wiener tasted refreshingly gamey and was much firmer than an ordinary hot dog. We liked it, but we wouldn't recommend it to older fans who don't have their original set of choppers. The Hebrew National kosher dog was also delicious as was the Jumbo Georgia Dog, which came topped with coleslaw and a sweet Vidalia onion relish.

Try as many different dogs as you can. After all, if you can't find a frankfurter you like at Turner Field, here's betting you just don't like franks. And if that's the case . . . well, then . . . shame on you.

BEST OF THE REST

Did we say the best ballpark pizza in the Majors is found at the US Cellular ballpark in Chicago? If so, we take it back. The New York-style pizza sold at Turner Field's **Italian Market** is a clear cut above any other pie in the big leagues. Large thin slices come heaping with sauce and cheese.

"New York pizza isn't even this good in New York," Josh said, folding his large slice in half as he'd learned to do while visiting the Big Apple earlier on the road trip.

"It tastes like real pizzeria pizza," Kevin added.

"That's because it is," Josh said, pointing to the large ovens behind the counter.

The Italian Market also offers calzones and meatball subs. If you'd like a whole pizza delivered to your seat pull out your cell phone and dial (404) 614-1469.

If you acquired a fondness for Cuban fare while visiting Miami and Tampa Bay, we recommend the Cuban sandwich available at the **Cubans and Reubens** stand. The tasty Turner Field Cuban consists of a spicy mix of grilled ham, sausage, and cheese served on grilled bread.

Desperate to sneak some veggies into his diet after a week on the road, Josh ordered an ear of roasted corn on the cob from the **Country Fare** stand behind the Terrace seats on the third-base side. The corn attendant removed an ear—still in its husk—from the smoking chamber, then shucked the husk off, seasoned the ear with salt, pepper, and butter and handed it over. It wasn't the sweetest corn Josh had ever tasted (that being the butter-and-sugar corn he grows in his backyard field in Maine), but it was very tasty and cooked properly.

The Braves also offer two solid options for those wishing to have a sit-down meal at the ballpark. The **Top o' the Chop** is located on a patio in right field above the main restaurant. The menu is less expansive here than at the more formal Chop House down below, but the view of the game is better. If you have the misfortune of holding an outfield upper-level ticket, visit the Top o' the Chop to upgrade your view for a few innings while you sip a beer. And when you get hungry, hunker down on a smoked turkey leg or a barbecued pork sandwich.

Downstairs, the **Chop House** offers a number of menu items that aren't available on the roof like baby back ribs, fried popcorn shrimp, and different salads. Expect to spend more time here though, and unless you happen to get a seat near the window, expect to miss a good part of the game.

BALLPARK BREW

The Braves sell twenty-four-ounce cans of macrobrew in assorted varieties. Hey, it's not quite a forty, but it's a good-sized gulp. **Tomahawk Amber Lager** is the local choice on tap.

SPORTS IN AND AROUND THE CITY

DISTANT REPLAYS
(324 E. Paces Ferry Road)

SELLING REPLICA UNIFORMS, hats, and other apparel representing all four major American sports, Distant Replays is worth a visit if you're looking to locate that elusive crap-brown Padres jersey or Popsicle-orange Astros cap to round out your collection. We had fun just browsing and being reminded of the uniforms worn by the heroes of our childhood. We found a Braves cap with the lower case "a" on it, a Brewers hat featuring the Milwaukee glove and then another adorned with a beer barrel, a stovepipe-style Pirates hat, a Kansas City Monarchs jersey, a Pittsburgh Crawfords hat, and more. And that was just in the baseball sections.

The Turner Field Experience

With some not-so-subtle prodding from the stadium-effects crew, the Turner Field fans make a lot of noise when their team is closing in on the postseason and during the playoffs. You've surely noticed the Tomahawk Chop and its accompanying ritualistic chanting while watching a game on TV.

As for the atmosphere inside the park: well, it's a little too corporate for our tastes, considering the many nods to Coke and AOL Time Warner, which still owned the team as of this printing. When we visited, a bank of TVs on the center field plaza was showing all of the stations owned by AOL/TW simultaneously. Meanwhile, Cartoon Network characters blend with baseball culture. For example, the souvenir stands sell a doll that depicts hippy-icon Scooby Doo shamelessly wearing a Braves jersey.

Kevin: "What a bad dog. What a sellout."

Josh: "Don't blame the pooch. You can't expect him to bite the hand that feeds him."

Kevin: "At least Shaggy hasn't sold out yet."

Josh: "Maybe they'll make a Daphne doll one of these days. That's one I'd actually consider buying."

Kevin: "Umm . . . yeah."

TOMAHAWK CHOP

Controversial: perhaps. A rip-off from the Florida State Seminoles: maybe. Unique in the universe of Major League Baseball: yes. Braves fans are famous for their Tomahawk Chop and the chant that goes along with it. Oh, oh-oh-oh-oh-oh, ooooh ooooh oh.

All right, maybe the ritualistic chanting doesn't translate well into text. But it does blanket the ballpark with an eerie tribal-war-is-about-to-begin sort of atmosphere when fans start making the guttural sounds for which they're famous. The Chop usually begins with prompting from the stadium organist and from the twenty-seven-foot-long flashing neon tomahawk above the scoreboard.

If the fans start chopping when you're in town, don't panic. You can do this. It takes very little coordination. Just raise your right arm, extend your hand and hold it flat and perpendicular to the ground, then bend your arm at your elbow. Then bring your forearm back up to its original position. If you're not sure about your pacing, keep an eye on the fans to the left and right of you and follow their lead.

JUST THE GOOD OLD BOYS . . .

You're in the Deep South, so don't be surprised when the *Dukes of Hazard* theme song plays over the Turner Field PA system, much to the pleasure of the fans in attendance.

Desperate to find a Braves superfan, we were on the lookout for Uncle Jessie or Boss Hog, but all we spotted were a few pairs of Daisy Dukes. We're not complaining.

Braves neon sign

Photo by Kevin O'Connell

HOT DOG BINGO

Fans play along with the Jumbotron, striving to become wiener winners between the first and second innings. With all the different types of dogs available here, Turner Field is a perfect place to play Hot Dog Bingo. Yes, we realize the game is a thinly veiled stunt designed to compel little Johnny and little Janie to ask mom and dad to buy them a dog. Well, it worked on little Joshie and little Kevie too. And we weren't sorry that it did. The dogs were excellent, and bought on our publisher's dime!

THE TY COBB MUSEUM AND THE TY COBB MAUSOLEUM (Royston, Georgia)

You may have heard that Cobb's bite was even worse than his bark. Well, here's your chance to do a little bit of firsthand research. The Ty Cobb Museum houses, among other things, Cobb's famous dentures, which fetched $7,500 at a Sotheby's memorabilia auction in 1999. Now, that's just weird.

We were also impressed by the Georgia Peach's Shriner's fez and one of his original fielding gloves. As you might have guessed, Cobb's mitt was quite a bit smaller than the Ken Griffey, Jr. model basket glove Kevin wears, however grudgingly, since Junior departed Seattle.

The museum is in Royston, Georgia, about one hundred miles northwest of Atlanta. From Atlanta, follow I-85 for ninety miles, then take Highway 17 south for about five miles into the center of Royston. The museum is inside the Joe A. Adams Professional Building of the Ty Cobb Healthcare System and is open twelve months per year. For details, call (706) 245-1825.

After our visit to the museum we followed Highway-17 South to the nearby Rose Hill Cemetery, where we found Cobb's mausoleum. We peaked through the glass doors to see his vault and those belonging to his mother, father, and sister but that's as close as we got to his corpse. Honest. In life, Tyrus was a notorious tough guy. And his mother shot his father to death as he sneaked through the bedroom window one night. Those are three ghosts we wouldn't want messing with us.

NOTE TO RICHARD CASSINTHATCHER IV: Josh and Kevin kept their word and included you in the manuscript, only to see you deleted by the evil editor.

—E. E.

ST. PETERSBURG,
FLORIDA

230 miles to Miami
440 miles to Atlanta
750 miles to St. Louis
920 miles to Cincinnati

TAMPA BAY DEVIL RAYS, TROPICANA FIELD

Sun Coast Baseball—Indoors

TROPICANA FIELD was designed to provide baseball players and fans as close an approximation of an old-style ballpark as possible. The fact that the field is situated inside a domed building certainly hampers this effort in many regards. Nonetheless it is admirable that the ball yard in St. Petersburg identifies itself as Tropicana Field and not Tropicana Dome, and even more admirable that in many regards the facility succeeds in effecting an old-time ballpark atmosphere, despite its roof and artificial grass. The Trop looks like a bona fide baseball park that happens to be encased by a dome, whereas all of the other domes we've visited resemble vast expanses of indoor space where people for some reason born out of necessity play and watch baseball.

The Trop's field dimensions are loosely modeled after Brooklyn's Ebbets Field in an apparent nod to the many transplanted New Yorkers who have chosen to spend their retirement on Florida's "Sun Coast." The eight-story rotunda, which makes up the main entrance to the ballpark, is another nod to Brooklyn. It was built from the same blueprints that were used in the construction of the famous Ebbets rotunda in 1913. While we appreciate this very thorough approach to preserving our memories of a beloved old-time ballpark's rotunda, we do wonder if advances in ballpark rotunda architecture haven't improved by leaps and bounds in the last ninety years. On the floor of the Trop's rotunda lies a twenty-foot-in-diameter baseball laid into the floor with the words "Devil Rays" written across its middle. Four models of actual devil rays—which are a type of saltwater fish in the shark family—hang from the ceiling. Other than that, there really isn't too much to recommend the Rays' rotunda—a few display cases half filled with Tampa Bay memorabilia, but that's about it. The base structure may be the same, but here's betting the rotunda in Brooklyn was a lot classier with its marble floor and crystal baseball-bat chandelier.

But there is plenty else that is special about the Trop. Since it opened for baseball in 1998, the facility has made use of a revolutionary new artificial playing surface called Field Turf or Astroturf No. 12, which consists of blades of longer-than-normal plastic grass combined with a patented mixture of sand and ground rubber that simulates the dirt that normally exists beneath ballpark sod and makes the field more forgiving. Use of this surface results in fewer "turf-doubles" shooting up the outfield gaps than at most artificial turf fields and in fewer skinned elbows and knees for diving outfielders. Believe it or not, the rubber portion of Field Turf is made from recycled NIKE athletic shoes. Where they collected all those shoes, we have no idea. Perhaps hanging from telephone wires in New Jersey? Maybe the turf mixers just wanted to be able to say that their artificial turf is the most environmentally conscious artificial turf out there. Or maybe they just wanted to be like Mike. In any event, Field Turf has since been installed at three National Football League stadiums (Detroit, Seattle, and New York) and at several big-time college football fields. We like it and see no reason why it shouldn't replace the current plastic mats at the Metrodome and SkyDome. However, there is no replacement for the kind of grass that grows, and the kind of dirt that is made of . . . well . . . dirt, not tennis shoes. There's gotta be a genetic engineer out there somewhere who can make grass grow indoors, under stadium lights. Don't laugh. Fifty years ago people said there'd never be such a thing as a seedless watermelon.

And just look how far we've come as a civilization.

The Trop's field is also unique among today's other artificial turf fields in that it features a full dirt infield, rather than merely dirt sliding pits around the bases. However, lest yo neophytes think this too is a new trend in field design, we remind you of the Astrodome that had a similar infield from 1966 to 1971, and San Francisco's Candlestick Park (1971) and St. Louis's Busch Stadium (1970–1976), which also experimented with a full dirt infield despite their faux grass.

While the roof may not appear exceptional at first glance, it too adds a new twist in the lineage of dome evolution. On nights when the D-Rays post a win at home, it lights up a bright glowing orange.

Josh: "My friend Joe would love this. He's obsessed with the color orange."

Kevin: "It looks like a giant jack-o'-lantern."

Josh: "Yeah, Joe pretty much does too.

Kevin: "No, this looks like a rotten pumpkin. The back side's all caved in."

That's right, the roof slopes significantly from one side to the other. This, to reduce the

view from above

Courtesy of Tampa Bay Devil Rays

volume of air inside and save on air-conditioning bills, while also helping to hurricane-proof the building. The roof is the largest cable-supported roof in the world and is famous for its four catwalks that spiral toward its top. Unfortunately the lowest two catwalks come into play fairly often. This is not a high dome. It's just 225 feet high at its apex. When he was playing for the Devil Rays, Jose Canseco hit a ball into a catwalk and it never came down. For this, the steroid-juiced slugger was awarded a double. But Josh's most memorable catwalk moment occurred in 2002 when Boston's Shea Hillenbrand won a game for the Red Sox with a ninth-inning grand slam that hit a catwalk in left field and then bounced all the way back to the infield. Homers seemed a lot more romantic back in the days when they used to disappear into the bleachers. But Hillenbrand was awarded four bases just the same, as per the local ground rules.

The concourse on the first level is colorful and festive and wide enough to accommodate the meager crowds that normally turn out for the ball game. There is an arcade for the kids and a number of drinking establishments, food courts, and shops for the adults. Clearly, the

Trop was designed to get people into the park early and keep them there late. As such, the facility has been dubbed a "mallpark" by some fans.

The dome was constructed by the city of St. Petersburg in the late 1980s specifically to lure a MLB team to Tampa Bay. When it opened in 1990 it was known as the Florida Suncoast Dome. It became the Thunder Dome in 1993 when the National Hockey League's Tampa Bay Lighting took to the ice for the first time. It was renamed Tropicana Field in 1996, when orange-juice company Tropicana committed to pay $45 million over the life of a thirty-year deal with St. Pete.

In 1996, the dome hosted the largest crowd in NHL history—more than 28,000 fans for a playoff game against the Philadelphia Flyers. It also set the record for the largest crowd ever at an Arena Football League game when twenty-eight thousand plus attended a Tampa Bay Storm game. The dome also holds the records for most fans to attend a Davis Cup Tennis tournament and for the most fans to attend an NCAA Men's Basketball Final Four. But the biggest crowd to date turned out in 1990 to see a New Kids on the Block concert.

Kevin: "Wait a minute, didn't we mention the New Kids in the Toronto chapter, too?"

Josh: "Yup . . . it's something about them and domes. They go together like hot dogs and ketchup."

Kevin: "Word."

Josh: "I'll pretend I didn't hear that."

In any case, it's too bad residents of the Sun Coast haven't supported their baseball team as well as they've supported other events at the dome. Attendance has gone steadily downhill since the Devil Rays drew 2.5 million fans during their inaugural season. In 2002, the team drew just 1.06 million fans, registering a lifeless average of only thirteen thousand per game, good for twenty-eighth in the Majors ahead of

interior

Courtesy of Tampa Bay Devil Rays

only the Marlins and Expos. Some observers believe the dome should have been built forty-five minutes away in the city of Tampa, clearly the area's population center. St. Pete is a much nicer city in our opinion. Its buildings are older and quainter and the town is not as built up as its sister city. But attendance has flagged, and maybe the locals have a point. Like they say, "location, location, location."

Another popular theory on why the Rays have struggled to build a fan base points to the fact that Tampa Bay is Yankee country. The city of Tampa has been the Grapefruit League home of the Bronx Bombers for more than four decades, and with so many retired New Yorkers living in Florida, the Florida State League Class A Tampa Yankees are a hot ticket during the summer. Some have even gone so far as to suggest that the Class A Yanks could give the Major League Devil Rays a run for their money on the diamond. We tend to think not. Although the Yankees' farm team might give the Rays a good fight in the attendance column if its ballpark were bigger. We were tempted to go watch an outdoor game rather than a dome game on the beautiful night that we visited Tampa Bay. But on one point, the local prevailing sentiment does not waiver. The Devil Rays fans we talked to seemed to agree that a dome is a necessity in this region of the country because of the frequent afternoon thunder showers and extreme summer heat.

The biggest problem for the Rays, in our opinion, is that they haven't had a winning season yet. Only then will the team have a true barometer of fan interest. We also do put stock in the Yankee country explanation: a lot of older folks would prefer to stay home and watch the big league Yanks on satellite TV or listen to them on the radio rather than watch the hapless D-Rays play in person. Further solidifying Tampa's image as Yankee country is the daily

presence of George Steinbrenner, who lives in Tampa year-round and who arranged a deal with a local radio station to bring the voice of Yankees announcer Bob Sheppard into homes along the Sun Coast all summer long.

Ironically, it was the success of the rookie-league and Spring Training Yanks that convinced Major League Baseball that Tampa Bay could be a viable big league market. In the late 1980s, the Chicago White Sox began threatening an escape to St. Petersburg if the Windy City wouldn't help fund a new Comiskey Park. Held hostage as such, Chicago eventually caved in and showed the Pale Hose the love they demanded. Next, the Mariners seemed on the verge of going cross-country in the early 1990s before plans for Safeco were finalized. And in 1992, Vince Naimoli thought that he and a group of investors had acquired the San Francisco Giants for $115 million. Naimoli planned to move the team from the West Coast's favorite bay to the East Coast's, before the other National League owners vetoed the deal. Finally, in March of 1995, the Sun Coast got its big league team when Tampa Bay and Arizona were granted expansion teams. Naimoli paid the other Major League owners $130 million for the right to join the American League.

On November 18, 1997, the Devil Rays and Diamondbacks held an expansion draft in Phoenix, Arizona that furnished each team a roster of thirty-five players, selected from the twenty-eight preexisting teams' forty-man rosters. After having doubtless watched the cross-state Florida Marlins become the quickest expansion team to ever claim a World Series title in the fall of 1997, the Devil Rays took the field for the first time with high hopes in the spring of 1998. Having given the dome an $85 million face-lift, hired former Marlins pitching coach Larry Rothschild to be the team's skipper, and signed Tampa native Wade Boggs to play third-base, the Rays were ready to follow in the Marlins' footsteps.

After suffering an 11–6 loss to Detroit before a hometown crowd that exceeded forty-five thousand people in the first game in franchise history on March 31, 1998, Tampa Bay bounced back to win ten of its next fifteen games. With a 10–6 record, Tampa Bay became the first expansion team ever to be four games over .500 in its first season. But the club came back to earth quickly, finishing the year 63–99. But there was no shame in that. Lots of expansion teams stink in their first year. The problem is, the Rays haven't gotten much better since. And meanwhile, the Diamondbacks, who entered the league at the same time, already have a World Series trophy in their display case. It turned out the D-Backs and not the D-Rays was the team destined to break the Marlins' record for quickest expansion team to win it all.

The Rays were doomed from the start. General manager Chuck LaMar foolishly built the team around aging sluggers like Boggs, Fred McGriff, Jose Canseco, Greg Vaughn, and Vinny Castilla, all of whom signed lucrative free-agent deals with the team well after their prime. The result: a team that hit a fair number of homers, struck out in droves, and hit for a low batting average—not exactly the recipe for hardball success.

The good news for Rays fans is that there's been a changing of the guard in the team's management, with the departures of LaMar and Rothschild. The new regime seems committed to building through the farm system and to fielding a team that can pitch and play defense as well as hit the occasional long ball. And the Rays finally got a qualified big league manager in the person of lifelong Tampa resident Lou Piniella who joined the organization to start the 2003 season. Here's hoping it all comes together for the Rays, and that more fans turn out to support them.

Getting a Choice Seat

As it currently stands, the Devil Rays draw throngs of transplanted New Yorkers and Bostonians to the Trop when the Yankees and Red Sox are in town, and sparse crowds otherwise. By throngs, we mean crowds in the thirty-thousand range so even when these two teams are in town, there's still no urgent need to order tickets in advance. Each game fits into one of three different pricing levels: regular, prime, or value. It seems to us like every game should be a value game until the Rays start averaging at least seventy wins per season, but we don't make the rules, we just report on what we see (and add an occasional editorial aside).

The building is small by dome standards and in general the seats on all three levels are appropriately angled to point toward home plate. For those seated in the upper deck, the under-hang is not as much of a factor as it is at most domes, but fans seated in the Terrace Boxes below will find their views obstructed by the overhang of the deck above.

Something to remember on all levels: all even-numbered sections are on the right field side of home plate, while odd-numbered sections are on the left field side.

┌─────────────────────────────────────┐
│   **TRIVIA TIMEOUT**   │

Tangerine: Name the only two players in Major League history to make their three-thousandth hit a home run.

Orange: Name the Pittsburgh businessman who played a pivotal role in bringing spring training to Florida in the early 1900s. (Hint: the Devil Rays' Grapefruit League field in St. Pete is named after him.)

Look for the answers in the text.
└─────────────────────────────────────┘

Catchers Club (101–108)

Catchers Club seats, as the name might suggest, are located right behind the catcher in the first three rows of Sections 101–108. For our money, these seats are grossly overpriced. Remember, you're at Tropicana Field, not Fenway Park or Yankee Stadium, and that's Joe Kennedy starting on the mound for the home team, not Pedro Martinez or Mike Mussina. Sit ten rows farther back, and use the $150 that you save per seat to treat yourself to a night on the town after the game.

Field Box (101–128)

These are found in the first few rows of what are otherwise called the Lower Box sections, spanning from the visiting bull pen in left field behind the plate, and out to the Rays bull pen in right. Sure, they're slightly better than the seats behind them. Duh! But are they worth three times the money? Season ticket holder Dick Vitale may think so, but Josh and Kevin say, "No way."

Lower Club Box (Sections 101–120, 127, 128)

Much more reasonably priced than the Catchers Club and Field Box seats located just in front of them, the Lower Club Boxes provide an excellent view of the interaction between pitcher and catcher. Shoot for Sections 101 and 102 behind the plate and you won't be disappointed.

The only Lower Club Boxes we don't recommend are those in Sections 127 and 128 immediately behind the bull pens (which really aren't pens but rather mounds in foul territory down the left and right field lines). Here, the lone sections of Club Box seats that appear— one on each side—are no better than the Lower Boxes on either side of them, except for the views they afford of relief pitchers warming up.

Sellout Index: 0% of games sell out
Seating Capacity: 45,360
Ticket Office: (888) 326-7297
www.devilrays.mlb.com

Diamond Club Box (Sections 203–222)

These Club seats are elevated a deck higher than the field level seats, on the same deck that also houses the Press Box directly behind the plate and the Beach section in left field. As is usually the case with club levels, the view is far better from the Trop's Lower Boxes for less money. If you really need the ego trip that comes with the "club experience," why not splurge and pay $5 more to sit in the Lower Club Boxes behind the plate?

Lower Box (Sections 101–132)

Except for the first few rows of seats on the infield, called the Catchers Club, Lower Club Boxes, or Field Boxes, all of the first-level seats are priced the same between the foul pole in left, around to third-base, behind the plate, out to first-base, and out to the foul pole in right. As such, shoot for tickets behind the plate (Sections 101–114) or near the bases where the Lower Club Box seats leave off (Sections 121, 122).

The Lower Boxes begin at Row A and continue to Row Z, before starting again at Row AA and continuing until Row JJ in most sections. The aisles that run toward the field vertically are extra wide, so folks in aisle seats needn't worry about their view being obstructed by a logjam of aisle traffic.

As mentioned above, the Rays have done a nice job of angling most of the seats toward the plate. The only sections we didn't like in this price range were 123–126. The seats in the sections on the infield and outfield sides of these are more squarely aimed at the infield.

Terrace Box (Sections 107–130)

Located behind the sunken walkway behind the Lower Boxes, the Terrace Boxes begin with

Row PP and continue back to Row XX. Here, the overhang of the Club Deck is a major factor. Only fans in Rows PP, QQ, and RR are able to see the full flight of fly balls from most of these sections. The fact that the team has mounted TVs on the bottom of the Club Deck for fans to watch the game in progress shows that management is aware of the problem. Yet, these tickets aren't cheap. And they're still called Box seats. It doesn't make sense to us. Except for the very first few rows of Terrace Box Sections 107–118, we recommend spending less money to sit in the outfield seats, which may not be as close to the plate but aren't hampered by any sort of overhead obstruction. You're here to see the game, right? Well, unless a pair of sinker-ball pitchers are on the mound, you ain't gonna see much of it from the Terrace Boxes.

Josh: "I'd pay to sit in these seats to see Derek Lowe pitch against Bob Stanley."

Kevin: "Impossible, they both play . . . or played . . . for the Red Sox."

Josh: "I meant Derek Lowe back when he pitched for Seattle."

Kevin: "I'd just about blocked that trade out of my memory. Lowe and Jason Varitek for Heathcliff "freakin" Slocumb. Man, did my M's get hosed."

Outfield (Sections 133–150)

The outfield seats in straightaway left and right fields provide excellent vantage points from which to watch the game. The fences aren't too far from the plate, thanks to the Trop's 370-foot-deep power alleys, and consequently the seats out here are relatively close to the infield. The best sections are 141–145 in left field and 142–146 in right field, which are aimed squarely at the infield. The angle of the seats is not as good in the sections on either side of these. In most sections, the first row of seats is Row T. After Row Z, the next row is

Row AA and so on, all the way to Row YY. But even the back rows don't feel too terribly removed from the action.

Here's something you won't see anywhere else in baseball: Rows PP through YY of Sections 135–141 and 136–142 feature comfortable, cushioned, airplane seats, with extra legroom. The seats have been installed courtesy of a promotional deal with a major commercial airline. It's funny that we call these airplane seats comfortable in comparison to the ballpark seats, isn't it? It just goes to show how everything is relative.

To gain an appreciation of what the outfielders are up against trying to track fly balls against the off-white-colored Tropicana Field roof, head out to the left field seats during batting practice. Looking up from Section 141 or 143 you'll also see just how close long fly balls often come to hitting the catwalks. During one of our visits, Boston's David Ortiz drilled a speaker that was mounted on a catwalk with a batting practice drive that would have otherwise left the yard.

Josh also snagged a BP homer hit by Manny Ramirez after it slammed down against the seat next to him (Section 147, Row CC, Seat 21). The score represented Josh's fourth free ball of the road trip.

Kevin: "You're a human ball magnet."

Josh: "That's what I tried to tell Mr. Haeblar."

Kevin: "Who?"

Josh: "My high school baseball coach."

Kevin: "He wouldn't play you?"

Josh: "He let me keep score."

Kevin: "Hey, that's important, too."

Josh: "That's what he kept telling me."

Upper Reserved (Sections 300–324)

As we've already said, Tropicana is smaller than most domes. And even in the upper deck we didn't feel too far away from the game. As far as upper levels go, this is a low one. Sure, we wouldn't want to be stuck in the uppermost seats, but hey, the Trop is never full, so that's not a legitimate concern.

The first row of each section is Row A. Then, after Row Z, the rows start over at AA. Some sections like 310 and 319 have bleachers instead of seats in the very back rows—we're not sure why. Rows A to D are best, located below the concourse that spans the entire upper level. These are akin to what are called "upper boxes" at most parks, but here they're sold at the same price as the seats behind the concourse.

After the concourse, avoid Rows E and F where walkway traffic is a distraction. But rows G to M are excellent, especially behind the plate.

Because the upper deck is set back an ample distance from the field, there is no under-hang obstruction to worry about.

SEATING TIP

IF YOU DON'T like your upper-level seat, head on down to the Batter's Eye restaurant on the first level in center field. Grab a barstool on the outdoor patio and milk a beer or two while enjoying a first-rate view of the game.

The Beach (Sections 341–355)

The left field bleacher seats on the Club level belong to an area known as "the Beach." These dirt-cheap tickets are sold on game day only. They go on sale two hours before game time at Gate 6. Fans who buy these tickets must enter the ballpark through Gate 6 and must stay at the beach until the seventh inning before scoping out other levels of the ballpark. As far as we're concerned sitting on these uncomfortable metal bleachers is no day at the beach. From many of these sections the under-hang below hides the left field warning track from view. This is less of a factor in the sections near

the foul line, like 341 and 343. These sections are also closer to the action than sections like 353 and 355 in center field which are approximately one hundred feet farther from the plate.

As for the beach theme: the cement behind the bleachers is painted sky blue and supports a few pieces of tacked-up cardboard thatch. This may be more of an effort to make the area festive and fun than what the Marlins offer in their Pro Player's "Fish Tank" section, but it's still not much. Why not do more? Heat lamps would be a nice touch. And maybe some sand. And seaweed. And beach umbrellas.

The Black Market

If you're hell-bent on haggling with a scalper, head to Tampa and visit the Tampa Yankees' Legends Field. Otherwise, buy a ticket from the Trop box office and stay in St. Pete to enjoy a cheap Major League game in what will likely be a pretty decent seat.

Before/After the Game

While the streets around the dome may not be steeped in baseball history, they offer plenty of attractions worth visiting for those fans looking to stretch their legs and soak up some sunshine before the game. Hey, you're going to be inside all night, so why not get some fresh air while you can?

Getting to Tropicana Field

From the south or west take I-75 to I-275. As you cross the bay the dome will come into view on your right. From this vantage point, it looks something like a crushed soda can. Stay on I-275 after crossing the bay, keeping the Trop on your left. Then take Exit 22 for I-175 east which leads right to the Dome.

The team lots on First Avenue South charge $10 per game. A bit farther down First Avenue is a $5 lot. Near the ballpark, the street spots on

Central Avenue are two-hour parking until 11:00 P.M.—no help for those wishing to watch a baseball game that begins at 7:00. Follow Central away from the dome, however, until you pass under the highway overpass. Here, past the intersection of Central and 18th Street, the street spots are limited to two-hour parking only until 6:00 P.M. at which time they become unlimited parking. A five-minute walk from the dome, this is an easy place to score free parking for those arriving at 4:00 P.M. or later.

Outside Attractions

BASEBALL (PLATE) BOULEVARD

Follow the bronze home-plate plaques that begin outside of Tropicana Field's Gate 1 and lead to Central Avenue and you'll soon find yourself at Al Lang Field, the spring training home of the Devil Rays and home ballpark of the Class-A Florida State League Rays.

The series of inscribed home plates makes up Baseball Boulevard, a walking tour that chronicles the history of baseball in St. Petersburg. The path is well landscaped, passing over a small river past some old railroad tracks and along a number of aromatic perennial beds. When the path led us into a tunnel underneath a bridge near the ballpark, we encountered a lone violinist playing a sad tune.

Chronologically, the walk begins with a plaque outside of Al Lang Field celebrating Lang's efforts to lure the St. Louis Browns to the Sunshine City. The final plaque at the time of our visit was the one celebrating Wade Boggs's three-thousandth hit at Tropicana Field in 1999. In between plaques remember the contributions of some of the game's brightest stars (Babe Ruth, Joe DiMaggio, Tom Seaver, Cal Ripken) have made to St. Petersburg over the years. They also commemorate the efforts of Vince Naimoli and others who never gave up the dream of making St. Petersburg a big league city.

Dirt

Always dreamed of running your fingers through the red clay on the Devil Rays' infield? Rather than running out on the field and getting hauled off by security to spend a night in the pen, we suggest visiting Parking Lot 6A right outside the main entrance of the ballpark. Here, a bin of the surplus red dirt sits in reserve waiting for the grounds crew to come collect it when needed. On one hand, it seems kind of bush league for a Major League team to have a big bin of dirt in plain view right outside of its main gates. On the other hand, what a thrill it was to touch the storied infield dirt of Tropicana Field.

Man, Them Mannequins

Mounted high above the concourse on the facade of the stadium, a larger-than-life Devil Ray mannequin wears uniform number 98, symbolic of 1998 when the team joined the league. The plastic player reaches out to catch a fly ball, and he does so, quite frankly, with a horrified look on his face. If he hasn't pooped in his pants yet, it seems as if he's about to very soon.

Al Lang Field, aka Progress Energy Park

If you have time to catch a Florida State League game while you're in town, we highly recommend it. After watching a game indoors at the Trop, a visit to Al Lang Field (aka Progress Energy Park) really hits the spot. And even if you don't have time to watch a game, we recommend walking or driving down to the waterfront to check out the old concrete ballpark perched above the bay. The park offers striking views of colorful sailboats bobbing in the harbor and is right near St. Petersburg's trademark Pier.

Legends Field (Tampa)

Another spring training field worth visiting is Tampa's Legends Field, home of the spring Yankees and Florida State League Tampa Yankees.

Legends Field features identical outfield dimensions to Yankee Stadium, a facade that resembles Yankee Stadium's, and a monument park similar to "The" Monument Park in the Bronx that provides details concerning the careers of all of the Yankees who have had their numbers retired. They even play Sinatra's "New York, New York," over the PA system after the game, just like they do in the Bronx.

Legends was built at a cost of $30 million and opened in 1996. Every game is a sellout during spring training but tickets to the Tampa Yankees games are often available. The ballpark is located next to Raymond James Stadium, home of the National Football League Tampa Bay Buccaneers. From St. Petersburg, take I-275 to Exit 41B, then follow the signs on Dale Mabry North to the ballpark, which is on Steinbrenner Drive.

The Pier (Second Avenue, Waterfront)

Located a short walk from Al Lang Field, the Pier has been a St. Petersburg landmark since 1899. The small beach and scenic green lawns offer ideal places to play a game of catch, while those with more ambitious designs for an afternoon can rent bicycles or fishing rods. Using fiddler crabs for bait, a fisherman had just landed a small pompano when we visited. Amberjack, snook, flounder, and sea bass are also reputedly lurking below the surface. The **Pier Bait House**, which is usually encircled by pelicans looking for a handout, rents rods and reels for $10 daily. The small tackle shop has been a fixture at the Pier since 1926.

Inside the inverted pyramid structure at the end of the Pier, a food court offers boardwalk staples like ice cream, corn dogs, and steak sandwiches, while **Captain Al's Waterfront Bar and Grill** provides a slightly more formal dining

---

AL LANG, GRANDFATHER OF THE GRAPEFRUIT LEAGUE

AL LANG played an integral role in creating the Grapefruit League. In the early 1900s Major League teams customarily brought their players to Southern states like Georgia, Alabama, and Arkansas before the start of the season to shed the weight they'd put on over the winter and prepare for the season. But baseball was without a central spring training location.

In 1911, Lang, a Pittsburgh businessman was stricken ill and told by doctors that he didn't have long to live. Though he was a relatively young man—in his mid-40s—Lang accepted this sad fate and moved to Florida to spend his last few months alive in the sunshine.

After settling in St. Petersburg, Lang experienced a remarkable recovery and soon became mayor of the small fishing town. In 1914 he lured the St. Louis Browns to town to prepare for the season. Robert L. Hedges, president of the Browns, was attracted to St. Pete because of its great sports fishing and the fact that it was

a dry town and as such would offer limited temptations to visiting players.

Playing under the direction of another baseball visionary, manager Branch Rickey, the Browns lost to the Cubs 3–2 in their first Florida game.

By 1929, ten of the sixteen Major League teams had established spring camps in Florida, including three—the Browns, Boston Braves, and New York Yankees—who trained in St. Petersburg. The Yankees reportedly fled their former training camp in New Orleans after Babe Ruth wore out his welcome in the city.

When St. Petersburg replaced the aging Coffee Pot Park with a new ballpark in 1946, the park was named in honor of Lang. Al Lang Field would house the spring Yankees (1946–50 and 1952–61) and Cardinals (1946–97) before the Devil Rays moved in for the 1998 season. As for Lang? He enjoyed spring baseball in St. Pete until the ripe old age of 89. And you probably thought the Fountain of Youth was only a myth.

experience. An assortment of tourist shops operate inside, for those road-trippers looking for just the right souvenir to bring home to their honey, while a small aquarium upstairs offers those too lazy to find their fish the hard way glimpses of some specimens.

Watering Holes and Outside Eats

Tampa is better known for its wild nightlife than St. Petersburg is, but we found a number of fun places to eat and drink in both cities. As for watering holes near the ballpark, there are a few. And while they may not be great, they are convenient and certainly adequate. Perhaps if the Rays someday start attracting thirty-thousand plus fans per night, a more diverse sampling of bars and restaurants will spring up in the streets around the Trop.

Tampa

MALIO'S STEAK HOUSE
(301 South Dale Mabry Highway)

Lou Piniella, who grew up in West Tampa with owner Malio Iavarone, is a regular here, as is Tampa resident George Steinbrenner. The Boss has his own private suite at the rear of the restaurant complete with his own phone line. From this room, the Big Stein spins his twisted webs all aimed at league domination. It was at Malio's, we've heard, that the Yankee brain trust hatched the plan to pry Roger Clemens away from the Blue Jays after the 1999 season. The upscale restaurant is certainly convenient to Yankees personnel, located just two miles from Legends Field. It is also within a mile of three strip clubs, including Tampa's renowned Mons Venus.

When we visited Malio's a sign out front read "Lou, Lou, Lou," in support of the new Rays manager. Inside, however, Yankee memorabilia dominated the walls. A signed photo of Wade Boggs doing a horseback victory lap of Yankee Stadium after winning the 1996 World

Series sent chills down Josh's spine. Other autographed photos included those of Yankees Derek Jeter, Whitey Ford, and Paul O'Neill; Buccaneers coach John Gruden; former Dallas cowboys Coach Jimmy Johnson; and Major League managers Tony LaRussa and Sparky Anderson. Also displayed is a signed sketch of Burt Reynolds who played college football at Florida State University before beginning his acting career.

Lunch entrées—we're guessing that you probably can't afford dinner—range from $12 to $22. The Yankee pasta, which comes topped with crabmeat, is a house specialty. The four-to-six-person appetizer platter is a good value at $28. It features coconut shrimp, calamari fritti, Sicilian cheese bread, seared sashimi tuna, a CrabMeat cocktail, and steak tartare.

DAMON'S GRILL (7700 Courtney Campbell)

Located inside the **Radisson Bay Harbor Hotel**, this casual restaurant used to be known as "The Yankee Trader." Despite its name change, the hosts still wear Yankee garb, plenty of autographed Yankees memorabilia adorns the walls, and the Bronx Bomber Breakfast plate is still featured prominently on the menu.

Owned by the Big Stein himself, the Radisson serves as Yankees headquarters during Spring Training, so if you're in Tampa during the Grapefruit League season, stake out the lobby with a Sharpie and stack of baseball cards.

BERN'S STEAK HOUSE (1208 S. Howard Avenue)

Serving what very well may be the finest steaks in the Southeast, this Tampa restaurant is famous for its red meats and fine wines. The steak is aged eight weeks, and the wine cellar houses more than half a million bottles, representing more than six thousand varieties. Bern's isn't cheap, but if you're looking to treat yourself (on your publisher's dime), have at it.

YBOR CITY (9th Avenue and surrounding streets)

The area of Tampa known as Ybor City is a National Historic Landmark District that was once recognized as the undisputed Cigar Capital of the World. A romp through Ybor (pronounced: E-bore) City today brings one back to another era. Wrought-iron balconies combine with globe streetlights, brick walkways, and the prolific architecture of the old cigar factories to paint a portrait of a decadent time in Tampa history.

Ybor City was built by immigrants from Spain, Cuba, Italy, Romania, and Germany. And this heritage is still reflected in the district's cultural and culinary offerings. Don't worry, even though today's Ybor City is known predominantly as an entertainment district, it still features its share of hand-rolled stogies.

We recommend **The Ybor City Brewing Company**, which brews Ybor Gold; **The Columbia**, the oldest Spanish restaurant in the United States; and the **Green Iguana Bar & Grill**.

St. Petersburg

FERG'S SPORTS BAR & GRILL
(1320 Central Avenue)

Directly across the street from the St. Petersburg police station, Ferg's offers fans a more than adequate pre- or postgame watering hole near the ballpark. The expansive bar features an upstairs nightclub with blaring DJ music as well as a covered outdoor patio with large electric fans that provide a breeze on hot days. We settled onto a pair of barstools on the patio where beer bottles sat in buckets of ice waiting to be plucked, TVs showed games from around the league, a few young ladies sported camel toes, and folks chowed down on cheap wings and burgers.

BOOMER'S EXTRA INNINGS BALLPARK CAFÉ
(Central and 18th)

If you take our tip and park for free on the corner of Central Avenue and 18th Street, this will be a convenient bar for you to visit. Trust us, it looks better on the inside than it does from the street. Housed in an old theater, Extra Innings is a solid choice for those who want to grab a pregame beer or to watch the West Coast games after the Rays game ends. Tiered seating gives everyone in the bar a good view of the big-screen TVs mounted above the old stage.

In the lobby a wall displays ballpark pictures painted on mirrors. In order from left to right, the five classic ballparks displayed here are Yankee Stadium, Wrigley Field, Tropicana Field, Fenway Park, and Tiger Stadium. All right, maybe they're not all classics. We found it hilarious to see the Trop arranged as the centerpiece of these hallowed ball yards.

The exterior display windows are decorated with pictures of baseball legends like Ty Cobb, Walter Johnson, Babe Ruth, Ted Williams, Lou Gehrig, and—Aubrey Huff. Just kidding. The displays honor only the Hall of Famers, no Devil Rays.

DAN MARINO'S TOWN TAVERN
(First Street and Second Avenue)

Part of a popular Florida restaurant chain, this Marino's edition is just a short walk from the Pier and Al Lang Field. The reasonably priced menu ranges from steaks to ribs to pasta plates.

SPIZZICO'S PIZZA (First Avenue and 15th Street)

Right across the street from the ballpark this casual joint offers homemade Italian food at dirt-cheap prices. Josh tried a slice of cheese pizza that was large and much tastier than the pizza available inside the park. Then he tried a delicious meatball sub that came on homemade Italian bread, stuffed with homemade balls, and slathered with homemade sauce. If you're in the mood for Italian, we highly recommend visiting Spizzico's before the game. Beer, wine, and Italian ice are available for those in need of something chilly.

Inside the Trop

Considering what they had to work with—namely, a domed facility—the D-Rays have done an excellent job of arranging the playing field and dressing it up to create the illusion of a real field. A bit of natural light seems to penetrate through the roof in the hour or so before sunset and this makes the environment feel a bit more natural as the game begins. As for the Field Turf, not only does it provide a playing surface that more closely resembles the texture of a real grass field, but its color is also a truer, paler shade of green than that of the nearly fluorescent rugs that have appeared elsewhere. The outfield fences are wallpapered an attractive dark green, with this background broken up occasionally with the images of swimming devil rays, oranges, orange leaves, and palm leaves—all very appropriate Florida symbols. The catwalks are also decorated to minimize their obtrusiveness. We like the outfield dimensions—not too deep and not too shallow—and the proximity of fair territory to most of the seats.

Our only major complaint regarding the field layout and design has to do with the positioning of the bull pens, presently located parallel to the outfield foul lines in right field (Devil Rays) and left field (visitors). Really, these are not bull pens. They are merely practice mounds in foul territory. Now, we're willing to cut teams some slack in cities like Chicago—where the Cubs and their opponents have no choice but to warm up their pitchers down the foul lines because of ballpark space considerations—but in Tampa Bay this is inexcusable. You see, the Trop contains two areas separate from the field—one out by the foul pole in left field, the other in the right—that would seem ideally suited to house a couple of legitimate bull pens. Instead the Rays use these spaces to accommodate private parties and groups of fans. The Bullpen Café in right field was populated with about twelve people when we visited, while the Bullpen Party Area in left field was completely empty, apparently not reserved on the day we stopped by. Relief pitchers deserve a space that's all their own and it's not like the Trop has any shortage of restaurants, so hopefully the Rays will reconsider and make better use of the space they have after reading our book.

Ballpark Features

CATWALKS

In time for the start of the 2003 season, the D-Rays decorated the two lowermost ceiling walkways with long orange banners. This is very well done, but it's not the most interesting aspect of the catwalks. We were intrigued by the mini foul poles that extend from the three outfield catwalks to help umpires judge whether balls striking these structures are fair or foul. Follow the regular foul poles up toward the ceiling with your eyes and you will see these yellow markers. This must be the only baseball field in the history of the world with eight foul poles.

CATWALK GROUND RULES

Because balls frequently bounce off the catwalks, we thought it might be helpful to run down the ground rules in case these structures come into play during your game at the Trop. This way you'll know why the umps are sending a runner back toward second base or circling their fingers in the air to signify a home run.

Without further ado, here's the list:

➤ A batted ball that hits a catwalk in foul territory will automatically be ruled a dead ball and called a strike.
➤ A batted ball that hits a catwalk in fair territory will be judged fair or foul depending upon where it hits the ground on the field.

If the ball hits the catwalk in fair territory and lands in fair territory or is touched by a fielder in fair territory, it is a fair ball. If the ball strikes the catwalk in fair territory and is caught by a fielder in fair or foul territory, the batter is out.

➤ A batted ball that hits the catwalk and remains on the catwalk in foul territory is a foul ball.

➤ A batted ball that hits the catwalk and remains on the catwalk in fair territory is a ground rule double.

➤ A batted ball that hits either of the lower two catwalks in fair territory is a home run.

A YELLOW SEAT—ICK!

Head out to Section 144 in right field and find the seat where Wade Boggs's three-thousandth career hit landed in 1999. After becoming the first player to enter the 3,000 Hit Club with a home run, The Chicken Man circled the bases then got down on all fours and kissed home plate. Josh kept waiting for him to will himself invisible (as Boggs claimed to have done during a Spring Training incident while with the Red Sox when he was robbed at knifepoint outside a bar) but it didn't happen.

As for being the only member of the exclusive hit club to enter with a flourish—well Boggs didn't keep that distinction for long. Rickey Henderson turned the same trick just two years later, hitting a big fly for his number three thousand. No, Rickey didn't will himself invisible either.

In any case, Boggs's gold seat is located in Row B of Section 144. On it, a plaque reads "Site of Wade Boggs's 3,000th hit." A short distance away, the D-Rays lone retired number, Boggs's number 12 hangs high above Section 146.

MURAL

Wrapping around much of the first level underneath the stands on the concourse, a large mural depicts an old-time ballpark with wooden bleachers where fans watch a game. Riding the escalator from the lower to upper level, we spotted Abbot and Costello in the crowd, Humphrey Bogart, Lauren Bacall, and other well-known persons. Higher still, on the face of the second-level concourse cutouts appear of fans watching from the mural's upper deck. We spotted Devil Rays owner Vince Naimoli pasted in the back row of nearly all of these upper boxes.

Kevin: "If Vince wanted an old-time ballpark experience, why didn't he build an open-air ballpark down by the waterfront?"

Josh: "The paint job was probably cheaper. And besides, do you really think Abbot and Costello would have turned out to watch a game outside in the humidity? They've got to be pretty old, and most of the old folks I know can't stand the humidity."

Stadium Eats

We give the Devil Rays credit for offering fans plenty to choose from. The two food courts on the first-level concourse house a number of private vendors from the local community. The Rays should also be applauded for setting up no less than four different bars inside the dome.

EXPANSION DRAFT

BEFORE the 1997 expansion draft got under way, each of the preexisting twenty-eight Major League teams was allowed to protect fifteen players from its forty-man roster. Then, after a first round that saw both Tampa Bay and Arizona take fourteen players, teams pulled back three of their exposed players before the second round, which saw the new teams take an additional fourteen players each. The preexisting teams each pulled another three players back prior to the third round, in which Tampa and Arizona took seven players, giving both teams a total of thirty-five players.

YBOR CITY CUBAN SANDWICH
(Trademark Food)

The Columbia, a landmark in Ybor City, operates a satellite stand inside the ballpark. These folks have been making Cuban sandwiches since 1905, and the sandwich at the ballpark reflects these years of experience. The Cuban comes brimming over with spicy meat, grilled peppers, and gooey cheese.

LYKES HOT DOG (Dog Rating)
The Sixteenth Best Hot Dog in the Majors

This beefy frank has a firm texture that has to be respected. However, we like our dogs to have a bit more bite. The folks mixing the meat porridge in the Lykes jungle would be well served to throw caution to the wind and increase the spiciness of their frankfurters.

BEST OF THE REST

In 2002, PETA (People for the Ethical Treatment of Animals)—the left-wing vegetarian group that seems to have found its way into quite a few of our chapters—named the Trop the most vegetarian-friendly ballpark in the big leagues. Offerings like garlic knots, black beans and rice, and peanut-butter-and-jelly sandwiches earned PETA's commendations. A devout carnivore, Josh refused to try any of these menu items, while Kevin—who dabbled in vegetarianism in his early twenties before finding the craving for animal flesh too strong—tried a Bloomin' Onion from the **Outback Steak House** stand, then immediately ordered a Cuban sandwich to wash it down. As for the onion, it cost the same amount as the onions served at the Outback restaurants and was just as spicy. Where else in the Majors can you sit in your seat and eat a deep-fried onion? This is a good bet for those who come to the ballpark prepared to carry a ball of grease around in their stomachs for the rest of the night.

Want to play a mean trick on one of the kids? Ask Little Billy or Little Suzie if they'd like a corn dog, then hand them a jalapeno corn dog from the **Throwing Heat** stand.

Selling burgers by the bag full, **Pete and Shorty's** will remind folks of White Castle, with its tiny burgers.

We tried a bucket of ribs from **Atwater's Southern Cooking**. For $10, the bucket was filled with enough ribs to satisfy the two of us and our hungry St. Petersburg host, Aaron Fournier. The ribs were meaty and falling off the bone, although Kevin would have liked them better had the sauce been basted onto them during cooking. Instead the tangy BBQ nectar came in a side-cup. And Josh and Aaron kept double-dipping.

Ballpark Bars and Restaurants

The **Batter's Eye** is a three-story restaurant located in dead center field. Its tinted windows actually serve as the ballpark's batter's eye. One of these windows was cracked in a spider-web pattern when we visited, courtesy of a batted ball that had struck it down a few days previously. Seating is available on a first-come first-served basis and the buffet costs $24. We were already too full to try the food, but we did spend a few innings outside on the double-tiered deck beside the cameramen. We liked the view from here, practically hanging out over the field in left-center.

The **Cuesta-Rey Cigar Bar** is located on the upper-level concourse in center field behind the Batter's Eye. While it doesn't offer a view of the game, it provides leather couches, cigars ranging from $2 to $22 in price, and plenty of ashtrays. Strangely, none of the twelve people inside were smoking when we stopped in.

Adjacent to the Cigar Bar, the **Jack Daniels Billiards Hall** provides pool tables for fans wanting to play some stick. The table rate is $10 per hour. No one was playing when we visited, and understandably so—there was a baseball game going on outside.

By far the most heavily trafficked of the Tropicana Field watering holes, the **Budweiser Brew House** is located on the first-level concourse. Inside, it has the feel of a real sports bar, with a classy wooden counter and multiple TVs mounted overhead showing games from around the league.

SAY "NO, THANKS," AND WALK AWAY

The **Hooters** stand that serves the restaurant chains trademark wings at one of the first-level food-courts was a major disappointment. A group of middle-aged men manned the counter when we visited. That's right, no tight orange spandex.

The Tropicana Field Experience

Visiting Tropicana Field, we got the distinct impression that, like the Devil Ray team, the Tampa Bay fans are still very much in search of their collective identity. This was evident in the crowd's lack of enthusiasm. The fact that there were clearly more Red Sox fans in attendance at the Trop during the series we saw didn't help matters. The hometown crowd was often drowned out by the cheers of the visiting fans. It may take a while, but if the Rays can someday mount a championship campaign, they will likely then discover their version of "homer-hankies" or "halo-sticks," or whatever other tradition ultimately will distinguish them.

DICKY V. (Superfan)

Recognize a familiar voice emanating from the third-base lower boxes—high pitched, high strung, and bubbling over with excitement?

There it is again: "Awesome pitch, baby! Awesome!"

That's right, college basketball guru and Tampa Bay resident Dick Vitale owns a box of four season tickets right next to the visitors' dugout. And if you think Dicky V. whoops it up on ESPN, wait until you hear him at the ballpark. He's not exactly the Spike Lee of MLB though. Rather than riding opposing players, Dicky cheers for his Rays.

DANCE, DANCE, DANCE

Grounds-crew member McArthur "Mac" Church does an interesting boogie each night when the crew drags the infield in the seventh inning. Break dancing as the crowd cheers him on, Church leaps in the air, puts one hand on his hip and the other behind his head and makes like he's riding a bucking bronco. A member of the Rays original grounds crew, Church had stopped performing his act following the death of his father. But after a period of grieving, and after fans and fellow crew members offered their encouragement, he began dancing again in 2003. Church calls his undulations, a "Mac Attack."

RALLY RAY

We don't pretend to be marine biologists, but the team mascot, Rally Ray, looks more like a bloated manatee than a devil ray to us.

Kevin: "That fellow needs to have a sit-down with Tommy Lasorda."

Josh: "The famous Dodgers manager?"

Kevin: "The Slim-Fast pitch man."

ODD-BALL USHERS

It seems like every ballpark has a few unique spirits in their cadre of souvenir- and refreshment-hawking wanderers. At the Trop, these characters are just plain bizarre. The Riddler, decked out all in Green and speaking in rhyme doles out bottles of beer to patrons in left field, while one of his colleagues selling cotton candy is dressed as a Native American with a full headdress. See what we mean when we say the Rays are still searching for an identity?

BLOOD DAY

The Rays were advertising for an upcoming ballpark promotion when we were in town. For a whole weekend series, fans arriving early at the ballpark could get a free cholesterol check

SPORTS IN THE CITY

DERBY LANE DOG RACING

ST. PETERSBURG is home to the oldest continuously operated greyhound track in the world. The pooches have been running at Derby Lane since 1925, which according to our estimation equals approximately 340 dog years.

If your visit occurs before the end of June, why not spend an afternoon betting on the "little ponies?" On Mondays, Wednesdays, and Saturdays racing begins at 12:30 P.M., while evening racing takes place Monday through Saturday, beginning at 6:30 P.M. The track is on Gandy Boulevard, just west of the Gandy Bridge and east of 4th Street.

In 2001, actors George Clooney and Brad Pitt spent three days at Derby Lane filming part of the Warner Brothers film *Ocean's 11*.

in exchange for donating blood at Tropicana Field. What's next, inoculation day?

THE TED WILLIAMS MUSEUM

(2455 N. Citrus Hills Boulevard, Hernando, Florida) Okay, his corpse may be presently suspended upside down in an Arizona lab, cryogenically frozen by his bizarre son, but that's no reason not to visit the project that occupied much of the Splendid Splinter's time in his later years. Not only is the facility full of unique baseball memorabilia, like Ted's first professional contract, but it also includes plenty of stuffed fish from Ted's time spent angling in the Florida Keys. Check out the one-hundred-fifty-pound tarpon he once boated on fly fishing equipment, the thirty-one-pound permit he caught on live bait, and the bonefish that he caught on fly-equipment. They're all here, stuffed for your viewing pleasure. Ted's rifle and golf clubs are also on display. And there is plenty more memorabilia from around the Major Leagues to interest visitors here. Josh's favorite picture was one of Ted batting at Fitton Field on the campus of Holy Cross in Worcester, Massachusetts, during an exhibition game against the Crusaders on April 14, 1939. Kevin was partial to a portrait of all of the members of the 500 Home Run Club standing together at old Yankee Stadium

The centerpiece of the museum is the Hitters Hall of Fame that honors all of the classic big hitters (including Pete Rose and Joe Jackson who remain banned from the National Baseball Hall of Fame), as well as current players like Nomar Garciaparra, the kid Ted said had the best chance of hitting .400 among current players. Ted himself was inducted posthumously in 2003, a few months after his death.

The museum is open Tuesday through Sunday from 10:00 A.M. to 4:00 P.M. and admission is $5. It is about an hour-and-a-half drive from Tampa. Follow I-75 north for sixty miles to Highway 44 west. After several miles turn right onto U.S. 41 north. Follow 41 for several miles into Hernando, then turn left onto CR 486 (Norvell Bryant Highway). After four miles, the museum will be on your left. Be sure to watch out for the many small lizards that sun themselves in the parking lot. We accidentally squashed about a half dozen of them when we pulled the road-trip car—a Toyota Corolla with standard sized tires—into the lot (sorry, PETA). For more information, visit www.tedwilliamsmuseum.com or call (352) 527-6566.

FLORIDA MARLINS, PRO PLAYER STADIUM

A Baseball Gridiron in Miami

MIAMI, FLORIDA

206 miles to Tampa Bay
228 miles to Havana, Cuba
605 miles to Atlanta
924 miles to Washington, D.C.

P RO PLAYER STADIUM, the home of the Florida Marlins, is a great place to see a game. A football game, that is. The facility is more appropriately the home of the National Football League Miami Dolphins from September to December. When converted for baseball, the facility seems enormous, with its distant fences and expansive seating. So expansive in fact, that in the upper deck the outfield sections are closed off during regular season games; something we never like to see in a ballpark. The rectangular shape of the facility contributes to less-than-stellar views of the baseball field from most seating areas and completely encloses the action, offering no views of outside the stadium. But what Pro Player lacks in intimacy and charm, it makes up for in bravado, having already hosted two World Series, not to mention three Super Bowls.

Although the annual conversion of the stadium from football gridiron to baseball park is fairly well done, a distinct football aftertaste remains. It's kind of like the time Josh's dad tried to remodel the garage and turn it into a second living room. Although there were carpets and couches and even a few lava lamps, there was always the lingering odor of motor oil and turpentine. And even though it was built in the 1980s, Pro Player doesn't offer many of the amenities that fans have come to expect in new stadiums. Each corner of the stadium exterior is flanked by spiraling concrete ramps; huge walkways that are decidedly un-ballparklike. The stadium feel is heightened by the eight entry gates, designed for easy access to and from the wasteland of parking lots outside. These rolling fields of asphalt leave the landscape outside the park barren and desolate. The good news is that this dearth of pre- and postgame entertainment options has given rise to a lively tailgating culture. Not only can the parking lot accommodate fifteen

exterior

Photo by Kevin O'Connell

thousand cars and two-hundred-fifty buses, it even houses its own heliport. Maybe the Dolphins were expecting Deion Sanders to drop in? But the lot's sheer size leaves no room for bars, restaurants, shops, or anything else that would make Pro Player a bit friendlier to the urban baseball experience. It's a distant drive to anything interesting, and there's no wonder the Marlins are lobbying for a new facility.

Inside the stadium, the first row of seating is about ten feet above field level; again, great for football. Have you ever noticed that no one sits in the first few rows of college and high school football stadiums where the bleachers go all the way down to field level? It's because fans sitting down low can't see over the players standing on the sidelines. In any case, the low seats that would be best for baseball are terrible football seats, and therefore removed from the design. It's a shame the Marlins don't install temporary field-level seats for baseball, as many of the cookie-cutter parks of the past provided.

The outfield wall is deep and features a few quirky angles that cause balls to carom off it in

bizarre ways. The thirty-three-foot-high left field wall, known as "the Teal Monster," houses an out-of-town scoreboard. The wall is the second highest in baseball, second only to the Green Monster in Boston, which rises thirty-seven feet. Meanwhile just to the left of the center field wall is a protuberance known as "the Bermuda Triangle" that comes toward the plate at a dramatic angle, from four hundred thirty-four feet quickly in to four hundred ten. After starting out three hundred thirty feet from the plate in the left field corner and angling out to three hundred eighty-five feet away in the left center field power alley, the wall drops to only eight feet high in dead center and remains that height all the way to the right field corner, which measures three hundred forty-five feet from the plate. Though the fences are deep, the humid Florida air enables the ball to carry a few extra feet.

Pro Player was the only stadium of its era to be built exclusively for football then converted into a multipurpose facility that could also accommodate baseball. Well, now that's not exactly true. When construction began in 1985, Dolphins owner Joe Robbie suspected that baseball might be arriving in South Florida soon. So the grandstands were laid out in a rectangular fashion wider than necessary for a football-only facility. A few months before construction began on the stadium, the Major League Baseball owners had agreed in principle to accept two new expansion teams. But it wouldn't be until 1990 that South Florida would be officially listed as among the six finalists considered for new teams. The other areas on MLB's short list included Washington, D.C.; Denver, Colorado; Buffalo, New York; Orlando, Florida; and Tampa, Florida.

The movement to bring a team to Miami gained momentum in March 1990 when Blockbuster Video mogul H. Wayne Huizenga announced he intended to spearhead the city's quest for a team. For good measure, Huizenga purchased half of Joe Robbie Stadium, and 15 percent of the Dolphins. The effort to convert Joe Robbie into a stadium capable of hosting baseball began in January of 1991. But it wasn't until June of that year that Baseball Commissioner Fay Vincent confirmed that South Florida and Denver had been selected by the expansion committee. Oh, what a feeling for South Florida. The longtime home of ball teams during spring training would finally have its own year-round franchise. Baseball fans celebrated by dancing in the streets and drinking till all hours. Well, almost. Perhaps those folks were just spring-breakers who still hadn't made their way back North.

To the credit of all involved, at the time of its construction the funding for Joe Robbie Stadium came entirely from private sources. Robbie spent $115 million to build the stadium, financed mostly through the leasing of executive suites that would cost high rollers $30,000 to $90,000 annually. At long last we've found a use for football fans: to fund new baseball

parks! Let this occur across the country, but let's make the ballparks smaller and design them for baseball only, of course. Kidding aside, the designers of Joe Robbie had baseball in the backs of their minds all along, and so costs to renovate the stadium amounted to only $10 million. While Huizenga provided the extra cash, the architectural firm HOK of Kansas City drew up the blueprints.

In 1994 Huizenga bought the remaining interest in the stadium. The naming rights were sold in 1996 to the Pro Player brand, a division of Fruit of the Loom that makes athletic apparel.

Josh: "They should have called it the Tighty-Whitey bowl."

Kevin: "And if Ralph Lauren had bought the naming rights to PacBell in San Francisco he could have called it, 'the Polo Grounds.'"

The baseball modifications of the facility included building a press box into the southwest corner of the stadium to sit behind home plate. And the large retractable out-of-town-scoreboard was built into left field with retractable baseball-only seating above it. Dugouts were dug out (as they should be) and a rubber warning track was added. The pitcher's mound was built like those in other multiuse stadiums, on a hydraulic platform that allows it to sink and disappear when some stadium tech-dude throws the switch.

It's hard to believe that an area of the country like southern Florida that has produced so many great Major Leaguers didn't have its own MLB team until 1993. Like migrating birds each spring, northern teams have flocked to Florida for years to train in the warm weather. And minor league ball—Class A especially—has flourished over the years in the Sunshine State.

The colleges and universities of Florida have produced many big leaguers over the years. While winning four College World Series championships (2001, 1999, 1985, 1982) the University of Miami has turned out such Major Leaguers as Mike Piazza, Pat Burrell, Charles Johnson, and Greg Vaughn, just to name a few. Florida State University (Dick Howser, Deion Sanders, Paul Sorrento, Doug Mientkiewicz, Luis Alicea, Jeff Gray, and Jody Reed) and the University of Florida (David Eckstein, Herbert Perry, Brad Wilkerson, Mike Stanley, Haywood Sullivan, and Marc Sullivan) also field excellent squads year in and year out, although neither school has ever won the College World Series. High school ball also thrives in the Sunshine State.

In 1997, the Marlins attracted three million fans to Pro Player. But by 2002, the Fish were struggling to outdraw Montreal. The Marlins attracted 10,038 fans per game in 2002, while the Expos drew 10,025. And we all know what happened in Montreal. Then came the Marlins of 2003, who boosted attendance back up to a barely sustainable yield, for now. Perhaps the lack of fan support for the Marlins can be attributed to the many transplants in the area whose loyalties lie with the Yankees, Red Sox, and Dolphins.

South Florida is home to millions of Cuban expatriates, Puerto Ricans, and Dominicans— folks whose love for the game of baseball is unparalleled. The massive immigration of Cubans to Miami in the 1950s, and to a lesser degree ever since, solidified the area's passion for the game. From Minnie Minoso to Tony Perez, baseball drew much of its talent from the countries of the Caribbean, a tradition that continues. Cuban players such as Livan and Orlando Hernandez, and Dominican players such as Sammy Sosa and Pedro Martinez have come to dominate the sport. And let's not leave out Puerto Rico, which produced Ivan Rodriguez. The insatiable Caribbean love for the game of baseball, the passion of the fans of these countries, and their highly represented numbers among the great players of our time, continues to inspire fans of the game here in America.

Major League Baseball came to Miami for the first time on April 5, 1993. Charlie Hough threw the first pitch in Marlins history against the Los Angeles Dodgers before a sellout crowd of 42,334 at Joe Robbie Stadium. The Fish would go on to win the game 6–3. Pitching proved fruitful for the young Minnows as Al Leiter threw the team's first no-hitter on May 11, 1996. A year later Kevin Brown came within one out of a perfect game against San Francisco on June 10, 1997, as he tossed the team's second no-no.

Some key acquisitions, not the least of which included Bobby Bonilla, Gary Sheffield, Moises Alou, and manger Jim Leyland enabled the Marlins to earn the National League Wild Card in 1997. The Fish swept the San Francisco Giants in three stunning games to win the National League Division Series. Key hits by Alou and Edgar Renteria helped win Games 1 and 2, while a grand slam by Devon White in the sixth inning of Game 3 sent the little fishies jumping into a bigger pond. But the pundits predicted that the upstart Marlins would be no match for the dynasty the Atlanta Braves had assembled in the National League Championship Series. Atlanta's pitching was better, and key hits were the team's specialty. Or so the experts said. They were wrong. Rather, the live arms of rookie Livan Hernandez and Brown overpowered the perennial World Series contenders, as the two hurlers won two games apiece in the six-game series. Hernandez, who earned MVP honors, struck out a championship series record fifteen batters in Game 5 before a home crowd of 51,982.

Next up for the Marlins, the Cleveland Indians and a World Series that would defy the odds. Hernandez won two more World Series starts, both over Orel Hershiser, becoming the first rookie to win two World Series games in more than fifty years. Memories of the climatic eleventh inning of Game 7 make Cleveland fans weep to this day. Renteria slapped a two-out single off Chuck Nagy that scored Craig Counsell to break the tie and crush the hopes of Tribe fans. One of the two newest teams in baseball had become the very best in just five seasons.

The Marlins broke many records on their march to destiny. They became the first Wild Card team to ever win the World Series, coming from behind in eight of their eleven postseason wins. Game 4 in Cleveland proved to be the coldest World Series game ever played, at fifteen degrees Fahrenheit with the wind chill factor. Game 6 at Pro Player Stadium was played before the largest World Series crowd since 1954, attracting 67,498 fans. The Game 7 finale was just the third World Series Game 7 to go into extra innings. And Florida became the first team to ever draw more than half a million fans during a postseason, thanks in part to the extra games of the NLDS, and in part to the huge capacity of Pro Player.

However, the Marlins have faced tough times, snagged by the netting of their own team, city, and football-flavored ballpark. After stocking the Marlins with talent from the free-agent pool before the 1997 season, Huizenga auctioned off the team the very next year. Some players were lost to free agency, while others were traded away for prospects. In response Marlins fans didn't exactly stream into the ballpark. Having won his championship, Huizenga didn't waste much time to dispose of the franchise, selling the Marlins to eccentric millionaire John Henry in 1999. Henry made priority number one constructing a new baseball-only ballpark. The new ballpark he envisioned would be much smaller than Pro Player, and would have a retractable roof to counter the unpredictable weather in southern Florida.

Kevin: "The weather's very predictable. It rains every day at the same time."

Josh: "Yeah, game time."

From a total of six different locations, the Marlins chose a site known as Bicentennial Park, which offered beautiful views of Biscayne Bay, to house the new park. But the well-documented messiness of politics in Florida (remember the 2000 Presidential election?) became a hanging chad stuck in the machine, and lawmakers decided that a downtown spot on the Miami River would be more appropriate. While there were advantages to this location, land acquisition and preparation costs would have been much higher, and the majority of the Marlins fan base actually lived in Broward and Palm Beach counties, rather than in Miami-Dade. In other words, the folks who were going to pay for the park wanted it in their backyard, even though most of the fans lived elsewhere. In any case, the many proposals to find public funding for a ballpark in this part of town ultimately failed.

We have a suggestion: cater to the many retirees living in southern Florida and rename the team the Florida Blue Hairs. They could play at Retirement Park at Phase III of the Del Boca Vista condos. Arby's could get the concession deal. Kidding aside, the Marlins need to determine who their fans are, and build a ballpark accessible to them.

The Marlins dodged the threat of contraction when the new work agreement was signed between the players and management in 2002.

When we arrived at Pro Player on opening day 2003, prospects for the team had ebbed so low that not only were there precious few Marlin fans on hand for what is traditionally the biggest attendance day for baseball, but stories had been floating around that the only reason the Marlins had signed Ivan Rodriquez to a one-year, ten-million-dollar deal was so that management would have good reason to move the team at the end of the season. After all, if no new ballpark was on the horizon and management could point to the fact that they had put a quality product on the field and fans still did not attend the games, who could blame ownership for moving the team?

But over the course of a lengthy baseball season, a lot of things change. Led by 72-year-old manager Jack McKeon, who took over the Fish on May 11, the team sank to ten games under .500 by the 22nd. But the old skipper put his faith in his trusted veterans Pudge Rodriquez, Jeff Conine, and Mike Lowell, as well as shining newcomers Juan Pierre, Don-trelle Willis, and Josh Beckett. The Marlins became the winningest team after the All-Star break and netted a wild-card playoff birth. Everyone had written these baby fish off as too young, not nearly experienced enough to advance far.

San Francisco quickly found out that the Marlins were for real, as the Fish disposed of the Giants three games to one in the National League Division Series. Then against the Cubs the Marlins joined the Red Sox, Braves, and Royals as the only teams to rally from a 3–1 deficit to win the League Championship Series. Game 6 again proved to be the deal breaker, as the Cubs led 3–0, and the Marlins were down to their last five outs. Cub shortstop Alex Gonzalez booted an easy double play ball. Then left fielder Moises Alou was unable to pull a ball out of the stands and away from a young Cub fan, who we shall not name. And the rally was on. The Marlins had been reawakened and they rallied for eight runs in the inning—enough for an 8–3 win. After that crushing defeat, Game 7 seemed academic. Though some Cub fans will blame the Billy Goat curse, while others will blame the kid, it doesn't matter. The tough-as-nails Marlins, the never-say-die Fish, were ready for the Yankees and the World Series.

But these were big Fish now, and they didn't even need seven games to dispose of the Yankees. McKeon's decision to pitch twenty-three-year-old Josh Beckett on short rest proved to be a stroke of brilliance, as Beckett tossed a complete-game five-hit shut-out. Few moments in life are as satisfying as watching King George stew and fume in his luxury box as the Yankees, with a payroll over $184 million were expected to pay almost $12 million more in luxury taxes sank like a stone. The small-budget Marlins' payroll was a mere $54 million, only $6 million more than the Yankees paid in revenue sharing. Ah, sweet justice.

And winning the World Series has gone miles towards the building of a new ballpark in Florida. Though the deal isn't done yet, expect the Fish to have a new home soon. And though the Marlins may not be able to hang onto their expensive veterans, they have proved they can win the old-fashioned way, with willpower. The 2003 Marlin team of destiny was an exciting team to watch, and one that proved themselves to be tougher than getting Josh to buy a round of beers. And, in a break from the tradition begun with the Fish on '97, ownership has promised not to gut the team.

A great truth in sports is that as long as there are winners, there will be losers. And losing teams are generally not profitable. So those at MLB headquarters shouldn't be so quick to threaten losing teams with contraction or relocation just because they're not drawing fans. Don't make fans feel like their lack of support is going to cost the community its team. Create an economic system that allows all teams to enjoy an equal and fair financial footing (as in the NFL) then see if the fans come back. Here's guessing they will.

Getting a Choice Seat

Getting a ticket to see the Marlins in Pro Player in 2003 was amongst the easiest buys of all the Major League facilities. What about Montreal you ask? We said *Major League* facility. The Marlins only averaged 16,000 fans during the year. Frankly, we have no idea what the climate will be like in 2004. This team never ceases to amaze us. But given that Pro Player is such a huge facility, we're betting that getting in won't be the problem, but getting a choice seat will be. So pay close attention to the seating details below.

Founder's Club Box Seats
(Sections 1–03, 41–43, 56, 101, 142–156)

These first-row seats on the infield were presold to rich folks before most of you graduated from high school, so don't waste too much time getting tickets down near the field. The Founder's Boxes attempt to bring some of the premium seating closer to field level, but they're still too pricey and very makeshift looking. Close, but no cigar.

Infield Box Seats (Sections 101, 142–156)

Pro Player is a fairly lousy ballpark where you might want to spend a tad more dough on seats than usual to enhance your experience. Luckily these infield sections aren't outrageously overpriced. Just make sure to sit down as low to the field as possible, as the steep incline of the seating bowl leaves folks in the back rows feeling like they're in the Mezzanine, rather than the first level.

Club Zone A (Sections 243–256)

These Mezzanine-level seats are located on the infield. Section 250 is directly behind the plate, while Section 243 is parallel with first-base and Section 256 is even with third-base. For cheap club seats, these aren't bad. Considering the concession offerings in the rest of the park, this might be one place where a Club seat starts to look attractive.

Sellout Index: 0% of games sell out
Seating Capacity: 42,531
Ticket Office: (305) 623-6100
http://florida.marlins.mlb.com

TRIVIA TIMEOUT

Rowe: Which two teams played in the first Major League game at Joe Robbie Stadium?

Minnow: In 1997 Livan Hernandez became the second rookie ever to win the World Series MVP Award. Who was the first?

Marlin: Which active Tampa Bay Buccaneer defensive back is already in the Baseball Hall of Fame as a Marlin?

Look for the answers in the text.

Club Zone B (Sections 201–210, 240–242)

These Mezzanine sections extend from third-base out to the foul pole in left field, except for the three sections in right field (240–242) that appear after the Club Zone A seats leave off. Sections 205–210 in left field feel far from the plate and should be avoided, while Sections 201, 202, 241, and 242 are the best seats in the price range.

Power Alley—Club Zone C
(Sections 211–215)

What are billed as seats above the Teal Monster should be called Second Level Leftovers. Technically at Club level, these seats hang in open space above the outfield wall, like the mismatched outfield seats to be found at nearly all multiuse stadiums. The Marlins would do well to make the Teal Monster higher and cover these seats completely.

Terrace Box Seats
(Sections 102–110, 140–141)

All but Section 110 have views over the bull pens, which unfortunately are crude and temporary looking. Also, these seats point toward the fifty-yard line rather than home plate. Be prepared to look over your left shoulder on the right field side, and over your right shoulder on the left field side.

SEATING TIP

4 FOR $44

IF THERE ARE four rugged baseball wanderers in your road-trip party, the four for $44 deal is one you might like to consider. For $44 you and your buddies get four tickets to the Mezzanine Level, four hot dogs, four fountain drinks, and four small bags of popcorn. Seat-hop a bit, and this deal gets even sweeter.

Outfield Reserved (Sections 128–131)

Not only is the price more reasonable here than in many parts of the park, but the atmosphere is more like that you'd hope to find at a ball game. Fans here are more into the game, and there is a bleacherlike atmosphere. Plus you're on the first level.

The Fish Tank (Sections 125–127)

Without a doubt these sections are the choice of the cheap road tripper. Of course they're terrible, but they're less than five bucks apiece. The seats don't face the action, but do provide an excellent view across the stadium of Sections 101–103. Binoculars needed, of course. This is where the true Fish fans sit.

Upper Deck (Sections 401–405, 440–456)

The seats in the upper deck are only available on weekends and holidays. They are not good and should be avoided if at all possible. If there are no other options, these seats vary slightly in quality, but not in price. Sections 448–451 are behind home plate (way behind, but hey) and should be sought first.

Before/After the Game

Normally when we say there is nothing around a ballpark, we are exaggerating slightly. For example, even at Shea Stadium or the Ballpark at Arlington there is something of a neighborhood nearby, even if it takes a hike worthy of Odysseus to get there. But in the case of Pro Player Stadium we really mean it. There is nothing even remotely in the vicinity. Parking lots, freeways, and swamp; that's it.

Getting to Pro Player Stadium

Unless you're taking a group bus to the game, you'll be driving into town. From the north and west, follow I-75 south to Route 821 east. Exit 47 leads right to the ballpark. From the south (i.e., the city part of Miami), follow I-95 north to Route 821 west and get off at Exit 47. Finding a parking spot will not be a problem.

Outside Attractions

MIDNIGHT AT THE OASIS

Come in from the wasteland of parking lots to the palm-tree-lined oasis next to the stadium where statues honor Dan Marino, Joe Robbie, and the mythical Casey at the Bat. And that is the order in which they should be listed with regards to this facility. With these statues Pro Player shows appreciation for its football heritage first and foremost. The Dan Marino statue, though "smaller than life," is nicely done. Actually, it's life sized, but compared to the larger statues of Casey and Joe Robbie, it looks a bit puny.

FIESTA LATINA SATURDAYS

We recommend visiting Pro Player on a Saturday and joining the party near Gate H. Though technically inside the stadium, this fiesta is a salute to the Latin influence on American culture outside the realm of baseball. Enjoy the delicious variety of authentic Latin foods and music and even take a free salsa lesson.

Kevin: "She could meringue, and do the salsa! But that was 30 years ago, when they used to have a show. Now it's a disco, but not for Lola. Still in the dress she used to wear . . ."

Josh: "What?"

FAMILY SUNDAYS

Families will enjoy coming to the park early on Sundays to take part in the family-oriented atmosphere at Gate F. Kids food, entertainment, facepainting, and interactive games all contribute to the fun. And after the game, kids twelve and under can run the bases as long as the weather cooperates.

SPORTS TOWN

South of the Stadium are a series of tents known as Sports Town. This attraction features memorabilia kiosks, food vendors, interactive games, and a few barlike tents. While these places are a poor substitute for real sports bars, there are advantages. Two things Miamians never seem to grow tired of are scantily clad women and ostentatious displays of wealth.

Watering Holes and Outside Eats

There is no restaurant or bar even remotely in the vicinity of Pro Player Stadium. For this reason we recommend hitting some of Miami's hot spots before or after the game.

Floridians have improvised and put on a fairly good tailgate. After all, this is a converted football stadium. You can park your car on grass in some sections, and even in the shade of a palm tree if you're lucky. The smells of barbecue waft about the air and fans are allowed to walk around with beer in hand. So bring along your hibachi and basting brush and get them ribs a-cooking.

CALLE OCHO

Head down to 8th Street in Miami and hang out in Little Havana. You can play dominoes and talk baseball with the Cubans in this neighborhood. Also in Calle Ocho is **La Gloria Cubana**, a cigar-making museum located at 1106 SW 8th Street. On hot days, visit **King's Ice Cream** at 1831 8th Street, which features fruity flavors that are as excellent as they are unique.

SHULA'S STEAK HOUSE (5225 Collins Avenue, Miami Beach) or SHULA'S STEAK 2 (15255 Bull Run Road, Miami Lakes)

If you're a football fan, as well as a hardball fan, a trip to one of Don Shula's restaurants may be in order. Not only could he manage a gridiron squad, but apparently Don knows how to assemble a dynamite restaurant management team too. The red meat and seafood are excellent, although a tad on the pricey side.

DAN MARINO'S TOWN TAVERN (5701 Sunset Drive)

Are you getting the impression yet that this is a football town? This is one of several restaurants in the chain owned by the Dolphins Hall of Fame quarterback. The food may not be quite as good as it is at his former coach's joint, but the memorabilia is better and the prices are more reasonable. Josh recommends the marinated prime filet of sirloin, while Kevin gives the nod to the bar which features the Flee Flicker (Vodka with orange juice and a special sweet-and-sour mix with a sidekick of Black Haus and Blue Curacao), the Quarterback Colada (Malibu rum, a colada mix, and a sidekick of Midori), and the Shotgun (banana liqueur, orange, and pineapple juice, with a sidekick of Mad Melon). Just kidding, Kevin didn't really order one of these girlie drinks with football names. But Josh did order the steak and it was excellent.

WOLFIE'S (2038 Collins Avenue)

This classic Jewish deli offers great food for cheap bucks. And best of all, Wolfie's is open twenty-four hours a day.

JOE'S STONE CRAB RESTAURANT (11 Washington Avenue)

Specializing in stone crabs with a mustard sauce, and key lime pie, Joe's offers the ultimate Miami experience. A landmark in South Beach since 1913, Joe's isn't cheap, but it's sure to satisfy.

MULLIGAN'S (10805 Sunset Drive)

This unpretentious sports bar is the place to head if you're looking to kick back and enjoy as many games as possible at once. Mulligan's offers plenty of TVs, drink specials, and slightly better-than-average pub-grub.

Inside the Stadium

Pro Player Stadium is an excellent place to see a football game. The massive facility is square and built up in all four directions with embattlements of concrete like a football fortress. But for baseball, the orange wall of unoccupied seats is a predominant feature. And not in a good way. What's more, a shoddy blue tarp blocks off a large number of lower-level seats in center field to create a rather pathetic batter's eye. The retired numbers that surround the upper deck predictably honor great players in Miami Dolphins history like Larry Czonka, Bob Griese, and Dan Marino. There are two Jumbotrons that face each other—one behind the plate and one in right field so that fans in either end zone will be able to see the instant replays. And to cap it off, at the end of each row of seats appears the Dolphins team emblem—a leaping dolphin wearing a football helmet. Having said all that, there are some redeeming features to Pro Player. Well, there was one. The outer concourses are painted in very warm and soothing pastel colors. And every sixty feet or so the colors change, a nice relief compared to many other Major League facilities that have sterile concrete walkways. If it sounds like we were grasping at straws to find something we liked about this place, frankly we were.

Stadium Features
SINCE WHEN IS TEAL A BASEBALL COLOR?

An out-of-town scoreboard adorns the left field oddity known as the Teal Monster. Doesn't the name say it all? A Teal Monster is nearly as intimidating as a pink elephant.

Sections of the wall alternate between twenty-five and thirty-three feet high, often wreaking havoc with potential home run balls. A hitter's best chance to go yard is right near the left field foul pole where the Monster gives way to a wall that is a more manageable eight feet high. In the left field power alley resides a clock above the scoreboard that seems to want to rob hitters of home runs, attracting more than its fair share of balls bouncing off its face.

We recommend giving the Teal Monster a makeover. Make it forty feet high, then not only will it be a force to be reckoned with, but it would cover up the empty seats above it. As for the name, perhaps they could paint it Dolphins' Blue and call it the Baby Blue Yonder.

THE BERMUDA TRIANGLE

There's no respite for hitters in left-center. This triangular notch sucks up singles and doubles and just like its namesake does with airplanes, causes them to disappear. Some are never heard from again, while others survive oblivion as triples.

Kevin: "Beware, maties, and let me tell you tales of de Bermuda Triangle."

Josh: "Save it for Pittsburgh, will ya?"

WORLD SERIES MINI BANNERS

Pro Player may not be the best place to see a game, but this ballpark boasts things all the great ballparks covet: World Series Banners. Does your team have one? Rather inauspiciously displayed beside the left field foul pole, the Marlins' banners look a bit like advertisements. You'd miss them if you weren't looking for them.

COLUMBIA REMEMBERED

On the right field fence appears a small blue tribute to the brave men and women who lost their lives aboard the Space Shuttle as it disintegrated upon reentry into the earth's atmosphere in February 2003. The emblem on the wall next to the 385-foot marker is identical to the patch the astronauts wore on their flight suits during the mission.

Stadium Eats

In general, the food at Pro Player Stadium is quite poor. With the cuisine in Miami so unique, we had hoped to find great Cuban sandwiches at the park, or at least a decent seafood option. We found neither. Perhaps serving fish when your team is nicknamed "the Fish" is a no-no, but we see no reason why there isn't a Cuban sandwich on the menu. Cheeseburgers and chicken tenders are available—nondescript and pretty much the same as you might find at any football game, WrestleMania event, or tractor pull. Luckily we found a few decent exceptions to salvage our dining experience.

SARATOGA CHIPS (Trademark Food)

We waited in line for an insane amount of time to try these chips. But it was Opening Day, so we will forgive the Marlins eventually. Saratoga chips are French fries shaped like, and as thin as, potato chips. They come out of a vat of boiling oil sizzling hot and crispy. Sprinkle liberally with salt, douse with ketchup, and enjoy.

MARLIN DOG (Dog Rating)

The Twelfth Best Hot Dog in the Majors

On Opening Day 2002, the Marlins' concessionaires were embarrassed when they ran out of hot dogs by the fifth inning. Can you imagine, a baseball park running out of hot dogs? To make reparations, on Opening Day 2003 the Marlins offered free dogs to the first thirty-thousand fans who entered the park, at a cost of more than $100,000. Kevin and Josh were the proud recipients of two of those dogs. The wieners came premade and wrapped in aluminum foil, having been stored in large hot carts. Despite this mishandling, they were better than the average

MIAMI BASEBALL

EARLY MINOR LEAGUE teams thrived in southern Florida with colorful names like the Miami Magicians and Miami Beach Flamingos or the Fort Lauderdale Tarpons. These teams played in small facilities. But after World War II it became apparent that a larger facility was needed to accommodate the growing baseball culture in the region. And so Miami Stadium was built in 1949 by Jose Manuel Aleman, a former minister of education in Cuba. The beautiful nine-thousand-seat ballpark housed such teams as the Miami Sun Sox, Fort Lauderdale Lions, and West Palm Beach Indians. The first incarnation of the Marlins' name came in 1956 when Bill Veeck came south with a Triple-A franchise that had moved to Miami from Syracuse, New York. Veeck signed aging pitcher Satchel Paige, who was delivered to the mound via helicopter for his Opening Night debut. The Triple-A Marlins lasted only three seasons in Miami, however, departing for San Juan, Puerto Rico. Other minor league teams that enjoyed success in the area included the Miami Amigos, Miami Orioles, and the Miami Miracle.

dog. The bun was more like a roll than a soft hot dog bun—more substantial than normal—although it had dried out some while sitting wrapped in foil. And the dog was only lukewarm. Hmm. Maybe we only liked them because they were free.

BEST OF THE REST

Arepas are one sound Cuban option inside the park. What are arepas, you may be wondering? They are sweet round cornbread patties with cheese inside that are deep fried. Try one, they're great.

It's tough to go wrong with **Mrs. Fields Cookies**, even if they're a bit on the expensive side.

Okay, we lied when we said the Marlins don't serve any fish, but technically crab is a shellfish. The crab cakes are decent but no match for those in Baltimore.

The beef knish is also a unique offering, and not too shabby if you're a knish fan like Kevin who fell in love with knish for the first time during our trip to New York and then again in Miami.

SAY "NO, THANKS," AND WALK AWAY

A connoisseur of chicken wings, Josh wholeheartedly renounces these. And the wings were actually passable compared to the horrendous grilled chicken sandwich.

Also on our walk-away list at Pro Player is the **Pizza Hut** stand. Our pie tasted like a doughy brick, and who wants to eat a doughy brick?

STADIUM SUDS

What Pro Player lacks in food, it makes up for in cold drinks. Not only are there plenty of places to get a mixed drink inside the stadium, there are also beer gardens located on the outer concourses. We recommend the margaritas.

For beer lovers, there is a great variety. Kevin was pleased to find Yuengling Lager on tap, the brew of choice in his current hometown.

The Pro Player Stadium Experience

The Pro Player Experience is the experience of southern Florida itself. While there may be twenty-thousand to thirty-thousand hard-core Fish Fans in the area, it's difficult for all of them to make it to all of the home games. Say, five-thousand Marlins fans make it to each game, and another five-thousand folks who are better defined as "baseball" fans. More

SPRING TRAINING—GRAPEFRUIT LEAGUE

WANT TO WATCH Major League Baseball in a minor league environment? Sure you do. So why not visit the Spring Training homes of the Cardinals, Mets, Marlins, Expos, and Orioles? You get to see the same players in smaller ballparks, and get to sit that much closer to the field. The players are even friendlier, more willing to sign autographs, and less apt to punch out your camera lens. And tickets are a lot cheaper.

If you time your road trip right, you can begin with a few Grapefruit League games, then start your official trip on Opening Day in Florida. That's what we did in 2003. But don't fret if you're visiting Miami in the middle of the summer. During the regular season, many of these parks are used by Rookie League affiliates of the big league teams. For tickets and directions to these ballparks, visit the team Web sites.

The Orioles play at **Fort Lauderdale Stadium**, a beautiful park built in 1962 that seats 8,340. The ballpark is located at 1301 NW 55th Street in Fort Lauderdale. Call (954) 776-1921 for ticket information.

The Cardinals and Marlins both play their Spring Training games at **Roger Dean Stadium** in Jupiter. During the regular season, the Gulf Coast League Marlins call the ballpark home. Roger Dean seats 6,700 fans, but also has a grassy outfield berm that can handle a few hundred more. The ballpark is state of the art, complete with many of the amenities (luxury boxes, picnic areas) that MLB ballparks have. It is surrounded by a golf course. Roger Dean is located at 4751 Main Street in Jupiter. Call (561) 775-1818 for tickets.

The Expos play their Spring Training games at **Space Coast Stadium** in Melbourne. The ballpark, which seats 8,100, is the home of the Florida State League Brevard Country Manatees during the minor league regular season. The space coast theme, which honors NASA's nearby Kennedy Space Center, is noticeable throughout the park. Space Coast is located at 5800 Stadium Parkway in Melbourne. For tickets call the park at (321) 633-4487.

Thomas J. White Stadium is home to the New York Mets during the spring. The sports complex is surrounded by a swamp that is notorious for the many alligators it contains. The park is located at the St. Lucie County Sports Complex on 525 N.W. Peacock Boulevard in Port St. Lucie. Tickets by phone are handled through the Mets ticket office at (772) 871-2115.

when the Fish have recently netted a World Series. The folks in the latter group are mostly Miami transplants: fans who identify their city of origin by the gear they wear in support of other teams. We saw fans dressed from head to toe in Baltimore Orioles garb, in Toronto Blue Jays garb, in Yankees pinstripes, in Dodger Blue, and so on. While these transplants occasionally go to Marlins games, they don't go out of any love for the home team. They go out of their love for baseball in general—or worse, to support the opposing team. Even the vendors who walk around selling gear inside the park cater to the diverse taste of the fans, selling hats and shirts from around the big leagues rather than simply the home team's colors.

CRAZY PIN GUY (Superfan)

Louis Mendez is covered in Marlins pins. World Series pins, championship series pins, Opening Day pins: you name it, he's wearing it on his leather vest and hat. Mendez has been collecting Marlins pins since the inception of the franchise and is a worthy and true superfan. As we talked to Mendez, his wife stood nearby, though she wore no pins at all. Hmm.

Louis told us that his favorite Marlins player was Ivan Rodriguez, because Pudge is Puerto Rican like he is. On Opening Day 2003 when we visited Pro Player and met Louis, Pudge was making his Marlins debut. Sadly for Louis, Rodriguez lost to free agency after helping the Fish win the 2003 World Series.

ARE YOU READY FOR SOME . . . BASEBALL?

Before games, Marlins players introduce themselves—via taped shots on the Jumbotrons—during the announcement of the starting lineup. This is eerily reminiscent of the annoying feature on Monday Night Football where the starters introduce themselves during the opening drive for each team.

RAIN DELAY TRIVIA

During the many rain delays at Pro Player, the Marlins use a trivia game and other games to keep fans interested. On the day we were there, it was sunny and clear. But in honor of the rain delays that occur so often we will provide the answers to our own trivia questions here.

At the end of Spring Training on March 30 and 31 of 1991, the New York Yankees and the Baltimore Orioles played the first exhibition baseball games at Joe Robbie Stadium, shattering preseason attendance records by drawing more than 125,000 to the two games.

Livan Hernandez's two World Series victories as a rookie represented only the second time a rookie had won two Series games. The

Pin Guy

Photo by Kevin O'Connell

first hurler to garner a pair of World Series W's was Larry Sherry, who accomplished the feat for the Brooklyn Dodgers in 1959.

Before John Lynch became a Pro Bowler in the NFL, he was a pitcher for a Marlins Rookie-League team—the Erie Sailors of the New York-Penn League. After displaying a fastball that could reach ninety-five miles per hour at Stanford, Lynch was drafted in the second round, sixty-sixth overall, of the 1992 Major League draft. The right-hander threw the first official pitch in Marlins franchise history (a ball) and recorded a no-decision as the Sailors went on to lose 6–5 to the Jamestown Expos in thirteen innings. Today, Lynch's Marlins hat resides at the Baseball Hall of Fame at Cooperstown. When we visited Pro Player, Lynch took the mound again, this time to throw out the ceremonial first pitch of the 2003 season. Predictably his offering was high and outside. But fresh off his Super Bowl

CARIBBEAN WORLD SERIES

"BATS, LIKE BALLPLAYERS, don't like the cold weather," Ty Cobb once said. If you're jonesing to do some baseball road-tripping during the off-season, we highly recommend checking out the spicy bats swinging at the Caribbean World Series. The sunny beaches and aquamarine warm waters of the islands also provide a nice escape from the cold winter back home.

It's a quick jaunt by plane or boat from Miami to San Juan, Puerto Rico. At Hiram Bithorn Stadium you'll catch big leaguers playing winter ball. Tickets go for rock-bottom prices and the atmosphere of the games is electric, positively Latin, and unlike any other in the world. The ballpark is abuzz all game long. Nearly naked cheerleaders dance atop the dugouts, while vendors hawk spicy treats and mixed drinks.

victory with Tampa Bay, the NFL star received a nice round of applause from the crowd.

ST. LOUIS CARDINALS,
BUSCH STADIUM

Red Bird Baseball in the Gateway City

**ST. LOUIS,
MISSOURI**

260 miles to Kansas City
300 miles to Chicago
360 miles to Cincinnati
365 miles to Milwaukee

O N THE BANKS of the Mississippi River and in the shadows of the Gateway Arch, the Cardinals' nesting grounds would appear ideal for a classic ballpark celebrating baseball's glorious past in St. Louis. But unfortunately Busch Stadium belongs to the family of multipurpose cookie-cutter stadiums that rose to prominence in the 1960s. As far as cookie-cutters go, Busch is one of the best, thanks in large part to renovations during the 1990s. Having previously visited similar stadiums like Riverfront in Cincinnati, Three Rivers in Pittsburgh, and Veterans Stadium in Philadelphia, we arrived in St. Louis with low expectations. And those expectations sank even lower as we walked up to the Busch Stadium ticket windows. From the outside, Busch may be one of the most attractive of the cookie-cutters, but it remains one of the least attractive big league parks, rising high into the city with its multitude of spiraling concrete concourses. But once inside we were pleasantly surprised. The Cardinals have made a serious effort to promote an old-time ballpark feel at Busch and for that the team deserves major kudos. Aside from the biggest renovation—the switch from Astroturf to natural grass in 1996—the Cards also removed several thousand upper-level seats in 1997 to make way for a manually operated scoreboard that is flanked by flag courts commemorating the team's proud history. The hand-operated scoreboard in straightaway center field provides the line scores of every ongoing Major League game. The flag court to the left of the scoreboard flies a pennant for each of the Cardinals' nine World Series championships. Meanwhile, to the right of the scoreboard each of the Cardinals' retired numbers flies on its own pennant with the names of the players appearing on their respective flags' standards. These classy displays are done in a rich green motif that gives the superstadium a fairly authentic old-time look. Further enhancing the atmosphere are the die-hard Cardinal fans

interior

Photo by Kevin O'Connell

Cardinals will contribute $50 million to the project up front and will pay $14 million per year for a minimum term of twenty-nine years to the group of private investors who will own the park.

If any team in the National League deserves a new ballpark in the retroclassic mold that has swept over the American ballpark landscape in the past decade, it is the Cardinals. The Cardinals boast a history as rich as any team's in the Senior Circuit. In fact, the franchise dates from 1881, when the team played in the American Asso-

who fill the seats each day decked out in Cardinal Red. These knowledgeable fans form a veritable sea of red, while bringing enthusiasm and passion to every game. Our visit to St. Louis came after games spent at Florida, Tampa Bay, Atlanta, and Kansas City, and we were thrilled by the energy and appreciation for the game's finer points that we found in the St. Louis faithful.

Despite our praise for the St. Louis experience, we believe the Cardinals and their fans deserve a nest more in line with the great Sportsman's Park—the classic ballpark they called "home" for decades before flocking to Busch Stadium in 1966. And most of the voices in the St. Louis community seem to agree. At the time of this publishing St. Louis was moving forward with plans to build a new $325 million ballpark in time to host the 2006 All-Star Game. The ballpark architects at HOK were drawing up the blueprints for the privately financed ballpark that would be developed in conjunction with a $250 million mixed-use, five-block neighborhood called Ballpark Village. The

ciation as the Browns, short for Brown Stockings. When the American Association folded in 1891, the Browns joined the National League. By 1901, a new American League team had arrived in town, transplanted from Milwaukee, and that team also called itself the Browns. So the original National League Browns took the "Cardinals" as their moniker and that's the team that still exists in St. Louis today. In the past century, the Cardinals have won nine World Series, more than any other team except the Yankees. Think about that. That's equal to all of the titles won by the Red Sox and both Chicago clubs combined.

We give the Cardinals credit for updating and modifying Busch Stadium while simultaneously promoting their agenda to build a new ballpark. Other teams like the Tigers, Indians, and White Sox—just to name a few—didn't do the same for their fans as they lobbied for new ballparks in their respective towns. These teams purposefully let their ballparks fall into disrepair so that they could then point out the facilities' flaws to state legislatures and taxpayers in an effort to raise money and public sentiment for the new digs. But the Cardinals haven't left their loyal fans to suffer through such a transition. Rather, they've steadily improved Busch Stadium, while appealing more forthrightly for new digs.

The biggest change to Busch came in 1996 when the team ripped up the Astroturf that had covered the field since 1970 and laid down real grass. Ironically, before this move, the quick and often scalding Busch Stadium turf had given the Cardinals a decided home-field advantage. In much the same way that the Red Sox perennially stock up on right-handed power hitters and the Yankees build their line-ups around left-handed sluggers, the Cardinals crafted fleet-footed, smooth-fielding teams that could leg out triples and steal bases offensively and close gaps in the outfield and turn snappy double players defensively. Players like Lou Brock, Vince Coleman, Willie McGee, and Ozzie Smith all fit the Cardinal prototype that has showered the team with success.

Perhaps no team typified the Cardinals' approach so well as the 1982 edition, which won the National League pennant despite hitting just 67 home runs during the entire season. To put that in perspective: the Brewers, who eventually lost to the Cardinals in the 1982 World Series, clubbed 216 home runs that year. St. Louis's equalizer was its speed, as the Cards swiped a league-best 200 bases in 1982, while also leading the circuit in triples with 52, and in fielding average with a .981 percentage. The same formula proved successful again in 1985 when the Cardinals hit only 87 homers, but led all of baseball in steals (314), triples (59), and fielding average (.983) en route to another National League title. And it worked yet again in 1987 when the Cards finished last in homers (94) but first in steals (248) and fielding average (.982) on the way to capturing their third NL pennant in six years.

In Busch Stadium's early days the field featured a natural grass playing surface. But artificial turf was installed in 1970, except for the places where the dirt normally appears on a traditional infield, creating a diamond similar to the one that exists today in Tampa Bay. In 1977, the team switched to an all-plastic infield however, leaving only dirt sliding pits around the bases. The Busch Stadium turf was famous for how hot it would get beneath an August sun, often reaching upward of one-hundred-forty degrees Fahrenheit in the heat of summer. Finally in 1996 with the city's football team having moved to a domed stadium, the Cardinals planted real grass at Busch once again.

It seems hard to imagine Vince Coleman, or any mortal, stealing one hundred plus bases per season on a dirt track, as the young Cardinal did three years consecutively (1985–1987) on the plastic. The field treated Coleman rather harshly though on October 13, 1985, as the Cardinals prepared for Game Four of the NLCS against the Dodgers. With light rain falling during pregame warm-ups, the Busch Stadium grounds crew activated the electronically operated tarp used to cover the infield. No one noticed until it was too late that Coleman was standing next to first-base practicing leading off the bag. Before the fleet-footed leadoff hitter knew what had hit him, the tarp's metal cylinder had rolled over his left knee and up his leg. Screaming in pain, he was trapped under the tarp and cylinder for nearly a minute before being rescued and carried off the field on a stretcher. He suffered a bone chip in his knee and multiple bruises, which put him out of commission for the rest of the postseason. The Royals took the all-Missouri series in seven games. Who knows, if Coleman had hit leadoff for the Cards in the World Series against Kansas City, he might have been the difference between winning and losing.

Despite expansion, the lively ball of the 1990s, and the suspected use of steroids among some Major League players, Cardinals teams continued to struggle to reach the one hundred-homer plateau as recently as 1995. But all that changed in 1997, when general manager Walt Jocketey landed Mark McGwire in a trading-deadline deal with Oakland. The A's were afraid they'd lose McGwire to free agency after the season, and wanted to free a spot at first-base for an up-and-coming slugger named Jason Giambi. In exchange for the premiere long-ball hitter of the era, the Cards gave up a trio of right-handed pitchers—T. J. Mathews, Eric Ludwick, and Blake Stein.

Kevin: "Who?"

Josh: "Exactly."

Reunited with his former A's skipper Tony LaRussa, Big Mac hit twenty-four homers for St. Louis in the final fifty-one games of the 1997 season. But that was just a prelude of things to come. Playing his first full season in the Senior Circuit—long known as a fastball pitcher's league—Big Mac, who had always struggled to hit the many breaking balls in the AL, connected for seventy homers in 1998. What made McGwire's feat all the more remarkable was that he accomplished it playing half his games in a pitcher-friendly ballpark. Like all cookie-cutters, Busch Stadium features deep outfield alleys and expansive foul territory that aid pitchers who record extra outs on long fly balls and foul popouts.

Busch opened on May 12, 1966, with a 4–3 Cardinals victory over the Atlanta Braves in twelve innings. The $20 million stadium, which was to also house the city's football Cardinals, was built as part of the same urban renewal project that produced the trademark St. Louis Arch. The monument, visible from inside Busch Stadium, was originally to be built during the 1930s. An area encompassing forty city blocks was purchased by the city and all preexisting buildings were razed, but the country's involvement in the World War II effort suspended the project for more than a decade. In 1947 a group of citizens known as the Jefferson National Expansion Memorial Association, organized a nationwide competition for architects to submit designs for a structure to commemorate the westward expansion of the United States in the 1800s. Eero Saarinen won with a design for the now famous Gateway Arch, which stands six hundred thirty feet high on the banks of the Mississippi.

Kevin: "Hey Josh, did you know the Arch makes use of an inverted catenary curve structure, which is based on the catenary equation?"

Josh: "Really . . ."

Kevin: "Do you know the catenary equation?"

Josh: "No, but I know Wade Boggs's batting averages for all eleven years he spent with the Red Sox."

Kevin: "Each leg is an equilateral triangle with fifty-four-foot-long sides at ground level that taper to seventeen feet long at the top. Concrete fills the walls for the first three hundred feet up, then after that it's filled with steel supports."

Josh: "Where'd you learn that? From that man you were talking to on the bus?"

Kevin: "No, I read it on this plaque, right here."

Josh: "Thanks for sharing."

Busch Stadium replaced ancient Sportsman's Park, which had served as home to the Cardinals since 1920 and had served as home to the American League Browns from 1902 to 1953. This joint usage represents the longest cohabitation of two Major League teams at the same park in the history of the grand old game. The ballpark was of the classic ilk, featuring two seating decks around the infield and along the foul lines, and just one level of bleachers in the outfield. St. Louis baseball fans must have been in hardball heaven during the thirty-four seasons in which Sportsman's hosted a Major League game virtually every night. Plus, there was a burlesque club catering to fans, located beneath the center field bleachers. How good can life get? Well it got even better than that for folks who liked goats. A resident billy goat used to mow Sportsman's outfield grass before and after games.

Kevin: "How did the goat get the grass even?"

Josh: "Dual-action molars."

During the 1940s, a section of free seats in the far left field stands was available for kids. The inhabitants of this section were known as the Knot Hole Gang.

Babe Ruth hit three dingers in Game 4 of the 1926 World Series at Sportsman's to set a single-game Series record. The longest of the three broke the window of an auto dealer's shop beyond the right field fence on Grand Avenue. Ruth duplicated the feat in Game 4 of the 1928 Series, also at Sportsman's. The Yankees won both Series.

On a regrettable note, Sportsman's was the last Major League facility to integrate its stands. Until 1944 African American patrons were restricted to the seats on the right field pavilion. On the positive side, the St. Louis Stars won three Negro National League pennants: in 1928, 1930, and 1931.

The tenant Cardinals enjoyed considerably more success at Sportsman's than the landlord Browns, highlighted by the Cards' win against the Browns in the 1944 All-St. Louis "Streetcar World Series." While 1944 represented the Browns' only trip to the October classic, the Cardinals racked up nine World Series appearances in the 1920s, '30s, and '40s. The most famous of these teams was the "Gas House Gang" edition of the mid-1930s, known for its rowdy players and zany personalities. Brother

hurlers Dizzy and Daffy Dean stifled opposing teams, while shortstop Leo Durocher, first-baseman Rip Collins, and left fielder Ducky Medwick slugged their way to glory.

As the Cardinals thrived, attendance waned at Browns games. But the Browns did contribute a few lasting memories to baseball lore during their final days in St. Louis. In 1945 one-armed outfielder Pete Gray debuted for the Browns at Sportsman's. Gray, who made it to the Majors when many of the regular ballplayers were away at war, batted .218 in 234 at bats in his only big league season. After losing his right arm in a childhood accident, he taught himself to catch the ball and in the same motion, tuck his glove under the stub of his right arm. He would then grab the ball as it rolled out of the glove and unleash his throw. At the plate, he batted from the left side.

In 1951 Bill Veeck purchased the Browns and hired a hypnotist to convince the team's players they could hit. And the players responded, batting a combined .264, good for second best in the league. Veeck also sent Eddie Gaedel up to pinch-hit against the Tigers that year. Wearing the uniform number 1/8, the three-foot, seven-inch Gaedel walked on four pitches. Later that season, Veeck let the fans seated behind the Browns' dugout manage a game against the Kansas City Athletics. The fans would hold up "Yes," or "No," signs in response to questions posed on signs held up above the Browns' dugout like: "Bunt?" or "Steal?" or "New Pitcher?" Believe it or not, the Browns won the game.

When the Browns left for Baltimore to become the Orioles, they sold Sportsman's Park to the Cardinals. August Busch, owner of the Cards, renamed the ballpark "Busch Stadium," but only after Major League Baseball told him he couldn't call it "Budweiser Stadium." So you see, the idea of using a ballpark's name as a marketing device isn't all that new after all.

Busch also installed an eagle (yes, an eagle, not a cardinal) above the scoreboard in left field that would flap its wings whenever a Cardinal player hit a home run. And he drove a team of Clydesdales onto the field on a number of occasions, to the fans' delight.

Getting a Choice Seat

The most difficult tickets to come by are those for games against the Chicago Cubs, the Cards' greatest rival. As far as grudge matches go, a Cubs-Cards game ranks right up there with a Yankees-Red Sox matchup. Since Big Mac retired, tickets are available to most other games thanks to the size of Busch.

Stadium gates open one hour prior to game time except for Gates 2 and 7, which open two hours before the first pitch for fans wishing to watch batting practice.

Because the seats in most sections are rather far from the field and because the decks are not stacked directly on top one another, there are fewer overhang obstructions at Busch than at most ballparks. The expansive foul territory doesn't hurt the views in this regard either, allowing fans a clear view of the fair territory in the outfield corners from most seats.

Field Box: Infield (Boxes 133–166), Outfield (Boxes 126–132, 167–173)

Even before the game the Field Box seats—whether between the dugouts or past the first- and third-base bags—are accessible only to ticket holders in these sections. Fans who have legitimate first-level tickets enter the ballpark through special first-level gates, while those (like Josh and Kevin) who try to sneak through the turnstile with Loge or Terrace level tickets are politely reminded by the ushers to use the

TRIVIA TIMEOUT

Jacks: How many inches high is a regulation baseball mound?

Rummy: Who posted the lowest single-season ERA by a Major Leaguer in the modern era? What year did he do it? What was his ERA? (Hint: Cardinal).

Look for the answers in the text.

appropriate gate. Inside the park, the first level is no less impregnable. The corridors to these areas are strictly monitored by ushers even an hour and a half before the game. What a bum deal. In any case, the Field Boxes are affordably priced.

Much like the similarly circular first-level seating bowl of Shea Stadium in New York, the first-level seats at Busch are close to the field in the sections behind home plate. But the sections parallel to the first- and third-base bags position fans far away from the action. Then the seats come back toward the field in the sections nearing the outfield corners. We recommend sitting either behind the plate in Infield Field Boxes 137–162 or in Outfield Field Boxes 126, 127, 172, or 173.

Loge Box: Infield (Boxes 233–287), Outfield (Boxes 214–231, 269–288)

The Loge Boxes—which number Rows 1–4—are nestled behind the Field Boxes and in front of the Loge Reserve. When all of the seats are full of fans, these sections almost look like an extension of the field-level seats, especially behind the plate where the first row of Loge Box seats is only a few feet higher than the last row of Field Boxes. These are good seats, but they seem a bit overpriced in comparison to Field Box seats, which are only a few dollars

Sellout Index: 20% of games sell out
Seating Capacity: 49,779
Ticket Office: (314) 421-3060
www.stlouis.cardinals.mlb.com

more, and the Loge Reserve seats, which are almost 30 percent cheaper.

That said, we liked the Outfield Loge Boxes in right field (Boxes 214 to 218) and in left field (Boxes 282 to 286), which are closer to the field than the other Loge Box seats because they don't have any Field Boxes in front of them. The under-hang of the Loge deck blocks the view of the warning track below, but for the most part the view from these seats—hovering over the field—is excellent. Avoid Loge Box 219 in right field unless you want to contend with the obstruction of the foul pole and its accompanying screen. And the same goes for Box 281 in left field where the left field foul pole presents a similar obstruction.

Loge Reserve: Infield (Sections 234–266), Outfield (Sections 214–232, 268–286)

We spent the better part of a game in Row 9 of Section 250 of the Infield Loge Reserve and were very satisfied with our view from behind the plate. The Reserve sections actually begin with Row 5, so our seat in Row 9 was the fourth row after the concourse. Our seat was low enough to allow us to feel like part of the game, yet elevated enough to provide a clear view of the entire field.

We recommend these Loge Reserve seats behind the plate over the Loge Boxes located near the first- and third-base bags and in the outfield where the curve of the seating bowl takes the seats farther from the field. Just be sure to sit up front to avoid the overhang that disrupts the view of fly balls for fans in Row 15 and beyond of the Infield Loge Reserve. The overhang is not as much of a factor in the Outfield Loge Reserve in right field (Sections 214–226) and left field (Sections 274–286) where any seat in Row 20 or lower has a clear view. The under-hang blocks from view a small portion of whichever outfield corner your seat is closest to in Sections 214–230 and 270–286.

Terrace: Box (Sections 319–381), Reserve (Sections 301–397)

As far as upper decks go, this is a good one. While the round configuration of the seating bowls detracts from the quality of many Field and Loge level seats, it ensures that a minimum number of Terrace seats are adversely affected by the under-hang. And even the back rows don't feel too high. Compared to the upper seats in other multipurpose facilities like Shea Stadium, SkyDome, or the Metrodome, these seats aren't bad. The Upper Reserve only extends back twenty-three rows at Busch, far fewer than the number found in many stadiums. The under-hang of the deck below blocks portions of the field in Box and Reserve Sections 314–332 and 372–386.

We recommend sitting behind the plate in Sections 343–358 or in fair territory beyond the outfield foul poles where the seats are closest to the field in right field (Sections 314–318) or left (Sections 382–386).

The Terrace Boxes may seem a bit on the pricey side for upper-level seats, but they might be worth the extra money. The Reserve seats start about ten feet higher than the Boxes because of the concourse between the two levels, and the Reserve level feels that much farther from the field. We recommend avoiding the first three rows of the Terrace Reserve because there is a railing above the concourse that is somewhat of an obstruction.

SEATING TIP

KEEP IN MIND the contours of Busch's expansive foul territory and rounded lower bowl when you select your tickets. If you performed passably well in ninth grade geometry, you should be fine in St. Louis. At Busch, a diamond (the field) fits into a circle (the stadium). The best seats are in the sections where the points of the diamond come closest to touching the circumference of the circle.

Seats in Sections 301–311 and 389–397 in the outfield sell for Terrace Reserve prices, even though they are located on the same level as the Terrace Boxes on the rest of the deck. Not a bad deal, especially for those who want to call balls and strikes from Sections 397 and 301 in dead center. Here the underhang is least severe as fans are able to see the warning track everywhere except directly below their seats. The main drawback to sitting in these seats is that they don't offer a view of the Jumbotron or out-of-town scoreboard.

Bleachers
(Sections 505, 507, 509, 591, 593, 595)

These first-level home run territory seats aren't the most comfortable butt-holders in the ballpark. Most of the bleacher sections offer fans actual metal bleachers to sit on, except for Sections 505 and 595, which offer comfortable plastic seats. These two sections sell for the same price as the rest of the bleachers, so be sure to ask for a ticket there if you're forced to buy a bleacher seat.

When buying bleachers tickets, be sure to ask for a seat in Row 1–13, because the overhang of the Jumbotron and of several advertising signs mounted on the face of the Terrace deck obstructs the view of fly balls for those seated in the back rows. The good news is that unlike at some ballparks, fans holding bleacher tickets are free to roam throughout the rest of the ballpark, excepting of course the Field Box sections.

The Black Market

We observed a number of ticket scalpers operating along Eighth Street on the corners of Clark Street and Walnut Street. They had first-level seats on the market at face value for our April game against the Astros, but assured us that the same seats would sell

---

THE GREAT RACE

THE OUTFIELD SEATS at Busch were bombarded by home run balls in 1998 when Mark McGwire hit thirty-eight of his seventy home runs in St. Louis. Big Mac's home homers included his first eight long balls of the year; numbers sixty-one and sixty-two to tie and break Roger Maris's forty-seven-year old record; and his final five homers of the season which came in his last eleven at bats.

Just as Mickey Mantle pushed Roger Maris to greater heights in 1961, as both pursued Babe Ruth's single season record of sixty clouts, Big Mac benefited from the constant pursuit of the Cubs' Sammy Sosa who finished the 1998 campaign with sixty-six homers. The two sluggers weren't teammates like the pair of Yankee greats. Better yet, one wore Cubs blue, and the other Cardinals red: embodying opposite sides of one of the greatest rivalries in the game.

---

well above face during the summer months. And Cubs games, they told us, are their bonus days.

Before/After the Game

On the one hand, the area immediately surrounding the ballpark doesn't offer a wealth of restaurants and bars, but on the other hand it does offer plenty of touristy things to do. Pre- and postgame activities might include visits to the Gateway Arch and Museum of Westward Expansion on the banks of the Mississippi River, the Riverboat Casinos on the Mississippi, the nearby Anheuser-Busch Brewery, or the International Bowling Hall of Fame. That's right, the bowling hall is right near the ballpark—go crazy kids!

Getting to Busch Stadium

Busch is easy to reach by a number of highways that all provide ample signage for the ballpark. But if you somehow get lost, just look for the Gateway Arch and drive toward it.

If you're coming into town from the west, take Route 40/I-64, which passes right by the ballpark. From the south, take I-55 to I-70, which also leads right to the park. From the north, take I-70. From the east, I-70, I-64, and I-55 all merge on the way into town, leading right to the park. Busch is located at 250 Stadium Plaza, right off of 8th Street.

A large parking garage right across from the stadium on East Street charges $12. A bit farther away, on the corner of Clark Street and 11th Street, a garage offers $10 parking. Then just another hundred feet away, the City of St. Louis Municipal Garage on the corner of 12th Street and Clark offers $5 parking. But beware: the city garage closes one hour after the last out is recorded. We almost learned this lesson the hard way. After watching the Cardinals bull pen surrender two runs in the ninth to lose 2–1 against the Astros, we headed to the Bowling Hall of Fame to roll a few frames (yes frames, not strings). Then we visited the Arch to snap a few pictures. By the time we returned to the garage our car was the only one left and a less-than-thrilled city employee was pacing at the front gate, trying to decide whether to wait another five minutes or to lock us in for the night. Not only had this kindly gentleman waited for us, but he also gave us directions out of town. Gotta love the Midwest.

For night games and Sundays, the streets around the ballpark offer plenty of free-meter spots. Patrol Market Street and 7th Street and you should be able to nab a space. Just remember that street parking is prohibited between the hours of 3:00 A.M. and 6:00 A.M., so don't plan on staying out all night and getting your car the next morning. Chances are it will have been ticketed, booted, or towed.

For those staying in town, the Metrolink subway provides a convenient way to get to the game. For $1.25 per ride the train drops folks off at the Busch Stadium stop, right across the street from the ballpark.

Outside Attractions

THE ARCH

It wouldn't be a trip to St. Louis without paying an obligatory visit to the Gateway Arch.

Silver, shiny, and enormous, Kevin likened it to a giant croquet wicket. From the ballpark, walk in the general direction of the river and soon enough you will encounter a pleasant tree-lined path leading to the Arch. The walk is quite scenic, with classy globe lights illuminating the way. If you hear church bells tolling, look to the old cathedral, also known as the Basilica of St. Louis, a short distance from the Arch. Originally blessed in June of 1770, the cathedral became a basilica in 1914.

Walk up to the Arch and give it a few raps with your knuckles. It's not hollow. Next, check out the underground visitor center that contains the Museum of Westward Expansion, which celebrates the opening of the West. Here theaters show movies about the discovery and development of the American West and about the Arch's construction.

The thing we liked best about the complex was the Arch Tram, which for just a few bucks takes visitors on the ride of a lifetime. Okay, that may be overstating things. But the Tram does take folks on a very impressive ten-minute sojourn to the top of the Arch, sixty-three stories above the ground. Josh gaped in awe at the view of the expansive west, while Kevin discussed the catenary equation with an architect from Belleville, Illinois, named Butch.

CARDINALS HALL OF FAME

Proudly located inside the International Bowling Hall of Fame at 111 Stadium Plaza, the Cardinals Hall of Fame is right across the street from the Busch ticket office. The hall is open 9:00 A.M. until 5:00 A.M. except when the

Cardinals have a home game, in which case it stays open until 6:30. Admission costs $6.

Here, every current member of the Cardinals twenty-five-man Major League roster receives his due, as do Cardinal greats and members of the St. Louis Browns who made lasting contributions to the Gateway City's hardball memory bank. The team's most recent World Series trophies—1967 and 1982—are on display as are a number of MVP trophies won by Cardinal players.

Our favorite attractions were McGwire's 1962 Cardinal-Red Corvette; a picture of Joe Torre from his playing days when he had lambchop side burns that made him look like Meathead from TVs *All in the Family*, old seats and lockers from Sportsman's Park, Bob Gibson's shower sandals, and the most disgusting baseball cap we've ever seen—the one worn by Steve Kline in 2001 when he pitched in a team record eighty-nine games. It's dirty. Really dirty.

Consider the Cardinals Hall of Fame a must-visit if you're a Cardinals fan. Otherwise, it's a decent place to spend an hour before or after the game—better than the Braves Hall of Fame in Atlanta and the White Sox Hall of Fame in Chicago, but not as comprehensive as the Legends of the Game Museum in Arlington. But the Cardinals Hall has one thing going for it that the others don't: the $6 cost of admission also gains patrons access to the Bowling Hall of Fame, along with four free frames of ten-pin.

PLAZA OF CHAMPIONS

On the Plaza of Champions in front of Busch Stadium's Gate 6 reside a number of sculptures of former Cardinals players including Stan Musial, Albert "Red" Schoendienst, Bob Gibson, George Kissell, Lou Brock, George Sisler, Enos Slaughter, Rogers Hornsby, and Dizzy Dean. Negro League star Cool Papa Bell, who played for the St. Louis Stars, is also honored with a statue. The statues portray the players in action—diving to making catches, sliding into bases, throwing, and swinging— and are very lifelike.

STAN THE STATUE

A larger statue of Musial, located on the sidewalk just outside the Plaza of Champions, was unveiled in 1968.

Josh: "Wow, Stan was one severely disproportional individual."

Kevin: "The smaller statue of him is certainly more flattering."

The big statue of Stan depicts him with shoulders that seem too broad for the rest of his body. His eyes seem rather ghoulish too. See what you think.

Stan Musial statue

Photo by Kevin O'Connell

The quintessential Cardinal, "Stan the Man" collected 3,630 hits, including 475 homers, in a twenty-two-year career spent entirely with the Cardinals (1941–1963). A winner of seven batting crowns, Musial finished with a .331 career average and three MVP awards. He was a National League All-Star in each of his final twenty seasons. What many folks don't know is that Musial actually began his minor league career as a pitcher before an arm injury moved him to the outfield. At the plate he used an unorthodox stance that saw him coil his body in the left-handed batter's box, as if he were looking around a corner. He would hold the bat straight up, then uncork a mighty cut.

Though he didn't have quite as much power as his American League contemporary Ted Williams, many considered Stan the Senior Circuit's equivalent of the Splendid Splinter. Both players could hit for power and average but when they faced each other in the 1946 October Classic—which St. Louis won in seven games to capture its third and final World Series title of the decade—neither fared particularly well. Musial batted .222 with 0 homers and 4 RBI in what would be the final World Series appearance of his career, while Williams hit .200 with 0 homers and 1 RBI in the only World Series appearance of his career.

The difference in the 1946 Series was Cardinals southpaw Harry Brecheen who threw complete game victories in Games 2 and 6, and then came out of the bull pen to quell a Boston rally and earn a win in relief in Game 7. Brecheen was 3–0 with a 0.45 ERA in twenty innings in the Series. That, from a pitcher who posted a 15–15 record during the regular season for a team that won ninety-eight games.

CHAMPIONS ON DISPLAY

Nine flag standards surround the larger Musial statue. Each standard is engraved with the year of a Cardinals championship team and text describing the highlights of that year's World Series. The roster of each championship team also appears in this space. Atop the masts, a Cardinals pennant flies above the pennant of whichever American League team the Cards beat in that year's World Series.

BANNERS

Fans walking along the outdoor concourse that traces the perimeter of the ballpark can look up to see colorful banners that celebrate "Great Moments in Busch Stadium History." Aside from the advertising insignias and corporate logos on these, the banners are very well done. Each contains a date, a picture, and a few words such as, "Fans go crazy as Ozzie's homer beats Dodgers in playoffs. October 14, 1985."

Watering Holes and Outside Eats

Unfortunately there are not many places around the ballpark to eat and drink. The Cards must recognize this, because the plan for a new ballpark in St. Louis includes a neighborhood development component that would build a festive city block around the ball yard. In the meantime, don't despair. St. Louis is a big town with plenty of exceptional places to eat and drink. Just don't plan on walking to too many of these after the game.

PATTY O'S (7th Street and Gratiot Street)

This is one of the few places close to the ballpark. The large old warehouse is packed with Cardinals fans before and after games with DJs located both inside and outside on the sidewalk where people drink beers in a makeshift beergarden underneath the highway overpass. Inside, big-screen TVs show games from around the league, a full-scale airplane hangs suspended from the ceiling, and baseball memorabilia appears sporadically on the walls. We were particularly fond of the

Babe Ruth "Pinch Hit Chewing Tobacco" sign located in the bar's foyer. Patty's is definitely the best bet for fans looking for a happening spot near the ballpark.

PITCHERS (Broadway and Market Street)

Although it's just a block from the park, and though it bills itself as the "unofficial sports bar of Cardinals' baseball," Pitchers is located inside a Marriott Hotel. And it's a typical hotel sports bar with just a few quirks. Waitresses walk around dressed like umpires and the decor consists of Red Bird pennants, plaques, and pictures—big whoop!

MAX & ERMA'S (316 Market Street)

This franchise belongs to a chain of moderately priced restaurants that appear in cities throughout the Midwest. It's a decent place to grab a burger and a few beers, but nothing super, and is listed here by virtue of its proximity to the ballpark and by virtue of the colorful Cardinal mural that adorns a brick wall inside. Josh recommends the ten-ounce Garbage Burger, which comes topped with "everything but the kitchen sink."

ANHEUSER-BUSCH BREWERY
(12th Street and Lynch Street)

Two miles south of the ballpark, the Anheuser-Busch Brewery offers free tours Monday through Saturday 9:00 A.M. until 4:00 P.M. and Sunday 11:30 A.M. until 4:00 P.M. Tours of the one-hundred-acre plant are free, and include visits to the Clydesdale stables, beechwood aging cellars, brew house, and Hospitality Room. From the ballpark, follow I-55 south to the Arsenal Street Exit and then follow the signs to the Brewery. For more information, call (314) 577-2333.

SHANNON'S STEAK AND SEAFOOD
(100 N. 7th Street)

This upscale restaurant is owned by former Cardinals player and radio broadcaster Mike Shannon, who hit .255 with the Red Birds between 1962 and 1970. This is a family place with great steaks. Josh, whose wife, Heather, has two pet frogs named Steve and Jenny, was horrified, however, to find frog legs—lightly crumbed and hot broiled—on the menu.

OZZIE'S RESTAURANT AND SPORTS BAR
(645 Westport Plaza Drive)

Named after Cardinals Hall of Famer Ozzie Smith, this reasonably priced restaurant has a huge menu that ranges from All-Star steaks, to Hall of Fame pastas, to Grand Slam ribs, to Shortstop of the Border Mexican food. The decor is not surprisingly composed entirely of Cardinals memorabilia, with plenty of pictures of "the Wizard" featured throughout. Out-of-town sports fans will like the multitude of TVs and the satellite package that brings all the games to life. A free happy hour buffet is available from 4:30 to 7:00 P.M. Monday through Friday.

UNION STATION (1820 Market Street)

Undecided on what type of food you're in the mood for either before of after the game? Why not head to Union Station where there's something for everybody.

Follow Clark Street away from the ballpark for about a mile and you'll come upon the old Union Station, which has been converted into a mall. Aside from offering more than eighty shops, the Grand Hall features a number of restaurants, including: **The Route 66 Brewery and Restaurant**, **The MVP Sports Grill**, **Hooters**, **Houlihan's**, and a **Hard Rock Café**.

JOHN D. MCGURK'S IRISH PUB
(1200 Russell Boulevard)

With more than sixty beers to choose from, live Irish music, and a menu that includes such items as lamb stew, potato soup, and homemade chips, McGurk's offers the quintessential Irish pub experience. Arrive early on weekends to get a seat up front near the band.

AMIGHETTI'S: CHARLIE GITTO'S ON THE HILL
(5226 Shaw Avenue)

Located in southwest St. Louis on "The Hill" where Yogi Berra and Joe Garagiola spent their childhoods in the late 1920s and early 1930s, Amighetti's offers the authentic Italian dining experience—from homemade pastas and breads to fine wines and delicious Sicilian beef, pork, chicken, and seafood entrées. Expect to pay a few dollars but to go home feeling more than satisfied. And be sure to order the cannelloni for an appetizer.

The neighborhood known as "the Hill" is still largely populated by descendants of Italian immigrants who began settling in St. Louis in the 1850s. The lawns are well manicured, the community is close knit, and the many restaurants are top notch. Even the fire hydrants in this part of town are painted with the red, green, and white of the Italian flag.

TED DREWES FROZEN CUSTARD
(6726 Chippewa Street)

Don't miss out on this local dessert if you can help it. Frozen custard is incredible and nearly as famous as the St. Louis Arch. Remember Bill Cosby's pudding pops? Well this stuff's even better. Articles have been written in the *Wall Street Journal* and other national publications about Ted's, the city's favorite custard joint since opening in the 1930s.

Kevin: "It's so much smoother than ice cream."

Josh: "So, so smooth."

BALLPARK VENDORS

On the corner of 8th Street and Clark Street, we encountered a few vendors selling peanuts, Cracker Jack, and pretzels much cheaper than the same items sell for inside the ballpark. This is also a good spot to pick up a scorecard and game program for cheap bucks. The "Red Bird Review" costs just $1 outside the park, while inside the official program published by the team costs nearly five times as much.

Inside the Stadium

It seems like every nook and cranny of Busch Stadium is fashioned in some way to remind fans of the home team's proud history. Along with being recognized in the Plaza of Champions outside the park, championship Cardinals teams and famous players are honored with banners on the concourse underneath the stands, with outfield flag courts, and with writing atop the dugout roofs. The team is accustomed to winning, and isn't afraid to flaunt it. In this regard, St. Louis reminds us of a Senior Circuit version of the Yankees.

Ballpark Features

LITTLE ARCHIE

In line with the town's trademark Arch, the top of Busch Stadium is ringed with ninety-four miniarches. No we weren't lame enough to actually count these, but fortunately one ballpark wanderer who went before us was. Actually, we'll call it ninety-six arches, adding the two golden arches painted on the face of the Terrace deck in left field that appear with the words "Big Mac Land" in tribute to Mark McGwire.

GREEN OUTFIELD HEAVENS

Having removed the Terrace Reserved seats on either side of the center field scoreboard, the Cardinals maintain two classy green monument areas. High above right field, flag standards bear the nicknames Dizzy, Red, Stan the Man, and so on, and Cardinals whose numbers that have been retired by the team. Atop each standard flies a pennant inscribed with the number worn by the player. These include: number 1 for Ozzie Smith, 2 for Red Schoendienst, 6 for Stan Musial, 9 for Enos

Slaughter, 14 for Ken Boyer, 17 for Dizzy Dean, 20 for Lou Brock, and 45 for Bob Gibson. Flags also fly for owner August (Gussie) Busch, longtime Cardinals broadcaster Jack Buck, and Hall of Famer Rogers Hornsby, who played in the days before players wore numbers on their uniforms.

The scoreboard in center field provides the entire line score for every ongoing MLB game while the current National League Central standings appear near the scoreboard, listing the teams in the Cardinals' division from first to last. Team records don't appear here, just the order in which the teams rank. Hey, Bud! Milwaukee was in the basement when we stopped by Busch!

On the left field side of the scoreboard a separate flag court honors each of the Cardinals' nine World Championship teams. Each flag standards bears a year in which the Cards won it all, while a Cardinals pennant flies atop each of the nine flagpoles.

We really like what the Cardinals have done with these monuments. Removing the worst seats in the house was a good call. Now, rather than a sea of empty seats hovering over the field, fans can look up to be reminded of the team's great history. Another far more ambitious remodeling approach would have been to remove the outfield Terrace level entirely—similar to the renovation in Anaheim—creating an open view of the city. But with a new ballpark plan in the works, this probably would have cost a lot more than the Cardinals were prepared to spend.

THE LOWER LEVELS FLYING HIGH
Atop the stadium roof in center field are still more pennants. Lest anyone in the organization feel left out, here the Cardinals fly flags bearing the names of each of their minor league affiliates. These include the Rookie League Johnson City Cardinals, Single-A New Jersey Cardinals, Single-A Palm Beach Cardinals, Single-A Peoria Chiefs, Double-A Tennessee Smokies, and Triple-A Memphis Redbirds.

DUGOUT
The top of the home dugout is painted with banners that commemorate the years in which the Cards won the World Series. Meanwhile the top of the visitors' dugout lists the years in which St. Louis won the National League pennant but lost in the World Series. Considering all of the other nods given the Cards' top teams throughout the park, this seems like overkill to us—but who are we to judge? Our favorite teams—the Red Sox (Josh) and Mariners (Kevin)—haven't had too many championship seasons to celebrate in recent memory. So perhaps we're just bitter.

BUT WHERE'S THE WHIP?
Electronic display boards mounted above the bull pens—the Cardinals' in right-center and visitors' in left-center—show up-to-the-minute statistics for the two pitchers currently in the game. Fantasy baseball buffs will love this, as it spares them the mental undulations of multiplying their pitchers' earned runs allowed times nine, then dividing by the number of innings pitched while the game is in progress. On these display boards pitchers' season-long ERAs fluctuate to reflect each out recorded or run allowed.

THE BOB GIBSON MOUND
Notice that the Busch Stadium pitchers' rubber is exactly ten inches higher than the rest of the playing field. It should come as no surprise. That's the height of all regulation Major League mounds.

The mound was lowered from fifteen inches to ten after the 1968 season in which Bob Gibson posted a modern-era-record 1.12 earned run average in 304 innings pitched. Gibson completed twenty-eight of his thirty-four starts, including thirteen shutouts.

Despite his microscopic ERA, Gibson finished with a 22–9 record for a Cardinals team that won the pennant before losing to the Tigers in the World Series. The problem for Gibson was that most of his opponents weren't allowing too many runs in 1968 either. Baseball had become a pitcher's game. How much so? Denny McLain won thirty-one games for the Tigers in the American League that year, but his 1.96 ERA was only fourth best in the Junior Circuit. Boston's Carl Yastrzemski won the AL batting crown with a .301 average, the lowest ever for a league leader. Only five players in the American League batted better than .283, and the league-wide batting average was .230. The overall AL ERA was 2.98, the National League ERA, 2.99. Twenty-one percent of Major League games resulted in shutouts. The National League won the 1968 All-Star Game 1–0 on an unearned run in the first inning. And in the postseason it was more of the same, with the losing team scoring one run or less in five of the seven World Series contests.

After Gibson and McLain took home the Cy Young Awards in their respective leagues and league MVP honors to boot, MLB decided to lower the mound from fifteen to ten inches to encourage more offense. With less of a height advantage, pitchers would get less leverage, and pitch planes would be more level. In another adjustment, the top boundary of the strike zone, which had been raised in 1963 from the batter's armpits to the top of his shoulders, was lowered to its previous level.

These modifications, in tandem with the arrival of four expansion teams in 1969—the Kansas City Royals, Montreal Expos, San Diego Padres, and Seattle Pilots—tipped the scales back a bit in the hitters' favor. In 1969, the overall batting average climbed to .250 in the NL and .246 in the AL. And now, look how far we've come!

Purists at heart, Josh and Kevin suggest raising the mound back to its original height. But don't hold your breath. "Chicks love the

GOLDEN OLDIE

GIBSON'S lethal right arm wasn't his only claim to fame. He could "throw some leather" with his left hand too. The Hall of Fame hurler established a record for National League pitchers at the time by winning nine consecutive Gold Glove Awards between 1965 and 1973.

The Gold Glove was a relatively new phenomenon when Gibson began his streak because baseball glove manufacturer Rawlings Sporting Goods did not begin honoring baseball's best fielders until 1957.

During Spring Training of 1956, a survey of Major League players revealed that 83 percent of big leaguers wore Rawlings fielders' mitts. Noting that Hillerich and Bradsby, the Major League's leading bat manufacturer, had been doling out Silver Slugger awards for years and gaining free publicity in the process, Rawlings teamed up with the Sporting News to announce the establishment the Gold Glove Award.

After the 1957 season, a panel of Sporting News reporters named one Major Leaguer at each position a Gold Glove recipient, and Rawlings sent the winners actual fielding gloves made of a gold-tanned leather usually used to make women's slippers. In 1958 the voting was turned over to the players and the award was expanded to include a winner from both the AL and NL at each position. In 1965 the managers and coaches of each team assumed voting responsibility, which they still hold.

Incidentally, Greg Maddux has since overtaken Gibson on the all-time list for most goldie's by a National League hurler. Maddux won his first award in 1990, beginning a streak that was still active at the time of this book's publishing.

long ball." And weekend fans (among whom we count the current commissioner) do, too.

Stadium Eats

Every concession offering that we sampled at Busch Stadium was freshly made and tasty. Not only was the food of high quality, but the service was excellent as well. A veritable parade of roving vendors patrol all three of the ballpark's seating levels and, consequently, the lines are never long at the stands on the concourses. Attendance exceeded thirty-four thousand on the April day we visited Busch, yet we didn't see a single concession line with more than four people in it. This renewed our faith in ballpark concession stands after our miserable Saratoga chip experience at Pro Player Stadium in Florida.

SUPER SMOKERS BARBECUE (Trademark Food)

Operating outside the ballpark proper on a patio accessible from the first-level concourse in center field, Super Smokers features slow-roasted pulled pork and beef. The joint offers four different types of barbecue sauce, and if you're like Josh, you'll want to try them all. The flavors, in order of Josh's preference from favorite to least-favorite-but-still-damn-good: Texas Hot, Kansas City Style, St. Louis Style, and Tennessee Style. We tried a pork sandwich that was tender, moist, and lean, and clearly a cut above Boog's Barbecue in Baltimore, Manny's in Pittsburgh, and Gorman's in Milwaukee. Hey, you're in St. Louis, a place that claims to be the barbecue capital of the world. So fold your scorecard into a bib and sauce up a sandwich.

HUNTER'S DOG (Hot Dog Rating)
The Seventh Best Hot Dog in the Majors

We found the Hunter's dog spicy, juicy, and firm. And the Cardinals don't defile its casing with the Texaco-style silver rollers found in many ballparks. This dog is grilled, and it's delicious.

BEST OF THE REST

Toasted ravioli and fried beef cannelloni are St. Louis specialties. And we think Berra and Garagiola would approve of the job Busch Stadium does with this local favorite. The stadium concession stands offer both fried cheese ravioli and fried beef cannelloni. We tried the cannelloni and were happy that we did. The casing was nice and crispy and the ground beef inside melted in our mouths. We dipped our little bundles of flavor in a marinara sauce that was also of higher quality than we expected to find at a ballpark.

We also tried the Bratwurst, which was superb. Busch serves the spiciest brat we encountered South of Milwaukee. The only thing missing was some stadium sauce. Kevin settled for mustard instead, while Josh opted to top his brat with ketchup.

The Giant Pretzel also deserves props for being the giant-est giant pretzel in the Majors.

On a hot day, the stadium snow cone is a good call. These aren't the usual freezer-burned blocks of colored ice that you get at most ballparks. The snow cones at Busch are freshly made with chipped ice and syrup.

SPORTS IN THE CITY

THE WALK OF FAME
(6504 Delmar Boulevard)

"THE LOOP" on Delmar Boulevard features the St. Louis Walk of Fame, which honors famous St. Louis natives and residents with stars on the sidewalk and plaques that summarize their accomplishments. Among the folks honored are poets Maya Angelou and T. S. Eliot, cabaret starlet Josephine Baker, musician Miles Davis, and Tennessee Williams. And, oh yeah, an assortment of baseball players and broadcasters also have their own stars: Yogi Berra, Bob Gibson, Lou Brock, Cool Papa Bell, Stan Musial, Harry Caray, and Jack Buck.

STADIUM SUDS

Not surprisingly, the macrobrews inside the stadium all hail from the Busch family (Busch, Bud, Bud Light, Michelob, Michelob Light, etc.). For some reason, we found it hilarious to hear the beer vendors calling out, "Who needs a Busch? Who likes Busch?" That's certainly something you don't hear at any other big league park.

For those with more distinguishing palates, the **Old Timer's Brew Pub and Pretzelry** offers a number of microbrews behind the bleachers on the first-level concourse in center field. Shiner Bock, Amber Bock, Boulevard Unfiltered Wheat, Red Hook, O'Fallon Gold, Schlaflay, and Fat Tire are all available on tap. Kevin recommends the Red Hook.

The Busch Stadium Experience

St. Louis fans arrive at the ballpark early and stay until the last out is recorded. The percentage of Cardinals fans wearing the team color is amazing and rivaled only, perhaps, by the Yankees fans who form a sea of navy blue at the stadium in the Bronx. Cardinal fans maintain a tradition of being knowledgeable, enthusiastic, and fiercely loyal to their Red Birds. For our money, their intensity during games matches that of their counterparts in hard-boiled East Coast baseball towns like Boston, Philadelphia, and New York. The only difference is that the Cardinals fans cheer for their team without devolving into jerks. They're friendly Midwestern people, and seemingly much more stable than the seam-heads on the East Coast. They don't holler profanities at their own players when they're struggling and they usually don't call sports radio shows to deliver expletive-bleeped tirades when their team loses.

In almost every regard, the Cardinals fans are Kevin's kind of people. As for Josh . . . well . . . he still has the phone numbers for both of Boston's sports radio stations programmed into his speed dial even though he moved to Maine a while back.

CLYDE

In homage to the Budweiser culture that dominated Busch Stadium for years and in memory of the late Gussie Busch who would sometimes drive a team of Clydesdales around the warning track, in the eighth inning the Jumbotron shows a team of Clydesdales trotting along a country road. The "Budweiser Horses" trot to the tune of polka music.

FATHER TIME (Superfan)

Since 1985 Paul Pagano has been showing up at Cardinals games to spread good cheer. A St. Louis icon, Paul has also traveled as far away as Milwaukee for the Italian Festival and has marched in Chicago's Columbus Day Parade.

At Cardinals games you will recognize Paul as the older fellow decked out in the colors of the American flag walking around with a "No. 1 Fan" sign.

Known locally as "Father Time," Pagano, a retired produce merchant, has lived in St. Louis his entire life. When designing his outfit twenty years ago, he intended to combine the costume of the folklore character Father Time with a Fourth of July motif.

Before the game, Paul patrols the plaza outside the park and offers every fan he sees a boisterous "Welcome," and hearty handshake. He plays fifty tunes on his harmonica ranging from "God Bless America," to "Take Me Out to the Ball Game." As game time approaches, Paul passes through the stadium turnstiles free of charge, courtesy of the Cardinals.

"Don't forget," Paul told us, "When you go to the Cardinals Hall of Fame, look for me in the video reel of McGwire's sixtieth home run."

We looked, and we found him—in all his glory.

The Jim Dandys

Photo by Kevin O'Connell

THE JIM DANDY'S

Busch Stadium may not be an old-time ballpark, but St. Louis is still an ancient baseball town. And clearly, locals remember the game's good old days, back when the players made the same money as schoolteachers, bleacher seats sold for less than a buck, and small bands often serenaded fans inside and outside the parks.

Today, a five-man band called The Jim Dandy's often sets up on the pedestrian bridge above 8th Street outside the stadium. The Dandy's treat fans filing into the ballpark to a lively selection of Dixieland tunes.

With roots in St. Louis that date from the 1960s, the Dandy's try to attend at least one game every home stand. Bandleader Robert Souza plays the trumpet, while Steve Hoover plays the trombone, Joe Schulz the tuba, Dan

Stevens the banjo, and Joe Van Cando the clarinet.

Josh and Kevin say, "Every ballpark should have a group like this outside its gates adding to the pregame festivities."

FRED BIRD THE RED BIRD

Okay, the Cardinals' mascot doesn't have quite the cachet of the San Diego Chicken, but in our book he's more legit than Wally the Green Monster and Billy the Marlin. At least his species is recognizable upon examination. And he's got a following of children, men, and women who emulate him. Some St. Louis fans—young and old—wear foam Cardinal-head hats that come complete with feathers that flow down to their shoulders. They're pretty hilarious.

Kevin: "You're not actually going to wear that thing, are you?"

Josh: "I sure am."

One inning later.

Kevin: "Can I try it now?"

PERSONALIZED BAT

From birds to bats. At Busch fans participate in fashioning their own handmade bat on the first-level center field concourse. While Rawlings employees look on, fans use lathes to make their own hitting sticks. The cost is $50.

Josh: "I'm calling mine Wonder Boy."

Kevin: "How about 'Savoy Special'?"

KANSAS CITY ROYALS, KAUFFMAN STADIUM

A Ballpark in the American Pastoral

KANSAS CITY, MISSOURI

235 miles to St. Louis
408 miles to Minneapolis
554 miles to Denver
646 miles to Houston

A S THE SUN SETS on Kansas City and game time approaches, Kauffman Stadium glows in the gloaming of the Midwestern pastoral, under the luminescent canopy of the clear and sacred baseball sky. A visit to the heartland stands to remind all of us that small-market baseball can be a unique experience. From the horseshoe design of the seating bowl to the signature fountains bubbling beyond the outfield, Kauffman Stadium is one of those parks that can only truly be appreciated in person. And the park holds many warm memories for Royals fans, having brought the world championship to their town, one of the smallest in the big leagues.

Built smack in the middle of the cookie-cutter era, Kauffman Stadium somehow escaped the conventional thinking of its time in important ways. First, and perhaps most important, Kauffman is a baseball-only facility. No other single factor contributes as much to the perfection of its design. Kauffman—or Royals Stadium as it was originally known—was built outside of downtown as part of the Truman Sports Complex, which also houses Arrowhead Stadium, home of the National Football League's Chiefs. A freeway runs nearby and unfortunately there is no surrounding neighborhood to enhance the game-day experience, but in a way that seems to be the point. Before migrating to the city, baseball was a barnstorming game often played in green pastures in small towns. And Kauffman Stadium is the nearest big-league equivalent to that era in the game's history.

Completely symmetrical in every way, the ballpark originally had an artificial turf playing field instead of natural grass. For our way of thinking these two less-than-appetizing ingredients usually spell disaster. But Kauffman bucked the right trends at the right times and was renovated through the years to become one of the best parks in all of baseball.

game time

Courtesy of Kansas City Royals

The first-level concourse is wide open and provides views of the action for those out of their seats to get a hot dog. That's right, an open first-level concourse at a park that wasn't recently built. While other cities were building multisport monstrosities, the folks in Kansas City built two different facilities: one for football, and one for baseball. Then when other cities started building retroparks, the folks in KC renovated Kauffman, improving it, but sticking with the original design.

On television, the signature waterfalls and grassy embankment beyond the outfield fence may look like a minigolf course, but they are wonderful to behold in person. Tranquil and pleasing to the eyes and ears, sitting near the running water and grassy slopes calms the soul. And while beautiful, the embankment has also come to be regarded as one of the best hitting backdrops in baseball. The massive scoreboard in center field is also distinct, featuring the Royals logo and bearing at its top an enormous crown that lets all who visit know that baseball, Midwestern style, is king.

When the Kansas City Athletics left Kansas City after the 1967 season after spending thirteen years in town, the very next year the city was awarded one of the four expansion franchises that would begin play in 1969. Ewing M. Kauffman bought the team with the hope of bringing championship baseball to his city. Kauffman named the team the Royals, a moniker highly reminiscent of the Kansas City Monarchs, one of the best-known and most successful franchises of the Negro Leagues.

Kauffman, who had made his fortune as founder of Marion Laboratories, provided the vision and some of the funding for the new ballpark. But the majority of the $70 million price tag was footed by the citizens of Jackson County through a bond issue, and thus, the county would own Royals Stadium. The ballpark was not designed by the hometown ballpark architects at HOK, but rather by another local firm named HNTB. Kauffman took the shape of a cookie-cutter stadium but eliminated the worst two-thirds of the standard seating bowl. If the cookie-cutters look like concrete hockey pucks, then Kauffman looks like a hockey puck slashed in half diagonally, with the vital seats behind home plate remaining, as well as the lower-level seats down the baselines. As for the rest—that is, those upper-level seats in the outfield that proffer awful sight lines? The Royals simply didn't build out there.

After the Royals played their first four seasons at Kansas City's Municipal Stadium at the intersection of 22nd Street and Brooklyn Avenue, the first game at Royals Stadium was held on April 10, 1973, with KC crushing the Texas Rangers 12–1. More than thirty-nine thousand fans attended the game and watched Amos Otis record the first hit for the Royals. On May 15 of that year, California's Nolan Ryan struck out twelve Royals, logging the first of his seven career no-hitters. The All-Star Game also came to town during that inaugural season. It would be the last of Willie Mays's long career. Although Johnny Bench led the National League to a 7–1 victory, three of the five hits for the American League came from the Royals' Otis and John Mayberry.

Before the Royals' brief inhabitancy, Municipal had been the home of the Athletics during their layover in Kansas City, en route to Oakland from Philadelphia. Built in 1923, Municipal was originally named Muehlebach Field after George Muehlebach, the owner of the Double-A Kansas City Blues. The single-decked ballpark, which was built at a cost of $400,000, was also home to the Kansas City Monarchs from 1923 until 1950. It is difficult to overstate how important the Monarchs were to the community of Kansas City. As charter members of the Negro National League, the Monarchs won ten pennants and played in the first two Negro League World Series—both against the Hilldale Daisies. The Monarchs won the first contest, but dropped the second. In their history they only suffered one losing season, and that was when the team's roster was heavily depleted with players serving in World War II. The Homestead Grays was the only other Negro League team to claim ten pennants, and in the only meeting of the two dynasties the Monarchs swept the Grays in the 1942 World Series.

Ernie Banks, Satchel Paige, and Jackie Robinson are among the Monarchs' famed alumni, but there was a wealth of talent through the years. The tradition of championship baseball that the Monarchs brought to this small Midwestern city fueled the desire in local residents to bring a Major League team to town. And should anyone wonder at the similarity of the names, Monarchs and Royals—it is a fitting tribute.

When the New York Yankees acquired the minor league Blues in 1937, Yankees owner Jacob Ruppert renamed the ballpark Ruppert Stadium. After Ruppert passed away, the ballpark officially became known as Blues Stadium before being completely rebuilt and renamed Municipal Stadium in 1955 in anticipation of the A's arrival. At the cost of $2.5 million, a partially covered second deck was added, which nearly doubled the capacity of the park to more than thirty thousand.

When Charlie O. Finley bought the A's in 1960, he oversaw many innovative changes to the park. The team mascot was a mule named "Charlie O" who lived in the children's petting zoo behind the left field bleachers. The zoo also contained rabbits, monkeys, sheep, pheasants, and a few bats—or so we've been told. "Little Blowhard," a device that blew air across home plate so the umpire wouldn't have to dust it, also became a Municipal Stadium trademark, as did a mechanical rabbit named Harvey, who would spring up from the ground to deliver fresh baseballs to the home plate ump whenever they were needed.

Josh: "Finley was buttering up the umpires."

Kevin: "The way the A's played, they needed every advantage they could get."

But Finley didn't stop at these gimmicks. He also constructed a fence that reduced the right field porch of the ballpark to 296 feet, the exact same dimension as right field at Yankee Stadium. Dubbing the protrusion "Pennant Porch," Finley was convinced that the Yankees' success derived from their short home run porch in right, and felt his team deserved the same advantage. Unfortunately the American League only allowed Pennant Porch to stand for two exhibition games before passing a rule that all new ballparks must have fences no less than 325 feet from home plate.

Kevin: "Just another case of East Coast bias."

Josh: "Rooting for the Yankees is like going to Vegas and betting on the house."

Though the A's were never very successful in KC, attendance was good, and fans were treated to many memorable moments at Municipal Stadium. Early Wynn got a late win—late in his career, that is—as the Indians hurler notched victory number 300 on July 13, 1963 to finish up with an even 300 wins against 244 defeats.

Bert Campaneris accomplished the unthinkable against the California Angels on September 8, 1965, when he played all nine positions in a nine-inning game, becoming the first player in modern times to do so. Hey, nine positions, nine innings. We don't think that was a marketing idea. Not with a straight shooter like Finley at the helm. But perhaps playing all nine positions is second to playing one position well.

While today forty years of age is considered ancient for pitchers, a fifty-nine year-old Satchel Paige pitched three shutout innings for the Royals against the Boston Red Sox on September 25, 1965, twelve years after his official retirement. With the appearance, Paige became eligible to receive a Major League pension.

TRIVIA TIMEOUT

Duke: In his final game as a Royal, how did George Brett show his appreciation for Kauffman Stadium?
Earl: How long in feet is Kauffman Stadium's right field water display?
Monarch: Which Royal hit the longest home run in Kauffman Stadium history? For extra points, which team and pitcher did he hit it off?

Look for the answers in the text.

When the Royals came to town, they won their first game at Municipal, a 4–3 extra-inning affair over the eventual AL West division winners, the Minnesota Twins. Lou Piniella won Rookie of the Year honors for KC in that first season, batting .282 with 11 HR and 68 RBI.

Kevin: "I guess it wasn't a great year for rookies."

Josh: "It was a different era. Back then, if you batted .300 with twenty-five dingers you were hitting cleanup."

The real celebrations for the Royals would come at Kauffman Stadium. Who can forget Cookie Rojas and Fred Patek jumping into the water fountain after clinching the 1976 AL West Championship? But it is difficult to think of the Royals' success without thinking of their teams of the 1980s that were led by third-baseman George Brett.

After losing three straight American League Championship Series to the Yankees in 1976, 1977, and 1978, the Royals faced their arch nemesis again in 1980. That season Brett pursued the mythical .400 mark with a passion and vigor few had exhibited since 1941 when Ted Williams hit .406. Though he would finish the campaign with a batting average of .390, Brett kept baseball fans across the country checking the box scores at the breakfast table through September. And Brett gave folks something to talk about in October, too. His home run off Goose Gossage at Yankee Stadium lifted the Royals into the World Series at long last. Apparently in KC, the fourth time is the charm, not the third. After dropping the first two World Series games to the Phillies, the Royals won Games 3 and 4 at home, before losing games 5 and 6.

The Royals returned to the October Classic in 1985 and this time they would not be denied, not even by the St. Louis Cardinals. A bad call by the men in blue gave the Royals a huge boost in the bottom of the ninth inning of Game Six as they staved off elimination. First base umpire Don Denkinger ruled Jose Orta safe at first, when replays showed he was clearly out. The Royals rallied to score two runs and win the game, tying the series at three games apiece. Then Bret Saberhagen tossed a five-hit shutout in Game 7, leading the Royals to an 11–0 win. Afterwards, the twenty-year-old Saberhagen was named Series MVP.

On July 2, 1993, Royals Stadium was renamed Kauffman Stadium, in honor of the only owner in franchise history. A month later Ewing Kauffman lost his bout with cancer at age seventy-six. Kauffman had provided the club with vision and a winning attitude and had helped to guide the Royals quickly from an expansion team to a World Series champion. His mark on Kauffman Stadium goes much deeper than merely a name. He etched out a beautiful ballpark in countrified Kansas City, in an era that saw the arrival of nothing but bland cookie-cutters elsewhere.

And unlike most of the multipurpose stadiums, Kauffman Stadium stands to this day, over thirty years after its opening, following no trends, and offering the best that small market baseball can. Though in this era, it may take more than this great ballpark to keep Kauffman's dream alive, as the Royals try to hold onto talented young players and face many of the same restraints that other small-market teams do.

Sellout Index: 0% of games sell out
Seating Capacity: 40,793
Ticket Office: (800) 6-ROYALS
www.kcroyals.com

Getting a Choice Seat

Kansas City fans have supported their Royals in good times and bad and have packed Kauffman Stadium over the years, peaking at 2.5 million during the 1989 season. But the last few years the club has experienced the largest falloff in ticket sales in its history. Still, they will draw more than a million, which wasn't too bad in the sixties, but is not nearly enough to survive today as a franchise.

More than half of the seats in the ballpark are on the first of the three levels. Practically, this means that getting into the park is not a problem, but that more than likely, the very good seats will be taken. But seats are not expensive at Kauffman. And with perhaps the smallest amount of foul territory in the heartland, seats are that much closer to the action. So see a game at Kauffman before the Royals start winning again and those 1.5 million fans come streaming back.

Dugout and Crown Club Suites

Added to the ballpark during the 1999 and 2000 seasons, these seats are only available to you if your last name is Kauffman, Otis, or Brett. Not really, but unless you have a connection you'll be left to wonder (like we were) what the lifestyles of the rich and famous in KC are like.

Club Box (200 Level Seats)

Why people would pay more to sit in the 200 Level when they could spend less to sit in the Dugout Boxes is beyond us. But then again, we don't understand paying extra for just about anything.

Kevin: "Perhaps they offer free massages to those viewing the game?"

Josh: "They should offer them to the folks sitting in the outfield. They're the ones with the sore necks."

Dugout Box (Sections 100–124, Lower)

Perhaps the best deal left in Major League Baseball, these seats are highly affordable for road trippers. Seats in these sections run little more than $20, a third to a quarter of what comparable seats cost at many of the new parks. Here, you're on the field side of the midlevel concourse, so there is little foot traffic to worry about. If the road-trip fund has been managed well, we suggest splurging a little and sitting in the Dugout Boxes.

To be avoided, however, are Seats 6–8 in Rows AA and BB of Sections 107 and 108. Cameramen that set up in the aisle block what would normally be great seats.

Dugout Plaza (Sections 100–124, Upper)

While still decent seats, and very good for the money, we can't help but suspect that if you've got three dollars extra you'll be happier with the Dugout Boxes. Folks meandering along the midlevel concourse block views and the overhang from the deck above obstructs the view for those in Rows, RR, SS, and TT. Not surprisingly, folks tend to sit in the lower and middle seats of the sections first.

Field Box (Sections 125–138, Lower)

These boxes run down to the corners on the first level and also offer views unobstructed by the midlevel concourse. The gentle curvature of the ballpark keeps these seats pointed toward the action in Sections 125–128. For this reason and because we liked the atmosphere especially on the third-base side, we prefer these seats over the Dugout Plaza seats, which go for the same price. Sections 129 and 130 marginally point toward the outfield, a trend that worsens by Sections 131 and 132. These aren't bad seats, just be prepared to look over your left shoulder on the right field side, or over your right shoulder on the left field side.

Field Plaza (Sections 125–138, Upper)

The same that is true for the Dugout Plaza is true for the Field Plaza, only the seats are that much worse because they're farther from the field. Don't get us wrong, these are still decent seats for the money, it's just that only two bucks more will get you into the Boxes.

Josh: "You can't even buy a pretzel for two bucks. Five years ago, you could."

Kevin: "Who are you, Norman Greenspan?"

Josh: "I think you mean Alan Greenspan."

View Box (Sections 300–326)

These seats are the best the upper deck has to offer, located along the railing and with a nice view from above the action. Because the Club Level and Press Box share just a single level, these seats aren't as high as in other parks, and don't feel like they're tucked up into the rafters. The upper deck is, however, very steep, and not that easy to navigate for seat-hopping or ballpark guidebook writers.

Outfield Plaza (Sections 139–146)

For the road tripper who may have spent a tad too much of his bankroll at Arthur Bryants, we recommend the only true bleacher seats in Kauffman Stadium. These seats are mostly good. Fans in Sections 139 and 140 have a foul pole obstruction of the outfield, while Sections 141 and 142 have to deal with infield foul pole obstructions. And this foul pole is thicker than most, like a foot thick, so it's nothing to scoff at.

Josh: "Rich Gedman hit that right field pole one night and the ball was incorrectly ruled foul. Cost the Sox a game."

Kevin: "You Boston fans never forget any-thing, do you?"

The worst seats in the house are Rows J, K, and L of Sections 139 and 140. Do not buy a ticket for Row J, Seat 12, of Sections 139 or 140, as the foul pole will be right in your lap. These seats should probably be removed. Perhaps they have been left for their comedic value.

The best bet is to stick to Sections 143 and 144. Though the highest ten rows here will also have some obstruction, they are not that bad. The remainder of these sections are clear and great seats. Lower seats in Sections 145 and 146 are also good, but seats in the upper rows of these sections are blocked by the bull pens and the water feature.

View Level Infield (Sections 400–424)

Though there are almost no under-hang issues, these seats are not recommended. As intimate as Kauffman is throughout most of the park, these seats will not provide that type of desired effect, especially in the upper rows. The park takes on a decided cookie-cutter upper-level feel in the back rows in these sections, and indeed if the park had been continued all the way around at this altitude, the dreaded "CC" moniker would be well earned.

Hi-Vee View Level
(Sections 327–344, 427–442)

The only way we can recommend these seats is if budget is the *only* concern. Use them to get into the ballpark for a five spot, if you must. Though not as bad as in other parks, these seats remind us of sitting out on the wings of an airplane. The steep taper of the ballpark, however, is not as noticeable up in these seats as one might think. What is noticeable is that at the extreme ends of these sections there are no lights. It feels a bit like watching a concert in the dark from up here, so if you enjoy rollin'

SEATING TIP

→ IT'S HARD TO go wrong at Kauffman, but our best seating tip is to sit in the outfield bleachers for $10. Not only are these some of the coolest seats in the park, they're also some of the least expensive. Follow the seating guidelines above and you'll enjoy your $10 seat much more in the outfield than one in the upper deck.

a fatty while watching the game, this might be the place for you.

The Black Market

Resale of tickets is not permissible on the Sports Complex grounds, but we didn't see anyone in the Denny's parking lot across the street hocking tickets either. That's not to say this type of activity does occasionally take place. Remember, if it ain't considerably below face value, you ain't buying.

Before/After the Game

Being that Kauffman Stadium is the premier example of baseball in America's rustic Midwest, it is fitting that the park is surrounded primarily by pasture. Or the modern form of pasture—parking lots. Kauffman Stadium is part of the Truman Sports Complex and shares its parking lots with Arrowhead Stadium. One major downfall of this park is that there are no restaurants or bars nearby. But as stated before, baseball began in America's great pasture, so we can forgive. Tailgating before Royals games takes on the local flavor: ribs, steaks, and bratwursts. Though we found this one of the best tailgating scenes in the big leagues, we did not encounter much in the way of parking lot sports. Just as long as the Royals fans keep cooking those ribs though, Josh and Kevin will be along, 'round about five o'clock.

Getting to Kauffman Stadium

Unless you ride the bus, you're driving to the ballpark. Coming from the north or south, I-435 is the best route. Take Exit 63C to the Sports Complex. From the east or west, take I-70 to Exit 9, the Blue-Ridge Cutoff/Sports Complex Exit. Passers on I-70 are treated to a quick view into the ballpark.

The Metro Bus System services Kauffman with express runs on game days. Just look for the Stadium Express signs in downtown for the Crown Center and Country Club Plaza routes. Call (816) 221-0660 for more information. But seriously, do you really want to take a bus to the ballpark?

Sights Outside the Stadium

CONCRETE GALORE

While the exterior look of the ballpark isn't bad, it does little to convey to the approaching fan the array of baseball wonders inside. Since when did architects decide on the beauty and luxurious warm feel of cement? A facade of brick, greenery, or even paint would do wonders to enhance this ballpark's exterior.

Speaking of possible renovations, the "Com-

mish" has hinted that ballpark improvements are necessary to keep the Royals in Kansas City. (Again with the bullying, eh Bud?) Voters and the legislature are struggling over the issue, though we doubt much of the money thus appropriated would go to the exterior of the ballpark. It will most likely go toward finding a way to generate more money, like more club-level corporate bull. These suits have their priorities in all the wrong places.

BRETT STATUE

A statue of George Brett—the greatest Royal of them all—stands forever at bat outside Kauffman Stadium. The text on the base of the statue speaks to the important contributions Brett made during his career toward fund-raising efforts to find a cure for ALS (Lou Gehrig's Disease). Brett's children—Jackson, Dylan, and Robin—were on hand to unveil the statue on August 11, 2001.

The story of George Brett's career is the story of the Kansas City Royals. Few players in the modern era have shown more loyalty to a city and in a sense are synonymous with that one single place. You think of Ted Williams, you think Boston. You think of Stan Musial, you think St. Louis. Likewise, it's impossible to think of George Brett without thinking of KC.

In twenty-one seasons—1973–1993—Brett amassed a lifetime average of .305, and led the American League in hitting three times. His 317 career home runs and 1,595 RBI are tops in Royals history, as are his 137 triples. Brett, who had just slightly above-average speed could thank the expansive Kauffman Stadium outfield and its quick

George Brett statue

Photo by Kevin O'Connell

turf for helping him to a few extra three-baggers. He was an All-Star every season between 1976 and 1988, and garnered the MVP in 1980.

George Brett showed his appreciation for how good Kauffman Stadium and the fans of Kansas City were to him throughout his career by dropping to his knees and kissing home plate after his last game.

Watering Holes and Outside Eats

Unless Denny's or the sports bar in the Howard Johnson's lobby sounds good to you, you'll need to get into your car and drive to one of the many great places to eat in Kansas City. Before the game, we recommend sitting tight and enjoying one of the best tailgating scenes in baseball, then after the game head for a steak house or saloon.

FUZZY'S SOUTH (1227 W. 103rd Street)

This popular sports bar boasts seven large-screen televisions and fifty-three smaller screens. That may not sound too impressive to you, but remember, this is Kansas City we're talking about. Most Best Buy stores in the area don't even have that many TV sets in stock.

Aside from watching about a zillion games at once when we visited Fuzzy's, we also enjoyed putting on a show for the locals in the National Trivia Network game. Then when the music started up at about ten o'clock, we sat back and watched the joint turn into a meat market for middle-aged suburbanites.

MIKE'S TAVERN (5424 Troost Avenue)

By day Mike's is a fairly average local bar, but at night it turns into a happening hangout for the college kids from the University of Missouri at Kansas City. If you fit into this demographic, Mike's might be the place for you, otherwise, you might be well advised to stay away. If you stop in during the day, Kevin recommends the quesadillas and soft tacos, while Josh recommends the burgers.

STROUD'S (1015 E. 85th)

If fried chicken is your thing, then Stroud's may be the best you'll find on the road. Pan fried to a golden brown, then baked the rest of the way through, we found this fowl deliciously crisp and juicy. Serving family style, Stroud's provides plenty of chicken, potatoes, green beans, and cinnamon rolls to fill you up. Though not the cheapest place we visited in our travels, it was one of the best.

STEAKS IN KANSAS CITY

There are numerous places to get a prime cut of beef in Kansas City. We like the names of these places almost as much of the meat they serve. **The Golden Ox** at 1600 Genessee, and **The Hereford House** at 20th and Main Streets are two of our favorites. But the best place we found for the price was **Jeff and Jim's** at 517 E. 135th.

ARTHUR BRYANT'S (1727 Brooklyn Street)

Serving the best "Q" we sampled on our road trip, Arthur Bryant's is a must-visit. This is barbecue the old fashion way: lots of meat, lots of sauce. The ribs come piping hot and with a side of bread—nearly a whole loaf—to soak up the juice, plus beans and fries. Located just four blocks from the location of old Municipal Stadium, Art's is also only a few blocks from the Negro League Museum. So plan on making an afternoon of your visit.

BLUES AND JAZZ

The neighborhood of 18th and Vine was once among the most vibrant in the city and was a jewel of African American culture in America. With a baseball game going on at Municipal (22nd and Brooklyn) and all that jazz, the excitement was palpable. Jesse Fisher once stated that "if you came to Kansas City on a Saturday night it was like trying to walk through Harlem when there was a parade. It was really something to see. Everybody that was everybody was at 18th and Vine."

Today, blues and jazz are still on the menu in this part of town. We recommend **The Blue Room** at 1600 E. 18th, and **The Gem Theatre** at 1615 E. 18th. Both places are easily spotted from the Negro League Museum and well worth a visit. If you're a fan of the music, head to **The Grand Emporium** at 3832 Main Street, considered by many in the know to be the best blues bar in America.

Inside the Stadium

The Spectacular Waterfall and Fountain

While often imitated around the big leagues, this idyllic fountain and waterfall feature, a Kauffman Stadium trademark, has never been duplicated. The fountain display runs behind the right field fence for an incredible 322 feet, making it the largest publicly funded fountain in the world. A 10-foot-high waterfall flows from an upper pool to two lower pools, which feed the fountains. At night, colored lights shine on the waters between innings, providing a backdrop for the game that is as tranquil as it is in daylight. To complete the Kauffman dream of a championship team, the fountains are in the shape of the number "1". Surrounding the waterworks, tiered embankments of grass serve as the batter's eye, as well as landscaping to enhance the natural effect.

A Royally High Scoreboard

Above the water spectacular beyond the center field fence, a twelve-story high scoreboard tower stands in the shape of the Royals Crest, topped off with a crown. Adorned with lights that illuminate the night like crowned jewels, this scoreboard perfectly caps the design of the outfield, and makes for one of the most recognizable and beautiful backdrops in all of baseball.

Bo Jackson's first Major League home run, hit off of Seattle's Mike Moore, was the longest dinger in Kauffman Stadium history. The 475-foot shot clanked off the scoreboard on September 14, 1986.

RETIRED NUMBERS

Appearing on the bottom face of the center field scoreboard are the Royals' three retired numbers. From left to right these read number 10, number 5, and number 20. Number 10, which belonged to Dick Howser, was retired in 1987 shortly after the death of the longtime KC manager. Brett's number 5 was put on the shelf in 1994, and Frank White's number 20 went up in 1995.

Also retired is Jackie Robinson's Brooklyn number 42, as it is in all Major League ballparks. But in Kansas City it has a special significance in this regard. Robinson once played for the Kansas City Monarchs, a team that was a veritable factory of Major League talent after Robinson broke the color barrier. Monarchs manager Buck O'Neil was responsible for sending more than three dozen players up to the big leagues.

Pennant Porch Reborn

On the left field side of the outfield, huge white flags flap in the Kansas City wind, commemorating the years the Royals won the pennant. Not surprisingly, the largest flag in the middle is the World Series flag. Though not exactly the "Pennant Porch" that Charlie Finley envisioned, this incarnation of pennant porch is a classy touch.

Royals Hall of Fame

Located behind Section 107 on the Plaza Level, the Royals Hall of Fame is a must-visit for any fan of the Blue Crew. Here you'll find portraits behind glass of Ewing and Muriel Kauffman, and of Royals greats like Amos

Otis, Paul Splittorff, Cookie Rojas, Dan Quisenberry, Whitey Herzog, Steve Busby, Jeff Montgomery, and, of course, George Brett.

Josh: "Kind of a weak group other than Brett, don't you think?"

Kevin: "I don't know, Steve Busby had a few wins."

Josh: "Yeah, seventy wins in eight seasons."

Kevin: "Maybe you're right."

Josh: "He's barely worth naming a pork sandwich after."

Kevin: "Maybe that would be regal enough for the Royals.

Josh: "And where the heck is Bret Saberhagen?"

THIRTY YEARS AND GOING STRONG

SINCE THE BALLPARK opened more than thirty years ago it has undergone a few alterations. The Jumbotron arrived in 1990 and the dreaded turf was removed in 1995, in favor of natural grass.

The Crown and Dugout seats came as part of the 1998 renovations, which also included the removal of the ghoulish red-colored seats in the upper level, which were replaced with Royals Blue seats. The Royals Pavilion was also added, as were the clubhouses located on the club level, down the left field line.

TROPHIES ON DISPLAY

Also in the Royals Hall of Fame is the Royals 1985 World Series trophy.

Kevin: "See Josh, that's what the Holy Grail looks like."

Josh: "I didn't notice one on display at Safeco either, pal."

Royal Pavilion

Near as we could figure, this outfield picnic area is for large groups who reserve it for the game. In other words, not a place to upgrade your seat.

Kevin: "Hey, a party."

Josh: "Kev, wait! I think it's private."

Kevin: "They look friendly enough. I'm going in the hot tub."

Josh: "So I'll meet you outside the detention center area again?"

It's All about the Kids

Added in 2002, the **Little K Ballpark** is located in right field next to a small forest of pine trees. At this miniature ballpark kids swing for the fences during pregame home run derbies And one lucky kid each day is selected to swing for the fences live on the Jumbotron during the third inning. If he or she hits the ball over the fence, it's fireworks for everyone to enjoy!

Kevin: "Come on, kid . . . you can do it."

Josh: "No pressure kid . . . no pressure."

Popout. Whiff. Another popout.

Kevin: "You blew it!"

Josh: "Thanks for ruining our fun!"

Stadium Eats

On the whole, the food at Kauffman Stadium rates better than most ballparks. While you can still find grub that is bland, tasteless, and odorless, following the guide below will keep you into eats that taste more like treats.

GATES BBQ (Trademark Food)

Gates BBQ serves sandwiches and ribs that will make your mouth water. Located behind Section 112, it's the real deal and a Kansas City institution since way back. If you are only in town for a short while, Gates is a delicious option. But if your palate forces you to make a choice between Gates and Arthur Bryant's, we must recommend the latter. Unless of course you've got an iron stomach like Josh, and can eat barbecue three meals a day.

THE NEGRO LEAGUE MUSEUM (AND JAZZ HALL OF FAME)

THERE MAY BE no other baseball-related attraction on the road as worthy of a visit as the Negro League Museum. It began as a labor of love on the part of the great Buck O'Neil and other former Kansas City Monarchs players. They paid the monthly rent for the building that now holds the Negro League Museum and Jazz Hall of Fame until permanent funding was secured. Here you'll find not only the story of a baseball league that most experts now admit was as ripe with talent as the Major Leagues, but you'll also find the story of America itself. Forced into exile by the dreaded unwritten "gentleman's agreement" that formed in the 1880s, owners kept black players out of Major League Baseball for more than six decades. African American performers were allowed to entertain white crowds at hotels, but weren't allowed to stay in those hotels or eat in their restaurants. Like America, baseball was segregated. And that segregation hurt both blacks and whites. But out of this tragic injustice, the Negro Leagues grew into a tremendous source of pride for their communities. The style and flair of the Negro League players reflected their personalities and zest for life.

The Negro League Museum is a veritable warehouse of artifacts and information. Really, you need to visit for yourself to see the field of life-sized statues that depict the greatest Negro League players ever, all on the same field. It is really something to behold.

We walked the few blocks from lunch at Arthur Bryant's to the Negro League Museum taking in the sights of the old 18th and Vine neighborhood. With baseball and jazz being two of Kevin's primary interests, he bounded along like a kid going to see Santa Claus.

"This is going to be great," he said.

"Yeah," Josh eeked out.

Approaching the building, Kevin noticed a smiling old man sitting on a chair outside the museum. He looked very familiar, but Kevin couldn't place him. He imagined his wrinkled black face without the large glasses, then with a baseball hat on. He had an inkling, but he wasn't quite sure.

Finally, he said, "I think that guy is Buck O'Neil."

"I think you're right," said Josh, holding his stomach.

"Wow, Buck O'Neil . . . 'Ole Skip,'" said Kevin, a bit too starstruck to walk up to the man. "The first black coach in the big leagues. Didn't he coach for the A's?"

"Cubs," said Josh, wiping a profuse sweat from his brow with his shirtsleeve.

"Well, I've got to talk to him," and with that Kevin walked over to the living legend.

"Wait," said Josh, "your shirt." But in his condition he wasn't talking too loud, and Kevin didn't hear him.

"Mr. O'Neil?" said Kevin meekly.

"That's right, son," Buck said. His face beamed like Buddha.

"Well, I just wanted to say, that I'm uh, uh, uh . . ."

"Relax, son," Buck said. "What's your name?"

"Kevin. And this is my pal Josh.

"Hello there, Josh. You feeling all right?"

"Hi," said Josh, "I'm fine." He pointed to his stomach in an attempt to signal to Kevin to look down at the mess of barbecue sauce still on his own shirt.

But Kevin, thinking his friend was still suffering from overindulgence, was oblivious. "We're traveling across the country seeing all the big league ballparks," he said.

"That sounds like some trip," Buck said. "You know, when the Monarchs traveled, way back when, it was quite a thing for a man." Buck launched into a story about the old-time rails, telling it the way an expert hand-weaves a carpet. His joy in telling the story, and his captivating smile, made Kevin and Josh eager to hear more. We couldn't help but feel good when Buck O'Neil was talking. An aura of warmth and charisma surrounds this wonderful man and great ambassador for the game.

"That was some story," said Kevin.

"Yeah," said Josh.

"Would you like to hear about the time Nancy and I whooped the Grays?"

Kevin, now more aware of his friend's condition than ever, said, "We sure would, but I think we have to get Josh here some antacid."

"Or to a bathroom," Josh half said as they left.

"You been to Arthur's, I'd guess?" Buck called after.

"Is it that obvious?" said Kevin.

"Sure is," laughed Josh. "You could barbecue a chicken with the sauce you're wearing on your shirt."

Here are a couple of the more interesting things we learned and observed during our visit, to whet your appetite:

- Josh Gibson hit the longest home runs ever in many big league parks, including Forbes Field, Crosley Field, and Yankee Stadium. The Bronx shot reportedly left the building, a feat accomplished by no Yankee, or any other Major League player.

- From an article in the Wichita Beacon, June 21, 1925: "The Wichita Klan No. 6 baseball team played the all black Wichita Monrovians. The game came off without a hint of violence. The Monrovians beat the Klan 10–8."

- Leroy "Satchel" Paige was known as much for his crowd-pleasing charisma and phenomenal longevity as for his achievements on the mound. During the 1930s and 1940s he was perhaps baseball's biggest gate attraction. He was the ultimate showman, whose only MLB counterpart was Gashouse Gang

pitcher Dizzy Dean. Dean once boasted, "If Satch and I was pitching (on the same team), we'd clinch the pennant by the fourth of July, and go fishing until World Series time."

- In an effort to make games convenient for working folks, Kansas City Monarchs owner J. L. Wilkinson mortgaged his property to build baseball's first lighted field to facilitate night baseball. The first night game took place in March 1930, five years before the Cincinnati Reds came to the same conclusion and installed lights at Crosley Field in 1935.

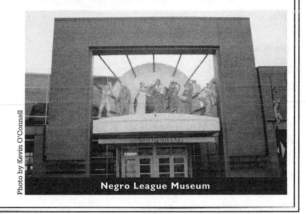

Photo by Kevin O'Connell

Negro League Museum

SCHWEIGERT HOT DOG (Dog Rating)

The Ninth Best Hot Dog in the Majors

A tradition in the upper Midwest, these Schweigert dogs have been heading south and east in recent years. They can be found deliciously grilled inside the stadium at many stands, but also on rollers at other stands. So avoid the roller dogs and get a grilled one.

BEST OF THE REST

Missouri and Kansas are in an area of the country where the South meets the Midwest, and that qualifies as "brat country" in our book. **Sheboygan** cased meats are slightly salty and quite delicious. Brats, Italians, and kosher beef dogs are available. The hot Polish brat is very hot and good, but if you're looking for Polska kielbasa, you've come to the wrong place. This

is a spicy spin on the old favorite with hot-pepper seeds right in the meat. Better get the large drink when ordering this one.

If you can order a meatball sub at a genuine Italian joint, you know it's authentic. **Torre's Pizzeria**, a KC favorite since 1978, is located behind Section 110. The pizza is better than your normal pie and well worth a try.

The **hand-squeezed lemonade** is just that...hand squeezed. Vendors carry these large drinks to fans in the stands. If you want to make sure it's the real thing, take a look for yourself. You'll find half a lemon floating in every cup.

SAY "NO, THANKS," AND WALK AWAY

The **Cantina at K** is a good place to get a margarita. Stay away from the other offerings, especially the tamales. These would have Fernando Valenzuela looking to the heavens for relief of a different sort.

STADIUM SUDS

Boulevard Pale Ale from the Boulevard Brewing Company is the most noteworthy beer on tap, among ubiquitous macrobrews.

Josh: "I like it: Not too hoppy and with a nice finish."

Kevin: "I need another sampling to make my final decision."

Josh: "You always need another sampling, don't you?"

The Kauffman Stadium Experience

Kauffman Stadium doesn't look like Wrigley or Fenway, and the fans aren't as actively involved as they are at those ballparks either. At Kauffman, baseball is to be enjoyed the way these folks enjoy life: at a calmer and much more laid-back pace. The park is mellow, and so are the fans. And while visitors from the East may consider the experience slower than the hardball in their hometowns, the passion for baseball runs deep in the Kansas City fans, even if they express it less vocally. So sit back, get yourself some barbecue, listen to the fountain, and enjoy.

SLUGGER

A lion with a mane that dips and rises like a golden crown, the Royals' mascot Slugger wears number 00 on the back of his home uniform. Slugger often brings the crowd to its feet with his Brat-cannon. This we liked. We were slightly disturbed however to later observe Slugger walking into a first-level ladies' room after the eighth inning. Slugger has a mane. That means he's a "he" lion. So what gives?

"BASEBALL IN KC"

Remember that tune from the early 1980s "Talkin' Baseball, Luzinski and Piniella?" Well, the song that has become popularly known as "Talkin' Baseball," was originally titled "Willie, Mickey and the Duke." It was penned by Terry Cashman as a tribute to baseball's golden era of the 1950s and came out in 1981. The Royals have their own version with lyrics modified to highlight Kansas City's baseball past, and they play it over the PA system before the game. We both liked the jingle and applaud the Royals for their creativity. This version needs updating though, as it still claims that the Royals own the "AL West." Hello? The team plays in the Central Division, now that everybody's favorite Bud has realigned the baseball world. The Royals haven't exactly "owned" the A.L. Central either.

THE COLLEGE WORLD SERIES, OMAHA NEBRASKA

Why not plan to be in Kansas City just before the last two weeks of June, so you can head to Rosenblatt Stadium in Omaha, Nebraska, and catch a few games of the College World Series? Though not all that close by, KC is closer than any other Major League city. And the CWS is a must for any serious hardball fan. Sure they use aluminum bats that make that annoying "dink" sound, and sure it may seem like Florida State, LSU, and Texas are always in it, but it's a fun trip and not too terribly expensive. And think how lucky the folks were who saw a younger (and slimmer) Roger Clemens seize the CWS stage and throw the fastball that would carry him to the big leagues and to the Hall of Fame after it brought his Texas Longhorns a College World Series title.

CINCINNATI REDS,
GREAT AMERICAN BALLPARK

A Ballpark Befitting the Senior Circuit's Eldest Team

CINCINNATI,
OHIO

220 miles to Cleveland
257 miles to Pittsburgh
250 miles to Chicago
311 miles to St. Louis

THE CINCINNATI REDS are the oldest team in professional baseball, dating from 1869. Now, with the 2003 opening of Great American Ballpark, the Reds have the best of the many baseball parks in their long history. Great American provides the natural playing surface, charm, and the intimacy of Crosley Field, as well as the festive location on the banks of the Ohio River that Riverfront/Cinergy Stadium provided. The river meanders just beyond the center and right field fences providing a rustic backdrop for baseball.

Perhaps the most distinctive feature of Great American is the Gap, a large notch along the third-base line that separates the upper deck into two sections. The Gap opens the interior of the ballpark up to the city, providing lucky folks who work in the buildings along Sycamore Street a peek in at the game from their offices.

There plenty more that's distinctive about Great American, starting with the fact that it is an incomparably better place to see a game than its predecessor. The first row of seats has been tucked slightly below the level of the playing surface. With innovations like this, it's easy to see that the architects designed the ballpark with the fans in mind. HOK of Kansas City again put its stamp on a ballpark built in Reds country, serving as the primary architects for Great American. HOK was assisted locally by GBBN architects of Cincinnati. These designers also built in a double-decked bleacher section in left field that is evocative of Crosley Field, as well as other parks built in that classic era. It remains to be seen if the winds off the river that helped right-handed hitters at Riverfront will be a factor at Great American, as the angle of the field still faces the river, but has been altered approximately twenty degrees.

The exterior of Great American Ballpark is much inspired by Jacobs Field in Cleveland. The main structure of the seating bowl is supported

homeplate

Photo by Meghan Coughlin

One reason the price tag was relatively high when compared with similar new parks built recently was that Great American was built on land directly adjacent to Riverfront. Though additional property costs were low, an enormous section from the left field foul pole to right-center field was removed from Riverfront to make room for the construction. For two full seasons the Reds played with a huge forty-foot tarp, known as the Black Monster, in right-center field. It's ironic that in order to make way for a new park, the destruction of this huge segment opened up the old cookie-cutter to the Ohio River, and with the addition of natural turf, Riverfront finally took on the look of an open ballpark itself. Cutting the stadium open was akin to the time Kevin cut the roof off his Corvair to make a convertible. But perhaps teams that are stuck with their cookie-cutters can take heed and come to the realization that much can be done to convert existing stadiums into more ballpark-friendly facilities.

It's sad that the oldest franchise in baseball had to play in perhaps the worst cookie-cutter stadium ever conceived. With four tiers of seating, Riverfront was as sterile a structure as any of its cloned brethren. But the architects, Heery, Heery, and Finch, managed to find ways to make it worse than most. Not only was it built on the edge of the beautiful Ohio River with no view of the water or downtown, but Riverfront had artificial turf for nearly all of its history. To make matters worse, the entire structure was shrouded with parking lots and was even built on top of an enormous car lot. That's right, cars were actually parked beneath

by huge white painted steel girders, while the surrounding buildings—only three stories tall—are made of red brick and cast stone, and separate the ballpark from the nearby freeway. Most fans enter the park through the Crosley Terrace, a sculpted plaza that features a pitcher's mound, statues, and landscaped grass that rises to the wall. Inspired by the old park, Crosley Terrace has recreated many of the eccentricities that made Crosley Field unique, but could not be recreated in the new park.

Financing negotiations for Great American dragged on for years, largely because the Reds were wary of spending great sums of their own money on the project. But in March of 1996 Hamilton County taxpayers approved a sales tax increase, one one-half cent per dollar, to finance separate facilities for the National Football League Bengals and the Reds. The original price tag for both was to be $544 million, but Paul Brown Stadium alone exceeded that amount. Great American came in at $297 million. The Great American Insurance Company paid $75 million to procure the naming rights.

the infield. Convenient, yes, ballparklike, no. Perhaps all these reasons prompted Cubs pitcher Jon Lieber to state after pitching the 2002 season opener at Cinergy, "Cincinnati is a great town. But that stadium . . . it's just like a big ashtray." And we must agree. In all of our travels, we've never found the multipurpose stadium that works, nor have we found the architect that has come up with the much sought-after design that successfully merges the rectangular gridiron with the triangle pitch of the baseball diamond.

Perhaps only in Seattle was there a bigger roar of cheers and mass cries of relief than in the Queen City, when Reds fans eagerly watched Riverfront implode on December 29, 2002. It took 1,275 pounds of dynamite and nitroglycerine exploded in successive blasts in a counterclockwise motion to bring the structure crashing down upon itself with an angry groan. The dust cloud from the exploding "ashtray" plumed up into the skies, as winds carried the smoke along the banks of the Ohio River. The entire process only took thirty-seven seconds.

But Riverfront was virtually packed to the rafters during many of its thirty-two seasons, and it was the site of the most exciting moments in Reds history. On June 30, 1970, the day Riverfront opened, Hank Aaron knocked out the first home run in an 8–2 Braves victory. The inaugural season would also witness the unforgettable moment when Pete Rose barreled over AL catcher Ray Fosse for the decisive run in the All-Star Game. That first season the stadium also played host to the World Series, which the Reds dropped to Baltimore in five games. But the Big Red Machine was just getting revved up.

Many sportswriters and fans point to the 1975 World Series as the best ever, as Bernie Carbo and Carlton Fisk lifted Josh's Red Sox to victory in Game 6, only to have the Reds rally from a 3–0 deficit in Game 7 on a two-run home run by Tony Perez and a single in the ninth inning by Joe Morgan to win the Series, in Boston yet. The Big Red Machine repeated as world champs in 1976 sweeping all seven playoff games, three versus the Phillies in the NLCS, and four against the Yankees in the World Series. The 1976 Reds led the Majors in an incredible ten categories that included batting average, stolen bases, doubles, triples, home runs, runs scored, slugging percentage, fewest errors, field percentage, and saves. Without a doubt, the 1976 incarnation of the Reds was the best team Cincinnati ever produced and ranks among the best baseball teams of all time. Reds fans feel there is no room to argue: they were the best ever. Period.

Over the years, Riverfront also witnessed the tying or shattering of two of baseball's most impressive records. On April 4, 1974, Hank Aaron hit his 714th home run there to tie Babe Ruth's all-time record. And then, on a kinder September 11th in 1985, Pete Rose broke the all-time hits record when he singled in the first inning off Padres pitcher Eric Show. It was the 4,192nd hit of Rose's stellar career, and Ty Cobb was rumored to have rolled over in his grave. Perhaps Cobb cursed Rose, because four years later "Charlie Hustle" was handed a lifetime ban from baseball for gambling.

Kevin: "I guess the 'Hustle' nickname wasn't for Rose's on-field heroics alone."

Josh: "Classy, as always."

After the Rose scandal, the Reds bounced back the following season to win the 1990 World Series over the heavily favored Oakland A's behind their "Nasty Boys." No, the Reds didn't invite a boy band to sing the National Anthem, the Nasty's were a trio of Cincinnati relievers—Norm Charlton, Randy Myers, and Rob Dibble. Their combined ERA in the Series was 0.00 in 8.2 innings pitched.

The success of the franchise while at River-front certainly wasn't predicted by owner Bill DeWitt, who before the stadium was built favored the idea of a baseball-only facility in the suburbs, à la Candlestick Park. But city officials were bent on a publicly funded stadium on the banks of the Ohio River that would also house the football franchise they were courting. When the NFL awarded Cincinnati the Bengals in 1966, plans went ahead for a multipurpose facility, the kind that was being built in so many cities across the country. DeWitt, a man of convictions, eventually sold the club rather than approve the Reds' lease at the new stadium. Riverfront would draw two million fans in eight consecutive seasons during the heart of the Big Red Machine dynasty (1973–1980). To put that in perspective, Crosley Field only drew one million fans four times in its eighty-six-year history.

Prior to Riverfront, the Reds had played in a great variety of ballparks, built and rebuilt on only a few locations. The undefeated Red Stockings of 1869 (57–0) called Union Grounds their home, currently the site of Union Terminal. The Reds wouldn't lose a game until 1870, going an amazing one-hundred-thirty contests in a row without a loss. Though some of those games weren't exactly against elite competition, the achievement is noteworthy nonetheless.

The Red Legs remained at Union Grounds until moving to Avenue Grounds on Spring Grove Avenue in 1876, the inaugural year of the National League. But in 1884 when the Queen City franchise of the upstart Player's League snatched up the lease on Avenue Grounds, the Reds had to move to an old brickyard at the corner of Western Avenue and Findlay Street. The yard was cleaned up and made ready for baseball. A grandstand was erected, and the brickyard was renamed League Park. The deepest part of the outfield in left had an incline that rose four feet up to the outfield wall. An underground stream caused the ballpark's signature deformity that eventually took on the nickname "the Terrace" when players began to hit the ball far enough for it to become a factor. The Terrace, as crazy and wonderful an outfield quirk as there ever was, remained until the park (by then named Crosley Field) closed in 1969. When Babe Ruth switched over to the National League at the end of his career, he fell flat on his face, confounded by his first experience with the Terrace at Crosley.

While it was still called League Park the ballpark's primary grandstands burned down on May 28, 1900. The Reds answered this problem by moving home plate out to where right field had been, thereby making use of the grandstands that hadn't burned. In 1902, perhaps because Cincinnati is named after the Roman dictator Cincinnatus (458 B.C.) the team erected a grandstand using Roman and Greek architectural elements, including columns, cornices, and arches. The new structure was dubbed "Palace of the Fans," and no ballpark had used these architectural elements prior or since.

Josh, who has watched the film *Spartacus* almost as many times as he has watched Ken Burns's baseball documentary, says, "Why the heck not? What a great way to make a park classic and new at the same time."

Nineteen "fashion boxes" adorned the Palace and each could hold up to fifteen well-to-do fans. It was the genesis of the luxury box. Directly beneath these seats were standing room sections called "Rooter's Row," where the less-fashionable fans could crowd on in. It is surely here that Josh and Kevin would have recommended fans spend the game, among their rowdy, odorous, beer swilling, penny-mongering brethren.

After the 1911 season, Reds owner Garry Hermann came to the conclusion that the

Palace of the Fans was too small for the team's rapidly growing fan base, and the structure was demolished. Yet another grandstand was built on the same spot, and this incarnation of the park was called Redland Field, a nickname of the former park. The Reds opened Redland Field a month after Fenway Park opened in Boston on May 18, 1912, with a 10–6 win over the Cubs. The improved ball yard had the look of the parks opening in great numbers across the country. The terrace still rose up to the outfield wall, but now there were bleachers in the outfield. Very much like Fenway, the bleachers in right center began with just a single seat, with rows added angling back toward a full-square bleacher section in right field. This angled point in right center was known as the "Sun Deck" (and later the "Moon Deck" during night games) and is a feature replicated at Great American Ballpark.

The infamous World Series of 1919 is a sticking point for many in the Queen City. Reds fans feel that the blemish of the Black Sox scandal tainted their very first World Series victory and feel the Reds would have won the best-of-nine championship series regardless of the supposed "fix" the Sox had on. Of course, what would you expect them to say? "We really should have been crushed and our World Series title is completely bogus"? Not likely, but the black mark on the Sox also has a flip side, a sadly tainted title for the Cincinnati team.

In 1934 Powel Crosley bought the Reds, and renamed the ballpark after himself. In order to attract more fans, the first night game in Major League Baseball history was played at Crosley Field on May 24, 1935. More than twenty thousand fans gathered to watch baseball beneath the glowing incandescent canopy provided by 632 lights. While day games had been averaging just over forty-five hundred fans, the new night games averaged more than eighteen thousand for the remainder of the season. The night-game experiment had worked.

On January 26, 1937, a local creek overflowed its banks and handed Cincinnati the worst flood in its history. Twenty-one feet of water stood atop the infield of Crosley when the creek finally crested. But two Reds pitchers, Lee Grissom and Gene Schott, used the opportunity to stage perhaps the most memorable stunt in Reds history when they paddled a rowboat along Western Avenue and over the waterfall pouring over the outfield wall.

Over the years several Negro League franchises made attempts at teams in Cincinnati, none with more than a few seasons of success. From 1934 to 1937 Cincinnati was home to the Tigers, who enjoyed moderate success as an independent team. The Tigers' most famous player was Ted "Double Duty" Radcliffe, who got his name because he would pitch the first game of a doubleheader, then serve as catcher in the second game. In 1942 the Cincinnati Buckeyes left after only one season for Cleveland. The Cincinnati Clowns played in 1943, then the Cincinnati-Indianapolis Clowns (no relation) played in the Negro American League from 1944 to 1945, calling both towns home. Indianapolis became the Clowns' sole home in 1946.

Crosley Field would continue to be expanded and touched up over the years. Double-decked outfield bleachers were constructed in anticipation of a 1938 playoff run that did not occur. But this feature of the park was so beloved that it has also been included in the left field bleachers of Great American Ballpark. In 1957 a new fifty-eight-foot-tall scoreboard, topped with the famous Longines Clock, replaced the existing board at Crosley and became the ballpark's signature piece. The scoreboard and analog clock at Great American Ballpark are reminiscent of the familiarly looming clock at Crosley.

Getting a Choice Seat

This ballpark is brand spankin' new and the Reds fans who have paid so dearly for it are enjoying it. And so are road-tripping ball fans. That said, sellouts have not occurred to a great degree in the early days of the ballpark, surely not to the degree that other new ballparks have enjoyed. Various reasons have been cited, but the results point to only one thing: getting a ticket at Great American is not very difficult.

Club Seats (Sections 1–6, 23–29, 122–126, 220–228, 301–307)

Never have we seen more club seating in a ballpark. But, we suppose all these richies pay a great deal so that us cheap-seat hunters don't have to. Sections 1 through 6 of Diamond seats go for two and a quarter bills (that's Franklins, bub, not Washingtons) but all the chicken wings and Milwaukee's Best you can put down are available at no extra charge. Damn, it's a good thing for the Reds that we can't afford Diamond seats because Josh can eat his weight in wings and Kevin can drink his weight in cheap beer.

Scout seats, Lower Club, Club Home, and Club Seating all go for right around $50 and offer access to the secret clubhouse. Just don't forget the secret handshake.

Terrace Level (Sections 107–121, 127–139)

The lower bowl has a medium grade to it, steep enough to see over a guy in front of you wearing a large hat, but not too steep. Seats in the first row offer fans the unique experience of having their feet lower than the field of play. We're not sure what this does to enhance the game, but at least you'll know you're that much closer to the action. All seats in the ballpark are red, which makes for a great deal of red when

Sellout Index: 10% of games sell out
Seating Capacity: 42,060
Ticket Office: (513) 765-7000
http://cincinnati.reds.mlb.com

TRIVIA TIMEOUT

Big: What did Reds management do to get the team expelled from the National League for ten years, from 1880 to 1889?
Red: Which Reds hurler is the only Major Leaguer to toss back-to-back no-hitters?
Look for the answers in the text.

the ballpark is not sold out. The overhang is not much of a factor on the first level, but we still recommend avoiding the back few rows.

Terrace Infield Boxes (Sections 113–133) all offer great views at a very reasonable price. Since many of the other seats in the park have some obstruction, these are the seats of choice for the discerning fan who cannot stand to have any obstruction at all.

One unfortunate thing about this ballpark is that it has a low rising wall along the right field side that blocks the view of the corner. Terrace Box Seats (Sections 110–112, 134–136) are good seats other than these minor blockages, though the wall is steeper on the left field side, and thus the seats on that side of the park suffer less.

The right field bull pen has been well placed near the foul pole to eliminate much of the obstruction that it often causes. Terrace Line Seats (Sections 107–109, 137–139) all have blockages of the corners, but Sections 138 and 108 have foul pole obstructions of the outfield, while 107 and 139 have the dreaded infield foul pole obstructions.

Mezzanine Level (Sections 408–419)

This seating section consists of the lower level of the double-decked seats running down the right field line. While in theory we like the idea of creating a replica of Crosley Field's double deck, some of these seats simply have poor sight lines.

The Mezzanine Infield Seats (Sections 415–419) are much preferred, though only Sections 417–419 are free from under-hang obstruction. If you cannot get into these three sections, and an under-hang bothers you, you might do better to sit along the right field side of the ballpark.

The Mezzanine Seats (Sections 408–414) have a variety of problems, and are only two dollars cheaper than the Mezzanine Infield Seats. Sections 408, 409, and part of 410 are obstructed by the lower seats of the Machine Room Grille. In the rest of Section 410 through Section 414 the left field corner is lost to the under-hang of the 400 level.

View Level (Sections 420–437, 509–537)

From the Gap out to right field are four different pricing structures, the best being the View Level Infield Boxes in Sections 420 through 431. These seats are a bit further from the field than their counterparts on the left field side (Mezzanine Infield Seats) but sight lines are perfect in all but the last section, 431. We prefer these seats to all seats on the Mezzanine level, except those in Sections 417 through 419, which are a bit closer for the same price.

The View Level Box seats in Sections 432–437 all have obstructed views of the right field corner, but less so than their left field counterparts. Plus there is the added bonus while sitting on the right field side of enjoying the breeze off the Ohio River on hot summer days.

Above these are the 500 Level View seats. Sections 515 through 531 are called View Level Infield Seats, and we can recommend them, except for Sections 515–516, and 531, which suffer from an appreciable under-hang.

Sections 511 through 514 and 532 through 535 are on the View Level, but offer the second worst views in ballpark. They're distant from

the action, and the under-hang issue increases in severity the farther out you sit.

Lastly and definitely least, are the ill-titled Outer View Level seats in Sections 509, 510, 536, and 537. By the time you get to those seats it will likely be the 5th inning. They're cheap, but bad, so you know the drill. Buy them for cheap bucks and sit somewhere else. Seat-hopping, especially on the third level is fairly easy.

Terrace Outfield and Bleachers (Sections 101–106, 140–146, 401–404)

Yes, we realize that Sections 101 through 106 and 140 through 146 are technically called "Terrace Outfield," but just because they call seats in new movie theaters "mezzanine," doesn't take them out of the balcony.

Josh: "The first-level sections all offer individual seats."

Kevin: "They're still bleachers to me."

Terrace Outfield Seats (Sections 140–146) on the right field side are the new incarnation of the Sun/Moon Deck from old Crosley Field. The steep uncovered section and the low right field wall offers great views of the action. We're not sure if we've seen any outfield seats as well done as these, even at the top of the section. Section 140 has a nice overview of the Reds bull pen. However, avoid seats in Row L and higher in Section 144, as they are severely blocked by the smokestack and paddle wheel feature in center. Otherwise, these sections feel very close and offer great views.

However, the same cannot be said for the Terrace Outfield Seats (Sections 101–106) on the left field side. Not only do these seats feel farther away than their right field counterparts, but there are other problems as well. The left field wall is an electronic out-of-town scoreboard and thus the seating section is significantly higher up. The pitch of the rows is not as steep, and there is an overhang for seats in the upper three rows (N, O, and P). Section 106 also has foul pole issues and should be avoided. The right field Outfield Seats are much better for the same price.

The second tier of the double-decked bleachers are actually called bleachers (Sections 401–406). Apparently the architects at HOK never studied marketing because labeling these seats as 400 level makes them seem even farther away. Though Crosley Field had double-decked bleachers, we doubt if they were as bad as their Great American replicas. Not only is even more of the outfield lost to the underhang, the glass barriers that are used to mark and protect the tunnels also do their fair share of blocking. Far better to pay the extra buck and sit in an unobstructed seat behind home plate in the View Infield Section.

THE BLACK MARKET

Plenty of scalpers hang out along Third Street and are easy to spot by the signage they wear.

SEATING TIP

AS A RULE it is best to sit on the third-base side on the first level of this ballpark. In the upper deck, unless you can get close to "the Gap" (see below) the first-base side is preferable. And as far as the outfield is concerned, it's no contest: right field is better than left.

The best seats for the price in our estimation are on the Mezzanine Level, Section 419, right next to "the Gap." One of the features of the notch is that along with providing excellent views of the city behind, it allows the smaller left field grandstand to be self-supported, and hung in closer. So take advantage of having a close view of the game, an elevated view across the river, and a view of the city through "the Gap," all for under $20. The seats directly across "the Gap" in Section 420 on the Mezzanine Level are the same price, but the section is smaller and doesn't offer as much of that "hanging out in space" feel. But if Section 419 is sold out, 420 is a good option, as are the upper Sections 519 and 520.

They must shop at the same place because all the signs were the same: white with red text that read, "I need tickets." Clearly they were both buying and selling. Scalped tickets for Great American will cost big dollars, at least for a few years, and the scalpers know they have the advantage. Patience is the only thing that can swing the advantage in the road tripper's favor. So hang around and wait them out. As the first pitch approaches, scalpers know their commodity cools off drastically, and you should reap the benefits of rapidly dropping ticket prices. Waiting too long while the Yankees are in town can cause tickets to sell out. This occurrence is otherwise rare, as scalpers buy far more tickets than they can sell. Anything above their profit margin is gravy, so it's easy to tell if they're moving tickets or not. If they pressure you, they need to move their tickets. If they don't pressure you, wait, and you can still get a price that won't clean out your wallet.

If tickets truly are sold out, another option is contacting a "legitimate" ticket broker. There are several located along Third and Fourth Streets. These ticket brokers are perfectly legal in Ohio, but expect to pay a healthy markup. Banks call this a transaction fee. Either way, you pay more.

Before/After the Game

In the days of the parking-lot-encrusted Riverfront there was no neighborhood surrounding the park. There wasn't room for any. The restaurant and bar situation has not improved greatly in the immediate vicinity of the park because, like its cookie-cutter predecessor, Great American is bordered by a freeway, the Ohio River, parking lots, and the US Bank Arena. But a quick venture either into downtown or across the river into Covington, Kentucky, can increase your prospects.

Getting to Great American

From U.S. 50 eastbound, take I-75 northbound or southbound or I-71 Northbound to the Second Street Exit. Turn onto Main Street or Vine Street for downtown garages.

From I-71 southbound or U.S. 50 westbound take the Third Street Exit, then take a left onto Walnut and a left again onto Second for the team garage. Or take the Third Street Exit, then turn right onto Main, Broadway, or Vine for downtown garages.

There is a team parking lot underneath the stands of the ballpark at the corner of Second Street and Pete Rose Way. Well, at least it's not under the infield.

The financial district of Cincinnati, like most financial districts, provides plenty of parking spaces. Garages offer game-time specials because all the suits are getting in their cars and heading home. But here's one better: at the edge of town near the park, after three o'clock, park in a metered spot, load up the meter and stay there all night for less than two dollars. After 5:00 P.M. street parking is free and you're in the clear until 8:00 A.M. the next morning.

The Metro, Cincinnati's bus system is also a great way to get to the park. Also referred to as SORTA, the Southwestern Ohio Regional Transportation Authority can be reached at (513) 621-4455, or on the Web at http://www.sorta.com, for rider information.

Outside the Park

CROSLEY TERRACE REBORN

No new ballpark has paid a bigger tribute to a ballpark of its city's past than Great American has to Crosley Field. The Crosley Terrace Plaza at the corner of Second and Main is the centerpiece of Great American's exterior, if not the entire park. Landscaped grass inclines up at the same grade as the terrace that led up to the outfield wall at Crosley. There are also inscribed bricks scattered about the plaza that helped to finance the park. If you feel like shelling out the coin, feel free to buy a brick while you're in town. Josh made his own for free with some chalk.

We like this area very much, but must point out that being so close to the ticket windows, it gets extremely crowded before hot-ticket games. So either get your tickets well in advance, or get to the ballpark right when it opens, like we do.

Future additions to the plaza are scheduled to include a pitcher's mound built to the dimensions of the day that will support a statue of Joe Nuxhall, who won 135 games—all but five for the Reds—in a sixteen-year career. Some sixty feet and six inches away will be a batter's box where statues of catcher Ernie Lombardi and Ted Kluszewski crouch and hit. Frank Robinson's statue will await in the on-deck circle. Somehow we think it's going to be a while before old Frankie gets to take a swing. Stone benches will be scattered about the plaza creating a parklike atmosphere and will be inscribed with stories and anecdotes of the Crosley Field era.

RIVER BOAT LANDING

Beyond the center field fence is a dock where riverboats drop off passengers coming to the game. There's even a gate beyond center field to let them into the park. The dock is highlighted by a sculpture that features a riverboat paddle wheel with a dozen smokestacks that emit blasts of steam high into the air that are visible from inside the ballpark. The sculpture is a gathering place for children who play in it as if it were a fountain.

The sculpture highlights the riverboating heritage of Cincinnati and is a wonderful incorporation of the continuing relationship between the city and the river. While sitting inside Great American Ballpark, riverboats continuously pass by, giving the ballpark a unique atmosphere. Some are passenger boats taking folks to the game, while others are gambling boats and pleasure cruisers.

HALL OF FAME

Opening in 2004, the Cincinnati Reds Hall of Fame is located at the east end of the ballpark. The hall connects with the ballpark via a bridge and is open year-round. Inside Reds fans will find traveling and permanent exhibits that honor great moments in the baseball history of the most historic team in the league. Carved numbers and plaques honor the Big Red Machine.

ACTUALLY, WE DID PROMISE PETE
A ROSE GARDEN

Located on the exact spot where Pete Rose's 4,192nd hit landed in Riverfront's left field stands a tribute to the man who broke Ty Cobb's all-time hit record. A circle of red roses marks the spot where history was made. And does this town ever love Pete? Cincy has renamed a road "Pete Rose Way" that runs near the ballpark.

Josh: "What are you doing down there?"

Kevin: "Praying."

Josh: "Do I want to know why?"

Kevin: "I'm trying to convince the baseball gods to change the commissioner's mind and allow Pete Rose into the Hall of Fame."

Josh: "But he bet on baseball, maybe even his own team."

Kevin: "I know, but not *against* his team. Plus, he's sorry now. Besides, we forgave Nixon, Jim and Tammy Faye, and even Winona Ryder. What must Pete do to gain entrance into the hall?"

Josh: "How about be sincere? Come on Charlie Hustle, get up off your knees."

WATERING HOLES AND OUTSIDE EATS

A freeway separates the ballpark from downtown Cincinnati, leaving little of that classic urban ballpark feel. Though there are a few places worthy of a visit, we recommend taking the short walk across the river into Kentucky, as there is much more to do there. But first we'll list a few watering holes that are worth stopping in if you're determined to stay in town.

IN BETWEEN TAVERN (307 Sycamore Street)

Directly across the freeway from Great American at the corner of Third and Sycamore is the In Between Tavern, offering patio seating for warm days, and complete with umbrellas and wait service. It's a no-frills kind of place and will be crowded on game days. Many pictures of old Reds players adorn the walls inside, as well as the famous "WE WIN" headline from the local newspaper. The food is typical pub grub fare, with burgers and chicken sandwiches in the $5 to $7 range.

HEAD FIRST SPORTS CAFÉ (218 Third Street)

This sports bar is small inside but does have pool tables and dartboards. Eclectic sports memorabilia hangs on the walls: everything from baseball to the Kentucky Derby to golf to college football. Catering much more to the Bengals crowd, this is the kind of place you go to if you want to see a lingerie show with your beer. But we're not promising anything.

TINA'S BAR (350 W. Fourth Street)

Though Tina's is a sports bar, it caters more to football and race fans than baseball fans, likely because Tina's is much closer to the new football stadium than it is to Great American. A nice offering from Tina's is the happy hour between 4:00 P.M. and 6:00 P.M. when drafts are $2. If you're thinking that perhaps this a good place to lube up before a night game, we agree. But it is a significant walk to the ballpark, so it depends on how much you like cheap beer. On the day we visited two guys in the back were playing a game with a beanbag that looked an awful lot like TossAcross.

MONTGOMERY INN (Boathouse, 925 Eastern Avenue; Original, 9440 Montgomery Road)

If the barbecue pork and chicken sandwiches at Great American Ballpark have you hankering for some serious barbecue ribs, why not head for the source? With three locations in the area, this longstanding Cincinnati institution has been Q'en it up right since the 1950s. Though on the pricey side of the ledger, the lunch menu is reasonable, and all entrées will tingle the taste buds. Upstairs at the Boathouse location is a room full of Cincinnati sports memorabilia.

FOR THOSE WILLING TO GO THE EXTRA MILE

For a better selection of bars and restaurants, we recommend taking the short walk across the bridge into Covington Landing, Kentucky, or parking there initially and then crossing the bridge to get to the game. Either way, this is the hot spot in the area. It may seem a tad seedy with check-cashing places, pawn shops, liquor stores, tattoo parlors, and strip clubs. Trust us, this is the place to go, especially after the game. Josh didn't feel nervous at all, and if Josh feels safe, most folks will *certainly* feel safe.

B AND J FISH BAR (336 Scott Street)

If it's fish you crave, the B&J has a whiting three-piece dinner with fries—nice and cheap. Other good choices are the cod, catfish, and perch combo meals. This order-at-the-counter fish bar is open Monday through Friday 11:00 A.M. to 9:00 P.M., so it's best to hit it on the way to the game.

JACK QUINN'S IRISH ALE HOUSE
(112 E. 4th Street)

Though not sports related, Jack Quinn's is one of the nicer Irish places in this part of Kentucky. It's a great place for a pint of Guinness and a bite of boxty. Kevin says, "And sure, Irish bars are brilliant for getting liquored up in, aren't they now?" Jack Quinn's is open until midnight.

SONOMA (Corner of East Third Street and Park)

Sonoma is a wine bar and a tad upscale. Definitely not a T-shirt and flip flops kind of place. Entrées start at $20, and feature Sonoma Valley filet, grilled steak, Atlantic salmon, and sesame-seared tuna.

T.G.I. FRIDAYS (1 Madison Avenue)

Okay, it's a chain, but this franchise is at a really cool location down on the riverbanks in an old converted riverboat. Kevin still disapproves.

Inside the Ballpark

Reds fans and baseball road trippers who visited Riverfront will be impressed with the improved experience that Great American offers. Ballparks that offer city views and those built near bodies of water hold a special place in our hearts. Great American offers both aplenty. Beyond the outfield fence, the Ohio River drifts past lazily, with its riverboats and bridges in full view. The Gap ties the city skyline with the interior of the ballpark. And while the Reds office buildings that surround the park aren't tucked right up next to the seating bowl, they serve a different purpose. Rather than being merely a brick facade intended to decrease the impact of a high seating bowl, the buildings at Great American are separate and give the folks inside the ballpark a bit of breathing space, while also acting as a sound barrier from the nearby freeways.

The Clock From Crosley

Though not the original Longines Clock that sat above the scoreboard at Crosley Field, the clock at Great American is a good re-creation. In this digital age, there is something very fitting about having an old-time analog clock looming above a baseball park, keeping our minds set to all the history and richness of the National Pastime. Well done, Cincinnati.

Grass and Glass Batter's Eye

The batter's eye at Great American is also a nice nod to Crosley Field. The lower section is comprised of several tiers of grass, recalling the Crosley Terrace outfield. Above the grass are large vertical segments of black glass. While the area is attractive, there's more than meets the eye. Behind the glass is a party room that can accommodate up to one hundred seventy people, and is available for rent. How much does it cost? More than we had between us.

BIG RED PARTY MACHINE

To completely contradict what we just said about the old-time feel of the clock, the Reds have installed a "celebration machine" in the outfield that stands sixty-four feet high and thirty-six feet wide. With two large smokestacks, a riverboat paddle wheel, and a misting machine located somewhere inside, this machine celebrates whenever something good happens for the Reds by shooting fireworks, making noise, and spewing mist all over the place. Sounds a little bit like how Kevin "celebrates" after he's had a few beers. While we are rarely fans of these types of attractions (aren't wins and home runs celebration enough in their own right?) the Big Red Party Machine (as we have dubbed it) is definitely a feature not seen in any other park, and one that reminds us of Bill Veeck's exploding scoreboard at Comiskey. Plus it acts as a misting station, cooling folks down on hot days.

Wide-open Concourses

Modern ballparks need wide concourses. Let's face it, we Americans aren't getting any thinner. And there are a lot of us these days. At Great American Ballpark most concourses are forty feet wide, as compared to the concourses that were twenty feet wide at Riverfront. In addition to their width these concourses provide excellent opportunities to keep an eye on the game while walking around the park, getting a dog, or taking care of other business. To top it all off, the upper deck has its own concourse that offer views of the field. This feature makes the upper deck feel more open and should be copied by ballparks everywhere.

Dedications to Immortal Reds

Just inside the main entrance of the ballpark are two tiled murals honoring the two most significant moments in Reds history. The first mural, titled "The First Nine," represents the 1869 Red Stockings, the first professionally paid baseball team. The second mural, "The Great Eight," honors the 1975 Reds. The Big Red Machine, which won one-hundred-eight games that year, is widely considered the best starting eight of all time.

Kevin: "The ninth guy on the team must be feeling not so great."

Josh: "The ninth guy was a different pitcher each night. The eight spots are for the position players."

Big Red Machine mural

Photo by Kevin O'Connell

Kevin: "Right. I knew that. Still."

Enriching the concourse's interior are photographs rendered in glass of great Reds moments, year by year. The second-level concourse features a quote band with entries from players all around baseball. One of our favorites is from Roy Campanella: "You gotta be a man to play baseball for a living, but you gotta have a lot of little boy in you too." Well said, Roy.

Retired Reds Numbers

Hanging from the exposed concrete just below the press level behind home plate, the team's retired numbers (in red) honor the great Reds throughout the years.

Number 42 belongs of course to Jackie Robinson.

Number 1 belonged to Fred Hutchinson, the manager who led the Reds to ninety-plus win seasons three times during his career, which was cut short, as his life was, by cancer. Hutchinson's number was the first ever to be retired by the Reds. See the Seattle chapter for more information on "Hutch."

Number 5 was the jersey Johnny Bench wore when he won his ten Gold Gloves, made fourteen All-Star appearances and collected two NL MVP awards. Bench is perhaps the most recognizable name of a catcher even to this day, as he led the Big Red Machine to consecutive World Series titles in 1975 and 1976. And he was a regular on Josh's second-favorite TV show of all time—*The Baseball Bunch*—to boot. "We have a hunch you'll love the baseball bunch."

Number 8 was second baseman Joe Morgan's number. Morgan, who won the NL MVP in both 1975 and 1976, collected 689 stolen bases, 1,133 RBI, and 268 homers during his twenty-two-year career.

Reds fans honor Number 18 Ted Kluszewski as their greatest left-handed first-baseman. On defense Big Klu led the NL in fielding percentage for five straight seasons, 1951–55. Surely he would have won the Gold Glove Award those years had it existed. He hit 1,028 RBI and 279 home runs in his career, including a whopping 49 in 1954. He finished his career with a batting average of .298.

Number 20 belonged to Frank Robinson, a twelve-time All-Star. Robinson hit 586 home runs in his career, fifth on the all-time tally. He hit 38 in his rookie season, easily winning the ROY award. In 1961 he won the NL MVP Award hitting for a .323 average, 37 HR, and 124 RBI.

Number 24 was worn by the heart of the Big Red Machine, Tony Perez. Playing for an amazing twenty-three seasons, Perez was a seven-time All-Star and MVP of the 1967 Midsummer Classic.

The Reds got into the retiring-of-numbers game a bit late, putting up the display for the first time in 1996. Perhaps this explains why most of the players retired are from the more recent era of baseball, when the team has such a long history. We wondered why Johnny Vander Meer's jersey hasn't been retired. After all, he threw back-to-back no-hitters for the Reds on June 11 and June 15, 1938.

Kevin: "Back-to-back no hitters: what does a guy have to do?"

Josh: "Well, it seems like a .500 record should be a prerequisite for having one's number retired. And even with his two no-no's the Dutch Master was only 119–121 in his career."

Kevin: "You looked that up on the Internet, didn't you?"

Stadium Eats

Great American offers a large selection of food options, though we have to admit being a bit confused at first. The signs on the stands ranged from the Fowl Pole Grill to Tex-Mex, though we found little correspondence to the items being sold. We don't know if it was simply because we went to the ballpark in its inaugural season and they hadn't worked out the kinks yet or what. But we quickly learned to ignore the signs above and simply read the menus to determine what each stand was selling.

Two restaurants in the corners of the ballpark cater to fans seeking varying price ranges. We found plenty of fans in **The Machine Room Grill and Microbrewery** before the game escaping the humid Cincinnati weather in the AC. Located on the 200 Level in the left field corner, the Machine Room is a better sports bar than you'll find in the area surrounding the ballpark, and one of the best places to see memorabilia of Cincinnati's Big Red Machine. The Machine Room is open before and after the game to fans with tickets.

Kevin: "And it's open on nongame days to fans . . . without tickets?"

Josh: "Guess so."

The other restaurant option for club members is the **Riverfront Club**, located in the right field corner. This place is more upscale, with tiered seating and white tablecloths. Not our scene. Another area for club members only is the **Fox Sports Net Club 4192**, located on the first-base side of the ballpark. All they have to say is "club" and we want no part of it.

MONTGOMERY INN BBQ (Trademark Food)
Barbecue pork and chicken sandwiches are available at the ballpark from this longtime Cincinnati griller. This was some of the best barbecue we had on the entire road trip. Tangy tangy tangy, with just a hint of spiciness, these sandwiches are served with a fork to eat the meat that comes piling out of the bun.

KAHN'S HOT DOG (Dog Rating)
The Twenty-seventh Best Hot Dog in the Majors
This Kahn's dog disappointed us quite a bit, though we're not sure the folks serving it gave the dog a fair shake. We were hard pressed to find a Kahn's dog that wasn't heated up on rollers. While there are grilled dogs at the park, this fact alone kept the dog in the bottom tier. Plus it was cold when we sampled it.

While we're not big fans of the Kahn's dog, there are plenty of other dog choices at Great American that are more than worthy. Kevin sampled a very tasty all-beef grilled kosher dog, from Best. It was one of the "best" all-beef grilled kosher dogs that he'd had. The Red Hot Smokey is another great dog option. The Skyline Cheese Coney Dogs are a big seller and could easily be a trademark food on their own. Piled over with chili and cheddar cheese, Josh could hardly control himself.

BEST OF THE REST
Cheese Fries are a nice option for those who like their deep-fried foods. Fried on the spot but not overly greasy, the fries were warm all the way to the bottom. And the cheese sauce had a nice spice to it. If it's the same cheese sauce that they use for the nachos and the pretzels, we can recommend those as well.

Davey's Cones offers many ice-cream options beyond just the average cone. Sundaes are available, and are pretty good. Clearly better than Dippin' Dots, ice cream of the future—whatever that is.

Another food choice that we'd never seen anywhere else before that is worth a mention

---

CINCINNATI STYLE CHILI

SKYLINE CHILI is a minor phenomenon in Cincinnati, as they prepare it their own unique "ways." Unlike Texas-style chili, which you've undoubtedly sampled before, the classic three-way Cincinnati style is served over spaghetti and covered with shredded cheese. Four-way adds onions or red beans to the three-way mix. Five-way adds red beans and cheese. While Skyline has stands at the ballpark, you cannot as of yet, get chili there, other than on a hot dog.

is the fried bologna sandwich offered at Great American. It's better than it sounds.

Josh: "Mmmm. Fried bologna, just like Grandma used to make."

Kevin: "It sounds gross."

Josh: "Come on, try it . . . I tried the Ichi-roll in Seattle."

Kevin: "No, if you'll recall, you did not try the Ichi-roll."

Josh: "Really, I thought I did."

SAY "NO, THANKS," AND WALK AWAY

Probably the worst food at this ballpark is the **Pete's Pizza**. Though we like the name (after Rose) the pizza itself should only be an option if you have a child who will throw a convulsive tantrum if he is not allowed to eat pizza at the game. In this case, go ahead, by all means, and buy some.

The wine and cheese stands represent something that ballparks should refrain from—catering to yuppies. This kind of food belongs in the luxury boxes, not out here among the real fans.

STADIUM SUDS

Great American Ballpark features much the same beers available everywhere else in the Western world with one exception: Redlegg Ale. This microbrew specialty is brewed by **Barrel House Brewing Company**, located at 22 E. 12th Street in Cincinnati.

The neighborhood is a bit dicey if you're planning to visit. But this brew is not too shabby, and we like the name.

Speaking of suds, the Redlegs were expelled from the National League in 1880, in part for selling beer at the ballpark. This outrage kept the Reds out of the NL for ten seasons. They were reinstated in 1890, and thus far they have stuck.

Kevin: "Did you know Sam Adam's, Boston's most famous microbrew, is actually brewed right here in Cincinnati?"

Josh: "It isn't. I've taken the tour of the brewery in Boston."

Kevin: "True, but a great majority of the product is brewed here."

Josh: "I hate you for telling me that."

The Great American Ballpark Experience

Reds fans are a serious breed, an army of devotees all donning their team colors. The Queen City accomplished big things in the 1970s and is looking to repeat that magical decade with another dynasty led by the often injured Ken Griffey. Great American is fairly unproven when it comes to how the ballpark will play. It hasn't been determined yet whether winds that can swirl off the Ohio River will play well for pitchers or hitters. And these factors will surely decide how the new-look Reds build their team for success.

Though the park has opened to mixed reviews, mostly stemming from the fact that sight lines are poorer than at other newer ballparks, one thing is certain: Cincinnati fans love their Reds with a passion that is infectious, and attending a game at Great American Ballpark will not disappoint—provided you have a copy of our book to help you get the most out of the experience.

GAPPER AND MR. RED

While most every Reds fan is rabid as heck and will talk your ear off to no end about the 1975 Big Red Machine and how it was the greatest team ever assembled, there are two fans who supercede all the rest.

Mr. Red is a seam-head if there ever was one. He's a mascot whose actual head is an oversized ball. Mr. Red cheers for the RedLegs during games, and attends functions all over Cincinnati while they're away. He has represented the Reds very well over the years.

Gapper is a much more recent addition to the Reds rooting crew. With a furry red face and

WHY NOT visit all four incarnations of Crosley Field? The first is Crosley Terrace, at the main entrance of the park. The second is a plaque located at the corner of Findlay and Western Streets that marks the actual location of Crosley Field. It's now a janitorial supply company, but six seats from the original park sit outside the front door.

The third and perhaps most comprehensive Crosley Field relic is located in Blue Ash, Ohio. Part of Crosley Sports Complex, the ballpark features replica baseball fields, including one of Crosley complete with the banked outfield: 328 feet to left, 370 to the gap in left, 383 to the power alley, 390 to straightaway center, 360 to the right field alley, and 366 feet down the right field line. And most impressively, the actual Longines Clock sits atop a replica scoreboard from old Crosley Field, looming above the outfield walls. Notice that the batting lineups for the final game at Crosley, June 24, 1970, against the Giants, are forever memorialized on the scoreboard. The ticket booths and a section of seats were brought over from the old park as well.

It's at this new Crosley Field that the Reds play their old-timers games, and the Big Red Machine games for charity. There's even a field built to replicate Riverfront, with its same dimensions.

Along the outside of the dugout are plaques dedicated to Dave Concepcion, Dave Parker, Johnny Bench, Caesar Geronimo, George Foster, Blue Moon Odom, Danny Ozark, Ken Griffey, Sr., Walt Terrell, Pete Rose, and plenty of others. Many plaques are autographed. Some players have written their uniform numbers as well as their names on their plaques, and some have drawn smiley faces. Josh tried unsuccessfully to trace several autographs onto a ball.

To get to the Crosley Sports Complex take Route 71 to Exit 15, which is the Blue Ash Exit. Follow Glendale Milford Road toward Blue Ash. Turn right onto Kenwood Road, another right on Cornell Road, then take a left onto Grooms Road. The address is 11540 Grooms Road.

The fourth Crosley Field existed across the River in Kentucky, but was torn down when the Blue Ash incarnation of the park was built. So maybe you shouldn't plan on visiting that one. But three out of four ain't bad, right?

---

a blue nose, Gapper appeals to the youngsters of all ages in the Great American crowd.

THIS PLACE IS JUST BATTY

Whether on your way to St. Louis or Kansas City, or just finding an extra day in the road trip itinerary, why not head down to Louisville, Kentucky, and pay a visit to the Louisville Slugger Museum and Factory? Located at 800 W. Main Street in Louisville, the museum is easy to spot. The world's tallest baseball bat, one-hundred-twenty feet high, leans up against the side of the building, and is the exact replica of Babe Ruth's own Louisville Slugger. Well, perhaps Ruth's was a tad smaller.

Inside the museum, there are plenty of actual bats used by players such as Hank Aaron and Ty Cobb and others, plus a fine collection of rare and period baseball bats and equipment. There's even an interactive exhibit that gives you the feel of standing in the batter's box while a ninety-mile-per-hour fastball whizzes past. After visiting the museum take a tour of the Louisville Slugger bat factory. Admission is $6 and everyone gets a free miniature bat. Call (502) 588-7228 for details, or check them out online at http://www.sluggermuseum.org.

PITTSBURGH PIRATES, PNC PARK

The Steel City Forges Hardball Haven

PITTSBURGH, PENNSYLVANIA

132 miles to Cleveland
290 miles to Baltimore
300 miles to Cincinnati
335 miles to Detroit

DURING THE 1970s the Pirates and the city of Pittsburgh loved their cookie-cutter Three Rivers Stadium. And though it looked like all the others, with its artificial turf and multisport adaptability, why shouldn't they have? The Pirates won two World Series during the decade and the NFL Steelers advanced to three Super Bowls, two of which they captured for Steeltown, USA. At the time, Three Rivers was widely considered the crown jewel in this little "City of Champions."

But as the saying goes, "Winning ain't everything." What was lacking wasn't championship rings or the community spirit that accompanies them. Pittsburgh baseball purists were haunted by the ghost of a beautiful ballpark they'd once enjoyed: their own steel green cathedral called Forbes Field. The brown dirt, the green grass, the blue seats, the brick walls, and the cozy confines Forbes had provided for so many years howled and moaned in the memories of old-timers seated in cavernous Three Rivers.

As the small-market Pirates steadily lost key players and then games to their wealthier rivals in the 1990s, attendance at Three Rivers dramatically suffered. And let's be honest, despite its rich baseball history, "the Burgh" has always been primarily a football town (despite the Steelers originally bearing the "Pirates" moniker). When the local nine failed to produce wins, folks stopped turning out to watch them play.

But how strange and wonderful the baseball gods can be. For Pittsburgh responded to its flagging attendance by building the most intimate, and perhaps most beautiful ball yard of the recent ballpark renaissance. On April 9, 2001, the Bucs opened PNC Park at North Shore, which not only brought back natural grass to the Burgh, but synthesized many elements of the old-time ballparks with the best elements of the

Allegheny River

Photo by Kevin O'Connell

new. PNC is the Pirates' fifth home and is very much an alloy of Pittsburgh's storied baseball past, combining features of the other parks the Pirates called home.

And equally as important, PNC was built with unique local materials. Steel has been used in every ballpark and stadium since the construction of Forbes Field, but it is a featured part of the beauty and strength of PNC. There is more exposed steel, decorative brushed steel, and featured steel design elements at PNC than at any other ballpark, and nowhere is it more fitting than in Pittsburgh, the city that made U.S. Steel king. A trademark yellow limestone called Kasota stone replaced the red brick that has nearly become a retro cliché, used in eight of the eleven retro ballparks built in the last twelve years. The distinctive warm color of this stone not only gives the park a unique look among its peers, but is also used in other buildings in Pittsburgh, helping to synthesize the ballpark and the city into one, building civic pride and beauty.

But perhaps most important, PNC was con-

structed as a baseball park, *not* a multisport stadium and *not* an amusement park. This makes PNC a no-frills place, and keeps the focus where it should be: on the ball game. That's right, no carousel. No rolly-coaster. No circus clowns. Heck, it took us twenty minutes to find the kiddie area—which, by the way, was tastefully done. What does all this add up to? A ballpark, built in the old style, with distinctive materials and modern amenities for the new era. PNC is a thoughtful return to all that was good about the small and glorious ballparks of yesteryear, without sacrificing the wide concourses and comfortable seating that make new parks comfortable. So as it was in the beginning, so shall it ever be, world without end, Amen.

But it all didn't happen quite so smoothly. With the Pirates struggling in the mid-1990s and some of the team's corporate owners wanting out, management threatened to sell the team to another city if a local buyer couldn't be found. Finally in 1996, a group led by Kevin McClatchy purchased the Pirates with MLB's condition that the city build a new baseball-only facility within five years. But as we've seen in almost every city that has built a new park, wanting new digs and figuring out who will pay for them are two different things. A sales tax increase was brought before voters to finance a new baseball park, a new football stadium, and a new convention center that city officials had long discussed. Taxpayers twice rejected the sales tax hike in all eleven counties in which it was proposed. But that would not stop progress.

Pittsburgh Mayor Thomas Murphy viewed the Pirates as a brand name of the city and drove the metaphorical stake in the ground to keep the stadium project moving forward. Even though taxpayers voted a resounding no, Plan B was put into effect. We're not being flip, it was actually called Plan B. Through the plan, the Regional Asset District Board, which administers the funds raised by 1 percent of the sales taxes already in place guaranteed the ballpark project $13.4 million dollars per year for thirty years, giving the new ballpark the anchor it needed to continue. The Pirates chipped in $44 million more, $30 million of which came from PNC Bank for the naming rights. And while we would liked to have seen the funding come totally from private sources, at least taxes weren't raised to finance the ballpark. Pennsylvania Governor Tom Ridge granted the remaining $75 million in a deal that brought new football stadiums and ballparks to both Pittsburgh and Philadelphia. As we've seen elsewhere, none of the politicians felt their careers could suffer the blame for the home team leaving because of finances.

The total cost of PNC was to be $262 million, with the construction timeline spanning an ambitious twenty-four months. On April 7, 1999, the groundbreaking ceremony was held for PNC Park and the Sixth Avenue Bridge was officially renamed Roberto Clemente Bridge. A very classy move by Pittsburgh, which had not always treated Clemente with the respect he deserved.

More than fifty-five thousand fans were on hand on October 1, 2000, to watch the Pirates play their final game at Three Rivers, a loss to the Cubs. It was the largest crowd ever to see a regular season baseball game in Pittsburgh. Three Rivers had served the Pirates since July 16, 1970, when they also lost to the Cubs. Baseball, like history, tends to repeat itself.

Three Rivers still holds many wonderful memories for Pirates fans and baseball fans alike. The Pirates fielded what is generally regarded as the Major League's first all-minority lineup on September 1, 1971. It is regarded as such because previously no one

Roberto Clemente statue and Clemente Bridge

Photo by Josh Pahigian / Kevin O'Connell

bothered to take this fact into account, and of course it depends on how we define minority. In any case, the Pirates make this claim.

The Pirates won a World Series the year after moving into Forbes Field in 1909, and in little more than a year as new residents of Three Rivers Stadium, they won their fourth October Classic against Baltimore in 1971. Clemente batted .414 in the Series, and hit a Game 7 homer while Steve Blass tossed a four-hitter. This series also featured the first night World Series game ever played.

Despite their cavernous ballpark the championships kept coming to the Pirates, who won the Series again in 1979, singing their memorable "We Are Family" anthem. Dave Parker and Willie "Pops" Stargell clubbed their way to fame, once again against the Orioles. Kevin, however, could never get past the "I got all my sisters and me," line in the song. Which one of those guys considered himself one of the sisters? Oh, well.

In 1992 Pittsburgh lost a heartbreaking NLCS to the Braves when the unthinkable occurred after starter Doug Drabek had pitched eight masterful innings in Game 7. Atlanta plated three runs against submarine-armed closer Stan Belinda in the bottom of the ninth to steal a 3–2 victory. This explains why manager Jim Leyland always looked so fidgety in the dugout (and maybe why he was sneaking butts in the runway). But Pirates fans took heart. With a roster that included Barry Bonds, Bobby Bonilla, Jay Bell, Denny Neagle, Tim Wakefield, and Drabek, fans knew the next championship was likely to come soon enough. But it didn't. One by one, the Pirates top players departed via free agency, and the team sank in the standings year after year.

In 1994 Three Rivers played host to its second All-Star Game (the first was in 1974). It was the largest crowd to see the Midsummer Classic, as 59,568 fans witnessed an 8–7 NL victory

that took ten innings to complete. You reading this, Bud? They finished the freakin' game.

As mentioned, Pittsburgh's hardball history ranks among the richest in the majors. Back in 1887, the Pittsburgh Alleghenies played at Recreation Park, a facility that seated fewer people than Wheeler Field, in Centralia, Washington where Kevin played his Babe Ruth ball. Not really, but it was small. It was there that the team garnered the name Pirates when a Philadelphia newspaper claimed the team had hijacked slugging second-baseman Louis Bierbauer away from the Athletics. There was no wrongdoing, but the name stuck.

In October of 1903 the Pirates played the Boston Pilgrims in the first World Series, but lost five games to three in the best-of-nine set. The Pirates did manage to win the first World Series game played in Pittsburgh, at Exposition Park, a small wooden facility on the north shore of the Allegheny River, spitting distance from the site where PNC Park would open a century later. A historical marker of the first Series stood in the parking lot during the Three Rivers days, but as of this printing it has not been reerected.

Way back in 1882, the old American Association Alleghenies played baseball in the open fields of Exposition Park. But the park flooded often and the league folded.

There were no outfield fences at the Ex and crowds respectfully lined up behind roped-off boundaries. Clearly this was another era for baseball fans.

It may not have had outfield fences, but an interesting innovation debuted at Exposition when the Pirates used a tarp to cover the infield during a rainstorm. Other cities quickly followed suit.

In 1909 Pittsburgh opened gorgeous Forbes Field, named after British General John Forbes, who in 1758 captured Fort Duquesne from the French and renamed it Fort Pitt. It was the first ballpark in the country built completely of steel and poured concrete. A beautiful structure with a stone facade and arched windows along its exterior, its most important feature was that its seats were close to the action. Forbes was a park of the grand old design, a rival to Wrigley and Fenway. The outfield was enormous and the park itself had a clunky shape. The flagpole in the left outfield was actually in play.

To commemorate their love for the old park, the Pirates designed PNC to imitate Forbes's blue steel, tall light standards, and blue seats.

In the first season at Forbes, Honus Wagner led the Pirates to their first World Series title, downing Ty Cobb and the Detroit Tigers in a series that went seven games. Wagner, whose tobacco card would one day fetch a record half-million dollars at a Sotheby's auction, had help in the Series from rookie hurler Babe Adams who won three games, including a Game 7 shutout in Detroit.

There were many other firsts and lasts at Forbes. The last tripleheader in major league history was played there on October 2, 1920, versus Cincinnati. The first radio broadcast of a baseball game emanated from Forbes Field in 1921. The first elevator in the Majors was built to shuttle fans up to the "crow's nest," bleacher seats. Also Forbes was the first stadium to install foam crash pads on its outfield wall.

In 1925 the Pirates claimed another championship, and this one they would win at home in storybook fashion. In the eighth inning of Game 7 with two outs and the bases loaded and fireballer Walter Johnson on the mound for the Senators, Kiki Cuyler laced a three-run double to propel the Pirates to a 9–7 win.

Another amazing Forbes moment occurred on May 25, 1935, when Babe Ruth—playing for the Boston Braves—hit the last three home runs of his career. Ruth's final blast, number 714, cleared the right field roof marking the first time a shot had left the Forbes yard.

In 1955 Forbes witnessed the debut of a twenty-year-old rookie from Carolina, Puerto Rico, by the name of Roberto Clemente. Number 21 would prove to be the last right fielder to play at Forbes for the Bucs, patrolling the post until the ballpark closed in 1970.

In 1960 Bill Mazeroski hit a shot in the bottom of the ninth to break a 9–9 deadlock and win Game 7 of the 1960 World Series against the Yankees. The legendary swat, which cleared the left field fence, gave the Bucs their third World Series title and first in thirty-five years.

Forbes provided Pittsburghers a beautiful place to experience a game. And much like the alloy of steel derives its strength by the fusion of two or more other metals, PNC Park has taken the best of what Forbes, Three Rivers, and Exposition Park had to offer into account, fusing them into a single structure. It is a ballpark of which the city and team can be proud. The only piece of the puzzle that remains is for the Pirates to return to their championship form. Though the opening of PNC hasn't brought this about as many had hoped, and attendance at the new park has dropped significantly since its inaugural season, don't

---

TRIVIA TIMEOUT

Iron: Who is the only player to ever hit the ball out of PNC park during a game and make the mighty splash down into the Allegheny River?

Aluminum: Who threw the first-ever Pirate no-hitter in the city of Pittsburgh? (Hint: it came in the five-hundredth game at Three Rivers Stadium.)

Steel: Which two Pirate hurlers pitched the first combined extra-inning no-hitter in Major League history? (Hint: at Three Rivers.)

Look for the answers in the text.

count out the Pirates. The fans will return once the team starts to win, and when they do, arguably the best new ballpark in the country will await them.

Getting a Choice Seat

Enjoy it while you can folks, because at the moment PNC offers one of the best and most affordable ballpark experiences in the big leagues. But it won't last forever. As soon as the Pirates start posting some wins, this ticket will be hotter than a cauldron of molten iron. But for now things are easygoing and serene, so get on out there and enjoy this beautiful place to watch a game, even if the home team is something less than competitive. PNC is the most intimate new park when it comes to seating, as is evident by the fact that the press box is up above all of the fans, even those who pay the least money. Luxury boxes hang from the upper deck rather than garnering their own level. There is very little foul territory, getting fans even closer to the action. And the seats all angle toward the action, with aisles that are lowered to prevent views from being blocked. The only problem with this feature is if you've gone to the game to gab with your buddies, the angled seats will have you talking over your shoulder at them. But who cares? Save talk until afterward over a few pints.

Sellout Index: 5% of games sell out
Seating Capacity: 38,127—second smallest park in baseball
Ticket Office: (800) BUY-BUCS
http://www.pirates.com

Home Plate Club (Sections 14–19)

We don't know anyone who can afford these seats. Sure they're better than outstanding, but in this park why spend $200 for better than outstanding, when you can spend $25 for outstanding? Move down to these in the eighth inning, once the rich duffers tucker out and the ushers lose interest.

Dugout Box (Sections 9–13, 20–24)

These seats will cost you at least double at almost every other park in the country. As Ferris Beuller said, "We recommend them highly if you have the means . . . they are so choice." Money seems to go farther at PNC, perhaps because seats cost half as much and are twice as close. With so little foul territory these seats are only forty-five feet from the bases.

Baseline Box (Sections 1–8, 25–32)

Again this is a "can't-go-wrong" situation. These seats are right on the hot corners of the park, so keep your eyes on the ball. At only $2 more than the seats in the sections behind them, you can't afford not to get these seats.

Infield Box (Sections 109–124)

Usually we'd say purchase elsewhere and move down, but these are only a few bucks more than the outfield boxes, making this price too good to pass up. Now is the time to put out a little dough, sit back, and have a dog and a few barley pops, without worrying about who might come along to claim your seat. Perhaps for the first time on your road trip, enjoy this seat because you paid for it. Feel free to ask others if they're in the correct seats, because for once, you are.

Left/Right Field Box (Sections 101–108, 125–132)

There are several advantages to the Left Field Box seats: in Sections 132, 131, and 130, try to get the seats closest to the infield side of the sections if at all possible. These seats feel right on top of the third-baseline and are well worth the money. As you get closer to the field, you're right at the corner as you would be in comparable seats at Fenway, but here the seats cost less than half as much as in Boston.

The seats in Section 129 angle slightly toward home plate, giving a nice view of the action. Sections 128, 127, and 125 angle toward the plate and are located just a bit off the third-baseline for a beautiful view. Even in the back rows of these sections the overhang is not a factor.

Right Field Sections 101–108 get much less direct sun than the right field bleachers (142–147), so keep that in mind if it's an extremely hot or cold day.

Outfield (RF) Reserve (Sections 139–147)

These are great seats, which we generally recommend, with two caveats. Seats in the center of Section 145 are blocked by the right field foul pole. In Sections 146 and 147 you may have a slight blockage looking across at left field. Try instead for Sections 139–144, which are clear of any obstruction. These are completely out of the sun, elevated, and nice for those looking to snag home run balls or long fouls.

Bleachers (Sections 133–138, 235–238)

The left field bleacher seats are a good place to stand during batting practice and a solid choice for the game. They offer a great view, facing home plate, and the very low wall is a great place to snag a dinger or BP ball. Just remember, the 200 Level seats cost the same as those on the 100 Level so try to get down close.

Section 138 is a mixed bag. While some seats are perfect, on the left side of the section the bull pen blocks part of the view of the outfield. We recommend Section 137 for the same price because it has completely clear sight lines.

Sections 235–238 are in straightaway left field. Here, the seats aren't up as high as the second level and they're well below the Club seats. They are about the same elevation as the uppermost seats of the first tier. Not too shabby. All of these left field bleacher seats face the sun as it sets.

Pittsburgh Baseball Club (Sections 207–224)

This is where the "party suits," uh, we mean where the party suites are located. There is no significant loss of sight lines on the 200 Club level or in the party suites, or in the 200 Level restaurants like Keystone Korner and Bierbauer's. The only thing to envy about having 200 Level access is that there are several nice displays of uniforms, memorabilia, and photos on this level. The best of these is the collection of bats, one from each Pirate batting title winner.

Pirates Cove (Sections 205–210)

These seats are an extension of the Club level and are available only for group purchase. So unless you're road-tripping with your fraternity,

---

SEATING TIP

→ THE RIGHT FIELD Reserve sections are more elevated than the left field bleachers (though they are the same price) giving a more downward sight line, which some people prefer. But there is an under-hang and you will lose a bit of the warning track from the seats in right. Plus the scoreboard is difficult to see from these seats. Also sitting in right, your back is to the skyline, which at this park is a bit like going to the Grand Canyon and facing the minivan the whole time. Advantages to the right field seats are that they have seat backs (making them not technically bleachers) and are closer: 320 feet from the plate, versus 389 for most sections in left.

Though the left field bleachers start 325 feet from home plate and the wall quickly runs out to 389, we liked them better than the right field bleachers because of the extremely low wall—just six feet—the lowest wall built in a new park. When a home run comes to the left field section it's exciting being down near the left fielder who may have to fight it out with a fan for the ball.

or in a very crowded Volkswagen microbus, forget it. Fear not, you can do much better.

Deck Seating (Sections 335–338)

Those who purchase a table seat at the Outback Steakhouse located on the second level have the option of sitting in the Deck Seating Sections. Tables can be reserved for parties of four ($52 per person), five ($43 per person), and six ($52 per person). All of these charges include a $25 food credit, making the seats actually $22 or $18. For the life of us, we couldn't figure out why the price didn't continue to go down when reserving a six-seat table. But then again we never go to restaurants inside ballparks anyway, unless there's no game going on and the restaurant is free admission and we want to catch a glimpse of the field and we're hungry and we need to use the restroom ASAP.

Grandstands (Sections 308–325)

These are perhaps the best second-level seats of any new ballpark in the country. That's right, we said second level. Don't let the 300-something on the ticket fool you. There is no true third level to this ballpark, making PNC the first two-tiered ballpark to be built in the Majors since Milwaukee's County Stadium in 1953. The highest row of seats is only eighty-eight feet from the field—that's closer to the plate than first-base. We recommend sitting in the second level and taking in the game from above—but not too far above.

There are some seats to avoid, however. Supporting the press box are seven small beams, which obstruct views for the seats behind them. These are in Sections 315–317.

As you enter the grandstands, the standards that support the stairwells have glass windows, so if you're seated behind those you'll have a minor obstructed view as well. It's best to sit up higher than Row 7 so you won't

be bothered at all. But until the Pirates become contenders again, you should be able to move back (or forward) with ease.

Left/Right Field Grandstands (Sections 301–307, 327–329)

The entire upper deck is close to the field and offers great views of the game and the city. With the Roberto Clemente Bridge stretching across the Allegheny and the sun going down over the river and buildings downtown, we suggest sitting at least one game in the upper deck (something we thought we'd never say) or at least taking a walk up there to see the view. With the three steel bridges lyrically repeating their spans across the river, it's quite lovely, and perhaps the best city view in all of baseball.

Sections 301 and 302 have the slightest under-hang in the right field corner due to a little terrace that juts out. But all in all, PNC has done a nearly perfect job of managing the overhang/under-hang issue. As for rainy nights, head for rows Q and higher to get under the small sunroof. Row Y catches a nice breeze off the river.

Left Field Terrace (Sections 330–333)

In these sections you lose a bit of the left field corner from sight. Avoid Section 333, as these seats are further obstructed by the steelwork of the Rotunda, which is beautiful, but blocks the view of the scoreboard. Better to spend an extra $2 to sit in the Right Field/Left Field Grandstands. Or better yet, buy these seats, move over to the third-baseline or behind home plate and use the extra cash to reward your cleverness with a beer.

Standing Room

The Rotunda not only allows fans to traverse from one level to another, but it also acts as a standing-room area, as people pause for extended periods to take in the magnificent view from all four decks. It's a wonderful arched-roof steel structure, painted blue and decorated with blue lights, standing as a beautiful tribute to Pittsburgh's steel-working heritage.

There is also a very good standing area with a few seats (it didn't make any sense to us either) above the "out-of-town" scoreboard and underneath the Right Field Reserved sections. You have to look through a screen, but it is a pretty cool view.

The Black Market

We spent ten minutes talking to a friendly scalper who gave us the lowdown on everything, from where to get good wings and cheap beers to what ticket prices were for that day. You heard right: a friendly scalper with time to kill. We didn't get the impression that his business was too hot right then.

What does this mean to you? If it's not a promotion night at PNC—fireworks or bobble-head dolls—there should be no problem getting tickets. The bad seats inside are few and far between, so be familiar with the guide above and if a scalper has the audacity to charge more than face value, chuckle knowingly to yourself and walk away. Or better yet, ask him if he can recommend a good wing joint.

Before/After the Game

Getting to PNC Park

PNC Park is located on the north side of Pittsburgh's Allegheny River, surrounded by General Robinson Street, Federal Street, and Mazeroski Way. If you have a map that predates 2001, Mazeroski Way may not appear, as it was created during construction of the ballpark. Though PNC lies just off of I-279, that's not all you'll need to know. Nearly every

option for getting to the park was created with some walking in mind to preserve an urban atmosphere. How unlike Three Rivers can you get?

Pittsburgh is a city of rivers and thus a city of bridges, and a city in which a wrong turn can be costly. Some of the bridges aren't accessible from certain freeways, while others enter tunnels without letting you off where you'd like. Don't simply look at the map and expect that a bridge or highway will get you where you need to be, because odds are it won't. A good rule of thumb is, if you're coming in from and returning to the north, then park in a lot or on the street north of the park. If you're coming in and returning to the east, south, or west, then you should park downtown, south of the ballpark, and walk across the Clemente Bridge. The downtown lots vary in price, but the Port Authority operates garages that will give you an after 4:00 P.M. rate of only $3.

If you're staying in town, you might be able to get to the game by bus or the light-rail/subway system, known as the "T." The Wood Street stop is only three blocks from the Clemente Bridge, but there are plans to service the north side soon. Call the Port Authority at (412) 422-2000 for information and schedules.

If you're on the south side, a great way to get to the game is by taking the Gateway Clipper, a passenger ferry system that departs from Station Square. You can park or take the "T" there, then ride a ferry that will take you across all three of "the Burgh's" famous rivers: the Monongahela, the Ohio, and the Allegheny. The line gets pretty crowded at the Station Square dock before the game and at the dock along the Riverwalk afterward, so plan ahead. But then again, there are plenty of places to go out in Station Square, and someone else is driving the ferryboat, so relax and have a brew or two during and after the game.

Ballpark Tours

PNC offers tours beginning in mid-April. You can schedule a tour by calling (800) BUY-BUCS, ext. 4700, or by e-mailing them at tours@pittsburghpirates.com.

Bridging Barriers (Absolute Must)

Whether or not you park downtown, walking across the Roberto Clemente Bridge is an essential part of the ballpark experience when visiting PNC. Formerly known as the Sixth Street Bridge, this steel cable-suspension bridge is one of three similar bridges that cross the Allegheny and date from the mid-1920s. They are collectively known as the Three Sisters and are part of the beauty of the skyline, all painted yellow. Josh wondered if there is so much yellow in Pittsburgh because all three sports teams feature it as their team color. "We can only hope," Kevin answered.

Before, during, and after each game the city closes the Clemente Bridge to car traffic, making it a pedestrian-only bridge, but really it becomes part of the ballpark. On it you'll find street musicians, people hawking tickets, peanuts, Pirates banners, shirts, and memorabilia. We'll be honest, we saw quite a bit of Steelers paraphernalia on display as we crossed, too. As you cross the Allegheny you're treated to a wonderful view of the park, the river, and the city. The bridge lets off right at the ballpark where stands an impressive statue of Clemente.

River Walking

Equally important as crossing the bridge is walking under it along the Riverwalk. This long stretch of developed embankment along the Allegheny will make you further appreciate the urban renaissance that the north side has undergone in the past few years. The bulkhead that embanks the ballpark was built during the construction of the park and is made of the same Minnesota limestone as PNC. Plus,

the walk is just beyond the right field wall and is the place players are trying to hit with long fly balls during batting practice.

We saw one lone kid with a glove standing along the Riverwalk before the game, waiting for a ball, but without success. Two balls had already bounced off the Riverwalk and into the Allegheny and sank.

"Do you know why in San Fran balls don't sink so fast?" Kevin asked the lad.

"Saltwater," the kid said somewhat sarcastically.

"If they don't bounce," Josh said, "you won't have to worry about them sinking."

"Thanks," the kid said, rather ungratefully.

In case you're wondering, Daryl Ward of Houston is the only player to hit a ball into the river during a game. His shot on July 6, 2002, traveled at least 443 feet to reach the water. As a comparison, a shot landing in McCovey Cove at PacBell in San Francisco need only be hit 352 feet.

Statues to the Three Great Ones

Outside the park there are statues of the three greatest Pirates to ever don the gold and black. Clemente's statue is the first one you'll encounter coming off the Bridge and originally was erected at Three Rivers. Engravings beneath his figure list important dates spanning his outstanding life and career, right up until the date of his tragic death in a plane crash. He was bringing relief supplies to earthquake-torn Nicaragua. Clemente was more than one of the greatest ballplayers to play the game. He was a great humanitarian and a graceful man who never forgot his roots—a citizen of the world, and one of those people who make you proud to be a human being. The Pirates have done well to honor him thusly.

Along Federal Street is the statue of Wilver "Willie" Stargell. Loved by the city first, and then by the nation, Pops is shown ready to put

Honus Wagner statue

Photo by Josh Pahigian / Kevin O'Connell

his ample frame fully into his mighty cut, as he did for a career mark of 475 home runs. Sadly, on April 1, 2001, PNC's Grand Opening Day and the statue's premier, Stargell passed away at sixty-one years of age from long-term health complications. "Pops" will never be forgotten, not as long as PNC stands.

Beneath Pop's feet are the "Bucco Bricks" that fans purchased for minimum donations of one dollar, that now bear their engraved names. All money gathered by the project went toward construction of the ballpark.

The final statue stands near the west entrance. Honus Wagner was perhaps the greatest Pirate player of them all. "The Flying Dutchman" won eight batting titles and was a member of the first class of inductees to the Baseball Hall of Fame, along with Babe Ruth, Ty Cobb, Walter Johnson, and Christy Mathewson. Not bad company. This statue stood in Schenley Park near Forbes Field, and at Three Rivers previously.

Banner Players

To honor the remaining Pirate greats, hanging banners extend around the entire exterior block, emblazoned with names like Ralph Kiner, Arkie Vaughn, Vern Law, Chuck Tanner, Tony Pena, and Bill Mazeroski.

John Candelaria has his own banner, too. The Candy Man threw the first-ever no-hit game in front of a Pittsburgh crowd on August 9, 1976, blanking the Dodgers 2–0. It was the five-hundredth game for the Pirates at Three Rivers.

Also honored on the banner walk are Francisco Cordova (nine innings) and Ricardo Rincon (one inning), who combined to hurl the first multipitcher extra-inning no-hitter on July 12, 1997, against the Astros before a capacity crowd at Three Rivers.

Watering Holes and Outside Eats

Along Federal Street several restaurants can be accessed from the outside of the park, as well as from the inside. Here you'll find **Outback Steakhouse**, **Seattle's Best Coffee**, **Ben and Jerry's**, and the **Sports Legacy Art Gallery** tucked neatly into the exterior walkway of PNC. Directly across the street at the corner of West General Robinson Street and along Federal Street are four bars that run the gamut in pre- and post game entertainment. There are also a few places worth a few extra blocks' walk.

FIREWATERS NORTH SHORE SALOON AND BBQ (120 W. Federal Street)

Firewaters, the closest bar to the park, is a sit-down place with some outside seating. It specializes in chicken wings with a variety of different sauces from buffalo to barbecue to honey. It also offers a large variety of other bar food like jalapeño poppers, fried provolone, and barbecue sandwiches. Firewaters lights an outdoor barbecue when the street closes off prior to the game, serving pork shoulder and lamb and beef brisket sandwiches.

The joint has an old oak bar with bunting around it—hey, baseball and bunting—and on the walls there are Pirate pennants and newspaper articles. The menu reads like it caters to baseball fans even though Heinz Field is only a few blocks away. Banners from all of the NL teams hang above the windows.

Over a few free beers (yeah, we know we have a tough job) the manager, Pete Shaffalo, told us that the place was previously a bar called Maggie May's, and prior to that the site was a brothel. If only these walls could talk.

Pete offered Josh a free bottle of Firewaters' homemade barbecue sauce to take home with him, which prompted Josh to later declare, "We're more popular than Jesus."

Kevin responded, "You mean Jesus Alou, right?"

HI-TOPS SPORTING NIGHTLIFE AND CAFÉ
(200 W. Federal Street)

Across the street from Firewaters is Hi-Tops. This place is a Wrigleyville original that has recently placed itself near the new ballparks in Pittsburgh and Arizona. They've wisely decked themselves out in the hometown colors. Hi-Tops also serves wings—though not nearly the selection of Firewaters, and you can get nachos, basic pub grub, cheese steaks, brats and Italian sausages, and mozzarella sticks. It's flashier and a tad corporate, so if that's your gig, have at it.

TRIANGLE 2 BAR AND GRILL
(208 Federal Street)

A bit farther down Federal Street is Triangle 2 Bar and Grill, specializing in a twenty-seven-inch battleship sandwich for $10. It offers a variety of other sandwiches made to order, as well as wings, appetizers, and cheese steaks. Triangle 2 is a transplant of a Pittsburgh bar

and after the game morphs into more of a dance club.

222 BAR (222 Federal Street)

Farther down Federal is the 222 Bar, which is an old-school dive in an old building. There are pool tables in the back as well as a variety of bar games. You know, your basic joint to have a cheap beer beside a rum-soaked local. Kevin started to get pretty comfortable here, while Josh lobbied for a return to Firewaters.

FINNEGAN'S WAKE IRISH PUB
(20 General Robinson)

Calling itself the biggest Irish pub in the Burgh, Kevin would be much happier if Finnegan's served the best pint of Guinness, which it does not. For Kevin, Irish bars are all about authenticity. Finnegan's Wake is about as authentically Irish as the horror flick *Leprechaun*. Still, Finnegan's is a large pub with live music and decent food, and people have a good time visiting, so where's the harm in that? So pull up a chair, have yourself some chicken wings and a Jägermeister, and sing along to "Danny Boy."

ROSA VILLA (Corner of 6th and General Robinson)

This is an old Pittsburgh establishment that has bottles of beer on the shelves older than Josh. But they've done quite a nice job upgrading the menu and sprucing up the joint to cater to the new folks that wander in from PNC.

JAMES STREET RESTAURANT
(422 Foreland Street)

Oddly not on James Street, this eatery is just a ten-minute walk to PNC and features a Cajun menu and two floors of live jazz. If you need a quick bite, try their buffet.

PLACES WORTH THE DRIVE

Pittsburgh is a great city with a lively nightlife. East Carson Street on the South Side Flats offers plenty of bars and clubs that are worth visiting. There are a bevy of great spots to have a beer or hear some music on this street including **Fatheads** for cheap eats, **Club Cafe** to catch some tunes, and **Smokin' Joe's Saloon** for an excellent beer selection.

Station Square is another place to park and get something to eat before the game or to go out for some nightlife afterward. Station Square is the place to head if you're interested in finding the local **Hard Rock Café** and places such as that. You can even take the "Monongahela Incline," sort of a cross between a ski lift and steep streetcar, up to the top of Mount Washington for a truly spectacular view of the city.

Another neighborhood with great late-night action is the Strip District, though Josh was disappointed to find its name misleading. At least he had plenty of one-dollar bills handy during the rest of the road trip whenever he wanted to buy a soda. This is a club-heavy, dance, and music scene for those who want to drop some cash to see bands or meet members of the opposite sex. On Penn Avenue visit **Mullaney's Harp and Fiddle**, one of Pittsburgh's best Irish bars.

PRIMANTI BROTHERS (Four Locations)

Whether you find yourself in the Strip District, Oakland, the South Side, or downtown, you should make some time to stop into a Primanti Brothers sandwich shop. The specialty of the house is "working-man sandwiches," for the men who worked in the mills and had no time to fuss with side dishes. With fries and coleslaw piled high right into the sandwich, along with your choice of meat and cheese, these sandwiches will disappoint no one, except Josh. When he ordered the number two bestseller, "steak and cheese," he was expecting Philly style. The Pittsburgh-style Salisbury steak did not "agree" with his delicate palate. But Kevin's Cappa Colla was delicious. And they're open late.

Josh: "Is that a cigarette she's smoking?"

Kevin: "The one making sandwiches? Yeah, I think so."

Josh: "Isn't that some sort of health code violation?"

Kevin: "Shut up and eat your number two bestseller."

THE ORIGINAL HOT DOG SHOP
(3901 Forbes Avenue)

The "O" is another place not to be missed. It is located in Oakland near the University of Pittsburgh and is a quick jaunt away if you're headed to see Forbes Field. "O" dogs are legendary in Pittsburgh and Kevin recommends the big kosher. Perhaps these delicious dogs are only outdone by the "O" fries. Pittsburghers adore French fries, even as a main course, and these are served nice and greasy with salt and cups of cheese, vinegar, and Heinz ketchup for dipping. Each heaping order overfills its paper container. Don't get the large unless you're in a group or can eat like Willie Stargell.

PIEROGIES PLUS
(342 Island Ave, McKees Rocks, PA)

In Pittsburgh you can get these tasty little Eastern European treats just about anywhere. Though they're great inside the park, our favorite place for pierogies is Pierogies Plus. It's an old gas station where you can get your drive-through pierogies in a Styrofoam container. Now Josh just needs to convince Heather to wear a babushka.

THE CRAWFORD GRILL (2141 Wylie Avenue)

This club not only has great ambiance and authentic jazz, it also has a great Pittsburgh baseball connection. You see, there is a good reason that the Crawford is decorated with black-and-white photos of Negro League teams and ballparks. Gus Greenlee, the same man who opened The Crawford Grill was also the owner of the Pittsburgh Crawfords. Greenlee also built Greenlee Field, the home of the Crawfords and eventually the Grays. Greenlee's ownership of both the team and the ballpark put him in very elite company at the time among black men in the country. His ballpark reflected this fact, offering locker rooms and showers—necessities that were not provided to black teams that played in white ballparks.

That said, this bar has cheap drinks, great jazz, and good food, although it is located in an area of town known as the Hill District. While the Hill used to be a rough neighborhood, it's not so bad now. But still, we wouldn't advise walking around alone here at night, unless you're "Bad" in the Michael Jackson sense of the word.

Inside the Park

PNC Park is about one thing: the game of baseball. That's it. Its class comes from the fact that there are not too many frills. PNC has the design and feel of an old park, with all that you'll want in a brand new facility. You'll find no merry-go-rounds for the kids, no gigantic corporate promotions that masquerade as entertainment. Other than a fizzing sound made by in the right field bleachers by a cola company that we refuse to name, there are few distractions at PNC. Rather you'll find good old-fashioned baseball in its most natural environment. In making the park a two-level-only facility, keeping a very limited amount of foul territory (seats behind home are only fifty-one feet from the batter's box), and by putting the press level above all the others, they have clearly set the priority on the fans, and the action of the game. Though Josh still prefers to think of Camden Yards as the best of the new parks built, Kevin is quick to point out that PNC has ten thousand fewer seats.

PITTSBURGH CRAWFORDS VERSUS HOMESTEAD GRAYS

BOTH OF these clubs can lay claim to having been the most successful Negro League team in history. Interestingly, they do so claiming many of the same players as alumni.

The Homestead Grays were founded in 1910 and played their games at West Field in Homestead, Pennsylvania, and later in Pittsburgh at Gus Greenlee field and at Forbes. They won the Eastern Championship defeating the New York Lincoln Giants in 1930. Then they won it again the next year as Josh Gibson hit for a .367 average and belted seventy-five home runs. But the onset of the Depression threw hard times at the Negro Leagues and it would take the Grays years to reestablish their dominance, but by then the franchise had moved to Washington, D.C.

When Gibson jumped ship to the crosstown Pittsburgh Crawfords in 1932, so did the championships. But this time he had the help of the great Satchel Paige. The Crawfords played home games at Ammon Field and Greenlee Field in the Hill District, and finished a single game behind the Chicago American Giants in the first half of the 1933 Negro National League's split season. The second half was never completed and Greenlee, who was also the league manager, awarded the Crawfords the disputed Negro National League championship. The Crawfords went on to defeat the New York Cubans in 1935 for their first undisputed pennant in one of the greatest series the Negro Leagues ever played. They also claimed another confused pennant in 1936. During the '30s Gibson routinely hit better than .400 while also banging in home runs at a staggering pace, and with Paige winning twenty-five to thirty games per year, it's no wonder the Crawfords are widely regarded as the most successful team in the history of the Negro Leagues. For a bit of this history, a marker stands at 2217 Bedford Avenue designating Ammon Field and some of Gibson's accomplishments.

At PNC they've also done a good job prioritizing modern amenities—wide concourses, lots of different places to eat, and a lot of good food set on the outside of the concourse to protect the walking view, again to not get in the way of the game. Ironically, the team stinks, giving fans the best view of some of the worst baseball in the big leagues.

As we stated previously, what we like best about the park is its use of local and unique materials: steel everywhere and limestone and yellow brick on the outside facade and in decorative places inside, adding beauty and local flavor. Much steel was used in the construction of the park, not only for the Rotunda concourse that takes you up and around, but also in the lighting fixtures and the steps in the stairs. In order to hang the luxury boxes under the second deck rather than give them their own level, thicker steel I-beams were necessary and are fastened with huge exposed bolts, adding beauty along with support.

A Fitting Tribute

If you come into the park through the Left Field Entrance you'll be impressed to see the tribute to the town's Negro League players and teams. The team has hung oversized fiberglass bats above the entrance bearing players' names and the names of their teams. Beneath the Crawfords are listed the names of Josh Gibson, Oscar Charleston, Judy Johnson, and Satchel Paige. The Grays' list includes Buck Leonard, Smokey Joe Williams, Sammy Bankhead, and Cool Papa Bell.

If you know that Josh Gibson and Cool Papa Bell played for both the Crawfords and the Grays, consider yourselves more "in the know" than those who approved this tribute. But know, too, that Oscar Charleston, Judy Johnson, and Sammy Bankhead played for both teams as well.

Retired Numbers

Retired numbers for the Pirates hang at the bottom of the second deck and above the boxes and light up in neon, a way that we haven't seen before. Down the right field line is Jackie Robinson's number 42, Roberto Clemente's number 21, Bill Mazeroski's number 9, Pie Traynor's number 20, and Ralph Kiner's number 4. Down the left field line is Billy Meyer's number 1, Honus Wagner's number 33, Willie Stargell's number 8, and Danny Murtaugh's number 40.

Straight Out of Forbes Field

Though the hanging luxury boxes and the press box attached to the roof clearly draw from the beauty of Wrigley Field, the influence of Forbes Field on the city of Pittsburgh and the design of PNC cannot be overstated. Fans of the old park will quickly recognize the seven vertical steel light towers of blue painted steel surrounding the park, and the choice of blue seats, all heavily influenced by Forbes. But there are a few others we'd like to point out that might not be so obvious, unless you were there. (We weren't.)

"21"

The right field wall is twenty-one feet high. Why? If you can't guess this one you haven't been paying attention. Number 21 patrolled right field for the Pirates for more than eighteen seasons. Fans loved him, his teammates and the world respected him. It seems fitting that the Pirates honor him in this wonderfully understated, but ever-present fashion.

OUT-OF-TOWN SCOREBOARD

Not only does the old-fashioned electric scoreboard on the right field wall provide the scores of all the games, it also tells what inning the game is in, how many outs there are, and how many runners are on base, with a cool retro-lighted diamond system, just like they used to have at Forbes Field. Our only suggestion for improvement: give us the number of who is pitching for each team so we'll know how our fantasy teams are doing.

When a ball hits this scoreboard a tinny clanking sound rings out, so we're not too sure what it's made of, but it's one of several surfaces that a ball could hit, including chain-link and exposed concrete. Right fielders will have to deal with the ball bouncing differently depending on where it hits this scoreboard. In case you're wondering, the team slates are manual, but the rest is updated electronically over the wire.

EVERY NOOK AND CRANNY

There is a nook in left-center that is reminiscent of the deep left-center of Forbes, which was 457 feet and helped Owen "Chief" Wilson set the Major League record for triples with thirty-six in 1912. The bull pens extend out to the right of it, which gives it a bit more naturally occurring feel than some of the other manufactured oddities in ballparks recently built.

THE DREYFUSS MEMORIAL

This memorial that used to be in play in center field at Forbes was moved first to Three Rivers and now sits inside the home plate entrance to PNC. It honors Barney Dreyfuss, the Pirates owner who built Forbes Field. At the time, the public sentiment was that Dreyfuss was building the park too far from downtown. Thus, many people referred to Forbes as Dreyfuss's Folly in its early days. But the ballpark survived to outlive many of its detractors.

Kids Not Left Out

Behind left field is a nice little picnic area, a place to scarf down some food, and a kids' play area, complete with a small jungle gym. There is also a tiny replica of the ballpark—complete with the limestone that adorns PNC's exterior.

Hey, Nice View

We noticed that the Pirates dugout is on the third-baseline, visitors on the first. Perhaps even the team wants to take in the beautiful view of downtown while its players wait to take the field. If you're interested in ambience, sitting along the left field bend is best, because in right you lose the view of downtown a bit with the outfield bleachers above the high right field wall. And the downtown view is one of the best in baseball: the skyline, Clemente Bridge, and the boats sailing past. In Kevin's book, it ranks right up there with Pac-Bell for best ballpark view. Josh is still partial to Shea Stadium's jetset panorama.

We Require . . . Shrubbery

In straightaway center is the batter's eye—a large green blockade of the river and downtown area that prevents the distraction of the hitters. Beneath this wall grows six Norway pines from Indiana County, Pennsylvania, that look very much like Christmas trees and are edged with mountain laurel, Pennsylvania's state flower. The well-known Pittsburgh "P" has been sculpted into the grassy knoll 399 feet away, beyond the center field fence.

Extra, Extra! Pirates Ahead 5–4 in the Sixth

Venders roam the park hawking the *Pittsburgh Post-Gazette* like they were selling beer, a first for us. We took it in as all part of the ballpark atmosphere and proof once again that baseball is America's pastime, not sport. After all, could you really afford to look away from a Steelers' game to read the paper?

Technologically Speaking

Often it is best to improve on quirks of an older park. Such as the sound system at Three Rivers, which was located in center field and was often inaudible. PNC has a top-notch system that can be heard everywhere in the park.

Also the Jumbotron at PNC cost $2.1 million, more than the entire cost to build Forbes Field. It includes a full entertainment package that features the Pirate Parrot, a scurvy-ridden pirate, and all the bells and whistles imaginable. And underneath the scoreboard is a small closed-captioned scoreboard for the hearing impaired that prints out everything the public address announcer says. Nice touch.

In Case of Encroaching Boredom . . .

If the game is dull and you've already bought and read the newspaper, look across the river into the city and you should be able to make out what looks like a movie screen mounted atop one of the buildings. It's actually a plasma screen courtesy of the Art Institute of Pittsburgh. The screen projects different colored shapes and designs for your own interpretation.

What You Won't See

The Pirates clubhouse inside PNC is eighteen thousand square feet, as opposed to the four thousand square foot room the team used at Three Rivers. It too has much steel in the design, as well as old-style wooden lockers. Next to the clubhouse is a warm-up mound and batting cages so that players can stay loose during rain delays. The floor of the cages is covered with the artificial turf from Three Rivers.

Inside Eats

There's a lot to try in Pittsburgh, and much of it is tough to find in other places, so dig in. We found some of the best and most unique food in baseball in this park.

KAHN'S HOT DOG (Dog Rating)
The Fourteenth Best Dog in the Majors

This is a pretty good dog and it's affordably priced. We've had Kahn's franks in other parks, and this dog is fairly typical of Kahn's. But you can do better. We recommend instead getting the Hebrew National dog at the Federal Street Grille (inside the park)

PIEROGIES (Trademark Food)

They're little Eastern European pasta ravioli that are stuffed with potatoes, cheese, onions or garlic. You sure as heck aren't going to find these anywhere else, so eat up. We suggest butter, salt, and pepper to top them off, and watch out, they're steaming hot!

PRIMANTI BROTHERS SANDWICHES
(Trademark Food)

While Josh was partial to the pierogies, Kevin fell in love with this Pittsburgh treat so we decided to award two trademark foods. Primanti Brothers is located behind Section 310. These sandwiches come piled high with your choice of meat and with French fries and coleslaw piled right in. There are no special orders at the Primanti Brothers stand until after the sixth inning. The sandwiches are good if you get them early, being that they're premade. But they fade in quality as the game goes on and they cost a buck and a quarter more inside the park than at their shops in town. So if you're heading toward one of their locations, we recommend getting your sandwich from the source. Or wait until after the sixth inning and ask for a sandwich sans the slaw, which will be made for you on the spot.

CHICKEN ON THE HILL

TEAM ANNOUNCER Bob Prince is primarily responsible for coining this phrase. Once when Willie belted a homerun, Prince began shouting "Chicken on the Hill!" having claimed earlier that Stargell owned a chicken restaurant in the Hill District that was going to give out free chicken if he homered. Of course they weren't, but the phrase "Chicken on the Hill" became a trademark Prince used whenever Pops went deep.

PLENTY OF OLD BALLPARKS

SINCE THE PIRATES have had so many ballparks, why not visit them all? Or what's left of them. The closest, Exposition Park, was located in the parking lots in between PNC Park and Heinz Field. Look for the historical marker because that's all that's left.

Recreation Park was located in the historic Allegheny West District of town, near Allegheny and Pennsylvania Avenues. There is nothing left to even indicate that a ballpark once stood there.

The remains of Forbes Field on the University of Pittsburgh campus offer the most to see of the former Pirates homes. The outfield wall still has ivy growing over the brick, and the flagpole that was "in play" is perhaps the most fitting remnant of an old park that we've found yet. The numbers marking the distances are still painted on the brick in white (457 feet to the flagpole in left-center, 436 to right-center). Follow the brick outline of the ballpark wall that runs across the street, marking the location of the left field fence, until you reach the plaque dedicated to Bill Mazeroski. Die-hard fans gather here once a year on October 14 to listen to the radio broadcast of the 1960 World Series, when "Maz's" shot sailed over these very walls and brought another championship to the Pirates over the New York Yankees.

Inside the lobby of the Joseph M. Katz Graduate School of Business building across from the wall you will find Forbes's home plate. Walk around looking at the ground and you'll see it resting peacefully under Plexiglas in its original location. The skyscraper across the street is Pitt University's Cathedral of Learning. While an impressive blend of Gothic and modern architecture, the cathedral also provided a view right down into Forbes Field, and during the World Series (and other crowded games) held the honor of being the highest bleacher seats in baseball history.

For fans of the Negro Leagues, Pittsburgh is a veritable Mecca. Though the historical marker at 2217 Bedford Avenue is all that remains of Ammon Field, it is a nice tribute to Josh Gibson. There is a ball field still on the location, in Ammon Park, behind the Macedonia Baptist Church.

Greenlee Field was just a few blocks down Bedford, along the 2500 block. There is very little remaining of the ballpark that was once the pride of the Negro Leagues. For a peek at some old photographs, head to the Crawford Grill at 2141 Wylie Avenue. Plus you'll get a chance to see the jazz club where John Coltrane, Mary Lou Williams, and Pittsburgh's own Art Blakey once performed.

A historical marker dedicated to the Homestead Grays stands on Amity Street, near Fifth Avenue in Homestead, detailing just a slice of the team's accomplishments. Very close by, at the corner of 6th and Amity once stood the SkyRocket Lounge, the owner of which owned the Grays for a time.

But it is West Field, located in the town of Munhall, along Main Street between 19th and Orchard and behind the Munhall Borough Building, that is truly something to see. Huge rusted metal light stanchions and ornate masonry surround this decaying ballpark, letting visitors know what a grand baseball palace once stood on the grounds. The seating bowl is still in use, and the field, though a tad shabby gives the feeling that great deeds were accomplished here. We sat in the ragged dugouts where Josh Gibson and Cool Papa Bell used to sit, and it gave us shivers.

Unlike Ammon Field and Greenlee Park, West Field remains still in use. Though it is in disrepair, it's not too far gone to be saved. Behind the park, the old entrance is now used as a storage and salvage grounds.

Any account of the mighty Homestead Grays will tell you that this ballpark was once a jewel. With as much of the ballpark still intact as there is we could not figure out why it is not registered as a National Historical Site, as it should be. With a bit of effort, money, and political will, the surrounding cities of Munhall, Homestead, and West Homestead (or one of our readers) could put forth the effort to restore this hallowed ground and return it to its former glory.

Why should this ballpark be restored? Because of the nine players immortalized in bronze on the miniature field at the Negro League Museum (considered the greatest nine to have played in the Negro Leagues) five played a majority of their career with Pittsburgh teams, and four are Homestead Grays: Josh Gibson, Judy Johnson, Buck Leonard, and Cool Papa Bell. Three more players who played a while with the Homestead Grays (Smokey Joe Williams, Bill Foster, and Martin Dihigo) are immortalized in the Baseball Hall of Fame in Cooper-

stown. If you include two more Hall of Famers, Pittsburgh Crawford Oscar Charleston and the time that the great Satchel Paige spent in a Crawford uniform, it's clear that this area of the country has fielded some of the greatest talents in the history of the game. Surely, the legacy of these great players is worthy of the restoration of West Field. We think so.

BEST OF THE REST

Super Fries stands offer cheese fries, garlic fries, and chili fries. They're tasty and greasy and deep-fat fried—just how we like 'em. Since there's no Major League ballpark in Buffalo, we also recommend getting some hot wings from **Quaker Steak and Lube**. Their large bucket of wings goes for $18, but "dere's like forty wings in dere."

Pops' Plaza is an area of Willie Stargell-themed eateries, off the main concourse on the first level. Head for the blue neon near the Rotunda in left field and see if you can guess all the Pops' references. **Pub 475** serves Penn draft and Premium draft as well as pub grub. **Familee BBQ** is better than Manny's BBQ in the outfield. **Pop's Potato Patch** has freshly cut French fries with toppings including chili, nacho cheese, garlic, chives, and sour cream. **Chicken on the Hill** has two-, three- or four-piece dinners. **Willie's Hit** offers New York kosher style hot dogs, sauerkraut, chili, nachos supreme, and hand-rolled pretzels—plain, salt, cinnamon and sugar, and garlic.

As for **Manny's Barbecue**, former Pirates catcher Manny Sanguillen operates this barbecue in center field and serves up sandwiches and platters of pit beef and smoked pork. We tried the pork, which was very tasty, healthy on the barbecue sauce but perhaps a bit too salty. It was also pricey for our liking, but good nonetheless.

The **Benkovitz** fish sandwich is one of the holdovers from Three Rivers' mediocre fare that we like. That is, if you're into fish. The raw bar looked good enough, but we decided to wait till we got somewhere close to the ocean.

SAY "NO, THANKS," AND WALK AWAY

The **Outback Steak House** Blooming Onion fits this category best for us, unless of course you enjoy indigestion. It may sound like a good idea, but then again so did getting five margaritas at US Cellular Field. The onion isn't bad for the first five bites or so. It's the finishing that kills. An entire deep-fried onion can be tough to digest. And yes, Kevin found that one out the hard way.

Another place to avoid is the **Pizza Outlet**. Why, oh why, can't ballparks get pizza done right? Perhaps because they prepare their pies three days in advance then zap them in the microwave? Can someone please help us!

BEERS OF THE BURGH

Pittsburgh has more than a few of its own breweries that offer beers at PNC. **Penn Brewery** has a nice selection that includes Penn Lager and Augustiner, a dark bock-style beer. The brewery is on the North Side and is worth a visit. But for the old-time Pittsburgh beer drinkers, Yuengling is still what it's all about. This very tasty beer originates from the oldest brewery in America dating from 1872. Iron City is yet another macrobrewery for which the

interior

Photo by Kevin O'Connell

way, in a competition between the pierogies of "The Burgh" and the sausages of Milwaukee, the pierogies won out. See the Milwaukee chapter for more details on "Sausage Gate."

STILL HUNGRY? STRAPPED FOR CASH?

Watch for hot dogs being fired out of an air gun by the **Pirate Parrot** up into the crowd. The Pirate Parrot is the team's mascot and is usually patrolling the park between innings offering promotions that you might find in a minor league park. During play, look for him to roost atop the Pirates dugout.

Burgh is famous. Try an IC Light if you're counting calories.

The PNC Experience

WE'RE SENSING A THEME HERE

The same limestone and yellow brick used on the exterior of the park also line the opening to the tunnels leading to the seats and are visible along the low wall behind home plate. This ties the entire park together in a unified theme. But behind home plate it can actually affect play. If a wild pitch gets past the catcher, the uneven angles of the limestone can send the ball in crazy directions and lead to extra bases, or even runs. Here's hoping the hometown Bucs figure out these nuances and play them to their advantage.

PIEROGIE RACES

All ballparks have some kind of racing entertainment between one of the innings. We're not sure why. In Pittsburgh it's a pierogie race. Jalapeño Hanna, Cheese Chester, Sauerkraut Saul, and the highly intelligent Oliver Onion are the pierogies in the running. First they compete on the scoreboard, then they finish as actual characters racing out onto the field. By the

UNDER THE BRIDGE DOWNTOWN

Also worth seeking out in the city is the intersection of Ross Street, Court Place, and Second Avenue under a bridge overpass. A wonderful mural has been painted here honoring all of Pittsburgh's baseball players from the Pirates to the Crawfords and Grays. The Art Institute of Pittsburgh presented the mural to city in 2000. It features Honus Wagner, Willie Stargell, Roberto Clemente, Josh Gibson, and many others all standing together on the same field of dreams.

IF YOU HAVE A FEW EXTRA DAYS

The Altoona Curve, Erie Seawolves, and Buffalo Bison are minor league teams that won't take you too far out of your way. But also check out the Washington Wildthings—perhaps the funniest minor league team name since the Toledo Mudhens. An affiliate of the Pirates, the Wildthings just opened a new park, Falconi Field, just twenty minutes away, in the town of Washington, Pennsylvania.

CLEVELAND INDIANS, JACOBS FIELD

The Jake by the Lake

CLEVELAND, OHIO

96 miles to Detroit
132 miles to Pittsburgh
190 miles to Toronto
220 miles to Cincinnati

IF YOU HAVEN'T SEEN the movie *Major League*, go rent it. It's the one where Charlie Sheen is an Indians pitcher with control problems whose nickname is "Wild Thing." The one where a failing baseball team in a failing baseball park in a failing baseball city decides to shock the world and make a run at the pennant. Ah, how like art, how like life.

When the Cleveland Indians moved into their new home, Jacobs Field, in 1994 it may have appeared to the casual observer that they enjoyed instant, overnight success, just as in the movie. This may be a bit of a stretch. But the truth is that Jacobs Field has done for Cleveland what every Major League city hopes a new ballpark will do. It helped bring new life and energy to the franchise, fan base, and city, selling out its first 455 games. This provided the Tribe with the capital to sign its talented young players to long-term deals and to dip into the free-agent market for quality veterans. The ballpark also anchored the economic revitalization of Cleveland's flagging Gateway District and provided Clevelanders with a ballpark they could be proud of. The Jake certainly wasn't the only post holding up the tepee, but it was a major component of what has become known in MLB as the "Blueprint for Success."

Jacobs Field has come to symbolize the rebirth of the Indians. And why not? It's a great ballpark. Though it seats more than forty-two thousand people, most areas of the park feel very intimate, with only a few sections being too far away from the action. The field is eighteen feet below street level, which helps give the exterior more the look of a ballpark, while providing room for the interior seating capacity of a small stadium. From street level, the ballpark only rises 120 feet in the air, not including the lighting towers.

The Jake was designed with grandeur in mind, as well as baseball. Therefore, it is unashamedly a larger facility than some of the other new ballparks. The Jake's exterior looks rather like Cleveland itself, with light towers reminiscent of the town's smokestacks, and steel girders that match the many bridges that cross the Cuyahoga River. The ballpark's pale yellow brick combines with the exposed steel to endow Jacobs with the elements of many classic ballparks past, as well as of postindustrial stadiums.

exterior

Photo by Kevin O'Connell

Asymmetrical field dimensions are always nice, but since all new parks are putting these in, what we really like to see in a ballpark is distinctiveness, and Jacobs Field is brimming with local flavor. Rising above the outfield scoreboard is the city of Cleveland, a wonderful backdrop that wraps the ballpark in Clevelandness from the left field corner around past the home bull pen. Few other cities can offer this kind of skyline view and it's a definite improvement over the Indians' old digs. Also unique, the Jacobs infield consists of gray dirt, something not found elsewhere in the big leagues. And the mini monster in left field provides an added dimension for pitchers, hitters, and especially outfielders to consider.

Looking at the beauty of the field, it's hard to believe that the original ballpark proposal called for a domed stadium. Voters turned down the ballot measure that would have raised their property taxes to fund the ill-conceived notion. In turn, team owner Richard E. Jacobs went to HOK, the Kansas City architectural firm, for the design of Jacobs Field. The sticker price would top out at $175 million, a veritable steal compared with subsequent ballparks that would open. Jacobs himself earned

naming rights when he funded 52 percent of the new ballpark. The remainder was publicly funded through a so-called "sin tax," a fifteen-year increase in alcohol and tobacco sales tax in Cuyahoga County. That means if you buy a beer at the game you're paying for the park. Hey now, we can understand taxing smokers—but why alcohol? No fair, especially when doctors say drinking a beer or two a day promotes good health. But anyway, at least it's a voluntary tax—for most people. The Indians also presold all of Jacobs Field's luxury boxes, and sold tax-exempt bonds to cover the remaining construction costs.

Before the Jake, the Indians played in Cleveland Municipal Stadium, an enormous structure that seated quite a bit more than seventy-thousand people. The ballpark often seemed totally empty and cavernous, even when a respectable crowd of, say, thirty thousand were on hand. Municipal Stadium was meant to be the Yankee Stadium of Cleveland, built with high hopes that crowds would fill the place. In our baseball journeys we have found other cities (Toronto) that have pejoratively nicknamed their stadiums the "Mistake by the Lake," but clearly the one in Cleveland, built seventy-five years ago where it would be exposed to the brutal winds of Lake Erie, was the originator of this infamous moniker.

There are conflicting reports about the reason Cleveland built Municipal, which was originally known as Lakefront Stadium. Sources abound, claiming that Municipal was part of a failed effort to draw the 1932 Olympics to town. This theory would further the "Mistake by the Lake" mythos, but we found this to be unsubstantiated. As far as we can tell Los Angeles had already been chosen as the site of the 1932 Games when ground was broken on Cleveland's superstadium. Lakefront—a veritable cookie-cutter prototype—was built to house baseball, football, and other functions under one roof, or in this case, beside one windy and icy cold lake. Optimistically, the city thought it might draw eighty thousand people to a baseball game, and publicly funded the $2.5 million project— the first publicly funded stadium ever built in the Major Leagues (this during the Great Depression no less).

Municipal was declared ready for play on July 1, 1931. But the Indians had yet to agree with the city on the terms of a lease, so the first game wasn't played at the park until July 31, 1932. The team made the new park its home for the remainder of the season and for the full 1933 season. But the optimism that had led the city to build such a huge facility soon proved unfounded. The ballpark was frequently empty, and so beginning in 1934 the Indians played there only on Sundays and holidays when larger-than-usual crowds were expected. The high costs of operating the huge facility made it preferable for the Indians to play most of their games at League Park, their former and much more intimate home.

League Park, the first home of the Indians, sat on the corner of 66th Street and Lexington Street, in the heart of what was once Cleveland's most prosperous area. Though the team underwent several name changes, Cleveland was one of the original members of the American League when it formed in 1901, along with Chicago, Boston, and Detroit. The "Cleveland Blues," as they were known that year, became the "Broncos," then the "Naps" in honor of star player Napolean Lajoie. The Indians name was chosen as the team's moniker in honor of Louis "Chief" Sockalexis, the first Native American known to play professional baseball. Sockalexis had great talent but his years in Cleveland (1897–1899) were marred by personal problems, and his performance on the field fell off dramatically after a promising rookie campaign in which he batted .341. Before his Major League career Sockalexis attended the College of the Holy Cross in Worcester, Massachusetts, Josh's alma mater. (By the way, the Worcester Brown Stockings were an early National League team that left town to become first the St. Louis Browns, and then eventually, the current Baltimore Orioles.)

On October 2, 1908, Cleveland's Addie Joss tossed a perfect game against Chicago. Tragically Joss would die three years later of spinal meningitis. A benefit game for the Joss family was held at League Park in 1911, featuring many of the great players of the day, including Ty Cobb, Walter Johnson, Tris Speaker, Cy Young, and Lajoie. The game would be the forerunner of today's All-Star Game, raising nearly $13,000 dollars.

Baseball had a convoluted history in Cleveland before League Park. The city played host to a National Association team called Forest City in 1871 and 1872. From 1876 until 1884, Cleveland had an entrant in the National League, and in 1886 and 1887 a Cleveland team played in the American Association. The year

1890 saw two Cleveland outfits in action, one in the NL and one in the upstart Player's League. When the Player's League disbanded after the 1890 season, the NL held a monopoly on baseball in America.

On May 1, 1891, the Cleveland Spiders led by Cy Young played their first game at League Park. Though the Spiders never led the NL in wins, the "arachnids" did earn passage to the Temple Cup, the equivalent of today's World Series, three times—in 1892, 1895, and 1896, winning the 1895 cup with a victory over Baltimore. But the team's fortunes took a turn for the worse when in 1899 owner Frank Robinson transferred all of the team's best players to the St. Louis Browns, which he had recently purchased. After the departure of players like Young, Jesse Burkett, and first-baseman/manager Patsy Tebeau, the Spiders posted an all-time-worst 20–134 record that season, finishing eighty-four games behind first place Brooklyn. After the season, the Spiders were cut, as the NL contracted from twelve to eight teams. There are now rules against holding controlling interest in more than one Major League Baseball franchise simultaneously. Except for the fact that all the owners now hold a share in the Expos.

League Park was an odd square-shaped structure, with its deepest corner just left of center field at an amazing 505 feet from home plate. Prior to construction owners of surrounding properties refused to sell their land and buildings to the city, accounting for the odd shape. The right field corner was very shallow at 290 feet, so a forty-foot high wall was constructed. Atop the wall rose twenty feet of chicken wire that kept balls in play. A sixty-foot wall? Now that's what we call distinctive.

The AL Indians took the World Series from the Brooklyn Dodgers in 1920, in a battle of two teams that had never won it all. Under Tris Speaker the Tribe disposed of the Dodgers five games to two in the best-of-nine series. Game 5, which the Indians won 8–1 to go up three games to two, saw Elmer Smith hit the first grand salami in World Series history. Also in the game, Jim Bagby, who led the AL with thirty-one wins that year, hit the first homer by a pitcher in Series history. And perhaps most remarkably, Indians second-baseman Bill Wambsganss pulled off the only unassisted triple play in Series history in the fifth inning. With runners on first and second, Wambsganss snagged a line drive for one out, stepped on second to double off one runner, and tagged the runner coming from first-base to second to retire the side. All this on October 10, 1920, at League Park.

Cleveland had perhaps more teams attempt to form a franchise in the Negro Leagues than any other, with the Buckeyes being the only one that lasted for more than a few years. This list of names is long for a city this size; it includes the Bears, Browns, Buckeyes, Cubs, Elites, Giants, Hornets, Red Sox, Stars, Tate Stars, and Tigers. The Buckeyes played at League Park from 1943 to 1948, winning the Negro League World Series in 1945 when they swept the Homestead Grays.

The Indians finally moved into Municipal Stadium full-time in 1947 under the guidance of owner Bill Veeck. Yes, that Bill Veeck. Veeck had been at the helm for less than two years when in 1948 he brought the World Series title back to Cleveland, as the Tribe beat both Boston teams in the playoffs. How so in the days before playoffs, you ask? Behind the hitting of Larry Doby (the AL's first African American player, picked up from the Newark Eagles in 1947), and the pitching of Bob Feller and Satchel Paige, Cleveland was tied at the end of the regular season with the Red Sox. Both teams had identical 96–59 records. A historic one-game playoff was instituted and won by the Indians at Fenway

Park, thus robbing Boston of its chance for an all-Beantown World Series. In the World Series the Indians defeated the Boston Braves, four games to two. After that great moment in time, Veeck left town for St. Louis where he attempted to resurrect the Browns. Nonetheless, the Indians returned to the World Series in 1954 to face the New York Giants. But the Tribe lost in a four-game sweep.

Originally 470 feet to center, the dimensions of Munic-

home plate

Photo by Kevin O'Connell

ipal were toned down a bit over the years, to 404 feet. Still, no batter ever put a ball in the center field bleachers of the stadium. But even if no one could "reach the bleach," and the Indians were sliding down to become one of the worst franchises in baseball, there were plenty of other hijinks to keep people occupied. When the Indians were mathematically eliminated from the pennant race during the 1949 season, Bill Veeck and the Tribe ceremonially buried their 1948 pennant in center field before a game.

During the seventh inning of a double-header dubbed "Nickel Beer Night," Indians fans threw bottles on the field and at the umps, and the home team ended up forfeiting both games. On May 15, 1981, Lenny Barker tossed a perfect game against the Blue Jays that is still replayed in local bars on the anniversary. And it need be mentioned, only 7,290 fans were on hand to see it live. Once, the Oakland A's Jose Canseco drifted back in left field after a deep fly ball, which bounced off his head and over the wall for a "ground rule" home run.

Then there was Boston pitcher "Oil Can" Boyd's much-publicized quote about the sta-

dium. When a game was called off because of fog in 1986, the Can quipped, "That's what you get for building a ballpark next to the ocean." Oh, the humanity. In Oil Can's defense, John Kruk made a similar statement, and there is a movement to rename the Great Lakes "the great north salt-free ocean," but it is a rather small group of folks leading the movement and they belong to the Lake Erie Institute for the Not-So-Clever.

Municipal Stadium would close its doors for good in 1993 after the Indians played their last game of the season, and the National Football League Browns left town to become the Baltimore Ravens. But Cleveland baseball would have its revenge on Baltimore by pilfering many of its coaches and players, including Eddie Murray, Dennis "El Presidente" Martinez, and Jose Mesa. The added pitching and Murray's bat helped put the Tribe atop the AL Central and into the World Series in both 1995 and 1997. In the 1995 Series the Indians met an unstoppable Atlanta Braves team. The 1997 Series loss to the Marlins was much more heartbreaking for Tribe fans, because the team was *so* close to winning it all. It was, dare we say, Bill Buckner-esque. Cleveland was within two outs of victory in

TRIVIA TIMEOUT

Scout: What percentage of Indians tickets for the 1996 season sold before the season began?

Warrior: What Cleveland-area native dreamed of buying the Indians, then went on to become one of the most notorious owners in baseball history elsewhere?

Chief: In what year did Major League teams first begin wearing uniform numbers?

Look for the answers in the text.

Game 7 when Craig Counsell hit a sacrifice fly against Mesa to tie the game at 2–2 and send it into extra innings. In the bottom of the eleventh, Florida's Edgar Renteria singled over Chuck Nagy's head with the bases loaded to score Counsell and end the game. The Marlins became the first wild card team to ever win the World Series. The fact that Florida was dismantled by a cost-conscious owner immediately after the Series did little to salve inconsolable Tribe fans.

But just because the Indians have yet to recapture the Series, their success is no matter for dismissal. Though they had the dynasty in place and have been closer than most teams ever want to get to the Series (without actually winning it), they have transformed themselves into one of the most dominant baseball franchises of recent history. By 2001, the Indians had won the AL Central title six out of seven seasons. Their management, farm system, and fan base had all improved by leaps and bounds, from mediocre to top notch. Then in 2002 things fell apart when management seemingly surrendered by trading ace Bartolo Colon and losing Jim Thome to free agency. Not surprisingly, the team's 2003 edition was one of the weaker squads in the league. But Indians fans, take heart. The team is stocking the farm system

with young talent and has its mind set on making a championship run in the future. When that long-awaited return to glory does come, let's not forget the role Jacobs Field has played in the Indians' return to respectability. For many years, this team was the laughingstock of the American League, until the Jake gave it, and its fans, a new life.

Getting a Choice Seat

This was once the hottest ticket in baseball, selling out an MLB record 455 straight games. Wow! That's five-and-a-half seasons worth of games. Luckily for road-tripping fans things have cooled off in Cleveland. Though tickets are not as hard to come by as they once were, games still occasionally sell out. And while there are plenty of good seats, there are plenty of lousy seats that should be avoided.

The Indians are one of the teams to adopt the "Showcase Series" ticket model, which means that tickets to Yankees, Reds, and other select games cost significantly more than normal games. Comparatively these primo games make tickets for regular games seem cheap. The Indians actually lowered the prices for bleacher and upper-deck seats before the 2003 season—a telltale sign that tickets aren't exactly flying off the shelf—or out the ticket window, as it were.

Sellout Index: 30% of games sellout
Seating Capacity: 43,345
Ticket Office: (866) 48-TRIBE
www.indians.com

Field Box (Sections 136–167)

Ah, yes, the good seats. Expect to pay for these seats dearly, however. The entire lower bowl offers a fairly gradual pitch, which can make the top of these sections farther from the action than expected. The lowest rows of these sections are called the **Diamond Box** seats, but are season-ticket seats, and thus usually unavailable except through ticket brokers. Though there is a large amount of foul territory directly behind home plate, it decreases down the lines, making the seats in Sections 136, 138, 165, and 167 very close to the action. But these are all good seats. Avoid Rows AA and higher in Sections 136–149 if you don't like the overhang. Behind home plate and on the left field side (Sections 150–167) the overhang is not an issue.

Lower Box (Sections 116–134, 169–179)

These are almost all good seats, nice and wide, and angled toward the action. The first few rows are called Baseline Boxes, and are more expensive, but are only significantly better seats in certain sections. Sections 115 and 116 are behind the right field foul pole and best to be avoided. Section 117 is only mildly affected by the pole. Section 119 is oddly detached from the rest of the bowl in the right field corner and feels removed from the field. Sections 120 and 121 in right are fine, but in Sections 122 to 134 an overhang obstructs the back five rows, so stick with Rows A–Z and avoid the double-letter rows.

On the left field side get into Section 168, as it's the only pure section of these seats as far as sight lines are concerned. Seats in Section 170 lose the tiniest bit of the left field corner beneath the foul pole. In Sections 171, 172, and 173 this loss of sight line is not too noticeable except for only the very particular (in other words, Josh was miffed), but the loss of the corner increases until Section 176, where the left field wall is lost and all of the corner. In Sections 177 and 178 the blockage is fairly severe, and seats along the high back rows of 178— Rows W–Z, AA–GG—have significant blockage of sight lines and should be avoided, if at all possible.

Infield Lower Box (Sections 250–267)

Rather than being their own level (as the 200 Level numbers would indicate) these are really just the farthest reaches of Field Boxes. And like their lower counterparts, there is only an overhang in the back few rows, and even then only slightly. When we were sitting in our seats, it was barely noticeable.

Lower Reserve (Sections 101–113)

These seats have backs and so are not technically bleacher seats, but for our money, they're bleachers and are the ones that you want at the Jake. The tiniest bit of the field is lost here with the low wall, but it's nothing compared with the other bleachers. These seats get a lot of sun, and angle nicely toward the plate. Section 101 for the most part is a good section, but avoid the top four rows (Y, Z, AA, and BB) as the view is obstructed by trees growing in the batter's eye. All in all there is a gradual pitch to these seats giving a decent view.

Club Seating (Sections 326–348)

The three-story Club level situates the upper deck above it much higher than it should be. Thanks for nothing, suits.

All of the triangle windows down in the left field corner belong to the Terrace Club Restaurant, which has delicious food for mucho dollars.

> **SEATING TIP**
>
> ➡ THE FIRST-LEVEL SEATS on the left field line are far superior to their right field counterparts for the same price. The right field seats are obstructed by an overhanging Club deck while the left field seats are not. The left field seats also get afternoon sun, while the right field seats are more often in the shade. For being only a handful of dollars more than bleachers, these are much better, and we recommend them.

Mezzanine Seating (Sections 303–317)

Located in straightaway right field, the seats in Sections 303–317 are much better than the 400–500 Level seats above them. And some sections are not too bad compared with the bleacher seats down below. Seats near the rail, in the low-numbered rows of Section 304 have the foul pole to deal with, but the sight lines are still good. Section 311 has no foul pole obstruction except for foul territory, but that's not a problem. The under-hang is not a factor, but there is a low outfield fence that blocks only the tiniest bit of the field, versus the high wall in the left field bleachers that blocks much more of the sightlines.

Section 303 is pretty far away and should be avoided. The seats kind of hang out there in space, and too much of Sections 101, 102, and 103 are visible from up here, thus leaving you envious of how infinitely better their seats are.

View Box (Sections 436–468)

We're not quite sure what the Indians are thinking with the pricing structure of these. They're decent enough 400 Level seats, but the same coin will fetch Baseline Box seats. For this kind of dough it's better to get into a low-level seat in Section 168. Also, avoid Sections 436 and 437 because of under-hang issues that cause the loss of much of the right field corner.

Upper Box
(Sections 420–434, 469–478, 537–567)

These seats are high above the field for "boxes." Sitting in Section 477, the corner near the left field foul pole is lost from view. Sections 420–429 all have some portion of the field blocked by the right field foul pole. Section 567 is obstructed by the scoreboard, which shaves from view the foul line.

All of the 500 Level seats above Row S are a long way away from the action, even the seats directly behind home plate. We recommend

getting seats in rows as low as possible, otherwise there is a loss of that "right-atop-the-action" feeling that makes sitting in the upper deck enjoyable.

The best of these seats are the **Infield Upper Boxes** (lower rows of Sections 537–567) which are definitely worth the extra dough.

Upper Reserve
(Sections 403–419, 522–533, 570–577)

Like most upper decks, the seats in many sections have spots of blockage—with the railings, the extended corners of the tunnels, the glass safety structures above the tunnels, and such coming into play. There are also under-hang issues, as the deck below one's feet blocks the left field corner in Sections 564–572, although the view improves farther from the plate in Sections 575–577.

In Section 533 the right field corner disappears almost totally from view because of the under-hang. The foul pole is nearly completely blocked, and all of the right field foul territory and most of the right field corner are blocked.

The seats in Sections 528–525 angle more toward the plate, and the whole right field side offers a sweet view of downtown. We recommend the first-base side of the Upper Reserve highly over the third-base side, as opposed to the lower level where the left field side is preferable. But once you get out to the outfield—forget about it. The Upper Reserve seats in deep right field are pretty terrible. We recommend avoiding any section numbered lower than Section 411. Better to sit closer and higher up than way out there in the Upper Reserve.

"Hey, wake up," said Kevin nudging his road-weary friend.

"I'm awake, I'm awake," Josh replied groggily. "I never sleep at ball games. It's a sin, I think. I don't know if it's the sunshine up here, the chicken, or the thin air. But I am beat like a Chuck Nagy fastball."

"ZZZZZZZZZ," said Kevin drifting off.

"Hey, wake up," said Josh. "Game's on."

"I never sleep at ball games," said Kevin.

"Yeah, me either."

Reserve General Admission (Sections 504–521)

How can these seats be general admission and reserved at the same time? Stupid name.

Many of these sections don't angle toward the action on the infield, which adds to the feeling that they are a long way from the ball game. We recommend avoiding Sections 521 and all of the sections around the bizarre corner until Section 518, unless it's Game 7 of the World Series and your TV's on the fritz.

We must admit, there is a nice breeze in the upper seats of the upper deck and an almost 360-degree panoramic view of downtown around the ballpark.

We'd rather sit in Sections 516 and 514 than in 518–521 as the former sections angle more toward the action and feel closer. Section 511 again begins to feel a long way away. The only people out there on the day we visited were slumming.

Bleachers (Section 180–185)

Normally we love the bleachers: hanging out in the sun, standing in the cheap seats, drinking beers with no shirt on. It's great. But unfortunately tickets to these bleachers restrict inhabitants from other sections of the park, so if you're only in town for one day to see the Jake, you probably don't want to be trapped out there. In addition, the upper seats in these bleachers have blocked views and aren't that cheap—though they were significantly lowered in 2003. The lower seats are called field bleachers and aren't too bad. If you're going to pop twenty bucks, it would be better spent in the Lower Reserve (really bleachers without sight lines blocked), or better still, buy a cheap Reserve General Admission (oxymoron) seat and sit on one of the patios. Then again, if you want to sit near the "drum guy" the bleachers may be your pick.

Standing Room Only

These tickets go on sale only after the crap seats in the Reserve General Admission sell out. It would be much preferable to just stand in the SRO area anyway, which consists of the Home Run Porch in the left field corner and the Back Yard Picnic Plaza in center. Luckily at the Jake, this is possible. Arrive early to secure a picnic table.

Black Market

Scalpers lurk on the street corners surrounding the park. They're not hard to find, and we saw a few doing business in clear view of Cleveland's finest, so legality doesn't seem to be a problem. Tickets are not at a premium any more, so use this to your advantage.

Before/After the Game

Jacobs Field is the cornerstone of the "Gateway District," and is part of the downtown sports complex that also includes the Gund Arena, parking garages, and plazas. We don't traditionally like sports complexes, but the Jake is also nestled into downtown nicely, giving it the feel of an urban ballpark. Strange as it is to say, it's a mixture of both ideas, depending on which angle it is viewed from. Keeping the park close to city streets has allowed the area around the park to flourish with bars and restaurants, while building it into the sports complex provides plenty of parking. It's a good system, combining the best of both worlds.

As distinctive as the exterior facade of the Jake is, it fits well into its surroundings. Bucking the red-brick trend of most retro ballparks, the Jake's exterior consists of huge white trusses connected to one another by Atlantic green granite, Kasota limestone, and a nearly white-colored yellow brick. It's distinctive, and it looks like Cleveland.

Getting to Jacobs Field

Most folks drive to the Jake, as it sits in the confluence of Interstates 90, 70, and 71. Finding the ballpark from whichever direction on these three interstates is fairly hassle free, as Jacobs Field has its own exits and signs guide cars right to the parking lots. If you're not taking the freeway, and are looking at a map that doesn't have the Jake on it, head your Dodge Dart for the area between East 9th Street, Carnegie Avenue, Ontario Street, and Eagle Avenue.

Most of the parking lots around the Jake charge about $10, but keep looking. On Ontario Street we saw a $4 lot, and on Huron Street we found a $3 lot at the Cleveland Tower City Center parking. Though a dingy lot that looks like something out of the movie *Rocky* it is a cheap option and pretty close. Take the elevator up to the Tower Center Mall and it will take you to Prospect Street, which is close to the ballpark. When coming in off of Huron Street, aim for the large guitar of the Hard Rock Hotel and you will run into the parking lot.

If you're like us, and you want to find any way possible to get to the park without driving, try taking the Rapid Transit Authority or the bus from your hotel. For schedule and route information visit RTA's Web site at www.rid-erta.com.

Check It Out

"ROCK-N-FELLER" PLAZA

Named for the greatest Indian pitcher of them all, and located just outside of Gate C, Feller Plaza is a great place to enter the game. A

Bob Feller statue

Photo by Kevin O'Connell

statue of Bob Feller looms above the plaza, honoring a man who pitched three no-hitters for the Indians (one on Opening Day of 1940) and led them to two World Series, one of which they won. Feller was an eight-time All-Star and won twenty games in six different seasons. Many folks—mostly Indians fans—consider the right-hander the best pitcher in history. We think that might be overstating things a tad. But there's no denying that Feller, who finished with a career ERA of 3.25 and 266 wins, was one of the best pitchers of his era.

A closer look on the plaza reveals marble benches scattered about that don't look like much on first glance, but are actual letters that spell out "Who's on First." They're pretty clever fellers.

Kevin: "That wasn't a Bob Feller routine, that was a Penn and Teller routine."

Josh: "Do you ever shut up?"

"HELLO CLEVELAND!"

Many cities across America have recently instituted public art projects, which consist of a series of the same animal or fish, all painted differently. Some towns have done a series of carp, others have done pigs, dogs, and elephants. Josh's home town, Charlton, Massachusetts, even did a series of painted aardvarks.

Cleveland's answer to this trend in urban art: oversized painted guitars—perhaps to cement the city's reputation as the rock-'n'-roll capital of the world. The project is called Guitar Mania and benefits the Make-a-Wish Foundation, United Way, and other charities. Now you could travel all over the city to see these decorative rock icons, but one in Feller Plaza was done by Omar Vizquel. Not only is "Little O" a magician at shortstop, he is also quite deft with a paintbrush, as his guitar dons names such as "Lemon Lofton" and "Frozen Alomar" and "Boudreau Ramirez." Lou Boudreau was the Indian player-manager who invented the "Ted Williams Shift" employed by many infields today to defend against prominent left-handed pull hitters. This is the maneuver where three infielders shift to the first-base side of the field.

SEE THE GAME FOR FREE

Between Gates A and B on Eagle Avenue off of Ontario Street is a tall iron gate from where the public can actually look down into the ballpark and see the field. It's a great place to catch a glimpse, or watch for a while longer if no one hassles you. We know what you're thinking. However, the only problem is once the standing-room area fills up during the playoffs you won't be able to see a thing, unless you brought a step ladder.

Watering Holes and Outside Eats

A vibrant little bar and restaurant scene has sprouted up around the Jake, comprising established joints in the area that have enjoyed the recent renaissance along with some new places. The Gateway offers much variety—from dance and blues clubs to country-and-western joints. And with the Gund Arena nearby, many of these places have the benefit of not having to do all their business during the baseball months, so they're likely to be around a while.

PANINI'S BAR AND GRILL (840 Huron Road, and Many Other Locations)

Panini's (literally "little bread") is our favorite place in Cleveland for great food and cheap beers. It features a variety of delicious fresh bread sandwiches, loaded with meat, cheese, tomato, and with French fries and cole slaw piled right in there, much like Primanti Brothers in Pittsburgh. The franchise near the ballpark offers outdoor seating, as well as two large rooms inside, each with its own bar. And Panini's offers dollar drafts on game days. One catch: during the game only.

COOPERSTOWN (2217 E. 9th Street)

Directly across 9th Street from the Jake is a place called Cooperstown, and we were instantly intrigued. When we found out Cooperstown is owned by Alice Cooper—yes, "No More Mr. Nice Guy" himself—we were doubly excited by the prospects. After all, Alice Cooper was Marilyn Manson before MM was born, removed two of his ribs, and started painting his face. But as uniquely rock 'n' roll as this joint may have sounded, we were a bit disappointed to find out it is a chain. Still, Cooperstown is very close to the ballpark, and it has a large food-and-bar menu with items cleverly named with baseball and classic rock music in mind. So until there's one outside every ballpark in America, we give Cooperstown and Alice the thumbs up. We also enjoyed the loads of sports and rock memorabilia hanging on the walls. On game days it will be packed with people, as it's a tad touristy: a bit like the Hard Rock Café meets Applebee's.

THE WINKING LIZARD TAVERN
(811 Huron Road)

The Winking Lizard advertises its fare as "Great American Food" and we agree: it is a great place for cheap food and drinks. The joint doesn't overextend itself with too many offerings: just sandwiches, burgers, salads, wings, and barbecue. Most menu items are in the $5 to $8 range. Better arrive early on game day, as it's packed before and after the ball game.

THE CLEVELANDER BAR AND GRILL
(834 Huron Road)

A favorite of our friend Dave Hayden, the place is much like the man himself: no frills, and a tad hokey. The name may sound upscale, but there is always country music on the jukebox and happy hour runs from 4:00 P.M. to 7:00 P.M. The food menu is inexpensive with nothing over $7. With a back-alley entrance that leads to the Jake, this joint is close to the ballpark and only started to get rockin' as we were leaving to catch the first pitch. We didn't take it personally.

THIRSTY PARROT (821 Bolivar Road)

Tucked behind two parking lots in a back alley close to the park, the Thirsty Parrot features loud music, outdoor seating, and a Caribbean Cantina. This is definitely the place where Jimmy Buffett and his parrot-headed fans would congregate in Cleveland. You know, a place to drink fru-fru drinks and cruise for girls who are wearing leis and grass skirts. But those are just the waitresses. The Cantina seats many and does a good job of blasting its tunes toward the Jake.

HARRY CORVAIR'S (810 Huron Road)

This is not a place to go before the game, but more like a dance club. It shares the same warehouse building that houses the Thirsty Parrot.

NEW YORK SPAGHETTI HOUSE
(2173 East 9th Street)

This is a top-notch family-style dinner place. In other words, you'll get a ton of food. Josh highly recommends the meatballs.

FERRIS STEAK HOUSE (2120 E. 4th Street)

This long time Cleveland establishment is the place to go when someone else is footing the bill. In other words: good food, high prices. The restaurant has roll-up windows that gives it an open-air feel on warm days, plus a few TVs behind the bar showing the game.

FAT FISH BLUES (21 Prospect Street)

On the corner of Prospect and Ontario is a place called Fat Fish Blues, and like its name suggests, it's a great place to get a fat piece of Creole-cooked fish, or to hear some phat Cajun tunes. Sandwiches can be had for $7, but entrées range from $11 to $18. From cat-in-a-bag to shrimp étouffée, this joint is a little bit of the French Quarter in downtown Cleveland. And it's open until 2:00 A.M. on weekends.

PLENTY OF VENDORS

After a bite to eat and a few pints, you'll find plenty of vendors hawking their wares outside the Jake, from guys selling peanuts to sports apparel. A funny thing we noticed: the plethora of orange and brown banners and T-shirts that read "Pittsburgh Sucks." Now since the color scheme was way off for the Indians and since the two teams don't play in the same league, we knew these were Browns-Steelers inspired. The only problem was that we also saw in Pittsburgh yellow and black gear with "Cleveland Sucks" plastered everywhere. For hating each other so much, these two towns have an awful lot in common.

Inside the Jake

The Jake offers a festive game-day environment

both outside and inside the park. Tribe fans are rabid and it's clear they enjoy their downtown digs. Although it seats nearly the same number of people as Camden Yards, the Jake feels larger inside, perhaps because of the three levels of club seating/press levels that push the upper deck a bit too high. It's reminiscent of US Cellular Field, but not nearly as bad. There are some great features of the ballpark that you won't find at other parks, so be sure to spend some time walking around and taking in all the sites.

Perhaps the most distinctive feature inside the park is the outfield wall. It truly ties the entire park together. Directly below the left field bleachers—down the line at 325 feet in the corner and out to 370 feet in left-center—is a 19-foot wall known as "the mini-green monster," because of its similarities to the left field wall in Boston. Straightaway center field logs in at 410 feet at a corner where the two major walls of the outfield meet to form the deepest part of the park. Above deep center is the batter's eye, which consists of a nice grouping of decorative trees that blend in well with the rest of the park. Tucked behind the trees is the four-tiered Davey Tree picnic area. In right-center, nearly 400 feet from the plate resides the Indians' elevated bull pen, which allows fans to easily see who's warming up. Right field features an angled set of bleachers between the bull pens, as the visiting pen is situated in the right field corner at 325 feet from the batter's box.

Don't Try This At Home

Perhaps the most distinctive feature of the Jake is its trademark gray dirt. Used on the mound, in the infield, and on the warning track, there is no dirt of this color used anywhere else in the Majors. The first time Kevin saw this on television, he futzed with the color-control knob on his set, but once seen in person, the gray dirt is wonderfully unique. Dredged from the Ohio River, not only is this

playing surface the only one of its kind, it's also a local treasure. We'd like to point out that we're not advocating that every ballpark in America comes up with its own color of dirt— orange dirt for Baltimore, teal dirt for Miami, and so on. This isn't the NBA.

What a Lovely Day for a Picnic, er, Ball Game

The Jake features two prominent picnic areas in its outfield. The first is the Davey Tree Picnic plaza in straightaway center. For those seated in the picnic area, the small forest of trees as well as the walls of ivy enhance the shady atmosphere. This beautiful and organic dual use of the batter's eye is far superior than, say, a large wall stuck up for no reason such as the one at Coors Field in Denver.

The four-tiered levels of the picnic area are nicely sculptured into the ballpark and don't dominate the look of the outfield as in other parks. The lower levels are often reserved for large groups, but sometimes open up if they have not been reserved. The Picnic Pavilion food court supplies the food to this area, offering the same fare available in the rest of the park.

Back behind the left field wall on the first level is "the Patio," sponsored by a major beer company. The Patio is the perfect place to get a beer and enjoy the game in the sunshine, and upgrade your seat.

Davey Tree sits just above the Indians bull pen and has a low railing where fans can watch the pitchers warming up. This is designed much better than some of the other bull pen areas in the league. Fans are not down on the same level as the pitchers, nor do they look in on them like animals at the zoo. The pitchers have their own area and fans have their area to watch the game or watch the pitchers warm up. It seems more respectful, while still allowing the fans a unique view of the action.

Three Bulls in the Pen?

The Jake's bull pens are much different than those of most parks. First off, they're perpendicular to the outfield wall. For those of you who slept through geometry class, that means they don't run alongside the wall, but rather the pitcher throws toward home plate. Reminiscent of Dodger Stadium, we like this because it gets more outfield seats closer to the action. The pens are also elevated so everyone can see who's warming up a bit better. Also they feature real grass, while the visitors are relegated to artificial turf. Well, we suppose there has to be some hometown advantage.

But what we couldn't fathom were the three mounds and three plates that both the Indians and the visiting pens house. Why do they need to have three? One for the left-hander, one for the right-hander, then what? We spoke with an usher who said in all his years at the Jake, he'd never seen three pitchers warming up at the same time.

Josh: "Maybe it's so they can warm up two lefties and a righty, or two righties and a lefty, and perhaps confuse the other team."

Kevin: "Do you think each team has three bull pen catchers?"

One Large Scoreboard

While we usually don't wax rhapsodic about scoreboards or Jumbotrons, the scoreboard above the left field bleachers at the Jake deserves mention. It has the distinction of being the largest scoreboard in the big leagues. Being so large however, we wonder if it wouldn't have been better to have a smaller scoreboard elsewhere in the park, and let the view of downtown Cleveland loom into the park to a much greater degree.

Retired Numbers

Above the right field bleachers hang the numbers of the Indians who have reached the Happy Hunting Grounds. While most of the retired numbers are standard, there is one that is pretty cool. Number 455 has been retired for the fans, as thanks for selling out the first 455 games at The Jake. After the 1995 American League pennant, the Jake had the distinction of selling out every single home game for the 1996 season, before it even began. Now our memories of twenty-five hundred people watching a day game at Municipal are officially erased.

The other numbers retired include: number 19 Bob Feller, number 21 Bob Lemon, number 3 Earl Averill, number 14 Larry Doby, number 5 Lou Boudreau, number 18 Mel Harder, and as always, number 42 Jackie Robinson.

Incidentally, the Indians were one of the first two teams to play a game with numbers on their backs when they took on the Yankees on May 13, 1929. Babe Ruth and Lou Gehrig led the Bronx Bombers to a 4–3 win.

MiniMonster

This nineteen-foot-high wall in left is more than reminiscent of Fenway's thirty-seven-foot-high Green Monster. And Cleveland's monster has always had bleacher seats above it, something Fenway's Wall didn't have until 2003. It creates a nice effect, having the wall there for balls to bounce off, and also having bleachers directly above for powerful home run shots to be snagged by lucky bleacher creatures.

Circle Up the Wagons

Because the bleacher seats in left field are cordoned off from the rest of the parks, you can't walk all the way around the Jake, which is unfortunate. The bleachers in left field are for bleacher ticket holders only and ushers do not allow other fans to walk through them. While this point seems small, we like to walk the whole park 'round and see it from all

MOMENTS OF GLORY

SURROUNDING the outside of the first-level concourse hang lighted signs that commemorate famous and popular Indians moments. We liked this idea and took note of our favorites.

- The first game at the new Cleveland Stadium in 1932 was one of the city's greatest sporting events, with a total attendance of 80,184.
- Frank Robinson's player-manager debut on April 8, 1975, made him the first African American manager in MLB history. He began his charge in grand style hitting a homer in his first at bat.
- Cy Young's five hundredth win came in 1910 as a member of the Cleveland Naps. He had previously pitched for the Cleveland Spiders from 1890 to 1898.

Here's one moment of glory that we didn't find commemorated on a banner: George Steinbrenner was an Ohio native who hoped to own the Tribe but settled for the Yanks. That's right, the leader of the Evil Empire himself was born in Rocky River, Ohio. His dream to own the Indians almost came to fruition, but he was cut out of the deal by Nick Mileti for reasons only Mileti knows, but we can speculate on. The Big Stein went on to buy the New York Yankees and form one of the most infamous dynasties in Major League history.

angles. The way the Jake is, inevitably you have to double back.

Fireworks on the Roof

We haven't enjoyed fireworks on top of the garage since high school. But at the Jake fireworks are shot from the top of the parking structure across Eagle Avenue that is attached to the ballpark. We saw the kind that shoot flaming colored rockets into the air and the cannon-fire-with-big-boom kinds. The team fires them off after the end of the National Anthem, when the Indians hit a home run, and when the Indians win.

Stadium Eats

While we rate the food inside the Jake somewhere between moderate to less than satisfactory, it's just the kind of food that makes a book like ours necessary. While there are some tasty options, it's best to know what they are before you waste a load of cash on something that tastes like crud.

INDIANS DOG (Dog Rating)
The Thirteenth Best Hot Dog in the Majors

This isn't the best dog in the world of MLB but it certainly isn't the worst either. The taste is right there with the top big league weenies, but the texture is a bit off. Topped with the right mustard though, this dog is sure to satisfy.

STADIUM MUSTARD VERSUS
BALLPARK MUSTARD (Trademark Food)

As far as the great rivalries go, there has always been the Red Sox versus the Yankees, Cardinals versus Cubs. In the 1980s it was the Lakers versus the Celtics, and in college hoops Kevin's Gonzaga Bulldogs versus the NCAA selection committee. But there is perhaps no rivalry in sports more ferocious than that of Stadium Mustard versus Ballpark Mustard in Cleveland. Both of these brand names are widely available at Cleveland grocers, but only Stadium Mustard is available at the Jake, and thus garners our vote for trademark Cleveland food. Yes, we are aware that it's really only a condiment. But whether you put it on your dog, a Polish, or on a brat, nothing will make you feel more like you're in the land of Cleve, than biting down into something (anything) in a bun, slathered in Stadium Mustard. Now while it would be our preference to have both mustards at the Jake (as was the case at Municipal), such is life. Why not pick up a container of both on your way into the ballpark and conduct your own taste test?

Best of the Rest

Though at first he was slightly offended by the name, Kevin tried the Irish Delight, a corned beef sandwich piled high atop savory coleslaw. It was pretty tasty, but then Josh tried the Shaved Roast Beef, which we both agreed (yes, we share sandwiches) was much better. These treats are available at the **Deli**.

The Jake features deserts galore. You cannot go wrong with a **Krispy Kreme Doughnut**, regardless of cost. Better still, we thought they only sold bulk candy by the pound at the supermarket, but it's available at the ballpark in Cleveland. Exceptional Ruggles-brand premium ice cream is available in Moose Tracks, Mint Chocolate Chip, Rocky Road, Butter Pecan, and Cookies and Crème.

The ballpark's freshly-cut fries are also tasty if you get them when they're fresh. You know our theory: everything is better when deep fried. Just beware: those heat lamps can wilt the zip right out of your delicious snack.

SAY "NO, THANKS," AND WALK AWAY

We eagerly sampled the three-piece fried chicken dinner on our quest for perfect ballpark chicken, but sadly, we were unimpressed. This bird went from frozen solid, to a greasy mess, to bone dried for hours under orange heat lamps. It left us longing for the disgusting truck-stop chicken that Josh kept picking up on the road.

Steer clear of the chicken fajita salad as well. It's not authentic Mexican, not very fresh, and we're not even completely convinced that it was chicken.

While we don't necessarily put the Johnsonville brat in the "Say 'No, Thanks,' and Walk Away" category, we must include a word of warning: these brats are a bit spongier than we usually like and taste a bit more like an Irish breakfast sausage than the hearty sausages available throughout much of the midwest.

STADIUM SUDS

Other than the standard macrobrewery options, the Jake offers "Beers of the World" at kiosks throughout the park. But Killian's Red they have mistakenly called an Irish beer, and as Kevin points out, it is brewed by Coors. Not only that, but we are aware of many microbrewery beers that hail from the Great Lakes region, so why aren't they represented here?

The Jacobs Field Experience

There is the prevalent feeling among Indians fans that the Supreme Being will not allow any team from Cleveland to win a sports championship because "God hates Cleveland," for some unspecified reason. Josh takes umbrage at this attitude, claiming the Tribe had won two World Series since his beloved Sox last triumphed.

But conversely, there is also a Midwestern optimism that brims in Indians fans each year during spring training, and a Brooklyn Dodgeresque "wait until next year" attitude when things don't pan out so well for Wahoo Nation. Prevalent as well among Tribe fans is a sense of fraternity. After all, Indians apparel

---

JOSH'S THRIFTY EATER'S TIPS

GO TO THE KIDS' concession stands to get the same dogs and drinks, only cheaper. It's a great idea and will only last until this book is published and they figure out our evil plan. And here's another tip. The Jake is the only park in the big leagues that houses three separate designated-driver booths. You'll find one Guest Services stand on the upper level behind Section 518, one on the lower level behind Section 175, and another on the lower level behind Section 121. All you need to do is print your name on a sheet of paper and you get a coupon for a free twelve-ounce soda. Josh got three freebies for a $7.75 value.

WHY NOT pay a visit to the park where Nap Lajoie played at League Park Center, the former site of League Park? The address is 6601 Lexington Avenue, at the corner of Lexington and 66th. This once great neighborhood has suffered much dilapidation in recent years, so we recommend visiting during the day.

Public youth ball fields sit on the old grounds, but a great deal of the old park remains, more than any other old park we found. The actual ticket booths are intact as part of League Park Community Center, as is a very large part of the intricate left field exterior brick wall. The old ballpark almost takes shape as you look at the brick facade. There are efforts under way to restore the site, but the city should get on this one fast. It would be a shame to let it deteriorate any further. League Park is definitely worth a visit and a photo for anyone who is a fan of old ballparks.

Visiting League Park reminded us that it was the setting for one of the most disputed batting titles in history. In 1910 the Chalmers Automobile Company pledged to give one of its cars to the AL batting champ, and as the season wound down, it became clear that either Ty Cobb or Nap Lajoie would be driving home in style. Cobb skipped the last two games to protect the lead he enjoyed. Nap's last two games came in a doubleheader against the St. Louis Browns, and he took full advantage, bunting six times for hits, and ending up going eight for nine on the day, his lone blemish being an error charged on a throw to first. The bunt hits proved enough to give him the lead over Cobb.

There was a problem, however. The reason Nap bunted so often was that a rookie named Red Corriden was playing a deep third-base for St. Louis. After the game, Corriden said his manager Jack O'Connor told him to play back, because one of Nap's line drives might otherwise take his head off. O'Connor was a former Cleveland Spider, and teammate of Lajoie. Also it was reported that Browns coach Harry Howell tried to bribe the official scorer with a new suit, if he were to change the error to a hit, but the scorekeeper declined.

Cobb fans and Tiger president Frank Navin were furious when the papers the next day declared Lajoie the winner. But as despised around the league as Cobb was, not everyone was upset. Eight of Cobb's friendly Detroit teammates sent a telegram to Lajoie congratulating him on his victory. AL president Ban Johnson conducted an investigation of the events and determined that O'Connor and Howell had done nothing wrong, but soon after they were both removed from their positions, and were never involved with baseball again.

The *Sporting News* settled the dispute when it listed the official averages as Cobb .3850687 to Lajoie's .3840947. Chalmers gave cars to both players, but legend has it that Lajoie's car always ran better.

But there's more. In the 1980s baseball historian Paul McFarlane discovered two hits with which Cobb had been incorrectly credited during the season, giving the posthumous title to Lajoie. But Baseball Commissioner Bowie Kuhn did not revoke Cobb's 1910 title, thus preserving his streak of nine consecutive AL crowns.

---

has never reached critical mass in "coolness" across the country, and you'll rarely see the latest hip-hop star donning Chief Wahoo on a cap. Rather, if you see someone wearing the Chief Wahoo hat, dirtied and road weary, you know that person has a Cleveland connection. He has either lived in Cleveland, has relatives there, went to school there, or recently saw his first ball game in the land that boasts Bob Feller, Halle Berry, and Jesse Owens as its own.

This sense of brotherhood all comes together at the Jake to create a great game-day atmosphere. Wahoo Nation is an excited and friendly faction. Fans are crazy, mostly about their Indians. The atmosphere is infectious, so don't be surprised to find yourself rooting for the home team no matter who the Tribe is playing.

"TOM, TOM" THE DRUM GUY (Superfan)

The movie *Major League* made this guy one of the most famous superfans in the bigs. And despite his fame he's still out there for every home game. Sitting in the worst seat in the left field bleachers, he beats the drum to rally Indians hitters. He has an arrangement with the team that dictates when he is free to bang away. He only hits the drum when the Tribe has runners in scoring position and he always quits well before the pitcher delivers the ball. He sits in a nice shaded spot underneath the scoreboard with his wife.

Kevin: "What do you think it's like to be Tom-Tom's wife?"

Josh: "Why do you ask me questions like that?"

A SUPERFAN THAT "TOPS" ALL OTHERS

The 1949 season saw Indians fan Charley Lupicia gain national superfan status. With the world champion Tribe in lowly seventh place, Lupicia climbed sixty feet in the air to a perch atop the flagpole on his Cleveland deli, vowing to remain up there until the Indians either clinched the AL title or were eliminated from the pennant race. His vigil saw him atop the pole for 117 days, where he missed the birth of a child, but garnered national newspaper and magazine coverage.

Never missing a marketing opportunity, owner Bill Veeck sent a truck to transport Lupicia—still sitting atop his flagpole—to Municipal Stadium on September 25, the day the Indians were officially eliminated from the pennant race. As Lupicia finally descended, a crowd of thirty-four thousand was on hand to cheer him on. Don't ask us how he went to the bathroom during his time spent in the clouds.

DETROIT TIGERS, COMERICA PARK

A Motor City Makeover

FOXTOWN,
DETROIT, MICHIGAN

180 miles to Cleveland
260 miles to Toronto
270 miles to Cincinnati
280 miles to Chicago

A ONCE PROUD and highly successful franchise, Detroit hit rock bottom in the 1990s. The Tigers were perpetual cellar dwellers. Once-glorious Tiger Stadium had fallen into disrepair. And even loyal baseball fans cringed at the thought of visiting the crime-addled streets of Tiger Town. Something had to be done.

Now, you know we're normally purists and advocate the restoration of the classic ballparks whenever possible. And you may have noticed that we usually praise those teams that have revitalized urban neighborhoods with new ballpark projects. But in this case, we think Tiger ownership made the right call. While it may have been feasible to renovate the old yard or build a new one adjacent to it, our visit to the Tiger Stadium hood in 2002 convinced us that it had been, indeed, time for Major League Baseball to bid the area adieu.

Beautiful Comerica Park opened on April 11, 2000, with the Tigers beating Seattle 5–2, in thirty-four-degree weather. Thanks to the new ballpark, Tiger fans and management began the new century with a new lease on life. But Comerica did little to improve the team's performance on the field, though it did increase interest in the team and dramatically boost gate attendance.

Little Caesar's pizza maven and Tiger owner Mike Ilitch played a lead role in the ballpark's design. And though amusement rides, liquid fireworks, and other distractions sometimes make the ballpark seem like a more ideal setting for a carnival than a baseball game, Comerica also presents a warm and festive environment for true fans. Once you get past the kiddie attractions and reach your seats, it feels almost as if you're at a classic ballpark. The dirt path from the pitcher's mound to home plate, the steel and brick construction, the center field ivy, and the open view of downtown Detroit, all contribute to a very pleasing old-time atmosphere.

fountain

Photo by Kevin O'Connell

The 60 percent privately funded ballpark project totaled $300 million, one thousand times the $300,000 it cost to build Tiger Stadium. Now that's what we call stadium inflation. But hey, at least the unions must have made out.

Comerica's main entranceway has become one of the most distinctive in the big leagues. Eighty-foot-high baseball bats flank the gates and a massive tiger sculpture lurks in the courtyard. On the face of the ballpark itself, drain spouts sculpted to look like enormous tiger heads chomp down on oversized baseballs. Clearly, these are not the happy-go-lucky cartoon Tigers you knew and loved in the 1980s and '90s. These angry cats announce to all visitors that the bite is back in Motown. They seem to wait patiently, along with local fans, for the team to start playing that way.

The batters' eye in center field is made of mesh and ivy, an obvious attempt to replicate the ivy at Wrigley Field and Oriole Park. A walkway behind the ivy doubles as a mist tent on hot days, connecting right field and left field,

and allowing fans a peek—but just a peek—of the action between the vines.

When a Detroit player hits a home run, liquid fireworks explode out of the ivy in celebration. The water show, which comes complete with a tacky corporate logo atop the ivy, is no match for Kauffman Stadium's classy outfield fountain. If the Tigers don't homer, don't despair, we were treated to a postgame water show after the last out, even though the home team lost. But root for a hometown homer, because that way you'll also get to see the eyes of the colorful tigers atop the scoreboard light up.

Realism collides with art on the left field pavilion where statues depict several Tiger heroes in action. These include the Mechanical Man, Charlie Gehringer; "Hammering" Hank Greenberg; the Georgia Peach, Ty Cobb; Willie "the Wonder" Horton; and Al Kaline, the only player without a nickname on his plaque. These large metallic statues are not meant to be entirely true to life. The movement of one player's bat whipping through the strike zone is simulated by a long blur of batlike steel material. Another statue depicts three balls coming off a bat, and another shows turf flying into the air as a player runs. All five statues were sculpted by the husband-wife team of Omri Amrany and Julie Rotblatt-Amrany, the same Illinois artists who created the Michael Jordan statue outside of Chicago's United Center.

For a teaser before your road trip, check out the interactive Web cameras accessible through the Tigers home page, www.detroit.tigers.com. These operate twenty-four hours per day, 365 days per year, allowing fans a peak of game action, a view of the skyline, and a view of the streets immediately surrounding the ballpark. Just click and drag to direct the camera wherever you like.

The Detroit Tigers joined the American League as founding members in 1901. But the franchise actually existed before the formation of the league. The early Tigers were in Ban Johnson's Western League, which evolved into the AL, and played on "the Corner," a Detroit hardball hotbed starting in the early 1890s. Bennett Park stood on the corner of Michigan and Trumbull Avenue, complete with elm and oak trees in the field of play in the outfield. The trees, which predated the American Revolution, were removed in 1900 as the Tigers prepared to join the Major Leagues.

Tiger Stadium was originally called Navin Field, in honor of team president Frank Navin. It opened April 20, 1912, the same day as Fenway Park in Boston. The Tigers capped the historic day by downing the Cleveland Indians, 6–5.

Like many other parks of its era, Tiger Stadium was constructed to fit into an actual city block, giving the field its quirks organically, and not as a matter of design. The distance to straightaway center field originally measured 467 feet. While the 125-foot-high center field flagpole was technically on the field of play, it didn't come into play very often. In 1938 the center field fence would be brought in to 440 feet, where it would remain.

Milestone moments at Tiger Stadium included Ty Cobb's three-thousandth career hit (August 19, 1921), Eddie Collins's three-

thousandth (June 3, 1925), and Babe Ruth's seven-hundredth home run (July 13, 1934). Ruth's blast cleared the right field roof and left the yard entirely.

The only All-Star Game won by the American League between 1962 and 1983 was played at Tiger Stadium in 1971. A mammoth third-inning homer by Reggie Jackson struck a light tower above the right-center field roof, propelling the AL to a 6–4 win.

Tiger Greats statues

Photo by Kevin O'Connell

Kevin: "The NL's continuing success in the All-Star Game was proof of its superiority."

Josh: "Yeah, but AL had a better record in interleague play."

Kevin: "In your dreams . . . Bud."

While twenty-three home runs cleared Tiger Stadium's right field roof, only four batted balls carried over the more distant left field roof. The culprits: Harmon Killebrew (1962), Frank Howard (1968), Cecil Fielder (1990), and Mark McGwire (1997).

On September 27, 1999, legendary Tiger broadcaster Ernie Harwell delivered a touching eulogy to a sellout crowd after the Tigers beat the Kansas City Royals 8–2, in the Tiger Stadium

TRIVIA TIMEOUT

Model-T: Which Tiger player holds the record for being the youngest batting champion in Major League Baseball history?

Town Car: The famous headline, "We Win!" appeared in the *Detroit Free Press* in what year?

Cadillac: Name the three Tiger pitchers who have won the American League MVP award. (Hint: One won the award more than once. Another won it after eclipsing the thirty-win mark. And the other was a relief pitcher.)

Look for the answers in the text.

finale. Then, with the assistance of a police motorcade and several Tiger players, home plate was driven one mile to Comerica's construction site.

Getting a Choice Seat

The Tigers sold out nearly a quarter of their home dates in Comerica's inaugural season. But tickets have been easy to come by in the past few years. Your trip to Detroit should offer an excellent opportunity to treat yourself to a premium seat for cheap bucks. And we really do advise doing so, because the cheap seats at Comerica—and there are many of them— aren't good.

Instead of stacking two steep decks on top of each other to keep the fans in the back rows close to the field, Comerica's designers strove to keep fans low to the field. As a result, both the lower- and upper-seating levels extend away from the field very gradually, leaving the fans in the back rows far from the action. We're no proponents of treacherously steep upper decks, like the ones at Shea Stadium or SkyDome, but there must be some

sort of happy medium between the designs of those parks and that of Comerica.

On-Deck Circle/Tiger Den

On-Deck Circle seats are located in the first few rows between the dugouts. If available on the black market, consider ODC seats if they're in the first few rows.

The Club level, called the Tiger Den, features moveable wooden seats, which are wide and padded, as well as a menu identical to the one found in the Beer Hall (discussed below). Because the Tiger Den is located behind the infield boxes and under the roof of the upper deck we found it too far from the action for our tastes. We were big fans of the padded seats though, so we stuck around for a few innings. Four thousand miles behind the wheel had taken its toll.

Infield Box (Sections 118–137)

These are all good seats for the money. Pay attention to what row number you're purchasing, however, as the boxes go all the way up to Row 35, and the gradual incline of the lower seating bowl leaves fans in the back rows far from the field.

The opportunity to sit right behind home plate for $30 is appealing. And sight lines throughout this section rate above average. Because of the gradual slope of the stands and larger-than-average amount of foul territory on the playing field, only small portions of the outfield corners are out of view from any seat.

The wide and open concourses behind these sections would allow a nice glimpse of the field to those waiting in line or walking about, but a multitude of mobile concession stands often block the view. This is not the best use of their open-air concourses, but at least

Sellout Index: 0% of games sell out
Seating Capacity: 39,168
Ticket Office: (248) 25-TIGER
www.detroittigers.com

it's an easy fix for any Tiger execs who might be reading this. Step one: move the pretzel carts to the back side of the concourse. Step two: move the hot dog carts. Step three: move the beer carts . . . well, leave the beer carts. Actually, leave hot dog carts too. But all the other stuff can go.

Kevin: "Josh, have you ever considered a career in feng shui?"

Josh: "Sushi? No way, man."

Outfield Box (Sections 138–143, 112–117)

The Outfield Boxes are located between the Infield Boxes and Pavilion (in left field) and bleachers (in right field). If the Infield Boxes are sold out, consider Outfield Boxes in Sections 138, 139, 117, 116, and 114 which are angled nicely toward the infield. If these sections are unavailable, we recommend passing on the remaining Outfield Box sections and opting for a straightaway view of the action from home run territory in the right field bleachers for a third of the money, or from the left field Pavilion for nearly half the money.

Section 115 is probably the worst section in the lower bowl as its position makes it impossible to see much of the right field corner. So avoid it like Kevin avoids yuppie bars.

Row 37 of these sections is behind a walkway, so try for seats in Row 36 or lower to avoid the traffic. Any row higher than Row 40 is under the overhang of the upper deck, which, if nothing else, provides a nice umbrella on rainy nights.

Pavilion (Sections 144–151)

Located in home run territory beyond the left field fence, the Pavilion is lower to the field than the right field bleachers. It is also a bit farther from home plate than the bleachers because of the ballpark's irregular dimensions. As the result of these two factors, the view from the Pavilion is not as good as it is from the

bleachers. So why are Pavilion tickets more expensive? Well, the Pavilion offers real seats, while the bleachers consist of numbered benches. We recommend buying the cheaper ticket and bringing along one of those attachable seat backs you see people using at high school football games. Really, they work. And the geek factor isn't that high, or so Kevin told Josh when he ran back to the car for his.

If you're still hell bent on sitting in the Pavilion (say, to heckle a certain left fielder), try for Rows A–V as Rows AA and higher are behind an aisle and farther from the field.

Remember, parts of Section 144 are screened by the foul pole.

Pepsi Bleachers (Sections 101–106)

Each ticket for the right field Pepsi Bleachers comes with a voucher for a tiny soda and the choice of Major League Baseball's twenty-fourth best hot dog (according to our tireless research) or a slice of Little Caesars pizza.

And while Kevin had to struggle to accept the corporate-sponsored name, he liked the view from the bleachers and applauded the Tigers for offering them at such a low price. Most of the seats in Section 101 are partially obstructed by the center field wall, as fans can't see part of the center field pasture. But otherwise these sections check out fine, even 104–106 behind the tiered bull pens.

By making the Pepsi Bleachers the "family section" the Tigers encourage kids and families to sit here. Drinking is prohibited, but you can stand not far behind the Pepsi Bleachers and enjoy a clear view of the game while having a brew or daiquiri. If Comerica ever sells out again, this would be a nice standing-room-only area.

The only drawback to the Pepsi Bleachers is that the Tigers seem to take the family atmosphere a bit too far for our liking. Stadium security swarmed upon the only beach ball that fans (okay, it was Kevin) tried to send aloft the day we were in town. Even a simple bit of ball bopping was apparently too rowdy for management's taste, which led us to wonder if too much family atmosphere might be a bad thing. If you've ever seen the look on a six-year-old's (or a thirty-five-year-old's) face when an usher tears a beach ball out of his hands and rips it to shreds, you know what we mean. Should security be focused on keeping people safe rather than being the fun police? We think so, as through all our research we found nary a single beach-ball-related accident at a sporting event of any kind. So, lighten up, ball patrol.

Naming Rights and Wrongs

Josh: "The Pepsi Bleachers? Aren't there any tickets left for the regular bleachers?"

Ticket-selling lady: "The Pepsi Bleachers are the regular bleachers."

Josh: "But you just said they were the Pepsi Bleachers."

Lady: "They are the Pepsi Bleachers."

Josh: "What planet am I on?"

Lady: "Little Planet Caesars Earth."

SEATING TIP

BUY A Pepsi Bleacher ticket and then sell your hot dog and soda coupons to some tee-totaler for 75 percent of face value (face = $4.50, you do the math). Take the dough and put it toward a brewski. Or skip the entire deal, get a regular ticket, and buy food that you like. It's a free country.

Buying Tickets Can Get Complicated

Our plan upon arriving in Motor City was to buy a pair of $8 Pepsi Bleacher tickets. Kevin set out to snap some photos and Josh headed to the ticket window. And quickly after that, the plan fell apart. Kevin became distracted when he struck up a conversation with a nice

man named Roger from Toledo who was in town for a symposium on urban ruin.

Josh meanwhile had trouble communicating with the ticket-selling lady and was disappointed to find that all of the bleacher seats were "family" seats. Since the Yankees were in town looking to clinch the AL East with another victory, Josh was afraid the Pepsi Bleachers would provide too mellow an atmosphere for his Yankee-hating heart (translation: he planned to heckle Bernie Williams all game long and didn't want any small children seated nearby to inhibit him). So the bleachers were out.

The $5 Skyline seats looked like a deal. But the ticket-selling lady talked Josh out of those.

"You can do better," she said. "You deserve better."

"Really," Josh said. "You think?"

Ultimately, we wound up with a pair of seats in the Upper Reserved for $12 each. Located in Section 344, each ticket came with coupons for a small Pepsi and either a hot dog or slice of Little Caesars.

Afterward we realized that the cheaper Skyline seats were located right beside our section. And we would have had an additional $7 each to spend on food, minus the $5 gain apiece in coupons, for a net screwup of $2 each. Yeah, we got scammed. That's our job, to take the hit so you don't have to.

However, we're happy to report that in the end, the joke was on the ticket-selling lady, Mike Ilitch, and the entire Tigers organization. We seat-hopped all the way over to Section 327 behind the plate and drank our minuscule "free" Pepsis from Upper Box seats. Then we headed down to field-level seats in the Pepsi Bleachers. Justice was served (with a small Pepsi and a mediocre hot dog to boot).

Upper Club/Upper Box

The first row of the upper deck is located in the airspace directly above the very last row of the Infield Boxes. The deck extends very gradually away from the field. If you are afraid of heights and shudder to recall your recent trip to the upper deck of Yankee Stadium or Comiskey Park, you might like this. Otherwise, you probably won't care much for it. The seats may be low, but they are distant from the field.

The Tigers call the first few rows of upper-deck seats on the infield Upper Club seats and charge an extra $5 for them. The seats and aisles are a bit wider than elsewhere but that's it. No waitress service or special concession offerings. Nada. We think there should be uniform rules governing what can and what cannot be called a "Club" seat. We also think the pitcher's mound should be raised, the DH abolished (except for Edgar Martinez), and the amateur draft expanded to include the entire world. But those are issues we're currently negotiating with Bud Selig. He's a tough nut to crack, but we think he's coming around. Either that or he thinks there's a chance he might be able to sell us a used car somewhere down the line.

But back to Comerica's upper deck. The Upper Boxes represent the upper-level seats on the infield (321–337) behind the so-called "Club" seats. These are decent but we recommend buying lower-level Infield Boxes for only 33 percent more money if they are available.

Upper Box Left Field/Upper Box Right Field

The Tigers call the first five rows of the left and right field upper levels "Box Seats" and charge extra for them. Avoid these seats, especially the so-called Box Seats in Section 345, where ticket holders pay $20 to sit one row in front of Skyline ticket holders who paid $5. This is the biggest rip-off in the park.

The Upper Box seats behind the plate are better, even if they're not in the first few rows.

Mezzanine (Sections 210–219)

Because the suite level does not extend past first-base, the Tigers opted to construct an intermediary level, in between the lower level and upper deck, in lieu of a right field upper level. Fifteen feet lower than the 300 Level, the 200 Level consists of four thousand seats. However, this deck is sloped even more gradually than the 300 Level and as a result we felt exceptionally far from the action here. Hey, there's a reason all of the movie theaters are adopting "stadium seating," you know. The Tigers ought to have looked into it.

At the very least, avoid the first row of the Mezzanine seats (Row 5, since the first four rows of this deck constitute Upper Box Right Field seats) because of the railings and glass plates that obstructed sight lines. Also beware: fans sitting in Sections 210–213 will not be able to see the right field corner.

Upper Reserved (Sections 338–344)

Similar to many new parks, railings and glass plates above all upper entranceways obstruct the views of fans in a number of seats behind them. In Rows 6–8 throughout the upper level, avoid aisle seats numbered 19–24 or 1–5 to avoid this obstruction.

Because of the under-hang of the upper deck, the left field corner starts to disappear at Section 336. This becomes worse as you continue toward the outfield.

The sunroof above the upper level will keep you in the shade if you're in Row 17 or higher.

Skyline (Section 345)

Kudos to the Tigers organization for getting you into the park for a five spot. Just remember you don't want to actually sit in these seats unless you have binoculars, X-ray vision, or only a mild interest in the ball game.

So here's your plan. Score a $5 seat in 345 and hop into the Upper Boxes behind the plate.

There are usually plenty of empties and ballpark staff doesn't seem to mind folks moving around (within reason).

Follow general seat-hopping protocol and you should be fine: wait until the bottom of the second inning, load your arms with food and drink, then stumble toward an open seat while pretending to study your ticket stub to make sure you're in the right section. And don't get greedy. If you're going to head for a front-row seat, you might as well just tell the usher on your way past that you don't have a ticket.

The Black Market

Reselling tickets at any price is illegal in the neighborhood surrounding the ballpark. We doubt this law had anything to do with it, but we couldn't find any scalpers during our visit to Detroit. Tickets are cheap and plentiful at the box office. And Detroit's bad boys have bigger fish to fry on the mean streets of Motor City— or at the nearby casinos.

Before/After the Game

While the neighborhood surrounding old Tiger Stadium seems to be steadily sliding toward the abyss, Comerica Park has been a revitalizing force in its neighborhood. As long as you stay within a few blocks of the ballpark in the area known as Foxtown, you should feel comfortable and safe. However, getting to the ballpark does require driving through some of Detroit's shady streets, and we don't mean Slim Shady. So make sure the road-trip car is running well before heading into town, and roll 'em up whenever you're in doubt.

Though Detroit's reputation for inner-city despair preceded our visit, we were still astounded by the grim reality we encountered. It was worse than we expected. The craziest sight of all was on Montcalm Way, where a completely burnt-out building stood right next to a fully operational fire station, with a couple of trucks in the lot and all. It sure made us want to buy American. Here's to baseball doing its share to bring better times to the Motor City.

Getting to Comerica

Follow I-75 north to the Grand River Avenue Exit. Off the ramp, cross Grand River and take a right onto Woodward Avenue, which will take you to Comerica.

Most of the parking lots in the area charge $15 to $20. As tempted as our visions of urban apocalypse may make you, don't bite. Instead, find Madison Street near the ballpark, take a quick right onto Witherell, then a left onto Adams, and there's a ramp for an underground lot about one hundred feet from the park that only charges $5. It's the closest and the cheapest. How 'bout that?

The People Mover monorail moves its people to the Broadway and Grand Circus Park stations, both near the ballpark. But we recommend driving to the game. No offense to the locals—but downtown Detroit doesn't conform to the tourist-friendly Midwest mold that you'll find in Milwaukee, Minneapolis, and Cleveland. Adding insult to injury, the town seems a bit short on bratwurst, too.

Outside Attractions

WHEN CATS FLY

Perched atop the marquee for the Fox Theatre at 2211 Woodward is a pair of winged lions that predate by seventy years construction of Comerica on the border of Detroit's cultural arts district. William Fox, founder of Twentieth Century Fox Pictures, built the theatre in 1928. In 1987 the Ilitch family purchased the building and restored it.

Josh: "I wonder if you get a slice of pizza and a Pepsi if you buy seats in the balcony."

Kevin: "You mean 'seats in the *Pepsi* Balcony,' right?"

WITH GOD ON OUR SIDE

A few blocks away, at 8850 Woodward, stands St. John's Episcopal Church, a beautiful example of neo-Gothic architecture. The church was constructed in 1927. When we visited, a large banner on its side read, "Pray here for the Tigers and Lions." Perhaps a bit on the tacky side, but unique, to say the least. And who knows, maybe one of these days it'll work and the Tigers will have a winning season. It might actually take divine intervention for that to happen, with the team Detroit's been putting on the field lately.

FORD FIELD

Both an easy place to visit and an easy place to walk past without noticing, the new home of the National Football League's Detroit Lions resides beyond Comerica's left field seats on the corner of Adams Street and Brush Street. The sixty-four-thousand-seat domed stadium is remarkable for blending in so well with the urban landscape. Because its playing field is forty feet below street level, fully 45 percent of its seats are actually underground. Thus, the building does not rise excessively high into the skyline. Though we didn't make it inside, we were impressed. Football stadiums don't usually look this innocuous. Way to go Detroit! Now, if Lions fans pray real hard, maybe their team will put together a winning team, too.

Free Standing Room

Because Comerica's field is below street level, the view of the action is surprisingly good from Adams Street behind the left field Pavilion where a number of gates allow a peak for those on the extremely low budget, or those like Kevin who lost their ticket money at the casino before the game.

Watering Holes and Outside Eats

Foxtown offers a few decent sports bars and restaurants. And for truly daring folks (in day-light hours) we recommend venturing a bit deeper into Detroit. Hey, we did and got away with it, so you can too—probably. (Disclaimer: Joshua R. Pahigian, Kevin T. O'Connell, and The Lyons Press shall bear no legal responsibility for any misfortune that befalls readers in any part of Detroit, or anywhere else for that matter.)

ELWOOD GRILL (Adams Street)

With indoor and outdoor seating, the Elwood looks like a diner from the 1950s. Buy a beer on the patio. Shoes and shirt not required! Well, shoes may be, but we saw a topless patron (unfortunately male) seated on the patio when we visited. It was a hot September day.

Inside, the atmosphere is a bit more formal with a full bar and waitress seating. Entrées and sandwiches are named after Tiger players. Kevin's Ty Cobb Salad didn't have any corn in it, rather featuring a generous portion of grilled chicken atop romaine lettuce.

HOCKEY TOWN (Woodward Avenue)

Located beside the Fox Theatre, Hockey Town offers your best bet for a quality pre- or postgame meal. Entrées range from $15 to $25.

The three-story bar and restaurant is all hockey, all the time. Busts of famous Detroit Red Wings include Gordie Howe, Ted Lindsay, Sid Abel, and a number of others. Trophy cases display old Stanley Cups and other pieces of Red Wing hardware.

Kevin tried his hand at some of the interactive hockey games for the kids and was happy to win back some of the money he had lost at the casino. The parents of the kids were none too pleased.

THE TOWN PUMP TAVERN
(100 W. Montcalm Way)

On the fringes of the Foxtown comfort zone a few blocks from the ballpark, The Town Pump Tavern is located on the ground floor of what must have been a pretty nice apartment building at one time. The casual rectangular bar has a nice old-time feel to it. Local brews include Motor City Ale, Oberon, and Belles Amber and the menu features cheap appetizers, pizzas, and sandwiches. Our favorite apps were the grilled hot and spicy chicken strips and the parmesan-topped breadsticks with dipping sauce. Both checked in at less than $4. Kevin dug the atmosphere and Josh dug the prices. A road tripper's delight.

LINDELL AC (1310 Cass Avenue)

We do not recommend seeking out Lindell AC after dark, on foot or by car. The Michigan stop of the People Mover is right nearby, but we don't necessarily recommend that either. This neighborhood is hurting. However, this is one of those classic joints, like Murphy's Bleachers in Chicago or the Cask 'n Flagon in Boston, that deserve a visit just for the sake of saying you've been there.

We're not sure how Lindell AC gets away with billing itself as the oldest sports bar in the country, but that is what it proudly proclaims on its sign out front. For our money, it's not even the oldest one in town. It was founded in 1948. Hockeytown, just a few blocks away, claims to have been founded in 1926. See the problem? Maybe it depends on how you define "sports bar," or maybe the folks at Lindell are using a different calendar than the rest of us.

With a faded Billy Martin *Sports Illustrated* cover in one window, a Rod Carew autographed bat in another (odd choices considering neither has any Detroit connection), today the bar attracts mostly regulars. But through the years it has been a favorite hangout of visiting and hometown athletes, a fact made clear by the many autographed eight-by-ten photos adorning the walls. The atmosphere inside is that of an aged but friendly dive,

making it much more of a Kevin place than a Josh one.

Josh: "Where are all the TVs? Where are the boneless buffalo wings? Why's that weird guy staring at me?"

Kevin: "Barkeep, another round."

Inside the Park

In this era of long-ball-friendly parks, juiced baseballs, and juiced baseball players, Comerica initially offered a variation of the game more akin to the one our fathers knew and loved. Yet homer-happy fans and players complained the outfield was too spacious. You may remember Juan Gonzalez's 162-game sulk in the ballpark's opening season. And the Tigers finally caved in to the pressure in 2003, moving the left-center field fence so that it now measures 370 feet from the plate, instead of its original 395. At 365 feet to the alley in right-center, 422 to the center field ivy, and 330 down the right field line, the field is still spacious by today's standards, just not as much so as it was in the park's first three years when the Tigers hit sixty-two home dingers in 2000, fifty-eight in 2001, and sixty-two in 2002. The last straw came when Detroit's right-handed batters combined to hit only sixteen home runs in 1,288 home at bats in 2002. That's one long ball every 80.5 at bats. Sure, blame the ballpark, not the lousy hitters.

We knew it was indeed a deep center field when lead-footed Robin Ventura tagged up on a fly ball to left-center and advanced from first-base to second during our visit.

Now, we like homers as much as the next guy. Really, we do. But isn't a gap triple more exciting than a 350-foot rinky-dink homer? In our book it is. And Comerica is a double and triple hitter's paradise, with its expansive outfield gaps. We hope it doesn't shrink any more in the years to come.

Ballpark Features

ONE DECADE AT A TIME

The walking museum on the first-level concourse features monuments dedicated to each decade in Tiger history, beginning with the 1900s and continuing through the 2000s. The display cases are on wheels with big tires, embracing the car culture that, like baseball, is as American as it gets.

The 1930s exhibit was Josh's favorite. Not only does it feature memorabilia from the 1935 World Series but also a number of cartoons from the Series, including one of a tiger killing a cardinal with a baseball bat. Okay, perhaps the '30s exhibit should be rated R, and Josh should get into some anger management sessions.

A history buff, Kevin liked the 1940s monument and its Baseball Answers America's Call exhibit, featuring Tiger players who went to war. Hank Greenberg, Virgil Trucks, and Dick Wakefield all appear in their military uniforms. It's odd, because Kevin isn't a fan of the military at all. Josh knew better than to ask him about this contradiction, though.

The 1950s monument salutes Al Kaline, who became the youngest batting champion ever when he hit .340 in 1955 at age twenty.

The 1960s pillar displays the famous *Detroit Free Press* headline, "We Win!" celebrating the Tigers' 1968 World Series win against the Cardinals.

THE CARNY COMES TO TIGER TOWN

Behind the home plate concourse you will find Major League Baseball's most elaborate kiddie area where children and adults ride a fifty-foot-high Ferris wheel in baseball-shaped carts or ride bareback on colorful tigers on the carousel.

If you're scrounging for loose change, or feeling ripped off after spending your hard-earned money on a disgusting Tiger Gyro (more on this later), check out the Wishing Well at the mouth of the Big Cat Court. Roll up those

Tiger Ball

Photo by Kevin O'Connell

sleeves and dive in like Kevin did. Or join with Tiger fans in wishing for a hometown win and cast a coin into the water yourself.

CASTING CALL: PREDATOR III

Remember the monster in the movie *Predator* that could blend in with its surroundings? The camouflaged cameramen who stand on a platform amid the center field ivy do a pretty good imitation. Well, they do when water isn't cascading onto their equipment when the liquid fireworks display erupts. There has got to be a way to fix that. Call the good folks at Disney, er, we mean Anaheim.

We were also intrigued by the puddles that quickly formed on the center field warning track whenever the fountain squirted. We couldn't help but think of our trusty Baltimore tour guide Irv and his porous rubber. Shouldn't there be a union for that type of thing?

THE TIGERS won the AL pennant in 1934 with a 101–53 mark, setting a team record for the winning percentage (.656) that still stands. First-baseman Greenberg hit .339 during the season with 139 RBI, second sacker Gehringer hit .356 with 127 RBI, and player-manager Mickey Cochrane won the AL MVP with a .320 average and 76 RBI.

The Tigers' bid for their first World Series title proved unsuccessful, however, as they lost to St. Louis's Gas House Gang in seven games. If you think Yankee Stadium is rowdy today, you should have been at Tiger Stadium for Game 7. After the Cardinals hung seven runs on the scoreboard to break a scoreless tie in the third inning, Tiger fans began to throw debris on the field. Then, after Cardinal Joe Medwick slid spikes-up into Tiger third-baseman Marv Owen in the sixth, all hell broke loose. As Medwick headed out to his position in left field for the bottom of the inning, frustrated Tiger fans threw bottles, partially eaten frankfurters, and batteries (and a Walkman had really big batteries back then) at him. The game was delayed for nearly half an hour before Judge Kenesaw Mountain Landis (previously of Black Sox fame) ordered Medwick to leave the game.

The Cardinals went on to win 11–0 behind the shutout pitching of Dizzy Dean. Dizzy combined with his brother Daffy to post a 4–1 record and 1.43 ERA in the Series. Remarkably, the Dean boys pitched forty-four of a possible forty-five innings in their five starts.

The loss represented the fourth time the Tigers had come up empty in their hunt for a world championship. But the very next year, they redeemed themselves, winning the AL behind the play of league MVP Greenberg and beating the Cubs four games to two in the Series. They beat the Cubs again ten years later to win the October Classic in 1945, a year in which Tiger pitcher Hal Newhouser won his second straight American League MVP award. They won their third title against the Cardinals in 1968, the year Denny McLain won thirty-one games en route to claiming the league MVP.

Detroit's fourth and most recent title came in 1984 when it beat San Diego. The Tigers began the regular season 9–0, finished April 18–2, and eventually amassed a 35–5 record. Closer Willie Hernandez won the Cy Young and MVP awards.

In every championship Tiger season, a Detroit player has won the league MVP.

GEOMETRY

The dirt from the pitcher's mound to home plate leads to a pentagon—or home-plate-shaped—patch of dirt that surrounds the entire batter's box, catcher box, and umpire circle. This, opposed to the dirt circle found at most parks. It's a nice touch, but it's also a really big plate.

POLE POSITION

The flagpole in left-center field is huge and it is in play, just like the one that resided 440 feet from home plate in Tiger Stadium at the time of its closing. This flag is approximately three feet from the outfield wall.

Using his compass, a protractor, a slide rule, the backside of a hot dog wrapper, and a blue Sharpie, Josh calculated its height to be 123.5 feet. During the entire three-inning ordeal,

Kevin just kept shaking his head and muttering, "We can look up the height on the Internet when we get home."

THE BRICK OF FAME

On the brick wall beside the bleachers in right-center appear the names and numbers of several legendary Tigers deemed not quite worthy of left field statue status. Among the names is that of broadcaster Ernie Harwell. During the course of our 2002 road trip we were in Detroit for his next-to-last home game, then in Toronto for his last game ever. Fare thee well, old friend—fare thee well!

SCOREBOARD

We don't usually get excited over scoreboards, but this one is in a class by itself.

Two tigers prowl atop the left field board and an old-style clock with the Tigers logo on its face appears in the middle. It has a nice old-time feel about it.

The scoreboard also leaves plenty of room for advertising and we absolutely love being bombarded with advertising while at the ballpark. You never know when you're going to glance up—say to see how many outs there are, or who's batting—and discover a whole new kind of shaving razor or cola that just might change your life. Well done!

AT SEA LEVEL

The upper-deck seats behind the plate offer the best view of the downtown Detroit skyline. The most prominent building is the Broderick Tower, which looms over right field displaying a 65-by-180-foot undersea/above-sea mural. The mural was painted by internationally renowned marine life artist Wyland (a Detroit-born fellow who goes by a single name, much like Madonna, Ichiro, or Hammer).

This is number seventy-six in a series of one-hundred proposed mural projects in the United States, Canada, Japan, Australia, Mexico, France, and New Zealand.

CANADIAN, EH?

During our September visit we were horrified to find many of the TVs on the Comerica Park concourse tuned in to a Canadian Football League game between Saskatchewan and Edmonton.

Josh: "Sweet fancy Butkus, they're punting on third down!"

Kevin: "Welcome to the Great White North."

Stadium Eats

As mentioned above, fast-food magnate Mike Ilitch owns the Tigers. Despite this, or perhaps because of this, the offerings at Comerica are rather generic and of poor quality, much like fast food in general. This, despite a diverse

food court that initially gave us hope. Sorry, Mike, we tried everything. It just wasn't that good.

Factoring in the limited offerings outside the park, Detroit ranks at the bottom of Major League binge-eating cities.

LITTLE CAESAR'S PIZZA (Trademark Food)

We generally try to avoid ballpark pizza unless we're in Chicago's South Side. But since the Tigers and Little Caesars share the same owner, and since we had coupons for free slices, we gave it a try. It was decent, but nothing special. Perhaps the crust was a bit less cardboardlike than that of the usual ballpark pie, but just barely.

Slices sell for $2.50 while whole pies sell for $13.50. The menu offers three different whole pie options: cheese, pepperoni, or the triple play (pepperoni, ham, mushroom).

TIGER DOG (Dog Rating)

The Twenty-fourth Best Hot Dog in the Majors

Ah, the dreaded silver bag.

We'd like to meet the man or woman who originally came up with the idea to take freshly cooked processed meat and soft buns and put them in tin foil bags to be sold anywhere from five minutes to six hours later. We're betting that person is a vegetarian, because no dog lover would ever commit such a breach of wiener etiquette.

Hello. Earth to stupid dog guy (or woman), the dogs become rubbery and if left to sit long enough, green. And the buns get soggy. We hope you're proud of yourself.

Best of the Rest

Your best bet at Comerica is to arrive at the park early and visit the **Beer Hall**, a reasonably priced sports bar located beside the Big Cat Court. This becomes a much less appealing option once game time arrives, because with waitress service and no view of the field, a trip to the hall will keep real fans away from the game for far too long.

Entrées, all of which are under $10, include roasted herb chicken, St. Louis pork ribs, and Southern chicken tender fritters. All come with curlicue fries and coleslaw. Sandwiches include a half-pound burger that rated above average on Josh's burger scale and a Santa Fe chicken wrap sandwich, which Kevin found a refreshing light choice after days of eating nothing but bratwurst and dogs.

Hard lemonade and wine are available for the ladies and lightweights while the bottled beer list includes Labatt Blue, Molson Canadian, Heineken, Corona, Sam Adams, Killian's Red, and Guinness Stout. Yes, that's right folks, honest-to-goodness Guinness at the ballpark—Kevin was MIA from innings two through seven.

With its industrial look and pictures of Tiger greats, we found the Beer Hall a decent place to eat or have a few brews.

Our favorite selections from the **Big Cat Court** included the twist and shout hand rolled pretzel, which we seasoned with cinnamon and sugar. Clearly, this hand-rolled pretzel is one of the best in the big leagues.

We also tried the **Hot Dog Stand** in the food court. The stand specializes in Chicago Style or Coney Island-style dogs, which cost a dollar more than the regular ballpark dog. This natural-casing Kowalski brand dog was grilled and tasty. Unfortunately the Coney sauce was creamy and not so good. But if you're in the mood for a dog, it's worth the extra buck to buy a frank here, rather than from the regular concession stands. Just remember: yes to onions, no to Coney sauce.

New Orleans-style Daiquiris are available on the concourse behind Sections 134 and 142. Flavors include Purple Raspberry, 190 Octane, Blue Sky, Jungle Juice, Green Apple, Strawberry, Piña Colada, and Margarita. Kevin tried the strawberry and found it a refreshing choice—effeminate, but refreshing on a balmy September day.

SAY "NO, THANKS," AND WALK AWAY

Kevin likes gyros and he likes Greek food. And Detroit is known for its Greektown. But the Gyro Kevin bought at Comerica was just plain horrible. The sauce was way too watery and dripped all over his favorite road-trip shirt—a San Francisco Giants jersey (Josh was happy it would finally get a washing). The tomatoes weren't fresh, and the lamb was dried out. The total package rivaled the Wrigley Pig for worst food in the Majors.

We'd also like to take this opportunity to pan the McDonalds located beyond the right field seats. A Micky D's inside a ballpark? Grimace.

BALLPARK SUDS

Since Detroit is actually north of the Canadian border (check out MapQuest if you doubt us), Labatt Blue is the local favorite. It comes in a twenty-five-ounce cup while Miller Light can be had in a thirty-two-ounce tub. That's almost a forty!

Do frosties come bigger than that anywhere in MLB, you wonder? Nope. Only in the minors, where the Springfield Isotopes do better, with a sixty-four-ounce Duff.

DESIGNATED DRIVER PROGRAM

Visit the Guest Services office behind Section 130 to claim your free DD soda. This freebie is actually larger than the free soda that comes with Pepsi Bleacher or Upper Reserved seats, twenty ounces versus twelve.

The Comerica Park Experience

Tiger fans are exceptionally tame. Perhaps this is because the ballpark caters to the interests of families and children, or perhaps it is because the team is rarely within spitting distance of first place.

TIGER STADIUM (MICHIGAN AVENUE)

WE VISITED the old Tiger Stadium, which looks like it hasn't been touched since it closed its gates for the last time. It looks as if the old yard will be left to slowly deteriorate as the city, which owns it, has yet to come up with a plan to raise the estimated $5 million to demolish it. At one time, there was an effort to find a developer who would renovate the facility and convert it into a residential and entertainment center, with lofts, shops, ice rinks and an Olympic-size swimming pool. But that failed to materialize when the only developers to express interest were those wishing to bring bullfighting (is this legal?), dog racing, boxing, and off-road racing to Tiger Stadium.

From the outside, the stadium reminded us of Wrigley Field, only bigger. We looked in to see fading advertising and concession signs for Little Caesars, Fox Sports, and Miller. A neon sign on the stadium's exterior was lit up to read "Tiger Stadiu," the "M" having long since retired.

The stadium is surrounded by a number of bars, several of which went out of business when the team moved. Those remaining look pretty scary. There is one of particular interest, O'Malleys. Back when Tiger Stadium was in operation, and long after the neighborhood had gone south, there was a doorbell that patrons needed to ring to gain entrance. A bouncer would stick his head out the second-story window, then buzz you up if you looked okay to him.

We were also unable to uncover any baseball-specific rituals that make the park unique, which led us to the conclusion that Comerica is still struggling to find its baseball identity.

FRIDAY NIGHT FIREWORKS
All season long the Tigers put on a free postgame fireworks display after Friday night home games. That must make the Fourth of July seem awfully special, eh?

BRING YOUR BASEBALL CARDS
Before every Saturday home game, current Tigers sign autographs for children and adults alike at designated locations throughout the park. Josh was thrilled when Brandon Inge signed three rookie cards for him.

"See Kev, I told you to bring your cards."

"You were right, Josh. You were right."

SUNDAY IS FOR THE KIDS
Children under the age of fourteen ride the Ferris wheel and carousel for free on Sundays. And after the game they are allowed to run the bases on the field, along with gangly thirty-five-year-olds who manage to convince Tiger management they need to do so as part of the research for their book—gangly thirty-five-year-olds who callously do so without securing equal permission for their writing partners.

CHICAGO,
ILLINOIS

6 miles to US Cellular Field
90 miles to Milwaukee
280 miles to Detroit
300 miles to St. Louis

CHICAGO CUBS, WRIGLEY FIELD

The Friendly Confines

FOR ANY STUDENT of the game and its history, Wrigley Field is as good as it gets. The weathered green steel of the ballpark's exterior may not present quite the regal edifice that Yankee Stadium projects to the world, but inside the essence of class abounds—not in a retro, overdone, twenty-first-century way, but subtly and genuinely. Wrigley Field is authentic. And while it may be the *second* oldest ballpark in the Majors, it feels much older than any other park in the current American ballpark landscape—and not just because the men's room (and possibly the ladies' room for all we know) still features cattle troughs. Unlike the ballparks in Boston and the Bronx where traditions have been updated over the years, Wrigley still offers players and fans alike a strikingly similar environment to the one it offered at the time of its opening in 1914. Sure, it has been renovated to add more seating, but the fact remains that a Jumbotron remains inconspicuously absent at Wrigley. Also left out are the electronic advertising, overpowering sound bites, and modern amenities that allegedly make the newer parks "fan friendly." The only sounds inside Wrigley are those emanating from an old-fashioned pipe organ, the crowd, or the unobtrusive PA announcer.

Upon entering "the Friendly Confines," as Cubs fans call the park, our attention was immediately drawn to the green grass and red dirt of the infield. The focus is where it should be: on the field. And watching the game, we felt as though we were sitting in 1920. We felt a kinship with our fellow fans as we sat elbow-to-elbow celebrating the game we love. If this isn't heaven, it's got to be pretty close.

Wrigley Field exemplifies the vital role that a ballpark can and should play in the American city. Nestled in festive Wrigleyville, this ancient gem presents hardball purists a vision of baseball the way it ought to be, while also serving as cornerstone of a vibrant entertainment district. Even when there isn't a game, tourists come to see the ballpark and sample the neighborhood restaurants and saloons.

Wrigley was built on the site of a former seminary for the meager cost of $250,000. At the time of its opening on April 23, 1914, it was called Weeghman Park and it served as home not to the Cubs, but to the Chicago Whales of the Federal Baseball League. The "Feds" folded a year later—no small wonder given the league's uncanny knack for accepting teams with completely inappropriate nicknames. Whaling in the windy city? What a gas! Or perhaps local history ignores the fact that was there a time when humpbacks frolicked in Lake Michigan? Sounds like a conspiracy to us.

In 1915 Charles Weeghman, former owner of the Whales, purchased the National League Cubs and moved them to Weeghman Park. This represented the vagabond Cubs' sixth home park since becoming a professional franchise in 1870.

On April 20, 1916, the Cubs played their first game at Weeghman, posting a 7–6 victory against the Reds. Ten years later, in 1926, the ballpark was renamed Wrigley Field in honor of new owner William Wrigley, Jr., a chewing-gum entrepreneur who had purchased the team in 1921. The Cubs would remain in the Wrigley family for sixty years before being sold to the Tribune Company in 1981.

In 1870 the Cubs franchise was a founding member of the National Association. Known as the White Stockings, the team was forced to drop out of the league in 1872 and 1873 because the Great Chicago Fire had destroyed

exterior

Photo by Kevin O'Connell

its ballpark, uniforms, and equipment. In 1875 White Stockings president William Hulbert led the charge to form a new league, and the National League was born.

Chicago won the first NL championship in 1876, outscoring its opponents by more than five runs per game. In the late 1890s and early 1900s the franchise tried on a number of new nicknames reflective of the team's youth, including the "Colts" and "Orphans," before settling on the Cubs.

In 1906, the Cubs and crosstown White Sox squared off in the World Series, which was won by the Pale Hose in six games. The Cubs rebounded to win the Series in 1907 and 1908, both times against the Tigers. They have not won a World Series since, despite having had seven opportunities, the most recent one in 1945. Unlike in Boston, however, where Red Sox fans gnash their teeth with the passing of each drought-lengthening season, Cubs fans seem content.

During the first two decades of the twentieth century, the Cubs fielded what is still regarded by many to be the most prolific trio of

scoreboard

Photo by Kevin O'Connell

defensive infielders in baseball history. The second baseman was Johnny Evers; the shortstop, Joe Tinker; and the first-baseman, Frank Chance. The third-sacker, Harry Steinfeldt, was no slouch either, leading the league in fielding average in 1906, 1907, and 1910. But "Tinker to Evers to Chance," became a familiar refrain among Chicago fans, who delighted in watching the ball zip around the horn to complete one double play after another.

Two of the most dramatic home runs in baseball history were hit at Wrigley. During Game 3 of the 1932 World Series, the Yankees' Babe Ruth stepped to the plate in the fifth inning with the score tied 4–4. After yelling something to Cubs pitcher Charlie Root, Ruth pointed his bat toward center field, and on the next pitch smacked a titanic homer into the center field bleachers, right where he had pointed. The "Called Shot" propelled New York to a four-game sweep in the Series. It was Ruth's fifteenth and final World Series home run.

When it comes to this bit of lore, Kevin is somewhat skeptical. But Josh is a believer all the way.

On the next-to-last day of the 1938 season, Cubs player-manager Gabby Hartnett hit his legendary "homer in the gloaming," to break a 5–5 tie against Pittsburgh. The walk-off shot that put the Cubs one game ahead of the Pirates in the standings garnered its name because it came with two out and no one on base in the bottom of the ninth inning when, because of the encroaching darkness, the umpires had announced they would rule the game a tie after Hartnett's at bat whether he made out or got on base. But it never came to that as the shot sailed off Hartnett's bat and into the fall night. The echoes of screaming fans could by heard all night along Waveland Avenue, and even the next day as the Cubs won the pennant.

One of the best-pitched games in baseball history was spun at Wrigley. On May 2, 1917, the Cubs' Jim "Hippo" Vaughn and the Reds' Fred Toney posted matching goose eggs for nine full innings. That's zeroes as in no-hits. Then, after former Olympian Jim Thorpe broke the scoreless tie with a bunt single in the top of the tenth, Toney finished his no-no, retiring the Cubs in order.

Bill Veeck originally planted the ivy that grows on Wrigley's brick outfield walls in 1937. Veeck, who would later own the White

---

TRIVIA TIMEOUT

Easy Breeze: Which former Cub once played for teams representing all four Major League divisions in a single season?

Blustery Gust: Name the only two Major Leaguers to play in parts of five different decades.

Gale Force: In what city was the original Wrigley Field located? (Hint: it began as a minor league park, then served as home to a Major League expansion team.)

Look for the answers in the text.

Sox, Cleveland Indians, and St. Louis Browns, managed a hot dog stand at Wrigley while his father served as Cubs general manager. The original vines consisted of 350 Japanese bittersweet plants and 200 Boston ivy plants. When the ivy debuted, eight Chinese elm trees accompanied it, growing out of large pots in the bleachers. But leaves started falling in the outfield and the trees had to be removed.

The scoreboard also dates from 1937. It remains today virtually unaltered. The clock face at its top was added in 1941. In its day, the scoreboard was a giant, rising eighty-five feet above the field. It appears drab and small by today's standards, but charming nonetheless. Listen for the rhythmic clicking sounds it makes when the numbers change. No one has ever hit the board with a batted ball, though a shot by Roberto Clemente once came close.

What better place to fly a flag than in the windy city? After each home game, the Cubs raise a banner bearing either the letter "W" or the letter "L" to let commuters on the "L" Train know how the home team has fared.

Wrigley was the last ballpark in the Majors to welcome night baseball, adding lights in 1988. But it wasn't always meant to be that way. The Cubs were set to begin installing lights in late 1942, but owner Philip K. Wrigley donated the lights to the World War II effort a few hours after the Japanese bombed Peal Harbor.

Wrigley would wait and wait for night baseball, then it would wait one more day. The first night game was rained out, making the first official evening affair an August 9, 1988, Cubs' win against the Mets. The day before, the Cubs and Phillies had played three innings before the heavens opened. While many Cubs fans cringed at the arrival of night

baseball in Wrigleyville, tickets to Wrigley's limited night games are among the first to sell out each year.

Wrigley has always been a home run hitter's paradise thanks to a trio of factors. First, there is the steady breeze that blows out toward left field in the summertime. Second, Chicago is a hot city and the ball travels farther when it is warm. And third, the ballpark is located at an altitude of more than six hundred feet above sea level. Lower air pressure allows the ball to fly longer (See the chapter on Coors Field for the physics-in-baseball lesson).

Getting a Choice Seat

Be sure to order your Cubs tickets well in advance, as many games sell out before opening day. The two hottest tickets are against the archrival Cardinals and crosstown White Sox. bleacher tickets, which account for 3,315 seats, sell out well before most other sections.

Starting when tickets go on sale in January, the Cubs Web site lists how many regular seats and bleacher seats are available for each home game, a nice feature that we wish other teams would copy. But then again, perhaps only teams that sell out most of their games need worry about this.

Don't ask us why they call the sections "Aisles," they just do.

Bleachers (Aisles 143–153, 246–249)

If you're looking for the quintessential Wrigley experience, be sure to spend at least one game in the bleachers. We speculate that the frat-house atmosphere in the Wrigley outfield may have something to do with the many graduates of Big Ten schools who settle in Chicago after college. Look for Ronnie Woo Woo posing for

Sellout Index: 95% of games sell out
Seating Capacity: 39,111
Ticket Office: (773) 404-CUBS
www.cubs.mlb.com

WE WERE SURPRISED to find so many young women in the bleachers during our September visit. In fact, a number of bachelorette parties were taking place around us—something we hadn't seen at any other ballparks. A rather hilarious episode that sums up the Wrigley bleacher scene unfolded involving one of these parties, some drunken middle-aged men, a Brit, and his son.

It all started when a gaggle of party gals spent the first few innings squirting each other with phallic-shaped water guns. By the top of the fourth, a quartet of middle-aged men seated nearby had started taking turns trying to throw peanuts down the women's shirts. Rather than inhibit the bachelorettes, this overture actually encouraged them. They bought a round of beers. Then the midlife crisis crew bought a round. And all were merry.

As Cub great Billy Williams led the crowd in the singing of "Take Me Out to the Ball Game," during the seventh-inning stretch, one of the girls pulled up her top to flash her appreciable bosom as is customary for drunken bachelorettes at Wrigley. And with that gesture, the floodgates opened. One by one, her friends flashed their breasts, much to the approval of the howling men. This would have been amusing enough in its own right, but what made it even more hilarious was that all afternoon, a dapper English gentleman and his ten-year-old son sat in the midst of these fun-loving hooligans. They sat prim and proper, watching the game and the father did his best to shield his young son's eyes from the squirting plastic penises, topless women, and drunken bleacher bums. Apparently, nobody had prepared him for what a day in the Wrigley bleachers might proffer. Observing the father's uncomfortable glances and the son's wide eyes was almost more fun than seeing one of the girls—a brunette with a locomotive tattoo on her right bicep and a medusa on the small of her back—autograph in lipstick one of her new male friend's bare buttocks in the top of the eighth inning. Ah, the Wrigley experience.

Finally, as the ninth inning began, the Englishman shifted in his seat and started rummaging through his coat. We assumed he had seen enough and was preparing to drag his traumatized son from Wrigley, never to return again. Instead, he removed a pack of long thin cigarettes from his coat pocket and lit one up. He took a relaxing puff, then another, and then before he could take a third, a ballpark security guard descended on him, grabbed the fag from his mouth, and barked "Sir, there's no smoking in Wrigley Field!"

"You must be jesting," the Brit said, aghast.

And to see the look on the bewildered fancy lad's face, as the bachelorettes continued squirting each other made the moment all the more poignant.

This amusing but true tale is not a rarity for the bleachers of Wrigley. In fact, it's unusual not to witness such good-hearted (if not a bit lewd) behavior when visiting the bleachers, which leads us—devoted baseball fans that we are—to our single complaint about the ballpark in Wrigleyville. No one seems to give a rip if the Cubs win or lose. Yankees fans live and die by the loss of their beloved boys in pinstripes. Philly fans woefully long for the days when the Phil's were contenders, and for when they will be again. Winning is important to them. But Cubs fans seem to have accepted that their team is going to lose, yet they love their day at the ballpark nonetheless. Doesn't the game mean anything at all to these folks? Wouldn't they rather see a Cubs win than some woman's breasts? While we're both fans of the female form, we can't help but feel that something has gone terribly wrong here.

pitchers, wooing into cell phones, and playing it up to the crowd. Chant "left field sucks," or "right field sucks," depending on where you're sitting, and treat yourself to a few Old Style brews.

The bleachers are general admission, so arrive twenty minutes before game time to claim a spot in the first level of benches for the best view and the best chance of snagging a home run ball. The left field seats usually fill up first.

A downside to the bleachers is that Wrigley policy prohibits bleacher patrons from entering other sections of the park. Also, when the bleachers are full, it is difficult to find your way to the exit ramps to buy a brew or visit the latrine because of the narrow walkways of the old ballpark. An upside: if you're looking to get lucky, start in the bleachers and work your way to the bars. Ballpark scoring has never been easier.

Club Box (Boxes 3–39)

The infield Club Boxes (9–34) are available almost exclusively to season ticket holders. But don't despair. They may be great seats, but the atmosphere here is exceedingly tame. Because the Cubs play so many day games, and because the park and team are so old, they attract a lot of older fans as season ticket holders. Nothing against the gray hairs, but if this is your once-in-a-lifetime trip to Wrigley, you might find yourself wedged between grandma and grandpa.

For those not daring enough to brave the bleachers, or those attending with children, we recommend the Outfield Boxes in left (3–8) or right (35–39).

Field Box Infield (Boxes 110–132)

Located directly behind the club boxes on the infield, these are prime seats that offer a great view of the playing field, skyline, and rooftop bleachers. They are exceptionally hard tickets to come by, however.

Field Box Outfield
(Boxes 101–109, 142–132)

If given the choice, pay the extra two bucks to sit in the infield boxes, but if that isn't happening, these are quality seats as well. In sections 101–105 in left and 139–142 in right, you won't be able to see a parcel of fair territory in the nearest outfield corner because of the rising brick wall. Even so, we recommend boxes 101, 102, 141, and 142, which are angled nicely toward the infield.

Terrace Boxes (Boxes 205–239)

The Terrace Boxes are located in the first few rows of the 200 Level. They are under the overhang caused by the luxury boxes but the view of fly balls is not obstructed. The seats are priced the same whether they're in the outfield or behind the plate, so be sure to ask for seats in the 213–228 range.

Terrace Reserved (200 Level)

The Terrace Reserved seats are located behind the Terrace Boxes on the 200 Level and account for the largest seating section in the ballpark, with 12,200 seats. The good news is that many of these seats are close to the action on the field. The bad news is that unless a pair of ground-ball pitchers are toeing the rubber, you might miss much of the game. Many of these seats are obstructed by the overhang of the luxury boxes, which were added in the 1980s. This obstruction is more of an issue for fans sitting in the high-number rows and is worst behind home plate in Aisles 215–219 because of the ramp to the luxury boxes. As a rule, try for seats no higher than Row 15. We liked the right field seats (235–238) where there is no overhang because the luxury boxes end in the airspace above Aisle 235.

SEATING TIP

FAMILY SECTION (AISLE 101A)

IF YOU'RE ONLY in town for one game and you want to check out Wrigley from all the angles, we recommend buying a Family Section seat in Section 101A. This catwalk section was added in 1985 and is the only section in the ballpark that allows you to access the main seating area and the bleachers. Technically, these ticket holders are not supposed to enter the bleachers, but it's more of a one-way restriction. Bleacher fans can't get in, but you should be able to pass freely into bumsville then safely back again when you show your stub.

As in older parks, many seats in the Wrigley Terrace are obstructed by support poles. We counted twenty-six poles in all. Kevin wasn't sure why Josh felt the need to count them, but Josh said it seemed necessary, kind of like counting TVs in a sports bar. Unfortunately there is no hard-and-fast rule as to what row number is safe. Any seat in front of Row 22 is in front of the pole and safe in left field's Aisle 202, whereas you'll need to be in front of Row 5 to be safe in Aisle 222 behind the plate. And with most games being sellouts, you'll have less opportunity to seat hop at Wrigley than at other parks.

Upper Deck Box (400 Level)

The press box is not located between the lower and upper levels as is the case at many ballparks, and there is no distinct luxury level because the private boxes actually cling to the underside of the upper deck. Consequently, Wrigley's upper level keeps fans low to the field and close to the action. At the same time, there is no under-hang to block the view of the field. Beware, however, if you buy seats in the upper deck you may wind up going home with a stiff neck. These seats are not angled toward the plate. If, for example, you're sitting in Section 434 in right field, you'll be looking over your left shoulder all day to see the infield.

Upper Deck Reserved (500 Level)

As with the lower level, all you can do is hope and pray you don't wind up behind one of the many support poles. On the plus side, there is no under-hang and the first row is not obstructed by concourse traffic thanks to a steep grade between the 400 and 500 Levels.

We suggest paying half the price of a 400 Level seat to sit in the 500 Level behind the plate. This is one of the best upper-level seats in the bigs. If given the choice, we would rather

sit in the Upper Reserved than in any seat behind Row 15 of the 200 Level. You can follow the whole flight of the ball from here, catch a bird's-eye-view of the interesting rooftop parties, and there's even a nice breeze on hot summer days. Plus with binoculars you have a perfect view of any topless happenings in the bleachers, er, um . . . oh, yeah, we said that wasn't cool, didn't we?

Like the Terrace seats, these are the same price all the way around the bowl of the upper deck, so shoot for the 515 to 525 range to be near the infield.

Avoid Aisle 532 where the view is obstructed by the upper-level scoreboard.

Standing Room

SRO tickets are sold for $10 when all other seats have sold out. Because of the overhang, there isn't much of a view from the standing area, located behind the 200 Level. We recommend seeking a scalper before the game instead.

Scalper Scene

Be prepared to pay at least double face value or more to sit with the bleacher bums, and a bit less for all other sections. You shouldn't have trouble finding a scalper on the streets around the ballpark. Just take a stroll down Waveland and they'll come to you. Somehow, like Santa Claus, they always seem to know.

Before/After the Game

While Wrigleyville may not offer a wealth of parking places where parking lots might ordinarily reside, there are scores of unique restaurants and bars surrounding the ballpark. Not a bad trade-off, if you ask us. This is easily the most festive ballpark neighborhood in the Majors, so plan on spending some time here before or after the game.

Getting to Wrigley

Wrigley is located between Sheffield Avenue, Waveland Avenue, Clark Street, and Addison Street. Take I-90 to the Addison Street Exit and follow Addison west into Wrigleyville. Or take I-290 east, to Route 55 north, to Lake Shore Drive, to Irving Park Road, to Clark Street.

If staying in town, we highly recommend taking the "L" train to the game. Get off at Addison Station, right across from the park. Because of the large postgame crowds on the platform, be sure to buy a token for your return trip in advance, or if you forget, follow the tracks to either the Belmont or Irving Park stops, which are a short walk away in either direction.

Another public transportation option is the Cubs remote parking program, which offers lot spaces at the DeVry Institute near Addison and Western, and a shuttle-bus ride to and from Wrigley Field, all for $5. For more information, call (773) 836-7000.

If driving is your only option, there are small parking lots on the corner of Waveland and Sheffield Avenue and on North Clark Street. These charge around $16 for a "full game" spot, which means that you arrive early, get boxed in, and cannot leave until well after the last out, or $25 for "easy-in, easy-out" service. We also found a $10 lot a ten-minute walk away on Cornelia Avenue off of Clark.

Unless you're attending a Sunday game, don't bother looking for a street spot in the neighborhood. Most spots are marked residential parking, while others have two-hour meters. Warning: Chicago parking authorities aggressively monitor and tow violators from these spots. On the Christian Sabbath, look for a meter spot on Sheffield or Clark. Also, we observed that some residents on Sheffield sell spots in their driveways, an option if the limited lot spaces near the ballpark are full.

Outside Attractions

ROOFTOP BLEACHERS

Walking along Waveland Avenue behind the left field bleachers, look up to see more bleachers perched high atop privately owned apartment buildings. One rooftop has a foul pole, aligned with Wrigley's left field line, and a 460-foot marker. Rooftop patrons belong to clubs such as the Lake View Baseball Club and pay annual dues for roof privileges. Many of the rooftops are also available to be rented out for corporate outings.

The rooftops have been at the center of a neighborhood-versus-ball-club controversy in recent years as the Cubs believe a portion of rooftop proceeds should be theirs, since they provide the attraction on the field. The owners of the buildings say, "No way. What's part of the view from our property is ours to look at freely." In response to the proliferation of rooftop viewing locales, the Cubs added twenty-foot high spite screens in 2002 to block a portion of the view. When we were in town, locals told us that according to rumor the team was planning to raise the screens even higher, and possibly add view-blocking helium balloons above them as well. The balloons sound like a disaster waiting to happen if you ask us. "Sosa drives one high and deep to left field. Way back! Way back! And it is . . . out of here! Wait a minute, the ball appears to have punctured one of the helium balloons. It's losing air. It could be! It could be! It is! It's deflated and falling into the bleachers. My God, the humanity!"

Whether or not the balloons ever come to fruition, the Cubs are also pursuing legal action against the owners of the rooftop establishments, claiming that the rooftop owners violate copyright laws and directly compete with the club for ticket sales. The lawsuit seeks compensatory damages and a share of the rooftop owners' profits. It also seeks to prevent them from marketing the Cubs without the team's expressed written consent. The two sides were due to meet in court right around the time of this publishing, with a date before a judge set for February 23, 2004.

Rooftop viewing is not a new phenomenon in Wrigleyville, which makes the team and its owner, the Tribune Newspaper Group, look even greedier for trying to shake down the locals. The tradition of watching Cubs games from outside the ballpark actually dates from the 1929 World Series when the Cubs themselves erected temporary bleachers on Waveland and Sheffield to accommodate large crowds. They did the same again for the World Series games in 1932 and 1935. Over the years, local fans would sometimes catch some sun and watch the games from atop their buildings. Then organized rooftop viewing swept through the neighborhood in response to the Cubs' magical 1984 season when they claimed the National League Eastern Division championship. And it's been here to stay ever since.

Being that it is a wonderfully distinctive feature of Wrigley, and that the Cubs sell out practically every game anyway, we say, "Long live the Rooftops." Lighten up, Trib.

BATTING PRACTICE BLISS

Like clockwork, two hours and twenty minutes before game time, an avid legion of ball hawks assembles at the corner of Kenmore and Waveland behind the left field bleachers.

Wearing gloves and toting duffel bags, they wait for Sammy to smack one clear out of the yard and then scramble like fire ants on crack to claim the souvenir as their own.

Josh spent an afternoon jostling for position among the regulars and was impressed by their numbers and enthusiasm. One fellow, named Kenny, claimed to have more than eight hundred balls at home. Another, Ray, claimed to be the best at catching balls on the fly.

Because the wind was blowing in toward home plate on the day Josh visited, the regulars predicted few if any balls would escape the confines. And they were right.

HAVE CHAIRS WILL TRAVEL

Though he didn't get a ball, while waiting on the sidewalk beyond the bleachers Josh did meet an avid Cubs fan named Doug who made him an offer he couldn't refuse.

A longtime ball hawk, Doug explained that the team was selling used Wrigley Field stadium chairs for $25 a pop or four for $75 in the pro shop. And he reasoned that if Josh and he pooled their money to purchase four chairs, they could each walk away with a pair of chairs for only $37.50 apiece.

"What do you say?" Doug asked. "Are you in?"

"You had me at 'hello,'" Josh said, already trying to think of the words he would use to convince his wife the chairs would look wonderful in their living room.

Josh and Doug met after the game to complete the deal. And Heather let Josh keep the chairs in the living room—for about a week. Now they're in the garage between his square of Boston Garden parquet and his piece of Foxboro Stadium goal post.

Kong

The Mets' Dave Kingman hit the longest homer in Wrigley history on April 14, 1976. The 550-footer smashed a porch railing on Kenmore.

Kingman, who would join the Cubs in 1978 and a year later hit forty-eight dingers for them, became the answer to an interesting trivia question in 1977 when he played for teams in all four Major League divisions—a record that with the new six-division format will surely never be broken. Kingman began the season with the New York Mets in the National League East, before being traded to the San Diego

Padres in the National League West, then to the California Angels in the American League West, and finally to the New York Yankees in the American League East. Keeping things in perspective, he may have played in four divisions, but only two states.

Much later, King Kong would become the answer to another trivia question: which eligible player hit the most career home runs but was not elected to the National Baseball Hall of Fame? Kingman's 442 homers weren't enough, and here's betting Jose Canseco's 462 won't be either, especially since he admitted to using the juice. We predict the Material Boy will take Kong's dubious mantle when he becomes eligible for the Hall in 2006.

HUNG LIKE A HORSE

On the corner of Sheridan and Belmont stands a statue of Civil War General Philip Henry Sheridan on his horse. The horse has very large testicles and it is a National League tradition for visiting teams to haze their rookies by making them paint the horse's balls in the team's colors on their first road trip to Chi-town each year.

You think that's bad? Imagine being the guy whose job it is to clean off those testicles the next morning?

"Mommy, what's that man doing to that horse?"

HARRY

Outside Gate D, pay tribute to one of baseball's all-time great broadcasters, where a monument memorializes the great Harry Caray. The beer-guzzling Caray was famous for leading fans during the seventh-inning singing of "Take Me Out to the Ball Game," and for coining such phrases as "Holy Cow," and "Cubs Win! Cubs Win! Cubs Win!"

The monument displays a bigger-than-life Harry towering over a miniature version of Wrigley Field.

Caray's broadcasting career actually began in St. Louis in 1945. After twenty-five years in the Cardinals booth, he moved to Oakland for one season in 1970, then became the White Sox play-by-play man in 1971. In 1982, he moved across town to Wrigley, where he would remain until his passing in 1998.

YESTERDAY: "WHERE THE PAST MEETS THE PRESENT" (West Addison/North Racine)

Okay, the name doesn't make a ton of sense according to rules of the time-space continuum, and it may look a bit run down, but this is a top-notch memorabilia shop and a must-visit for the serious collector.

Josh told shopkeeper Tom Boyle that he was a Red Sox fan and within ten seconds Boyle had produced a table full of baseball cards, photos, autographs, game programs, and other sundry relics all related to the Boston Nine. He found Josh a Carl Yaz card from when the Captain had the big sideburns, a circa-1957 Ted Williams button, a Sox roster from the 1960s, Red Sox newspaper articles from the 1930s and 1940s, and much more.

Watering Holes and Outside Eats

As mentioned above, Wrigleyville offers dozens of great restaurants and bars, the best and most varied selection of pre- and postgame activities in the big leagues. Whether you consider yourself a yuppie, slacker, bohemian, or karaoke queen, there's something for you. So do enjoy.

THE BILLY GOAT TAVERN AND GRILL
(West Madison Street) (Trademark Food)

If you're looking for a quick bite before the game, nothing beats a burger at the Billy Goat.

Topping its fried beef patties with a few slices of pickle, a slab of onion, and a sprinkle of history, the Goat is sure to satisfy.

This is the joint that John Belushi made famous with his "Cheezeborger, Cheezeborger," skit on *Saturday Night Live*. But this isn't the original Billy Goat—that one is located downtown and is actually much seedier. The Goat is one of many trademark Chicago eateries that have satellites in Wrigleyville.

Josh tried the double cheezeborger for under $3. Cheap, tasty, and a little on the greasy side. Just the way Josh likes 'em.

It was at the Billy Goat that we encountered famous Cub fan Ronnie Woo Woo sitting in full uniform, drinking a glass of milk, and eating a burger between two slices of white bread.

Just remember, "No fries! Chips!" And, "No Pepsi! Coke!" And don't even think about trying to order a grilled-chicken sandwich. (If you don't get the joke, catch a rerun of the old SNL skit on Nickelodeon.)

GIORDANO'S
(Belmont Street and Kenmore Street)
Gooey cheese. Thick, rich tomato sauce. And loads and loads of toppings. More toppings than you've ever seen on a pizza before. Chicago is famous for its deep-dish pizza and Giordano's makes one of the best pies in town. The pizzas are served with marinara atop the cheese, an interesting and not in the least bit regrettable culinary innovation. If you're a pizza lover, eat up.

THE WIENER CIRCLE
(Clark Avenue/Lincoln Park)
A bit of a walk from Wrigley, but exceptional dogs, Chicago-style, of course.

In case you don't know, a Chicago dog is a char-grilled all-beef natural-casing Vienna weenie served on a poppy-seed roll and topped with mint, green relish, chopped onion, crushed red tomato, a spear of dill pickle, hot peppers, celery salt, and mustard. Just remember, folks don't call their dogs, "dogs" in these parts. They call 'em "red hots."

Kevin also recommends getting an order of fries topped with cheddar.

We should warn you. Be prepared to be treated viciously by the foul-mouthed waitstaff. This place is famous for after-dark shouting matches between drunken patrons and the help. All in good fun, of course.

CLARK STREET DOG (Clark Street and Halsted)
A convenient place to grab a pregame dog or to try an Italian dipped-beef sandwich. A dipped beef is a hot roast beef sandwich, loaded with sautéed green peppers and onions, then doused, and we do mean doused, au jus. This soaking bread and beef makes one delicious mess of a sandwich.

THE CUBBY BEAR LOUNGE
(Clark Street and Addison Street)
A Wrigleyville mainstay, the Cubby Bear offers a spacious open-atmosphere bar area, pub grub, a roof deck, and live bands. If you like to run with the yuppie crowd, this might be the best place for you in the immediate vicinity of the ballpark.

MURPHY'S BLEACHERS
(Waveland Avenue and Sheffield Avenue)
This favorite hangout of the bleacher bums is located right outside bleacher Gate N. With outdoor seating and a limited menu centered around cased-meat products, this is one of those places that's worth stopping into, just to say you've been there.

If you're looking to grab a quickie before the game, order up a plastic cup of Old Style, then hurry across the street in time for the first pitch. If you're looking to get lucky after the game, stick around a while.

SLUGGERS (North Clark Street)
This spacious bar features the best sports decor in Wrigleyville and an upstairs game-room that offers patrons the chance to take a few swings in real live batting cages. When we visited, our friend Ronnie Woo Woo was cutting the rug with an attractive blonde.

THE RIVALRY HEATS UP

After a few frosties, we headed upstairs to Sluggers' batting cages where, for just $1 for twelve balls, fans line up to see if they're really cockeyed after their Wrigleyville binge. Native son John Cusack was allegedly once a regular in the "Major League" (eighty to eighty-five miles per hour) cage.

We tried the "Triple A" seventy to seventy-five miles per hour cage. After stretching, strapping on a helmet, and doing his best Nomar impression, Josh stepped up to the plate and slapped a few weak liners to right field. Then Kevin took his turn, which turned out to be much less successful. He fouled a few pitches off, but couldn't put the ball in play. Afterward, he whined that the strike zone was calibrated for someone significantly shorter than he was.

While Josh certainly hadn't torn the cover off the ball, he had proven slightly more successful than Kevin, a stroke that his ego sorely needed after his buddy had shown him up in Philadelphia, touching an electric sixty three miles per hour on the radar gun. So if Josh was a slightly better hitter, and Kevin a slightly better pitcher, we wondered, which one of us would enjoy more success hitting against the other? Later on our road trip we would find out in Los Angeles that throwing the ball is a lot easier than hitting it, and that we're both pretty awful with the stick.

GOOSE ISLAND (North Clark Street)

Located directly across the street from Sluggers, this local microbrewery abides by the slogan "Get Goosed!"

The Island is worth a visit if for no other reason than to check out the first-floor mural that depicts a number of all-time statistical leaders standing side by side: Hank Aaron, Joe Jackson, Babe Ruth, and many others.

And hey, there's karaoke—which is big in these parts—too.

THE BILLY GOAT'S GRUFF

THE BILLY GOAT earned its place in Chicago lore long before Belushi made it famous, and long before Ronnie Woo Woo made it his pregame hangout of choice.

The Legend of the Goat dates from 1945. It explains how the Cubs got to be cursed and why they've gone longer than any team but the White Sox without winning a World Series title.

The story goes something like this. A gentleman by the name of Bill Sianas owned a billy goat named Murphy that he tried to take to a 1945 World Series game at Wrigley. Apparently Murphy was a big fan. And Bill was, too, but when the goat was denied admission to the ballpark, an irate Sianas tried to appeal to Pete Wrigley himself, who upheld the ban on the grounds that the goat would stink up the place. When the Cubs lost the series to Detroit in seven games, Sianas sent a telegram to Wrigley asking, "Who smells now?" Sianas then put a curse on the Cubs. "Goatless, they will remain winless," he said. The Cubs have not returned to the October Classic since. It's been so bad, they've had only fourteen winning seasons since 1945.

Bill's nephew, Sam Sianas, now owns four Billy Goat Tavern locations in Chicago. In 1984 he tried to lift his uncle's curse, parading a goat onto the field on Opening Day as thousands cheered. The Cubs responded by winning the NL East that year, but fell to the Padres in the NLCS. The curse still lived!

Josh: "See, they're cursed just like the Red Sox."

Kevin: "There's no such thing as curses."

Josh: "How do you explain all those crushing losses then?

Kevin: "The other team was better?"

Josh: "Fine . . . I cast a curse on you: Goatless, you will remain womanless."

Kevin: "I'm already married."

GINGER MAN TAVERN (3740 Clark Street)

For Bohemian Cubs fans or simply for those tired of drinking their suds out of plastic cups, we recommend the Ginger Man Tavern. While not a sports bar, this is a cool place to avoid the ball game crowd, and a favorite hangout of Kevin's friend Paul who served as our tour guide during much of our Windy City stay. Kevin says they pour a decent pint of Guinness.

TRADER TODD'S ADVENTURE CLUB
(North Sheffield and Belmont Street)

Check out this friendly place, just try not to get lost in the side stories.

First off, everything inside the bar is for sale, from the assorted neon beer signs, to the mirrors, to the arcade games.

Second, the owner, Todd, personally mobilized fans in the days leading up to the near strike of 2002 and continues to forward fan mail to the commissioner's office as he receives it at his Web site, www.mlbfu.org. The "fu" stands for fan's union, of course.

Third, you can trade in your ticket stub for a free basket of chicken wings after the game.

Fourth, this is one of Chicago's premier karaoke clubs.

And finally, this is your best bet in Wrigleyville to trade barbs with a bona fide Chicago-based movie star. Don Gibb, who played Ogre in *Revenge of the Nerds*, is part of the management team. He had just had his belly button pierced when we caught up with him.

Todd gave Josh a valueless but interesting souvenir—a Vegas betting slip from Mandalay Bay for a $5 bet he had placed in March giving the Cubs 12-to-1 odds to win the 2002 World Series. Todd gave Kevin a free pint of Trader Todd's home-brewed Sunset Red Adventure Beer. We liked Todd.

WILD HARE (Clark Street and Eddy Street)

The Hare's a swinging reggae bar. You dig, Mon?

THE ULTIMATE SPORTS BAR
(9 W. Division Street)

Good prices, plenty of televisions, honey-bear waitresses, and hey, it's the *ultimate*, so it's got to be good.

Inside the Park

Sure, it's a bit cramped on the concourses beneath the stands. And yeah, parts of it look old and even a bit dingy. And yes, we are aware that the seats at many of the newer parks all face the general direction of home plate and are not obstructed by support poles. But if they ever tear this place down, they'll be making a huge mistake. It really is perfect, not in spite of these imperfections, but because of them. It's a time machine, so sit back and enjoy the ride.

When we conducted our ballpark draft prior to our trip and took turns picking which ballparks each of us would play the lead in writing, Josh selected Wrigley with the secret intention of comparing it to his beloved Fenway. He knew Wrigley would be a treat, but he expected it would fall somewhat short of the jewel in Boston. But it absolutely won him over. The Wrigley experience is right there with the one to be had in the Fens. If the Chicago fans were as intense and into the game as those in Boston, then Wrigley would be the clear-cut choice as the best ballpark to experience a game. As it stands currently, though, it's a toss-up between the two oldest parks in the Majors.

Ballpark Features
WRINKLED LINES

You know you're at a ballpark with extremely limited foul territory when the bull pen mounds located down the right and left field lines actually spill into fair territory. Take a look at the foul lines and you'll see that a sizable portion of fair territory rises to accommodate the mounds. Curved foul lines— these will definitely will be a determining factor in an important Cubs game someday. Here's hoping the ball bounces the Cubbies' way.

DISTANT POLES

Though its power alleys are rather shallow, Wrigley boasts the deepest outfield in the big leagues down the lines, at 355 feet to the left field foul pole and 353 feet to the one in right. A flag honoring Ernie Banks flies atop the left field pole and a flag honoring Billie Williams atop the right field pole.

Banks, who became the first National Leaguer to win back-to-back Most Valuable Player Awards in 1959, played shortstop for the Cubs from 1953 to 1971. Mr. Cub hit 512 long balls back in the day when middle infielders just plain didn't hit home runs. He was elected to the Hall of Fame in 1977.

Williams burst onto the Major League scene in 1961, winning the National League Rookie of the Year award on the strength of his twenty-five homers and eighty-six runs batted in. He would play left field for the Cubs for another fourteen years, before finishing his career with two seasons in Oakland in 1975 and 1976. A six-time All-Star who registered 426 home runs in his career, Williams was elected to the Hall of Fame in 1987.

DOUBLE YOUR PLEASURE, DOUBLE YOUR FUN

In 1925, before Chicago's Weeghman Park had changed its name to Wrigley Field, the Cubs' minor league affiliate in Los Angeles dedicated its own "Wrigley Field" on Avalon Boulevard. Mimicking Weeghman Park, the original Wrigley sported deep outfield foul lines and power alleys only five feet deeper at 345 feet to left- and right-center.

The expansion Los Angeles Angels played their inaugural season at Wrigley in 1961, and combined with their American League opponents to set a new big league record with 248 home runs in eighty-one games at Wrigley.

Look in the Los Angeles Dodgers chapter for info on yet another ballpark named Wrigley Field.

FROM TOP TO BOTTOM

Six flagpoles stand atop the scoreboard ranking the Major League teams in all six divisions according to their current place in the standings. Variations of this feature have since surfaced at Camden Yards in Baltimore, as well as other places.

EVEN MORE FLAGS

Hey, we weren't kidding when we said the Windy City was an ideal place to fly a flag.

Appearing on the roof of the upper deck on the right field side are pennants bearing the initials, nicknames, or uniform numbers of famous Cubs. A "Hawk" flag for Andre Dawson, "Ryno" for Ryan Sandberg, "Sammy 66" for Sammy Sosa, Santo for Ron Santo, "FJ" for Fergussen Jenkins, and so on.

On the left field side are flags commemorating pennant-winning seasons.

SILHOUETTE HARRY

Above the WGN window in the press box, you'll see the cartoon likeness of Harry Caray looking down at the field, watching the game like a sentinel.

Josh: "Harry seems thinner than I remember him being."

Kevin: "Indeed. And not quite as three-dimensional."

WHO

Visit Aisles 538 and 503 of the upper deck to find the ornamental plastic owls perched in the rafters. Judging by the number of feathers remaining on their wings, they look like they hail from the Ernie Banks era. We know these are meant to keep the pigeons away, but they didn't seem to be working when we visited.

Not to get off on an ultramodern new-age jag in a chapter dedicated to an old-school haunt like Wrigley, but Josh has always wondered why pro sports teams and their stadium managers don't rig the upper levels with electricity to shock the winged rats into the high heavens, or why, at the very least, they don't poison them. "Because that's cruel," Kevin says.

Stadium Eats

The food at Wrigley is rather poor. But remember, you're visiting the Confines for old-time ball and a few brews. And the neighborhood is full of places to eat before and afterward.

ARMOUR HOT DOG (Dog Rating)
The Nineteenth Best Hot Dog in the Majors
We found our Armour experience affordably priced but only mildly tasty. Maybe we were spoiled before the game by the fine dogs at **The Wiener Circle** and **Clark Street Dog**.

If the frankfurter hankering hits you, and waiting to get a dog outside the park after the game is not an option, we recommend shelling out a bit more money and picking up a Chicago Style Hebrew National dog at one of Wrigley's specialty stands. This is a far superior dog to the Armour one. First off, it's grilled, second it comes on a poppy-seed roll, and third it comes with tasty grilled onions. Someone should take a few of these onions and mail them to the food services manager at SkyDome in Toronto. They'll see what we're talking about.

BEST OF THE REST
We picked up a slice of **Connie's Pizza**. It didn't seem as hot or fresh as the Connie's slice we sampled at Comisky the day before, but it was still a solid offering. For the real thing, though, visit **Giordano's** before or after the game.

We also tried the Italian sausage/Italian beef combo, which is available at the Italian Market beneath the grandstand. For a soggy mess of pork and beef, it wasn't bad. Just make sure you have plenty of Maalox on hand.

On a hot day, we highly recommend a Frosty Malt, a tasty frozen treat that you eat with a wooden spoon.

SAY "NO, THANKS," AND WALK AWAY
In this case, it's "say, 'no, thanks,' and run like hell." We found **The Wrigley Pig** the worst ballpark food in the big leagues, even worse than Kevin's awful Motor City gyro. This sloppy atrocity consists of a chopped and processed pork patty topped with sautéed onions and way too much barbecue sauce. The aftertaste lingered for hours and we were still picking bones and hoof chips out of our teeth the next day in Cleveland! "Yuck!!!" Kevin said, "Anyone who orders this will either voluntarily or involuntarily, *throw it back, throw it back!*" His friend Paul dubbed the Pig, "the Upton Sinclair Special," because it's right out of *The Jungle*.

Checking in as a distant runner-up is the ballpark burger, which was dried out, tiny, and just plain lousy. Instead, get a double burger for less money at the **Billy Goat Tavern** before or after the game.

STADIUM SUDS
Two words. Old Style. We found people of all ages, shapes, and sizes drinking this stuff. So reach for the beer your grandfather loved—or perhaps your grandmother, and enjoy the game.

The Wrigley Field Experience

As mentioned above, for the optimum Wrigley experience, bleacher seats are in order. It's all about having a good time here. Whether the home team wins or loses, fans enjoy the game and have entirely too much to drink. Maybe the reason the outcome of the game plays second fiddle to having fun has something to do with the fact that Wrigley is usually full of folks who skipped out of work to spend an afternoon in the sun. A bad day at the ballpark beats a good day at the office.

THROW IT BACK

Wrigley is where the tradition of "throwing back" home run balls hit by the opposing team began. And though we love the tradition, this is where we feel it should remain.

If you're sitting in the bleachers and you catch a dinger hit by the visitors, you have only two options. One: throw the ball back onto the field before the crowd turns violent. Or two: tuck the ball into your shorts and run like hell for the ballpark gates. PS: You won't make it out of the park.

CALLING ALL TENORS

Each day, a different guest conductor leads fans in singing "Take Me Out to the Ball Game," during the seventh-inning stretch. Cubs Hall of Famers Ernie Banks and Billy Williams played the part of maestro during our visits. Celebrities who have taken a turn behind Harry's mick include *Wheel of Fortune* letter-gal Vanna White and Olympic figure skater Nancy Kerrigan. They get bona fide celebrities too sometimes. Honest, they do.

RONNIE WOO WOO (Superfan)

Wrigley Field is home to one of the most famous superfans in baseball, the gregarious Ronnie Woo Woo. Ronnie is so well known and well regarded that when Cubs rookies get called up to the bigs, they often ask him for his autograph, rather than the other way around. Spend five seconds with Ronnie, and you'll understand where he got his nickname. His distinctive high-pitched "Woo Woo" yelp can be heard eighty-one games a year, resonating in the bleachers and in the streets surrounding the ballpark.

As we walked down the street with Ronnie prior to a game between the Cubs and Pirates we quickly came to realize that everyone knew Ronnie. People shook his hand, asked him to pose for pictures, and asked him to "Woo" into their cell phones for friends to hear.

Ronnie, who told us a group of filmmakers are currently making a documentary about his life, rides his bicycle to Wrigley clad in an official Cubs uniform that says "Woo Woo" on the back. He attended his first Cubs game in 1947 to see Jackie Robinson play.

SPORTS IN THE CITY

CRYPT CREEPING IN THE WINDY CITY

WITHIN the Chicago city limits, you have the chance to visit the gravesites of no less than four Hall of Famers. Red Faber who won 254 games in a twenty-year career for the White Sox is buried in Acacia Park Cemetery, which is located at 7800 W. Irving Park Road. He rests in the Rose Section, Block 5, Lot SE2, Grave 2. William Hulbert, the White Stockings president who played an instrumental role in founding the National League, is buried in Graceland Cemetery at 4001 N. Clark Street. Cap Anson, who recorded 2,995 hits in a twenty-two-year career spent mostly with the Cubs, and Judge Kenesaw Mountain Landis, the commissioner who banned Joe Jackson and seven of his Black Sox teammates, are buried in Oak Woods Cemetery at 1035 E. 67th Street. Anson rests in Section E, Lot 4, Grave 10, and Landis in Section J, Lot 1, Grave 123. Happy haunting!

When we were in town, Slammin' Sammy was only two home runs shy of five hundred for his career, and Ronnie had his heart set on catching number five hundred. He claimed to have a magnetic connection with the ball and said he wouldn't be surprised if number 499 landed in his lap as well. When Sosa came up for his first at bat in the bottom of the second inning, we spotted Ronnie outside the ballpark on Waveland Avenue, down on one knee with his hands outstretched, as if expecting a ball to drop from the heavens. After Sammy grounded out, Ronnie came inside for the rest of the game.

Much to Ronnie's, and our, dismay, Sammy didn't homer during our two-day visit at the end of the 2002 season. We did have a ball hanging out with Ronnie though, beginning with pregame burgers at the Goat and ending at Sluggers a good three hours after the last out.

We were just about to bid him farewell, when he sucked us back in, as Ronnie has a way of doing.

"Stick around," he said. "And I'll introduce you to some players." He then escorted the latest in his long line of partners to the dance floor.

By players, we were not sure what Ronnie meant.

"I think he means . . . like, cool cats," Josh said, finding it exceedingly hard to envision any present or former Major Leaguers rubbing elbows with the locals at Sluggers.

"No, he means baseball players, and I'll bet you he delivers," Kevin said, his faith in Ronnie having grown stronger and stronger throughout the day.

"I'm not betting, but I don't think so," Josh said.

Kevin shook his head. "Don't you wonder what it would be like to have a little faith, just once in a while?" he asked.

"Yeah, I sometimes wonder," Josh said. "But I'm a Red Sox fan, remember?"

"Point taken," Kevin said.

When Ronnie finally relinquished the dance floor, sure enough, he proceeded to lead us to the bar and introduce us to the ageless Minnie Minoso, who had been sitting in our midst all along. Minnie, a friend of Sluggers' owner, is a frequent visitor on game days.

In case you need a quick memory jog, Minnie tied Nick Altrock's Major League record by playing in parts of five different decades with the White Sox, Indians, Senators, and Cardinals. He shook our hands, posed for a few pictures, and wished us well for the rest of our road trip. He said his favorite ballpark to play in was Tiger Stadium in Detroit.

Josh looked up Minnie in his baseball encyclopedia upon returning home and was shocked to discover that Minnie was more than eighty years old. He truly didn't look a day over sixty. A native of Havana, Cuba, Minnie began his big league career in 1949 and initially retired in 1964, before returning to the White Sox for Bill Veeck end-of-the-season fan-pleasing appearances in 1976 and 1980. He made it six decades in pro ball when he stepped to the plate for Mike Veeck's St. Paul Saints of the Independent Northern League in 1993.

Minnie has hit .298 in his Major League career to date (we're not ruling out one more comeback), and actually recorded a base hit in 1976 at age fifty-four.

Before we parted, Ronnie summed up his evolution as a superfan and his philosophy on life, quite eloquently. Said Ronnie, "I didn't know fifty years ago that I was going to be Ronnie Woo Woo. It just kind of happened. I try to make people happy. It's great to be healthy and to be outside in the sun for the games. The most important thing, as far as I can tell, is to just be yourself and let life come to you." Great advice from a man who knows.

CHICAGO WHITE SOX,
US CELLULAR FIELD

Born Too Soon on the South Side

CHICAGO,
ILLINOIS

7 miles to Wrigley Field
90 miles to Milwaukee
280 miles to Detroit
300 miles to St. Louis

I N BASEBALL, as in life, all things must pass eventually. Just as we are warmed by the wonderful memories we've treasured when a favorite player retires, we are likewise haunted by that same marking of time—the all-too-quick passage of seasons that retirement represents. These mixed emotions can only be assuaged when we reminisce with others who were there, and reflect on the player's contributions to the game. And so it is true with baseball parks. Eventually, one way or another, whether we like the idea or not, the game leaves our favorite parks in the past. We can only care for and preserve the old parks for so long. Then we must turn out the lights.

And so that fateful day of reckoning came to the south side of Chicago and to the White Sox organization in the early 1990s. The day when beloved Comiskey Park, a jewel of the American League could be expanded, refurbished, and polished no longer. Its era had come and gone, and as painful as the idea was to all, a new Comiskey would have to be constructed, one that would accommodate the Sox and their fans in the twenty-first century. Most folks among the White Sox faithful accepted the painful truth with the optimism and forward-thinking vision that has made Chicago one of the greatest cities in the world. And after all, this was to be a new and improved Comiskey: one that would bear the old-school look of its predecessor along with the conveniences of modernization.

But as our friend Jim Kauss—a lifelong White Sox fan and one of our tour guides when we visited Chicago—so aptly put it, "After all the hype and all the media coverage, you can't imagine my profound disappointment on Opening Day here, as I walked through these gates. From the blue seats that should have been green to an upper deck that is so sterile it looks like it belongs at a football stadium, I was completely deflated."

During our visit to Comiskey, Jim expressed often his longing for the old ballpark that once sat just across the street. Clearly, Comiskey, Jr. does not share much of its father's DNA. Perhaps the milkman is responsible.

Making matters worse for White Sox fans, just two short years after their new ballpark opened, HOK, the architectural firm that designed the park, unveiled Oriole Park at Camden Yards. Baltimore's new ball yard offered all those features that the new Comiskey didn't, features that the Chicago faithful were clamoring for—like an intimate playing environment, old-time feel, and striking views of downtown beyond its walls.

The new Comiskey Park was built for $167 million, nearly all of which came from a 2 percent sales tax on hotels in the city. In 1986 a bill was passed by the Illinois General Assembly to fund a new ballpark to be built across the street from the old Comiskey. This bill came in response to White Sox owner Jerry Reinsdorf's threat to move the team to Tampa Bay. The pressure created a harried environment and so the rush was on to build a new South Side ballpark as soon as possible. In 1989 Chicago Mayor Richard M. Daly—son of the former Mayor Richard J. Daly and die-hard Sox fan—helped break ground on new Comiskey. And optimism swelled in the hearts of White Sox fans.

But instead of a second Comiskey that borrowed from the best of the old, the folks on the South Side got a glorified stadium. While many of old Comiskey's attractions and idiosyncrasies have been imitated or duplicated in the new park, the only thing brought directly over from the old park was the infield dirt. What

exterior

Photo by Kevin O'Connell

was to be the first-baseball-only facility built in the American League since 1973, turned out to be overly huge, unfriendly to fans, and sterile. The first row of seats in the upper deck sit farther from the field than the last row of upper-level seats at the old park.

With the return-to-retro trend that Camden Yards started, the since-renamed US Cellular Field now stands in memoriam to the last of its kind: a large, suburban, multidecked stadium that has little charm and even less neighborhood surrounding it. Perhaps that is why in 2003, the Comiskey name that had been synonymous with baseball on the South Side of Chicago for eighty years was changed, and the stadium took on its new corporate title.

On April 18, 1991, more than forty-two thousand fans poured through the gates with high hopes for the first game at the new park, and their disappointment was palpable as Opening Day saw the Sox get demolished by the Tigers 16–0. Our friend Jim joked that he wished it was the new stadium that had been demolished. Buck up Jim, White Sox tradition is still long and glorious. And thanks to the novelty factor the Pale Hose set a new team attendance record in that inaugural year when nearly three million fans came to see the new ballpark.

Perhaps the sweetest home run at the new park came on Opening Day of 1993 when Bo Jackson, coming off hip-replacement surgery, crushed the first pitch he saw into the right field bleachers. Jackson had previously dedicated the game to his mother, who had recently passed away. The Sox went on to win the American League's Western Division that year, their first divisional title in ten seasons. The next year, Chicago led Cleveland by a single game in the AL Central standings when the strike ended their playoff hopes.

In 1997 interleague play began and the new Comiskey hosted the Sox and Cubs for the first regular season "L Series," so named for the "el"-evated rail that connects the two ballparks, and oh, yeah, the rest of the city as well. The Cubs nabbed the opener 8–3, but the Sox won the final two games to take the series, which drew two of the biggest crowds in the new park's history.

But despite these few highlights, the general consensus among fans is that US Cellular field just isn't good enough to accommodate their baseball needs. And as a testament to Sox fans' love of the game, the team, and their city, ordinary folks are getting involved with the team and taking responsibility to improve their ballpark. Donning their hard hats and work boots, the residents of the City of the Big Shoulders are working with the team to desterilize the new park, to make it cozy and intimate. Committees have been formed, opinions have been proffered to management, and the team has responded by tinkering with the stadium. The White Sox are a Chicago institution, and they are taking the right attitude toward their still-new stadium. We have seen how preservation can work with an old park— over-the-years upkeep, remodeling, and care

for the structure—and will be interested to see how this approach works with a newer park. Only time will tell if tinkering with US Cellular Field will be able to recreate the magic old Comiskey had. And here's hoping that the $63 million US Cellular paid for naming rights will bring about some much needed improvements.

In baseball, as in life, most things that are worthwhile take time to accomplish. The American League was formed in Chicago originally in 1899, then officially in 1901 when the Junior Circuit expanded to a 140-game schedule and declared itself a second Major League. In 1900 Charles Comiskey had bought the St. Paul Saints and moved them to the South Side Grounds at 39th and Princeton, where they played their games in a small wooden stadium and captured the pennant by defeating the Cleveland Blues. This park, which doubled as home of the American Giants, Chicago's Negro League team, was torn down in 1940 to make way for housing projects.

The White Stockings kicked off the 1901 season by playing the first "official" game of the new American League, winning again against Cleveland 8–2. They also won the pennant that inaugural season.

Nixey Callahan tossed Chicago's first no-hitter against the Detroit Tigers on September 20, 1902. On October 14, 1906, the Sox won the only "All-Chicago" World Series, downing the crosstown Cubs in six games. Sox fans still brag about this one the way Yankees' fans shout "1918" at Josh.

A green cornerstone for the new ballpark, which was known as "the Baseball Palace of the World," was laid at 35th and Shields Avenue on Saint Patrick's Day in 1910, thanks in no small part to the Irish who lived in the South Side neighborhood known as Bridgeport. White Sox Park opened its "palatial" gates just three-and-a-half months later on July 1, 1910. It didn't take long for the new park to take on its third moniker, that of Comiskey. And it wasn't just owner's pride from which the park drew its name. Comiskey financed the entire structure and helped in its design, along with architect Zachary Taylor Davis and pitcher Ed Walsh. Perhaps the fact that a pitcher had a hand in the design was one reason why the field was 362 feet down each foul line and 420 to straightaway center.

But current baseball owners take note: if you pay for a new ballpark, you can name it anything you want. Toot your own horn. Name the place after your daughter like that hamburger guy did. Fans will love you all the more for it. But can you imagine George Steinbrenner designing a new "Steinbrenner Grounds" in New Jersey? It would probably be 175 feet down the right field line, and then he'd corner the market on left-handed hitting and left-handed pitching. In any case, the Sox lost 2–0 to the St. Louis Browns in their Comiskey debut on July 1, 1910.

The fans who turned out at old Comiskey witnessed the rise and fall of a sweet-swinging hick named Joe Jackson. "Shoeless" Joe signed his name with an X and sometimes shagged balls barefooted, just like he used to growing up in South Carolina. But he could sure punish a baseball. In 1915 he joined the White Sox via Cleveland, signing a contract for $31,000 a year—huge money in those days. Two years later, the Sox picked up their second World Series title, downing the New York Giants four games to two.

Tragedy struck a few years later when eight White Sox players were suspended by Comiskey for allegedly conspiring to fix the 1919 World Series, which Chicago lost to the Cincinnati Reds five games to three. The players were later found not guilty in the "Black Sox" trial, which stained the reputation of the National Pastime nonetheless and shook the confidence of American values to their very core. Despite the verdict, after the 1920 season Baseball Commissioner Kenesaw Mountain Landis banned all eight players from baseball for life, including Shoeless Joe, though his numbers for the Series were outstanding. The debate over his guilt or innocence carries forth to this day, and the scandal is well documented in the movie *Eight Men Out*, directed by John Sayles.

In 1927 a double-decked outfield grandstand was constructed at Comiskey, completely enclosing the park while accommodating more than twenty-three thousand new seats. Though it seated many, the enclosure gave Comiskey an intimate feel that most folks from the South Side remember fondly. The first ever All-Star Game was played at Comiskey on July 6, 1933. See what renovation and modernization, done well, can accomplish? But the Sox weren't done improving the grounds yet. Lights were added in 1939 to facilitate night games. Then on July 5, 1947, lights of a different kind went on in Comiskey when Cleveland's Larry Doby broke the American League color barrier pinch-hitting against the White Sox. Doby struck out in his first at-bat but went 1–5 the next day, starting at first-base.

The All-Star Game returned to the grand old park in 1950 in the form of a thirteen-inning marathon that saw the National League win 4–3. White Sox shortstop Luke Appling would retire later that year after playing 2,422 games in a Chicago uniform. In 1951 Minnie Minoso became the first African American player to take the field for the Sox, and he did so in grand style, homering off Vic Raschi of the Yankees in his first game. Who knew then that fifty years later Minnie would meet Josh and Kevin in Wrigleyville when their road trip brought them to Chicago?

In 1958 the first Bill Veeck era began, one that would bring the White Sox many of their current traditions and many enhancements to the old ballpark. Veeck would become a baseball marketing legend, to the extent that South Shields Street is today known as Bill Veeck Drive. There are too many interesting stories about Veeck's wacky promotions to list them all, but we'll do our best in the pages ahead to hit some of the high (and low) lights. If Veeck's style catches your fancy, we suggest reading his autobiography *Veeck, as in Wreck*, or the simply titled biography *Bill Veeck*, by Gerald Eskenazi.

interior

Photo by Kevin O'Connell

The Sox quickly flourished under Veeck's inspired leadership, winning the pennant in 1959 to end a forty-year postseason drought. Unfortunately for the Sox, Veeck was forced by ill health to sell his interest in the team in 1961. He would later reemerge as owner in 1975. In between the Veeck years some even crazier things happened on the South Side, but none held any comedic value to Sox fans. The low point came when in a decision to bolster flagging attendance the Sox played one "home" game against each of their AL opponents in Milwaukee at County Stadium. They had losing records both years, and fears that the team might permanently make Milwaukee its home made Chicago fans mighty nervous. Also, in 1969 Astroturf was laid at Comiskey. The team responded to the plastic grass by having its worst season ever in 1970, losing 106 games. Ouch.

But by 1973 the Sox were on the rebound. A May 20th doubleheader against the Minnesota Twins drew a Comiskey record 55,555 fans. And by 1975 Veeck was back at the helm, and the high jinks and fun picked up where they had left off, even if the Sox still couldn't bring

home a World Series title.

As another Sox fan and tour guide of ours—Douglas Hammer—pointed out, the White Sox World Series drought has lasted longer than that of Josh's beloved Red Sox—a fact that does little to lessen Josh's anguish and pain.

Kevin told both of them that "if losses make for better stories, you two ought to have some of the best stories in the big leagues."

Then they turned on him. "At least our teams have been to the World Series and actually won a few!" they said simultaneously.

Kevin retorted, "Or so your great-grandfather's have told you."

In 1976 natural grass came back to Comiskey. "Thank you, Lord." Perhaps the secret to success for an owner comes in knowing what features not to mess with in order to preserve the history of the game alongside being adventurous enough to try something new. Veeck tried morning baseball: first pitch 10:30 A.M., to accommodate third-shift factory workers. Another innovation that didn't catch on. In 1978 Larry Doby replaced Bob Lemon as manager, becoming the second African American manager in AL history and the first for the Sox. On July 12, 1979, in a move *way* ahead of its time, Veeck sponsored "Disco Demolition

TRIVIA TIMEOUT

Big Manly Shoulders: Which White Sox hurler holds the record for most wins in a season during the last one hundred years, and how many victories did he post? (Hint: think 1908.)

Atlas's Shoulders: Who hit the first home run that set off Bill Veeck's exploding scoreboard?

Frank Thomas's Shoulders: How many All-Star Games have Comiskey Park and US Cellular Field hosted?

Look for the answers in the text.

Night," during which fans were encouraged to bring disco records to the ball yard for their destruction between games of a double-header. Good idea, Bill—at least on paper. After fans sent thousands of records Frisbee-ing onto the field, the nightcap against the Tigers was forfeited.

Perhaps Disco Demolition Night was the beginning of the end, because Veeck sold the team to Jerry Reinsdorf in 1981. In 1982 a new exploding scoreboard, with improvements such as a color video board, was constructed, as were new dugouts and luxury suites. In 1983 Comiskey hosted the All-Star Game, played on July 6. Fifty years earlier to the day, on the same field, the first All-Star Game had taken place with the American League prevailing 4–2. In the Golden Anniversary game, the AL won 13–3, paced by a Fred Lynn grand slam. Lynn's blast was the first grand salami in the history of the Midsummer Classic. The Sox would go on to clinch the AL West title that year and win the division by twenty games—a MLB record that stood until 1998 when the Yankees finished twenty-two games ahead of the Red Sox. But the Sox fell to Baltimore three games to one in the ALCS. In 1984, the longest game in American League history was played at Comiskey against the

Milwaukee Brewers. The game lasted twenty-five innings and spanned two days, before Harold Baines ended it with a walk-off home run to give the Sox a 5–4 win.

Getting a Choice Seat

Unless the hated North Side Nine are in town, getting a ticket on game day shouldn't be any hassle. Unless the Sox are making a playoff run, they don't sell out too many of their games. And US Cellular Field has an expansive upper deck, so getting into the yard is not as much of an issue as procuring a good seat.

Infield Box and Club Level (Sections 121–143, 312–357)

Forget about these seats unless you have a Chi-town connection. They're available for season ticket plans only. But if you can find them from a broker or on the streets they are quite good. Sections 131–133 are right behind home plate, in case there's any discrepancy with the scalper who's trying to make a deal with you. A crooked scalper in Chicago? Get outta here!

Lower Deck Box (Sections 109–120, 144–155)

These are the best seats we plebes are allowed to buy, and they are pretty good. It feels spacious inside US Cellular Field, likely because the upper deck is pushed back away from the lower level. There's no overhang problem at all, which is good for the lower level, bad for the upper.

A very low retaining wall separates the fieldlevel seats from the field, which is great for autograph hounds or for those wishing to lean over to snag a ball along the third-base side

Sellout Index: 10% of games sell out
Seating Capacity: 45,936
Ticket Office: (312) 674-1000
www.whitesox.mlb.com

during batting practice. Josh got a ball from Red Sox third-baseman Shea Hillenbrand during infield warm-ups after only five innings of pestering.

The lower bowl has more rows than most parks, twenty-eight by Josh's count. Again, good if you can get them. You may have to take a rather lengthy hike to find the men's room or get another beer, but find a seat in these sections if you can. There are times on a baseball road trip to open up the wallet and let some of the road flies out. US Cellular Field is one of them as the good seats are pretty good, but the bad seats are horrible.

Another thing about the rows on the first level, they rarely go more than seventeen seats across without an aisle break, and the aisles are nice and wide. So with only eight or fewer seats to either side of you, it's almost like everyone has a box seat.

Lower Deck Reserved
(Sections 100–108, 156–159)

If you buy your tickets from the window on game day, these will most likely be the best seats available. So make the most of the situation. Avoid Sections 156 and 108 as they have foul-pole obstructions. Also steer clear of Sections 100 and 101, as the batter's eye and the massive concrete patio in center field wreak havoc on the sight lines. In Section 101 sit only in Row 15 or lower, and in Section 100 don't get caught behind Row 10.

Other than that, the advantage of building a field with fairly symmetrical dimensions is that the sight lines are largely preserved. And old Comiskey had symmetrical dimensions, too, so we're not arguing with that decision. That's not the problem here. Candidly, we feel one of the main problems with US Cellular Field is old Comiskey Park. People who don't remember how intimate the old park was (or who grew up watching the Mariners

play in the Kingdome) don't have nearly as much to say about how large and sterile the new park is.

Bull Pen Sports Bar and Patio Seating

Situated in right field, the Bullpen Sports Bar is located behind the visiting bull pen and separated by a glass wall that also offers a view of the rest of the field. You can have an Old Style and watch the relievers warm up. We found it amazing to see how much snap is on the ball from this close. But honestly, the setup smacks a bit of the monkey cage at the zoo. The players know you're there but won't look at you. It's awkward for both sides and probably should be altered a bit.

> ### SEATING TIP
>
> ➜ THE SEATS in right field are farther away than in left because the patio area in right pushes the seats back about twenty feet. We recommend left field Sections 157–159 over any in right. Section 159 is prime as it is lower to the field and closer to the action.
>
> The bull pen in left field is elevated and a see-through outfield fence allows the pitchers and fans seated near ground level to see through the mesh. Though initially against the idea, it did add to the experience for Josh. The benefit of chain-link is that it diminishes what would be an obstructed view.

Inside, a wooden bar sits in a cinderblock locker room. There are plenty of tables and places to sit, but not all of them offer views of the field. They should. And the place lacks the warmth that a bar should offer. Picture putting the bar from *Cheers* inside your high school locker room and you've got the idea. Now this may have seemed like a great idea when you were sixteen, but when Kevin was sixteen he also thought it would be cool to cut the roof off his car to make it a convertible—unfortunately, he was living in rainy Seattle at the time and his upholstery got ruined.

Both the Bull Pen Sports Bar and the Patio in right field have been dubbed "the Party Area" by the signage. If you have crappy seats, by all means head on down. Even if you don't pop the $10 extra to get from the Bull Pen Sports Bar to the Patio area up above (which provides much better access to the players to snag autographs) you'll be upgrading your seats at no charge. But beware. The Patio has only eighteeen tables with four seats at each that cannot be seen from inside the Pub, so if seating is a priority for you like it is for us, scope it out from up above before you pull out the green down below.

Bleachers (Sections 160–164)

The seats in left field home run territory are actual bleachers seats, but on the plus side they have contoured seat backs and there is enough space in between the numbered sitting spots to give your rump some room to breathe. All in all these are pretty comfortable for bleachers, so we're not sure why they're two bucks cheaper than their right field counterparts (Sections 100–103) that are the same distance from the plate. And while you're out here don't expect the shenanigans of the cross-town team's bleachers. That kind of funny business doesn't fly on the South Side, except when Josh is using the public shower on the concourse.

Section 164 in left field has serious visual obstructions caused by the cement of the batter's eye, unless you're in Rows 1–12, which are okay.

Upper Deck Box and Reserved (Sections 506–558)

We learned a great deal about ballparks visiting US Cellular Field. For the most part, the first levels of nearly all ballparks offer pretty good seats. It's what the architects do with the problems of the upper deck that make a ballpark distinctive and what it will inevitably be judged on. If the upper deck hangs out a great distance above the lower, thus providing a steep but close upper level, it will then be compared to Yankee Stadium. If the upper deck is small, not terribly steep, and tucked close to the field, as on the North Side, a "Wrigley-like," quality will be observed. If neither strategy has been used, and the upper deck is high up, not hung close to the field in any way, and still very steep, the park will unfortunately be dubbed "US Cellularesque."

We cannot stress this enough: if at all possible, stay away from the upper deck at US Cellular Field. The first row of these seats is farther from the field than the last row was at old Comiskey. Not only is there a level of luxury boxes and a Club Level, but also a level for the press in between the lower and upper decks. We do not recommend sitting in the upper deck at all. Between the decks is almost sixty feet of sterile concrete. What the architects were thinking building an upper deck like this, we have no idea, except perhaps to keep it back and eliminate all overhang for the lower levels. Spend the extra two bucks and sit in the bleachers.

Our friend and tour guide of the South Side was Mr. Murphy, who was part of a neighborhood focus committee investigating what could be done about the upper deck at US Cellular Field. After confirming rumors we'd heard that bullet holes had been found in the seats from stray gunfire, Mr. Murphy informed us that the team was working toward improvements. Because the field was not below street level, the upper deck rises that much higher, giving from the outside the impression of a cookie-cutter-style stadium.

Can the upper deck be torn down and rebuilt: doubtful. So, to Mr. Murphy and the rest of the dedicated Sox fans who care enough to try to improve US Cellular Field, we wish you the best of luck. Remember, Rome wasn't built in a day, so stick with it.

Scalper Scene

There is a sign outside the park that reads, "Resale of tickets at any price is prohibited." That said, we did see a few folks walking around, and we don't think they were selling Girl Scout cookies. By now you should know the drill, but beware, it is against the rules.

Before/After the Game

There used to be a neighborhood surrounding Comiskey, before the Dan Ryan Expressway was built and before the project buildings arrived. The South Side had an inner-city ball-yard neighborhood much like the one the cross-town team now enjoys. It seems urban renewal is not always a good thing. So, in an effort to recapture what they once had, the team has discussed tentative plans to develop the parking lot behind the left field wall, making it inhabitable for a restaurant and bar scene. But at present, a lengthy walk is in order to get to any nearby pubs and eateries.

Getting to US Cellular Field

There really isn't any street parking during ball games in the residential neighborhoods. Don't waste time looking like we did. Folks have been scoping out the neighborhood for secret spots for more than eighty years. There aren't any left. US Cellular Field is one of those places where drivers need to bite the bullet and park in the team lot. And truthfully, it's probably best to do so, if you want the road-trip car to be in one piece after the game. US Cellular Field is located just off the Dan Ryan Expressway at 35th Street. You'll see it from the freeway.

We took the "L," Red Line train, to the game. Get off at the Sox/35th stop and US Cellular Field will be on your right as you come up to street level above the Dan Ryan. If you're leaving by way of the "L," use the same protocol that you'd use in the Bronx. Get on the train soon after the game ends, before the crowd disperses.

Tailgating, Uh, Yeah

The team Web site claims that tailgating in the parking lots is encouraged in White Sox Parking Lots A–E. While the only tailgating we saw was on the Dan Ryan, we are not ones to cast aspersions. And perhaps we were a bit biased because we had just come from Milwaukee, where tailgating is an art form. There was no parking lot bowling. There were no bratwursts being handed out. Then again. There aren't many bars in the neighborhood, so if you feel like making your own party, tailgate your brains out.

Outside Attractions

OLD COMISKEY PARK-ING LOT

Rather than tailgate, why not seek out some of the history of the old park that used to be right across the street? In the parking lot just to the north of the ballpark resides old Comiskey's home plate. White lines mark the location of the batter's box and where the baselines once ran, whereas yellow lines tell you where to park your car. Imagine the players that walked the grass of that once glorious park. Imagine the home run that Al Smith hit to set off the exploding scoreboard for the first time. Imagine the five glorious All-Star Games that were played here. No, you say? Your count is different? Well, there was the inaugural game in played in 1933, the 1950 All-Star Game, the Negro League All-Star Game in 1933, the fiftieth anniversary All-Star Game was played in 1983, and the seventieth anniversary game was held across the street in 2003. If you want to imagine White Sox pitcher Ed Walsh winning forty games in 1908—a feat no one has matched since—it might be more inspiring to visit 39th and Princeton, the site of the old Schorling's Park, five blocks to the south.

THE SHOT HEARD 'CROSS THE BLOCK

Amour Square Park to the north of the old ball-park was the supposed landing site of a ball Jimmy Foxx knocked completely out of old Comiskey in 1932. Today, the park is a good place to have a catch before the game as it sits right next to Lot B. The park was established in 1904 and the Sox are working with the city to spruce up the grounds.

THE BABE'S BOTTLE

Just to the left of the Gate 4 ticket window, vines of ivy grow on the side of US Cellular Field. This location used to be just across the street from old Comiskey, and there used to be a bar here called McCuddy's, an infamous joint where legend had it Babe Ruth used to go between innings to toss back beers when the Yankees were in Chicago. It's a romantic image, isn't it? Imagine how well "the Sultan" could have swatted if he'd played the game sober. Then again, perhaps he hit better after a few belts. Kevin plays pool better, as long as he's well within the "beer window," a sliding scale of beers where improvement is notice-able within its confines. Before or after, well, that's another story.

GRANDSTAND, LTD (600 W. 35th Street)

This memorabilia shop features more White Sox gear than we found anywhere else, includ-ing inside the park. They have street signs bearing the current players' names (Frank Thomas Way, Paul Konerko Boulevard) as well as autographed balls and shirts, old packs of baseball cards to fill out your collection, and

AMERICAN GIANTS

SCHORLING'S PARK was also the home of Rube Foster's American Giants—Negro League World Series champs in 1926 and 1927. Andrew "Rube" Foster was the father of the Negro Leagues who as a pitcher won fifty-one games himself during the 1902 season with the Chicago Union Giants. He posted an unimaginable 54–1 record in 1903 with the Cuban X-Giants. Prior to forming the Negro National League, his American Giants won every championship from 1910 to 1920. He excelled as player, manager, and league administrator before suffering a nervous breakdown and dying in 1930. He was named to the Baseball Hall of Fame in 1981.

Chicago was also home to many other Negro League teams including the Columbia Giants, Leland Giants, Unions, Union Giants, Lelands, and, of course, the Chicago Giants. For complete information on the teams of the Negro Leagues, we recommend *The Bio-graphical Encyclopedia of the Negro Baseball Leagues*, by James A. Riley.

more. Kevin was excited to find a Ken Griffey, Jr. uniform, from his days as a Mariner.

Watering Holes and Outside Eats

Chicago is a meat-and-potatoes town, a shot-and-a-beer town. And though most of the places we found were a healthy walk from the park, they were definitely worth the extra steps. If you don't want to walk, hail a cab.

MORRIE O'MALLEY'S HOT DOGS (Corner of 35th and Union)

We tried to figure out the Irish hot dog con-nection that is famous in Chicago. We failed. But O'Malley's features charred Vienna beef dogs that are damned tasty. Also the joint has four green seats from the old Comiskey out front that patrons can use while they eat. Remember, never put ketchup on a hot dog in Chicago. Josh disregarded this local prohibi-tion, much to the dismay of management and other diners. In this town dogs come loaded with pickles, tomato, relish, kraut, and more if you ask for it, and at O'Malley's all for less than two dollars. O'Malley's also serves Italian beef, and an assortment of other treats sure to raise your cholesterol.

SCHALLER'S PUMP
(3714 block of Halstead Street)

We have one word for this type of White Sox hangout: old school. Wait, that's two words, but in any case, Schaller's was a haunt of Mayor Daly the elder, a famous fan of Bridgeport and the White Sox. Inside you'll find friendly people, a smoky atmosphere, and cheap beers served in the can. The bar feels like an American Legion bar, with aged regulars downing Old Style. A must-visit if you're in the neighborhood and a great place to down a few on the cheap before the game.

TUFANO'S (1073 W. Vernon Park Place)

A good Italian restaurant with a liquor license to boot! It's not really a White Sox place but it is a quality Italian place to eat close by the park.

MARIO'S CANTINA (3938 N. Ashland Avenue)

This is the place to go for Italian lemon ice on a steamy summer afternoon or night.

JIMBO'S (33rd and Princeton off Shields Street)

Look for the decrepit black fire escape and the small Jimbo's Lounge sign. Jimbo's is your basic sports bar. There's not too much to distinguish it other than a signed Tommy Lasorda picture and a picture of Babe Ruth in street clothes.

DONNIE'S (3258 S. Wells Street)

One block from Jimbo's toward the corner of Wells Street is Donnie's New York-style pizza. Affordable and nearby, this place is not a dive. We repeat: not a dive, it's clean looking, trendy and modern, and is a favorite of our friend and tour guide Douglas Hammer. Donnie's offers gourmet pizza by the pie or slice, pasta dinners, deli subs and homemade sandwiches on freshly baked bread, paisanos (baked not fried), and calzones. Josh recommends the Pizza Paisano, a whole Italian sausage wrapped in pizza crust with mozzarella cheese and red sauce.

HUFFER'S (3356 S. Halstead Street)

With open-air windows and a long wooden bar this slightly more upscale bar still sells peanuts in bags as well as potato chips and popcorn to other patrons. But Kevin wasn't interested in the snacks. He went for an apple martini for $3.

Kevin: "It sounded interesting."
Josh: "You should be ashamed of yourself."
Kevin: "You're right. I know."

PANADERIA BAKERY
(corner of 33rd Street and S. Halstead Street)

Specializing in French pastry, Panaderia bakes French bread, pastries, and muffins. If you're afraid of temptation, stay away. This place smells so good from the outside you won't be able to walk past.

FIRST-BASE (3201 S. Normal Avenue)

Look for the baseball diamond on the awning. Inside, a square bar offers limited seating. This is a "drink 'em while you stand and don't talk to anyone" kind of place. Plan on spending about as much time here as most runners spend at—first-base.

KEVIN'S HAMBURGER
(Wallace Street and Pershing Road)

Hey, it's a twenty-four-hour breakfast joint and it has Kevin's name on the door. How bad could it be? Well, we wouldn't go there after dark. According to a sign on the front door, patrons must pass through a metal detector after 10 P.M., and another sign reads: "No soliciting of prostitution." Enough said?

DOX GRILL (Wallace Street and Pershing Road)

Located across the street from Kevin's Hamburger, Dox specializes in Italian beef. See Kevin's Hamburger for dress code.

AL'S ITALIAN BEEF (1079 W. Taylor)

"You gotta' try Al's Italian beef over dere by Taylor Street," our friend Jim told us. Italian dipped-beef sandwiches are something to see. Italian beef is a hot steak sandwich drowned au jus. The bread soaks up the juice turning the whole thing into one big sloppy delicious mess.

MAXWELL STREET HOT DOG STAND (Corner of Damen and Diversey)

While you can expect good dogs from this longtime hot dog vendor, the specialty of the house is the pork chop sandwich. Loaded with grilled onions, mustard, and served dripping with grease, this sandwich is another Chicago original. Though Kevin claims he's sampled them in Butte, Montana, as well.

LA PASADITA (1140 N. Ashland)

After the game why not try a burrito that is as big as your head, and tasty too? La Pasadita is open until 3 A.M., so after the bars close this is a solid choice. We were told these burritos would help allay the inevitable next-day hangover.

For Those Willing to Go the Extra Mile

GENO'S EAST PIZZA (633 N. Wells)

Not only is this town divided over baseball, there's also a pizza war between deep dish and stuffed, both Chicago originals. Though the battle lines are a bit less clear, we suggest you try them both. Geno's is a stuffed-pizza lover's dream.

GARRETT POPCORN SHOPS (670 N. Michigan Avenue, Other Locations)

Sure it's a touristy thing to do and you're going to be standing in line with a bunch of blue hairs with cameras hanging from their necks and

with short pants exposing their aged spotted legs. But this here is some good corn.

HAROLD'S CHICKEN SHACK (550 W. Harrison)

You should try to hit this regional chain (and institution) before you leave town. The fried chicken at Harold's is something else, and the people-watching especially after dark is even better than the eats.

Inside the Park

As stated, US Cellular Field has been no small disappointment to White Sox fans, despite attempts to bring over much of the character and charm of the old park. But the Sox are working on the situation. And there is more going on here than at most parks, so take some time to walk around and see the many sights.

A Grand Entrance

Upon entering the park on the first level, you will notice that the ballpark designers attempted to re-create the facade at old Comiskey with elegant glass windows. While the old park was done in brick, these windows are about as regal as you can get when a precast colored concrete frontage is used in imitation. Banners commemorate great White Sox players as well as other great players from around baseball, providing some of the game's more famous quotes.

Entering at street level we had to use an escalator to get to the first concourse. Talk about instantly dismissing the mystique of the old park. Why couldn't they have dug down below street level so fans could enter at the same level as the first concourse? This problem doesn't seem fixable, unless they tear down and completely redo the upper deck.

Upon first glance, seeing the blue seats—Dodger Blue to be specific—we couldn't help but feel let down like our friend Jim. Why did

Jerry Reinsdorf, a former Dodger GM, give the okay to Dodger Blue seats over the traditional Comiskey Green? The seats do come equipped with cup holders, but this is still a poor decision that makes Reinsdorf seem like a carpetbagger. But wait, Jerry, we may have a solution for you. We noticed in our travels to the North Side that Wrigley has green seats although the Cubs' team color is blue. Perhaps a massive seat swap can be arranged?

Changes Are in Order

When the park opened, the field was even bigger and more symmetrical than it is now. After the 2000 season, the left field fence was brought in from 347 feet to 330 and right field wall moved in from 347 to 335. Center field stayed at 400 feet, while the power alleys were moved in a tad in right-center from 375 to 372 feet, and out a tad in left-center, from 375 to 377 feet. We're not sure how these changes affect play, but we applaud management for making them, even if they look a bit reactionary to the Camden phenomenon.

With these changes, seats were added along the foul lines, the bull pens were redesigned and the outdoor terrace was added, and under it the Bullpen Bar.

Cozy Concourses

A major complaint when US Cellular opened was that although the concourses were very wide, the sterile feeling of the fluorescent lighting and concrete inside left folks unimpressed. In recent years management has added better lighting, brick walls, and decorative lighting sconces that have gone a long way to give the concourse a more intimate feeling. In addition, renovations have enclosed the Club Level concourse and added air-conditioning and heat, as well as carpeting for the comfort of those spending the extra buck.

Members Only

That large-windowed monstrosity in the right field corner of the Club Level is the members-only Stadium Club, available to folks who are season ticket holders. The menu is better than in the rest of the park, the waitresses are cuter, and they probably have dollar bills available for use in the toilet stalls. We don't know, we're just speculating. But these types of amenities belong on airplanes, not in ballparks, as far as we're concerned.

FUNdamentals

Now this is more like it. During every home game coaches from the Sox training center conduct a baseball clinic for kids—and it's free! After their lessons, kids hone their skills in batting cages and on practice pitcher's mounds. Why oh why didn't they have this when we were kids? Josh tried to convince the attendant he was thirteen, and the guy almost bought it until Josh went into a rant about "kids today" throwing too many pitches in Little League and trying to throw curve balls too soon.

Anyway, to get to FUNdamentals, enter US Cellular Field at Gate 3, or ask a Guest Services Representative for directions if you're already inside the park.

Retired Heroes

Look up between the decks to find the many retired numbers of White Sox greats. In the order they were retired, the numbers belong to (4) Luke Appling, the Sox all-time leader in hits, runs, walks, at bats and games; (2) Nellie Fox, a twelve-time All-Star; (9) Minnie Minoso, the only Major Leaguer to play in five different decades; (11) Louis Aparicio, a ten-time All-Star and nine-time Gold Glove winner; (16) Ted Lyons, a 260-game winner; (19) Billy Pierce, a seven-time All-Star; (3) Harold Baines, who played for the Sox on three separate tours and had to have his number taken down upon returning the third time; (42) Jackie Robinson, whose number is universally retired; and (72) Carlton Fisk, who spent thirteen seasons behind the plate for the White Sox and holds the MLB record for games caught and home runs by a catcher.

It's a Hall of Fame. No, It's a Gift Shop.

The White Sox Hall of Fame is located behind home plate on the first level. Actually, it's located inside the ballpark gift shop. The hall is small but impressive. We enjoyed the old-time pictures of old Comiskey and Schorling's Park and the autographed team balls going back all the way to the 1940s. There's a great memorial to the first All-Star Game, dubbed the "Game of the Century." There's something for every Sox fan, old and new here, including baseball cards, featuring such White Sox as Fisk, Eddie Farmer, Jorge Orta, and Baines.

Inside the gift shop portion of the area you'll find the actual lockers from the old park, from such players as Robin Ventura, Frank Thomas, Fisk, Ozzie Guillen, and others, with bats and other equipment inside them. Also in the shop you'll find the original showerhead that Bill Veeck installed on the center field concourse of the old park so fans could cool off on hot Chicago days.

The Patio and Batter's Eye

The batter's eye in center field has also been renovated, transformed into a multitiered, ivy-covered terrace to give hitters a green background. The top level now features a semi-transparent screen that fans can see through from the patio behind without affecting the hitter's vision. The patio behind the batter's eye has picnic tables and chairs and is a large area where fans can sit and enjoy their meals and still see the game through the mesh.

Never to Return

Originally there was a ball-return screen behind home plate that ran back to the press box and blocked much of the view for fans in Sections 130–134. A new vertical screen was installed in 1992 that is much less distracting to fans and allows for more souvenirs.

Old Comiskey Flavor

Behind Section 158, murals honor famous White Sox players. We found it odd that there is a portrait of the infamous 1919 team here. A picture of Eddie Cicotte and Joe Jackson highlights the display, and there is a team picture in the center. These are very cool old photos, but didn't these guys throw the World Series for cash? On the other hand, gambling was rampant in the decades prior to 1919.

How Does It Keep On Exploding?

The idea for an exploding scoreboard was one of Bill Veeck's best and one that has been successfully brought over from the old park. Though today's scoreboard is in fact a new one, its festive rolling pinwheels and fireworks are similar to those that have lit up the Chicago night for years now whenever a Sox player homers. We watched a Joe Creed dinger set the scoreboard ablazing, and though we're not usually ones to wax rhapsodic about a bunch of lights (we think scoreboards are for keeping score) we thought the exploding board at US Cellular Field was really something to see. It adds a spectacular and heroic, Roy Hobbs-type aspect to the show that's very appealing.

The Rainmakers

Sure enough, there is an outdoor shower on the left field concourse behind Section 158. The showerhead is sponsored by the plumbing council of Chicago and is a replica of the one installed at Comiskey by Bill Veeck. If a cold shower isn't enough to cool you off on those

"BARNUM BILL" VEECK

WE'VE MENTIONED some of the memorable promotions and traditions that Bill Veeck brought to Comiskey. Now we thought we'd mention some that were less successful. Sox fans may find these a bit embarrassing. But we love Bill, and after all, no one bats a thousand, right?

- The famous little people. Veeck would routinely send onto the field a trio of small folks dressed up in carnival garb. One time they came out as tiny Martians in silver space suits complete with baseball bats and equipment.
- In the 1970s Veeck had ex-Bears quarterback Bobby Douglass suit up and take a tryout for the Sox pitching staff. A sports writer suggested that opposing batters could protect themselves from ever being hit by Douglass simply by donning number 88, because clearly Douglass couldn't hit anyone wearing a wide receiver's number. Swing and a miss, Bill.
- Perhaps the most embarrassing moment of all came on August 8, 1976, when the White Sox came out for the first game of a doubleheader wearing shorts. Yes Martha, shorts for a baseball game. After Kansas City's John Mabry quipped, "You guys are the sweetest team we've seen yet," the Sox put on long pants for the second game.

We fully appreciate the efforts of Bill Veeck and everyone else who over the years have tried to improve the ballpark experience without disrupting the game too much. Rather than corporate-sponsored crap, why don't teams take a few thousand pages outta Bill's book and bring back some of the promotions, stunts, and gags that made baseball fun?

Dog Days of August, there is also a Rain Room behind Section 104. It's a misting station that provides for those poor souls whose sweat glands don't work.

Dogs and Cats Living Together

Also brought over from the old park is the Pet Check area behind Section 157, in case Buster can't bear to be left home alone. Remember, only bring your pet on special pet days. Sweet Fancy (John) Moses, what has happened to this game we love?

Stadium Eats

We found the food at US Cellular Field to be above average, and because many of the places to go out in the neighborhood are quite a walk, finding quality eats inside is important.

SOX DOG (Dog Rating)
The Eighteenth Best Hot Dog in the Majors

We refuse to eat a dog in any ballpark or stadium that has a pet-check area! Just kidding, US Cellular features a tasty dog. But Morrie O'Malley's offers way more toppings for their dogs, which are half the price of the dogs inside the ballpark. So if you're going for value, this might be one ballpark treat you'll want to pick up on the way to the ballpark, rather than once you arrive.

TRADEMARK FOOD

Though every pizza stand is named after a different former manager, they all serve Connie's Pizza. Thick and tasty, Connie's comes in three varieties: cheese, sausage, and pepperoni. We tried sausage with a liberal sprinkling of grated Parmesan cheese on top and rate it excellent by any standard. While most ballpark "za" tastes like ketchup and cardboard, this ballpark pizza does not disappoint. It may very well be the best ballpark pie in the big leagues.

BEST OF THE REST

Chico Carrasquel's dogs and Polish sausages are awfully tasty. We like how all these stands are named for players.

Also the chicken dinner was quite good. We were happy to have finally found both good chicken and great pizza at a ballpark. We can finally cross those off our lists.

We also must include in this section the excellent corn off the cob. It may sound odd, but a woman slices the corn off the cob right in front of you, then mixes it with whatever you'd like—butter, sour cream, mayonnaise, garlic, cheese, lime, or chili. Perhaps it tasted so delicious because we had been eating processed meat exclusively for ten straight days. Or perhaps it was really sweet corn. But in any case, we rate the corn as delicious as it is distinctive.

If you have kids or immature eating habits, head for the Kids Korner, behind Section 100. Alongside the play area and kid-size gift shop, you'll find the sure-fire, always-a-hit-with-every-kid-in America meal, good old-fashioned PBJs (if you were born in Russia, these are peanut butter and jelly sandwiches).

SAY "NO, THANKS," AND WALK AWAY
The enchiladas may have been better than we expected, but our expectations were awfully low. Best to save your appetite for these for when you're in the Southwest.

STADIUM SUDS
In Milwaukee we drink High Life. In Chicago we drink Old Style. Sure, it tastes like the dog's breakfast, but after you down a couple, you hardly even wince any more.

Or why not try a margarita? José Cuervo himself will come by with a barrel of tequila strapped to his back and a hose in his hand that will deliver you a margarita. Okay, it's not really Mr. Cuervo, it's some pimply faced college kid trying to make a few bucks over the summer.

Kevin: "How 'bout we skip the Margarita stuff, and you just hit me with a shot of tequila? There'll be a little something extra for it."

Josh: "Please do not give him any tequila."

Kevin: "Why not?"

Josh: "Remember what happened in San Diego?"

Kevin: "No, what?"

Josh: "My point, exactly."

The US Cellular Experience
White Sox fans are enthusiastic and loyal. And for the most part they're good folks. But in 2002 and 2003, two of the uglier on-field incidents baseball has seen in recent years occurred at US Cellular. First, in September 2002, Kansas City Royals first-base coach Tom Gamboa was assaulted by two fans who ran onto the field, pushed him to the ground, and began kicking him. Players from both teams swarmed the drugged-out father and son, but not before Gamboa had been badly bloodied and beaten. The next April, with the Royals again in town, a fan again assaulted someone on the field. This time umpire Laz Diaz was ambushed by a fan who tried to tackle him from behind. Diaz, a former Marine, quickly drove his assailant to the ground with a series of cool martial-arts moves. Then players from both teams came to the ump's defense. But the fact remained that for the second time in thirty games, White Sox security had failed to prevent crazy fans from reaching the on-field personnel. Clearly, this is unacceptable. The good news is that the majority of White Sox fans are fine people. The bad news is, the crazies are apparently out there, lurking in the US Cellular stands, and the team has a spotty track record in controlling them. So keep your ears and eyes opened when you head out to the ball game in Chicago. If the players and umpires aren't immune from being attacked, you can bet that fellow fans aren't either.

CLASSY DR. FAUST
Nancy Faust has been the White Sox organist since the early 1970s, spanning the Harry

Carey era and every one since. She's a hip tickler of the ivories who is very clever about what she plays, such that you have to pay attention. If number 8 John McDowell comes to bat up she might play "Eight Days a Week," by the Beatles, or if Nomar (number. 5) steps into the batter's box and starts playing with his batting gloves she's likely to play "Take 5" by Dave Brubeck. When Johnny Damon comes up she might play "Johnny Angel." She also plays either "Runaround Sue" or "Forever in Blue Jeans" after "Take Me Out to the Ball Game."

THE GET-UP GUY (Superfan)

A south suburban policeman has become the unofficial mascot for the White Sox. Known as "the Get Up Guy" this very large fan with an even larger voice, sits behind home plate and roars for the Sox. How Mr. Get Up got his name is a good story. A few years ago, the Sox came back home after a great road trip where they went 7–0 against Cleveland and New York, and returned to play Cleveland on a Monday night—a half-price night, which was a sellout. A Monday night sellout was unheard of. Before

THE K&J GUIDE TO FAN ETIQUETTE

AFTER SPENDING good portions of this book telling players, owners, and management what they can do to make the game better for fans, we thought this would be a good opportunity to list what fans need to do to keep baseball from turning into something ugly.

1. Do not go on the field for any reason. Sure, it was funny back in the day when some lunatic would run around on the field at Yankee Stadium, eluding inept security for as long as possible. But those days are now officially over. If you go on the field now, not only are you risking your own neck, but also those of everyone involved.

2. Do not interfere with a batted ball. If you reach down out of your first-row outfield seat to scoop a rolling ball off the ground, you run the risk of depriving the entire crowd of seeing the batter go for a triple. If the catcher throws aside his mask and runs toward the front row of seats to catch a foul pop-up, get out of his way. If you reach out your hand to snatch it before he does, chances are you'll only deflect it, and it will wind up hitting you, the player, or another fan in the face. Remember what happened in Chicago's North Side in the 2003 playoff.

3. After getting treats or using the can, wait until there is a break in the action before you move through the aisle to your seat. People seated on the aisle have had to deal not only with you, but hundreds of other people in your section streaming past them, and it's rude. With all the standing room at these new ball-

parks, watch the action from the top of the concourse and wait until an out is made, then head back to your seat. You'll thank others for their courtesy when you have seats on the aisle.

4. For folks with seats behind the plate: STOP WAVING and stay off of your cell phones. The "miracle" of television has been with us for years now, so don't distract the pitcher, or the fans seated near you, or the home-viewing audience, by acting like a fool. If you want to wave to the camera and act like a baboon, go stand outside the *Today Show*.

5. Do not, after drinking ten or twelve beers, get it into your head that you're going to start the Wave. While you're running back and forth on the concourse yelling "one . . . two . . . three . . . wave!" everyone else is trying to see around you and wishing you'd drop dead, because—get this—they're trying to watch the game. Besides, the Wave is for football.

6. When you see a player outside the ballpark, be respectful. Don't do rude things, like interrupt a player while he's eating dinner and grovel for an autograph. How would you feel if people were always bugging you while your mouth was half full of linguine? Bugging players at inappropriate times does nothing but widen the gap between players and the fans. If you really want an autograph that badly, wait until the player is done eating, then ask nicely. Who knows, he might even take a picture with you.

the game started everyone in the crowd stood and applauded for three or four minutes before the team came out onto the field. After that it became a nightly pregame ritual and Get Up Guy took it on as his mantra as well, sitting behind home plate, wearing his sign that said "Get Up," yelling "Get up, get up," to keep the dream alive. See how easy it is to be a super-fan? The tradition continued for a while but has since died down a bit, perhaps to be revived when the Sox win another seven in a row on the road or when they make the play-offs again.

ANDY THE CLOWN (Superfan)

Though never an employee of the White Sox, Andy the Clown came to games at old Comiskey for years dressed in full clown regalia and brought people joy, we think. You see we're not sure because when the new park opened Andy wasn't invited to return. Perhaps some traditions ought to "go gently into that good night." But we thought we'd mention Andy for his many efforts.

CROSS-CHI RIVALRY

We learned a lot about Sox history during our visit, and this seems as good a place as any to talk some more history, for the Pale Hose have history coming out their ears. The rivalry is still fierce between the North Side Nine and the South Side Hit Men. A recent billboard advertisement above the L train outside Wrigley Field portrayed "the Big Hurt" pointing his formidable bat back toward US Cellular Field. It read "Real Baseball, only 7 miles back."

But our pal and tour guide Douglas Hammer took great issue with the false notion that because the Cubs routinely sell out their games,

---

SPORTS IN THE CITY

MONSTERS OF THE MIDWAY

THE SOUTH SIDE is a short distance by car from the Midway. What's the Midway you ask? Ever heard of the term Monsters of the Midway used to describe the Chicago Bears? Well, though it's only a field, check out the Midway where the World's Fair was once held and where those Bears were once mighty and victorious and may one day be again.

---

they have more loyal fans than the Sox. According to Hammer, team loyalty is split fifty-fifty in Chicago, and the attendance disparity is more due to tourists and college kids looking for a good time in the Wrigley bleachers.

The South Side was once divided into Irish and black neighborhoods, both of which supported the Sox. But when many of the Irish left for the suburbs during the white flight of the 1970s, Sox local support suffered and caused a situation in which many people in the fan base chose to stay at home to watch the team on TV. Now we are left with the notions that further divide the baseball fans of Chi—that Sox fans are poor black South Sider's and that Cubs fans are white, yuppie, Big-Ten fraternity punks. Neither of these stereotypes is true.

BLACK SOX TRIAL LOCATION

An office building at 54 West Hubbard Street was at one time the Chicago Criminal Courts Building and is where the infamous Chicago eight were found not guilty of all charges by a jury. A plaque outside marks the court's role in the Black Sox Trial, as well as other famous trials in the history of Chicago.

MILWAUKEE BREWERS, MILLER PARK

A Space-Age Brew City Ballpark

MILWAUKEE, WISCONSIN

90 miles to Chicago
295 miles to Minneapolis
328 miles to St. Louis
438 miles to Kansas City

BASEBALL IN MILWAUKEE has always been something of a roller-coaster ride: a rapid succession of ups and downs, often exciting, sometimes terrifying. In good times Milwaukee has enjoyed explosive fan support and great team success. But in bad times fan attention has waned and teams have closed up shop and departed town.

The latest "up" for this city was the building of Miller Park, a modern ball field, huge in almost every way, and whose most distinctive feature is a space-age retractable roof that opens and closes in a fanlike motion. The roof dominates both the interior and exterior of the park. To Kevin, the roof looks like the gills of some huge space fish. To Josh, who lacks quite the same imagination, it merely looks distinctive. It weighs twelve thousand tons, spans 10.5 acres, and can withstand twelve feet of snow, or roughly 170 pounds of snow per square foot. When the roof is open the park has a remarkable open-air feel to it. When closed, the building can be warmed up to thirty degrees Fahrenheit higher than the outside temperature. Behind home plate there are three control buttons: Open, Close, and Stop. The roof takes about ten minutes to open or close.

At the top of the roof arches, the park is 330 feet tall, roughly three times the height of its predecessor, County Stadium. And Miller Park feels very big inside. But in its largeness, parts of the park feel very open to the outside world as well. The exterior is a red brick facade that is nearly the only nod to giving the park an old-time feel.

So the designers of Miller Park clearly were going for a grand stadium design, rather than an intimate ballpark. Intimate is not ever going to be a word used to describe the place. Not with its ten escalators and nine elevators, its four seating levels, and multiple under-hangs obstructing the views of fans seated in the upper stratosphere. But those in the best two-thirds of the seats sit closer to the game than they did in comparable seats at County Stadium. So says a computer study by a design company from Dallas.

Upon first entering Miller Park, with brat in hand, the field is as beautiful as it is big. A drainage system under the expansive field of immaculately groomed grass can handle twenty-five inches of rainwater per hour just in case the roof ever breaks. Miller has tried to include many of the features that have become standard for new parks. The concourses are wide, there are patios and restaurants, club-level seats and luxury boxes. But of all the new parks we've visited, only US Cellular Field has done a poorer job of combining the intimate feel of a ballpark with the amenities expected in a modern large facility.

Like many other new parks, Miller's journey into being was long and arduous. Just when attendance was dropping and the Milwaukee baseball roller coaster appeared readying to dive perhaps for a final time, funding for the new park was secured when Senator George Petak changed his vote on the third try, at 5:00 A.M. no less. Later, in the parking lot of County Stadium, Governor of Wisconsin Tommy Thomson signed the Stadium Bill into law, which guaranteed construction of a new baseball park, and that the Brewers would stick around for at least another thirty years.

There were also a few debacles with the financing, as the funding plan had to be restructured once it became apparent that the Brewers didn't have the collateral to insure the loan. An ongoing dispute with Mitsubishi over the actual costs for building the roof may smack of creative accounting on someone's part, or perhaps simply poor communication. It wasn't pretty, or graceful, but the pieces are again in place for happy days to return to Brew City, provided that the Brewers can field a competitive team one of these years.

Controlling interest in Miller Park is owned by the State Stadium Board because the taxpayers of five Wisconsin counties paid $310 million of the $400 million sticker price. A .1 percent sales tax raises roughly $20 million per year to insure the bonds on the loan. The Brewers own 23 percent of the ballpark, having chipped in $90 million, most of which came from Miller Brewing Company for the naming rights.

Ground was broken for Miller Park on November 6, 1996. The outfield dimensions were designed with help from Brewer Hall of Famer Robin Yount and former general manager Sal Bando. Yount's intention in deepening the outfield wall from power alley to power alley was to increase the frequency of what he

roof

Photo by Kevin O'Connell

considers the most exciting plays in baseball: the stretching of doubles into triples. Although the Brewers had always been in the American League, Miller was not to be an American League park. In 1998, when the Tampa Bay Devil Rays joined the AL and the Arizona Diamondbacks joined the NL as expansion teams, the Brewers were realigned and sent to the newly created National League Central Division. Why was a team added to the NL to bring it to sixteen teams while a team was taken from the AL to leave it at fourteen? Because if both leagues had had fifteen teams, an uneven number, that would have meant one team in each league would have been left with no one to play during every day of the season, excepting of course during interleague play. However, some speculate that it was advantageous for the Brewers to move because Bud Selig thought National League ball would do better in Milwaukee, since the Twins—who for some reason he viewed as competing with the Brewers' fan base—are an AL team. These backroom decisions bother us too. And these suspicious manipulations must be remembered when owners start speaking about contraction and other such nonsense.

The final game at County Stadium came on September 28, 2000, and was an event attended by Henry Aaron, Robin Yount, Rollie Fingers, and Warren Spahn, among others. Milwaukeeans had been waiting for more than four years, until April 6, 2001, for the Brewers to complete construction of Miller Park. A crane accident that killed three men during construction cost a hefty $100 million in repairs and set the timetable back a year. The four-year wait proved worthwhile when the Brewers defeated the Cincinnati Reds on an eighth-inning blast by Richie Sexson on Opening Day.

In the first year in their new digs, the Brewers drew more than 2.8 million fans, setting a new franchise record. In 2002 Miller Park played host to the All-Star Game, a contest that will forever be considered a Major League debacle because it disappointingly ended in a tie when Bud Selig declared the game over rather than let it go past the tenth inning.

Professional baseball had a vibrant life in Milwaukee prior to the arrival of the Brewers and Braves. The first incarnation of the American League Brewers came in 1901 when Milwaukee was granted a franchise. The team played its games at Athletic Park, a site that is now covered by I-43. But the Brewers lasted only one season and left town to become the St. Louis Browns. The Brewers name would return in the years 1902–52 as a minor league team in the Double-A American Association. In 1919 Milwaukee's own Otto Borchert bought the Brewers, and Athletic Park was renamed Borchert Park. Borchert was an oddly shaped park, square with the power alleys on the corners. Its dimensions were 266 feet down the lines, 395 feet to straightaway center, and considerably deeper in the power alleys.

In 1941 the "Suds" were purchased by a young Bill Veeck—yes, *that* Bill Veeck—his first stab at management. Veeck, wasting no time, began the promotions that would garner his nickname, "Barnum Bill." Some of the more memorable were giveaways such as livestock, ladders, and vegetables, and the institution of morning games for the enjoyment of third-shift workers. Veeck was also responsible for installing a right field retractable retaining fence, used to keep balls in the park. Problem was, Bill only retracted the fence when the home team was at bat, and thus it was banned after only one day's use.

In 1923 the Milwaukee Bears—the city's entrant in the Negro National League—played at Borchert Field. But the Bears couldn't make a go of it either and didn't finish the season. Another rise and fall for baseball in Beertown

Our best seats EVER!

Photo by Kevin O'Connell

were the beloved Milwaukee Chicks of the All-American Girls Professional Baseball League, which enjoyed much success during the war years. But sadly the league declined once the men returned, eventually folding. The Chicks also called Borchert Field their home for twelve seasons.

Major League Baseball returned to Milwaukee in 1953 when Boston Braves owner Lou Perini decided to stop trying to compete with his more successful cross-Beantown rivals, and moved the franchise west. The Braves were the first franchise to change cities since 1903 when Baltimore moved to New York. Many baseball historians point to the Braves' move as the beginning of a new era in baseball. This type of modernity we're not too sure we like, however. In 1953 the Milwaukee Braves broke the National League record for attendance drawing more than 1.8 million fans to Milwaukee County Stadium. Surely the Brooklyn Dodgers, New York Giants, and Philadelphia Athletics, who would all head West in the following few years, were aware of the money that almost two million fans could bring to a franchise, ailing or not. Brooklyn, you can blame Boston for starting the trend.

Josh: "Ah, they're New Yorkers, they deserve what they got."

Kevin: "The Braves won a World Series only four years after leaving Boston. Maybe the Red Sox should move, too."

The Braves' attendance record was no small feat, considering County Stadium seated only thirty-six thousand fans in 1953, and eight thousand of those seats were temporary. Built on the site of a stone quarry, County Stadium resembled Tiger Stadium in its exterior, its eventual size, and its roof, which was supported by steel poles that obstructed views. It had a deep rounded outfield with dimensions that ran from 320 feet in left field to evenly rounding out to 404 in dead center. Year by year, seats were added in the bleachers, the fences were altered, and the park was spruced up, literally. Spruce trees were planted in 1954 behind the center field fence and became known as Perini's Woods.

And for Milwaukee, the roller coaster was still on its way up. Led by young Hank Aaron, the Braves won the 1957 World Series, defeating the Yankees in seven games. The Braves also won the NL pennant in 1958, but lost a heartbreaking World Series to the Yanks. No one really knows why attendance began to fall off so rapidly after that. Perhaps because Milwaukeeans had been to the highest heights so quickly and figured it was better to get off the ride before it reached bottom. For whatever reason, folks stopped coming.

A year after purchasing the team from the Perini Corporation in 1962, John McHale and six former White Sox stockholders offered 115,000 shares of the Milwaukee Braves to the public. The IPO was withdrawn, however, after only 13,000 shares sold. Rock bottom came for

Milwaukee in 1966 when the Braves left town for Atlanta, only twelve years after moving from Boston.

Well documented in the Seattle chapter are Kevin's feelings about the moving of the Seattle Pilots after only one season to Milwaukee. But he doesn't want his bitterness to poison Milwaukee fans (who he considers among the best in baseball), because he was only three at the time, and perhaps because the Mariners have done so well in recent years he is willing to forgive what happened. This is how it went down. A few days before Opening Day 1969 was scheduled in Seattle, Bud Selig and Edmund Fitzgerald acquired the Pilots. The Pilots were renamed "the Brewers" in honor of the city's reputable beer-brewing heritage. Today, Kevin enjoys drinking a fine Milwaukee-brewed beverage very much while he watches his Mariners, so all's well that ends well.

But the Milwaukee baseball roller coaster had a few more ups and downs in it yet. In 1972 when the Washington Senators moved to Texas to become the Rangers, the Brewers were shifted from the American League West division to the East. After a snowstorm buried Milwaukee, the 1973 season opener had to be delayed four days. In 1975 County Stadium was expanded to seat 53,192. In 1976, Hank Aaron—who had been acquired in a trade with the Atlanta Braves—hit his 755th and final home run against the Cleveland Indians at County Stadium.

After much rebuilding and a few years of playoff flirtation, the Brewers met the St. Louis Cardinals in the World Series of 1982, dubbed "the Suds Series." (We're told St. Louis also brews beer). The Brewers, though smooth and hoppy in the first six games, lost in the seventh, 6–3. But 1983 was another blue-ribbon year

(pun intended) as the Brewers broke the two-million mark in attendance.

The Brewers would get close to the AL East title in 1992, falling to the World Series-bound Toronto Blue Jays.

It remains to be seen if in their new home the Brewers can field a competitive team and live up to the great success that Milwaukee has enjoyed in the past.

Getting a Choice Seat

Miller Park is three decks worth of enormous, and for quite a while now the Brewers have not put a team on the field worthy of huge attendance. Let's be honest, the Suds have been downright skunked like a six-pack left in the road-trip car trunk all summer long. So don't worry too much about getting a seat, but rather use this opportunity to spend some hard-earned cash on a good seat at Miller. The bad seats can be awfully bad, and if you're not a seat-hopper, you'd do well to spend at this park to increase your enjoyment.

Field Infield Box (Sections 110–125)

Why use the word "field" twice? Though screaming to be renamed (we'll just call them

Sellout Index: 2% of games sellout
Seating Capacity: 42,900
Ticket Office: (414) 902-4000
www.milwaukeebrewers.com

TRIVIA TIMEOUT

Yeast: What baseball movie was filmed at County Stadium? (Hint: it's not a Brewers or Braves movie.)
Barley: Who is the only player to ever hit the ball out of Milwaukee's County Stadium?
Hops: We all know the 2002 All-Star Game at Miller Park ended in a tie. Name the only previous All-Star Game to end in a tie.

Look for the answers in the text.

Infield Boxes), these, of course, are the good seats. And they're not outrageously pricey. In this park, where the upper deck is really up there, you might be wise to spend some extra cash.

The pitch of the Infield Boxes and of the whole lower bowl is fairly gradual, putting fans a little farther from the action than if it were steeper. But, conversely, they are not as high up. It's a trade-off, but a low grade means there will be overhang issues, as the upper decks must be hung out farther over the lower bowl. Why can't there be gradual grade with no overhangs, you might ask? Because then you would wind up with the US Cellular Field design, and that's not good for anyone. We were able to finagle our way down to these seats, with a little help from a friend, but more on that later.

Field Outfield Box
(Sections 106–109, 126–131)

Again, bad name. Section 126 on the left field side is the place to sit, as it is significantly cheaper and just as close as Section 110 (an Infield Box) on the opposite side of the park. There is little foul territory here, which puts fans close to the action. The way the park angles from Section 126 out along the third-base side, combined with the high outfield wall, causes a sight line loss of the fair territory in the left field corner. But these are still great seats.

The seats in Sections 127–129 do not angle toward home plate, but Sections 128 and 129 remain parallel to the arching of the concourse, which does set you looking toward the action. This oddly seems to make 128 a better section than 127.

In Sections 131 and 106 along the walls, rather than a low wall, the Brewers have opted for a slatted fence. If you are sitting in the seats right next to this fence it will be a factor. Fans seated here are forced to look through the slats, where a few seats farther back from the fence is not an issue. Though the experience is like sitting in a front-row seat in some ways (angled, however, away obliquely) as the fence doesn't block too much of the view, and if you're like us, you'll stand up anytime a ball heads for the outfield anyway.

Loge Diamond Box (Section 210–227)

The Loge Diamond Box (first five rows of the sections) are more expensive but are not significantly better seats. There's no aisle traffic to worry about, so if that's important, pop the extra cash.

Loge Infield Box (Section 210–227)

There is a low overhang that does not obstruct the view of the field much, though it blocks high fly balls for those seated in Row 18 and higher. As you proceed from Section 215 toward the higher-number sections you lose more and more of the outfield corner from view.

Loge Outfield Box
(Section 206–209, 228–232)

Beginning in Section 209 you lose a certain amount of the corner to the under-hang of the Loge level. In Section 208 it is moderately annoying and in Section 207 any play to the corner is blocked. We had to watch any play here on the big screen. Even in the front-row seats of the deck, huge sections of the corner are still missing. We recommend the bleacher seats instead which are much better, and go for half the price.

Club Infield Box (Sections 314–343)/Club Outfield Box (Sections 306–313, 344–353)

All of the seats on the Club level have a slightly obstructed view. These seats are the same price as the Field Boxes and not half as good. So sit down in the stands with the real fans.

Terrace Box (Sections 404–439)

These seats are in the first few rows of the third level. But we don't recommend the Terrace Boxes. In fact, if you consider yourself a baseball purist (like we do) and must see every blade of grass, every inch of dirt, do yourself a favor and do not sit anywhere in the upper Terrace Level of Miller Park. Even directly behind home plate the view is not completely clean, as the bottom parts of the foul poles on either side are not within view. Many seats in the upper deck only a have small amount of field blocked from view, but who knows, an important play might take place out there late in the game. Rather, head for the Loge bleachers or, better still, the Field bleachers, which are far superior for less cash.

Terrace Reserved (Sections 404–439)

We had trouble grappling with the phenomenon of an upper deck without any pure sight lines. Now, we realize that in building a ballpark, trade-off decisions have to be made. Not every seat can be perfect. In the case of Miller Park the Brewers clearly decided to build a multilevel stadium with stacked decks that hang over one another. Fine, but this is a three-level stadium that feels like a five-level stadium. The third-level seats are affected by not one, but two under-hangs. This, it seems to us, could have been avoided by eliminating a few hundred (or thousand) seats, making the Terrace level smaller, and tucking it in closer to preserve sight lines. But of course, that would have meant less revenue for the Brewers for each (sold-out) game.

Also in the Terrace level, some seats are stuck in the place that would (should) normally be the aisle, making it difficult to walk all the way around the park and seat-hop. Crossing over someone's legs and suffering those annoyed looks add additional barriers to wandering the upper level at Miller Park.

The only piece of positive advice we can offer about this level is that if you prefer the shade, sit down the right field line. The sun favors the left field line. All sections beyond the outfield walls are in the shade, even when the sun is shining. Beyond Section 437 the foul pole becomes a factor. In Sections 438 and 439 it cuts the view of the field in half.

Field Bleachers (Sections 101–105)

Most of these seats are decent, comfortable, and offer a good view, though there are some blocked views because the loge deck above is supported by pillars. We thought the days of pillars at the ballpark were over, but Miller Park has them—not too many and not blocking too many seats—but there are some. Also, there is a loss of the tiniest bit of the warning track from these seats, but all in all, the action is not lost. Thus, we recommend them. These seats feel a ways away, but at least they're first-level seats. Sections 101, 102, and parts of 103 offer a view right down into the bullpen, with no obstructions.

Remember, Loge bleachers cost the same and are up a level higher. So definitely take Sections 101–105 before 201–205.

The major criticism of Sections 101–105 being directly above the outfield wall is that there is a gully that separates the fans from the fence. Home run balls may clear the gully and reach the bleachers, but more often they just disappear into oblivion, which is much less satisfying for the fans. The manual scoreboard, which can be seen by all the other fans in the park, is operated from this gully, but this is just a case of poor planning. The scoreboard could have been built into the bleachers and operated from underneath them. We have one word of advice to offer here: remodel.

Loge Bleachers
(Sections 201–205, 233–238)

The Loge level bleachers provide almost as good a view as Section 206, but go for half the price. Sections 204–205 are not as affected by the under-hang, which is still a factor, but really only the wall is blocked from view.

At the bottom of the aisles all along the Loge level grates rise up and obstruct the view slightly. Basically anything higher than Row 16 or lower than Row 3 is poor.

Bernie's Terrace (Sections 440–442)

Even though the kids may want to sit here to catch a glimpse of Milwaukee mascot Bernie Brewer, Bernie's Terrace seats are pretty terrible. Many seats in Section 442 are actually directly behind Bernie's Dugout, which is no small obstacle, and are worse than the Uecker

BERNIE'S CHALET AND BEER STEIN

IN TIME for Opening Day 2003 the Brewers upgraded Bernie Brewer's digs to include an air-conditioned enclosure. Score one for the drunk guy! But in the old days of County Stadium, Bernie Brewer, the lovable mascot of Beertown, spent each game in a wooden chalet. Whenever a hometown homer was hit, Bernie in his drunken exuberance, would slide down his slide and land in a giant stein of beer to cool off. Some things are better when they're less-politically correct. If you're interested in seeing the old Chalet and slide, head for **Lakefront Brewery** (details below).

seats. We understand that many kids would rather watch Bernie than the game, but they'll be disappointed by the seats in Bernie's Terrace. Kid-friendly Bernie can be better seen from nearly every other part of the park. Seems as though better planning could have backed up Bernie's Clubhouse about fifteen feet, taking up the space of these seats to protect some of the sight lines in these sections.

The concourse up here is desolate, looking like a corridor out of a sci-fi movie. There are no close concession stands or bathrooms. Worst of

UECKER SEATING TIP

➡ WE RECOMMEND out-Ueckering the Uecker seats. Pay a buck for these crap seats, then seat-hop over to some good seats, or at the very least sit in the patio, and thus Uecker them the way they tried to Uecker you. Or sit in your Uecker seats and get Uke'd up, spending the money you saved on tickets for beer.

all, perhaps, is that these seats feel about 100 miles from the game.

Uecker Seats (Only a Dollar)

The saying "You get what you pay for," clearly applies. The $1 Uecker seats are just plain bad. Not only do these seats fight multiple deck under-hang problems, but there is also the right field foul pole in the way, which is fairly wide and divides the view down the middle. Still, they're only a dollar.

These seats do have a certain comedic value, except when you have to sit in them. They were named after the always-entertaining Bob Uecker. Uke's Miller Lite commercials gave us the memorable lines, "I must be in the front row," and "He missed the tag, he missed the tag!" that he shouted from his seat in the very back row. Here's a line Josh thought up while sitting in the Uecker seats, "From the Uecker seats, right field is a myth and center field is a rumor."

Black Market
(Another Scalping Lesson Learned)

The local rules state, "No scalping within 800 feet of the ballpark," so follow the bridge over the river and into the far parking lot, where the scalpers reside 801 feet from the ballpark.

Scalping 101: know the exact bills in your wallet and have the amount you intend to spend at your fingertips. In Milwaukee Josh talked a scalper down from $20 to $15 per ticket, but only had two twenties. The seasoned scalper wouldn't make change for him, so we wound up paying the higher price. Learn from our mistake.

At a large park like Miller, with a poor team like the Brewers, the consumer is in the driver's seat. Act like it, and be rewarded by paying less.

Before/After the Game

Before we left on this road trip, we never thought we'd say what we're about to say. We thought every park that wasn't tucked into a neighborhood was third-rate and unworthy of our adoration. But we learned a few things while out on the road.

We (gulp) recommend driving to Miller Park and parking in one of the team-run lots (gulp, again) outside the stadium. Game day is all about the tailgating in Wisconsin, and what we experienced during our late-season visit beat any college football game. Little kids played catch with their dads, college guys threw the football around, and tailgaters participated in nontraditional sports that included a ring-toss game that was much like horseshoes and parking-lot-bowling using real bowling balls, ten pins, and one drunk guy named Lenny who kept getting knocked down only to stand back up and resume his spot as the seven pin. Many of these folks had brought their kids along to shag beers and reset the pins. We also saw parking lot volleyball, hopscotch, and people playing games with food used as balls, and as the goal. All of this, of course, was brought on by the copious amounts of beer.

The people in Wisconsin are among the nicest in the world. Walk around and talk to folks and don't be surprised if someone hands you a brat or offers you some of grandma's pickled dilly beans. Tailgating etiquette states that you, too, must bring along something to the party to toss on the grill. Do we suggest stopping off and picking up some cased meat to throw on the hibachi. Then sit back and talk to your neighboring tailgaters. It won't take long to make friends in this tailgating nirvana.

Getting to Miller Park

From the east or west, take I-94 to Miller Park Way and take the Miller Park Exit.

From the north, take Highway 41 south to the Miller Park Exit, or take Bluemound Road and access Miller from Story Parkway or Mitchell Boulevard.

From the south, take 43rd Street/Miller Park Way north and take the Miller Park Exit.

Friendly men with fluorescent clothing will guide you into your tailgating locale. Parking is not a problem as there are plenty of lots surrounding the park. The general parking price is $6 and the lots are all named after teams in the National League. Professional tailgaters know where and when to enter to get where they need to be, but you ain't one of them.

The Milwaukee Country Transit System bus stops right outside the ballpark. Riding the bus allows you to set up your mobile tailgate unit anywhere you like, but it also means that you have to schlep everything with you on the bus, then leave it in the parking lot, unattended during the game. The city also offers a trolley for fifty cents that runs along the Lake Route to the ballpark. For information call (414) 344-6711 or visit www.ridemcts.com

Outside Attractions

HAVE A CATCH, OR PLAY A FULL GAME

Beautiful Helfaer Field was built in the connecting lot to Miller Park, roughly on the grounds where County Stadium once stood. Local teams play Little League baseball games at this wonderful little diamond in the rough, as well as girls' softball, and even men's baseball, except the grown-ups use mush-balls to soften the blow. Fences are only two-hundred-feet deep all the way around and the same grounds crew that works on the big league field cares for Helfaer.

Informative murals surround Helfaer Field loaded with facts and trivia about baseball in Milwaukee. Reading them we learned that "Bud the Wonder Dog" used to chase seagulls out of right field at County Stadium.

COUNTY STADIUM MEMORIALS

Behind Helfaer you'll find a memorial to County Stadium as well as one for the World Series-winning Braves of 1957. It's not hard to picture County Stadium standing on this very spot. But it is hard to visualize how vast it was, and that fateful game when Detroit's Cecil Fielder became the only player to ever hit a ball completely out of the expansive park.

Josh: "It should have landed right about there, where that guy is choking on that brat."

Kevin: "Naw, over there, near where that woman just knocked down all the pins but Lenny."

The day we visited, a tour group from Japan was listening to a tour guide reverently talk about the history of the great "Hammerin' Hank Aaron." Now, while we could make an easy and cheap joke about how funny it was to hear a Japanese tour guide say "Hammerin' Hank Aaron," we had a better idea. How about translating *The Ultimate Baseball Road-Trip* into Japanese and letting these folks hit the road sometime themselves?

HAMMERIN' HANK AND ROCKIN' ROBIN

Outside the ballpark gates stands a memorial to Robin Yount, who played his entire career as a Brewer—a feat rarely seen in the free-agent era. One of the youngest players ever called up to the big leagues, Yount notched 242 games while still a teenager. He won the MVP at two positions and was an instrumental member of man-

ager Harvey Kuenn's "Wallbangers," who advanced to the 1982 World Series. Yount banged out 3,142 career hits and was an easy first-ballot selection to the Baseball Hall of Fame.

A Hank Aaron statue stands nearby. While there is nothing about Hank Aaron we could say that hasn't been said better by someone else, we'll try. The player who broke Babe Ruth's home run record could not have been a more different man from the Bambino. Understated and humble, Aaron both began and ended his career in Milwaukee, hitting his first big-league home run as a Brave and his last as a Brewer. Elected to the All-Star team in twenty-one of his twenty-three seasons, many people forget that he also won two batting titles and four Gold Gloves in right field. Averaging thirty-three home runs a year and never

Robin Yount statue

Photo by Kevin O'Connell

hitting more than forty-four in a season, perhaps the durability and consistency of Aaron's physical achievements are what will forever be the hallmark of his great career.

Aaron broke the Braves' color barrier in 1954. And as he approached Ruth's record of 714 long balls, he received hate mail and death threats. He weathered these like a true champion and gentleman, never once letting on to the world how it must have affected him. As Aaron's career progressed he continued hammering and became a more vocal critic of the treatment of blacks in baseball and in management. Today, he is an executive with the Atlanta Braves. Any argument that concerns who was the greatest baseball player of all time, must include Aaron.

MEN AND WOMEN AT WORK

Another statue in front of the main entrance to the ballpark stands in dedication to the laborers who built Miller Park, and is a fitting memorial to Jeffrey A. Wischer, William R. DeGrave, and Jerome W. Starr, the working men who died during its construction. "Big Blue," the largest crane operating in North America at the time, collapsed on the roof of Miller Park, taking the lives of these three men and injuring five others. The families of the deceased were awarded a negligence settlement, and the faces of the men have been memorialized in bronze.

The statue of the work crew is a nice tribute to the city's working-class heritage, as well as to the diversity of its progressive work force. Sadly, three men also died during the construction of County Stadium: Carl Walter, Fred Maypark, and Joseph Wicks.

Watering Holes and Outside Eats

The best way to enjoy Miller Park is to tailgate. No doubt about it. Why drink in a bar when you have to drive into the parking lot anyway?

THE SAUSAGE HAUS

If you're like Josh and you're too timid to mooch 'em like Kevin, this is your only option in walking distance of the lot. The brats we tried at the Sausage Haus were the same quality as inside the park, but slightly more expensive. But Josh recommends the Italian sausage, which he rated even higher than the Italian inside.

OUTSIDE THE LOT

One thing Milwaukee is not short on is pubs and you won't have to look far to find a watering hole. Be it an old brewery-sponsored bar, a new microbrew house, a traditional bar, or a corner joint that looks like it used to be someone's living room, the beer is flowing in Brew City. The Water Street area has a lot of pubs within walking distance of each other and is a nice area for dining and nightlife. Walking over the Milwaukee River offers the opportunity to identify one of the famous "Seven Smells of Milwaukee." Also try the East Side neighborhood for some great joints, dive bars, and local hangouts.

WATER STREET BREWERY
(1101 N. Water Street)

This is your standard microbrewery, with reasonably priced food. Sandwiches run $6–$8. The bar's Honey Light Lager and Old World Oktoberfest have won medals at the Great American Beer Festival. But what we really liked was the huge collection of brew memorabilia. Some of this stuff would fetch quite a price on *Antiques Road Show*.

BUCK BRADLEY'S (1019 Third Street)

Buck Bradley's, in the Water Street area, boasts the longest bar east of the Mississippi River. Buck offers a decently priced lunch menu, but by dinnertime the prices are a bit too rich for our blood.

LAKEFRONT BREWERY
(1872 N. Commerce Street)

Though a bit off the beaten path, this micro-brew-haus is a good spot to hang out on its own, with a terrific selection of homemade beers. They have about any flavor of beer there is, but we recommend trying the Big Easy, Cream City, or the Golden Maploroot.

The Milwaukee Brewer ambiance is greatly enhanced by the fully assembled Bernie Brewer's Chalet and Slide from old County Stadium. The only thing that we suggest: let patrons slide down into a huge stein of beer.

THURMAN'S 15 (1731 N. Arlington)

If you're tired of all the yuppies at the micro-brew scene why not hang out with hippies? This is the kind of joint where you might find yourself talking to a beautiful local hippie chick, or just as easily to some old booze-hound. Probably the booze-hound.

WOLSKI'S (1836 N. Pulaski)

This is a place to drink a PBR (Pabst Blue Ribbon) in true Milwaukee fashion. Stick around until closing and the bartender will hand you an "I Closed Wolski's" bumpersticker for your road-trip car. After we got ours we started seeing them everywhere. Unfortunately, when we turned the rental car back in to Hertz, they were not happy. And we lost the sticker forever.

LANDMARK LANES (2200 N. Farwell Avenue)

This pool hall, brew pub, and bowling alley combination is an East Side attraction and we describe it as disgusting and fabulous. Incidentally, Miller Park weighs 500,000 tons, which is roughly equivalent to 62.5 million bowling balls (sixteen-pounders, not those little candlestick balls Josh rolls in the alley beneath Fenway).

VON TRIER (2235 N. Farwell Avenue)

Just down the road from Landmark you'll find a true German-style beer garden, and a hell-of-a-place to sing along to "Beer Barrel Polka." There was no music when we visited, but Kevin sang along anyway, while Josh slowly inched away from him and scanned the crowd for "new friends." The beer-garden owners are still waiting for the Brewers to get back to the World Series so they can hold the biggest Octoberfest since 1982.

HOOLIGAN'S (2017 E. North)

Head to Hooligan's for tasty pub-grub, or on the day after for great Bloody Marys.

THE UP AND UNDER (1216 E. Brady)

This is an authentic blues bar: no frills, just good music. And if you arrive early you can get in "up and under" the cover charge. When inclined, the band will jam from atop the bar.

Inside the Stadium

When we entered Miller Park on the first level and walked around the concourse we thought we may have found Baseball Heaven. When the roof is closed it has the feel of a retractable roofed stadium. When the roof is open, the park really comes alive and feels very much like an open-air ballpark. The wall beyond the outfield remains open at all times, and when the roof is opened, from some angles it's like there's no roof at all. As you sit in different seats around the park you do begin to notice the fanned-out segments and design of the roof, which is a featured part of the ballpark. Sitting behind home plate it looks all wedged up like the gills of some beast from *20,000 Leagues Under the Sea* and is clearly the most interesting of all the retractable roofs built to date. The roof is also quite functional on those chilly April snow days when the wind whips off Lake Michigan.

Though we had a fantastic experience at Miller, we began to notice many of the flaws and inadequacies that make a book like ours possible when we left the first level for higher ground. The first level is the only level where you can walk around the entire park, but even on this level much of the concourse is stuck behind the seating, offering no view of the game. This dismantles the outdoor feel of the open roof and left us feeling like we were again indoors, walking in a domed ramp or cookie-cutter stadium. Kevin even had a flashback that he was back in the Kingdome during his grunge days. This was bad on many levels.

Continuing around the park we walked behind the batter's eye, which blocks even more of the view for the wandering fan. Again, this could have been better thought out, and needs to be renovated.

The glass windows that run above the seating along three sides of the park allow in much-needed light, but sadly are frosted about a quarter of the way up, which effectively blocks out the views. It's unfortunate because in the other roof parks like Seattle, Arizona, and Houston there is always the opportunity to check out the view.

The Hot Corner

This area down at the end of the third baseline is a collection of shops and restaurants and memorials. While we like the latter, the former felt like a mall.

Friday's Front Row Sports Grille in the Hot Corner features darts, billiards, bowling, soccer, and lacrosse. You can sit in the restaurant at seats with a windowed view of the action on the field. But there are many more seats on the inside with no view of the action on the field, so be careful. The placement of the restaurant forces the concourse to run behind it so fans walking on the concourse can't see a thing. Not impressive at all, as far as design goes. We would have liked the ballpark designers to prioritize the fans walking around the park ahead of a chain restaurant.

Sticks by Stan, a vendor in the Hot Corner across from Friday's, custom-makes bats for fans on the spot and offers a variety of other bats for sale. Also in the Hot Corner hang the **Walls of Honor**, which pay homage to Wisconsin's MLB baseball players, Negro League players, and members of the Girls' Professional Baseball League. The walls are actually display cases that offer a nice collection of balls, caps, uniforms, and bats, as well as photographs and statistics. The Negro League display honors all players of the Negro Leagues nationwide, not just the Wisconsin Bears.

Autograph Alley features newspaper clippings and a memorial to Frank Seneca whose collection of 280 baseballs bearing 3,420 autographs of Major League players forms the basis of the exhibit. Most of Seneca's autographs were collected for him by Harvey Kuenn, the 1953 American League batting champion and manager of the great '82 team. Many of the great names are here including Babe Ruth and Ty Cobb, Satchel Paige and Joe DiMaggio. The collection is still seeking Lou Gehrig though.

From 1926 to 1940 Seneca was a pitcher and a shortstop for a number of Double-A and Triple-A baseball teams. In his fifteen-year

---

A LEAGUE OF THEIR OWN

IN ORDER TO keep baseball alive during World War II, fast-pitch softball evolved into overhand hardball. The movie *A League of their Own* pays special tribute to this era, which lasted from 1943 to 1954. Ten teams played in the American Girl's Professional Ball League, which drew 910,000 patrons at its height in 1948. The local gals club was called the Milwaukee Chicks, and starred Thelma Tiby Eisen and Connie Wisniewski.

Another movie filmed in Milwaukee was *Major League*. Even though the ballpark in the film is supposed to be Cleveland's Stadium, all the interiors were shot at Milwaukee County Stadium.

career he hit .330 and usually struck out fifteen or more batters per game—this from a newspaper article that appeared in the *Milwaukee Post*. We wonder how with numbers like those Seneca never made it to the big leagues?

The Brewers Fan Zone within Autograph Alley has some nice autographs and offers fans the opportunity to add their own. So if you're a Brewers fan who wants to memorialize your name among other Wisconsin greats (where your fastball could not accomplish the task) this is the place to go.

Retired Numbers

These numbers are not easy to find and cannot be seen from many areas of the park. Look up above the huge open area beyond the outfield walls and on either side of the scoreboard. There are little baseballs with the numbers inside honoring Brewer greats. Number 44 belongs to Hank Aaron, 4 to Paul Molitor, 34 to Rollie Fingers, 19 to Robin Yount, and 42 to Jackie Robinson.

A Brady Bunch Bull Pen?

The bull pens do not have grass in them. Rather they are covered with artificial turf with a little grate in the middle for drainage. How cheesy is this? Bud? Was this your idea? This is an easy fix, however, and we suggest, respectfully, that the Brewers get on it ASAP.

Speaking of Bull Pen Debacles . . .

Miller Park played host to the 2002 All-Star Game. While the game itself was a success on many levels, it will undoubtedly go down in history as one of the biggest black eyes of Bud Selig's tenure as baseball's commissioner because he allowed the game to end in a 7–7 tie. In order to make sure every player got into the game, there were no pitchers left in the bull pens for either team when the game went into extra innings. So the commish decided not to penalize teams in playoff contention whose

pitchers would have to remain on the mound indefinitely. Strangely, Kevin sides with Bud on this one. Well, perhaps not so strange: the last remaining AL pitcher was Freddy Garcia, of his beloved Mariners.

But the St. Paul Saints rose to the comedic occasion when they sponsored "Tie one on for Bud," night. On July 10, 2002, the Saints gave away Allan H. "Bud" Selig memorial neck "ties," complete with a picture of "Bud" himself in the center. We suppose this promotion was in better taste than one sponsored by the Saints later in the year that awarded fans seat cushions featuring pictures of the faces of Selig and players' union head Donald Fehr.

Incidentally the only previous All-Star Game to end in a deadlock was the 1961 Midsummer Classic played at Fenway Park in Boston. Because of heavy rains, the game was called off after nine innings with the score tied 1–1.

"Brewing" Aaron and "Papermaking" Yount

Well-done "Home to Heroes" murals can be found all over the park. These intertwine the region's heritage of brewing, manufacturing, tourism, papermaking, and agriculture, alongside baseball players from all eras. Adrienne Wiess, Corp. of Chicago created the designs.

Stadium Eats

If you haven't had your fill of brats, and Italian and Polish sausages in the parking lot, fear not. This is the land of the spicy encased meats, and those inside the park do not disappoint. The remaining fare is just that, fair. So enjoy the brat and sausage Mecca that is Milwaukee.

BRATS WITH SECRET SAUCE (Trademark Food)
Leave the chicken, pizza, and nachos to the other parks, and enjoy the best brats and sausages that baseball has to offer. What do you expect from Milwaukee, America's home of the spicy salt-cured meats?

SPORTS IN THE CITY

DOWNTOWN along 4th Street between Kilborn and State is the **Milwaukee Sports Walk of Fame**, which features any sports figure however remotely attached to Milwaukee. Natives who played for teams in other cities and players who played for the teams of Wisconsin are honored here. And it is a most impressive and numerous list of folks. Bronze placards pay tribute to such Milwaukee greats as Earl L. "Curley" Lambeau, Oscar "the Big O" Robertson, Elroy "Crazy Legs" Hirsch, and of course the immortal Vincent T. Lombardi. Baseball greats include Warren Spahn, Aaron, and Uecker.

While it's true that there is no substitute for a home- (or parking lot-) grilled brat of your own design, these ballpark beauties come awfully close. And whether you get your brat inside the park or outside, they come with the trademark Secret Sauce, which we thought was a lot like Arby's sauce. It tasted ketchupy and vinegary, with perhaps a dash of horseradish thrown in. Remember to bite down all the way through the natural casing, or you might get Secret Sauce all over your new Brewers jersey like Kevin did.

We tried the Italian. Spicy and hot, it is one of the better Italian sausages that you can get inside a ballpark. Kevin recommends getting a drink to wash it down, as it is spicy.

After eating the spicy sausage, with much glee, Josh went to partake in the designated driver program and receive his free Coke, only to woefully discover that he did not have his parking receipt on his person, and therefore could not participate. Kevin tried not to laugh, he really did, but to no avail. Josh would have to open his wallet and pay for a soda.

KLEMENTS HOT DOG (Dog Rating)
The Twenty-second Best Hot Dog in the Majors
The Klements stadium dog was squishy rather than firm, bland and lifeless. This dog isn't worth your time, or appetite—especially when so many other great cased-meat products are grilling nearby.

BEST OF THE REST
Gorman's Corner stands behind the right field bleacher seats, complete with uniforms on display from the famous Milwaukee Brewer and Seattle Pilot Gorman Thomas. Like Texas and the man Gorman himself, everything at this place is big. The stand features the Stormin' Gorman—a smoked beef brisket sandwich prepared by Chef Bobby Dean. It comes with a bag of chips and a slice of pickle. The Stormin' gives you lots of meat and a tangy sauce, but our one criticism is that it is very fatty. Also worth trying is the foot-long brat (Why didn't we think of this? Pure genius!).

After you eat all these brats, Italians, and beef briskets, your tummy might need a little cooling. Ours did and so we tried **Home Sweet Home**, an ice-cream place that offers soft serve in a dish or waffle cone, in a root beer float, or in a chocolate or strawberry sundae. We're not sure if after weeks on the road we were simply in need of some dairy in our diet or what, but the cream tasted great.

Freshly squeezed lemonade and smoothies on the first level are available and very refreshing on hot days.

THE .300 CLUB
While normally we could not give a crap about Club level restaurants filled with crab Louis and bananas Foster, this one burns our butt. Like many new parks, Miller has a Club level designed to make certain people feel like they're better than everyone else. They sit in better seats, eat better food, and probably drink better beer for all we know, and all for a lot more money. So is the case with the .300 Club, a glassed-in, two-hundred-seat, tiered dining room for the muckety-mucks to entertain their

wealthy clients. While normally we'd sneer at these dorks from our cheap seats and find comfort in yelling "real fans sit in the bleachers and eat brats!" our trip to Miller brought us great distress when we found out that the .300 Club bar is open until an hour after the game. Now this we find to be just plain classist.

Josh: "Hey, we'd rather tailgate with the common folk after the game anyway."

Kevin: "That's right. Free brats and dilly beans, you bastards."

Josh: "I wonder what bananas Foster tastes like."

SAY "NO, THANKS," AND WALK AWAY
An Italian place called **"Catch"-a-torries** you'll recognize by the logo of a mitt catching a tomato and by the overpriced mediocre pizzas. The marinara sauce is ketchupy, and should be avoided.

STADIUM SUDS
All the beer for sale inside Miller Park bears— you guessed it, the Miller label. Nothing else is available, which is a shame considering the many national beers Milwaukee produces. But from Miller's perspective, why invite in the competition?

The Miller Park Experience
HAVE A BARREL OF FUN
Now here is a Brew City tradition from County Stadium. Instead of playing "Take Me Out to the Ball Game," a rousing rendition of "Roll Out the Barrel" can be heard throughout the park during the seventh-inning stretch. Ushers dance the two-step while the crowd cheers them on. Unfortunately the barrel isn't being rolled out, it's being rolled up. At the end of the seventh inning all beer sales cease.

Kevin: "Even during day games?"

Josh: "Yes, Kevin, even during day games."

SAUSAGE RACES
At Miller there are daily Sausage Races, where a Brat, a Polish, an Italian, and a Klements Hot Dog all make their way from the video screen onto the field. In the race we saw the Brat won, the Italian finished second, the Polish third, and the Hot Dog finished last. We found much wisdom in the races that day, because the order in which they finished is exactly the order we would rank them for your eating pleasure.

As a sidebar, during a game in 2003, Pirates first baseman Randall Simon knocked over one of the sausages with his bat. While the video of this looks as if Simon was trying to hurt the sausage racer, this was really a case of a joke that went bad. But nevertheless, Sausage Gate was born, causing strife between Pittsburgh and Milwaukee fans.

BERNIE BREWER'S DUGOUT
Hey, what gives? Bernie Brewer, the team's infamous drunken mascot from the old days, used to live in a chalet and slide down into a huge

Sausage Racers
Photo by Kevin O'Connell

stein of beer whenever there was a Brewer home run. So why the change? Now Bernie lives in an air-conditioned dugout (on the third level) and slides down to a lower level, all of which block views.

Bernie still casts hexes on the opposing team and hangs K's when Brewer pitchers strike out opponents. But what happened to the old Bernie? This is a tradition that should have been brought over from County in full force.

We don't mean to keep going on and on about how things were better at the old park, it's just that we can't really understand some of these decisions. The distinctions and traditions that made the old park great should have been preserved in the new park. That not only makes the transition easier for fans, it keeps the heritage alive. We ask you, does the Smithsonian throw out old exhibits simply because they open up a new building? Heck, no. And baseball, America's historic game, ought to preserve the game and its rituals, especially those that work.

BOB "THE VOICE" UECKER (Superfan)

There is no greater athletic supporter (just kidding, Bob) for the Brewers than "the Voice," Mr. Bob Uecker. A Milwaukee native who made good, Uecker has turned a very mediocre career as a catcher and his tremendous personality into great celebrity, perhaps culminating in his hit television series *Mr. Belvedere*. Plus just the name "Uke" carries with it as much meaning as "Noonan!" does for fans of the movie *Caddyshack*. Because Uke is the radio announcer for the Brewers you won't be able to hear him from your seats, so cruise on into the bathroom where he can be heard all game long. How appropriate (just kidding again, Bob). But seriously, aside from being an actor, entertainer, and fabulous storyteller, Uecker is a very solid play-by-play man. In July of 2003 he was honored with the Ford C. Frick Award and entered the broadcaster's wing of the Baseball Hall of Fame at Cooperstown.

HOG CROSSING

Harley Davidson motorcycles are made in Milwaukee and a biker dude takes a lap around the warning track every time a new pitcher is brought in mid-inning. The Harley hogs used to actually ferry in the relievers, but now the gesture is purely symbolic. But if a player hits for the cycle, he wins a motorcycle. This hasn't happened yet, but it's something to watch for.

TAXI ANYONE?

The "Safe Ride Home" program Miller Park offers seems like a necessity for a number of reasons. The park is isolated by its own off-ramp from the freeway, and other than the bus, there is no way in or out except by car. The team name is the Brewers and the park is named after a major beer company. Tailgating is encouraged (in true Wisconsin fashion) and the team mascot is a drunken brewmeister. The team plays "Roll Out the Barrel" instead of "Take Me Out to the Ball Game." The beer culture that permeates Milwaukee has no shortage when it comes to Miller Park, so giving free rides home seems like a bit of a no-brainer. The rules state that a cab will be called for you at the discretion of management.

Josh: "Does this mean if you're turned down, you can have a few more beers and try again?"

Kevin: "I dunno. It's worth a shot."

MINNEAPOLIS,
MINNESOTA

250 miles to Field of Dreams
400 miles to Milwaukee
450 miles to Kansas City
1,650 miles to Seattle

MINNESOTA TWINS, HUBERT H. HUMPHREY METRODOME

Baseball in the Land of 10,000 Lakes

DESPITE THE many changes to Major League Baseball's landscape in recent years, the classic ballpark era is still well represented by Fenway Park, Wrigley Field, and Yankee Stadium. The cookie-cutter era continues to hang its proverbial hat on Shea Stadium and Busch Stadium. And the era of the dome—well, in the purest sense, the Metrodome is all that remains. Sure, there are the new retractable-roof stadiums, and there's a new dome in Tampa Bay, complete with a dirt infield and a trademark "I-can't-believe-it's-not-grass" playing surface. And there's the soon-to-be extinct Olympic Stadium in Montreal. Soon only the Metrodome will remain from hardball's concrete glory days that spanned the late 1960s through the early 1980s. Domes were the rage back then: the best stadiums under the sun, though you'd never know it under their various roofs. Perhaps ten thousand years from now archeologists will study the massive concrete pillars of the Metrodome and try to learn something about our culture in much the same way that they currently study the monoliths at Stonehenge. We just hope they won't think this was the quintessential baseball facility that our culture could offer.

Bloated, artificial, and oddly bursting with an enthusiastic crowd that seems more befitting of a midwinter monster truck rally, the Metrodome delivers a game-day experience unlike any other in the big leagues. Is it the best place to see a ball game the way the baseball gods intended? Unequivocally, the answer must be "no." But fans in the Twin Cities don't care. Their team has won two world championships in this dome they call home, and they have reason to believe the Twinkies will soon win another.

We found the Metrodome extraordinarily unique. Even if it isn't the best place to catch an afternoon game, consider the Homer Dome a must-visit on your ballpark tour. You won't find anything that even remotely resembles it anywhere else in the bigs. Therefore a visit becomes mandatory if you're someone who would like to one day say you've seen and experienced the game in all its many forms.

In architecture, there's an old saying, "form follows function." The engineering firm that built the Metrodome—the same one that constructed the Silverdome, Kingdome, and Vancouver Dome—clearly understood this concept. The Metrodome was designed to accommodate a wide variety of functions, ranging from baseball, football, and basketball games to fishing shows to three-ring circuses. And in that sense, the dome has been a huge success. It is the only stadium to have hosted the World Series (1987, 1991), the Major League Baseball All-Star Game (1985), the Super Bowl (1992), and the NCAA Final Four basketball tourney (1992, 2000), all under one roof.

The Twins must have thought they were getting a pretty good deal back in 1982 when they signed a thirty-year lease with the State of Minnesota Sports Facilities Commission. They would never have to worry about mowing the lawn, or watering and grading a huge infield, or dragging the tarp out every time rain or snow crept onto the Minnesota weathermen's Doppler screen. They would never have to worry about running out of tickets, except if they made the playoffs, and that wouldn't be such a bad thing. And they wouldn't have to put up with being labeled a second-class Major League city for another minute. The dome was massive, state-of-the-art, and ultra-useful. It was the very vision of all that the future might hold.

But a funny thing happened in the Twin Cities. Just a few short years after the Metrodome peaked—drawing a franchise-record three million fans in 1988, and hosting a walk-off victory party in Game 7 of the World Series in 1991—the nearby St. Paul Saints began frequently outdrawing their Major League neighbors. The Saints, who belonged to the Independent Northern League. The Saints, who played in a sixty-three-hundred-seat open-air ballpark situated beside a junkyard. Something had gone horribly awry. Baseball under the big top had suddenly fallen from favor.

Once considered beautiful because it was utilitarian, the Metrodome in just twenty short

exterior

Photo by Kevin O'Connell

interior

Photo by Kevin O'Connell

years had come to be considered a blight on the face of Major League Baseball. You see, the downside of utilitarianism in the form-follows-function debate, is that though the dome may be able to hold a monster truck rally on Saturday night, a football game on Sunday, and then kick off a baseball series on Monday, it can't do all of this well. Something suffers. And it is baseball that surely suffers the most in multipurpose facilities. We're yet to see a cookie-cutter or dome design that favors baseball over football.

But, did the Metrodome change, or did we? Surely, the latter. And as fickle as we humans are, who's to say that in some future era we won't frown at today's retroclassic ballparks and retractable roof stadiums? Who's to say we won't pine for a return to the age of the dome? Well, we do. Domes are a bit like flair-leg pants or Swatch watches. They were hip at one time, but it will take another generation and mind-set to make them hip again. We've already lived through this trend once and we're confident we won't have to experience it again in our lifetimes. And as far as we're concerned, that's all

that matters. If the unlucky saps in the future have to figure it out for themselves that domes just ain't the way to play—then so be it.

"Who knows," Kevin says, "Maybe someday the threat of acid rain will force all teams to play inside."

Josh asks uneasily, "You're not trying to scare me into making another contribution to that environmental group, are you?"

But back to your generation and the game as you know it. If you want to someday shed a nostalgic tear as you tell your grandson about the "cavernous concrete beast" you visited in your road-tripping glory days, the time to visit Minnesota is now. Because one way or another, we don't see too many more Opening Days in the Homer Dome's future. As native Minnesotan Bob Dylan so eloquently put it, "The times they are a' changin," in the Land of 10,000 Lakes. It remains to be seen whether the Twinkies will end up in a new ballpark in the greater St. Paul/Minneapolis area, in some far-off corner of the country, or if the commissioner and owner of the team will once again try to delete them from the Major League Baseball universe. By the way, we consider any option that doesn't keep the Twins in the Twin Cities to be morally reprehensible and distasteful. They won two World Series in this town. You can't just erase that from the history books because you don't like the Metrodome, Bud.

The high attendance garnered by the magical season of 2002 notwithstanding, most in the Twin Cities agree that a replacement for the Metrodome would be a good thing. The problem is, as always, that no one wants to pay for a new facility. Billionaire owner Carl Pohlad would happily make the problem go away by accepting a buyout from MLB to move the Twins to another city—or to eliminate them. And nothing would make commissioner Bud Selig happier than contraction. As best as we can tell, Bud sees the Twins as competing with his "daughter's" team, the Brewers, for the Midwest fan base. Hello, earth to Bud. First off, four hundred miles separate Minnesota and Milwaukee. Second, the Brewers aren't attracting fans to Miller Park because Wendy consistently puts an atrocious team on the field. Third, Miller is the worst of the new ballparks when it comes to sight lines. Fourth, you are not our bud! Fifth, we still appreciate your city's fine bratwurst. Keep up the good work if you have anything to do with the brats.

Getting back to the problems in Minnesota. While the Twin Cities and state appreciate the economic importance of keeping the Twins in Minnesota, the legislature has been unable to approve a public financing plan that taxpayers will accept. Unlike Pohlad and Selig, most taxpayers want to keep the Twins in Minnesota. But Minnesotans also want to keep their tax dollars in their own pockets, especially when they have a fully functional stadium already in use. Tough to argue with that kind of good old-fashioned Midwestern horse sense. And as no-nonsense former Governor Jesse Ventura echoed, tax money doesn't pay for the state to replace its schools after just two decades of use, so why should it pay to build a new baseball park?

Perhaps this is a good time for us to point out the unsavory side of much of the ballpark construction that has taken place in the past decade. A lot of questionable politics have been involved and some unfortunate precedents have been set. While we thoroughly enjoy traveling to the new baseball yards, we think just because a community votes against paying for a new, retractable-roof, air-condi-tioned, locust-proof, six-hundred million-dollar ballpark, that doesn't mean the local folks don't appreciate baseball in their town. Yet today's owners frequently hold fans hostage by threatening to relocate the home team if fans don't step up to the plate and pledge their loyalty at the ballot box. What happened to the days when the owners built the ballparks and named them after themselves? Wrigley, Comiskey, Shibe, et cetera? Those owners deserved the profits garnered by their ballparks because they had spent the capital as investment, just like every other businessman in America. Today's owners stand to make fortunes when their teams succeed or when their merchandise becomes ghetto-fabulous, so why should the public pay to upgrade their facilities? We say end this unfortunate trend of corporate welfare that has become the norm.

Whew! That said, let's talk a little history. The Metrodome opened for baseball on April 6, 1982. Previously, after migrating to Minnesota from Washington in 1961, the Twins had played at Metropolitan Stadium, in Bloomington, Minnesota.

The Metrodome followed the Astrodome and Kingdome in becoming the third fixed-domed facility in baseball. (We're not counting the atrocity in Montreal, because it was technically a retractable-roof stadium, even though the roof usually refused to contract.) To this day, the Metrodome remains the only air-supported structure in the league. The ten-acre roof measures just 1/32nd of an inch thick. It is made of Teflon-coated fiberglass and is kept aloft by 250,000 cubic feet of air pressure per minute, supplied by twenty electric fans, each of which check in at ninety horsepower. The change in air pressure is noticeable upon entering or exiting the building. Our ears popped a few times on our way in as we walked up the runway. And Josh's sinus allergies acted up for a few minutes. After that, things were fine.

The Metrodome was named after Hubert Horatio Humphrey, the thirtieth vice president of the United States. After serving as second in command to Lyndon Johnson, Humphrey received the Democratic nomination for president in 1968, but lost to Richard Nixon. During his tenure as VP, the fire-breathing liberal served as chairman of the National Aeronautics and Space Council, so perhaps Minnesotans thought it fitting that their "space-age" ballpark should bear his name. Or maybe they just wanted to honor a local man, who after graduating from the University of Minnesota, served as mayor of Minneapolis and then represented Minnesota in the U.S. Senate. After Humphrey passed away in 1978, he was given a funeral worthy of a head of state. His body lay in the Capitol rotunda in Washington, and President Jimmy Carter eulogized him. A short time later, the city of Minneapolis announced that its new stadium would bear his name.

Though the Twins lost the first game in their new digs, 11–7, to the dome-savvy Seattle Mariners, the Homer Dome quickly earned a reputation as one of the most difficult venues for visiting teams. And not just because of the loud fans and poor acoustics.

The Twins enjoy the advantage of practicing inside the dome and mastering its quirks. Perhaps trickiest of all is the roof, which is nearly identical in color to the white rawhide of a baseball. Visiting outfielders often lose sight of fly balls as they look up into the roof and/or into the low banks of lights on the first- and third-base sides of home plate. Fair balls occasionally bounce off of the speakers suspended just 180 feet above the field. Fly balls to right field swish against the Hefty Bag—a twenty-three-foot-high plastic curtain that serves as an outfield wall—and barely carom anywhere at all, dropping straight down to the warning track. A low liner just eludes the second baseman's lunge, then suddenly

scoots up the right-center field gap for a triple. A bloop hit bounces over the left fielder's head and rolls all the way to the outfield wall for extra bases. A runner advances from first to third on a wild pitch when the ball caroms off the backstop and rolls away from the catcher toward first-base. Welcome to the world of arena baseball.

Due in part to these eccentricities, the Twins posted an 8–0 home record in winning the 1987 and 1991 World Series against the Cardinals and Braves. In both October Classics they went 4–0 at home and 0–3 on the road. In 1991, the Twins won Game 6 on an eleventh-inning walk-off homer by Kirby Puckett, then won Game 7 on a tenth-inning walk-off single by Gene Larkin. Native son Jack Morris, who was born in Saint Paul, went all ten innings for the 1–0 victory. Great stories spun by the hardball gods.

In 2002 the American League Central Division Champion Twins were not quite as indomitable at home, posting a 1–1 record against the A's in the American League Division Series and a 1–2 record against the Angels in the American League Championship Series. But Minnesota was nearly unbeatable in the first games of home series during the regular season, going a remarkable 22–3.

TRIVIA TIMEOUT

Puddle: What current American tourist attraction is now located on the site of Minnesota's old Metropolitan Stadium?

Pond: The Twins display five retired numbers at the Metrodome. Name the two numbers that belong to players who have not been inducted into the National Baseball Hall of Fame.

Lake: Who hit the longest home run in Twins history? In which ballpark did he hit it? How far did it travel?

Look for the answers in the text.

Speaking of the 2002 season, the Twins used the opening game of the 2002 ALCS to make a Hall of Fame pitch to the Baseball Writers of America. Three former Twins whom the organization believes worthy of induction tossed out the ceremonial first pitches: Bert Blyleven (287 wins, 3,701 strikeouts, 3.31 ERA), Jim Kaat (283 wins, 2,461 strikeouts, 3.45 ERA), and Tony Oliva (1,917 hits, 220 home runs, .304 average). We say, "yes," to Blyleven, "not quite," to Kaat (who needed twenty-five seasons to amass his totals), and "no way," to Oliva (who doesn't have the numbers).

On April 14, 1983, the roof collapsed under the weight of heavy snow, forcing the Twins to postpone their game against the California Angels, the only postponement in stadium history. Another game in April 1986, also against the Angels, was delayed for nine minutes when high winds tore a hole in the roof. Perhaps the Angels have an ear with a higher power when it comes to playing at the Met.

Air-conditioning arrived halfway through the 1983 season and not a moment too soon. It arrived only after much complaining, sweating, and stinking up of the joint by the fans and players alike.

On May 4, 1984, A's slugger Dave Kingman hit a ball right through the roof. For this tremendous feat, he was awarded only a double. Bogus! Another famous big swinger, Rob Deer, hit the roof with pop-ups in consecutive at bats in 1992. Both balls were caught for outs by Twins shortstop Greg Gagne.

The first professional football game at the Metrodome was played between the Vikings and Seattle Seahawks, August 21, 1982. The Vikings won 7–3. Currently the Vikings are lobbying for a new football facility in Minnesota that they would share with the collegiate Minnesota Golden Gophers.

Getting a Choice Seat

Despite the obvious drawback to seeing a game in Minnesota—the Metrodome is not a baseball park—there are a number of pluses. And one of those is the seating situation. Most seats offer unobstructed sight lines. Tickets are as affordable as they are plentiful. And large general-admission areas on both the lower and upper levels allow early arrivals the opportunity to choose the seats best suited to their particular needs and interests. There is a sense of equality about the Metrodome that we can appreciate. All of the seats are the same color and width, regardless of their price.

Better yet, there is no overhang obstructing the view of fly balls for those seated on the first level. The view from the second level is somewhat less impressive, as the underhang claims large portions of the field for those sitting in the outfield corners.

There are no box seats at the Metrodome, so even the best seats may leave you getting up and down frequently to let people out of your row. If you're sitting down near the field, it's a long walk (36 rows) up to the concourse to get a snack or use the bathroom.

Something else to keep in mind when ordering tickets: in each section, the first and last rows are identical in price, meaning that on the first level, a seat in Row 1, right on the field, costs the same as a seat in Row 36, all the way in back. So don't automatically assume that a ticket in Section 133 for example, is preferable to one farther from the infield in 134. The seat in Section 133 might be in the last row, and the one in 134 in the first or second.

Sellout Index: 0% of games sell out
Seating Capacity: 48,678
Ticket Office: (800) 33-TWINS
www.twinsbaseball.com

Lower Club (119–131)

Located between the dugouts, these seats are elevated about fifteen feet above the field. We liked the view but didn't feel as much a part of the action as when sitting behind the screen at most other parks where the first few rows are generally lower to the field.

Diamond View (118, 132)

Located at first- (118) and third-base (132) between the Lower Club and Lower Reserved sections, these two sections for some reason merited their own price range in the eyes of Twins management. Instead of these, we recommend spending a third less money for seats one section over in the Lower Reserved.

Lower Reserved
(Sections 113–117, 133–139)

There is a big disparity in seat quality within this price range. Shoot for Section 117 on the first-base side or 133 on the third-base side as these are nearest to the infield.

In left field, avoid Sections 136–139, which aim seat holders toward the Hefty Bag in right rather than toward the plate. Instead, buy general-admission seats and sit in home run territory in straightaway left.

In right field, Section 115 is angled more toward the infield than 116. In 117 and 118 part of the right field corner is obscured from view. The first row of Section 114 is Row 9—unless of course you're in town for a football game, in which case we imagine the ninth row of Section 14 is Row 9. See what we mean about these domes catering to football first? In any case, Section 14 is angled nicely toward the plate and creates a cozy little porch above the bull pen. Just don't look for a ticket for Rows 1–8, which are folded up like the bleachers in a high school gym during baseball season.

Lower General Admission
(Sections 100–106, 140, 141)

Sections 140, 141, and 100 offer a great view of the action from straightaway left. They fill up as game time approaches, so be sure to arrive half-an-hour early or so.

The folded-up football seats in left-center field aren't just an eyesore, they also create an under-hang issue, blocking the view of center field from Sections 104 and 103. Avoid these sections. And avoid Rows 24–28 of Sections 105 and 106. Here, the center field cameras block the view. These sections are up very high and don't offer the same field-level feel that the seats in left field do.

So stick with the seats in left. Just be sure to avoid seats 8–12 in all rows of Section 140 where the foul screen (we refuse to call it a pole) blocks the view.

Bouncing Balls

The left field general-admission sections are a popular hangout for pregame ball hawks. This is one of the best batting-practice parks in the Majors as the shallow left field, short fence, and bouncy rubber warning track provide plenty of opportunities to claim a free souvenir.

Also benefiting fans is the fact that during BP batters hit off a green mat that is rolled out over home plate. In most natural-grass ballparks, the BP plate is located well behind the real plate so that players don't disturb the groundskeeping. Here, there is no groundskeeping, and thus no extra distance is added to would-be batting-practice dingers, thereby increasing their numbers.

The hockey-style Plexiglas that once shielded fans in left field has been removed, so bring your mitt and set up camp in Section 100. Just don't lose sight of a ball in the roof or you may leave the Twin Cities with a lump on your noggin.

Upper Club (Sections 217–224, 226–233)

Because there is no luxury box level between the lower and upper decks, the upper level in general is not particularly high or steep. The problem is that it keeps rising up and away forever, all the way back to Row 31. If you can score an upper seat in Rows 1–10 of Sections 220–228 on the infield, you'll be doing very well; if not, consider going with a field level seat in the Lower General Admission section for the same price.

Seats located in Row 27 or higher may be partially obstructed by the concrete trusses that rise up to support the stadium.

Avoid Section 219, Row 24, unless you crave attention. The Jumbotron is just half a foot above these seats. Feel free to walk right in front of it and do a little disco dance for the onlooking fans like Kevin did. Hey, you're in a dome. It's hip to be square.

SEATING TIP

➤ KUDOS TO THE TWINS for putting the Family Section (no alcohol) right behind the plate in Section 225 and not way out in the outfield as is the case at most ballparks. Not only are these the best upper-level seats, but each ticket comes with a coupon for a free soda, or "pop" as they call their carbonated beverages in the Midwest. So even if you plan on boozing, buy a Family Section ticket, then scalp your soda coupon to some thirsty kid, seat-hop over one section, and put your profits toward a tasty brew.

Upper General Admission (Sections 200–203, 212–216, 234–239)

Upper-level tickets confine their holders to the upper level, a policy strictly enforced by ushers who monitor the entrance gates and ramps to lower-level stairways. And don't plan on slipping into the lower level well before game time, as there are separate turnstiles for upper- and lower-level ticket holders.

If you purchase an upper-level seat, then find yourself disappointed, visit the ticket upgrade booth behind Section 205 on the upper concourse where you can upgrade to a lower-level seat.

In right field Sections 213–217, the underhang blocks the view of the Hefty Bag and a significant portion of right field. In the back rows, even the right fielder is hidden.

The left field Upper General Admission seats are not as bad, but they're not much better either.

If traveling on the cheap, your best bet is to buy an Upper General Admission, then seat-hop into the Upper Club seats above the infield, which rarely fill up. Or plan to arrive early and beg one of the ramp guardians to let you down to the first level for batting practice. Just don't leave, even to get a soda on the concourse, because you won't be allowed back.

The Black Market

Josh knew Minnesota wasn't going to eat him for lunch when the first scalper he encountered was sporting a stylish leather fanny pack. He asked the fellow if it was European, but the guy only shrugged.

Tickets are cheap enough at the box office, and always plentiful, but if you like to feel like you're getting a good deal, or want primo seats for around face value, stop by the corner of Park Avenue and Sixth Street, or the corner of Sixth and Chicago Avenue. As always, bargain your way down. And don't be afraid to throw in the "Hey, bud, I can get tickets at face at the window. This is Minneapolis, not New York City."

Before/After the Game

We found the greater Minneapolis/St. Paul area friendly and easy to navigate. Both cities are clean and safe and small enough that they aren't overwhelming. And while we'll stop short of calling the nightlife great in either town, it offers plenty to keep you entertained between games. The locals pointed us toward the Warehouse District and Hennepin Avenue when we asked for directions to the best late-night spots.

Getting to the Dome

The Metrodome is located between Fourth and Fifth Streets at the intersection of 11th Avenue in Minneapolis's Industry Square neighborhood. From the east, take I-94 west to the Fifth Street Exit. From the west, take I-394 to the Fourth Street Exit and follow Fourth for about ten blocks. From the north, take I-35W south to the Washington Avenue Exit. From the south, take I-35W to the Third Street exit.

The best option is to find an open meter on the street. We plugged one on Fifth Avenue (between Fourth and Fifth Streets) for $1.50. But watch out. The streets running perpendicular to the Metrodome—such as Fourth, Fifth, and Sixth Streets—contain meters that require constant feeding between the hours of 8:00 A.M. and 10:00 P.M. (kind of like Josh), while the meters on the intersecting avenues shut off at 6:00 P.M. There are also eight-hour meters on Chicago, Park, and Portland Streets. We noticed that as we got farther away from the dome, the meters reverted to two-hour limits.

The parking lots closest to the dome charge between $7 and $10. A better option is the $3 lot on South Sixth Street between Fifth Avenue and Portland Street.

Outside Attractions

CAMP SNOOPY (Killebrew Drive, Bloomington)
No visit to the Twin Cities would be complete without a trip to the Mall of America, the world's largest covered shopping mall. The Mall of America is in nearby Bloomington. Take Route 35W north to Route 5 east, then look for Killebrew Drive.

Yeah, we know, malls are to shopping what domes are to baseball: covered, sterile, and all remarkably similar to one another. But this jumbo mall has a bona fide ballpark connection. It seems only fitting that in this land of the dome, old Metropolitan Stadium (or what's left of it) is now an indoor venue. That's right. It's inside the mall.

Head for Camp Snoopy, a festive amusement park located smack in the middle of the mall. Named after native son and Peanuts creator Charles Schulz's lovable pooch, the Camp resides where "the Met" stood from 1956 until its demolition in 1984. The ballpark attracted twenty-two million people in twenty-one Major League seasons. The mall now attracts more than thirty-five million people per year from all over the world.

Inside the Camp, we found a man-sized and slightly mangy Snoopy wearing a Twins uniform with the number 1 on his back. He was very friendly and willing to pose for a picture with Kevin, but he kept lifting his leg, so we couldn't get a shot. All in all, he was a good dog, though. It took him a few moments of sniffing to lead us to the spot where the Met's old home plate resides between the Hunters Paradise shooting range and Ghost Blasters haunted cave. Snoop Dog also showed us the lone outfield seat mounted high above the Log Chute water ride some 534 feet from the plate. The seat commemorates the landing spot of Harmon Killebrew's team-record longest homer. Stand at the plate and see just how far Hammerin' Harmon's shot traveled.

After taking Snoopy for a walk, we had lunch at **The Stadium Club** sports bar and grill, on the second level of Camp Snoopy. Josh ordered the barbecue chicken sandwich, which came topped with cheddar and bacon. Kevin tried the barbecue shredded pork. We agreed that like the restaurant's atmosphere, the food was just average. But, hey, we were at the Mall to meet Snoopy, see the remnants of the Met, and stock up on such road-trip necessities as camera film, deodorant, and new underwear; and in those regards our trip was successful. Nonetheless, we were glad we hadn't come all the way from Japan to see the mall, like a nice man Kevin met named Hideki had.

THE ORIGINAL BASEBALL HALL OF FAME MUSEUM OF MINNESOTA (910 Third Street)

First off, we should tell you that this little museum, located a few steps from the Metrodome's Gate A, is designed to get folks into its souvenir shop. Even so, we found it an interesting place to visit.

The free museum was founded by former Washington Senator batboy Ray Crump. When the Senators moved to Minnesota in 1961, Ray traveled to the Twin Cities with them and became the Twins' first equipment manager. After retiring from the organization in 1984, Ray wanted to share some of the artifacts he had collected through the years, so he opened the museum.

We enjoyed seeing autographed baseballs and photos, clubhouse books, and a display case dedicated to Kirby Puckett. The shop also featured memorabilia from the Beatles' 1965 trip to Minnesota. The song "Norwegian Wood," you may recall, made John and the boys favorites in these parts where any and all things Scandinavian are still revered.

NICK'S SPORTS WORLD

(Seventh Street and Second Avenue)

Another shop worth ducking into is Nick's, which is more a pro shop than memorabilia store. We liked the old-school Twins jerseys— you know, the powder-puff-blue pajamas.

Our favorite offering though, was a T-shirt bearing the words, "Selig is not my bud!" Here, here!

Watering Holes and Outside Eats

We found plenty of eating and drinking establishments within a few blocks of the dome. But being part of the downtown business district, few put forward any real effort to embrace the local baseball culture.

HUBERT'S BAR AND GRILL

(601 Chicago Avenue)

Located right across the street from the stadium, this metrodome mainstay is your best bet to grab a quick beer and bite to eat before the game. Spacious and featuring a square bar like the one on *Cheers*, the establishment is complimented nicely by an assortment of interesting Minnesota sports memorabilia. We enjoyed looking at pictures from the 1965 World Series between the Twins and Dodgers, University of Minnesota football relics, and the regularly updated Big-Ten Standings board.

MURRAY'S (26 South Sixth Street)

This upscale steak house is as notable for its gaudy orange sign as it is for its daily happy hour from 4:00 P.M. to 7:00 P.M. With entrées in the $25 to $45 range, however, Murray's priced us out of an extended stay. Perhaps this would be a good pick if you're road-tripping with your well-to-do parents, or on the company's dime.

LYONS PUB (Sixth Street)

A more affordable happy hour is to be had at this pub, which has no affiliation with our publisher—we swear. At 4:30 P.M. the price of tap beers drops by $1 and appetizers become half-priced. We enjoyed a few bowls of free popcorn as well.

Did we mention the name of our pub (short for publisher)? That's right. Lyons. Here's to our next book together!

GABE'S BY THE PARK

(991 North Lexington Parkway, St. Paul)

This blue-collar sports bar is a favorite hangout of Saints fans before or after the game.

HALF TIME REC (1013 Front Avenue, St. Paul)

If you'd like to take in a bit of St. Paul's rich Irish culture after a game at the Metrodome or Midway Stadium, stop in for live music and smooth Irish whiskey. Josh had to practically tear Kevin from his seat.

KIRBY PUCKETT PLAZA

This food court and fun zone is located just outside the Metrodome's entrance ramps. Aside from some very tasty food, we liked seeing interactive batting games for the kids, and a twenty-foot-high Twins jersey that fans could sign for $1, with proceeds benefiting the Twins Community Fund.

We highly recommend ordering some hickory-smoked St. Louis style ribs at **Famous Dave's Legendary Pit Barbecue (Trademark Food)** before the game. You can order these tangy treats by the slab or individual bone. The baked beans, which came with chunks of kielbasa in them, were also exceptional. And the cornbread wasn't half bad either.

Afterward, we bought a bag of cinnamon roasted almonds from another stand in the plaza. The nuts made for a nice dessert.

The liberal open-container law allows fans to purchase a beer or hard lemonade on the plaza and to drink it outside. But whether opened or unopened, fans are not allowed to bring these into the Metrodome. At least that's what the vendor working the cart told us. And why would he lie?

Inside the Dome

The Metrodome presents as artificial a playing environment as there is in Major League Baseball. The Astroturf is Brady Bunch green, and the outline of a football gridiron gives the impression that it needs to be ironed. The outfield walls are flimsy canvas sheets eerily reminiscent to the tarps Josh uses to cover his backyard woodpile. And the foul poles are actually nets, suspended somewhat less than perpendicularly from the upper deck. The dugouts are hardly dug out, but are rather rectangular pens with benches all level to the ground, similar to those found at city softball fields. The sound system is loud and muffled, stealing much of Hall of Fame announcer Bob Casey's thunder.

The twenty-two-year-old stadium is showing wear and tear beyond its years. Beneath your seat you'll likely find plenty of mildew, caulk, discarded chewing gum, and other regrettable specimens of uncertain origin growing on the concrete, which itself is stained and pitted. Several of the temporary baseball railings look like they could be pushed over by a sturdy ten-year-old.

Ballpark Features

THE BANNERS

Huge banners hang above the upper-level outfield seats honoring players whose numbers have been retired by the Twins. These include Harmon Killebrew (3), Rod Carew (29), Tony Oliva (6), Kirby Puckett (34), and Kent Hrbek (14).

Killebrew, Carew, and Puckett are members of the National Baseball Hall of Fame. Oliva and Hrbek hadn't made it as of this printing, and we don't expect they ever will.

THE WALK OF FAME (ABSOLUTE MUST)

To learn about a wide spectrum of famous and not-so-famous Minnesota athletes, we suggest taking a stroll along the upper-level concourse where plaques honor members of the Minnesota Sports Hall of Fame. Sure, you'll find Killebrew and the other likely suspects here, but we rather enjoyed the plaques paying tribute to forgotten heroes like Jean Havlish— member of the National Bowling Hall of Fame and owner of a 189.89 lifetime average, and

Robert Dunbar—the most acclaimed curler of the late 1800s. Yeah, that's right. We said "curling." Don't knock it till you've tried it.

THE BLIMP

This is certainly something you won't see anywhere else in the big leagues.

Sponsored by the Minnesota State Lottery, a radio-controlled helium-filled blimp drops T-shirts down on fans.

When we visited, Paul Moore, one of four rotating blimp operators, was working the controls. He was sitting in Section 217. Paul, an electrical designer by day, said his previous experience in radio-control flying clubs helped him land his part-time job. Sometimes he said, he uses a spotter who sits in Section 2 on the first level and communicates with him by walkie-talkie to let him know what part of the stands the blimp is presently over (depth perception can be a problem at such high altitudes). But most days Paul and his colleagues just take their chances and let the T-shirts drop where they may.

For weekday games, the blimp flies before the game, in the top of second inning, and the top of fourth. On weekends it adds an extra flight during the seventh-inning stretch.

TURF-BONI

Surrounding the dirt of the pitcher's mound is a darker than normal octagonal patch of artificial turf. Before the game a member of the grounds crew drives onto the field on a machine that looks like a tiny Zamboni and uses the machine to clean up any dirt that has spilled off the mound onto the turf during batting practice. Kevin, who has seen these machines in other domes, wonders if they come with the indoor baseball assembly package, along with the Astroturf, rubber warning tracks, and foul pole netting. And if they are available, can you get them on eBay?

THE WATER BOY

They water down the minuscule dirt patches on the infield prior to the game. But not with the conventional garden hoses found in other ballparks. Here, a guy comes onto the field with a tiny water truck and hand pumps a fine mist onto the dirt.

MEN'S ROOM TROUGHS

Most parks have phased out the old urinal troughs, but they still remain at old-time parks like Wrigley Field and the Metrodome. Wait a minute. What's wrong with that picture? They were still installing these things in the 1980s?

Take a squirt if you dare, just hope the fellow next to you is a straight shooter.

Stadium Eats

As a whole, the food inside the Metrodome does little to distinguish itself, with one BIG exception. One BIG JUICY exception.

HORMEL JUMBO DOG (Dog Rating)
The Fifth Best Hot Dog in the Majors

Easily the equivalent of four normal-sized hot dogs, this processed behemoth is thick, long, and heavy. Kevin speculates that it must weigh at least ten ounces. Its sheer size earns it a top-ten rating. Its salty wholesome taste bumps it all the way into the top four. And it costs less than a regular-sized dog at Yankee Stadium.

For a few dollars less, a more manageable-sized dog is available. One day a week during the season (usually Wednesdays) these are available for the low price of $1. The only catch to Dollar-Dog Night is a two-dog-per-person limit.

BEST OF THE REST

The waffle-cut fries were plentiful and tasty. The waffle-cone ice cream was cold, hard, flavorful, and affordably priced.

The waffle-cut pizza was . . . okay, we're just kidding, but the waffle-cut fries and waffle-cone ice cream were both solid choices.

And you're still in brat country. The Metrodome bratwurst doesn't quite compare to the ones in Milwaukee, but it was tasty and firm and still beat the brats in most parks. A kraut-scooping station came in handy, too.

SAY "NO, THANKS," AND WALK AWAY

A number of stadium employees advised us to avoid **Blimpie's Subs**, but were we going to take their advice? Hell, no. We had made a promise to our readers. After smelling the fast-food greasy odors originating from Blimpie's, however, we decided we weren't that dedicated. Sorry.

Papa John's Pizza epitomized stadium pizza: a sprinkle of cheese and a dab of sauce atop a piece of cardboard. Is your mouth watering now? Or do we need to continue?

STADIUM SUDS

A **Beers of the World** stand behind Section 140 offers a wide range of brews. Bacardi Breezers are also available if you're into that kind of thing. Kevin had to hold Josh back, but only a little.

The Metrodome Experience

Kevin, who grew up in Seattle and considers himself something of a dome expert, rates the Metrodome higher than the Kingdome, the Astrodome, and SkyDome (when closed). The Metrodome seems intimate compared to these larger facilities, and though it goes against most conventional thinking on what a ballpark should be, there are things about it that are done right. For kids and grown-ups alike there is a spectaclelike quality to the place. A visit to the Metrodome is like a trip to the circus. The action in the center ring (the game) is often overshadowed by the peripheral goings on: the loud theme music offered each hitter as he approaches the plate, innovative use of the Jumbotron, and interesting promotions. These combine to keep fans on the edge of their seats waiting to see what will come next. It's an arena show, all right.

Proud and Loud

Homer Hankies were back in 2002, pulled out of the closet for the first time since 1991. These white-and-red snotrags became a symbol of the wild atmosphere inside the dome when fans began pulsing them en masse during the 1987 championship run.

Josh bought five for a dollar apiece at the pro shop inside the stadium.

Should a hanky find its way into your hands during your visit to the Twin Cities, here's a quick tutorial on how to properly use it. Don't swirl the hanky—it's not a Terrible Towel. If you're going to do that, you might as well be wearing a leather fanny pack. Rather, hold it above your head and pump it forward with quick little punches, sort of like a fly-fishing motion. And don't ever blow your nose in one. To die-hard Twins fans, such a gesture is akin to letting an American flag touch the ground.

T-W-I-N-G-O

To keep things moving along during the game, fans often play twingo—a variation of bingo—sponsored by a local restaurant chain. Cards are available for free on the concourse. When the official scoring of the last out of each half inning appears on the Jumbotron, fans look down at their cards to see if they have a match and if so, X-out a box. Five in a row makes for a winner. We were unable, however, to get a straight answer on what the winners received. It must have been something good though, because lots of folks were playing, especially the blue hairs. This is a great way to keep the bingo-loving grandma in your family occupied while you try to enjoy the game.

Jumbo Laughs

The Twins do a number of creative things on the Jumbotron to make the Metrodome experience interactive for fans. At most parks, they give the basic treatment, scanning the crowd with a camera to look for scantily clad ladies or homely kids. Here, they take it a step further.

One trick is to show a fan and then distort the image of his or her head so it looks like it might explode.

Another feature is the Twin Cam, which takes one person and splits him in half to make Twins with a reverse image. It's a tad trippy, the whole making-everyone-into-twins thing. Thank goodness there's a ban on human cloning. We'd like to keep our stem cells to ourselves, thank you very much. Although, it has occurred to Josh that if he did have a double he could eat twice as much processed meat during his ballpark touring, which wouldn't be an altogether unattractive proposition. Kevin: "One of you is enough to deal with. Trust me."

The Kiss Cam shows two fans with the outline of a heart overlaid around them. At this prompt, the fans are supposed to kiss for the camera. Hilarity ensues when mismatched "couples" appear on screen. The thing is, once you're shown, you really have no choice but to kiss. It's kind of like catching a visiting team's homer in the Wrigley bleachers. Follow the protocol, or be subject to the wrath of the mob, even if the guy next to you is a hairy biker named Bubba who quite obviously ate a liver, tuna, and garlic casserole before the game.

Fishing Races

Appropriately in the Land of 10,000 Lakes, the Jumbotron hosts nightly fishing races. Cartoon characters Bob the Bass, Tina Trout, and Sleepy Pete compete to see who can fill their buckets with fish the quickest. On the night we visited, everyone in Section 118 received a free salted nut roll when Tina Trout won.

Freebies

At the Metrodome, every night is giveaway night. That's right, all eighty-one home dates. We got a team photo when we passed through the gates. Other promotions from last season included Fishing Weasel night, Bat night, Hat night, Umbrella night, Mug night, Bobble-Head Doll night, Backpack night, Lunch Box night, and many more.

Josh suggests a Minnesota Twins *Ultimate Baseball Road-Trip* night. Hey, why not? Maybe a hotel chain or airline would like to buy twenty thousand copies and distribute them for the free advertising such an act of beneficence would offer.

Magic Number Guy (Superfan)

Benjamin Kruse, also known as Magic Number Guy sits in right field's Section 216, with an assortment of other Twinkie-lovin' diehards who never miss a game. He attended Opening Day on 2002 with a sign reading, "Twins Magic Number: 163." He had reached 0 by the time we visited in September. As we interviewed Ben, he was attempting to learn to keep score of the game on his palm pilot. Baseball enters the high-tech age.

A few seats over from Ben, we found Chris Thompson, publisher of www.twinsdugout.com, one of the team's unofficial fan pages.

The general consensus among the superfans in Section 216 could best be summarized

Magic Number Guy

Photo by Kevin O'Connell

as thus: Public Enemy Number 1: Bud Selig. Public Enemy Number 2: Carl Pohlad. Public Enemy Number 3: Wendy Selig Priem. Public Enemy Number 4: Public Enemy. They're not crazy about rap in these parts. But seriously, these fans have fought back against the commissioner's plan for contraction, against an owner they believe lied to them about interested buyers in the Carolinas, against the strike of 1994 and the near-strike of 2002. These fans are loyal, perhaps to a fault. But we admire their dedication to the hometown team.

On Our Way to Minneapolis

We Made Like Ray Kinsella and Shoeless Joe

That's right, on the way from Milwaukee to Minnesota, we stopped by the *Field of Dreams* movie site in Dyersville, Iowa. The field, which has been visited by nearly a million people since the movie debuted in 1989, is 185 miles from Milwaukee, 210 miles from Chicago, and 260 miles from Minneapolis.

Fans are encouraged to bring their gloves and play a game of catch on the field. Use of the field and parking are free. Just watch out for the power lines that bisect the diamond, running ten feet above the field from third-base out to center field. What? You didn't notice those in the movie? Neither did we. Camera tricks and airbrushing, we suppose.

Interestingly, two different families own parts of the field and maintain their own separate tourist centers/souvenir stands.

The Lansing family, headed by Don Lansing who has lived his entire life in the white farmhouse in which Ray and Annie made their home in the movie, owns the infield and right field. Don, who along with his sister was an extra in the movie, used to grow beans and tobacco on the site of the ball field. But since Universal Studios came knocking he grows nothing but corn. Don told us Universal was looking for a white farmhouse with a long lane leading to it. The Dubuque Chamber of Commerce helped make the match. He recounted his meeting with the chamber as being much like scenes from the movie. "You want to build a ball field, out here?" he asked. Once Don accepted Universal's offer, in a matter of days the land was leveled, sod planted, and lights erected. The field was ready for filming.

Don mows and fertilizes his portion of the field only. He told the story of how he moved the bleachers about six inches once and suddenly distraught tourists were telling him that it wasn't quite like it was in the movie. Now he is very careful to leave everything in its proper place. Don has fought to keep the field from becoming too commercialized.

The owners of "Left & Center Field of Dreams," the Ameskamps, wishing to develop the area a bit more, have added some gimmicky, nonbaseball-related features such as a corn maze—or "maize" maze as Josh's brother Jamie might call it—to their portion of the site. But on the plus side, in 1991 the Ameskamps founded The Ghost Players, a barnstorming group of locals (many of whom played extra ballplayers in the movie) who dress up in circa 1919 White Sox uniforms and play exhibition games on the field. We have to admit, this is pretty cool.

Inside the Left & Center Field of Dreams souvenir store is a map of the United States with pushpins showing where tourists have come from in the current year. Every state, including Hawaii and Alaska was represented with pins when we visited. And there were also business cards tacked to the board belonging to folks from France, Chile, Japan, Spain, Australia, England, Norway, Holland, Scotland, Germany, and Switzerland. They built it—and they came.

The wind was really blowing on the day we played a game of catch on the field and the air

MIDWAY STADIUM, HOME OF THE ST. PAUL SAINTS

ACROSS THE Mississippi River from the Metrodome Kevin wanted to see the birthplace of F. Scott Fitzgerald, but Josh talked him into visiting one of the most successful minor league franchises in the country.

Since joining the independent Northern League in 1993, the St. Paul Saints have filled 6,329-seat Midway Stadium to more than 98 percent capacity. And with good reason. The team is owned by Mike Veeck, son of baseball promotions guru, Bill Veeck, and comedian Bill Murray who sometimes coaches third-base. Management, players, and fans embrace the Saints' "fun is good" motto.

Tailgating begins in the parking lot three hours before game time. The team CEO, a nine-year-old girl, greets fans as they enter. Once the game begins, a barber cuts hair behind the plate, a pot-bellied pig delivers fresh balls to the umpires, a seventy-year-old nun gives massages, fans float in an outfield hot tub, a ferry boat looms behind the left fielder.

Former Major Leaguers such as Leon Durham, Daryl Strawberry, Matt Nokes, Minnie Minoso, and Jack Morris have played for the Saints, as have future big leaguers like Kevin Millar, J. D. Drew, and Rey Ordonez.

We met Tom Farrell, director of food services at Midway. Tom pointed out that hot dogs are only $1.50 and brats $2.50 and that beer comes in three sizes, priced $1.50, $2, $3. This all sounded very fair to us,

after we had been spending all of our writing advance on steep stadium suds (Kevin) and grub (Josh). We also talked to Bob Klepperich, director of stadium operations for the city of St. Paul's Division of Parks and Recreation, which owns the team. Bob gave us a tour of the park and told us to look for him later that day at the Twins game. And sure enough, we ran into Bob outside the Metrodome as we were chowing down at Famous Dave's Barbecue. Great coincidences like this happen on baseball road trips.

A beautiful mural outside Midway celebrates Minnesota's baseball history, depicting Puckett, Hrbek, Oliva, Blyleven, Carew, Frank Viola, Dave Winfield, and Paul Molitor. The wall also honors Women's League stars who played for the Minneapolis Millerettes, and Negro League players like Bobby Marshall and Rube Foster who both played for the St. Paul Gophers. The Chicago-based Foster, who later founded the organized Negro Leagues, often pitched for the Gophers as a ringer in key games during the 1910s.

Midway is located at 1771 Energy Park Drive. From the west, take I-94 to Highway 280 to the Energy Park Drive Exit. Head east on Energy for one mile and you'll be at the ballpark. From the east, take I-94 to Snelling Avenue north to the Energy Park Drive Exit. Head west on Energy for a quarter-of-a-mile. Tickets are $3–$8 and parking is free. For schedule and ticketing information, visit www.saintsbaseball.com or call (651) 644-3517.

was ripe with the scent of manure, but we were glad we visited. If you have the time, this place sure beats the Spam Museum (Austin, Minnesota, (800) LUV-SPAM), the memories of which still give us strange-colored goose bumps.

From Milwaukee, en route to Minnesota,

take I-94 west to 151 west to 20 west to 136 north to Third Avenue. Follow Third for three miles, then turn right onto Lansing Road.

As you pull into the driveway, listen for the voice of James Earl Jones saying, "If you build it, he will come," emanating from somewhere within your imagination.

HOUSTON,
TEXAS

245 miles to Arlington
800 miles to Atlanta
800 miles to Kansas City
860 miles to St. Louis

HOUSTON ASTROS, MINUTE MAID PARK

Post-Dome Baseball in Houston

W HEN HOUSTON unveiled baseball's first domed stadium in 1965, many billed the Astrodome the Eighth Wonder of the World. And when Minute Maid Park replaced the aging dome a few years ago, many Houstonians dubbed the new retractable-roof facility the Ninth Wonder of the World. Certainly, that is overstating the significance of Minute Maid Park on the Major League Baseball landscape. Minute Maid was not the first ballpark to be built with a retractable roof, nor does it make use of technology that is superior to the retractable-lid parks in Phoenix, Milwaukee, and Seattle. Nonetheless, it is understandable that folks in the humidity capital of the world are proud of their new downtown ballpark.

Smaller than its sister stadiums, Minute Maid provides a great environment for a ball game, whether the roof is closed or opened. Old-time brick arches rise up beyond the outfield fence, a giant window above left field allows fans a glimpse of the stars at night, and quirky field dimensions often influence the outcome of the game. And best yet, the playing surface is natural grass. Even in the land where Astroturf was invented, it has been forsaken. Are you reading this Toronto? Minnesota?

It will come as no surprise to those who have visited a number of the recent additions to the MLB ballpark scene that Minute Maid was designed by HOK, the architectural firm that specializes in neo-retro ballyards. Concrete and steel are featured prominently in the ballpark's interior and exterior design along with brick. The facade is made of limestone, while the top two stories are nicely done in brick with arched windows. The facade juts out every one hundred feet or so with a building-type edifice, giving the ballpark more of the look of an office building than a typical ballpark. The roof is a color significantly paler than traditional ballpark green; perhaps HOK was going for a corroded copper look. In any case,

roof

Photo by Kevin O'Connell

it resembles the green that we see frequently on highway overpasses: not terribly attractive, but not off-putting either.

The main entrance—located at the corner of Texas Avenue and Crawford Street—is one of the most distinctive in all of baseball. The entrance uses Houston's preexisting Union Station, which the new structure was built around. The classy marble pillars and regal arches inside the main entrance were originally envisioned by Whitney Warren, the same architect who designed Grand Central Station in New York City. Built in 1911, Union Station was once the hub of Houston's bustling railroad industry. Today, along with providing an entrance to the ballpark, it houses an Astros souvenir store, a café, and the Astros' executive offices.

Complementing the old-time motif anchored by Union Station is a tall tower that rises up from the ballpark's edifice. From atop this perch emanates the sound of chiming bells (not real bells, but a good sounding imitation) playing "Take Me Out to the Ball Game," as if calling baseball worshippers to mass.

Large windows beside the Union Station entrance to the ballpark furnish fans with a street-level peak at the sunken playing field inside. Meanwhile, above, a replica of a nineteenth century locomotive chugs along an eight-hundred-foot track atop the arches running from center field to left field. The train weighs more than fifty-thousand pounds and comes complete with a linked coal-tender's car that is loaded with faux oranges that are in fact big enough to be pumpkins.

Inside the park, in tribute to the Texas oil industry, a gigantic gas pump that resides on the left field concourse perpetually updates the number of home runs the Astros have hit at Minute Maid since its opening. When we were in town, no Astros homered so the meter remained stuck at 336.

The by-now-familiar embankment in center field is reminiscent of the classic ballpark era when many fields featured outfield knolls—Crosley Field in Cincinnati and Fenway Park in Boston just to name a couple. Houston's embankment, named Tal's Hill after team president Tal Smith, rises at a twenty-degree angle, measures ninety feet at its widest point, and spans one hundred feet of outfield fence. You don't realize just how big it is when watching the game on TV. While we think this is an interesting and unique touch, we dread the day when a $10 million-a-year outfielder tears an ACL stumbling after a long fly ball, or worse, runs full speed into the flagpole that is in-play atop the hill. We're thinking Tal's Hill won't be very popular after that. And if an Astros player gets hurt, Tal Smith might not be either.

The roof, which is similar in its three-panel design to the roof in Seattle, allows for the largest open area of any of the sliding-roof ballparks. It weighs eighteen million pounds and covers more than six acres. Unlike the umbrella in Seattle, however, the Minute Maid roof seals up airtight to keep the heat and humidity out and the air-conditioned air in.

The aforementioned window in left field—which is actually a fifty-thousand-square-foot sliding wall of glass—offers fans a view of downtown Houston when the roof is closed. When the roof is open, the window is, too, retracted into the bowels of center field. This design element, combined with the ballpark's relatively cozy confines compared to the other roofed yards makes Minute Maid a vast improvement over the Bank One Ballpark and Miller Park, which also seal up airtight. While Safeco in Seattle may be larger than Minute Maid, it maintains an outside feel even when the roof is closed. And that's worth major points in our book.

Besides the roof and sliding door, the grass on the field is also specially designed to mitigate Houston's sweltering summer days. A special Bermuda hybrid grown in Poteet, Texas, the grass was genetically engineered to allow for survival in extreme heat. What this means is that it won't burn out like the crabgrass does in Josh's front lawn every July.

In Houston, all of these weather-related modifications are necessities. The average daily high temperature during the month of June is ninety-one degrees Fahrenheit. In July, it's ninety-four, August ninety-three, and September eighty-nine. But to reiterate an old and annoying cliché, it's not just the heat—it's the humidity. With summer dew points perpetually hovering in the mid-70s and an average monthly rainfall of 4.3 inches during the six months of the baseball season, Houston would be a sticky place to watch, much less play, outdoor baseball.

After several years of mounting dissatisfaction with the Astrodome (on the part of fans, players, and management), rumors began swirling in 1995 that the Astros were pondering a move to northern Virginia. Fearful of losing the 'Stros, the City of Houston began exploring new ballpark possibilities, and in November 1996 voters approved a referendum to construct a new downtown ballpark. Financing was provided through a combined effort from the private and public sectors with a partnership of fourteen Houston-area businesses contributing $35 million in the form of an interest-free loan to the city. The entire project cost $250 million, comparatively little considering the price tags of Safeco Field in Seattle ($500 million) and Bank One Ballpark in Phoenix ($350 million). Heck, even the roofless Comerica Park in Detroit cost $300 million and that's not counting the expensive Ferris wheel!

interior

Photo by Kevin O'Connell

We're not sure if the Astros cut corners, used nonunion labor, or supported the roof with discount steel. However they did it, we say, "well done!" The savings are reflected in the ballpark's reasonable ticket prices. And if a few unattractive HVAC ducts—exposed on the ceiling of the first-level concourse—are the price to pay for cheap tickets, we say that's a fair trade.

Construction began on October 30, 1997, and was completed in time for Opening Day 2000. After a preseason game between the Astros and Yankees, the ballpark made its regular season debut before a sellout crowd on April 7, 2000, with the Phillies downing the home team 4–1.

In its first two years of existence the new ballpark sported three different names. It was originally called Enron Field, thanks to a thirty-year, $100 million naming rights deal with Enron. But when the "Infamous E" filed for bankruptcy in 2002 amid a world of scandal, the Astros did everything they could to disassociate themselves with the beleaguered energy company as quickly as possible. The team paid $2.1 million to buy back rights to the ballpark's name and temporarily renamed the park Astros Field. Just a few months later, the Astros announced a deal with local orange juice company Minute Maid, a subsidiary of Coca-Cola, and renamed the yard Minute Maid Park. In effect the Astros replaced the name of one juice company on their marquee with the name of another (trading electricity for fruit pulp). And you thought only the players and balls were juiced these days!

Kidding aside, Enron's collapse actually benefited the Astros. The new deal with Minute Maid was much more lucrative, paying the 'Stros $170 million over twenty-eight years, or $6.07 million per season. At the time of this printing, this represents the biggest naming-rights contract a big league team has scored. However, given today's market $6 million a year only purchases a third or fourth starter.

While the Astros and their fans are ecstatic to have a new ballpark to call their home, they are still proud of their former digs—and perhaps that is why the Astrodome has yet to be demolished. The advent of the Astrodome represented a defining moment in baseball and all of sports. While looking back on it we now see the dawning of a regrettable era of artificial playing fields and sterile, oversized facilities. But in its day the dome was a real marvel, an example of a team reaching for the stars and raising the bar in the architecture of sports. Though its duplication came to represent an ugly era for baseball, the Astrodome originally symbolized American decadence. From the cushioned seats and comfortable air-conditioned environment, to the shoe-shine stands behind home plate, to the ballpark lighting system that required more electricity than a city of nine thousand homes, the Astrodome represented American opulence. Elvis played the Astrodome. And the Rolling Stones. And Billy Graham led huge Bible-thumping crusades there. For a number of years, the Astrodome was the world's ultimate entertainment venue. It stood for something bigger than just Houston. It was a monument to American industrialism, workmanship, and vision.

Most important to local baseball fans, the Astrodome brought Major League hardball to Texas. When Houston was awarded an expansion team in 1960, the dome was already in the works. Had Houston not had specific plans for a weatherproof ballpark underway, it would have never been granted a franchise. The Houston Colt .45s—as the Astros were originally called—joined the National League with the Mets in 1962. While the Mets would go on to capture a World Series title before the end of the decade, Houston continues to seek its first World Series appearance. The Astros are currently the longest existent Major League team to have never won a championship.

In their first three seasons, the Colt .45s played in a thirty-two-thousand-seat temporary facility called Colt Stadium, which was dubbed "Mosquito Heaven" by locals. With its humming-bird-sized mosquitoes and oppressive heat, the ballpark didn't draw well. Houston averaged just 789,000 fans per year in its first three seasons.

When the Harris County Domed Stadium was completed in 1964 and promptly renamed the Astrodome in recognition of Houston's contribution to the U.S. space program, the team too was renamed. And fans started turning out to see the local nine. More than 2.15 million fans visited the Astrodome in its initial season.

Kevin: "That's impressive."

Josh: "Not when you consider that the Astrodome had a seating capacity of about one million."

Kevin: "Actually, the Astrodome seated 54,370."

Josh: "And the 'Stros drew about 26,500 fans per game, which means the dome was more than half empty on most nights."

Kevin: "Point taken."

As for Colt Stadium, it was disassembled in the early 1970s and shipped to Torreon, Mexico, for use in the Mexican League. Its old footprint is now buried beneath asphalt in the Astrodome parking lot.

Many have mistakenly called the Astrodome the first weatherproof American ballpark, which is not exactly correct. It was indeed the first dome, but the New York Cubans of the Negro National League played at a ballpark beneath the 59th Street Bridge in Queensboro, New York, during the 1930s. The field was entirely covered by the bridge.

TRIVIA TIMEOUT

Big Dipper: Which pitcher holds the Astros single-season strikeout record?

Orion: Which pitcher recorded the most wins for the Astros in his career?

Look for the answers in the text.

Kevin: "I bet the ushers and groundskeeper didn't wear funky silver space suits like they did at the Astrodome though."

Josh: "I'm thinking you're probably right."

Another thing many people may not remember is that initially the Astrodome had a real grass infield that featured special Bermuda grass engineered for indoor play. The grass field necessitated a see-through glass roof that let in the sunlight. When the glare from the see-through panes gave infielders fits on pop-ups, the roof was painted white, and as a result the grass died (Duh! Photosynthesis!). The trademark plastic grass dubbed "Astroturf" was laid down in 1966. At first, the team left the normal amount of dirt on the infield, but in 1970 the switch was made to virtually maintenance-free dirt sliding pits, a model that would become the norm at domed stadiums and multipurpose stadiums across the nation.

The Astrodome hosted its fair share of memorable moments—including several no-hitters, Willie Mays's five hundredth round-tripper and Nolan Ryan's four-thousandth strike out. On April 15, 1968, the Astros beat the Mets in twenty-four innings at the Astrodome in the longest 1–0 game in history. Later that year the National League beat the American League 1–0 at the Astrodome in the first one-run All-Star Game in history. On May 4, 1969, the Astros turned seven double plays on the slick turf to set a new Major League record.

On September 25, 1986, Houston's Mike Scott clinched the AL West title at the Astrodome with a no-hitter against the Giants.

Scott then shut out Dwight Gooden and the Mets 1 0 in the opening game of the National League Championship Series at the Astrodome, and pitched a complete game three-hitter in Game 4 at New York to even the Series at two games apiece. But Houston lost gut-wrenching twelve- and sixteen-inning affairs in Games 5 and 6, and Scott never got a chance to start Game 7.

The Astrodome also had its share of wacky moments, like the time in 1965 when Mets announcer Lindsey Nelson broadcast a game from a gondola suspended from the apex of the dome; or the time in 1965 when the Mets accused the Astrodome groundskeepers of manipulating the air-conditioning system to blow toward the outfield when the Astros were batting and then reversing the currents when the visitors were at the plate, thereby helping the Astros' fly balls travel farther and knocking down fly balls hit by the Mets. In 1974, a fly ball hit by Philadelphia's Mike Schmidt struck a PA speaker in center field. The slugger was awarded only a single, even though the speaker was 330 feet from home plate and 117 feet high and the blast would have certainly cleared the fences. In 1976 a game was rained out, or "rained-in" as some said, when flooding in the streets prevented players and fans from getting to the dome.

By the 1990s just about everyone agreed that the Astrodome had outlived its era. Cavernous, dark, and sterile, it wasn't conducive to festive ballpark revelry. Though conceived with the future in mind, its time had passed. Minute Maid Park—a real jewel—arrived just in time to give Houston fans the breath of fresh air they craved and inject new energy into the Astros franchise. Only time will tell if the ballpark will also play a leading role in the team's first championship season.

Sellout Index: 10% of games sell out
Seating Capacity: 40,950
Ticket Office: (877) 9-ASTROS
www.astros.mlb.com

Getting a Choice Seat

A small ballpark by today's standards, Minute Maid contains plenty of excellent seats. Most of the field-level sections provide a good vantage point from which to watch the game. The upper-level seats are also decent thanks to the fact that the deck only extends back seventeen rows. In another good call, the upper deck was constructed to minimize the number of upper-level seats in the outfield.

As for pricing, the box seats around the infield seem underpriced compared to similar seats at other MLB parks. Meanwhile the outfield seats seem too expensive. What commonly pass for bleachers in most ballparks are called "boxes" here. For this reason, Minute Maid is a park where fans wanting to sit on the first level should treat themselves and spend a few extra dollars to sit on the infield.

Club Seats (Sections 205–236)

These second-level seats provide a clear view of the action, with the only significant obstruction being the protrusion of the Field Boxes in left that cost fans in Sections 205–209 a sizable chunk of the left field corner.

The food up here may be a cut above the concession offerings in the rest of the park, and the ushers may call you "sir," but ask yourself: Is it ever worth sitting in the second level when first-level seats are available for less money?

Dugout Seats (Sections 112–126)

The architects were no doubt going for an old-time feel when they designed Minute Maid's lower bowl. The seats begin low to the field and close to fair territory, and extend back in rows that rise at a very low pitch. The stadium-seating effect is minimal, putting Row 2 only about six inches higher than Row 1 and so on.

This won't be an issue for tall guys like Kevin, but fans under six feet, like Josh, will find themselves having to sit on the edge of their seats all game long to see over the head of the person seated directly in front of them.

Keep in mind that the seats extend back thirty-nine rows on the first level. And it's the same price to sit in Row 1 as it is to sit in Row 39, so don't take it for granted that a Field Box seat is going to be right on the field. Those seated in Rows 34–39 won't be able to see the full flight of fly balls because of the overhang of the Club deck and the huge HVAC pipes.

One flaw in the ballpark's design—that reminded us of the fiasco in Milwaukee—is that fans seated directly behind home plate on the first level can't see the entirety of fair territory. From the dugout seats, the left field corner is a black hole courtesy of the Field Boxes that jut out midway down the left field line—reminiscent of the left field stands at Fenway Park in Boston. The left field grandstand at Minute Maid rises much higher than the grandstand in right field as it straddles the foul line. Thus the left field corner is only visible from Sections 122 to 134 on the right field side of the diamond, but by then the view of right field line has begun to wane. The view of the right field corner is obstructed for those seated in Sections 129 to 134. So, considering these two factors, only the seats in Sections 122 to 128 allow a view of the entire field. If this isn't enough to convince you to shoot for seats on the first-base side, rather than third, consider that fans seated in right field also enjoy a view of the setting sun and then later of the stars through the window above left field.

Field Boxes (Sections 105–11, 127–135)

Beginning after the first- and third-base bags and extending out to the foul poles, the sections in this range nearest the infield provide good views, while the ones out near the foul poles are rather average. We especially recommend Sections 127 to 129 on the first-base side. Sections 110 and 111 on the third-base side are also good. Be sure to avoid Section 108, which is tucked behind Sections 107 and 109 and doesn't contain any seats close to the field.

Before buying tickets in Sections 134 deep in the right field corner, consider that a seat in Section 151 of the Bull Pen Boxes is 33 percent cheaper while providing a better view of the field thanks to its straight-on orientation.

A fairly significant obstruction affects Section 105 in left field, where you'll want to stay in Row 28 or lower to avoid losing much of center field from view because of the Crawford Boxes that jut out in home run territory.

As with the Dugout Seats, try for tickets in Row 33 or lower to minimize the effects of the overhanging Club deck.

Crawford Boxes (Sections 100–124)

Named after Crawford Street, which runs along the ballpark's left field perimeter, these home run territory seats are relatively close to the action because the left field foul pole is just 315 feet from the plate. The twenty-five hundred seats in this price range are elevated. But because the Crawford Boxes jut out into left field, they don't provide a very good view of the very deep center field. Fans have to look back over their left shoulders to see plays in center. Due to the height of these boxes, fans seated in them can't see plays up against the left field wall, or anywhere on the left field warning track for that matter.

For the most part, we say these seats are overhyped. They have an old-timey name and are few in number, but really they're glorified bleacher seats and not much more. The worst of the lot is Section 104 where the foul pole blocks much of the view.

Bull Pen Boxes (Sections 150–156)

The bad news is that the so-called boxes in right field are no better than the "boxes" in left. In fact, they're not as good. These seats are very far from the plate and they're low to the field, which makes it more difficult to see balls on the infield. Making matters worse, the Mezzanine deck casts a significant overhang above a large portion of these sections. Unless your seat is in Row 10 or lower don't plan on seeing the tops of any fly balls. So take your pick, would you rather contend with the overhang that afflicts these first-level right field seats, or the under-hang that hampers the left field Crawford Boxes? We give a slight nod to the Crawford Boxes.

Sections 155 and 156 provide a nice view of the action in the Astros bull pen. But for the most part, we take a pass on these seats that angle fans toward the left field line rather than toward home plate. One other thing to keep in mind: because of the space the home bull pen takes up, the first row of Section 155 is numbered Row 8. Yet the first row of Section 156—parallel to Section 155's Row 8—is numbered Row 1. Go figure. In any case, it's better to sit in Rows 1–8 of Sections 153 or 154 where Row 1 really is the first row, and Row 8 really is the eighth row. At least then you'll be able to find your seat if you misplace your ticket stub after making a beer run.

Mezzanine (Sections 250–258)

The Mezzanine seats in right field home run territory are located on the same second-level deck that houses the Club seats. Extending from the right field foul pole out to right-center field, not only are these seats cheaper than the Bull Pen Boxes below, but they also provide a clearer view of the action. The Mezzanine's slight under-hang affects views from that level but is far preferable to the overhang that obstructs views from many of the Bull Pen Boxes. We recommend Sections 252 or 253 in

straightaway right field, which are much closer to the plate than the seats out near center field in Sections 258 and 257.

Terrace Deck (Sections 305–338)

Both the 300 Level Terrace Deck seats and the 400 Level View Deck seats are located on the upper deck. The difference between them is that the Terrace Deck seats hang down below the concourse, like the seats called "upper-boxes" in some stadiums, while the View Deck seats are located above the concourse. Here it's definitely worth spending a few extra bucks to sit closer to the field in the Terrace Deck.

The Terrace Deck seats are all the same price, whether they're located in the outfield or behind the plate, so be smart and shoot for Sections 311–329 for the best view. Avoid Sections 305 to 307 in left field where the under-hang blocks a good portion of left field from view.

View Deck (Sections 409–431)

Beginning about fifteen feet higher than the Terrace Level, the View Deck in Houston still isn't all that bad. Encompassing only seventeen rows, the View Deck isn't half as expansive or high up as some upper decks in the big leagues. Unlike the ungodly heavens in Toronto and Arizona, which seemed to keep going and going forever, Houston's highest seats seem to end at just about the right spot.

Sections 413–425 behind the plate are best, while the quality quickly declines in the sections leading to the outfield View Deck sections. The under-hang isn't much of a factor in any of these infield sections. We recommend Rows 3–8, which are high enough to allow fans a view unobstructed by the grate that runs along the first row over the concourse, and low enough to keep fans in the flow of the game.

In some of the level's upper extremities a number of seats are situated behind the lighting banks. Thus, it can get rather dark in these back rows. And it can get loud too, as PA speakers hover above many of the back rows.

Inexplicably, metal bleachers appear in lieu of actual seats in the back rows (15–17) of some upper sections. Obviously, they are less comfortable than the seats.

Outfield View Deck
(Sections 405–408, 432–438)

Located in the outfield before the foul poles, these upper-level seats are to be avoided, unless you're just trying to get into the park cheap and then move down to one of the standing areas. The under-hang obstructs the view from all of these sections in varying degrees. Here again, the jutting out of the first level's grandstand in left blocks the view of the left field corner for those sitting on the third-base side of the Outfield View Deck. This effect is most noticeable in Sections 405–408, which house the worst seats in the ballpark. In right field, Sections 432–438 contend with a less dramatic obstruction of the right field corner.

Standing Room

The Astros put a limited number of standing-room tickets on sale before otherwise sold-out games. These are worth buying, as there is ample standing room on the Home Run Porch that serves as the left field concourse.

The Black Market

Scalping is illegal in Houston but we observed a fellow waving people into one of the parking lots near the ballpark while holding a sign that read, "I have tickets." This made us think that maybe there is good reason for so many bail-bond shops operating in the streets around Minute Maid.

Before/After the Game

Despite the half-dozen bail-bond businesses within a few blocks of the ballpark—owing to the nearby courthouse—the neighborhood around Minute Maid feels both safe and festive on game days. By constructing Minute Maid in a once-forgotten corner of Houston, doubtless the city was hoping to use the ballpark project as an impetus for the revitalization of the area. And by all accounts, the plan is working. We observed plenty of new construction projects on the ballpark side of the highway overpass, while the other side of the freeway looked like it's been slower to respond to the economic benefit of two million fans visiting the neighborhood each year. A number of preexisting Chinese restaurants had not quite caught the new ballpark wave and had either gone out of business and left their buildings dormant or appeared on the verge of going under. Hopefully the ballpark's effect will eventually spread to this area of the city as well.

Getting to Minute Maid Park

From the north, take I–45 south to the Scott Street Exit, then take either Pease Street or St. Joseph's Parkway and follow the signs to the ballpark. From the east or west take I-10 to the

---

SEATING TIP

FREE UPGRADES—FOR THOSE WHO DON'T MIND STANDING

IF YOU don't like the view from your upper-level seats, head on down to the home run porch located to the right of the Crawford Boxes in center field. The porch provides ample standing space beneath the brick arches that support the train tracks above. The view is actually better from this center field location—where more of the field is visible—than in the Crawford Boxes in left. If it feels like you're hanging out over the field while standing on the porch—it's because you are. Enjoy this unique location to watch a game.

U.S. 59 South Exit, then take the Hamilton Street Exit to downtown.

A multitude of privately owned parking lots operate near Minute Maid, charging $6–$10. The cheapest parking we saw was a $5 lot on the corner of Crawford and Congress Streets. Be sure to shop around. Or better yet, find a spot on the street. Almost all of the streets near the ballpark offer two-hour meters that can be plugged until 6:00 P.M. and then become free for the night. Congress, Fannin, and Carolina Streets are all worth a look-see. We should mention that we saw two tow trucks patrolling the perimeter of the ballpark neighborhood, tire-booting cars in front of expired meters. So be smart.

The local Metro Bus is another option for those staying in town. It stops at the ballpark's main ticket window on Texas Avenue.

Outside Attractions

THE PLAZA

Named Halliburton Plaza after the construction company that played a lead role in building the ballpark, a brick courtyard outside the Crawford Street entrance flies pennants to remember Astros teams that were National League Central and previously National League West division winners. Of course, the 'Stros have never won an NL title, but if they ever do there's plenty of room in Halliburton Plaza for additional pennants.

Plaques honor great Houston players like Jose Cruz, Mike Scott, Doug Jones, Don Wilson, Jim Umbricht, Nolan Ryan, and Larry Dierker, as well as pitcher Darryl Kile who died during the 2002 season of congenital heart failure at age thirty-three. Additionally, plaques acknowledge a team MVP for each of Houston's seasons. The Colt .45's logo—a pistol with the word "Colt" written parallel to its shaft—appears on a number of the team's early plaques. If the NBA had to rename the Washington Bullets to satisfy the new rules of political correctness, we're guessing the Colt .45's wouldn't have lasted for the long term either.

The Colt emblem wasn't the strangest thing we found on the plaza, however. The Astros display two slightly larger-than-life-sized statues here of current players Jeff Bagwell and Craig Biggio. Customarily players aren't so honored outside ballparks until after their playing days have ended. Stretching off first-base, Bagwell reaches as if to take a throw from Biggio who steps across second base as if turning a double play.

CLOCK TOWER

Reminiscent of the clock tower at Ebbets Field, a tall clock tower is built into the ballpark facade to the right of the home plate gate. Unlike the tower in Brooklyn, however, the face of this clock is designed to resemble an orange-colored baseball and comes complete with a green stem at its top. This orange-work turns what could be a classy element of the ballpark's design into a cheesy marketing device.

MAN OF STEEL

As a tribute to the Houston blacksmith shop that was founded on the ballpark site in 1902 and then grew into a global corporation known as Stewart and Stevenson, a statue of a steelworker forging a horseshoe resides on the sidewalk not far from the plaza. Dedicated in 2002 on the hundredth anniversary of the company's founding, the statue is called the "Forging the Future" monument.

BALLS OF CONCRETE

On the sidewalks surrounding the park appear large baseball designs done in brick, with each red brick serving as a stitch in the lacing of the ball. There is also baseball stitching "stampcrete" here that breaks up the brickwork every ten feet or so. This subtle touch makes the sidewalks around the ballpark unique.

Watering Holes and Outside Eats

Contributing to the festive ballpark neighborhood is a row of bars located across the street from the main ticket window on Texas Avenue. It ain't Wrigleyville, but it gets the job done. And for those wanting to score some quality eats, we found a few gems near the ballpark.

IRMA'S (22 North Chenevert Street)

If you're looking for an authentic Mexican meal served with a side of atmosphere, we highly recommend Irma's. This Houston institution is famous for attracting visitors from around the world.

You may recognize owner Monica Galvan from her appearances on the Food Network, and from her appearances on many other cooking shows. While she is a familiar face nationally, in these parts she is more than that—she's also a respected voice in the community. When the Astros were lobbying to build the new downtown ballpark, Galvan flew to Austin on one of Enron's private jets to testify before the state legislature on how she believed the project would benefit the local community. Despite Enron's collapse, Irma's continues to be a popular hangout among city and state politicians.

Located among the old warehouses, the New Orleans-style building offers a porch and outdoor patio overflowing with lush green plants. Inside, Irma's is no less quirky—a collage of collectibles adorn the walls, and the men's room urinals brim with crushed ice and fresh-smelling lemon peels. Chances are, Irma's john will be nicer than the hotel room you stay at while in Houston.

Menu items are affordably priced, reflecting a full range of homemade Mexican entrées. From the ballpark, drive North on Crawford Street, then take a left on Ruiz Street, which will run right into North Chenevert. You'll know you're getting close when you find yourself in the old warehouse district. The restaurant is open Monday through Friday 8:00 A.M. until 3:00 P.M., except on game days when it stays open until 7:00 P.M.

IRMA'S SOUTHWEST GRILL

(1314 Texas Avenue and Austin)

Closer to the ballpark we found another Irma's—this one owned by Monica Galvan's son, Louis. We really can't say enough in the way of praise for Irma's Southwest Grill. When we reached Houston, it was the seventh city we'd visited in ten days and we were road weary. Believe it or not, we were both getting a bit tired of eating the hot dogs and bratwurst we were sampling each night at the ballparks and the fast food we'd been getting along the road. Like finding an oasis in a hot desert, we stumbled into Irma's.

Everything we tasted was superb, from the homemade fresh fruit lemonade (Kevin had five glasses) that came complete with floating strawberries, grapes, and melon, to the chile con queso and chips and two homemade salsas we tried, to Josh's beef enchiladas and Kevin's Chilean sea bass and shrimp.

Other interesting entrées included Southwest rainbow trout, shrimp fajitas, and chicken mole enchiladas.

Unlike many Southwestern Mexican joints, Louis told us that Irma's doesn't cook with grease. Every dish is prepared in a manner to ensure that patrons will head home without a lump of lard festering in their stomachs.

Louis's restaurant is a bit more chic than his mother's and a bit more upscale, but the prices are still quite reasonable, with most entrees in the $10 to $15 range. As for who serves the better food, Louis or his mom—we got the impression that there is a friendly rivalry between the two. We echo their mutual praise for one another.

A subtle baseball theme prevails, with an autographed Nolan Ryan painting courtesy of

Leroy Neiman highlighting the decor. Above the long bar appear a small collection of baseballs autographed by regular customers like Hall of Famer Juan Marichal, Astros first-baseman Jeff Bagwell, and Astros CEO Drayton McLane.

Like the other Irma's, this restaurant is also open Monday–Friday, 8:00 A.M. until 3:00 P.M., except when the Astros have a home game, in which case Louis keeps the doors open until game time.

When you stop in to eat, tell Louis that Josh and Kevin sent you. He treated us well.

THE B.U.S. (Chenevert Street and Texas Avenue)

With a wide-open window front on nice days, the B.U.S. is a good spot to grab a quick one before heading into the game. The music is loud, seating is limited, and the crowd is on the younger side.

HOME PLATE BAR AND GRILL
(Chenevert Street and Texas Avenue)

Serving basic ballpark food, Home Plate is a convenient place to have a quick burger, hot dog, or chicken sandwich before the game. The appetizer menu is anchored by wings, pretzels, chili, and jalapeño peppers. The upstairs patio, called The Drink, is a nice place to catch a breeze on a warm day.

TEXAS BARBECUE HOUSE
(Texas Avenue and Dowling Street)

Though a bit farther away from the park than the other Texas Avenue watering holes, this is a solid choice for those craving saucy meat and fixings before the game. Josh recommends the chopped barbecued beef.

JAMES' CONEY ISLAND HOT DOGS
(Fifteen Locations)

A Houston institution since 1923, James' Coney Island has fifteen different Houston locations. From the ballpark, head north on I-45 and within a mile you'll see a large neon sign for one of James's locations on the left. We thought the Vienna franks were of excellent quality but the chili sauce was a bit watery. And of all the places in the world where we might have expected to find watery chili, Houston wasn't one of them.

Inside the Ballpark

The playing field at Minute Maid is top notch. We like its quirky angles and dimensions. Hal's Hill in center field—a knoll of grass, appearing on the "other side" of the dirt warning track, gives the field a look that is unique in all of baseball. The left field home run porch is shallow, while center field is monstrous at 436 feet at its deepest point. The American flag in center field flies on a pole that rises up from the field of play, while the Texas state flag and Houston flag fly atop masts that rise from just behind the outfield fence. The Astros' bull pen in right field is well done, featuring real grass and an old-style wooden bench for the pitchers to sit on while they watch the game. The visitors' bull pen is another story. It exists tucked halfway underneath the center field stands, partially illuminated by fluorescent lights and sporting artificial turf. It seems like the ballpark designers could have done a better job with this. Perhaps if center field weren't quite so deep, some room would have been left over for the out-of-town pitchers.

The brick arches that extend from center field to left, above the playing field, are a classy touch that looks great on TV, but we were slightly disturbed by the asymmetry created by the one double-sized arch in left field, which is extra big so that it can accommodate an advertising banner strung across its top. This especially offended Kevin's sense of aesthetics.

Some parts of the interior—mostly those hidden from the TV cameras' lenses—could be made more attractive, such as the overhead wires, tubing, and HVAC ducts on the first level concourse, and the concourse beyond the outfield fence that remains completely unfinished. But for the most part the ballpark is a clean and comfortable place to watch a game.

Ballpark Features

LOCO

To say the Minute Maid locomotive "runs" along its track—from center field to left field—may be overstating things a bit. The train crawls along like the Little Train That Could—but just barely—then stops, and drives in reverse back to its normal resting point in center. An actual conductor drives the train, which chugs along its track as the final notes of the National Anthem fade into the night.

When the roof closes and the left field window slides into place, the support beams for the window actually slide past the train on either side of the track, briefly encasing it, before reaching their destination in left field. The conductor, for his part, sits in the train looking slightly uncomfortable while all of this is going on around him.

HOME RUN ALLEY

The first-level concourse behind the seats in center field—called Home Run Alley—offers a couple of interesting displays. One exhibit holds two-dozen bolted-down baseball bats that belonged to former and present Astros players. The thickest bat handle of all was on a bat that had belonged to Cesar Cedeno, while the thinnest was on the stick swung by Jose Cruz.

The other exhibit we especially liked consisted of bronze casts of the gloves worn by former and current Astros players.

HOME RUN PUMP

A replica of an old-fashioned gas pump sits on the Home Run Porch in center field, keeping track of the homers the Astros have hit at Minute Maid since the park's opening in 2000. Hey, this is the oil capital of the country, what did you expect?

While fans can see the pump from anywhere in the ballpark, it's impossible to read the very small numbers that reflect the current homer tally from anywhere but right beside the pump.

Kevin: "The numbers should be big and bold for all to see."

Josh: "It's a gas pump, not a billboard."

Kevin: "Actually, if you want to get technical it is a billboard. It's got a corporate logo on it."

Josh: "Point taken."

PAINTED PENNANTS

Above the Crawford Boxes in left field appear the outlines of pennants painted on the brickwork, commemorating years in which the Astros won their division. Why painted pennants and not real flags? Well, there isn't much of a breeze inside Minute Maid, especially when the roof is closed. Also here, a painted white baseball appears inscribed with the initials DK in memory of Darryl Kile. It seems odd to us that Kile is remembered this way, while the premature deaths of two other Astros hurlers resulted in their numbers being retired by the team.

RETIRED NUMBERS

Mounted just below the roof in left field are the franchise's retired numbers: number 25 for Jose Cruz, 32 for Jim Umbricht, 33 for Mike Scott, 34 for Nolan Ryan, 40 for Don Wilson, 49 for Larry Dierker, and 42 for Jackie Robinson.

Statistically, this is not a remarkable group of Colts and Astros.

The only Astros hitter to have his number retired, Cruz played thirteen seasons in Houston. He finished with 2,251 hits and a .284 batting average in nineteen total seasons.

Umbricht's number was retired posthumously after he died of cancer in 1964. The right-hander won eight games for the Colts in two seasons.

Scott registered 110 of his 124 career wins in nine seasons with the 'Stros.

Ryan won 106 games (of his 324 total) in nine seasons with Houston.

Wilson won 104 games for Houston before dying in 1975 at age twenty-nine of carbon monoxide poisoning in his garage.

And Dierker earned all but two of his 139 career wins with Houston before going on to manage the team in the 1990s. With 137 Ws Dierker ranks first among Astros pitchers all time.

SCORES, HOWEVER FLEETING

Below the Crawford Boxes on the left field wall a hand-operated scoreboard provides the full line score of every Major League game in progress. But for some reason, once a game ends, they take down all of the inning-by-inning numbers, leaving up only the final score. This is no good if you're a fantasy baseball owner wondering how one of your pitchers did in a game that started earlier in the day. Sometimes knowing that a team won 6–5 is not enough. You want to know if the team scored five runs in the

---

SLINGING HEAT

WHILE RYAN may hold the MLB record for career strikeouts, the most he ever notched in his seasons with the Astros came in 1987 when he led the NL with 270 Ks to go with a circuit-best 2.76 ERA and a misleading 8–16 record.

J. R. Richard actually holds the team record for most whiffs in a season with the 313 he recorded in 1979. Scott also registered more punch-outs than Ryan ever did with Houston when he fanned 306 in 1986.

---

bottom of the ninth to steal a win for one of its relievers, or if the team staked its starter to an early lead that he carried all game long.

Kevin: "Maybe they need the 0's to use elsewhere on the board?"

OIL

Talk about an "only-in-Houston ballpark feature," on the face of the right field Mezzanine deck, an electronic display board shows the current selling prices of crude oil, unleaded gasoline, heating oil, and natural gas. Oil was going for $28.81 per barrel when we visited Minute Maid.

BROADCAST ALLEY

The first-level concourse behind Section 119 houses a bank of TVs that is supposed to show the other Major League games in progress. Josh was disappointed that the Red Sox weren't on any of these tubes when we visited, though. Instead CNN was tuned in, as well as a couple of hockey games.

Stadium Eats

Aramark has the concession deal at Minute Maid. As such the offerings reminded us a lot of the Aramark food we ate in college while studying to be creative writers together at Emerson in Boston. We wish Houston would bring in some outside vendors to coexist with Aramark. The way the Red Sox have things set up in Boston provides an excellent example of how things could work in Houston. At Fenway Park Aramark serves the dogs, peanuts, pretzels, sodas, and other ballpark staples, while privately operated specialty stands sell food items inside the park, including a local steak house, seafood restaurant, and a Chinese restaurant. Houston should do the same. As it stands now, the ballpark basics are okay at Minute Maid, but just okay, while the slightly more ambitious offerings aren't very good. This is one of those

WE TOOK a drive to check out the Eighth Wonder of the World, which stands across the street from a Six Flags Over Texas amusement park, just off the southwest corner of the I-610 loop that circles Houston.

Expecting to be blown away by the shear size of the Astrodome, we were disappointed to find it currently dwarfed by Reliant Stadium, which is right beside it. Reliant, home of the National Football League Houston Texans, sits in a larger footprint than the dome and rises quite a bit higher into the sky. The football field, which opened in 2002, is NFL's first retractable-roof stadium.

In any case, we were also disappointed that the dome is located in the same gated-off sports complex as Reliant Stadium and Reliant Arena. So Josh wasn't able to give it a wrap with his knuckles, and Kevin wasn't able to snap any up-close pictures.

parks where we recommend eating a good meal in town before the game.

SHERIFF BLALOCK NACHOS (Trademark Food)

While certainly not the best nachos you'll ever taste, these are a cut above the usual ballpark fare. A good-sized portion of chips comes topped with grated cheese, the Sheriff's (greasy, canned) chili, and jalapeño peppers.

DECKER DOG (Dog Rating)

The Seventeenth Best Hot Dog in the Majors.

This is the same Decker dog as the one served in Arlington—cooked on the dreaded rollers. The saving grace of the dogs at Minute Maid lies in the number of different toppings available. The trademark Texas Dog comes loaded with chili, grated cheddar, and jalapeños. For a few bucks more, the Super Dog is easily twice the size of a regular dog and comes similarly loaded with toppings. The New York dog (sauerkraut) and Chicago dog (poppy-seed roll and all the fixings) are also popular sellers.

Sheriff Blalock's Most Wanted dog comes loaded with pickles, chili, and onions.

BEST OF THE REST

Thicker and juicier than the normal ballpark burgers, the Nolan Ryan burger comes topped with fresh lettuce and a slice of tomato.

The jalapeño sausage ranks right up there with the Hot Polish in Kansas City for spiciest sausage in the big league honors.

The Astros Grand Slam Sundae is served in a bigger-than-usual plastic replica helmet. With four scoops of Dreyers ice cream, chocolate sauce, or hot caramel, the sundae is a good value.

One of two new restaurants to open inside Minute Maid in 2003, **Nine Amigos**, may be the best bet for dinner inside the park. The only problem is that folks can't see the playing field from within the restaurant. Large glass windows allow fans a striking view of the concourse behind the right field seats. There is limited patio seating closer to the field, where fans can catch a glimpse of the field alongside Section 156, but the overhang is significant and the area is far from the infield. Inside, Nine Amigos is relatively upscale, with waiter service. Don't plan on being able to get in and out without missing much of the game. You'll likely spend at least three innings here. The menu of upscale Mexican food ranges from $12 to $24 per entrée. Red Snapper Veracruzano and Carne Asada Chimichurri Steak are popular choices.

The other new joint to open in 2003, **Larry's Big Bamboo**, behind home plate on the first level replaced Ruggles Grill, which lasted only a few seasons at Minute Maid. Named after Larry Dierker's favorite Spring Training watering hole in Kissimmee, Florida, the Big Bamboo resembles a Florida beach hut, complete with surfboards adorning the walls. With TVs above the bar, the Big Bamboo offers a full bar and appetizers like hot wings and chili cheese fries.

Dierker, whose jersey hangs on the wall, has no financial stake in the business.

SAY "NO, THANKS," AND WALK AWAY

We had high hopes for **Round House Pizza**. After all, it features DiGiorno's famous rising crust. The crust may be thicker than that of the average ballpark pie, but let us ask: would you rather eat a one-quarter-inch-thick piece of cardboard topped with bland sauce and dried-out cheese, or a three-quarters-of-an-inch-thick piece of cardboard with the same toppings? Our pizza had been sitting under a heating lamp since the ballpark was called Enron Field. The crust was horrendous and the cheese was burnt to a crisp.

The **Home Plate Burrito** also fits in this sad category. Kevin took two bites of his chicken burrito and then tossed it in the trash. What fat and spoiled Americans we are, eh? But this burrito was bad. Still-frozen grated cheese, hot sauce, rice, beans, wilted lettuce, dried-out chicken, bammo—$8. And when Kevin asked for an extra scoop of guacamole, the counter-woman told him it would be an extra $2. Say what?

STADIUM SUDS (AND SPIRITS)

Glasses of Robert Mondavi's finest vintage are available from a stand on the first-level left field concourse. Daiquiris, frozen and fruity, are also available throughout the park.

As for beer, twenty-four-ounce bottles of Corona and Dos Equis are unique to Houston. On tap, Shiner Bock and Shiner Blond are the local choice. Kevin tried the Bock and called it "microbrew for beginners."

The Minute Maid Experience

As far as the Minute Maid experience goes, we liken our visit to Houston's new park to opening a new carton of orange juice only to discover that it's pulp-free. The taste may still be right, and the color, and in general it may be pleasant. But there's not a whole heck of a lot of substance to it. A fairly large contingent of fans were on hand for our game, but most of them were still wearing whatever clothes they had worn to work that day, not the team colors. The crowd seemed conspicuously quiet even when the Astros had a rally. It was hard to figure.

"Maybe after so many years spent visiting the sterile Astrodome, they don't know how to act at a real ball game," Josh suggested.

"And as for not wearing the team colors," Kevin said. "Who can blame them? I don't know anyone who wears orange by choice."

"I know one person," Josh said, "but he's very odd."

"Maybe you should buy him some Astros gear," Kevin suggested.

STRETCH TIME

After singing "Take Me Out to the Ball Game," during the seventh inning stretch, the Astros play "Deep in the Heart of Texas" over the PA system and a handful of oddball fans sing along. So be prepared to carry your section.

PYROTECHNICS

Don't freak out when the person performing the National Anthem gets to "and the rockets red glare," and fireworks come shooting out of left field—even when the roof is closed. It's standard procedure at Minute Maid.

BIRDS OF A FEATHER

Bring your binoculars if you fancy yourself a bird-watcher because we observed plenty of birds of assorted types flying around inside Minute Maid, even though the roof was closed.

Kevin: "Hey, birds are better than bats, right?"

CLOSED CAPTIONS

A display board in right field provides the text of everything the stadium PA announcer says.

ARLINGTON,
TEXAS

224 miles to Houston
454 miles to Kansas City
544 miles to St. Louis
660 miles to Denver

TEXAS RANGERS, THE BALLPARK AT ARLINGTON

The Ballpark That Feels Like a Stadium

THE SAYING "Everything's bigger in Texas," could have been penned exclusively about The Ballpark at Arlington. If this is a ballpark, it's the biggest one we've ever seen. But Texans have a reputation for being fiercely independent in their thinking and for doing things their own way. The Ballpark at Arlington is in reality a stadium masquerading as a ballpark; an impressive structure with an exterior facade that gives the impression of being a baseball fortress complete with turrets at its beveled corners. The walls do not attempt to mask the seating bowl or minimize it, but rather corral the structure, giving it plenty of room to spare. There is no pretense of intimacy from the exterior, though within, The Ballpark has more than its share of good seats, personality, and charm.

The Ballpark at Arlington is reminiscent of several parks built during baseball's classic era. A roof-topped, double-decked outfield porch in right field is quickly recognizable to fans of Tiger Stadium. The out-of-town scoreboard set into the left field wall is clearly a nod to the original at Fenway Park. The white steel filigree adornment surrounding the upper deck would please any fan of Yankee Stadium. And the many irregularities of the outfield fence are clearly patterned after those of Ebbets Field. The granite facade combines the red brick and retro turrets of Camden Yards with the arches of the original Comiskey Park.

But the five-level park is also distinctly Texan. Lone stars and longhorn steer-head gargoyles adorn the exterior walls and are visible throughout the ballpark. While many of the ballparks built during the retro renaissance have since opened up their outfields to allow for city views, the Rangers enclosed the ballpark with a four-story office building in center field, and made it part of the ballpark's signature look. Consisting primarily of glass, the building has a white steel multilevel facade, which provides porches for the offices and a unique backdrop for baseball. This white decorative steel also adorns the roofline of the ballpark, both on the interior and exterior to tie the entire structure together nicely with a unified theme.

The office building, along with the windscreens mounted on top, temper the strong Texas winds that would otherwise wreak havoc with fly balls. The playing surface was also sunk twenty-two feet below street level to minimize the effects of the wind.

Between the office building and the center field bleachers is a grassy picnic area for fans to enjoy. And clearly fan enjoyment was primary in the minds of the facility's designers. Residing next to the Six Flags Over Texas amusement park, the Ballpark at Arlington offers the complete game-day experience. As well as the restaurants and shopping facilities that have become almost standard fares in newly built "retro" ballparks, a full baseball museum called Legends of the Game resides within The Ballpark's walls, containing the largest collection of baseball memorabilia out-

side of Cooperstown. A children's learning center teaches kids in such subjects as science, history and math, using baseball as the teaching tool. How we yearned for teachers like these.

The Ballpark is the centerpiece of an area known as the Metroplex. While the sports complexes in many cities feature a baseball field, football stadium, and basketball/hockey arena, Arlington's Metroplex is purely baseball. This is somewhat ironic in an area where football—from the high school game to the Dallas Cowboys—reigns supreme. But there is plenty outside the park to keep baseball fans interested. A youth ballpark, the Rangers Walk of Fame, two small man-made lakes, a river walk, and a natural grass amphitheatre surround The Ballpark.

The Ballpark rises up from these environs beckoning fans to come inside where a lush green baseball diamond will quench any ball fan's thirst for the sport. "Sunset red" granite that was mined at Marble Falls, Texas, is the most distinctive local material used in the park's construction. Decidedly Texan scenes

exterior

Photo by Kevin O'Connell

facade

Photo by Kevin O'Connell

from settling and ranching to space exploration are etched into white murals that appear between the two levels of exterior arches.

The funding for the ballpark came primarily from public sources, as the citizens of Arlington voted on January 19, 1991, for a one-half-cent sales tax increase to finance up to $135 million of the $191 million needed to complete the project. The remaining $56 million was provided by the Ranger ownership group, which included a Texan named George W. Bush. "Dubya" would go on to become governor of the Lone Star State and would eventually travel to Washington, D.C., to become president of United States, retracing the path of the Rangers franchise, which in 1972 had made the reverse trip after starting out as the Washington Senators.

This is just one of many connections that the Rangers share with the nation's capital city. David M. Schwartz Architectural Services of Washington, D.C., was chosen to design the ballpark, while Dallas firm HKS, Inc., was the architect of record.

Josh: "What's the difference?"

Kevin: "Well, you see, the architect of record is the one who would actually be responsible for the day-to-day ins and outs of the implementation of the construction of the project, while the designing architect would provide the original and overall design."

Josh: "If you don't know, just say so. Don't just make up an answer."

In any case, construction began in the spring of 1992 and took a total of twenty-three months.

In their first appearance at the new ballpark the Rangers lost an exhibition game to the Mets on April 1, 1994. The regular-season opener ten days later proved no kinder to the home team, which fell to the Brewers 4–3. Though their start was rough, the first season in the new park signified a time of great optimism for the Rangers, who until that point had a long history devoid of postseason appearances. Kenny Rogers, "the Gambler" himself, highlighted the good fortune a new ballpark can bring to a franchise when he threw the first perfect game in Rangers' history, a 4–0 blanking of the Angels on July 28, 1994. With the gem, Rogers became the first left-hander in American League history to achieve perfection.

Speaking of history, Texas is one of two American League teams that can lay claim to having originated as the Washington Senators. The Minnesota Twins are the other team. But the Rangers of old, perhaps, best exemplified the hapless Senator spirit. When the longtime Senators left Washington, D.C., in 1960 to become the Minnesota Twins, the city was awarded an expansion franchise the very next year. And that franchise would eventually become the Rangers.

President John F. Kennedy threw out the first pitch for the new-look Senators at Griffith Stadium on Opening Day 1961, before a 4–3 loss to the White Sox.

On the site of Griffith Stadium there had previously existed several ballparks under many names dating from as far as 1892. For a number of years the wooden ballpark was known simultaneously as National Park, League Park, and American League Park, depending on whom you were talking to. (And we thought politics in Washington were confusing.) The park with three names burned down in 1911 and was rebuilt out of concrete and steel, and was once again named National Park. Then in 1920 it was renamed Griffith Stadium in honor of Senators owner Clark Griffith.

But Griffith Stadium wasn't a stadium at all. It was a clunky old ballpark that at its peak seated only thirty-two thousand fans. Perhaps the most noticeable of the ballpark's many quirks was a huge center-field wall with an irregular indented and squared-off segment that cast two right angles protruding into an otherwise regular field of play. Beyond this thirty-foot-high wall were five houses outside the park, whose owners had refused to sell their property to Griffith when the ballpark was being built. And so the backyards of these homes were just beyond the wall. In one backyard a huge oak tree's branches and leaves rose up over the fence and into the field of play. According to lore, Babe Ruth lodged a few home runs in that tree. A flagpole also stood atop the fence, to add to the irregularity of it all. Plus the park was simply shaped funny. Not only were its bull pens in fair play, but the left field wall was 407 feet from the plate, while right was only 328 feet.

Walter "the Big Train" Johnson's career with the Senators was to be one of great personal success, and one of much team disappointment. In twenty-one seasons from 1907–1927, Johnson won 417 games, struck out 3,509 batters, and authored an amazing 2.17 ERA. But despite boasting one of the most dominant pitchers of the era, the Senators managed only two trips to the World Series, winning the October Classic only in 1924.

The Senators' incarnation that would later become the Texas Rangers only played one season at Griffith Stadium. Newly built DC Stadium was ready for the Senators by 1962, where they won the first game at the cookie-cutter, 4–1 over Detroit. The 1962 All-Star Game was also held at DC Stadium, resulting in a 3–1 National League victory. DC Stadium was renamed RFK Stadium in 1969, in honor of the late Robert F. Kennedy. Ted Williams managed the Senators of 1969 to a winning record—the first in their history as an expansion franchise—and won AL Manager of the Year honors in the process. And the All-Star Game was held at RFK in 1969, another NL victory, this time by a score of 9–3.

But RFK had all the trappings of the cookie-cutter it was, and fan attendance steadily declined as the Senators dabbled in mediocrity. In 1972 the Senators left D.C. for Texas. It is somewhat ironic that RFK, which contributed little to the glory of baseball in the D.C. area, became a featured player in 2003 in the movement to bring Major League Baseball back to the city. Those working to bring the Expos to D.C. reasoned that the facility could provide the transplanted team with a spacious place to play until a new ballpark—probably with many of the quirks of Griffith Stadium—could be built.

Who knows? Maybe the third time will prove the charm in Washington. It's hard to imagine that D.C. lost two baseball teams in twelve years, and that the actual senators had such anemic political pull that they couldn't keep the team named after them in town. Either that or maybe they just didn't care. But many fans in D.C. cared. In the final Senators game on September 30, 1971, with two outs in the bottom of the ninth, fans poured onto the field at RFK and refused to leave. Though the Senators were leading 7–5, the game had to be called and was forfeited to the Yankees. But the last game not withstanding, the fan support in D.C. was not sufficient to keep a franchise. The Senators drew just 824,000 fans in 1970 and only 655,000 in 1971.

Meanwhile Arlington was attempting to lure a Major League team to town. Two years after an attempt by Kansas City A's owner Charlie O.

Finley to move his team to Arlington failed, construction began on Turnpike Stadium in 1964. The ten-thousand-seat facility opened in 1965 and became the home of the minor league Dallas-Fort Worth Spurs of the Texas League. But Arlington would fall short once again, when on April 19, 1968, the National League approved Montreal and San Diego as cities for National League expansion franchises.

But the push to bring baseball to Arlington gained new momentum when Robert E. Short, the Democratic National Committee treasurer, bought controlling interest in the Senators at the winter meetings in San Francisco in 1968. Turnpike Stadium was expanded to seat twenty thousand in 1970. And at the end of the 1971 season, Short received permission to move the Senators to Arlington for the beginning of 1972.

Turnpike Stadium was again renovated, this time to accommodate more than thirty-five thousand fans, and was renamed Arlington Stadium, because Arlingtonians felt Turnpike Stadium did not sound like the name of a big league ballpark. They were right.

After a long and arduous struggle to bring Major League Baseball to the Dallas-Fort Worth area, local fans prepared for the arrival of big-time baseball in Arlington. And then a player's strike delayed the first game. But eventually the games began and though the new Texas Rangers lost their first regular-season game on the road against the California Angels, they won their first home date, defeating the Angels 7–6.

Arlington Stadium had been reconstructed several times before its opening, and the resulting patchwork of misfit sections and bleachers shared more than a passing similarity to the ballpark's D.C. counterpart, Griffith Stadium.

Arlington also had the reputation for being the hottest place to play a game in the Major Leagues, as temperatures rarely dipped below ninety degrees during the summer months. Unlike Griffith, the seats at Arlington were completely uncovered, so fans were exposed to the unforgiving Texas sun during day games. For this reason, most games were played at night, even on Sundays, and the Rangers were the first team to forego the use of flannel uniforms.

The field at Arlington Stadium was forty feet below street level, and before yet another set of bleachers in the upper deck was constructed, fans entered the stadium at the highest level. The Stadium had the most expansive bleachers in baseball, which gave it a symmetrical and very bowl-like outfield look.

The most distinctive feature of Arlington Stadium was its massive scoreboard, a large section of which featured a cutout of the state of Texas. But the many billboard advertisements gave the park a minor league feel that it never seemed to overcome. Much like the Ballpark at Arlington, the signs at Arlington Stadium covered huge windscreens that were installed in 1983 from foul pole to foul pole. One advertisement of note at Arlington Stadium was an enormous disaffected Marlboro Man, leaning, smoking, standing watch like a sentinel, and seemingly caring about nothing, certainly not the action occurring on the field down below. And this is perhaps typical of how many Texans feel about baseball. In Dallas-Fort Worth, if you're not wearing a blue star on your helmet, you might as well be playing hopscotch. Football is the Texas religion, and the Cowboys are the local prophets. And the Rangers didn't help their case much when in their first twenty-two seasons, they never once appeared in the postseason. What's more, Arlington Stadium was never chosen as the site of an All-Star Game, a fan-building tool often used by MLB to showcase new facilities.

But the true seam-heads in Arlington were treated to plenty of great players and wonderful baseball moments, under such colorful managers as Ted Williams, Whitey Herzog,

Billy Martin, and Don Zimmer. One such moment came when eighteen-year-old pitching phenom David Clyde made his Major League debut, beating the Twins 4-3, just twenty days after graduating from Houston's Westchester High School in 1973. Another was the time Dave Nelson stole second-base, third-base, and then home—all in one inning, on August 30, 1974. And who could forget August 4, 1993, when forty-six-year-old Nolan Ryan beat the stuffing out of Chicago's Robin Ventura, who had charged the mound after Ryan beaned him.

But Ryan did much more damage to batters while they were still in the batter's box. Ryan holds a special place in the hearts of Texas sports fans, even football fans. Ryan is a Texan, and the most overpowering pitcher of his generation and arguably of all time. When Ryan pitched, fans packed Arlington Stadium. The hard-throwing right-hander treated the home crowd to his seventh and final no-hitter, as well as his five-thousandth strikeout.

Recent Rangers history has been more kind to the club from a wins-and-losses point of view. The move to The Ballpark at Arlington coincided with some of the Rangers' greatest successes, and most bitter playoff disappointments. Led by players like Rafael Palmeiro, Kevin Brown, Will Clark, MVPs Ivan Rodriguez and Juan Gonzalez, and manager Johnny Oates, the Rangers became a force in the American League West. A dynasty was in the making. The Rangers clinched their first AL West division championship on September 27, 1996. Things were looking up in Arlington as the Rangers defeated the Yankees at home in their first-ever postseason game, a 6–2 win on October 1, 1996, in the Division Championship Series. But the specter of the Senators' postseason past hung somewhere in the air over Texas, as the Yanks took the next three games to win the series.

The Rangers would get a second chance against the Yanks in the 1998 Division Series, but were swept, with the final insult coming at home, a 4–0 beating. The next season the Rangers and Yanks were back at it in the play-offs, and again the Yankees swept three in a row from the Rangers marking their ninth straight playoff victory over Texas.

Josh: "That's almost three sweeps in a row."

Kevin: "Nearly."

Josh: "Three-Sweep. I like that. Maybe I can get a trademark on that."

In December 2000, the Rangers decided that the way to put an end to their playoff drought was not by finally building a pitching staff that could compete with the big boys, but by signing another big hitter. Owner Tom Hicks signed former Mariners shortstop Alex Rodriguez to the biggest contract in history, a ten-year deal worth $252 million that also assured A-Rod a salary increase if anyone else in baseball ever got more. This signing looked good to only a few people even at first and represented a watershed moment, as teams' purse strings have been cinched-up ever since from such high-dollar figures. There have been big deals since A-Rod's signing, just not as big. And some experts have suggested that the "Pay-Rod" deal, as well as the discrepancies between the richest and poorest teams, caused the owners to insist on a salary cap in the 2002 labor negotiations.

Kevin: "Why didn't the owners just give A-Rod the team?"

Josh: "You're still bitter that he left Seattle, aren't you?"

Kevin: "$252 million, that's ludicrous. It's more than many organizations are worth."

While the Players Association has managed to avoid a salary cap in the strictest sense of the term, the Rangers' financial constraints have prevented them from signing any other marquee players to play on Alex's team. Paying one player so much (especially in a football town) has left no room to surround A-Rod with sufficient pitching, and all the hitting in the world hasn't helped either. In fact, the Rangers couldn't come to terms with fan-favorite and perennial All-Star Ivan Rodriguez, losing him to free agency. The team has not returned to the playoffs since the signing of A-Rod, nor has it been able to climb out of the cellar of the admittedly competitive American League West.

During the 2003 season, A-Rod, frustrated with losing, announced he would be open to a trade. A potential deal to Boston for Manny Ramirez was eventually blocked by the players union.

Kevin: "Some union."

Only time will tell if the A-Rod signing will be the salvation or the downfall of a franchise that took so long to achieve success. But one thing is certain, with A-Rod in town, even if he is untradeable, there will be no shortage of baseballs flying out of The Ballpark at Arlington, whether the Rangers win or lose.

Sellout Index: 2% of games sell out
Seating Capacity: 49,178
Ticket Office: (817) 273-5100
www.rangers.mlb.com

Getting a Choice Seat

This was once the hottest ticket in baseball, literally. And while the temperature in Arlington may still be soaring, ticket sales have sagged in the last few seasons as the Rangers have fallen to the bottom of their division. Though the ballpark is a new "retro" facility, the upper seats in the highest deck are the farthest away in all of baseball. So getting a prime seat becomes paramount.

Trying to make sense of the chopped up seating sections of the Ballpark is like trying to decipher the Dead Sea Scrolls. There are plenty of differing types of seating sections to choose from at a great variety of prices. The park offers a reasonable average ticket price, but don't let

that fool you into thinking that the average seat is well priced. The average ticket price is lowered by the fact that there are a great number of bad seats.

Commissioner's Box

So pricey they don't even have section numbers, these seats beside the Rangers' dugout are reserved for the likes of the Bush sisters, while they're at the game. Food is free and so are the drinks, if you're of age, or accompanied by the Secret Service.

VIP, Premium, and Lower Infield (Sections 18–34; Sections 16 and 17, Lowest Rows)

The best seats the ballpark has to offer are broken down into three pricing tiers. The way we see it, if you're going to spend this kind of money for seats, don't stop short and get the ones in the back of the section. If you have the means, go for the best.

The incline of the seats on the first level is steeper than at most parks, and though the section appears to be very wide, it's really an illusion (see Lower Box).

Club Infield (Sections 222–230)

Sure these are great, if you like to be pampered, coddled, and have your hand held. We've said it before and we'll say it again: real fans sit down near the action, not up where people have one eye on the game and the other on the latest oil prices.

Lower Box (Sections 14–17, 35–38, 115–136)

This hodgepodge of pricing represents two kinds of seats, those infield seats just beyond the bases, and the seats just behind all the infield seats on what appears to be the first level. We say this because the seats in Sections 115–136 are actually on the first level, but can

TRIVIA TIMEOUT

Longhorn: Name the only Major League player to have his number retired by three teams. And name the teams.

Filet Mignon: How did the term "Texas Leaguer" come to signify a bloop hit in baseball vernacular?

Look for the answers in the text.

only be accessed by an upper concourse. They are located immediately behind the section in front of them, and thus the illusion is created that they are part of the same section, yet there is no access to them from the first-level concourse.

While we like this idea very much, there are only nine rows of seats in the upper (Lower Box) sections. It seems as if it would have been a much more effective system for fifteen to twenty rows of seats.

Seats in Sections 14–17 and Sections 35–38 are excellent but pricey compared to the comparable seats at other ballparks. They are angled nicely toward the action, even more so than the seats in the lower bowl, which begin to angle away on the right field side, but not on the left.

Club Box (Sections 217–221, 231–235)

Overheard in this section: "The firm who 'comped' me these seats can't afford the Club Infield." Also overheard in Sections 217 and 235: "Did anyone else notice that the seats one section over are half the price?"

Corner Box (Sections 10–13, 39–42, 112–114, 137–139)

Here is another hodgepodge of sections, thrown together more by price than by the fact that they're in a similar area of the park. These are probably the best value for the money on the first level. Getting seats in the lower rows of Sections 13 or 39 will not disappoint you.

The other important factor with these seats is that (except for Sections 41 and 42) they are all clear of any foul pole obstructions, while the bleacher sections nearby have obstruction issues. If this is important to you, spend the extra five bones to stay in the clear.

Terrace Box (Sections 201–216, 236–245)

Josh: "Why would anyone pay the same price for seats one entire level higher than the seats directly below?"

Kevin: "Because they didn't buy our book."

Just take a look at Sections 201 to 209. They are second-level seats that go for the same price as the seats down below. On the plus side, the general seating on the Terrace Level is closer than the Club seating on this level, which can be attributed to the design of the decks. But that still doesn't make them great seats. Sections 213–216 on the left field side are the pick of this litter.

Lower Reserved (Sections 3–9, 44–49)

A distinctive and kitschy section to sit in is the double-decked grandstand, a roof-covered area in right field. If you want a unique experience, remember not to sit in Section 44, which is not under the roof. The aisles are built around the pillars, and the pillars themselves are narrow, so the inevitable blockage of view is not terrible and it does provide a nice "old-time" feel to the experience. Sit in the center of the sections and down low if you want to avoid the "experience" of sitting behind a pole, regardless of the kitsch factor involved.

Sections 3 to 7 are elevated above the out-of-town scoreboard. These sections lose just a tad of the warning track and seem a bit far away for the money, but all in all they're not bad. A small gully separates the first row of seats from the outfield wall.

Kevin: "Prevents fan interference with potential homeruns, I suppose."

Josh: "It's aesthetically unsatisfying and overly hygienic."

Kevin: "What?"

Josh: "It's ugly and ruins the bleacher experience."

Kevin: "I agree. Fan interference is part of the game. Except when it harms our teams."

Josh: "Of course. Then it's totally unacceptable."

Sections 8 and 9 are not great. The upper seats of these sections are under a significant overhang, and the field of view is cut in half by the foul pole. The lower seats in Section 8 are not too awful, but most of Section 9 has some obstructions. Paying this much for obstructed-view seats really leaves a bad taste in your mouth.

Upper Box and Upper Reserved (Sections 313–338)

The best seats of Sections 316 to 335 are in the Upper Boxes. These are okay, but not great. As for the Upper Reserved, we don't know who they would be reserved for, as they are fairly horrible. These seats are distant and pricey, and the wind blows up here like it did in the barbecue scene in the movie *Giant*.

The Rangers have done a few crazy things with the upper deck to make it the farthest from the action in baseball. The second deck is hung a bit over the first-level bowl, but the third deck is pushed back behind the second deck. And with the Club and Press levels also between, these seats are up in the stratosphere. The sky at night sure is big and bright (deep in the heart of Texas) from this level.

In a ballpark where you can't even see every blade of grass even when seated behind home plate, these seats really suffer. And we wouldn't mind all this if they were priced cheap. But they're not. Teams should either provide seats that are close and expensive, or distant and cheap.

Sit in the lower seats of Sections 313 to 315 for the best value in the upper deck. You'll pay four dollars less than the cost of a seat in the Upper Boxes and have just as good a view. The seats on the right field side in Sections 336 to 338 are not as close to the field as their left field counterparts.

Upper Home Run Porch (Sections 246–252)

If there is an Upper Home Run Porch, then mustn't there by necessity be a Lower Home Run Porch? Well, it doesn't exist by that name, but rather consists of the Lower Reserved Sections 45–49.

As far as the Upper Home Run Porch is concerned, almost every seat will have some kind of obstruction from the poles, which support the roof. The good news is that the poles are small, and that if you stand up and lean you can see any play around them. These seats are far better than anything on the 300 Level, and much cheaper than any seats on the 200 Level. They are one of the better deals in the ballpark. The downside is that a very large part of the right field wall is lost to the under-hang.

Bleachers (Sections 50–54)

The full bench bleachers were brought over from Arlington Stadium (they had plenty) and put into use at the Ballpark. If you can get into the lower seats of these sections you will do better, as the upper seats lose much of the corners.

Grandstand Reserved (Sections 301–312, 339–345)

There's no way around it: These seats stink. To qualify the level of sucky-ness, we would only pay money for seats in Section 301 if it were Confederate money. You can't see the left field wall or corner at all, and a huge chunk of center field is blocked by the white steel facade of the building. Sitting in Sections 302 to 305

SEATING TIP

➡ WE DON'T really need to spell out that it's better to sit closer to the field, do we? Not for the benefit of our very intelligent readers. But the folks who made the pricing decisions at this ballpark were apparently not aware of this fairly obvious conclusion, and thus a number of price discrepancies exist. Terrace Box seats in Sections 201 to 208 go for the same price as the seats one level below them in Sections 3 to 9. Obviously getting a good seat in the lower section in preferable. The center field bleachers (Sections 50 to 54) go for the same price as the Upper Reserved (Sections 313 to 338) but are three levels closer to the action. Likewise, Lower Box seats on the field level (Sections 14 to 17 and 35 to 38) go for the same price as Club Box Seats (Sections 217 to 221 and 231 to 235).

(unless you're in the first three rows) will also prevent you from seeing the wall and corner. In Sections 306 to 312 the wall becomes visible but the corner is still blocked. The under-hang is not a factor on the left field side.

In general, the right field sections of the Grandstand Reserved are better than the left field sections. But only Section 339 is fairly clear of the under-hang issues on the second deck.

The Black Market

If you feel like haggling, chances are you'll encounter a scalper or two on the walk from your car to the ballpark. As is usually the case at ballparks that rarely fill up, look for a seat at or below face value. Otherwise, buy your tickets from the team.

Before/After the Game

The Ballpark at Arlington is surrounded by the Metroplex, which means lots of parking. Whether your pregame ritual includes a picnic by a man-made lake, or a ride on the roller coaster at Six Flags, baseball is only one of the many entertainment options at the Metroplex. Though it feels a bit forced, at least it's not merely fields of concrete and asphalt deep in the heart of Texas.

The problem with the Metroplex is that there aren't any restaurants or bars within a convenient walk of the place. And since tailgating is not a popular choice when the pregame temperature is 120 degrees, the pregame atmosphere is a tad on the sterile side and the postgame atmosphere is nonexistent.

Getting to The Ballpark at Arlington

On-site parking is plentiful and most folks drive to the game. Coming from Fort Worth take I-30 east to the Nolan Ryan Expressway Exit. Follow the Ryan Express to Randol Mill Road and turn left. Coming from Dallas take I-30 west and exit at Ballpark Way south.

Follow Ballpark Way into the parking lot. The different parking areas are lettered, with each letter representing a famous Texan. The "A" lot is also called the Stephen F. Austin parking lot, while the "H" lot has been named after Sam Houston, and so on.

Free parking is available about two miles away in Arlington, if you don't mind the walk. Another option is parking at one of the privately owned Star Parking Lots, which range between $3 and $5, depending on how close they are. None are more than five blocks away. But remember, these are Texas blocks, and everything's bigger in Texas.

Outside Ballpark Attractions

RANGERS WALK OF FAME

Along the north and west sides of The Ballpark brick panels are laid into the walkway featuring the rosters of each Rangers ball club since 1972, the year the Senators moved to Texas. There are special markers for Gold Glove Award winners, Most Valuable Players, and other various award winners. Fans can have their names etched in clay, with the purchase of a brick to be placed near the year of their choosing. Each panel is made of 2,600 bricks. Josh counted, while Kevin fibbed to passersby, asking them to steer clear of the walkway so Josh could find his "contact lens."

LEGENDS OF THE GAME BASEBALL MUSEUM AND LEARNING CENTER

Located inside the ballpark (though admission is separate) this interactive attraction boasts the largest collection of baseball-related artifacts outside of Cooperstown. More than 140 items from the Hall of Fame are actually on display here, so if your road-trip plans don't include a pass through upstate New York, this may be a good substitute.

The Legends Museum does an excellent job of providing exhibits that cover all aspects of baseball history, including the state of Texas's own ballplayers, Negro League greats, women in baseball, and famous ballparks.

Josh: "Ballparks? Hey, that's our gig."

Kevin: "You would think they'd have at least called us."

Most of our favorite items were from other faraway parks and cities. After all, having a Rangers Hall of Fame is a bit like having a Gold Glove Award for the DH. Our favorite exhibits were:

➤ A seating display that furnishes actual seats from many of the extinct classic ballparks such as Tiger Stadium, Forbes Field, Crosley Field, and the Polo Grounds.
➤ Billy Martin's cowboy boots from 1974.
➤ A room full of electronic display boards of all major offensive and pitching statistical leaders and record holders for a single season, a career, and for the Rangers. Of course Josh, the stat-lover, was in heaven here. He kept muttering that if only his friend Joe Bird, a fellow stat-lover, could have been

there, he might have set up a tent and stayed a week to undertake the demanding but worthwhile chore of memorizing "everything on the wall."
➤ Computer terminals loaded with information on all of the current ballparks, including the seating charts (which are virtually impossible to acquire licensing rights for) and pictures of the fields from different angles.
➤ Upstairs on the third floor resides a Learning Center that links baseball with history, geography, math, and science. The center provides educational programs and a story time for kids, as well as an after-school program, and space for birthday parties and even sleepovers.

LEGENDS OF THE GAME THEATER

"I hope they're showing *Bull Durham*," said Kevin, sitting in his seat anxiously.

"Or maybe *Eight Men Out*," Josh said. "I do love D. B. Sweeney."

"Gentlemen you'll have to leave now," said a gruff and rather portly security guard. "This theater is for corporate audiovisual presentations only."

That's how we found out that this stadium-style theater with 275 real ballpark seats and a thirty-foot presentation wall and deluxe sound system is available for rental only. In fact the entire museum is available for rental, and the Rangers will even do the catering.

YOU CANNOT BE OVER THIS TALL . . .

Designed for children twelve and under, a kid-sized ballpark named after a cola company resides outside the ballpark, on the other side of the man-made lake. The park is a replica of The Ballpark at Arlington, and is available for rental. Complete with a PA system, lights, decorative steel, and a scoreboard, the park is also used for Rangers instructional camps and baseball clinics. The little guys' ballpark closes an hour prior

BASEBALL VERNACULAR

ONE THING we learned while visiting the museum was the origin of the term "Texas Leaguer." A Texas Leaguer, of course, is baseball speak for a bloop hit that lands out of reach of the infielders, but too shallow for the outfielders to reach. Because the sun baked the fields of the Double-A level Texas League, they were very fast (to borrow a golf term). So in order to not get burned for extra bases, outfielders in the league would play deep to prevent balls from shooting up the gaps. The result: there were many bloop hits in the Texas Leagues. Today the term has become as much a part of baseball jargon as "Baltimore Chop" or "Can of Corn."

to each home game. Not far away, Punch Wright Park provides a great spot for a picnic.

Watering Holes and Outside Eats

There simply aren't any unique bars close by the ballpark. The city of Arlington is itself a huge strip mall that provides one set of restaurant-and-bar chains after another, and the Metroplex area is no exception. Places like **Hooters** and **Joe's Crab Shack** are only a short drive away, as are many others of a similar ilk. Forgive us if we don't review all of your favorite chains and seedy sports bars that are available within the endless miles surrounding the ballpark, but honestly, we wouldn't have the space (or desire) to do so.

But do remember that along Collins Street and Copeland Road, there are also a great variety of Mexican and Salvadoran restaurants and taquerias. The nice thing about places like this is that you can get a huge helping of good food at a reasonable price.

HUMPERDINKS RESTAURANT AND BIG HORN BREWERY (700 Six Flags Drive)
Humperdinks tries to be all things to all people. A sports bar with many TVs, a brew pub with

its own handcrafted brews on tap, and a restaurant with an expansive menu. In a land where chain restaurants are king, we think Humperdinks succeeds. Being only eight blocks from the ballpark, this may be your one-stop-shopping place for pre- and postgame entertainment.

The menu features everything from burgers to calzones to seafood and steaks. The cuisine varies from Tex-Mex options, as well as Cajun, to good old-fashioned American diner food.

A full list of national beer and wines is available, plus a selection of home brewed micros. Josh sampled a Texas Blonde, while Kevin enjoyed a Total Disorder Porter. Humperdinks boasts the tallest barroom ceiling in Texas, which we guess is worth something.

BOBBY VALENTINE'S SPORTS GALLERY CAFÉ (4301 S. Bowen)
If you've been taking our advice, you may have already been to the Bobby V's in New York, and even the one in Connecticut. Here's your chance to visit the third in the baseball manager's growing chain in the city where Valentine's big-league managerial career began.

Two things distinguish this Bobby V's from the others: first, the raised boxing ring in the middle of the dining room that allows folks at a few select tables to eat inside the ropes, and second, the exceptional chili that comes served in a bread bowl.

FLYING SAUCER (770 E. Road to Six Flags in Lincoln Square)
Decorated like a German Beer House, the Flying Saucer's interior is covered with decorative plates. This chain is not a sports bar by any means, but rather a beer lover's paradise, with more than 80 different beers on tap, and another 120 available in the bottle. Whether your international favorite is Asahi Super Dry from Tokyo, or Delirium Tremens from Belgium, or Rogue Dead Guy Ale from Newport, Oregon,

or Murphy's Stout from County Cork, you're likely to find it on the menu here. But be careful when ordering: prices range from $2.75 (Bud and Coors) to $75. (Chimay, Belgium) per pint. Yikes!

CARSON'S LIVE (17727 Dallas Parkway, Dallas)

A popular hangout for Cowboys fans both during and out of football season, this large bar offers live music and a happening singles scene. If this sounds like your type of fun, give it a try. As for us, it was a little too *Walker, Texas Ranger*-esque for our tastes.

BEN'S HALF YARD HOUSE

(7102 Greenville Avenue, Dallas)

If you visit this hard-core Dallas sports bar on a Sunday in September, see if you and your friends can out-gain the Cowboys' offense drinking half yards of beer. The menu is decent and there are pool tables and darts to keep you occupied. We much preferred the laid-back atmosphere at Ben's to that of Carson's.

MESQUITE CHAMPIONSHIP RODEO

(I-635 at Military Parkway, Mesquite)

For a real Texas experience, drive about half an hour out of town to visit the rodeo. Mesquite has it all, including bull riding, bronc riding, tie-down roping, and of course, lovable rodeo clowns. But most of all, Kevin enjoyed the unique Texas music, and Josh enjoyed Sonny Bryan's famous chuck wagon barbecue. During baseball season the ranch is open Friday and Saturday nights. Tickets range from $5 to $30. We were tempted to conduct our usual seating survey, but decided against it. For more information (and to request a stadium seating map) call (972) 285-8777.

Inside the stadium

Inside the main entrance gates, the square shape of the vast entry level makes the concourse feel more like a plaza. The gated arches cast shadows across the concrete floor and give the plaza a charming baseball feel. But the real personality of this ballpark is down near the field. The Ballpark at Arlington is instantly recognizable.

Ballpark Features

GREENE'S HILL

The batter's eye is a slope of green grass in dead center that was named for former Arlington Mayor Richard Greene. Fans gather in the bleachers on both sides of the hill during batting practice, while the players attempt to launch their pregame blasts toward the knoll. When a ball strikes Greene's Hill, a mad scramble ensues for the souvenir. Then fans politely return to the bleachers and await the next shot. Yes, Josh scrambled onto the hill after a Juan Gonzalez blast touched down, but he was beaten to the ball by a gangly thirteen-year-old. Probably just as well.

HOME RUN PORCH

The double-decked grandstand section in right field is the signature feature of The Ballpark. The pillars that support the upper deck and roof give the outfield the distinctive look of a classic park. This may make the ballpark look old-timey, but in reality the seats aren't anything to write home about. Think about it, you're in Texas where the stars at night are big and bright. Do you really want to sit under a roof?

BEST "FANS" IN BASEBALL

Overhead electric fans hang from the roof of the covered Home Run Porch, cooling folks seated in these sections on hot days.

Josh: "Fans sometimes hang from the rafters at Fenway too."

Kevin: "What do you mean 'sometimes'?"

Josh: "Well sometimes they oversell the standing room sections, and folks hop up on

batting practice

Photo by Kevin O'Connell

AUTOMATIC FOR THE INFIELD

Mounted on hydraulic lifts and stored beneath ground level on the third-base side, the infield tarp used to cover the field during rain delays runs without the help of the grounds crew.

VANDERGRIFF PLAZA

Located between the office building and the center field fence, Vandergriff Plaza is a fun place to visit before or during the game. The plaza is an interactive sports park, where kids and the young at heart play Wiffle ball. On the day we visited, youngsters were attempting to jack Wiffle balls into the upper levels of the white steel facade of the office building.

In the center of the plaza, a statue honors native son Nolan Ryan, the only player in Major League history to have his number retired by three teams. (Yes, we know that Jackie Robinson has had his number 42 retired by all thirty teams.) The first team to honor Ryan was the Angels, who retired his number 30 California jersey in 1992. Next were the Rangers who retired the number 34 Ryan wore for them on September 15, 1996. Exactly two weeks later, the Astros retired the number 34 Ryan had worn during his days in Houston, completing the trifecta. Ryan showed his fondness for his final team, the Rangers, by entering the Hall of Fame wearing a Rangers cap.

each other's shoulders, then hang from the piping behind Section 28."

SAVE THE FOUL POLES

Perhaps the only things from old Arlington Stadium worth saving were the foul poles. Other than the bleachers in center field, all of the other features that resemble the old Stadium were re-created, such as the State of Texas cutout between the American and Texas flags in center.

BULL PEN CONFIGURATION

The home bull pen is located in right-center field and causes the outfield wall to jut back toward the infield, creating difficult angles for center fielders. We like this configuration and applaud the designers.

Not so well done is the visiting bull pen. With the seats for the pitchers located underneath the outfield grandstands in left-center field, hurlers must walk behind the manual scoreboard to get to the throwing area. While this quirk might be acceptable, the hurling pen itself is oddly shaped, such that it gives the impression that it was an afterthought. While we realize that dissing the opposing team is part of the game, this just looks shoddy.

AUTOGRAPH WEDNESDAYS

Autograph hounds like Josh are going to want to plan to be at The Ballpark at Arlington early on Wednesdays. After batting practice fans line up along the main concourse

A POPULAR old vaudeville saying went: "The Washington Senators: first in War, first in Peace, and last in the American League," as the Senators were more often at the bottom of the standings than the top. But Griffith Stadium did manage to host three World Series: in 1924, 1925, and 1933. Only the 1924 set would prove successful for the Senators, when in Game 7, New York Giants catcher Hank Gowdy tripped over his own mask and missed an easy pop-up. This gaff set the stage for a come-from-behind win for the Senators when Earl McNeely chopped a grounder over the head of third-baseman Fred Lindstrom to score the winning run in the bottom of the twelfth inning.

A couple of interesting traditions also began at Griffith Stadium. The first was in 1910, when President William Howard Taft threw out the first pitch of the season. During the remaining time the Senators played in Washington, D.C., and continuing now at Oriole Park at Camden Yards, the president is always on hand to toss out the first ball of the season. The seventh-inning stretch was also born in Griffith.

where players and coaches sign for a limited number of people. Josh was thrilled to walk away with a signed Marcus Texiera rookie card.

Stadium Eats

Let's face it: ballpark food is not meant to be exactly gourmet. Don't worry, in Arlington it's not. The Ballpark offers the basics, with a few unique twists. The menu isn't great, but it isn't horrible either.

TEXMEX EXPRESS (Trademark Food)

Normally, we pass on nachos at the ballpark: stale chips slathered in a limp cheese sauce that was once a powder. But the Nachos Supreme at the TexMex Express come loaded with jalapeño peppers, taco meat, shredded cheese, lettuce, salsa, and black olives. Not too shabby. The Taco Salad is also a big seller, and the lines for these stands are the longest in the park. While this isn't the most authentic Tex-Mex you'll find (get that outside the ballpark) it's pretty good.

DECKER HOT DOG (Dog Rating)

The Twentieth Best Hot Dog in the Majors

The Decker Dog was a bit of a disappointment. Though it wasn't the worst dog we tasted on the southern swing of our road trip, it was far from the best. Perhaps we didn't get the freshest sample, but we have to rate the Decker Dog on the lower end of the scale. If you're dying for a dog, go for the foot-long Coney or Chicago dog instead of the ballpark basic.

BEST OF THE REST

The catfish and chips is an excellent option, and if it's piping hot and right out of the fryer, it could contend for the Trademark Food.

The smoked turkey leg is quite good, as is the barbecue sandwich, both from the **Red River Barbecue Stand** behind Section 136.

On a hot day try the Big Kahuna Giant Chocolate Chip Cookie Sandwich.

SAY "NO, THANKS," AND WALK AWAY

Josh was tempted by the aroma of sizzling meat, onions, and peppers and lured to the grill in right field where he ordered a chicken fajita. It was only after he ordered that he realized that his fajita would not come fresh off the grill, but rather from the stash of premade fajitas wrapped in aluminum foil under the counter. Not good.

Kevin tried the soft taco, which was passable, but nothing special.

FRIDAY'S FRONT ROW GRILL

How they named this place the Front Row is beyond us. The restaurant actually begins behind the last row of the second deck.

Josh: "Is it the front row of the third deck?"

In any case, this is a Friday's restaurant, with little view of the ball game. You can find the same menu and the same decor at a Friday's much closer to your house.

STADIUM SUDS

All manner of macrobrewed beer is available, but the popular choice on a hot day are the foot-long margaritas. At least we saw plenty of the ladies drinking them.

The Ballpark at Arlington Experience

Texans are a vocal bunch. We came to this conclusion after just a few innings of our first game at the ballpark after observing folks yelling like East Coasters, sparing no one, not the players, umps, or batboys. So we thought we'd found another baseball mecca, an oasis in the desert of football and NASCAR. But we were wrong. With the game tied and going into the top of the seventh inning, fans began to leave. And not just a few, in droves and droves.

Kevin: "The game was tied before you got here!"

Josh: "Yeah, why bother coming out?"

That said, the fans who remained were into the game, and seemed to take it seriously—or at least as seriously as we did.

COWBOY WAYNE (Superfan)

Scan the front row of box seats on the third-base side and you're apt to spot Cowboy Wayne—a veritable Kenny Rogers look-alike—just beyond the visitors' dugout. He'll be wearing a big old cowboy hat, sporting a baseball glove on his left hand, and holding a colossal green fishing net in his right hand. This guy wants a ball.

A season ticket holder, Wayne has been getting plenty of foul balls in recent years. He started bringing the net to games in 1995 and claims to have scooped up hundreds of balls since then. Don't worry, as soon as Wayne sees

lightning in the sky, he puts the aluminum-framed net under his seat.

THE TEXAS TWO STEP?

After "Take Me out to the Ball Game" the Rangers play square-dance music over the PA system. It sounded a lot like the theme to *Hee-Haw* to us. It wasn't but people sure were yelling "Yee-Haw!" as they grabbed their belt buckles and did a bowlegged two-step.

TEXAS RANGER

The Lone Ranger theme song ("William Tell Overture") and video clips from the old television series rally the crowd when the Rangers are trying to mount a late-inning rally. Hey—at least it's not the Anaheim Angels' Rally-Monkey.

FRISCO? THOUGHT THAT WAS IN CALIFORNIA

But if you're a baseball purist like the two of us, another option is to catch a Frisco Roughriders game. The Roughriders are the Double-A Texas League affiliate of the Rangers. Their brand new ballpark in Frisco, Texas, is considered one of the most beautiful in all the minor leagues. Buck Showalter described it to us as "unbelievable." With a season that runs from April to August, there should be plenty of opportunities to catch a game.

NOLAN RYAN THE RANGER

TWO OF Ryan's most memorable feats came in a Rangers uniform at the end of his career. When the old man threw his final no-no on May 1, 1991, against the Blue Jays, he was forty-four years old, the oldest ever to turn the trick. Both Ryan's final no-no and five-thousandth strike-out came at the expense of Oakland's Rickey Henderson. Ryan struck out Henderson to record K number five thousand. Then on the same day that Rickey broke Lou Brock's all-time stolen base record in a game against the Yankees—a huge achievement—Ryan gobbled up headlines, by topping Henderson's accomplishment with his seventh no-hitter.

MICKEY MANTLE BOULEVARD

If you're on the way from Arlington to Kansas City or heading from Colorado to either big league town, why not drive a few hundred miles out of your way to visit the town of Commerce, Oklahoma (population 3,700), where Mickey Mantle grew up. The Mick was born on October 20, 1931, in Spavinaw, Oklahoma, but his family moved to a modest home in Commerce, a lead and zinc mining center, when he was three. His boyhood home is still standing, but of even greater interest to tourists will be the new Mickey Mantle Museum that will hopefully be getting ready to open by the time our book comes out. The Mickey Mantle Memorial Trust, a nonprofit organization formed in 2002, was still working to find a site in town for the museum in 2003. Commerce is located in the northeast corner of Oklahoma's Green Country on U.S. Highway 69.

SPORTS IN THE CITY

FOOTBALL FOOTBALL FOOTBALL

PLANNING your road trip so that you will be in Texas during football season is worth considering. Irvine, Texas, where the National Football League Cowboys play, is just a twenty-minute drive from The Ballpark at Arlington.

While We Were in Arlington

WE ACTED LIKE GIDDY SCHOOLKIDS

When we wrote to the Texas Rangers telling them of our epic baseball road trip, we hoped they might send us a few free tickets to a future game. But the Rangers did us one better. They gave us field-access press credentials for batting practice. Of course, we didn't know how we were supposed to get onto the field or where we'd be allowed to stand once we got there. So we milled around in the stands for five

minutes before Kevin mustered the courage to ask a tough-looking security guard, in his own fashion, just how the whole deal worked.

"Not a bad detail to pull," Kevin said.

"I've had worse," the guard smiled, and with that we were off and running. Kevin can talk to just about anyone. The guard told us which gate to use to access the field and where we were allowed to go. Basically, as long as we stayed in the foul territory on the infield between the first- and third-base bags, we'd be okay.

The Rangers had already taken their BP and the Oakland A's were hitting. So we scampered out onto the field, trying to look cool, like we'd done this a thousand times before. We stood behind the batting cage and rubbed elbows with Jermaine Dye and Terrence Long, while Miguel Tejada raked away in the cage.

We stared in amazement at each hitter, like we'd never watched anyone hit a baseball before. Man, did the ball ever jump off those bats. And standing that close, the pitches, considered "meat" in the big leagues, looked unhittable to us. Likely, they were.

Josh spent most of his time trying to pilfer a ball.

"Will you knock it off?" said Kevin, highly annoyed.

"What?" asked Josh innocently.

"You think that looks professional, resting your foot on a ball like no one's going to notice?"

"Well," answered Josh, "we aren't professional."

"This I realize," said Kevin.

"So I'm getting myself a ball."

Just as Josh was bending over to pocket his prize, Rangers manager Buck Showalter came bounding up the dugout steps and gave him a look of consternation. Nervous and attempting to recover his dignity, Josh tossed the ball out toward the mound and snapped into reporter mode, asking Buck if he could have a few minutes.

"Sure," Buck said.

"What are your favorite ballparks?" Josh asked.

"Yankee Stadium's at the top of the list," Buck said. "I also like Baltimore a lot." He paused, then said smiling, "And I like the ballpark here in Texas. Wrigley Field . . . Fenway . . . I coached in the old Comiskey. I'll tell you the one I really like—I've broadcast from the new ballpark in Pittsburgh, and I think that's a new park that will really stand the test of time."

The dubious start aside, the interview was a real thrill for Josh, as was being down on the field for both of us.

DENVER,
COLORADO

605 miles to Kansas City
855 miles to St. Louis
900 miles to Phoenix
925 miles to Minneapolis

COLORADO ROCKIES,
COORS FIELD

Rocky Mountain Baseball High

THE ROCKY MOUNTAINS are the backdrop beyond Coors Field's left field and center field walls, and are they ever spectacular. As the sun sinks behind the snow-capped peaks, an orange glow illuminates baseball's magical twilight hour. There may be no more beautiful sight in all of sports. With this breathtaking view well worth the cost of admission on its own accord, fans at Coors Field receive the added bonus of getting to see a baseball game. And not just any game. At Coors fans are guaranteed an entertaining game fueled by offense. Runs will be scored, often in bunches, home runs will

exterior

Photo by Kevin O'Connell

be swatted, and no lead will be safe until the final out is recorded. This is mile-high baseball where all things offensive are possible. So, sit back and enjoy the show.

For a large facility, Coors maintains an intimate atmosphere that allows both players and fans to enjoy a day at the ballpark uninterrupted by the barrage of sound bites and flashing advertising that distract them at many of the newer stadiums. Despite its size, Coors feels like a ballpark, and not a stadium. And it's a good thing it does, because Coors represents an important link in ballpark evolution. At the time of its debut in 1995, Coors was the first new National League ballpark to open since Montreal's Olympic Stadium in 1977, and the first baseball-only facility to be unveiled in the senior circuit since Dodger Stadium in 1962. Coors appeared on the MLB landscape a year after the Indians and Rangers opened their new ballparks in the American League, and two years before the Braves would open Turner Field. Coors fits well in this retro-classic lineage, blending into its warehouse district neighborhood with an attractive facade made of Colorado limestone at street level and red brick up above. If any ballpark has the right to feature red brick in its construction it is this one in Denver, Colorado, which once belonged to Mexico. In Spanish, Colorado means "colored red," a nod to the state's many auburn rock formations.

As mentioned already, slugfests are the norm at Coors on account of the thin mountain air, which turns long fly balls into home runs and home runs into feats of earth-shattering power. After the expansion Rockies spent their first two seasons at Denver's Mile High Stadium, the first game at Coors was played on April 26, 1995, against the Mets. Appropriately, the two teams combined to hang twenty runs on the board, with the Rockies prevailing 11–9 in fourteen innings. And that was just the

beginning. In the ballpark's second season, the Rockies and their opponents set a new Major League record, smacking 271 homers in eighty-one games. And the 1998 All-Star Game set a Midsummer Classic scoring record as the American League posted a 13–8 win behind an MVP performance from Roberto Alomar, after Robby's older brother, Sandy, had won the award the previous year. In 1999 the Rockies and their opponents broke the home run record again, walloping 303 Denver dingers. And all this occurred in a ballpark that measures a deep 424 feet to right-center field, 415 to straightaway center, and 390 to left-center. Even the foul poles—350 feet away in right and 347 in left—are distant.

With the home run derbies piling up, it quickly became undeniable that the altitude had a significant effect on the flight of batted balls in Mile High City. Yet a few years earlier in 1993 no one had taken seriously Rockies manager Don Baylor's suggestion that special high-altitude balls be used for games in Denver. After a decade of double-figure scoring, the doubters were ready to listen, and the league approved the Rockies' request to bend the rules. In 2002 the Rockies started storing their game balls in a humidor at 40 percent humidity, hoping the soggy-centered balls (which are imperceptibly heavier and dry on the exterior) wouldn't fly as far. The drop-off in homers was negligible, but according to our sources several members of the home team smoked exceptionally dank stogies all season long.

The fact is a batted ball that travels 400 feet at sea level, flies 5 to 10 percent farther (420 or 440 feet) a mile above sea level in Denver. Further stacking the odds against pitchers, breaking balls don't break as sharply in the low-density air, allowing batters to tee off on curveballs and sliders that they might ordinarily fail to hit squarely. To make matters worse, batted balls speed to the gaps more quickly, making outfielders essentially lose a step in their pursuit. As a result, Colorado perennially ranks atop the NL in many major offensive categories like batting average and home runs, and at the bottom of the league in pitching categories like earned run average and opponents' batting average. These trends affect the Rockies' ability to compete financially with other teams in two ways. First, the Rockies must overpay to lure qualified free-agent pitchers to Colorado. Second, they must overpay their offensive players who expect big contracts after putting up monstrous stats that are largely the result of the eighty-one games they play each year in Denver. On the pitching side, the Rockies have shelled out big bucks to net top hurlers who have flopped in Denver. Accomplished veterans like Bret Saberhagen, Pedro Astacio, Darryl Kile, Denny Neagle, and Mike Hampton all brought lofty résumés with them to Coors but flamed out in the thin air. Especially after Hampton's meltdown, the thinking among big league pitchers now seems to be that if you sign a free-agent contract with the Rockies, you had better get an exceptional deal, because it's likely to be the last big contract you will get. As far as offensive players go, the Rockies have historically overpaid Jekyll and Hyde sluggers like Dante Bichette, Mike Lansing, Vinny Castilla, and Neifi Perez who made their living going two for four in virtually every home game and zero for four all season long on the road.

The thin air has also affected the way fantasy baseball owners across the country manage their squads. Smart (read super-nerdy) fantasy owners never draft Rockies pitchers, but load up on Rockies hitters. Once the season begins, the objective is to bench any pitcher on your roster whose (real) team is heading into a series at Coors, and activate any position player on your bench whose team is playing in Denver. Even when Randy Johnson—the one-time ace of Kevin's Seattle Slackers—is scheduled to pitch in Colorado, Kevin gives him the night off. It's just too much of an ERA risk to let even the Big Unit pitch in the City of Clouds.

But never mind the fantasy owners. How can the Rockies themselves compensate for this unique home field disadvantage? The soggy-cored balls seem like a step in the right direction, but what else can be done? Some might say, "move back the fences," but this would force outfielders to play deeper to defend the gaps, which would result in even more bloop singles and stretch doubles. Home-run stats would decline, but batting averages and ERAs likely would not. Josh suggests growing the infield grass ridiculously high to turn seeing-eye singles into ground outs and adding ten feet in height to the outfield wall in the form of a see-through chain-link fence to turn some homers into doubles. Kevin says take out the first few rows of seats (sorry high rollers) to expand the already expansive amount of foul territory on the infield and increase the number of foul pop-outs. No doubt, balls would still fly out of Coors, but with these modifications we think pitchers might at least have a fighting chance.

In the meantime, it seems fairly obvious that the Rockies should stop spending money on high fastball pitchers like Astacio, Neagle, and Hampton, and instead recruit ground-ball pitchers. In addition, the team should teach every pitcher in its minor league system how to throw a forkball/splitter long before they reach "the Show." After all, the first pitcher to throw a no-hitter at Coors was Hideo Nomo, master of the splitter, who turned the trick September 17, 1996, pitching for the Dodgers.

To put in perspective how altitudinous Coors Field is, consider that prior to the advent of Major League Baseball in Denver, Atlanta-Fulton County Stadium held the distinction of being the highest ballpark in the bigs at 1,000 feet above sea level. Coors is 5,259 feet above the waves, and that's after you subtract 21 feet because the playing field lies below street level. A row of purple seats amid the otherwise green seats of the upper deck—Row 20—marks the mile-high plateau. We know what you're thinking, and the answer is "no." The ballpark is too crowded a place to ever consider joining the "mile-high club" in its upper extremities, no matter how cute and/or willing she may be.

After Major League Baseball announced Colorado was one of six cities being considered for an expansion franchise, in 1990 Denver voters passed a .1 percent sales tax increase to finance construction of a new ballpark, should Colorado be awarded a team. The other expansion sites under consideration were Buffalo, New York; Orlando, Florida; Washington, D.C.; Tampa-St. Petersburg, Florida; and South Florida.

In 1991 Denver was chosen along with Miami, marking the first expansion in the National League since the Montreal Expos and San Diego Padres entered the league in 1969. The Rockies commissioned the architectural firm HOK, fresh off its success in Baltimore, to design a ballpark befitting Denver's downtown warehouse setting.

While Coors was being constructed, the Rockies played at Mile High Stadium, home of the National Football League Denver Broncos since 1960, and also of the AAA American Association's Denver Zephyrs, a Milwaukee affiliate. Denver was awarded a team largely due to its history of supporting the Zephyrs (1985–1992) and the Denver Bears before them (1955–1962, 1969–1984). After Denver broke ground on Coors Field in October of 1992, the Zephyrs moved to New Orleans to begin the 1993 season.

In their first season, the Rockies set a new Major League record for wins by a first-year team, racking up 67 Ws in 1993. But the big news wasn't the Rockies' sixth-place finish in the seven-team National League West. Rather, it was their place atop the MLB attendance ledger. Playing at Mile High, Colorado drew more than 80,000 fans to its first home game, an 11–4 victory against the Expos. By the end of the season 4,483,350 people had visited the converted football field to watch Major League hardball in the thin air. In two seasons at Mile

Rockpile seats

Photo by Kevin O'Connell

High, the Rockies averaged an astounding 57,000 fans per game. After the Broncos moved to brand new Invesco Field, Mile High Stadium was demolished in January of 2003.

But due to the Rockies' remarkable fan support at the converted football field, construction of Coors Field was modified to increase capacity from the originally planned forty-three thousand people to more than fifty-thousand, bringing the ballpark's total cost of construction to $215 million. Despite the work stoppage of 1994, which adversely affected attendance in many cities once baseball resumed, the extra seats in Colorado were filled night in and night out in 1995. And Colorado attracted more than three million fans in each of its first nine seasons before a dramatic fall in attendance in

TRIVIA TIMEOUT

Tree-line: Name the Rockies player who once posted identical stat lines in two consecutive seasons for home runs, runs batted in, and batting average?
Summit: What are Rocky Mountain oysters?

Look for the answers in the text.

2002. The Rockies had never played before a home crowd of less than thirty thousand before doing so thirty-eight times in 2002. The Rockies weren't a contender in 2002 like they had been in many of their previous seasons, and Coors Field was no longer a novelty. As a result, fan interest waned.

The truth is, interest in the team may never again match its levels of 1995 when the upstart Rockies became the quickest expansion team ever to reach the playoffs, earning a wild card berth. The Miracle Mets of 1969 had been the previous record holders, making the playoffs in their eighth season. Unlike the Miracle Mets, however, the 1995 Rockies bowed out of the playoffs in the first round, losing to Atlanta three games to one. Just the same, the impact that Coors Field has made on its neighborhood in lower downtown Denver cannot be overstated. What was once a shabby and crime-ridden area of the city now bustles with activity 365 days a year—and especially on game days. LoDo has become a trendy spot as Coloradans visit the many new restaurants and brew pubs that have opened in the old warehouse buildings. And the centerpiece of the whole neighborhood is a new building that looks almost like an old warehouse from the exterior—Coors Field. The ballpark offers the total game-day experience: a hip urban entertainment district, a festive pregame plaza, seats with great sight lines,

Sellout Index: 10% of games sell out
Seating Capacity: 50,445
Ticket Office: (800) 388-ROCK
www.colorado.rockies.mlb.com

and a ballpark rife with unique local flavor. So do enjoy your visit.

Getting a Choice Seat

What was once a hard ticket to find has become increasingly more available as the Rockies have spent their free-agent dollars poorly and the team has struggled. The Rockies average about thirty-three thousand fans per game these days. Although a crowd of this size may constitute a sell-out in Boston or Pittsburgh, at spacious Coors Field it leaves plenty of open seats.

So picking out a seat that suits your tastes and fits your budget should be easy, right? Think again. Not only do the Rockies divide the Coors stands into seventeen different pricing categories, but they also price these categories differently depending upon which opposing team is in town and what time of year it is. There are four different pricing levels: the Value Price, Division Price, Premium Price, and Classic Price. We'd need PhDs in statistics and economics to explain exactly what that means to you, the average American ticket-buyer. And between us all we have are two master's degrees in creative writing and Kevin's welding certificate. But figure that if the weather's nice and a quality opponent is in town, you'll be paying the maximum price. If the Pirates are in town for a game in September, you'll be paying the minimum. In a sense, we suppose this is equitable. But it can get confusing. One good thing is that the center field Rockpile seats are always $4—the same as they've always been. We appreciate consistency.

As a rule, the sight lines at the ballpark are excellent. The Club Level is set back far enough so as to avoid the overhang complications that afflict the back rows of the first-level seats at many parks. Likewise, the Upper Level is not back far enough from the field to prevent the under-hang below from being a factor in most sections of the top deck, with the exception being the Upper Right Field Reserved sections, which contain the worst seats in the house.

Field Level

INFIELD BOX (Sections 120–141)

Upon visiting Coors Field we were immediately struck by how wide the seats are as well as the aisles between the seats. This is true on the first level and throughout the ballpark. You really can't go wrong with a seat in these primo sections around the infield. Shoot for Section 131 or 132 if you want to set up camp right behind the catcher. Thanks to a low retaining wall between the first row of seats and the field, there are hardly any obstructed views on the first level. The outfield corners are visible from just about everywhere.

If you're haggling with a scalper on a rainy night, ask for tickets under the overhang of the Club Level in Rows 29–38 of the first level. As far as overhangs go, this is not a very obtrusive one, but if you're the type of fan who likes to see the whole flight of the ball on those Major League pop-ups, we recommend avoiding Rows 34–38.

Section 141 near third-base is a no-alcohol seating area. Wow, a no-booze section in the lower boxes. And we thought the upper-level family section behind home plate in Minnesota was a find! This is indeed a rarity, so if you're a teetotaler, do take advantage.

MIDFIELD BOX (Sections 116–119, 142–145)

Midfield? What is this, a soccer game? In one of the few gaffes committed in building and labeling their beautiful ballpark, the Rocky Mountain baseball neophytes chose to categorize the seating sections along the foul lines in medium-depth right field and left field as Midfield Boxes. But don't fret. As long as you don't have your hopes set on seeing a header or bicycle kick, you'll enjoy a first-rate view of the action from these field-level seats. A minor drawback to these sections is that the seats along the left field line point fans toward right field, and the seats along the right field line point fans toward left field, rather than toward the plate. The seats are angled, in an effort to provide fans a view of the infield, but we still both had stiff necks after sitting in Section 116 for the better part of a game.

As is the case in the Infield Boxes, the rows number 1–38. And the first row is the same price as Row 38, so shoot for seats down near the field.

OUTFIELD BOX (Sections 110–114, 146–150)

Deep in the outfield corners, on the foul side of the foul poles, are the Outfield Boxes. These are quality seats. But in our opinion they're priced a bit too high, given their proximity to the Pavilion seats in home run territory in left field and the Right Field Boxes in long-ball land in right, both of which provide straight-on views of the game for considerably less money. As a rule, the left field seats (146–150) offer a better view of the left field corner and entire field than the right field seats (110–114) do of the right field corner and field, because of the higher retaining wall between the field and seats in right field.

Right Field Box (Sections 105–109)

Located above the out-of-town scoreboard in home run territory, these seats provide an excellent view of the game. Seats in Rows 10 and back are beneath the overhang of the Club deck—good to know, if rain is forecast. The obstruction from the overhang is negligible.

We recommend avoiding Section 109 where the right field foul pole interferes with the view.

Seats 1–5 in all rows of this section provide a particularly poor view of home plate, while the pole blocks other portions of the field for those sitting elsewhere in the higher-numbered seats.

Pavilion (Sections 151–160)

If you don't mind sitting on a bleacher bench (with a back), rather than in your own individual seat, we recommend these seats . . . err . . . bleachers . . . over the Right Field Boxes. The Pavilion is not only lower to the field and cheaper, but it also offers a view of the out-of-town scores—something the Right Field Boxes do not.

Wisely, the ballpark designers did not place seats behind the left field foul pole, where instead there is a runway used for field equipment. As a result, the pole doesn't interfere with the view for fans in left. In another good decision, the top half of the outfield wall is composed of a chain-link fence, which allows fans seated in the Pavilion a clear view of outfielders making plays on the warning track.

We especially liked the Pavilion seats near the left field line in Sections 151–153, which are much closer to the infield than Sections 156–160 in deep left left-center.

Leave the Watermelon and Cabbage at Home

The Rockies' Web site lists a number of items that fans are prohibited from bringing into Coors Field. Among these are such no-brainers as illegal drugs, fireworks, weapons, animals, backpacks, and beach balls. Also, remember that any fruit or vegetable larger than a grapefruit must be sliced ahead of time. But the two taboos we liked best were confetti and wineskins. Wineskins? They must be talking about bota bags.

Second Level

CLUB LEVEL (Sections 214–247)

The Club Level, which shares a deck with the press box, is set a bit farther back from the field than the Club Level at most three-deck parks, but on the plus side the Coors Club is fairly low, which keeps fans in the flow of the game. Sections 221–227 on the first-baseline and Sections 234–241 on the third-baseline are the pick of the litter. However, we still say it's pure madness that these seats sell for more money than first-row seats down on the field level.

RIGHT FIELD MEZZANINE (Sections 201–209)

Beginning in right field where the Club seats leave off, these are excellent seats for the price. We recommend aiming for the first or second row, perched above the right fielder. Even in the back row—Row 12—the overhang of the upper deck is not a factor. In Rows 6 and back a minimal under-hang blocks the view below of the right field warning track, but it's not too bothersome.

ROCKPILE (Sections 401–404)

A comparable bleacher seat at Fenway Park will cost you more than $20. Here, bleacher seats in the Rockpile cost just $4, the same as they've always been. The view really isn't bad. Because the seats are well elevated and set back from the center field fence, the view of the field is not at all obstructed by the under-hang of the section or by the outfield fence itself. Though these seats bear the 400 Level stigma, they are actually located a full level below the 300 Level seats in right field.

The downside is that unlike the first-level bleacher sections, the Rockpile features plain old metal benches, sans the backrests. But unlike many teams, the Rockies do not confine fans who buy tickets to this cheapest section to the area. Rockpile fans are free to roam and visit the rest of the ballpark.

We observed a family atmosphere in these cheap seats—in contrast to the beer-guzzling atmosphere in the cheapies at many parks.

A limited number of Rockpile tickets are always available on the day of the game. Tick-

Kevin and Josh

Photo by Josh Pahigian / Kevin O'Connell

ets go on sale two-and-a-half hours before the game at the Gate A ticket office. If the game is otherwise sold out, be sure to arrive early to wait in line.

Vinny, Vinny

As we sat in the Rockpile waiting for a game against the Mets to begin, Josh flipped through a pack of 2003 Topps baseball cards, while Kevin made small talk with a nice man named Stagno from Utah who was in town for an accounting conference and to do some rock climbing.

Josh paused when he came across a card for former Rockies player Vinny Castilla, then butted his way into Kevin and Stagno's conversation. "This stiff killed my fantasy team last year when he was playing for Tampa Bay, so I traded him," he said holding up the card. "Then he got traded to Houston—in real life—halfway through the season and started hitting homers again. And all along I thought his success in the National League was due to Denver's thin air."

"Maybe he's just a National League hitter," Kevin said, eager to disengage Josh and tell Stagno more interesting facts about Rocky Mountain National Park.

"You can say that again," Josh said. "And speaking of being repetitive, did you know Castilla hit 40 homers, drove in 113 runs, and batted .304 in 1996, then posted the exact same numbers in all three categories in 1997?"

Kevin and Stagno both raised their eyebrows and admitted that they hadn't previously been aware of that bizarre statistical aberration.

"And his slugging percentage was .548 in 1996," Josh said, "and guess what it was in 1997?"

"Five-forty-eight?" Kevin and Stagno said in unison.

"Nope, .547," Josh said. "Ain't that something?"

"It sure is," Kevin said. "Anyway, Stagno, how do you get those spikes into the rock if you're not already up there to drive them in?"

Upper Level (301–346)

If you're in Colorado primarily to gaze at the snow-capped Rocky Mountains and baseball is your second priority, consider sitting in the Upper Level. The mountains are visible from all upper-deck seats, and particularly from those on the first-base side and right field side of the park. Ironically, the worst seats in the house—those in Right Field Reserved Sections 301–304—offer the most panoramic and breathtaking view of the mountain range.

Generally speaking, the Upper Level at Coors Field is steep and expansive. Rows 1–9 hang below the midlevel concourse and are called Lower Reserved seats—even though they're in the Upper Level. We found this a tad confusing. Most ballparks call their seats in this area "Upper Boxes" or "View Boxes." There's nothing "lower" about these seats.

The Upper Reserved seats begin behind the Lower Reserved seats and span Rows 10–25. Rows 19 and back are beneath the sunroof for those in search of a shady or dry spot—depending on the weather.

Even all the way out in Section 347 in left field, the Upper Level seats are free of under-hang obstructions. It's another story entirely, however, in right field, where Sections 301–315 are obstructed by the under-hang from the deck below. The right field warning track is hidden from view for those in Sections 311–315, while even more of right field and center field disappear for those in 301–310. These seats are to be avoided like Rocky Mountain Oysters—but more on this so-called delicacy in our food sections.

Scalpers Aplenty

We found no less than a dozen scalpers aggressively peddling their wares on the corner of Blake and 20th Streets. They all had wads of tickets in their hands and one even had a Coors Field seating map attached to a string that hung from his belt; how's that for service? Perhaps more ticket offices should consider this practice. In any case, scalped tickets were selling at about half of their face value. So keep that in mind, and don't overpay.

Before/After the Game

On the whole, Denver is a decidedly Western city. Though Los Angeles is farther west and is often billed as the center of the urban West, Denver epitomizes the Old West. You'll find stores in town where you can buy grain for cattle, a saddle for your horse, and chaps. Much of this can still be seen in LoDo, whereas deeper into downtown the city gets all white collar and stuffy. But Denver is perhaps the most Western of the big Western cities. The towns in Texas are very Western as well, but

they also have a Southern influence that Denver does not. So be sure to wear your Stetson hat and cowboy boots and to spit some "tobbaccy" juice when you're in town.

Coors Field is located at the corner of Blake Street and 20th Street in the area of downtown Denver known as LoDo—an area full of old brick warehouse buildings, which was pretty seedy before the ballpark was built. And it had been since the days when Jack Kerouac and Neal Cassidy, the original road trippers, roamed these streets, hooting and hollering into the mountain air.

Denver's ballpark has had as great an impact on its neighborhood as any of the new Major League ballparks have had on their respective locales. If Baltimore and Cleveland were the prototypes for the ballpark as vehicle-to-urban revitalization movement, Denver is the mother of all examples. Abandoned warehouses and pawn shops continue to reopen as yuppie bars and loft apartments.

Getting to Coors Field

The ballpark is easily accessible from I-25's Exit 213 (Park Avenue). From the east or west, take I-70 to I-25 first. Street parking is not a viable option as the metered spots on 19th and 20th near the ballpark offer only two-hour parking and remain active until 10:00 P.M. except on Sundays when they are free all day. The parking lots immediately around the ballpark charge $15 per game, with a tailgating lot on the corner of Blake and 22nd Streets charging $20. The Rockies fans we observed tailgating had gone all out: many stood over full-sized gas grills. Hey, if you're going to pay $20 to park just so you can cook, you might as well do it up right. The cheapest parking spot we found was on the corner of Curtis Street and 19th Street, where for just $4 fans can park on the roof of the Greyhound bus station. We should mention that the stairwell leading from the rooftop garage down to street level was urine-soaked when we visited, but for the price, we couldn't complain. Also, after the game fans must enter the seedy bus station and take the elevator up to the parking level, which made even the ultra-calm Kevin a bit nervous after the night game we attended. But for the price, Josh still couldn't complain. For a safer bet, try the $7 lot on the corner of Market and 18th Street.

The Regional Transportation Department (RTD) offers bus service to the ballpark throughout Denver. The Light Rail is another viable option, dropping fans off at the 20th and Welton station, a short walk from the ballpark.

Outside Attractions

BALLS, BALLS, BALLS—AND STILL MORE BALLS

Leading to Gate E, a colorful arch rises above a pedestrian bridge on Wynkoop Street celebrating the evolution of the ball, with artistic representations of baseballs, tetherballs, meatballs, mothballs, matzo balls, cheese balls, masquerade balls, crystal balls, beach balls, dust balls, snowballs, rubber-band balls, lacrosse balls, jai alai balls, soccer balls, pearl balls, screw balls, typewriter balls, ornamental Christmas tree balls, foosballs, volleyballs, snooker balls, bowling balls, punch balls, skittle balls, kickballs, fireballs, racket balls, tennis balls, baseballs, softballs, roulette balls, wrecking balls, laurel balls, eyeballs, ball-point pens, spitballs, billiard balls, skeet balls, and more. All this courtesy of an artist by the name of Lonnie Hanzon, who built the arch in 1995.

CLOCK TOWER

A brick clock tower rises above the home plate entrance on 20th Street. The numbers on the clock appear in Rockies Purple, while a purple sunshield provides a small roof over the clock face, and an American flag flies above. This wonderfully understated finishing touch to the facade reminded Kevin of Ebbets Field, and reminded Josh that it was almost game time.

ROCK GARDENS

Huge flower pots reside on the plaza outside the home plate gate in the shadows of the clock tower. These hold small spruce trees as well as piles of baseball-sized boulders that add a distinctive touch to the area.

Kevin: "Check it out. They're growing rocks."

BALLPARK TOURS

The Rockies offer a seventy-five-minute tour of Coors Field that takes fans into the Club Level, Suite Level, press area, visitors' clubhouse, and visitors' dugout. At the reasonable price of $6, tours take place Monday through Saturday, departing from Gate C. For more information, call (303) ROC-KIES.

While on the clubhouse level, check out the bronze stars between the home and visiting locker rooms that honor each Rockies player who has made the National League All-Star team. Repeat All-Stars have multiple stars.

SPORTS FAN (1962 Blake Street)

This top-notch memorabilia and apparel store features old-time jerseys and hats for all four major sports. If you've been looking for that heinous old-school Denver Nuggets jersey with the rainbow-colored band over the city skyline, this might be your best chance to pick it up. Negro League and college teams are also well represented. Our favorite items in the store were the Colorado Rockies salt and pepper shakers shaped like beer bottles.

For those looking simply for dirt-cheap Rockies gear—you know, the team logo airbrushed onto a Hanes T-shirt—we recommend instead visiting the **First Base Warehouse** on 21st Street.

Watering Holes and Outside Eats

Second among Major League neighborhoods only to Wrigleyville, LoDo houses scores of bars and restaurants. Some predate Coors Field, while others have sprung up as part of the urban renaissance the ball yard anchored. Offering open warehouse settings, a wide variety of foods, including eats in the Southwestern tradition and an array of local microbrews, the eating and drinking establishments of Denver's Lower Downtown form a baseball fan's paradise. Arrive early and stay late. Cruise down 20th Street, Blake Street, and Wynkoop Street and see what strikes your fancy. Hop from bar to bar, and eat hearty! Mexican food is very good in Denver, at least by east coast standards. While most folks back east wouldn't associate the Mexican influence with an area this far north, this land once belonged to Mexico and many of the menus in town still do. As was the case in Cubbie land, there are simply too many fine LoDo watering holes and eateries for us to do them all justice in this format. But here are a few of our favorites.

ABOVE THE DOVE (1949 Market Street)

Located above a restaurant called Pinetop Perkins, Above the Dove—a rooftop bar—was jammed with partying young people drinking bottles of cheap beer when we visited after a game. Sweaty chicks were pressed up against sweaty guys as the music blared. If that's your scene, have at it.

JACKSON'S HOLE (1520 20th Street)

This enormous warehouse hangout offers three first-level barrooms as well as an outdoor patio at street level and another up on the roof. The bar predates the ballpark by nearly twenty years and has long been a favorite of Denver sports fans. Jackson's may be your best to catch an out-of-town game on the big screen via satellite.

EL CHAPULTEPEC (Market Street and 20th Street)

This is our favorite place to eat in LoDo. Preexisting the ballpark by many decades, El Chapultepec (literally, "the hill of the grasshopper," according to Kevin who took three years of high

school Spanish) combines dirt-cheap Mexican food with live jazz in the late-night hour. A winning combination, to be sure. Josh tried a beef burrito and a bowl of green chili and his whole meal cost less than $5. Kevin tried a smothered burrito with a bottle of Fat Tire on the side. We were both blown away by the scrumptious food. Legendary names in jazz—ranging from Branford Marsalis to Bill Clinton—are well represented at this famous club by the autographed pictures hanging in the barroom.

THE LAUGHING DOG DELI (1925 Blake Street)

This is our second-favorite place to grab a bite before the game. A New York-style deli, the Dog's best offerings include the delicious chicken Parmesan sandwich, the Ellis Island special (prosciutto, roasted red peppers, fresh mozzarella, basil, and pesto Parmesan), and the Staten Island Special (smoked turkey, fresh mozzarella, basil, and pesto). As for the Laughing Dog's motto: "Eat well, play ball, take naps." What else is there in life?

LODO'S BAR & GRILL (1946 Market Street)

This warehouse joint offers the most expansive menu of cheap eats near the ballpark, and a rooftop patio to boot. But back to the food: from steaks and seafood, to barbecue platters, to burgers and hoagies and Mexican fare, there's sure to be something on the menu for you. Josh recommends the smoked buffalo link sausage, while Kevin gives two tumbs up—er, make that *thumbs* up—to the Manny Burger—a half-pound patty topped with sautéed mushrooms, bacon, cheddar cheese, and avocado.

BRECKENRIDGE BREWERY & PUB
(2220 Blake Street)

With its variety of home brews, Breckenridge serves an authentic taste of the Rocky Mountains. Kevin enjoyed the Avalanche Ale, an amber with a clean-as-Colorado finish, while Josh preferred the oatmeal stout, which tasted like a blend of dark-roast coffee and semisweet chocolate. The menu features a variety of burgers and chicken sandwiches, and Southwestern specials like burritos, tamales, and sizzling fajitas.

WYNKOOP BREWING COMPANY
(1634 18th Street)

Aside from brewing its own beer, Wynkoop also bakes its own bread daily. The "big-mouth burgers" and "two-fisted sandwiches" are trademarks. Billiards, darts, and the bar's very own comedy club keep patrons entertained.

The Railyard Ale and Union Hub Light Ale are engineered for perfection. Josh waited until Kevin had had more than a few of each and was past his "beer window" before challenging him to a game of darts.

Josh: "So tell me about your 'beer window' theory again."

Kevin: "There is a very small window of time, where you are actually a better dart player, pool player, trivia player—basically any pub game player—after a few brews."

Josh: "And what happens after the beer window closes?"

Kevin: "Never anything good."

OUTSIDE VENDORS

There's no sense paying $4 for a small bag of peanuts inside the park when you can buy a big bag right outside the gates on the corner of 20th and Blake Streets for just $1. Pistachios, bottled water, Gatorade, hats, T-shirts, and scorecards are also for sale on the plaza outside the park.

Inside the Stadium

Far too often something goes horribly wrong when the new designers of the parks decide to build outfield landscape displays as the ballparks' signature characteristics. Usually these either end up looking exceptionally fake (as in Anaheim) or being dominated by advertising for whichever Fortune 500 company is sponsoring the extravaganza (as in Detroit). But at Coors Field, the outfield fountain and surrounding rock garden add a classy and organic touch to the ballpark. True, the spring may be dry more often than not, because of the shortage of water in the region these days, but make no mistake about it, the red and gray rocks surrounding the spring bed are real Colorado Navajo ruby sandstones and granite marbled river boulders—not Styrofoam replicas. And the many small Colorado spruces, piñon pines, curl-leaf, mountain mahogany trees, and gamble oaks sent us flipping through our arbor guide. All they need to do now is toss in a few rattlesnakes, and the area will be about as authentic as it can get.

To appreciate this unique ballpark oasis, we recommend taking a stroll out to center field on the first-level concourse, which allows fans to look down into the area and abutting bull pens.

We thought it was pretty neat that there's no wall separating the visiting bull pen from the rock area. Then we saw Tom Glavine uncork a wild pitch during his pregame warmups, which prompted Mike Piazza to go traipsing through the rockpile like a Little Leaguer looking for a lost ball in tall grass.

As for the bull pens, they are elevated to allow fans all over the ballpark a view into them. On a wall above the home bull pen is a tribute to former Rockies pitcher Darryl Kile, who passed away while he was a member of the Astros. The remembrance is identical to the tribute to Kile at Minute Maid Park in Houston: an oversized white plaque bearing number 57 and the initials "DK."

Ballpark Features
SMOKING GRASS
No, we're not talking about the stuff you used

to pack in the homemade steamroller back in your college days. We're talking about the playing field that features forty-five miles of underground wire that serves as a heating system, melting any snow that accumulates in April. The lawn is also equipped with a drainage system that can handle up to five inches of rain per hour.

LAVA

The gray warning track—as opposed to the red infield dirt—consists of 90 percent crushed lava and 10 percent red clay to ensure quick drainage. We applaud the Rockies for not taking the easy route and opting for a porous rubber warning track, such as the kind that appear at too many big league parks these days. Are you reading this in Baltimore, Irv?

THE WILD, WILD WEST

Behind the batter's eye on the first-level concourse in center field, a long mural depicts a landscape that is uniquely representative of Colorado. The mural include images of red rock formations, such as the ones that we visited at Pike's Peak in nearby Colorado Springs, and such as the kind you probably remember from the old Road Runner and Wile E. Coyote cartoons. Also pictured on the mural are Native American tepees, buffalo, railroad cars, miners at work, brick buildings under construction, and Mile High Stadium. This is a well-done tribute to the state and its history, and we suggest taking a pregame stroll out to center field to check it out. For those of you who need a nutritional incentive, plan on picking up a bag of Kettle Corn when you get there.

BAD BOYS, BAD BOYS, WHAT-CHA-GONNA DO?

Speaking of the Wild West, a strange hobby among some Major League players was brought to light after a Denver drug bust went horribly awry in September 1999.

While executing a raid, Denver police mistakenly went to the wrong house. When the plainclothes cops broke down the front door, the surprised owner reached for a pistol and was promptly shot to death. During the ensuing investigation and wrongful death litigation it was revealed that Rockies second baseman Mike Lansing was seated in the police van outside the house during the entire incident partaking in a celebrity "ride-along."

In the days ahead, it was revealed that fellow Rockie Larry Walker had accompanied the Denver P.D. on various assignments and Dante Bichette admitted to driving around New York city with police officers. "What gives?" we ask. "Isn't playing Major League ball exciting enough for these guys?"

Stadium Eats

Coors Field offers a respectable array of concession offerings, ranging from traditional ballpark staples to local favorites such as Mexican food and Rocky Mountain Oysters. The food we tried was consistently good, though few items stood out as being exceptional. While there are plenty of points of sale on the concourses, there was a noticeable lack of roving vendors patrolling the stands when we visited.

ROCKY MOUNTAIN OYSTERS (Trademark Food)

These deep-fried balls of wonder may be a Denver trademark and a featured item at the **Outfield Grill Barbecue** behind Section 153, but we don't recommend them. You see, Rocky Mountain Oysters are Colorado's cruel joke on the rest of the world. The gag is on the unknowing tourists, in particular. Rocky Mountain Oysters are one of the reasons that a book like ours is not just a road-trip commodity, but a road-trip necessity for baseball wanderers.

After making a concession run, Josh arrived back at the seats with a cardboard tray loaded with food.

"Did you get me some of those oysters?" Kevin asked, eagerly eyeing Josh's haul.

"I sure did," Josh said.

"Wow, they're deep fried," Kevin noted. "I love deep fried oysters—and they're huge. These are the biggest oysters I've ever seen!"

While Josh suppressed a laugh, Kevin hungrily dug into the ample portion of greasy oysters.

"They sure are meaty," Kevin said. "And tasty." He popped another in his mouth.

Able to restrain himself no longer, Josh finally burst into a fit of hysterical laughter, a fit so severe that he nearly wet himself. Actually, he did wet himself a little.

"What?" Kevin asked, again, and again. "What?"

"You'd be unbeatable on *Fear Factor*," laughed Josh.

Finally Kevin started to put two and two together. He examined what he was eating, then retraced Josh's steps and found his way to the concession stand behind Section 153. After waiting in line for a moment, he leaned forward to discreetly ask the girl behind the counter, "Excuse me Miss, can you tell me what exactly Rocky Mountain Oysters are?"

Blushing, the girl replied, "Bull nuts."

"Do you mean 'bull' as in a male cow?" Kevin asked.

The girl replied in the affirmative.

"And do you mean 'nuts' as in testicles?"

The girl nodded again.

If you can get drunk enough to try these, God bless you. Otherwise, steer clear. And for the record, the only way Josh could buy Kevin's forgiveness was by buying him pints of Fat Tire for the rest of the night. And even then, it wasn't until the road-trip car rolled into Phoenix a few days later that Kevin let go of his grudge.

"They were pretty good, though," Kevin finally admitted.

ROCKIES DOG (Dog Rating)
The Eleventh Best Hot Dog in the Majors

Unfortunately the basic ballpark dog comes precooked and prewrapped in a tin-foil bag—and we just couldn't bring ourselves to throw away three dollars on it. So instead we tried a fresh-made foot-long Rockies Dog, which came topped with sauteed peppers and onions. We were very satisfied with our selection. The grilled dog was meaty and tasty.

For foot-long specialty dogs, visit the **Top Dog** stand, which offers a Chicago dog, New York dog, Tucson chili dog, and the Denver dog, which features green chili sauce, shredded cheddar cheese, and jalapeño peppers.

BEST OF THE REST

We tried the **Kettle Corn** from the stand located in right-center field near the Rockpile and were glad we did. Josh nearly splurged and bought the three-foot-long $7 bag. But the smaller bag, for half the price, turned out to be more than enough corn for the two of us.

Coors Field may not be home to the spiciest bratwurst in the big leagues, but it's surely home to the biggest. This grilled behemoth is a meal in and of itself.

Steak Escape offers a Philly cheese steak as well as a chicken cheese steak. Both come topped with onions and provolone. We tried the steak and thought it was decent, but nothing spectacular. As is the case at far too many sandwich stands in the big leagues, Steak Escape precooks and prewraps its hoagies, so the fare is something less than fresh off the grill by the time it makes its way into fans' hands.

Rather than a lukewarm dried-out chicken sandwich from Steak Escape, we recommend ordering a freshly made mesquite grilled chicken sandwich from one of the **Fanfare** concession stands. Tenderized in a subtle but unique marinade, the mesquite chicken ranks right up there with the best ballpark poultry sandwiches in the Majors.

Blake Street Burrito offers a taste of Mexico. The chicken burrito we sampled rated higher than normal on our big league burrito barometer, but was nowhere near as good as the food we ate at El Chapultepec before and—then again after—the game. Did we mention yet that Josh returned home from the West Coast leg of our trip seven pounds heavier than he was when he left?

SAY "NO, THANKS," AND WALK AWAY

The Pub Burger, available at the **Outfield Grill Barbecue**, is larger and thicker than the average ballpark burger. But don't be deceived, it's still a frozen burger patty. And its preparation leaves something to be desired. Once the grill attendant that we observed in action was satisfied each burger was thoroughly cooked, he dropped it into a vat of burger grease on the side of the grill to stay warm. Presumably this container had been collecting grease all night long after beginning the night as a plain old metal bowl. In any case, we didn't want to eat anything that had spent more than half a second submerged in its artery-clogging depths.

Kevin was also less than satisfied with the snow cone he purchased. It either had too much ice or not enough syrup. Instead, consider buying a Frozen Lemon Squishy for twenty-five cents less.

STADIUM SUDS

Predictably, Coors and Coors Light are the featured beers at Coors Field. But to the Rockies' credit a fair selection of other macro's are available. Right Field Red and Squeeze Play Wheat are the house brews. That's right, Coors Field brews its own beer on site at the **Sandlot Brewery**. In a town renowned for its many great microbrews, you can certainly do better, but both drafts are respectable and worth a try.

Rounders at the Sandlot offers patio seating with waitress service on the first-level right field concourse—where the view of the field is poor. There is also a Rounders sitting area outside the ballpark on a patio at the corner of Blake and 22nd Street; here too, the view of the city is less than remarkable. The Brewery Building actually predates construction of the ballpark, which makes it somewhat unique.

You may notice the glassed-in **Mountain Ranch Club** on the second level out in right field, but don't get any ideas. The joint is accessible to season ticket holders only.

DESIGNATED DRIVER PROGRAM

After scores of free sodas obtained throughout the road trip, Josh's designated driver scam hit a snag in Colorado. He was horrified to receive—upon visiting the Coors Field Designated Driver booth behind Section 142 and filling out the necessary paperwork—a coupon for a nonalcoholic beer.

The Coors Experience

Denver is a city composed largely of transplants from other parts of the country. It took us nearly three innings at Coors Field to find someone in the crowd who was born and raised in Colorado—and even then, it was the Rockies Barney look-alike mascot named Dinger the Dinosaur. Owing to the low percentage of genuine locals, and to the fact that the Rockies are a relatively new franchise, the fans don't bleed Rockies Purple the way fans in St. Louis bleed Cardinal Red or the fans in Los Angeles bleed Dodger Blue. We got the impression that most folks leave Coors happy—regardless of the outcome—so long as the Rockies and their opponents combine to belt a few home runs and hang a few crooked numbers on the scoreboard. Great baseball may not always be on the agenda, but games at Coors are rarely boring. So sit back and enjoy the barrage of homers. It's the Rocky Mountain Way.

FEELING PUKEY?

If you travel to Denver by way of road-trip car, chances are your body will gradually acclimate itself to the altitude as you wind and wend your way up to the City in the Clouds. But those arriving by plane should beware. Sudden immersion in the thin air often causes dizziness and nausea. Because the air contains less oxygen, you'll have to inhale and exhale all the more frequently to get your cells the oxygen they need. All this respiration can lead to a mild case of dehydration, as with each breath your body loses a bit of moisture. Beware of drinking alcohol as well, as a beer consumed at high altitude will affect you more than you might be aware.

To counteract these effects, be sure to drink plenty of water before and after arriving in town. If, like Josh, you fly into town two hours before first pitch with already low H_2O levels and drive straight to the ballpark, and then spend an hour trouncing up and down the aisles of the upper deck to scope out the sight lines for your readers, don't be surprised if you find yourself retching in the Coors Field men's room by the time the third inning begins.

Kevin: "Are you sure you didn't eat any of those Rocky Mountain Oysters?"

Josh: "Yes. Positive."

Kevin: "Maybe it was that Coors Cutter you drank?"

Josh: "I don't think so."

PLAY ME OR SPRAY ME

On hot days ballpark employees dressed in purple roam the lower level equipped with water tanks on their backs. As fans cheer them on, these kindly men and women hydrate the fans with wide streams of cold water. It's not quite the outdoor shower in Chicago, but it's not bad. And when you consider that most of

---

SPORTS IN THE CITY

COLORADO SILVER BULLETS

IN 1994 an all-women professional baseball team called the Colorado Silver Bullets took the field for the first time. Led by Hall of Fame manager and part-owner Phil Niekro, the team was formed to expand hardball opportunities for females of all ages by demonstrating that women could play on the big diamond and with the little white ball, and not just on the little diamond with the big white ball.

The team was actually originally based in Knoxville, Tennessee, home of its main owner, Whittle Communications. But when the Coors Brewing Company of Golden, Colorado, agreed to sponsor the team on behalf of its Coors Light brand, the Colorado Silver Bullets were born.

Barnstorming across the South, Midwest, and West, the Bullets made national headlines playing against men's minor league, semiprofessional, and college teams. The Bullets posted a 6–38 record in their inaugural campaign, playing in Major League facilities like San Diego's Candlestick Park, the Oakland Coliseum, the Seattle Kingdome, and Mile High Stadium.

The Bullets improved steadily in the ensuing four seasons until disbanding in 1998 when Coors, which had spent more than $3 million to back the team financially, opted not to renew its sponsorship agreement. There's no denying, however, that the Bullets pried the door open a little wider for women who want to play hardball at a high level of competition. Two of the team's alumnae, Lee Anne Ketcham and Julie Croteau, went on to play for the Maui Stingrays of the Hawaiian Winter Baseball League, a developmental league at about the Rookie League level. And in 1997, Ila Borders, a left-handed pitcher who posted a 4–5 record at Whittier College, became the first woman to pitch in a men's professional baseball game for the St. Paul Saints of the independent Northern League. Today, more than three million girls and three hundred-thousand women play amateur baseball in the United States.

the young women in Denver keep in excellent shape by hiking, rock climbing, and mountain biking, it's even better.

RASCALLY JON (Superfan)

He may not make quite the impression that the brass quartet does outside Busch Stadium in St. Louis, but the grizzly old veteran who sets up shop on his motorized wheelchair across from Coors Field on the corner of 20th and Blake makes quite a ruckus. He blows into a clarinet while playing the tambourine and high-hat with a foot pedal. His name is Jon and he told us he's been entertaining fans outside the park since it opened. We give him credit for multitasking if for nothing else.

RUN FORREST, RUN

The Rockies' bull pen attendant is a fan favorite among those seated in right field. Thin as a rail and wearing coke-bottle eyeglasses, he sprints out of the bull pen toward the infield whenever a new reliever enters the game to deliver the pitcher's warm-up jacket to the dugout. Then he sprints back to the bull pen at full throttle. His running form is less than smooth and the fans let him know it, cheering and mock-jeering all the while he's on the field.

ROCKY MOUNTAIN WAY

When the Rockies are one inning away from victory, the ballpark DJ cues up Joe Walsh's "Rocky Mountain Way" on the PA system and plays the first few power chords to rev fans up with each ensuing out. Then when the final out is recorded the song begins in full force.

Stick around for a minute and listen to hear the baseball reference in the later verses of the song. It goes: "the bases are loaded and Casey's at bat . . ."

GET INTERACTIVE . . .

Behind the bull pens on the first level is the Coors Field Interactive Area. Whether T-ball is your thing, the video batting cages, or speed pitch, this is a great place to work out some of that excess energy that's accumulated during all those hours riding in the car.

The IA also houses a Fantasy Broadcast Booth where fans can record themselves doing play-by-play for a half-inning while the game is in progress. Truthfully, this is easy enough to do at home. Just turn down the volume on the tube and press the little red button on your tape recorder. The same goes for the **Scoreboard Memories** stand that allows fans to superimpose their name on the scoreboard of any Major League Park. To save a few bucks just take a picture of the scoreboard next time you're at your favorite park. Then, after you get the photos developed, black out the scoreboard with a Sharpie and print your name in yellow highlighter.

CLEAN CATCH

Whenever a fan catches a foul ball or home run before it has made contact with another fan, railing, seat, or umbrella, the ballpark staff presents the fan with a special Rockies pin commemorating her fifteen seconds of fame. Batting practice grabs don't count.

ARIZONA DIAMONDBACKS, BANK ONE BALLPARK

Air-tight Baseball in the Painted Desert

PHOENIX, ARIZONA

298 miles to San Diego
335 miles to Anaheim
367 miles to Los Angeles
586 miles to Denver

"THE CLIMATE in Phoenix is too hot for baseball in May, much less August. The players would sweat like stuck pigs and collapse from heat exhaustion, and the fans would get sunburned, and the grass would burn out. And what's the point in building a dome? No one wants to watch baseball on artificial turf."

If Arizonans had listened to backward logic like this, the only time they would get the chance to see big leaguers play would be during Spring Training, or by taking baseball road trips. Thankfully, "cooler" heads eventually prevailed, and the so-called experts were proven wrong by Bank One Ballpark—and its retractable roof and massive air conditioners.

From the exterior, "the BOB" does not appear to be a baseball oasis in the Phoenix desert. It looks more like the oversized hangar in which NASA builds its space shuttles. The massive retractable roof, open or closed, is the centerpiece of the structure. The two ends of the roof close up toward the middle as each side is comprised of three telescoping panels that can be operated independently or in unison. Nine million pounds of structural steel make up the roof, which spans nearly twenty-two acres.

At ground level the brick and steel attempt the retro-warehouse look of other new ballparks, but because the roof rises up so very high—two hundred feet—the supportive structure that must rise above the brick is also considerable. Huge white panels of white and green support the roof and give the ballpark its hangar feel. The BOB conjures up not baseball's antique ballparks, but rather the bold statement of what can and must be done to provide the necessary playing conditions in the often blistering summer heat of the Valley of the Sun.

Once inside, the BOB does little to disrupt the external impressions. When the roof is closed the BOB has the conditioned-air feel of a dome. The sweetness of fresh air does not dance in the wind. In fact there is no

aerial view

Courtesy of Arizona Diamondbacks

wind, only the blast of air conditioners that could have cooled the Death Star. Kevin, having grown up watching baseball in the Kingdome, is all too familiar with stadium ball. The closed roof creates darkness where there should be light and the indoor feel that so many new parks have tried to avoid.

When the roof is opened up, things at the BOB are improved considerably. Sunlight seems to liven up the grass and dirt just by shining on it. A breeze can be felt tickling your arm hairs, and the ill feelings of indoor ball subside, almost completely. But the pundits were right about one thing: serious alteration of the environment was necessary to make Phoenix a baseball-friendly locale.

The BOB is the biggest of the retractable-roof ballparks, and it surely feels that way. Advertisements abound, even on the enormous window panels at the scoreboard level that

close to seal the park up tight. Sure there's the famous pool in right center, but "huge with a capital H" is the overriding phrase that comes to mind. Most of the seats are between the foul poles, but many of those feel very far from the action. A close seat at the BOB, between the bases on the first level, does give a feeling of intimacy. But the BOB is a daring structure, closer akin to the dome than the ball yard, more like Astrodome than Wrigley Field.

But there are many innovations in this bold ballpark. The BOB has a roof, air-conditioning, and natural grass, a combination that had never been seen before it opened, not at the Astrodome, not at SkyDome. The BOB will serve as the model for cities longing for natural-grass baseball—sometimes under blue skies, sometimes not, when severe weather requires a roof and climate control. Before the BOB, it was considered impossible. After BOB, new ballparks in Houston and Milwaukee follow the mold—though the opposite temperature extreme is Wisconsin's problem—and will most likely be the solution if baseball is to remain in Minnesota.

The folks who designed the BOB didn't listen to naysayers telling them what could and could not be done. They went ahead and did what was necessary. But how? One secret to their success is that the retractable roof is kept open as long as possible before summer games, so that as much sunlight as possible hits the grass, keeping it green and growing. After some experimentation with Anza grass, Kentucky bluegrass, and other different grasses, Bull's Eye Bermuda was installed before the All-Star Game in 1999. Why is it better? We have no idea. We just know that it has performed best under these conditions. The turf gets as much sunlight as possible without overheating the stadium. The dual-action panels of the roof can be opened in a variety of manners to put the most direct sunlight on the grass without raising the temperature of the concrete and steel support structures.

Three hours before fans arrive, the roof can be closed up and the AC cranked on full blast. By the time folks enter the ballpark, it is thirty degrees cooler than it was an hour ago. In a city that is usually over one hundred degrees Fahrenheit during the summer months, AC is not a luxury, it's a necessity to prevent heat stroke.

Contrary to popular belief, the entire ballpark doesn't fill with cool air. Because hot air rises and gets trapped up near the roof, it is only necessary to cool the air at the lower levels. An eight-thousand-ton cooling system makes use of an enormous cooling tower located on the south side of the ballpark. Then air handlers push 1.2 million cubic feet per minute of cool air past air coils containing water chilled to forty-eight degrees. The cool air is forced down where it is needed by the layers of progressively warmer air trapped under the roof. The result: a method that ensures only the seating areas and concourses are cooled.

Josh: "Warm on top, cool on bottom? Sounds like the recipe for a tornado to me."

Kevin: "Everything's not a disaster, just the teams we root for."

Long the spring home to many of MLB's western teams, for years Arizona failed to draw a bid for its own big league club because of the heat. But with the advent of the retractable roof, it became clear that a sustainable facility could be built in Phoenix. Not only a ballpark that would protect the players and fans from the oppressive heat, but one that would not toss aside the nuances that make baseball magical: natural grass and dirt.

To design an indoor structure, perhaps it is best to go with someone who is familiar with such facilities. The architectural firm chosen for this massive undertaking was Ellerbe Becket from Minneapolis, best known for Boston's Fleet Center; The Rose Garden in Portland, Oregon; and Madison Square Garden. The official cost of the BOB was $349 million, though some estimates tack on an additional $55 to $60 million. The residents of Maricopa County funded $238 million of the project with a quarter-cent sales tax increase, and are thus the owners of the building, which is leased to the Diamondbacks. The remaining $111 million came from the Diamondback ownership, with $2.2 million per season coming from Bank One for the naming rights.

Construction began in November 1995, and the ballpark was ready for its official opening on March 31, 1998. But the first game at the BOB was to be the last exhibition game of the Spring Training season. A full house of 49,198 fans crowded in under the roof on March 29, 1998, to see the White Sox defeat the Diamondbacks 3–0. After losing the trial run and the official opener a few days later, the Diamondbacks lost four more games before posting their first win. Andy Benes, the same pitcher who lost the opener on March 31, registered the first win in team history as Arizona beat the Giants on April 4, 1998.

To say that the Diamondbacks have thrived at Bank One is an understatement. After their first expansion season was understandably a losing effort, the D-Backs have posted a winning record every year since. Randy Johnson, perhaps the most dominant pitcher in recent history, came to the desert to pitch for his hometown team during the 1999 campaign.

Behind the bats of Matt Williams, Jay Bell, and Luis Gonzalez, the Rattlers not only won the National League West that season, they also won one hundred games in the process.

Josh: "How many years did it take Seattle to win one hundred games?"

Kevin: "A quarter as many as it's taken the Sox to win the World Series."

The New York Mets put an end to the Diamondbacks' playoff run in 1999 when Todd Pratt homered in the bottom of the tenth inning during the decisive Game 4 of the NLDS. Johnson, though plagued by mediocre playoff performances (according to the media), still managed to pick up the Cy Young Award.

After a disappointing 2000 season, the Diamondbacks acquired pitcher Curt Schilling, who turned out to be the perfect complement to Johnson. Now the Diamondbacks had in place the "one-two punch" necessary for a deep playoff run. Schilling became the first twenty-game winner for the D-Backs, while Johnson kept striking people out with an ERA lower than a snake in a wagon rut.

The 2001 NLDS matched Arizona against the St. Louis Cardinals, and the series went the full five games. And five games was all it took for the two dominant Diamondback pitchers to dispose of the Braves in the NLCS. The young

upstart, a team in only its fourth season, was now ready to take on the New York Yankees, who were gunning for their fourth consecutive World Series. The D-Backs took the first two games at home, the second behind a masterful

TRIVIA TIMEOUT

Sun Soaked: Name the first player to drop one in the drink (splash down in the pool).
Scorcher: How long was the batting practice moon-shot hit by Mark McGwire that bounced out of the BOB window, next to the scoreboard.
Sunblock and Chapstick: Name the Diamondback player who is from Kevin's hometown?

Look for the answers in the text.

three-hit complete game by Johnson that saw eleven Yankees go down swinging. When the Series returned to New York, the Yanks rallied at home (as they always seem to do) winning three in a row to take a 3–2 series lead. It appeared as if a New York Four-Peat was imminent.

In many World Series, Game 6 is truly the pivotal game. Coming back home to the BOB gave the Rattlers back their venom, and they bit the Yankees hard in a 15–2 pummeling. But instead of rolling over and dying, as many losers of Game 6 do, the Yanks came out swinging in Game 7. With a 2–1 lead going into the bottom of the ninth, and their nearly unhittable closer Mariano Rivera on the mound, the Yankees dugout was all smiles. They thought—strike that—they *knew* that the game and the Series were all sewn up. Everyone in America seemed to know that this World Series was a done deal. All the Yanks had left to do was get their champagne-popping thumbs ready to do some uncorking.

Everyone knew, that is, except for the Arizona Diamondbacks and their loyal fans. This time luck wouldn't go the way of the Yankees.

A strange thing happened. The untouchable Mariano Rivera became mortal, if just for that one inning, and the Diamondbacks got to him. In as dramatic a finish to a season as any in recent memory, with two outs Luis Gonzalez tapped a single to left that scored Jay Bell and put the finishing touches on a two-run ninth, giving Arizona the World Series Championship. Bank One Ballpark proved to be central to the home team's feat, as the D-Backs got all four games of their wins at home. Randy Johnson shook off any concerns of his ability to pitch in the postseason, as he and Curt Schilling earned co-MVP honors. For the season Johnson won his second straight Cy Young Award, while Schilling finished second among NL vote-getters.

Though the D-Backs lost in the 2002 NLDS to the World Series bound San Francisco Giants, their season was by no means a failure. For as long as the Diamondbacks can hold on to dominant pitching and above-average hitting, they'll be able to contend, and fans in Arizona will have reason to cheer.

Sellout Index: 5% of games sell out
Seating Capacity: 49,033
Ticket Office: (602) 514-8400
http://arizona.diamondbacks.mlb.com

Getting a Choice Seat

Getting a ticket at the BOB is not the problem. It's getting a seat that won't make your nose bleed, or like you're watching the game from atop the Camelback Mountains. If you're after that "every seat is intimate" ballpark feeling, we can only suggest driving on to Dodger Stadium. Joking aside, intimacy with the baseball surroundings can be achieved at the BOB by getting a seat on the lower levels between the bases. These are, of course, the toughest seats to come by, so do follow the guide below.

The seating bowl has a medium grade to it, not steep, but steep enough so that you'll be able to see over the guy in front of you, unless

that guy played in the NBA. (Don't worry, those guys have their own luxury boxes.)

Lower Level (Sections 100–145)

Being that there are eight divisions of "Lower" sections, we'll try to simplify things a bit. First off, by the time you read this, the best seats of Sections 113–129 will already be gone, sold to season ticket holders and other high-level muckety-mucks. And these are the most expensive seats in the ballpark, so there are really only five divisions with which to concern ourselves. See, we're making it easier for you already.

Seats in Sections 115–128 are between the bases, and at right around $30, should be sought after. These seats will cost much more at smaller ballparks, so snatch these up and your BOB experience will be enhanced.

Low walls in the corners provide clear sight lines for nearly all of the first level, so that is not a concern at the BOB as it is in other ballparks. In the upper reaches of each section a good rule for the entire first level is to avoid any row higher than thirty-nine. It's not that the overhang is that much of an issue, it's that the industrial piping clinging to the bottom of the second deck is huge, heavy duty, and can block the view.

Seats in Sections 111–115 and 129–134 are still pretty good seats, but there is a great variety between the closest sections and the farthest away. Sections 115 and 129 are very nice, giving you all the advantages of the more expensive seats one section over (116 and 128) for less coin.

As for the next cheapest group of first-level seats (Sections 109–106 and 134–138) we recommend avoiding these altogether with a few exceptions. Most sections will have foul pole issues, and feel a bit too far away to merit spending $20. But there are four sections that provide an interesting wrinkle. The lowest seats of Sections 108–109 and 135–136 put you right down close to the field, with the added advantage of having the bull pens right nearby. If you can get down into the first ten rows, we say go for it. If not, you'll be happier paying more and sitting much closer without obstruction, or paying significantly less and sitting in the bleachers, also without the foul pole to block your view.

The bleachers seats in Sections 101–105 and 139–144 offer the best seat for the money at the BOB. There is a sight-line loss of the warning track in the bleachers, but nearly none of the grass is lost. Also a tad unfortunate is the gully between the bleachers and the actual fence. While the D-Backs use this gully well for handicapped seating—which we applaud, and which the BOB has in spades—we're never really fans of space between us and our chance to interfere with the ball. All in all, the bleachers offer the best bargain seats on the first level.

Or you could choose to pay the same price and sit an entire level up. That's right, the picnic area seats, which amount to 200 Level seats, are the same price as the bleachers along the fence. We'd like to interview the brainiac that came up with this one. Plus there are two sections of seats on either side of the batter's eye that protrude from the outfield wall in straightaway center and hang out into the field of play. This idea is really very poor, causing the home run line to waiver haphazardly.

Though not really a "seating" area, parties of up to thirty-five people can rent the pool/hot tub area—which is sponsored by a major credit card company—for merely $5,000 per game. If you want the good food, it costs extra. The five Gs cover the price of admission, pool maintenance, and lifeguards only. Also in the pool area are TV screens, because it's hard to keep one eye on your drink and the other on the game.

Infinity Diamond Level (Sections 200–223)

Finally, here at the BOB the name "Diamond" used in so many other ballparks makes sense. While the seats are mostly good the boxes themselves are tucked awfully far under the third deck. This decision goes a long way toward protecting the sight lines of the upper decks, but would most likely anger us if we were the corporate folks who'd paid extra for the luxury accommodations. We say kudos to the BOB. Thanks for thinking of the little guy first!

Upper Level (Sections 300–332)

The Upper Level is also broken down into many pricing sections—titled Home Plate Lower and Upper, Foul Line Lower and Upper, Deep Foul Line Seats, and $1 seats. These

home plate

Courtesy of Arizona Diamondbacks

sections range from $20 for the Home Plate Lower, which is way too much money for a seat this far up in the air, to $1 for seats in sections so far away they should have never been installed.

While the Upper Level seats all have sight lines that are very protected and offer views unfettered by any under-hang problems, this

---

SEATING TIP

WHILE ALL the bleachers are better seats than their counterparts in the corners, the bleachers on the left field side are closer to the field than those in right, and don't have that annoying space separating the wall from seats. Sitting down low in bleacher Sections 140–143 will offer the best view of the twenty outfield and corner sections, and at the cheapest price. But be wary: seat hopping into this section can be a bit of a problem as the ushers usually check for tickets.

Also the Upper Level is rarely filled, so if you're an experienced seat hopper, why not spend a single bill on these crappy seats, then hop on over to the good seats behind the plate? Come on—everyone's doing it.

---

upper deck goes on forever, steeper and higher than many of the cliff sides in the surrounding mountains. Therefore we cannot recommend seats in the Upper Level higher than Row 20.

In the sections behind home plate—Sections 310–322—you could probably get away with sitting as high as Row 32, which is the highest row. The view is a tad eagle-eyed, so, appropriately, there are plenty of birds living in the rafters up here, snacking on old French fries.

As mentioned previously, the BOB's AC unit does not cool the entire air mass inside. The higher you go, the hotter it gets. Seats in rows higher than twenty-five are hotter than blazes on a typical Arizona day—and the money you save on tickets by sitting up here will be spent on sodas, beers, ice waters, frozen yogurt, slushies, and the like.

Seats in Sections 300 and 301 do have under-hang issues, severe ones. But when you're sitting this far away, who cares if the right field corner is missing? You're so far from the action you might as well bring a portable TV, otherwise you'll miss much of the game.

The Black Market

Being a scalper in Phoenix (when the Suns aren't playing) is a bit like being a snow-cone salesman at the North Pole. Having said that, there are determined folks who make their living plying hot tickets to a large ballpark that rarely sells out. Whatever you do, do not pay more than face value for scalped tickets, otherwise Suckers Anonymous will want to feature you as its new poster child.

Before/After the Game

The BOB is located in Copper Square, a historic warehouse district between Fourth and Seventh Streets, and Jefferson Street to the south. Copper Square is a cultural center, filled with shops, restaurants, and bars. Though there is plenty going on outside, nearly all the baseball-related happenings are inside the park.

Kevin: "Are you aware that Arizona was once known as the Copper State, and produced more of the precious metal than all the other forty-nine states combined?"

Josh: "Makes you wonder why they didn't call the team the Copperheads."

Getting to Bank One Ballpark

Access the BOB from the freeway by getting off at the Seventh Street Exit from I-10 or I-17.

Parking studies have shown that there are somewhere between eighteen thousand to thirty thousand parking places within a fifteen-minute walk of the BOB, depending on whom you ask. Whichever figure is correct, the Diamondbacks estimate that at full capacity, fans at the BOB will only use some fifteen thousand. Lots run as low as $8 dollars per game to as high as $20. For a night game we found a nearly unlimited number of two-hour meter spots within a few blocks walk of the ballpark that could be plugged with quarters until 5 P.M. when they become free for the night.

While Phoenix does offer public transportation to the ballpark through several types of bus systems (http://www.ci.phoenix.az.us/PUB TRANS/pubtridx.html), a unique way to get to the game, or back to your car, is the bike taxi—or as we like to call it—the modern form of the rickshaw. Poor slobs on ten-speeds will pedal and sweat in temperatures of one-hundred-ten degrees Fahrenheit while you and your pals recline in comfort waiting for your frozen water to melt. Phoenix is a nice flat city for this type of transportation, but man were those guys sweating on the day we visited.

Outside Attractions

THE ENTRY PLAZA

Phoenix has more than its fair share of street vendors and pregame hawkers. All this activity comes to a head in the plaza outside the main entrance to the BOB. Radio stations broadcast live, there are pitching games, and of course, more vendors. All in all the atmosphere is very lively, in large part due to the music blasting from McFadden's, a nearby bar that specializes in patio seating and top-heavy waitresses.

D-BACK PRIDE

The Arizona franchise isn't bashful about celebrating its recent success. A huge banner that must be forty feet high hangs on the face of the BOB, depicting the 2001 World Series trophy. It's a wonderful image for passersby who might not otherwise get the chance to see the actual trophy displayed inside on the rotunda. Fans need only to drive by to relive their team's most important victory one more time, over the Yankees.

Kevin: "I'm no D-Backs fan, but man I loved that World Series. When defeat seemed certain, they came from behind and stole the game from the Yanks."

Josh: "You told me you changed the channel to *Behind the Music: Vanilla Ice* once Rivera came in the game."

Kevin: "I can still love it in retrospect, can't I?"

In addition to the photo of the trophy, slightly smaller pictures hanging above the ticket windows commemorate great Rattler's such as Randy Johnson, Curt Schilling, and Louis Gonzales.

GUESS IT BEATS THE OLD-FASHIONED PIPE ORGAN?

An interesting piece of artwork with a semi-baseball theme resides on the plaza where a roller coaster/obstacle course for little balls is encased in glass. Balls roll along tracks, are picked up by twirling arms that lift them to other levels of track, are dropped off from heights, and then land into canisters that set them rolling along again. Basically we believe the piece is intended to completely amaze and hold in awe the viewer who realizes that the balls will continue to make it along their precarious course ad infinitum.

Kevin: "It makes me feel very small and insignificant in the grand scheme of the vast and timeless universe."

Josh: "Spot me a few bucks. I want to try one of those hot dogs."

As for the exhibit's baseball theme, it comes into play with little bats and ballplayers serving as part of the obstacle course. Also, the melody of "Take Me Out to the Ball Game" can be heard faintly.

MISSION STATEMENT

One thing outside the ballpark that we've never noticed at any other ballpark is the team mission statement that appears in bronze below a statue of a generic Diamondbacks player near Gate K. The Diamondbacks mission statement reads:

> The Arizona Diamondbacks mission is to establish a winning tradition that embodies the genuine spirit of baseball; an organization to which all Arizonans will point with pride, which conducts its business with integrity and community responsibility; so that Arizona's children will grow up knowing the rich tradition that has made baseball America's national pastime.

So far so good, Arizona.

Watering Holes and Outside Eats

The BOB's neighborhood of Copper Square is surprisingly better than the hoods outside of most big league parks. Though this town's city blocks are long—like Las Vegas long—there are no massive parking lots surrounding the BOB, so access to eating and drinking establishments is that much easier. And while many of the places are chains (such as **Hooters** at 445 N. 3rd Street and the **Hard Rock Café** on the corner of Jefferson and 2nd), a number of unique spots exist to have a beer and/or meal. Plus Phoenix offers some of the best Mexican Food in the big league circuit, so do partake.

MCFADDEN'S SPORTS PUB (201 S. 4th Street)

While this prime plaza location originally opened as Leinenkugels Ballyard Brewery, that venture has been replaced by McFadden's, an Irish-themed sports pub. While Kevin was busy making comments about how the food wasn't Irish, and about how if it were a true Irish sports pub it would have been showing road bowling or Gaelic football on TV, or at least Liverpool soccer, Josh was noticing something quite different. Let's just say McFadden's competes with Hooters when it comes to hired help. McFadden's is a large establishment with plenty of seating indoors and out. It's as close as you can get to the ballpark and has a very reasonably priced menu. McFadden's music dominates the plaza: good if you like the tunes, annoying if you don't.

JACKSON'S ON 3RD
(Corner of 3rd and Jackson Streets)

Jackson's is close to the park and better than most all of the other joints in the neighborhood when it comes to spots for beer drinking and pregame partying. With air-conditioning, TVs everywhere, multiple bars inside and out, and a vast selection of beers on tap, we were impressed. Unlike other so-called baseball books, normally we would not give a hoot about the number of TVs an establishment provides. But at Jackson's there were even TVs on the floor and above the urinals for fans who can't stand to miss even a moment of *Sports-Center*. We give Jackson's our recommendation as the best place to go in the area for pre- and postgame entertainment.

The menu has few surprises on it: burgers, chicken sandwiches, barbecue, and salads; but the prices are consumer friendly. We tried a great little microbrew called Kiltlifter, brewed by the Four Peaks Brewery, and it was definitely worth sampling. But nearly any other beer you desire will be available either on tap or in the bottle.

MAJERLE'S (Washington and 2nd Streets)

Fans of Phoenix Suns star Dan Majerle will want to visit Dynamite Dan's sports bar. Though Dan hasn't played for the Suns in more than ten years, this pub opened in 1992 and is still going strong. The menu is not as interesting as the photos and memorabilia on the wall that feature Dan and his famous friends. The back entrance farther down 2nd Street will most likely be the only one open after games so don't get discouraged if the front door is locked.

COACH AND WILLIE'S (412 S. 3rd Street)

For those willing to spend a few bucks more on dinner, Coach and Willie's is a sound choice. From wood-fired pizza to filet mignon, this wonderfully Arizona-decorated restaurant is sure to please. The patio and the balcony are nearly worth the price of admission in themselves. This is the kind of place where players are more likely to hang out.

BARBARA'S SOUTHERN DELI
(Between 3rd and 4th on East Jefferson Street)

A deli that features fried chicken, catfish, okra, and gumbo, this might be the best place to get a quick, cheap meal before the game. However, Barbara's is small, without many tables inside, and in Phoenix sitting inside can sometimes be vital to your dining pleasure.

JEFFERSON STREET BAR AND GRILL
(Corner of 4th and East Jefferson Street)

Just a few doors down from Barbara's is this close-to-the-park, but uninspired sports bar. Dark inside, Jefferson Street is the choice for local boozehounds, as well as sports fans on the fast track to one day becoming boozehounds.

SEAMUS MCCAFFERY'S IRISH PUB
(18 W. Monroe Street)

This place is an authentic Irish pub and is worth a mention because Kevin seems to get some special thrill at pointing out every Irish Pub in America. A great sports pub if you're into *football*: not our kind of football. When they say "football," they mean soccer. When they say "American football," they mean football. But more often than not, they only talk about football.

COOPERSTOWN (101 E. Jackson Street)

I'm eighteen and I like it! But you've got to be twenty-one to get into this joint, named after 1970s rocker and golf enthusiast Alice Cooper. Cooperstown best describes itself as a place "where jocks and rock meet." It's kind of like the Hard Rock Café and ESPN Zone rolled into one restaurant. But the barbecue is their specialty, and its pretty good, though not terribly cheap. And the musical acts that play on the live stage are impressive.

SOLD ON THE STREET

Vendors line the streets hawking all kinds of goodies, giving the ballpark a real baseball aesthetic. We found everything from souvenir programs to Cajun peanuts, which by the way were delicious. The Vienna beef dog stands are a great choice for a pregame snack, and Kettle Corn is always good. But what we couldn't understand were the venders selling bottles of frozen water. We had both always called frozen water "ice," but the vendors outside the BOB call it frozen water for some reason. Since visiting, Josh has taken to calling really hard cold water, frozen water.

Inside the BOB

Bank One Ballpark might have the most refreshing main entry of any park in baseball, misting stations that gingerly spray entrants with refreshing cool drops of water. But sadly, that's where the misting ends. When you get inside your body acclimates very quickly to the air-conditioning, and because its one-hundred-fifteen degrees Fahrenheit outside, that means that it's only eighty-five degrees Fahrenheit inside on the lower level, and hotter than that as you climb up to your seats on the upper level. Clearly seeing a game in the BOB's AC is nothing like going to a movie in the summer and coming out chilled.

With very wide and open concourses that keep fans in close contact with game, there is plenty to do at the BOB away from your seat. A wide variety of restaurants and vendors inhabit the concourses. And the upper level provides

all the same offerings that the lower-level concourses do, which we appreciate very much.

Though the BOB does not like to be called a
dome, when the arched roof is closed up, it truly
stretches the definition of a retractable-roof
stadium.

Inside, aside from baseball, it's advertising
as far as the eye can see. Unashamedly, the
Diamondbacks have catered to the corporate
world, and perhaps that is one of the keys to
their quick success.

Ballpark Features

THAT'S SOME ROOF

Of all the ballparks with retractable roofs, Bank
One feels the most domelike, that is except
SkyDome, which bills itself as such. But the
BOB roof differs from the other retractables in
other important ways. First off, it does not
open parallel to either of the base paths as the
parks in Seattle and Houston do. The BOB roof
opens from the middle, following an imagi-
nary line that runs from foul pole to foul pole.
When the roof is open the outfield feels more
exposed than the fields at the other retractable-
roof ballparks do. But the downside of this is
that seats at both ends of the park are still covered when the roof is open, making parts of the
ballpark always feel indoors. Both Seattle and
Houston have huge areas outside the ballpark
where their roofs can telescope when opened.
This allows those ballparks to open up that
much more.

SIGNS, SIGNS, EVERYWHERE A SIGN

Six huge advertising banners above the outfield walls reside on panels that open up to
the outside world when the weather allows.
Each of these measures about sixty feet high
and sixty feet wide. When closed, they help
seal the BOB up tight for maximum cooling
and add to the feeling that this ballpark has
oversold its sponsorships. When opened,

statues

Courtesy of Arizona Diamondbacks

they give the ballpark the feel of a complex
mechanism with many controls. Plus, opening the panels provides much better views of
downtown.

Josh: "Do you think the sponsors pray for
sun?"

Kevin: "I don't think they have to."

While visiting Phoenix with the Cardinals,
Mark McGwire once hit a batting practice
homer that bounced out of the BOB through the
window just to the left of the Jumbotron. The
shot was reported to be 510 feet.

TWISTIN' BY THE POOL

The pool is as mandatory to the everyday survival of folks in Phoenix as the subway is to life
in New York City. Life is simply more enjoyable—make that "bearable"—because of it.
But for the price they charge at the BOB, you
could have a pool and hot tub built in your
backyard. Clearly this is for the corporate types
who are trying to impress their clients.

Kevin: "You want to take a swim, don't you?"

Josh: "I feel like I'm a kid again and it's
summer and I'm trying to work an invite from
my next-door neighbor."

Future Arizona first-baseman Mark Grace
became the first player to hit a home run into
the swimming pool while playing for the Cubs

on May 12, 1998. Less than a week later, the Diamondbacks' Devon White became the first player to hit two homers into the drink. White "went pool" on May 16 and May 18.

When the home team hits a home run, fountains located above the pool spew streams of chlorinated water into the air.

REMODELING NEEDED

The outfield picnic area is an ill conceived and underused area of the ballpark that the Diamondbacks might want to rethink during their first remodel. The picnic tables are too far from the field to make attractive sitting places, and the tables that protrude out above the field on either side of the batter's eye do more harm than good when it comes to the ballpark's aesthetic.

The batter's eye itself is little more than a black wall that rises from the field all the way up to the scoreboard, with a yellow home run line drawn across it midway up that continues across to the picnic protrusions on either side. So all that separates a home run from any other ball hit off the center field wall is a painted yellow line.

Kevin: "I'd call that unromantic."

Josh: "I'd call it un-American."

Above this mess that flanks the Jumbotron appear large tributes to the home team's success: banners commemorating the D-Backs' NL West titles in 1999, 2001, and 2002, their National League Pennant in 2001, and their World Series championship of 2001.

THE INFIELD

There is plenty of foul territory at the BOB, more than at most ballparks. And at the time of its opening the BOB was the only ballpark with a dirt track running from the pitcher's mound to home, a feature common to ballparks of yesteryear.

Kevin: "What do you think that adds to the game?"

Josh: "Who do I look like, Ty Cobb?"

Another understated touch that makes the infield distinctive is a slanted walkway cut between each on-deck circle and the batter's box. These almost form the shape of the Arizona A, but not quite. Still, they are unique.

SECOND HIGHEST ELEVATION

At more than one thousand feet above sea level, the BOB is the second highest ballpark in the Majors. Other than making the nosebleed sections actually give people bloody noses, expect the ball to carry approximately seven feet farther than it would at others parks.

Josh: "Seven feet, that's about the length of Richie Sexson."

Kevin: "It doesn't seem so far when you put it that way."

I THINK WE'LL PUT THE BULL PENS—HERE

The bull pens at the BOB sit behind the foul poles, half in and half out of fair territory. What does this mean? Shots that wind up inside the pens can either be home runs, or very long fouls.

COX CLUBHOUSE AND ARIZONA DIAMONDTOWN

Located on the first level, Cox Clubhouse is a mini-hall of fame featuring tributes to baseball's history, as well as to the history of baseball in Arizona. There are a good number of exhibits.

While visiting we learned that Joe Black was not only a character in a very mediocre movie starring Brad Pitt, but also the Rookie of the Year in 1952, going an incredible 15–6 for the Brooklyn Dodgers. He lost both World Series games in which he pitched, one in 1952 and the other in 1953, both against the Yankees. Why does Arizona care so much for Joe? Because he spent his latter years in Scottsdale, before passing away on May 17, 2002. And when you're a young franchise like the D-Backs, dying nearby is almost as good as being born nearby. It makes someone a local.

The ten themed areas of DiamondTown on the first level evoke the best of the baseball history that an ultramodern facility can provide. Video walls, three-dimensional exhibits, and a baseball chronology all bring to the forefront a sense of the game's nostalgic past. Our favorite displays were tributes to the "We are Family" Pirates of 1979, and to the 1986 "One Strike Away" Mets (Kevin's favorite, not Josh's). But perhaps the best feature of all was the series of murals depicting the history of baseball parks, dating all the way from Elysian Fields in Hoboken, New Jersey in 1845.

ENTRY ROTUNDA

On the first level of the entry rotunda is a mural depicting an abbreviated history of sports, with pictures ranging from medieval jousting in Europe and games of Native Americans, to Ancient Greece and Rome. Of course the display concludes with the formation of the Diamondbacks in 1998, the crowning achievement in the history of sporting advancement, from an Arizonan's perspective at least.

Encircling the upper levels of the rotunda are painted scenes of the history of the Arizona area.

Kevin: "Can you name the five Cs of early Arizona's economic prosperity?"

Josh: "Cattle, Climate, Copper, Citrus, and Cotton. I read the historical marker, too"

PETER PIPER'S PLAYHOUSE

The area behind the batter's eye houses a team shop and a "little folks" food area called the peanut gallery. Also available for the young ones who may be tiring of the subtle game that is our national pastime is an arcade area known as Peter Piper's Playhouse. Old-style arcade games like Skee-Ball are featured here. And the clubhouse comes complete with wooden lockers that contain uniforms from players all around the NL. This is undoubtedly one of the better kiddie areas in all of baseball,

and one that has managed to tie in a baseball theme.

Kevin: "Boy, someone in the marketing department really screwed up."

Josh: "What do you mean?"

Kevin: "Well, they named this place Peter Piper's, thinking that Peter Piper was the guy who blew his flute and led all the snakes out of the fairy-tale kingdom. But that was the Pied Piper. Peter Piper is the guy who picked a peck of pickled peppers."

Josh: "You realize that Peter Piper is a local pizza company, don't you?"

Kevin: "Oh. My bad."

Josh: "And the Pied Piper led rats, not snakes."

Kevin: "Forget I mentioned it."

THE CENTRALIA CONNECTION

FORMER ARIZONA first-baseman Lyle Overbay hails from the small town—Centralia, Washington—that spawned Kevin O'Connell. In fact, the two played their youth ball at the same park in Centralia—Wheeler Field. Lyle played exceptionally well for the Centralia High Tigers, while Kevin sat at the end of the bench for the Kiwanis Babe Ruth team. Lyle currently plays for the Milwaukee Brewers.

Stadium Eats

The ballpark food at the BOB will not rock your world. But this is not one of those ballparks where we recommend bringing in all of your food from the outside either. A decent meal can be had at the ballpark, if you're selective. The BOB has done a good job of mixing it up by inviting in small carts from mom-and-pop places as well as big fast-food chains. Try to guess which ones we're going to recommend.

HUNGRY HILL SANDWICHES (Trademark Food)
With five different types of sandwiches made fresh before your eyes, Hungry Hill is the best

thing going at the BOB. The meatball with sauce and Parmesan is a treat. The homemade sausage with peppers and onions make the other ballpark sausages—available at the regular concession stands—taste grizzly and greasy. Also available are Polish sausage, bratwurst, and Italian beef that made us feel like we were back in Chicago. And to top it all off, these delicious sandwiches are reasonably priced: meaning they cost about what you might expect to pay outside the ballpark for a quality hoagie.

OSCAR MAYER DIAMOND DOG (Dog Rating)
The Twenty-third Best Hot Dog in the Majors

Prewrapping this weenie in aluminum foil ruins an otherwise respectable dog. Diamond Dogs are pretty tasty, as Arizonans know, and can be purchased across the state—in packages at grocery stores, or on rollers at 7-11s. The dog is made of all beef and weighs a full quarter-pound, both of which we like. But dogs need to be pulled off the grill right before our eyes to finish high in the rankings. Sorry, Oscar, it's a tough competition that leaves no room for lukewarm meat and crumbly buns.

BEST OF THE REST

The Coyote fresh fruit medley is a refreshing treat available at the BOB. Fresh melon, grapes, and berries are all combined to form a zesty mix. Meats and cheeses are available to complement your fruit, as are bean dip and chips or even strawberries and cream.

Kevin: "What is this? Wimbledon?"

Carla's Crazy Corn is also a unique ballpark snack that we enjoyed. Carla mixes four types of corn together: jalapeño, Cajun, Parmesan, and chili. We were highly impressed.

Ben and Jerry's ice cream is always tough to turn down. And the stand at the BOB offers fourteen different flavors, which makes it almost as good as visiting one of their stores.

The **Taste of the Majors** stand offers one type of ballpark fare each night from the visiting team's city. And while this stand is in no way an acceptable substitute for embarking on your own baseball road trip and sampling all these foods in person, we applaud the efforts of the Diamondbacks for thinking along the right lines. It was fun for us to see which items they had identified as the trademark foods in each city compared to our own selections. PS: our picks are the correct choices. For example, a barbecue pork sandwich for Pittsburgh? What about Primanti Brothers? The D-Backs did manage to get things right in Philly (cheese steaks), Chicago (Chicago-style hot dog), St. Louis (toasted cheese ravioli), Milwaukee (brats), San Diego (fish tacos), and San Francisco (garlic Parmesan fries).

SAY "NO, THANKS," AND WALK AWAY

Unless you have kids, there is no excuse for eating fast food at the ballpark. And even then we're not going to endorse the idea. Read the book *Fast Food Nation* for more on this. In any case, there is a certain burger place, a certain sub shop, and a certain pizza place that are all over the BOB and that we recommend avoiding like the plague. Not specific enough? Okay, steer clear of **McDonalds**, **Blimpies**, and **Peter Piper's**. Alongside these belong the sausages of all types made at the **Grandstand Grill**. They are relatively tasteless, premade, prewrapped, and placed under heat lamps for what must be days. Pay the extra fifty cents and enjoy a fresh sausage at **Hungry Hill**.

The other obvious place to steer clear of is the **Friday's Front Row Sports Grill**. Once again we have to point out that most of the seats in this place have no view of the game at all, and we're left to wonder how they can call it "front row" when it's on the second deck tucked back behind the right field foul pole. Besides, it's a Fridays. There are thousands of them, and they're all the same. The only time we'd

PHOENIX, along with Florida, is one of those places to begin your road trip in March. Why? Because Cactus League Spring Training brings twelve teams to the Phoenix area. You can see all these ballparks at the beginning of the trip before heading out to see the big league parks.

Though widely spread across the huge valley, everything in Phoenix is just about forty five minutes from everything else. So why not see some Major League ball up close and personal. For directions and maps and more information log on to: www.azcentral.com/ sports/diamondbacks/03cactus/cactusindex.html.

Hi Corbett Field

(3400 E. Camino Campestre, Tucson)
At the spring home of the Colorado Rockies, you can sit in the box seats for under $15 or out in the sand pile for an amazingly low $2. Bring your flip-flops but keep in mind that it's a healthy walk to the nearest beach. The ballpark is nestled in a scenic valley between the Rincon, Catalina, and Santa Rita Mountains.

Hohokam Park

(1235 N. Center, Mesa)
The Chicago Cubs play their home games at Hohokam Park. The $5 general admission seats on the grass are the road trippers' viewing location of choice.

Maryvale Baseball Park

(3600 N. 51st Avenue, Maryvale)
Big Brewers fan, are ya? Maryvale is home to the Milwaukee Brewers while it rains in the Wisconsin spring. At Maryvale you can see pretty much the same team that will be on the field at Miller Park all year: only twice as close, and at half the price. Thanks, Uncle Bud!

Peoria Sports Complex,

(16101 N. 83rd Avenue, Phoenix)
Hosting both the Seattle Mariners and the San Diego Padres, the Peoria Sports Complex is as intimate as it gets. Lawn seats cost only $4.

Phoenix Municipal Stadium

(5999 E. Van Buren, Phoenix)
Oakland A's baseball takes up springtime residence in Phoenix, where the ball park uses the light towers that once stood at New York's legendary Polo Grounds.

Scottsdale Stadium

(7408 E. Osborn Road, Scottsdale)
The San Francisco Giants play their Spring Training games at Scottsdale. Although three decks high this ball park is perhaps the most expensive of all the parks in the Cactus League. But, hey, you get to see Barry and the Giants.

Surprise Stadium

(15850 N. Bullard Avenue, Surprise, AZ)
The Kansas City Royals and the Texas Rangers are the newest additions to the Cactus League, as is their ballpark, Surprise Stadium. The lawn is huge but not terribly surprising.

Tempe Diablo Stadium

(2200 W. Alameda Drive, Tempe)
Angels during the regular season, Anaheim's players are transformed into devils at Diablo Stadium during the Tempe spring. A grassy knoll beyond the left field fence allows a place for families to open picnic baskets and ball-hawks to scramble after home runs.

Tucson Electric Park (2500 E. Ajo Way, Tucson)

The Arizona Diamondbacks and the Chicago White Sox call Tucson Electric Park their springtime home. We like the name of this one even better than Diablo. Sounds like something out of the 1930s when baseball first got lights. The park is located beside Davis Air Force Base, treating fans to glimpses of stealth bombers landing and taking off.

recommend patronizing this Friday's would be on a day when there was no game. At least that way you could get a peek inside the ballpark on your way back from the bathroom.

STADIUM SUDS

While there are some nice beers available at the BOB (Fat Tire, Fosters, Amstel Light) the true fan of brews will want to head to the **Beer-**

garden in the left field Upper Deck area above Friday's. This is a singles kind of atmosphere, with a DJ spinning discs and lots of young girls downing beers. Need we say more? But serious ball fans will shake their heads disapprovingly at this party patio full of folks more interested in the potential hook-up than in the baseball game taking place hundreds of feet below.

The BOB Experience

From folks wearing strings of purple and turquoise beads, to the rattling of Diamondback rattles during rallies, the Arizona fans have supported their D-Backs through thick and thin—mostly thick, as this team has had much success and little adversity. They may not be the most knowledgeable fans in the circuit, but they understand winning, something their team has done plenty of since entering the league.

OLD-TIME ORGAN

That's right, this space-aged ballpark features an old-time pipe organ. Tickling the keyboard since the BOB opened has been a fellow by the name of Bobby Freeman, who previously played for the Phoenix Firebirds of the Pacific Coast League.

"THE SUPERFAN"

Arizona's superfan is named Susan, but the players know her only as "the Superfan." With piles of platinum blonde hair and a very Phoenix tan, the Superfan is always adorned with plenty of D-Back paraphernalia. She always has the same seats, a few rows up from the home on deck circle. But what launches Susan into superfan category is that she arrives at the ballpark as early as 2:00 P.M. for 7:05

games and stakes out a spot near the players' parking lot. Susan can be identified by her deep and husky voice when she shouts "Go Louis!" or "All right Curt!" She knows where every player is from, what his birthday is, what his kids are named, and so on. Susan can be spotted at the parking garage that adjoins the player parking area before the game, at batting practice while the D-Backs hit, and in her seat during the game. Aside from home games, she attends Spring Training and many road trips.

The D-Back players know Susan so well that there have been tales spun as to how she can afford to come to the ballpark everyday without working. Some say she discovered a few rock bands, while others say she gets her money from her ex who made a fortune as a computer developer. All we know for sure is that Susan is the number one Diamondbacks fan, bar none.

D. BAXTER THE BOB-CAT (Superfan)

Named by young Brantley Bell, the son of Jay Bell, the mountain lion mascot of the D-Backs has been patrolling the BOB since 2000. Josh wishes the team had chosen a snake as its mascot. Kevin couldn't care two hoots one way or the other.

AUTOGRAPH HOUNDS

Autographs can be sought on the infield side of the D-Backs' dugout prior to the start of the game. It's a very organized autograph session that only features a handful of players and begins promptly at 5:20 P.M. for a 7:05 start and runs precisely ten minutes. The Jumbotron counts down the time so players don't have to be the bad guys when they sign their last hat, then turn to leave.

SAN DIEGO PADRES, PETCO PARK

A Baseball Park Alas, in Sunny San Diego

SAN DIEGO, CALIFORNIA

125 miles to Los Angeles
350 miles to Phoenix
530 miles to San Francisco
1,270 miles to Seattle

PETCO PARK combines the best of the old and the best of the new in ballpark design and comfort. Now surely we've already said that or something very similar about one of the other recently constructed parks, but Petco does a superior job of providing both the ambience of the classic ballpark era along with the amenities we've come to expect in the twenty-first century. The ballpark caters simultaneously to those fans seeking an intimate old-time baseball experience and to those in search of a new-age day at the ballpark complete with all the bells and whistles of modernity. By any measure, Petco is a vast improvement over multipurpose Qualcomm Stadium, the Padres' only previous home.

At street level "the Pet" embraces the beauty of San Diego's early Spanish missions. The ballpark facade is composed of sandstone, stucco, and brick as well as steel. Tiles of attractive Padres Gold sandstone plate the lower levels. Rising above are what must be the tallest palm trees in the world, located on the roof decks of the ballpark's upper-level towers. The grounds at street level are exquisitely manicured, featuring jacaranda trees, bubbling waterfalls, and a courtyard full of airy palms. Also technically outside the facility is the "park at the park," an elevated grassy knoll beyond the center field fence that can accommodate as many as twenty-five hundred surfer dudes and surfer babes who mingle on the lawn while watching the game with one eye. For years Cactus League fans have been sunbathing during Spring Training on the grassy embankments beyond the Arizona park's outfield fences. Regular-season sunbathers were long overdue in the Major Leagues. And what better place for them than in laid-back and always sunny Southern California?

As for the clash of modern technology with the pastoral grand old game, well it's really no clash at all, even though a number of seats come

construction

Photo by Kevin O'Connell

equipped with computer terminals that allow fans to surf the Web Net, access player stats, and order food to be delivered to their seats. We know this sounds like the kind of thing we'd normally pan. But c'mon. Stats and food made easy. Why not? Even if you still object, not to worry—your limited road-trip budget won't get you anywhere near these high-priced seats.

But your seats are likely to be pretty decent wherever you wind up sitting inside the Pet. A revolutionary "fractured" approach to the ballpark seating configuration creates clusters of independently angled sections that all point toward the batter's box at slightly different angles. This makes it impossible to walk the full circumference of the park on the upper levels, but having good sight lines will always be more important than being seat-hopper friendly in our book. And Petco Park offers quality views from all levels. This is something no one ever said about Qualcomm, at

least no sober person, and not when it came to baseball.

A few days after the Padres were swept by the Yankees in the 1998 World Series, the voters of San Diego approved a proposition to provide partial public funding for a new downtown ballpark. Under the plan, the city kicked in $304 million of the project's $457 million budget and the Padres contributed the rest. The ballpark cost $285 million to build, with the remaining portion of the price tag attributed to land acquisition and infrastructure. Most of the city's financial support came from newly issued municipal bonds to be paid back with the revenue generated by a new hotel tax. This makes good sense for the city and its residents. Let the tourists pay a little more when they're in town, and let the locals reap the benefits. We inconvenienced friends and relatives for places to stay during our road trip (and you should too), so the hotel tax didn't bother us one bit.

Petco Park was designed by HOK, the architectural firm that has surfed along the leading edge of the recent ballpark construction wave. Fans who have been to Baltimore will note the similarities between the use of Baltimore's B&O Warehouse and San Diego's landmark Western Metal Building in the two ballpark complexes. Both brick behemoths loom over their respective playing fields—the B&O over Oriole Park's right field, the Western Metal Building over Petco's left field. But unlike the B&O, part of the Western Metal Building actually juts out into the field of play at Petco. The building's southwest corner forms the left field foul pole. That's right, the ballpark was constructed, literally, around this old masonry building. If the ball hits one face of the building, it's a long foul, if it hits the other, it's a home run. The building also houses restaurants and observation suites for high rollers, as well as a rooftop standing-room area. What a unique trademark feature to build a ballpark around. And to think, we were starting to feel like we'd seen it all.

Petco Park was originally slated to open in April 2002, but several lawsuits brought against the city by citizens opposed to the hotel tax led to a construction halt in 2000. Since San Diego couldn't sell municipal bonds backed by the tax hike until the disputes were resolved, there was no money to continue the project. After construction resumed, the Friars struck a naming-rights deal with Petco, the familiar pet-supply retailer. Just a few days after announcing the twenty-two-year, $60 million agreement in January 2003, the Padres again faced resistance from the local community when PETA called for the Padres to cancel the agreement. PETA was boycotting Petco (the store, not the yet-to-be-completed ballpark) on the grounds that an unacceptable number of animals died each year from diseases and overcrowding while in Petco stores.

Josh: "PETA . . . are these the same soy-huggers who petitioned the Brewers to add a tofu-dog to the Milwaukee Sausage Races?"

Kevin: "Yup."

Josh: "And the same bean-fryers who forced the White Sox to provide a game-day pet-sitting service at US Cellular Field?"

Kevin: "That, I cannot verify, but I've heard rumors they may have been at the negotiating table."

After joining the National League in 1969 as an expansion team along with the Montreal Expos, the Padres played their first thirty-five seasons in the multipurpose, multinamed stadium that continues to serve as home to the National Football League Chargers. Padres management may have planted decorative palm trees beyond the outfield fences, but make

Qualcomm interior

Photo by Kevin O'Connell

no mistake about it, the stadium currently known as Qualcomm was one of the cookie-cutters. It wasn't the worst cookie-cutter to ever come down the pike, and it served the Padres well for many years, but in the end, it was wearing out its welcome for baseball. The stadium's main problem was that it was too gigantic to provide an authentic ballpark experience, especially after it was remodeled in 1983 to add ten thousand extra seats in right and center field for football. This expansion increased the stadium's seating capacity to more than sixty-seven thousand. Perfect for hosting Super Bowls, lousy for baseball. And lousy for regular season football too. The Chargers rarely sell out the four-level stadium, which means the city (as per an agreement with the team) must buy any unsold tickets from the Chargers. This really eats at local residents whose tax money is spent to subsidize the NFL.

From 1967 until 1980 the Chargers' present facility and the Padres' longtime facility was called San Diego Stadium, and from 1981 until 1996 it was called Jack Murphy Stadium in honor of the local sports editor who campaigned to bring a Major League team to San Diego. After Murphy championed a movement to garner support for a big league squad in town, a 1965 voter referendum approved construction of the $28 million stadium in Mission Valley. This suburban neighborhood had previously housed Westgate Park, which belonged to the Triple-A Pacific Coast League Padres.

If ever a city paid its dues before earning a team in the Show, that city is San Diego. The PCL Padres migrated to town from Salt Lake City, Utah, in 1936. In just their second season in Southern California, the PCL Padres captured the league championship buoyed by the play of slugging native son Ted Williams, just ninteen years old at the time. Theodore Samuel Williams was born in San Diego on August 30,

1918, just a few weeks before the Red Sox would win their last, or "most recent" as Josh prefers to say, World Series. Williams would fight in two foreign theaters of war and put the finishing touches on a Hall of Fame career with the Red Sox, before groundbreaking would take place for a new stadium in San Diego on Christmas Eve, 1965. A year and a half later, the Chargers dedicated the facility on August 20, 1967, with a preseason loss to the Detroit Lions. With a stadium in place, Major League Baseball awarded San Diego a National League franchise in May of 1968. Less than a year later, the Padres fielded their first starting nine.

Big league ball was not an immediate hit in San Diego. And while some might argue that hardball still hasn't captured the hearts of sports fans in this town to the degree that it has in other west coast cities, the baseball culture and interest in the team have grown considerably since the team's early days. The Padres didn't surpass the one million mark in home attendance in any of their first five campaigns and nearly jumped town for Washington, D.C., following the 1973 season. By early 1974 team owner C. Arnholt Smith had found a prospective buyer who planned to move the franchise to the nation's capital. New uniforms were being manufactured, and the team's front office employees were packing for the move. But at the last minute Ray Kroc, a San Diego native who had made his fortune building McDonald's fast-food franchises, jumped in and purchased the team. Kroc vowed to make the Padres viable in his hometown.

The team was atrocious before Kroc took the helm. In their first five seasons, the Padres never finished closer than 28½ games out of first place in the National League's newly formed West Division. The team averaged just six-hundred thousand fans per year during that time, or seventy-four hundred per home game. Ouch! Even the Montreal Expos, who entered the National League at the same time attracted a million fans in each of their first six seasons. And they were playing in the barren snowbelt known as the Great White North. It is important to note, however, that California baseball in general was not flourishing when the Padres entered the league. The Oakland A's, California Angels, and San Francisco Giants did poorly at the gate in the late 1960s and early 1970s, attracting less than a million fans per year themselves. Only the Dodgers thrived on the West Coast, routinely welcoming two million fans per season to Dodger Stadium.

In any case, the Padres finished last again under Kroc in 1974, forty-two games behind the first-place Dodgers, but attendance jumped from 611,000 the year before to 1,075,000, thanks to the ray of hope Kroc had provided. In the years ahead, the emergence of exciting rookies like Dave Winfield and Ozzie Smith, and the acquisition of veteran stars like Rollie Fingers, Gaylord Perry, Steve Garvey, and Goose Gossage finally gave the Padres a foothold in San Diego.

Josh: "Didn't San Francisco's Willie McCovey play his final season with the Pads?"

Kevin: "Yeah. 'Stretch' became 'Big Mac' at the McDonalds owner's insistence."

In 1984 a San Diego team led by Tony Gwynn, Kevin McReynolds, Graig Nettles, and the tireless Garvey won three straight games in the National League Championship Series to post a come-from-behind three-games-to-two win against the Cubs and advance to the World Series. But Detroit proved too powerful for The Friars in the Series. Jack Morris tossed two complete game wins, leading the Tigers to a four-games-to-one victory.

In 1998 the Padres tasted postseason champagne again after beating the Braves four games to two in the National League Championship Series. But the Yankees swept the Padres in the October Classic. Although the Padres lost both of their home games in the Series, including the clincher, the 1998 World Series would represent one of Qualcomm's greatest baseball moments. More than sixty-five thousand fans were on hand the night the Yankees closed out the Friars with a 3–0 shutout in Game 4.

Concrete and massive, Qualcomm offered very few features about which baseball fans might now wax poetic. Large parcels of the foul territory in the right field and left field corners were not visible from the infield due to the configuration of the seating bowl. The Jumbotron would get so hot that fans in the back rows would feel the heat burning through their shirts. The foul poles were actually two feet behind the outfield fences. But the stadium did play host to some memorable moments, like Willie Mays's six-hundredth career home run in 1969, and the ten innings of shutout ball pitched by the Dodgers' Orel Hershiser in 1988, which extended his consecutive scoreless innings streak to fifty-nine frames, breaking Don Drysdale's Major League record. Hershiser didn't pick up the win though, as the Padres prevailed 2–1 in sixteen frames. In 1995 another game went into extra innings tied at 0–0, as Pedro Martinez, then of the Montreal Expos, pitched nine perfect innings against the Padres before losing his perfect game and no-hitter in the bottom of the tenth. Martinez still got a 1–0 victory with help from his bull pen.

Perhaps Qualcomm's most ignominious moment came in 1990 when Padres management made the ill-fated decision to let actress Roseanne Barr sing the "Star Spangled Banner" before a game. After a purposely off-key rendition of the National Anthem, Roseanne theatrically grabbed her crotch and spit. Though the comedian claimed she was parodying the antics of ballplayers, her joke was lost on the crowd, which booed lustily as the hefty hussy was escorted from the field by then hubby Tom Arnold. The clip replayed on TV stations across the country for months, rarely alongside favorable commentary. At least Tom eventually moved on to bigger and better things with *The Best Damn Sports Show, Period.*

And now San Diego has moved on, leaving *its* bloated old girl—Qualcomm Stadium—in its past. Only time will tell if Petco Park and the increased revenue it generates for the team will propel the Padres to their first world championship.

Getting a Choice Seat

We didn't see a game at Petco Park during our 2003 road trip because the ballpark was not yet completed, though it was originally supposed to be ready by 2002. Blame it on those silly lawsuits back in 2000. But the good news is that we were treated to a sneak preview of Petco, which allowed us to check out the sight lines from a number of different seating areas. And we were very impressed.

Don't let that forty-six thousand capacity fool you. Petco is relatively small. There are actually only forty-two thousand fixed seats on the ballpark's three seating levels. The other four thousand spots are scattered between an outfield picnic area known as the "park at the park" and several standing-room locations.

Nearly every seat in the Pet is a winner. An extended cantilever supports the upper deck, bringing fans seated there closer than usual to the playing field, and the unique design of the seating bowl offers fragmented "seating neighborhoods" that all point toward the plate at their own angle.

Padres management is committed to leaving a number of Field Level seats available for day-of-game purchase only. We think this is a great idea and hope it catches on in other cities. So don't rule out the possibility of nab-

bing decent last-minute seats. But do arrive at the box office early, if you hope to score.

TRIVIA TIMEOUT

Flipper: Name the first player to enter the Baseball Hall of Fame with a Padres hat on his plaque.
Free Willy: When the Padres "hosted" the first Opening Day game ever played outside the United States or Canada, where did they play?
Shamu: Name the only two Cy Young Award winners to retire with losing records for their careers? (Hint: both won the award while pitching for the Padres.)

Look for the answers in the text.

Field Level (Sections 101–135)

The Field Level extends thirty-nine rows on the infield and forty-four rows in the outfield. Yes, this is a deep first level. There are nearly fifteen thousand seats on the first level between the foul poles at Petco, while Qualcomm offered only seven thousand such seats.

Sections 101 and 102 are behind the plate, with even-numbered sections continuing on the left field side and odd-numbered sections on the right. The first five rows of seats on the infield are reserved for members of the Padres Premier Club. The next best seats are in Rows 6–22 below the midlevel concourse in Sections 100–110, and those belong exclusively to season ticket holders. Further back are the Field Reserved seats (Rows 36–44) tucked underneath the Club Level. These should be avoided because of the overhang, which blocks the view of fly balls.

The best seats likely to be available to the average member of the ticket-buying public (read you) are in Rows 26–35 of the Field Reserved

Seating Capacity: 46,000
Ticket Office: (877) FRIAR-TIX
www.sandiegopadres.mlb.com

sections just beyond the first- and third-base bags. Row 26 is the first row behind the walkway, which is set down low enough to not ruin the view for "front-row" seat holders. We recommend Sections 111 and 112, just beyond the corner bags. If you want to get closer to the field with a lower row number and are willing to sacrifice your proximity to the plate to do so, shoot for Field Box Sections 116 to 124 in the outfield.

Sections 125 to 137 are located in right field home run territory—with two levels of seating above them. The foul pole obstructs the view of the batter's box for those in Section 127, and bisects the outfield for those in Section 125.

Sections 126 to 134 in left field not only offer fans the hope of catching a home run ball, but the chance to sit near legendary superfan Harry "the Heckler" Maker, and Josh's wife's cousin Michael Hernandez, a certified bleacher bum and Heckling Harry's protégé.

Club Level (Sections 201–235)

At fifteen rows deep, the Club Level contains more than five thousand seats, many of which come complete with waiter/waitress service. The level also houses four lounges. In our book though, an afternoon spent in the outfield bleachers easily trumps any Club experience. Although, we must admit this is a low Club level that offers excellent views.

Sections 225 to 235 are located in the second deck in home run territory in right field, while Sections 226 to 230 are in homer territory in left. Although these sections are on the Club Level, they do not come with Club privileges. The seats in right field seemed far from the action to us. And the foul pole blocks the view of the plate for many of the seats in Section 225.

Upper Level (Sections 300–328)

The first several rows of Petco Park's upper deck are called the Upper Boxes. These sell for $4 more than seats in the Upper Reserved (Rows 7–27) located behind the concourse. We suggest throwing down the extra four bills to sit in one of the deck's first rows. What's $4? You can't even get a hot dog at most parks for $4 these days.

The midlevel concourse is sunken adequately to allow fans in the first few rows of the Upper Reserved to see over the walkway traffic. The railings of the stairways leading to the Upper Reserved, however, present something of an obstruction for fans seated in Rows 9 through 11.

In the outfield, the under-hang of the deck below presents a slight obstruction. Expect to lose view of balls hit into the nearest outfield corner if you're seated in Sections 314 through 328. The worst seats in the house are in Section 328 where the Western Metal Building blocks most of left field.

If you'd like to call balls and strikes, stake out a spot in Section 300, directly behind (and above) home plate.

Bleachers

The bleacher section in right-center field provides benches in one of the deepest parts of the outfield. These are also behind "the Beach" party area. Situated as they are, these are exceptionally far from the infield. Heck, they're not even that close to the outfield. While usually we counsel fans to get as low to the action as possible, in this park we recommend upper-level seats on the infield rather than these bleachers.

SEATING TIP

THE FIRST ROW of seats in Section 124 near the Western Metal Building is Row 14. So if you want to sit down near the field, pass up that fifth-row seat in Section 120 or that third-row seat in Section 122, and aim for Section 114, Row 14. Just be advised that the large brick building immediately to your left may block your view of the left field fence.

Park at the Park

The grassy park beyond the outfield fence has room for twenty-five hundred fans. Quasi fans with short attention spans are encouraged to spread out a picnic blanket here or throw a Frisbee. As far as we know, however, volleyball nets and half barrels are prohibited. This is a unique place but it's not a quality locale from which to watch a baseball game. We appreciate the see-through outfield fences though that maximize fans' views of outfielders chasing deep fly balls.

Standing Room

The ballpark designers went to great lengths to ensure that fans have room to linger and lounge at Petco, whether by choice or necessity in the event of a sellout. Petco can accommodate fifteen hundred standing-room ticket holders in designated standing areas on all three levels. Our favorite standing area is on the roof of the Western Metal building, some eighty feet above the field.

The Black Market

As with any of the new parks, tickets will be somewhat hard to find for the first few years, then will become increasingly more available as the novelty wears off and fans realize the team still stinks. This may happen sooner rather than later in San Diego—a city that offers plenty of other tourist destinations, ranging from the beach to the zoo to the mountains to nearby Tijuana, Mexico.

Before/After the Game

The city of San Diego and its voters agreed to finance the lion's share of the new ballpark in the hope that it would anchor a massive urban revitalization effort. The newly minted Ballpark District consists of twenty-six blocks that just a few years ago represented one of San Diego's seediest neighborhoods. Keep in mind, however, that a "seedy" neighborhood in America's Finest City is still nicer than 75 percent of the urban hoods in the country.

Today, the Ballpark District is still seeking its ultimate identity. Some new businesses will open and thrive while others will open and fail. Likewise some of the district's old businesses will catch the wave of the new park, while others will splash down face-first into oblivion. Eventually, the streets will chisel out their own unique landscape—reflecting something of their previous roots and something of the baseball culture that has moved in next door. Hey, it worked in Cleveland and Colorado, so why not San Diego?

Getting to Petco Park

The ballpark is accessible from five major freeways: I-5, I-805, I-15, Highway 163, and Route 94. The intersection of Route 5 (which runs north and south) and Route 94 (east and west) is about a mile northeast of the ballpark. As part of the new ballpark initiative, San Diego has marked all of these roads with signs pointing fans in the direction of Petco. The ballpark is adjacent to the San Diego Convention Center, bordered by 7th Avenue, K Street, Harbor Drive, and 10th Avenue. L Street serves as a game-day pedestrian mall between 7th and 10th Avenues.

On-site parking is limited to five thousand spaces, which seems like a low number. Chalk it up as the price fans pay to have their ballpark located in an actual city neighborhood. Private lots provide another eleven thousand spots within the Ballpark District. And fans wishing to avoid the parking scene and traffic may take advantage of one of the several MTS light-rail trolley stations within walking distance of the ballpark. The Orange Line's Seaport Village, Convention Center, and Gaslamp Quarter stations are all within a few blocks of

Petco. The trolley is affordably priced at $1.25 per ride.

Watering Holes and Outside Eats

It will take time for local fans to make the transition from frequenting a suburban stadium in the middle of nowhere to frequenting an urban ballpark in a happening entertainment district. Many locals came of age as fans tailgating in the Qualcomm lot with their friends and relatives. It's all they know. It's all they want in the way of a pregame ritual. And some fans are threatening to continue tailgating at the Q after Petco opens, even if it means missing the start of the game to ride the trolley from the old park to the new one. Given time, we think even these diehards will become accustomed to going out for eats and drinks downtown. They might even find they enjoy not having to cook, and that they prefer fresh pints of microbrews rather than lukewarm cans of macrodraft out of their cooler. As baseball fans claim this area of the city as their own, their likes and wonts will dictate which preexisting downtown establishments become pregame hot spots. In the meantime, many fans will doubtlessly continue to frequent their favorite bars and restaurants near Qualcomm. So here are a few predictions as to which downtown joints will become popular among Friars fans in the years ahead, followed by a few of the old favorites.

GASLAMP QUARTER

The Gaslamp Quarter is an old warehouse and historical area that is already an established entertainment destination. It can be distinguished by the gas lamps that serve as streetlights. The neighborhood has been through hard times, but the city is committed to improving it. The ballpark and new convention center right across the street should go a long way toward accomplishing this. Stroll down Fourth, Fifth, or Sixth Avenues and you'll find scores of bars and restaurants from which to choose.

HENNESSEY'S (708 Fourth Avenue)

This reasonably priced local chain serves food until 1:00 A.M. The Pub offers an extensive menu of burgers and sandwiches, as well as entrées in the Irish and American traditions. The Baseball Steak is a thickly cut sirloin (roughly the shape of a baseball) served with burgundy wine sauce.

SAMMY'S WOODFIRED PIZZA (770 Fourth Avenue)

Another local chain, Sammy started serving his unique wood-cooked pizza pies in San Diego in 1000 with a restaurant in Mission Valley. Kevin waited until Josh had eaten half of his sausage pizza to tell him that it was actually Sammy's special *duck sausage* he was enjoying. Kevin considered it sweet revenge for Josh's Rocky Mountain Oyster gag in Colorado. But in all seriousness, Sammy's serves a refreshingly light wood-grilled pizza, similar to Bertucci's back east.

SUSHI-ITTO (409 F Street)

It wouldn't be a road trip to San Diego without sampling some sushi. At least that's what Kevin says. Sushi-Itto is probably the most cost-effective spot to wrap your lips around some raw fish. The chain also has locations in Europe, Central America, South America, and Mexico. For an upscale sushi party, visit **Sushi Bar Nippon** at 532 Fourth Avenue or **Octopuses Garden** on 5th Avenue.

THE FIELD (544 5th Avenue)

This is an Irish bar that was transferred over from Ireland. If Kevin says it's okay, you know it's got to be somewhat authentic, and Kevin gives it the thumbs up. Stop in for a pint of Guinness.

THE FIFTH QUARTER (600 5th Avenue)

This quality downtown sports bar has traditionally been more of a Chargers hangout. Expect hardball to gain in popularity with the infusion of Padres fans into the neighborhood. Aside from steaks, ribs, and wood-fired pizza, the menu also offers such exotic and healthy items as alligator and buffalo.

THE OLD SPAGHETTI FACTORY
(5th and K Streets)

Exactly like every other franchise in the chain, this edition offers the factory's decent Italian food. But it's still a chain, which drops it down a few pegs in our book.

THE GASLAMP STRIP CLUB (5th Street)

Don't get your hopes up. This isn't a "girls get naked" strip club but rather a place to order strip steaks and cocktails—unless there was a back room they weren't telling us about.

THE TIN FISH RESTAURANT (L Street)

This upscale fish joint couldn't be more conveniently located, right beside the new park. Look for it to become a players' hangout in upcoming years.

The Old Haunts

MCGREGGOR'S (10475 San Diego Mission Road)

Located near Qualcomm Stadium, this bar is still a favorite of players and fans alike. We expect that with the move to the new park, players will be dropping by less frequently in the years ahead, but who knows? Harry the Heckler told us this was *the* place to go if we wanted to meet the Padres players.

SEAU'S (1640 Camino Del Rio)

Junior's NFL career may have recently landed him in Miami, but here's betting the former Chargers linebacker will continue to operate this family-oriented pub in sunny San Diego. After all, Junior's roots in this town run deep. He was born in San Diego in 1969 and played his college ball at the University of Southern California. As for the Chargers-style lightning bolt atop the Seau's sign, well, Junior's new employer may just have to overlook that.

The restaurant offers plenty of memorabilia, an outdoor patio, and a cigar lounge. And the creatively named burgers and entrées are pretty good too.

SAN DIEGO BREWING COMPANY
(Zion Street and Mission Gorge)

Located in the midst of a strip mall near Qualcomm Stadium, this continues to be a favorite watering hole among Padres and Chargers fans. With its quality homemade brews and burgers, it's easy to see why. Josh's Uncle Joe and some of his friends ran into Ryan Klesko arriving for dinner after a game in 2003. But we didn't spot any players when we visited. Not that we were looking.

Eyeing the dartboard hanging on the far side of the hall, Josh waited as Kevin's voice got louder and louder with each pint of beer consumed. Then Josh challenged Kevin to a game of Clock Baseball.

After handing Josh an 18–12 loss, Kevin said, "Sorry, Manny, but I'm still within my beer window. Better try again later."

So Josh bought a round (a rarity), then tried again and lost again.

"How about another round," Kevin said, "then we can play a third game."

"Sorry," Josh replied, "but I'm outside my generosity window."

"Wow, that's some window," Kevin said. "It opens only $4 wide?"

CLOCK BASEBALL

In the days before baseball video games arrived to humor fans during the winter months and on those loathsome off-nights during the summer, the fans' game of choice was Clock Baseball.

Not to be confused with Dart Baseball, which is played on a special Baseball Field dartboard, Clock Baseball is played on an ordinary twenty-point-face dartboard. This is how it works. Each player throws three darts per inning. In the top of the first inning, the first player aims for the number one segment. A dart in either of the two large areas of the segment counts for one run. A dart in the double area (outer ring) counts for two runs and in the triple area (inner ring) counts for three runs. A dart in any other segment is an out. After three throws, the players clear the board and the second player takes a turn throwing at the number one segment in the bottom half of the first inning. Then, the first player shoots for the number two segment, and so on. To keep score, players build nine inning line scores identical to the type used to score real baseball games, sans the hits and errors columns. Whoever has the most runs at the end of nine innings wins. In the case of a tie, both players take aim at the number ten segment. It's a fun game. Give it a try!

Inside the Park

When it comes to comparing Petco and Qualcomm, it's really no comparison at all. The configuration of the new park makes games more interesting than they ever were at the generic cookie-cutter that previously served as home to the Friars. And the proximity of the seats to the playing field gives fans a better view of the game than they ever enjoyed in the past.

Petco features an asymmetrical outfield that offers a bevy of angles, nooks, and crannies. In left field, the corner of the Western Metal Building is 334 feet from home plate. The gap in left-center is 367 feet away, dead center is 390 feet, and the deepest part of the park in right-center is 409 feet. A spacious right-center field gap measures 387 feet away before tapering to just 322 feet down the right field line. How does this measure up to Qualcomm? The Q was 330 feet down both lines, 375 feet to the power alleys and 405 feet to center field, with its outfield wall taking one long and unwavering trip along the outer perimeter of the field: boring!

Petco's front row seats along the first- and third-base lines are just thirty-three feet from fair territory, as opposed to forty-four feet from the front-row seats at the Q. The first row of the Club deck is thirty-four feet above the field, as opposed to the forty-four feet above the field at the Q. And the first row of the upper deck is sixty-six feet high, as opposed to seventy-nine feet at the old park.

So be glad you're not seeing a game at generic Qualcomm, and enjoy the unique dimensions and quality views of this interesting new ballpark.

Ballpark Features

THE WESTERN METAL SUPPLY BUILDING

The ninety-five-year-old Western Metal Building had to be seismically retrofitted in order to comply with the new earthquake-proof standards of the day before it could be incorporated into the ballpark. Concrete was poured in all levels, including the roof, to accomplish this in early 2003. Then openings were created on each level to serve as ramps to the seating decks.

The Padres team store is on the first floor, as is a doorway leading to a standing-room area in left. The second floor and third floor house luxury suites, and the fourth floor houses a restaurant. There are bleachers and a standing-room area on the roof, eighty feet above the field.

PADRES HALL OF FAME

The San Diego Padres Hall of Fame honors players, coaches, and executives who left their mark in the Padres' history books. At the time of this printing six men had been inducted into the hall since it was created to honor the club's thirtieth anniversary in 1999. The group includes four players, two executives, and one broadcaster/manager.

The inaugural class included pitcher Randy Jones, who won ninety-two games in eight seasons with San Diego (1973–1980), outfielder Nate Colbert who averaged twenty-seven home runs per year in six seasons with the Padres (1969–1974), and former owner Ray Kroc (1974–1984).

In 2000 outfielder Dave Winfield, the only player to be enshrined in Cooperstown wearing a Padres hat on his plaque, was inducted into the Padres Hall. Winfield jumped right from the University of Minnesota campus into the Padres lineup in 1973 without playing a single game in the minors. He played eight seasons with San Diego, before joining the Yankees in 1981. Though his prime years were spent in the Big Apple, the slugger's distaste for George Steinbrenner and fondness for America's Finest City were taken into account when it came time for the Baseball Hall of Fame to make his plaque, which portrayed him in a Padres hat.

The team's first president, Buzzie Bavasi, and longtime radio broadcaster Jerry Coleman were inducted in 2001. Coleman, who has been calling Padres games since 1972, actually stepped out of the broadcast booth to manage the team to a 73–89 record in 1980, paving the way for broadcaster Larry Dierker to pull the same trick in Houston several years later with considerably better results. Coleman, you may also remember, won the 1949 American League Rookie of the Year Award playing second base for the Yankees.

Tony Gwynn, who holds nearly every Padres batting record, assumed his place in the Padres Hall in 2002 and will no doubt join the Baseball Hall of Fame when he first becomes eligible in 2007. "Mr. Padre" won a National League record-tying eight batting titles and was selected to fifteen All-Star teams. His .338 lifetime average is the highest by any Major Leaguer since Ted Williams. In a career that spanned 1982 to 2001, Gwynn recorded 3,141 hits. He also notched 1,138 RBI and 319 stolen bases. Today Gwynn is the head baseball coach at his alma mater, San Diego State University.

Stadium Eats

With a couple of exceptions that come courtesy of independent vendors, the ballpark food in San Diego has always rated pretty poorly. Consequently, fans built a strong tailgating culture during the Qualcomm years. These industrious Southern Californians got into the habit of bringing their own food to the ballpark and cooking it before the game, and then saying "no, thanks" to the eats inside. Sadly, with the new ballpark nestled in the downtown area where parking spots are limited, the tailgating tradition is apt to go the way of the dinosaur.

In any case, hopefully with the advent of the new park, the Padres will upgrade their concession menu and improve their food preparation techniques.

THE WIENERSCHNITZEL DOG (Dog Rating)
The Worst Hot Dog in the Majors

There's a reason why Padres fans used to stop at the Costco food court for hot dogs on their way to Qualcomm. Padres dogs are abominable. Prewrapped and stored in metal drawers beneath the concession counters, the meat is room-temp and the buns are stale by the time these flavorless Wienerschnitzels are handed to fans. And to think, Wienerschnitzel has the audacity to tout its franks as "America's Most Wanted Hot Dogs."

RUBIO'S FISH TACOS (Trademark Food)

A San Diego specialty, Rubio's Mexican Grill operates a multitude of stands in Southern California, including one at the ballpark. Ralph Rubio opened the first Rubio's stand in Mission Bay in 1983 after bringing the recipe to the States from San Felipe in Baja, Mexico. Inside the park, expect to pay about twice the ordinary going rate for these salsa-and-cabbage-topped, deep-fried fish tacos and burritos. If you

ON AUGUST 16, 1996, the Padres and Mets played the first regular season MLB game ever played in Mexico when a series between the two teams was moved out of San Diego to accommodate the Republican National Convention. Monterrey's Estadio Monterrey hosted La Primera Serie. Mexican native Fernando Valenzuela made the first game memorable, starting on the mound for the Padres earning a 15–10 Padres win. Fans chanted "Toro, Toro," Valenzuela's nickname in Spanish, throughout the game.

The next April the Padres hosted the Cardinals for a regular season series at the University of Hawaii's Aloha Stadium in Honolulu in an effort to reestablish a local following in Hawaii. From 1971–1983, the Padres' top farm team had been the Pacific Coast League Hawaii Islanders who played first at Honolulu Stadium, and then, beginning in 1975 at the brand new fifty-thousand-seat Aloha Stadium (currently the site of the NFL Pro-Bowl each February). But despite the historic connection, the Padres lost two out of three to the Cards in the Paradise Series. And *Magnum PI* star Tom Selleck wasn't spotted at any of the games.

The Friars weren't finished traveling to home games. In 1999 they returned to Monterrey to host the Rockies in a Sunday night season opener. Played a day before the rest of the 1999 season began and broadcast nationally, the Padres' return trip to Mexico was less successful than their first visit. The presence of Mexican slugger Vinny Castilla on the Rockies made Colorado a decided fan favorite. The 27,104 people who jammed tiny Estadio Monterrey cheered wildly for Castilla, who responded with four hits, leading the Rockies to an 8–2 victory. The game marked the first season opener ever played outside of the United States or Canada.

like fried fish and you like Mexican, you'll be happy you tried these unique treats.

BEST OF THE REST

The Mission Burger and garlic fries at the **Gordon Biersch** stand are respectable offerings. But if you've really got a hankering for vampire-repellent fries, we recommend saving your appetite for San Francisco where this treat originated.

We also stopped by **Randy Jones' Barbecue** where we not only sampled a tasty plate of Brush Back Ribs, but we also met former Cy Young Award winner Randy Jones. Randy was friendly and personable and took time out from running the stand to talk to us about our travels. Aside from the ribs, we also recommend the Fowl Territory plate, which consists of half a barbecued chicken with a choice of two side dishes.

If you're planning to pay Randy a visit, be sure to stop by his stand early as it usually closes up shop after the fourth inning. Initially, this upset us quite a bit. We're the type of fans who like to go back for seconds and sometimes thirds when we find food we really like. But we can't blame Randy and his crew for wanting to catch the last few innings of the game. A southpaw, Jones became the first Padre to win the Cy Young Award in 1976 when he posted a 22–14 record to go with a 2.76 ERA and twenty-five complete games. He remains the team's all-time leader in innings pitched (1,765), starts (253), complete games (71), and shutouts (18), and is a member of the Padres Hall of Fame. For his career, however, Jones was an unremarkable 100–123. He and another former Padre, Mark Davis, are the only two pitchers to finish their careers with losing records after winning the Cy Young Award. Davis, who posted forty-four saves and a 1.85 ERA to claim the 1989 Cy, hung up his spikes in 1997 with a career record of 51–84.

SAY "NO, THANKS," AND WALK AWAY

Here's hoping that by the time you visit Petco Park, **Carl's Junior** will be on the outside looking in. As we've said time and time again, folks can eat fast food any day of the week in just about any corner of the country. The ballpark is supposed to be a magical place with its own sights, sounds, smells, and flavors. And there's nothing magical about a greasy burger patty, no matter how much makeup Ronald McDonald wears or how grandfatherly Dave Thomas seemed, or how many cute little stars Carl puts on his sign.

BALLPARK BREW

San Diego offers the full gamut of macrobrews on tap and in bottles. Meanwhile, Gordon Biersch is the featured microbrew on tap. Bottles of Corona and Sam Adams are also available. If you're looking for local flavor, we recommend the Corona.

The San Diego Experience

Maybe it's because so many transplanted New Englanders live in Southern California, or maybe it's because the Friars came close to winning it all in 1998 before being decimated by the Yankees in the World Series, but we were surprised to find quite a few severely jaded Padres fans. It probably had something to do with how awful the team was in 2003. This bitterness, Josh liked. Being a Red Sox fan, he could relate to it. Kevin, on the other hand, was a bit affronted.

Some fans were just plain grumpy, like Josh's Uncle Joe, while others bordered on being surly. The fans seemed universally angry at management for not investing more money in on-field talent. And many season ticket holders complained that the team had shafted them, giving them far inferior tickets at Petco than they had had at Qualcomm. They said that instead of relocating the die-hard fans to quality seats, management had sold out to the corporate entities and rewarded the big companies with the best pickings. Yet despite a laundry list of complaints, a respectable number of fans had shown up at the park early to watch batting practice, then stayed for the entire game. We were impressed by their dedication to the team, even during a down year at a ballpark taking its final breath. It's like Kevin's cousin Jeremy says, "Being a Padres fan can become a chore."

HARRY THE HECKLER (Superfan)

One superfan sure to survive the move from the old ballpark to the new one is San Diego resident Harry Maker who has spent the better part of the last ten years making life miserable for visiting left fielders. When we spent a few innings sitting with Harry in the front row of Section 7 at Qualcomm, he told us the Padres had already promised him front-row seats at Petco. "Some of the other fans complain about my noise now," Harry said. "If the team moved me back (away from the field) at the new park, then they'd really hear complaints."

With his handlebar mustache, ponytail, yellow and brown Padres hat, and throwback Tony Gwynn jersey, Harry is perhaps the most hated fan in all of baseball among visiting players. The man was born with a healthy set of lungs and over the years he's learned how to use them to his team's best advantage. Visiting left fielders cringe each time they trot out to their position, because they know they're going to hear an earful.

Heckling Harry Superfan (at Qualcomm)

Photo by Kevin O'Connell

The great thing about Harry is that he keeps it clean and never gets personal. He doesn't have to resort to lowbrow heckling, because he does his homework. "I spend each off-season researching all of the left fielders in the league," he told us. "I look for their weaknesses as players—deficiencies in their games—and I write myself notes for when the season begins."

Harry's not a drinker either—at least not when he's at work inside the ballpark. He told us he drinks lemonade instead of beer because it's better for his vocal chords, which he needs to keep well hydrated if he's going to last the full nine innings. Did we mention this man is loud, very loud?

When we were in town, Harry was riding "Larry" (aka Chipper) Jones. Before the game, Chipper had sent a clubhouse attendant out to the left field seats to offer Harry an autographed bat as a bribe. Wow, now that's respect. But Harry gave Chipper the business just the same, complaining that the Braves star didn't hand deliver the bat to him but instead sent an errand boy out to do his bidding. "How do I know it's really your autograph, Larry?" Harry called to Chipper.

Bribing Harry is something many players do. He's gotten scores of autographed bats over the years. And he also gets more than his share of balls. As each inning begins, the Padres' left fielder tosses a warm-up ball to Harry. He keeps the ball in the first inning, then gives the remaining eight to the youngsters seated nearest him.

As for the player who gets most upset at Harry's act—hands down, Harry says, it's Barry Bonds. "Bonds swore he will kill me if he can ever get his hands on me," Harry said. "But I eventually wear on them all. Some players give me a lot of feedback, while others hardly give any indication that I'm bothering them at all. But I know I'm getting to them."

Harry lists Glenallen Hill, Travis Lee, Luis Gonzalez, and Moises Alou as other left fielders whom he has particularly riled.

The only visiting players Harry doesn't harass are out-of-town left fielders who previously played for the Padres. Harry gives them a break.

Whether you love him or hate him, Harry is a San Diego institution. As a kid in the 1960s he used to ride his bike to Westgate Park to watch San Diego's Pacific Coast League team play. Now as an adult, he's more than just a spectator but a player of sorts himself.

"It's one game between nine players and nine players, but it's another game between me and the one player in front of me," Harry said. "The grass in left field is my grass, and I let them know it."

THE SAN DIEGO CHICKEN

If any mascot has transcended his role as kiddie entertainer and become a veritable folk icon, it is the San Diego Chicken. *The Sporting News* recently named him one of the one hundred most powerful people in sports for the twentieth century, along with Muhammad Ali, Babe Ruth, Jesse Owens, and other great athletes. The chicken has appeared on baseball cards (Donruss and Upper Deck), shown up at rock concerts (Elvis, Doobie Brothers, Jimmy Buffet, Cheap Trick, the Ramones, Chuck Berry, Jerry Lee Lewis), and performed in all fifty states and eight foreign countries. But most of all, he is associated with the San Diego Padres.

The San Diego Chicken was born as part of a radio promotion in 1974 when Ted Giannoulas signed on to wear a silly suit which his mother had made, for $2 a day at the San Diego Zoo. Giannoulas was told to set up a nest at the zoo and hand out candy to kids as they passed through the turnstiles during the week before Easter. But this was not to be a one-week gig. The man inside the suit had a vision. He was

LAKE ELSINORE STORM

"STRANGE BREW" jokes aside, the Diamond—home park of the California League Lake Elsinore Storm—is worth visiting on your ride out of San Diego. Try to catch a game at this terrific minor league park if the schedule works out. Just an hour north of Petco, the Padres' Class A affiliate plays in a beautiful eight-thousand-seat facility. The Diamond features a grass berm sitting area beyond the right field fence similar to the "park at the park" at Petco, only a whole lot closer to the action. From San Diego follow Highway 15 north to the Diamond Drive Exit and follow Diamond Drive to the ballpark.

more than just a mercenary. He was an actor at heart, a showman with unparalleled flair. The crazy bird became famous.

The Chicken debuted at San Diego Stadium on Opening Day of the 1974 season during a game against the Astros and quickly became a mainstay at the ballpark, delighting crowds with his antics. *The Baseball Bunch* called looking for an interview, then the *Tonight Show*, and so the legend grew. Soon other teams started hatching their own mascots, but none—save perhaps the Philly Phanatic—won over the hearts of fans in quite the way the San Diego Chicken did.

Then in the late 1970s the Chicken almost lost his feathers when Giannoulas and KGB— the radio station that had originally hired him to wear the suit—had a contractual dispute regarding when and where he could perform.

Eventually KGB fired the Chicken. Later the California Supreme Court declared Giannoulas free of obligations to his former employer and he returned wearing a brand new chicken costume in June 1979. The return was memorable, to say the least. Flanked by a California Highway Patrol motorcade, he rode into San Diego Stadium inside a gigantic egg atop an armored truck. After the egg was lowered to the field by Padres players, the Chicken hatched out, to the roaring approval of the forty-seven thousand fans in attendance.

Given his hectic touring schedule, the Chicken only turns up at the ballpark these days a few times per year. His absence has given rise to a goofy clergyman known as "the Friar." This larger-than-life cartoon-type character stomps around the field in a brown robe. His humdrum antics may play well with the kids and neophytes, but for folks who remember the ingenious tomfoolery of the Chicken, the Friar doesn't have quite the same cachet.

MEN AND WOMEN IN UNIFORM

San Diego is a town that takes great pride in its servicemen and servicewomen. And the members of the Navy and Marines who are stationed in San Diego return this affection by going above and beyond the ordinary call of duty in their interactions with the greater community. Oftentimes on Sundays, a large number of Marines march into the ballpark to present the color guard, then spend the afternoon watching the game in uniform from the outfield seats. And sometimes on Sundays the Padres wear special-occasion camouflage jerseys.

ANAHEIM ANGELS,
ANGEL STADIUM OF ANAHEIM

Baseball, Orange County Style

**ANAHEIM,
CALIFORNIA**

25 miles to Los Angeles
100 miles to San Diego
380 miles to Phoenix
400 miles to San Francisco /
Oakland

W E DROVE to Anaheim from Los Angeles with decidedly low expectations for Edison Field, which was renamed Angel Stadium of Anaheim subsequent to our visit. We knew the ballpark had undergone extensive renovations in recent years, but we also knew that Disney had played a leading role in those efforts. And that gave us worries. What also concerned us was that the facility in Anaheim—formerly known as the Big A, Anaheim Stadium, and Edison International Field—had served as home to the National Football League Los Angeles Rams for many years prior to the team's exodus to St. Louis; this labeled Angel Stadium a cookie-cutter stadium in our minds. What's more, we rolled into town not expecting much from the Angels' fans who have long had a reputation for showing up in the third inning and leaving in the seventh.

Well, at least one our preconceived notions proved accurate. Many fans were indeed tardy in arriving. Everything else that we expected to find—or not find—in Anaheim failed to materialize. Angel Stadium is indeed a stadium and not a ballpark. There's no denying that. But it is one of the best stadiums in the game today. In other words, it's not Yankee Stadium, but it sure beats places like Network Associates Coliseum or Shea Stadium when it comes to showcasing a ball game. Not only are the sight lines superb from all three seating decks, but the soft earth tones of the facility and the lack of flashing lights and blaring sound bites promote an old-time ballpark feel. And the fans? Well, once they got settled into their seats they were loud and involved in the game. Yes, they are for some reason obsessed with the ridiculous monkey that serves as their team's mascot, but they stayed until the bottom of the ninth to watch the Angels post a come-from-behind win over the Orioles when we visited.

exterior

Photo by Kevin O'Connell

With the San Bernardino Mountains rising up in the distance beyond the left field fence, Angel Stadium provides some sweet views when the smog is not too thick. Inside the park, the Angels embrace the mountain theme with an outfield rock and water display that—while less impressive than the similar feature at Coors Field in Denver—is well done. The rocks and waterfall give this once exceptionally bland facility a trademark feature—something it had lacked for years.

Other than the outfield rocks and the fireworks that occasionally come shooting forth from them, Angel Stadium is not too overdone—in the Disney sense. We like that. Baseball is the main attraction, the way it should be. And the way it was during the 2002 postseason when the Angels shocked the baseball world by winning their first World Series. Who will ever forget Scott Spiezio's home run against the Giants in Game 6 of the 2002 World Series? Or Adam Kennedy's surprising power display against the Twins when he belted three dingers in Game 5 of the American League Championship Series? Or how about the Angels' eight-run fifth-inning uprising in Game 4 of the American League Division Series to smite the mighty Yankees? Or the crazy Rally

Monkey whose enthusiasm helped propel the Angels to an 8–1 home record during the 2002 postseason?

By claiming the 2002 championship, and doing so in such dramatic fashion at every step along the way, the Angels finally put Anaheim on the map as a bona fide big league town. Previously, Anaheim had not been regarded as much of a baseball town. Catching a game at The Big A—as Angel Stadium was previously known—was an option when the Dodgers were on an extended road trip. But as for the team, well, for many years most folks could take or leave "the Halos." Management usually put a good, but never great, squad on the field. So the fans came and left as they pleased, enjoying a few innings at the park, but caring little whether or not the home team won. But that was before the fourth-ever all-California World Series pitted the Angels against the San Francisco Giants. Now, the Angels have a World Series trophy to go with their remodeled stadium. And they even have a new owner. During the 2003 season MLB approved the sale of the Angels from the Walt Disney Company to Arturo Moreno in a deal worth roughly $185 million. With the purchase, Moreno became the first Hispanic owner in the Majors.

But back to the 2002 season. The magical campaign seemed like a fairy tale scripted by the heartstring-tuggers at Disney. How unlikely was an Angels' championship run? Consider that in 2001 the Angels had finished forty-one games behind the first place Mariners in the American League West. That's right, we said forty-one games back! And the Angels hadn't been a factor in the division since blowing a thirteen-and-a-half-game lead in 1995 and then losing a one-game playoff to the Mariners for the division title. In the years between the Angels' 1986 implosion against the Red Sox in their only previous American League Championship Series and 2002, the team went through six managers, four general managers, three logo changes, a ballpark makeover, and a geographic identity crisis that saw them change their name from the California Angels to the Anaheim Angels. Never mind the World Series, the Angels' 2002 American League Championship represented their first AL pennant in their forty-two-year history.

The Angels got off to a slow start to the regular season in 2002 but came on strong in the second half to end up with a 99–63 record—best in team history. But they still finished four games behind the Oakland A's in the AL West. After running through the Yankees and Twins to advance to the October Classic, they again found themselves facing long odds against the Giants. Trailing three games to two in the Series and 5–0 in Game 6, it appeared Anaheim was on the brink of elimination. But Spiezio ripped a three-run homer to right field in the bottom of the seventh inning to pull the Angels within 5–3. And then in the bottom of the eighth the Angels struck for three more runs on a Darin Erstad homer and a two-run double by Troy Glaus. The Angels prevailed 6–5 to force a seventh and final game. In Game 7 the Giants jumped out to a 1–0 lead in the top of the second, but the Angels tied it in the bottom of the inning and took the lead for good on a three-run double by Garrett Anderson in the third. Pitching on three days' rest, John Lackey went five innings allowing just one run to become the first rookie in ninety-five years to start and win Game 7 of a World Series. Troy Percival pitched the ninth inning to record the save as the Angels triumphed 4–1. And the crowd went wild in the Land of Disney. Angel Stadium rocked like it never had before.

Angel Stadium was originally known as Anaheim Stadium. The facility opened in 1966 and was expanded in 1979 to accommodate the NFL Rams. It was remodeled for a second time beginning in 1996 to undo much of what the 1979 expansion had wrought. Accomplished ballpark architectural firm HOK was assigned the task of making "the Big A" into a

left field with big A

Photo by Kevin O'Connell)

TRIVIA TIMEOUT

Michael: What two members of the Angels family are honored with statues at Angel Stadium? (Hint: neither played for the team)

Gabriel: Who was the first player selected by the Angels in the 1961 expansion draft?

Goofy: We've told you about the Wrigley Field locations in Chicago and Los Angeles. Now we ask, "Where was the third Wrigley Field located?"

Look for the answers in the text.

ballpark again in the wake of the Rams' departure to St. Louis. With some help from Disney, which footed the $100 million bill, HOK eliminated nearly twenty-thousand outfield seats, added a center field video board and an out-of-town scoreboard in right and created a fake mountainside in the outfield, complete with rocks, streams, geysers, and trees. During these renovations, the ballpark shed the name Anaheim Stadium and became Edison Field after a hefty payout from local energy company Edison International. The project was completed in time for the start of the 1998 season opener, a 4–1 Angels win against the Yankees.

Prior to opening the Big A in 1966, the Angels had spent their first five seasons as vagabonds, like the two of us on our road trip, crashing wherever they could find an open couch. The team was founded by movie star Gene Autry and former football player Bob Reynolds in 1960 and joined the American League as the expansion Los Angeles Angels in 1961. The Angels played their first season in Los Angeles' Wrigley Field, an expanded minor league ballpark that once belonged to the Cubs. How cozy was Wrigley? The seating capacity was 20,500. And the Angels and their opponents combined to hit a record 248 home runs in eighty-one games at the park that season. The next year, the Angels moved to Dodger Stadium where they played until Anaheim Stadium was completed in time

for the start of the 1966 season. With the move to Anaheim, the team changed its name to the California Angels.

After the 1979 remodeling effort to accommodate the Rams, folks took to calling the facility "the Bigger A" as the once-open skyline in the outfield was closed off by the addition of more seats. Now that these seats have been removed, Angel Stadium resembles the original Anaheim Stadium once again.

Angels ownership continued to be "all about entertainment," as the team passed from the estate of the Singing Cowboy to the Walt Disney Company in 1996. Shortly thereafter the team changed its name to the Anaheim Angels. After the Angels won Game 7 of the 2002 World Series, both the old and new ownership teams took part in the celebration. Gene Autry's widow, Jackie, stood beside Disney boss Michael Eisner on the field, and together they accepted the World Series trophy, along with Troy Glaus, the Series MVP. While Jackie Autry reached for the championship trophy with one hand, she held up her late husband's trademark cowboy hat in the other. And the fans went wild.

Autry was the anti-Steinbrenner, an aged fatherly figure who loved his team and players through good times and bad. As for Disney's short-lived reign? Well, not only did Eisner and company significantly hike ticket prices before raising the world champions banner at Angel Stadium in April of 2003, but they also had the gall to charge admission to the victory parade in October of 2002. Perhaps because Anaheim didn't have any buildings tall enough to have a true ticker-tape parade, or perhaps because Disney was out to make a buck, the victory parade was held at Disneyland. In any case, Disney had sold the Angels by the middle of the next season, bringing an end to its short but successful tenure as owner of the team.

As for historic moments, the Big A hosted plenty. On September 23, 1973, Nolan Ryan struck out sixteen Twins in his final start of the season to break Sandy Koufax's single-season strikeout record. The big Texan recorded his 383rd punch-out in the game's eleventh inning to best Koufax by a single K. Afterward it was revealed that Ryan had pitched the game with a torn thigh muscle.

In his final start of the next season, Ryan pitched his third career no-hitter and first in Anaheim, again baffling the Twins on September 28, 1974. But the Ryan Express was just getting started. The next season Ryan authored his record-tying fourth no-no, beating the Orioles 1–0 in Anaheim. He would pitch three more no-hitters before retiring after the 1993 season with 324 wins, an all-time best 5,714 strikeouts, and a 3.19 career ERA.

The Angels retired Ryan's number 30 in 1992. In 291 games for the Angels, Ryan posted a 138–121 record to go with a 3.06 ERA. The 138 Angels Ws were the most Ryan earned with any one team during a career that also saw him play for the Mets (29 wins), Astros (106), and Rangers (51).

When Anaheim hosted the All-Star Game in 1989, Bo Jackson and Wade Boggs made the first inning special, hitting back-to-back homers to lead off the bottom half of the first inning against forty-year-old National League starter Rick Reuschel. The Americans went on to win 5–3. Appropriately, Ryan, wearing a Texas uniform, earned the win in relief, making him the oldest pitcher to win the Midsummer Classic at age forty-two.

Two Hall of Famers joined the three-thousand-hit club in Anaheim, the Angels' Rod Carew (1985) and the Royals' George Brett (1992). The latter was picked off first-base by Angels pitcher Tim Fortugno after recording his three-thousandth. How embarrassing.

Reggie Jackson joined the five-hundred-homer club at the Big A, and Don Sutton recorded win number three hundred, as both Hall of Famers put the finishing touches on their seemingly interminable careers. Sutton pitched twenty-three seasons in the bigs, including two-and-a-half with the Angels. He won 324 games, or an average of 14 per season in the era of the four-man rotation.

Jackson, meanwhile, played twenty-one seasons, including five with the Angels. He hit 563 long balls but also struck out a whopping, or should we say "whiffing," 2,597 times, more than any other player in history. And Mr. October batted just .262 in the regular season. His teams did win eleven division titles, six pennants, and five world championships though.

Getting a Choice Seat

Until recently quality tickets for games at Angel Stadium were easy to find. Hey, there's always been a lot of other stuff going on in la-la land. Ticket sales were up dramatically in 2003, however, following the Angels' first championship season. This, despite the fact that the Angels responded to their success by raising ticket prices 20 percent and by designating several home dates "Premium Games" for which tickets cost an additional $5 each, excepting tickets in the outfield. Ah, the price of success, as always, footed by the loyal common fan.

Angel Stadium is perhaps the most vexing park in the big leagues for those hard-core, yet thrifty baseball fans who consider themselves accomplished seat-hoppers. You know, folks like us who buy the cheapest seats we can, and then sneak into the lower boxes for free.

In most parks, by the time the bottom of the second inning rolls around Josh feels daring enough to start his routine. He saunters past the

Sellout Index: 15% of games sell out
Seating Capacity: 45,050
Ticket Office: (888) 796-HALO
www.anaheim.angels.mlb.com

lower-level ushers with a dog in one hand and his ticket in the other, checking his ticket as if to make sure he's headed in the right direction. Then he settles into any open seat he can find after inspecting it, and then his ticket, as if double-checking that he's found his rightful seat.

This approach doesn't work so well in Disneyland, where late-game seat hopping is easy but early-game hopping resembles a hybrid of Russian roulette and musical chairs. No, the ushers aren't the problem, the other fans are. Many of the folks holding tickets for the good seats don't show up until the third or fourth inning. They live important lives, and do their best to fit the game into their busy schedules around such priorities as movie shoots, surfing parties, Wally World adventures, tofu tastings, power yoga, and God knows what else.

Adventures in Seat Hopping

Josh had spent almost three full innings in a primo seat in Section 124 when a dapper fan with plenty of gel in his hair showed up and started waving a ticket stub in his face.

"Umm, you're out-ie," the waiter/aspiring actor/director/producer said.

"Haven't you ever heard of squatter's rights?" Josh said playfully, as he gathered his ballpark accoutrements (glove, binoculars, baseball card case, ball bag, etc.) and prepared to rejoin Kevin in the cheap seats.

"What?"

"Squatter's rights."

"If that means what I think it does," the pretty boy said, scanning the crowd for an usher, "you'd better find some paper towels and clean my seat before you leave."

Just then, the dandy's cell phone rang, and by the time he could answer it, his beeper had started beeping. And then his palm pilot started to make a shrill sizzling sound. In a flutter, he was gone. So Josh sat back down and enjoyed the rest of the game.

The moral of the story: you're the real fan in this equation and if you see an open seat, do your best to get your butt into it. You deserve it.

We should mention that the Angels have a growing base of dedicated "real" fans who shake their heads with disdain at the fast-talking pseudofans who occupy (or fail to occupy as the case often is) many of the park's best seats. Now that the Rally Monkey is in town and the Angels have a world championship to their credit, the shift has begun. More and more baseball fans are showing up at Angel Stadium, and they're drowning out the status seekers who just show up to make an appearance.

Field MVP (Sections 123–126, 110–113); Terrace MVP (Boxes 43–54)

The first level consists of Field Boxes below the midlevel concourse and Terrace Boxes behind the concourse and beneath the overhang of the Club deck. All of these first-level seats on the infield are sold exclusively to corporate entities and season ticket holders. In other words, "it ain't happening for you."

Field Box (Sections 101–109, 127–135)

The closest to the plate that average fans can get on the first level is just beyond the first- and third-base bags in outfield Sections 109 (left field) and 127 (right field). The first row of seats is Row A, and the last is Row Z. The low retaining walls separating the stands and field on the right and left field lines contribute to excellent views of the outfield corners for first-level fans.

Close to the infield, the Field Box sections are pretty good. But strangely, the worst of these seats—those in the sections out near the foul poles—cost the same as those just beyond the dugouts. Don't get stuck with a ticket out near the poles. Sections 134 and 135 in deep right field are particularly terrible because the right field Terrace juts out to block the view of center field. Plus, there is a foul pole obstruction. If you're dying to relive Spiezio's dramatic Game 6 homer from the point of view of the fan in the first row of Section 135 who caught the ball, however, then this might be the place for you.

Sections 101 and 102 in deep left field are slightly obstructed by the protuberance of the Angels bull pen, but are much better than their equivalent sections in right field. The left field foul pole blocks a portion of the field for those seated anywhere in Section 102 and for those in Seats 13 through 21 in Rows N through Z of Section 101.

Closer to the infield, where the views are better, the seats still angle fans toward the outfield, rather than toward home plate, reminding us that this ballpark once was, and in some ways continues to be, a cookie-cutter facility—even if it is no longer multifunctional.

Terrace Box (Sections 201–209, 227–233)

To take the overhang of the Club deck out of the equation, you'll want to stay in Rows A–D of the Terrace Boxes. But those seated in Row A have to contend with the aisle traffic on the midlevel concourse, which should have been sunken a bit lower when the ballpark was constructed. On the whole, these are good seats that have the benefit of a roof overhead on hot and sunny days. Just be sure to avoid Sections 231, 232, and 233 in deep right field, which, like the Field Boxes below them, are obstructed by the jutting out of the right field Terrace; and these three sections are also afflicted by a significant overhang.

Club Loge (Sections 301–308, 344–348)

The only second-deck seats available to regular fans are these Club Loge seats way out near the foul poles. A first-level view down below can be had for less money. And a third-level view closer to the infield is also better. So who would pay top dollar for these seats?

Apparently not too many people, as the Club Loge sections were nearly empty when we visited Anaheim.

Lower View MVP (Sections 411–426)

These are the first nine rows of third-level seats, located behind the plate and extending to the first- and third-base bags. These seats are below the walkway. As far as upper box sections go, this is a rather deep one. At most parks, the upper boxes extend back about five rows, but all of these seats provide a solid, if not exceptional, view of the field.

Lower View Box (Sections 427–436, 401–410)

We don't recommend these seats. Not that they're awful, but the View seats (above the concourse) on the infield provide a better gander at the game and for less money. On the right field side, avoid Section 435 where the foul pole blocks the view of the pitcher's mound, and Section 436 where the pole blocks the plate. In left field, steer clear of Sections 401 and 402 for the same reasons.

View (Sections 501–540)

This is one of the best-designed upper decks in the Majors. The under-hang of this deck does not block the view of the field as is the case at most three-level stadiums and the deck does not extend back too far, continuing only until Row S. That's only nineteen rows, for nonmath majors (Kevin counted). And Row A is high enough above the concourse to take the aisle traffic out of play. In all regards, the Angels hit a home run when they built this deck. Angle for seats in Sections 513–529 and enjoy a bird's-eye- (or dare we say Angel's-eye) view of the infield. Sections 523–529 provide the best view of the San Bernardino Mountains beyond the left field wall. If it's a smoggy day, you may not see the peaks, but trust us, they're there.

┌─────────────────────────────────┐
│ **SEATING TIP**   │
└─────────────────────────────────┘

➡️ Josh: "Do your best to locate the beautiful people and then seat-hop as close to their box seats as possible. This is your chance to casually tell your pals back home in Sulphur, Louisiana, 'Yeah, I caught a game with Celebrity X, when I was in Hollywood.'"

Kevin: "Wow. You've been on the West Coast too long."

Josh: "You're just jealous I spent two innings sitting between Matt Damon and Frankie Muniz."

Kevin: "Yeah, I'm jealous of all that face time you got with Frankie Muniz."

Terrace/Club Pavilion (Sections 236–240, 351–358)

The Terrace Pavilion in right field provides a porch from which to watch the game. We highly recommend these sections for any fan traveling on a limited budget. The first row is Row A, and shoot for it, as there's no aisle to block the view for folks in the front row.

Tickets to the Club Pavilion sell for the same price as Terrace Pavilion tickets. Yet the Terrace seats are closer to the field and more desirable. The Club Pavilion was closed when we visited Angel Stadium as an usher quickly reminded Josh when he ventured into the area to scope out the view. That was just as well.

Left Field Family Pavilion (Sections 247–250)

These first-level seats in left field are lower to the field than the outfield seats in right, but are farther from the action because they are behind the bull pens, which run parallel to each other horizontal to the outfield wall. As such, the first row of seats begins at least forty feet behind the left field wall. Not good. The outfield fence in left-center field is also about fifteen feet farther from the plate than the fence in right-center, which makes these seats even worse.

The seats here are hard plastic fixed chairs that don't flip up or down like the more comfortable seats in the rest of the park. Section 250 should be avoided because the visiting bull pen screens the view of left field, and the first row of all of the Left Field Family sections should be avoided because of an obtrusive railing that blocks sight lines. Section 248, in the middle portion of the bull pens, provides the clearest view of the field. But we recommend sitting in the Terrace Pavilion instead for only $1 more.

The Black Market

Although we were on the lookout, we couldn't find any scalpers near Angel Stadium. Maybe they were all scalping tickets at a place that actually might sell out—Disney across town.

And the Rockets' Red Glare . . .

How desperate were the Angels to drum up fans prior to the enervating 2002 season? Well, before that campaign began the Halo's announced a new fourteen-game season ticket miniplan called (and we're not making this up) the Angels Pyro Pack. The plan provided pyromaniacs tickets for fourteen "Friday Big Bang Fireworks" games plus free tickets to the 2002 home opener. That's right, free tickets to the season opener. In one regard the plan worked as the Opening Day game was a sellout. But after Navy SEALs parachuted down from the heavens to deliver the ceremonial first pitch, Cleveland's Bartolo Colon shut out the home team 6–0.

Before/After the Game

The area immediately surrounding Angel Stadium will certainly never be confused with a festive downtown neighborhood. The sports complex, which houses both the ballpark and the Pond—home of the NHL Mighty Ducks, is surrounded by urban sprawl. On the plus side, several highways service the area and Disneyland is not far away. This is not a terribly pedestrian-friendly part of town, so once you park the car at the stadium plan on staying the rest of the night.

Although the ballpark is surrounded by tar, a number of palm trees and perennial beds create a visually appealing oasis for baseball fans closer to the park. And the subtle beige and green earth tones of the ballpark's exterior make it warm and inviting. In contrast to these natural effects, the remnants of the Disney regime stand bright, colorful, and larger than life outside the home plate gate. But somehow, rather than clashing, the two approaches seem to complement one another. Several other teams (Mets, Marlins, Blue Jays, etc.) could learn a valuable lesson from studying what the Angels have done to dress up what was once a multipurpose and fairly generic stadium.

Getting to Angel Stadium

If you're driving up the coast following a game in San Diego or Lake Elsinore, follow Route 5 to CA-57 north, then take the Orangewood Avenue Exit that lets off right near the ballpark. If you're coming from a game in Los Angeles, take Route 5 south to the Katella Avenue Exit. Follow Katella east for one mile, then take a right onto State College Boulevard and take a left onto Gene Autry Way. From the east, follow I-10 west to CA-60 west to CA-91 west to CA-57 south to the exit for Katella.

The stadium parking lot charges $8, but we found a private lot on the corner of Katella and Howell Street that only cost $5. Considering that Kevin ripped a hole in his new shorts climbing over the chain-link fence to get to the ballpark, in retrospect it probably would have been wiser for us to shell out the extra three bucks to park closer by. Or Kevin could have walked the extra block to get around the fence.

A Pacific Surfliner Amtrak station is located just a five-minute-walk away from the ballpark,

but the last train for L.A. leaves at 10:10 each night, not nearly late enough to guarantee fans will catch the entire game.

Outside Attractions

THE BIG A

Shortly after Anaheim Stadium opened in 1966 fans took to calling it the Big A on account of the 230-foot-tall A-shaped scoreboard behind the outfield wall that bore a halo at its top. The "A" remains today, transplanted to the parking lot beyond the fence in right field. It was moved in 1980 to allow football fans clear sight lines from the newly added upper-level outfield seats, although management maintained the move was made as an earthquake safety precaution. Right.

We were somewhat disappointed to find that an advertising banner now resides where the scoreboard used to appear midway up the "A." At least it was an ad for water conservation and not for motor oil or pesticide, but still, is nothing sacred in the modern day?

BIG HATS

Josh: "What do Carlos Quintana, Dwight Evans, and Rudy Pemberton all have in common?"

Kevin: "Easy. They all played right field for the Red Sox."

Josh: "Wrong. They each hit for a higher lifetime average than Reggie Jackson."

Kevin: "But they also played right for the Sox, right?"

Josh: "Yeah, I guess so."

Kevin: "So my answer was essentially right."

Josh: "Keep fanning that ego. You've still got a way to go to catch Reggie."

Kevin: "Let me guess. He refused you an autograph when you were twelve years old and you still can't let it go?"

Josh: "Wrong. The Jackson incident occurred when I was nineteen."

Whether or not you agree that Reggie Jackson's head was a few sizes too big for his helmet, you'll marvel at the two gigantic hats on display on the concourse outside the ballpark. If these were fitted caps, they would be size 649.5. That's what the tags on the inside rims say anyway. They also say 100 percent wool, however, when viewed up close it can be easily determined that the hats are made of metal mesh. Thank you, Disney. Don't let the door hit you on the way out.

BALLPARK BRICKS
Outside the home plate gate is an infield of brick. The grass portion of the diamond is represented by gray bricks, while the dirt portion is represented by red bricks. The bases and pitcher's rubber light up in fluorescent colors at night.

If you trot out to one of the infield positions, you will find the name and year of each Opening Day Angels' starter for that position inscribed on a brick.

Both the right-handed and left-handed batter's boxes contain bricks inscribed with the team's Opening Day designated hitters.

Fans have also left their marks, for better or worse, on the bricks located in the sixty feet, six inches between home plate and the mound in the form of personalized bricks. We found a few inscribed with the verse numbers of biblical passages (Hebrews 4:14 and Corinthians II 5:9), which struck us as just plain goofy. Another brick advertised a Web site address. Several others read like tombstones, noting the dates of birth and death for people whom we assumed were lifelong Angels fans.

If you want to leave something behind so that Angels and their fans will always remember your trip to the West Coast, consider shelling out $75 to buy a brick of your own. Or to save a little coin, just leave a wad of Big League Chew on the bottom of your seat like Kevin did.

BATS AND BALLS
Reminiscent of the entranceway at the Louis-ville Slugger Museum in Louisville, Kentucky, Angel Stadium's main gate is flanked by three gigantic bats and two cement balls that hold up the letters that spell the stadium name. Also here on the front facade are larger-than-life pictures of Angels stars like Garret Anderson, Troy Glaus, and Tim Salmon.

CLASS "A" CITY
At eye level beside the main gate, a bronze plaque is attached to the face of the stadium. It reads, "City of Anaheim, California, founded in 1857," and features orange trees in the foreground and the rolling hills of the city in the background. Unless there's a part of Anaheim we missed somehow, the depiction on the plaque is a whole lot nicer than the present reality of the place. But we assume the Orange County name came from somewhere nearby.

Watering Holes and Outside Eats

It seems like just about every chain restaurant imaginable is represented on State College Boulevard and Katella Avenue, ranging from **Denny's** to **Del Taco** to **El Torito** to **Flaky Jake's** to **Hooters**. But there are also a number of unique local establishments worth visiting.

THE CATCH (1929 State College Boulevard)
This restaurant's name and proximity to the ballpark may suggest that it's a sports bar, but in fact The Catch is an upscale seafood and steak restaurant. Steak and chop plates average about $25 per meal, while the fish dishes—such as pan-seared salmon, blackened Hawaiian ahi tuna, and Alaskan halibut fish tacos—are less expensive. The smoked salmon pizza and open-face crab melt are house specials.

On game days, The Catch features twenty-cent Swampfire Wings and a special $5 menu that includes prime rib chili, New England clam chowder, and fresh fish seviche. The Rally Monkey—a mixed drink—consists of Malibu Rum, banana liqueur, white cream de cocoa, and a banana chip garnish. Kevin doesn't go in for fru-fru drinks, but Josh drank three in about fifteen minutes.

J. T. SCHMID'S BREWERY AND RESTAURANT
(2610 Katella Avenue)

Maybe it's a California thing, but here's another fine brewery located within the confines of a strip mall. From the appetizer menu, we recommend the pot-stickers: chicken-filled raviolis, flash fried and served with a Mandarin orange sauce. For an entrée we tried the barbecue chicken quesadilla, also a solid choice. From the bar, we suggest the house-brewed Hefeweizen and Emil's Amber. There is ample outdoor seating in back on a lush green patio.

FRITZ: THAT'S TOO
(Lewis Street and Katella Avenue)

We're still trying to figure out what's meant by the name of this gentlemen's club. And to figure out what a seedy strip club is doing so close to Disneyland. What would Mickey and Minnie say?

CALIFORNIA COUNTRY CAFÉ SPORTS BAR
(1221 Katella Avenue)

This establishment looks and feels more like a diner than a sports bar. But it stays open until 2:00 A.M., offering country-fried steak, fajitas, and other cheap eats that are definitely a cut above the many fast-food joints in the area. There are a few autographs on the walls, including signed jerseys that once belonged to Ken Griffey, Jr., Tim Salmon, and Mo Vaughn.

PANDA EXPRESS (2055 Katella Avenue)

This is a popular chain in these parts, and there is a Panda stand inside the ballpark that does a nice job of providing fans with freshly cooked Chinese food. But if you have the time, why not eat here and avoid the markup inside the park?

DISNEYLAND BARS AND RESTAURANTS
(Downtown Drive)

Downtown Disney—a land of colorful make-believe houses and storefronts—is located about a mile from the ballpark, so why not stop by for an overpriced cocktail and a bite to eat? At least the help is always smiling and eager to assist. Don't worry, you don't have to pay the $47 amusement park admission fee to get into Downtown Disney. Heck, you don't even have to pay to park. A large lot on Downtown Drive offers free three-hour parking. Just don't overstay the three-hour limit, because it's $6 for each additional hour. If you manage your time wisely, this is a good place to get a taste of Disney without having to empty your wallet for Mickey.

Follow Katella to Disney Drive and take a right. Drive past the theme park, then take a left onto Downtown Drive and you'll drive right into the parking lot.

We stopped by the **Disney ESPN Zone** to watch the Red Sox play the Yankees on satellite. Kevin's brother, Sean, was happy to find the pour-job on his Guinness better than the average pint of Guinness in L.A. Sean also enjoyed a Bloody Mary. As for the two of us? Well, wary of these chain-type places, we played it safe and ordered pints of Bud Light the size of vats.

As far as ESPN Zones go, there's nothing too spectacular to check out in this one. The most interesting item is an American flag made of 383 red-white-and-blue baseballs—one for each of the strikeouts Nolan Ryan registered for the Angels in 1973. Each ball bears the name of one of Ryan's victims, beginning with number 1, Fred Patek, and ending with number 383, Rich Reese. We don't know what's more remarkable, the fact that Ryan struck out 383 batters in 1973, or the fact that he completed twenty-six games and still wound up three behind league leader Gaylord Perry who had twenty-nine.

Other eateries in Downtown Disney include the **House of Blues**, **The Rain Forest Café**, and **Ralph Brennan's Jazz Kitchen**.

Inside the Stadium

The latest round of renovations has returned the ballpark flavor to Angel Stadium, repairing the damage done by previous remodeling efforts designed to make the facility more grid-iron friendly. The open view beyond left field of the mountains goes a long way to improve the atmosphere and give the joint the character it had been lacking.

Angel Stadium clearly does not have the Hollywood cachet that Dodger Stadium does but it is still an attractive stadium. Even under new ownership, Angel Stadium retains a Disneyland type feel with ushers that are very courteous—almost too courteous—and exceptionally clean concourses, bathrooms, and seating areas.

Ballpark Features

EXTRAVAGANT INDEED

The fake-rock formation beyond the center field wall was created as part of the 1996–98 renovations to give Angel Stadium a trademark feature. Of course the trademark features that come about organically—like the Wall in Boston or the Ivy in Chicago—are always preferable, but we can't blame the Angels for trying something to dress up a once-drab part of their park. With its one-hundred-foot-high geyser, fireworks, and assortment of rocks, the "Outfield Extravaganza" is meant to resemble the rocky California coastline. The rocks at the top of the waterfall form the shape of a capital A, while down below, the center field cameramen hide in a cave.

Perhaps the display would look better had real rocks been used instead of Styrofoam. As actor/comedian/all-around-good-guy Robin Williams stated, "It looks like a miniature golf course on steroids."

And as writer/comedian/all-around-good-guy Kevin O'Connell remarked, "It looks and feels a lot like Disney's Country Bear Jamboree. All that's left is to install animatronic bears to play banjos and dance every time the Angels hit a homer."

In case you're wondering, Walt Disney Imagineering served as manager of the renovation project, while HOK Sports drew up the actual blueprints. So, as far as we can tell, blame Disney for the Styrofoam rocks and thank HOK for the tiered bull pens, widened concourses, and landscaped courtyards outside.

To the left field side of the rocks, red and white flags honor Angels teams that made the postseason: the 2002 world champions, and the 1986 and 1979 teams that lost in the American League Championship Series after winning the AL West. Appropriately, the 2002 flag is bigger than the other two.

STATUES

A number of ballparks display statues honoring the great players in their city's history. In Anaheim, the team founder and a player's daughter are memorialized in this way.

Inside the main gate on the third-base side stands a bronze statue of Gene Autry smiling, as if for the camera, and holding out his trademark cowboy hat.

On the first-base side there is a statue of Michelle Carew, holding a puppy dog in her arms. A beautiful bed of flowers surrounds the statue, which depicts Ms. Carew from the waist up. The daughter of Rod Carew—who poked and bunted his way to 3,053 hits in a nineteen-year career with the Twins and Angels—Michelle died of leukemia, but not before inspiring others to fight back against the disease. The base of her statue reads, "Her spirited battle against leukemia raised awareness for the national marrow donor program throughout this country and in the process her legacy has saved countless lives. When she went to sleep, she woke up the world."

RETIRED NUMBERS

Beneath the Jumbotron in right field appear the Angels' retired numbers: number 11 for Jim Fregosi who played for California from 1961–1971 and managed the Angels in 1978; number 26 for longtime owner Gene Autry, the team's metaphoric twenty-sixth man; number 29 for Rod Carew who not only played for the Halos but served as batting coach from 1992–1999; number 30 for Nolan Ryan; number 42 for Jackie Robinson; and number 50 for coach Jimmie Reese who began his seventy-year professional baseball career as a batboy for the Pacific Coast League Los Angeles Stars in 1917, went on to play for the Yankees and Cardinals, and finished his career hitting fungoes for the Angels from 1972 to 1994.

Josh: "Let me get this straight: Autry wasn't on his death bed or even sick when the team retired his number in 1982?"

Kevin: "Yeah, he lived something like another fifteen years after it was retired. What's the point?"

Josh: "Tom Yawkey never retired his own number at Fenway. It seems self-aggrandizing to me."

Kevin: "Yeah, even Steinbrenner hasn't pulled that stunt yet."

CHAMPIONS ON DISPLAY

The team store is located on the 100 Level concourse. You may not have $15 to shell out on a Rally Monkey, but you should drop down for a visit just the same. Outside the store a classy exhibit displays the 2002 World Series trophy and other mementos from the Angels' championship season such as a Rally Monkey, a "Yes We Can" halo stick, and a World Series ring. Not far from the display, a huge American flag is mounted on the concourse wall. The flag was flown over the U.S. Capitol at the request of congresswoman Loretta Sanchez in commemoration of the opening of the remodeled stadium on April 1, 1998.

TIME AND TIME AGAIN

On the 200 Level concourse behind home plate a lengthy Angels time line extends nearly sixty feet, reflecting in words and pictures the story of the Angels. The history begins all the way back in 1960 when Gene Autry went to the MLB winter meetings looking for a team to broadcast on his radio station and left as owner and chairman of the expansion Los Angeles Angels.

While most years get only one or two blurbs of text, no less than nineteen magical moments from 2002 are remembered on the time line.

While perusing this well-done display, we learned that Yankees pitcher Eli Grba was the first player selected by the Angels in the 1961 expansion draft. The right-hander, who had won eight games in two seasons with New York, went 11–13 with a 4.25 ERA for the Angels in their inaugural season.

Kevin: "Eli Grba. I'd like to buy a vowel."

THE CURSE

To Angels fans their team's curse is much more frightening than the supposed hexes hovering over the Red Sox and Cubs. In Boston and Chicago, the players have a history of losing. In Anaheim, they have a history of dying.

This caused Gene Autry and others to publicly consider rumors (that were never substantiated) that Anaheim Stadium resided on the site of a former Juanenos Indian burial ground and that angry Native American spirits were to blame for the Angels' awful luck.

Stadium Eats

There are many concession stands located throughout the park, with the basic ballpark items appearing on the first level beneath the stands and on the third level. The wide and airy second level concourse behind the Terrace

WALLY WORLD

REMEMBER Chevy Chase's (aka Clark W. Griswold's) epic quest for the perfect family vacation at the fictitious Los Angeles amusement park named "Wally World," in the movie *Vacation*? Wally World, of course, was a spoof on Disneyland.

Shortly after the movie opened, in 1986 a wunderkind named Wally Joyner emerged as the Halos' new first-baseman and fans responded by decking out the Big A with Wally World banners. As a rookie that year, the twenty-four-year-old batted .290 with 22 HR and 100 RBI. However, a mysterious allergic reaction to a bee sting limited Joyner to just three games against the Red Sox in the American League Championship Series that year, a series Boston won in seven games after rallying from a three-games-to-one deficit. The BoSox were one strike from elimination in Game 5 before Dave Henderson deposited a Donnie Moore fastball into Anaheim Stadium's left field seats to turn the momentum in the series. The Sox went on to win in seven games, setting the stage for an equally cataclysmic meltdown of their own against the Mets in the World Series. Tragically, Moore committed suicide in 1989, reviving an old Anaheim contention that the Angels were a cursed franchise.

houses a number of specialty stands, though few items that we sampled were very special. **Dominoes Pizza** has a stand here, as does **Carl's Jr.**, and there is a barbecue stand called **Autry's Smokehouse** out in left field. On the whole, we were disappointed by the Angel Stadium concessions and recommend eating at one of the many nearby restaurants before the game.

PANDA EXPRESS (Trademark Food)

Offering a limited menu of combination plates, Panda Express operates a stand on the first-level concourse in right field. We ordered the orange-flavored chicken/beef and broccoli combination plate that came with a healthy portion of fried rice and a fortune cookie that we split in half to share. The meal was freshly cooked, the beef was tender, and the broccoli was still a little bit crisp, the way it's supposed to be. The chicken was crispy and sweet, and the rice was decent. The other combo plates on the menu were orange-flavored chicken with mixed vegetables, and beef and broccoli with black-pepper chicken. While the menu is not expansive, the food is on a par with the Chinese food you'll find at most Chinese take-out joints.

Our fortune read: "Make use of your talents."

WIENERSCHNITZEL HOT DOG (Dog Rating)
The Twenty-ninth Best Hot Dog in the Majors

We didn't care for this brand of dog when we first tried it at the ballpark in San Diego. Yet we cut it some slack, figuring that had our Padres dog been prepared better it might have made a more favorable impression. Well, the preparation wasn't any better in Anaheim. Our dog was literally a pale shade of green and our bun was completely stale. Ah, the dangers of the pre-bagged ballpark dog. Be afraid, be very afraid.

BEST OF THE REST

If you're trying to do some artery clogging, the **Stadium Fish Bowl** on the 200 Level concourse offers a decent plate of fish and chips for a reasonable price.

The smoked turkey sandwich that we sampled from the **Main Street Deli** on the 200 Level was freshly made, and certainly a cut above the Blimpie or Subway sandwiches available at many parks. It seemed overpriced, however, at $8.25.

The ballpark malt is a good choice on a hot day. As long as they keep it adequately frozen, this is one item the Angel Stadium concession stands can't screw up. And ours was chilled nice and solid.

SAY "NO, THANKS," AND WALK AWAY

Although the idea of heading out to the center field patio to have an authentic Western barbecue may be appealing, avoid **Gene Autry's Smoke House**. Avoid it like the plague. Soupy and sloppy and soaked in its own grease, the pork tasted awful. The corn on the cob was overcooked and mushy, but the mashed potatoes were actually pretty good.

Like the hot dogs, the ballpark bratwurst and Italian sausage come precooked and pre-wrapped and aren't worth any part of your $6.

STADIUM SUDS

Angel Stadium offers Fosters and a number of macrobrews on tap. The micro-brew on tap is Pyramid Hefeweizen. The Tiki Bar on the 100 Level concourse offers frozen margaritas. And Woodbridge wine is available by the glass throughout the ballpark.

The Angel Stadium Experience

Anaheim offers a festive ballpark experience. When the home team is in contention—especially late in the season—Angel Stadium can be a raucous place to watch a game, with the fans opting not to sit back as simple spectators but to play a part in the action. What else would you expect in an area full of directors and wannabe directors? They're loud, they're sort of creative, and they're not bashful. They might be a bit late getting to the ballpark though. And maybe a bit early departing if the game's not a nail-biter. Like we said, they're A-type personalities on their way to fame. Hey, if that's what it takes to "make it," we say no thanks. We'll settle for nine full innings and a few cold frosties.

PRIMATES APLENTY

Leave it to an entertainment-driven city to get its mascot from such a high quality movie as *Ace Ventura, Pet Detective*. But if it works for them—who are we to judge.

The Rally Monkey phenomenon may look like nothing more than fun and games on TV, but there's actually a method to the madness in Anaheim. And Angels fans take this monkey business very seriously.

First, the Rally Monkey cannot make his first official appearance until the seventh inning has begun. Second, the Angels must be trailing in the game, when the monkey squeaks his first shrill cries of encouragement on the Jumbotron. Third, the Angels must have at least one runner on base before the monkey's spirit is invoked. Fourth, once he does appear, fans are free to whip out whatever monkeys of their own they may have brought with them to the game, or to start monkeying around if the spirit suits them (you know: picking bugs out of each other's hair, swinging from the rafters, and making general baboons of themselves).

Now just so we're clear, when we talk about the Rally Monkey we're not talking about that ridiculous twelve-year-old in the orange orangutan suit who kept running up and down the aisle behind home plate during the 2002 postseason. He was a poor excuse for a monkey, and a little too old to be dressing like that in public as far as we're concerned. We're talking about the real Rally Monkey. The one from the Angels TV commercials who lights up the Jumbotron with his effervescence and enthusiasm, kind of the way Kevin lights up a barroom when he enters. You'll know him when you see him: a crazy little bugger with a long tail and beady eyes.

It may be hard to understand how or why Angels fans get so excited over this moronic monkey, but they do. Whenever he appears on screen, they hold up their own $15 monkeys and wave them back and forth frantically. Whether you laugh at this ritual as we did, or buy into it, you have to admit that the power of the Monkey often proves legitimate. When we were in town the Angels scored two runs in the

THE BASEBALL RELIQUARY

TALK ABOUT odd-ball baseball. The Baseball Reliquary, a nonprofit organization based in Monrovia, California, surely qualifies. Offering exhibitions and programs at public libraries and art galleries throughout California, the Reliquary is devoted to bringing fans a slice of the game that might not otherwise be accessible to them.

Our visit coincided with an exhibition at the Pomona Public Library entitled "Culinary Baseball: Dishing Up the National Pastime," which featured artifacts and artwork exploring the relationship between food and baseball. Other recent exhibits have focused on the relationship between comedy and baseball, and the place of women in baseball.

The Reliquary owns such items as the jockstrap worn by Bill Veeck's pinch-hitting Eddie Gaedel; a scale model of Ebbets Field made of wood, clay, and cake frosting; a soil sample from Hoboken, New Jersey's, Elysian Fields where many believe the game of baseball was first played in the 1840s; a humanitarian award that legendary misanthrope Ty Cobb was awarded after donating $100,000 to the construction of a new hospital in his hometown, Royston, Georgia; and a cigar partially smoked by Babe Ruth that he left behind after departing a Philadelphia brothel. Classy, eh?

The Reliquary also manages the Shrine of the Eternals, an elite club that honors those individuals who have helped shape (for better or worse) the game of baseball. The 2002 class of inductees included Mark "the Bird" Fidrych, "Shoeless" Joe Jackson, and Minnie Minoso. Minoso, whom we met while touring Chicago, became the oldest player to ever get a base hit in a big league game when he singled for the White Sox at the Big A on September 12, 1976, at age fifty-three.

To find out what exhibits the Reliquary is sponsoring during your visit, call (626) 791-7647 or visit the Web site at www.baseballreliquary.org.

---

bottom of the ninth inning to complete a 7–6 come-from-behind win over the Orioles.

NUTTY

Hey, as long as you're embracing the circus theme, you might as well have some peanuts. The Angel Stadium ushers wear straw hats and old-style vests that are green on front and pin-striped on the back. During the seventh-inning stretch they stand on the field facing the crowd and with varying degrees of enthusiasm lead fans in the singing of "Take Me Out to the Ball Game." When it gets to the part in the song that goes, "Buy me some peanuts and Cracker Jack," they throw bags of peanuts into the crowd. When the song finishes, they take a bow. So weasel your way down to the front row seats by the middle of the seventh, and you might be in for a treat.

Kevin: "Almost as much fun as watching the ushers square-dance in Milwaukee?"

Josh: "I still prefer Toronto's stretch. 'Let's Go Blue Jays,' eh?"

Kevin: "Don't forget those cheerleaders, either."

FIREWORKS

The Angels really do it up with the fireworks when one of their players goes yard. Maybe the team is still getting Disney's leftover rockets and Roman candles, or maybe the new owner has stock in a pyrotechnics company. Most parks that use fireworks send two or three colorful rockets into the air when the home team has something to celebrate. But at Angel Stadium more like a dozen rockets take off from atop the rock display in center field when it comes time to party. When we visited, a first-inning home run by Garret Anderson produced a great light display that quickly turned into a billowing black cloud of smoke. During the course of the next inning, the cloud slowly wafted toward the infield. We wondered if the game would have to be stopped, but the Orioles and Angels played through it and none of the other fans seemed to mind. With all of the smog these folks tolerate on a daily basis, what's a little extra smoke, right?

HALO STICKS

The folks clapping Thunder Sticks in Frisco might argue otherwise, but Angels fans will tell you that the Halo Sticks on display during the fourth-ever all-California October Classic in 2002 were originally an Anaheim phenomenon. The noisemakers debuted in July 2002 during a series against Seattle. Either way, we think these things should be banned. They make the game annoying to watch, even on TV. This ain't NASCAR. It's baseball.

SANTA CATALINA ISLAND

From 1921 to 1951 the Chicago Cubs spent their preseasons on Santa Catalina Island, a 76-square-mile paradise twenty-five miles off the coast of Los Angeles. Cubs owner William Wrigley acquired majority interest in the largely undeveloped terrain in 1919, hoping to turn it into a resort. The chewing gum millionaire installed streetlights and sewers, erected hotels, and built the world's largest dance hall at the time—the Avalon Grand Casino. But with the Great Depression looming, the island failed to catch on as a tourist destination.

Santa Catalina did, however, provide the Cubs with an exotic Spring Training base for the better part of three decades. The island featured a practice field—named Wrigley Field—that matched the exact field dimensions of Chicago's regular season Wrigley Field. Even the famous Waveland Avenue rooftop viewing decks of Chicago's North Side were mimicked by clubhouse patios built into a mountainside overlooking the field.

Cubs players would get in shape by running along the Island's hilly goat trails. Then afterward they would soothe their burning feet with fresh eucalyptus, which grew on the island in abundance. A few weeks before the regular season was set to begin, they would leave the island to scrimmage other teams on the mainland.

But after several rainy springs, the Cubs left Santa Catalina in 1952 in favor of Mesa, Arizona.

Today, the beautiful island has finally become the beach resort Wrigley envisioned, offering visitors a glimpse of what California looked like two centuries ago: a wilderness of oaks, cactus, and sage surrounded by the sea. The island is just a fifteen-minute helicopter ride from Los Angeles and makes for an enjoyable day trip or a longer stay—especially if you're road-tripping with your wife or girlfriend and want to give her a treat after so many days spent in the bleachers and smelly road-trip car. For more information, check out www.ecatalina.com.

As for the ballpark? It was razed years ago, but the Wrigley Memorial remains—featuring a botanical garden and the Wrigley Mausoleum.

LOS ANGELES,
CALIFORNIA

36 miles to Anaheim
116 miles to San Diego
340 miles to San
Francisco / Oakland
367 miles to Phoenix

LOS ANGELES DODGERS, DODGER STADIUM

A Baseball Taj Mahal—with Plenty of Parking

THE MOST FORTUNATE of baseball teams find that elusive ballpark nirvana once in their history, that one hallowed plot of ground that not only provides the team a place where it can win championships before the hometown crowd, but also a place that defines the spirit of the franchise and city. The Dodgers have had the good fortune of finding two such houses of baseball perfection, one on each coast. And each embodies the spirit of those different Dodger teams perfectly.

Dodger Stadium is as much a part of Los Angeles as the in-ground swimming pool and the movie studio. For in L.A., image is everything. And Dodger Stadium provides the local nine with that perfect image of baseball in paradise. Carved into Elysian Hills in an area known as Chavez Ravine, the stadium stands like a shining beacon on the gloried hill of baseball success. And while no other baseball park in the Majors is built on a hill, the Elysian Hills of L.A. bring to mind that dreamlike ideal of an ethereal ball field in the heavens.

A more ideal setting would be difficult to imagine. The weather is nearly flawless, having accounted for less than twenty rainouts in the forty-year history of the stadium. The San Gabriel Mountains loom beyond the hills—snowcapped in the spring and fall—purple under the setting summer sun—and ring the outfield in an ever-glorious backdrop for the game we so love. Meanwhile, out the back of the stadium a breathtaking view of the downtown L.A. skyline rises from the valley below.

Dodger Stadium is a large facility for baseball, with expansive foul territory and five decks for seating. But still it manages to maintain a feeling of intimacy. The cliché "not a bad seat in the house" is almost applicable, as sight lines are outstanding for nearly every seat. And though it's completely symmetrical in every way, Dodger Stadium's wavy topped Pavilion roof and wonderful views of the action, scenery, and Hollywood stars make attending a game at Chavez Ravine an experience unlike any other in sports.

Contrary to popular belief, Dodger fans are savagely loyal to their team. But like baseball in other parts of the West, a more laid-back form of that loyalty is expressed. These folks can't understand why Easterners yell their heads off at ball games; it just doesn't seem to Los Angelenos that Easterners could be having a good time acting that way. Relax, have a Dodger Dog and beer, you can almost hear them say with their laid-back eyes. Enjoy yourself, the weather's good, and so is everything else, dude.

Dodger Stadium is rarely full when the first pitch is thrown, or when the last out is made. Fashion dictates that local fans arrive at the ballpark late and leave early. Josh cannot quite wrap his brain around the idea that there are fans who don't thrive on every pitch of the game the way he breathes in the very air around him. But in defense of the locals, the L.A. traffic is legendarily brutal.

Aside for their lack of punctuality, there is no shortage of other reminders that this is Holly-wood, the image factory, fans arrive wearing sunglasses (even during night games) and have cell phones pasted to their ears. Seeing and being seen are as important as watching the game. It's true what they say: the clothes are a tad skimpier, and the breasts are mysteriously bigger. For the life of us, we cannot figure out why. Must be all that wheat germ and yoga.

And to sustain that image, the Dodgers maintain their stadium with a tenacity envied by the wealthiest of Hollywood dream makers. Dodger Stadium is repainted every season, given a face-lift to keep any blight from fans' eyes. During the game the ballpark is kept more immaculate than Josh's bathroom. There is no cleaner or better maintained facility in all of sports than Dodger Stadium.

Alongside a grounds crew that tends to the field, a full-time crew of seven gardeners care for the three-hundred-acre site, comprising ubiquitous palm trees, lush bushes, and flower beds that surround the twenty-one landscaped and terraced parking lots. This obsessive attention to the sparkling image of the ballpark is a very L.A. phenomenon, and is as important to the team as winning ball games.

exterior

Photo by Kevin O'Connell

Kevin: "Recently their image seems more important than winning."

But winning has come in great abundance since the Dodgers moved west to L.A. Dodger Stadium transformed the team's attitude from "Wait till Next Year," to pennants and world championships accumulated at a rate exceeded only by the New York Yankees, and then only recently. The Dodgers have hosted nine World Series since moving to Los Angeles in 1958, and the Blue Crew has won five of them.

Team owner Walter O'Malley was the man responsible for moving the Dodgers west and out of Brooklyn. After a four-year wait for new digs after the move, the Dodgers celebrated the opening of Dodger Stadium on April 10, 1962, with a loss to the Cincinnati Reds, 6–3. The huge stadium seated fifty-six thousand, but was built to be expandable to eighty-five thousand should the team ever decide to continue the decks all the way around the outfield.

Plenty of misinformation surrounds the Dodgers' move to Chavez Ravine. Rumors that

the police evicted poor Mexican American families that were living in the area at the behest of the Dodgers organization are simply not true. The L.A. police did forcibly drag people out of their homes, but these heinous acts were with the city's intention to build housing at Chavez Ravine, and occurred long before the land was sold to O'Malley.

Captain Emil Praeger was chosen as the architect of the stadium. The Vinell Construction Company of Los Angeles built the structure at a cost of $23 million. O'Malley and his partners paid for all of the construction costs, making Dodger Stadium only the second ballpark to be entirely privately funded during the twentieth century. Yankee Stadium was the first (1923) and PacBell Park in San Francisco was the only other, built in 2000.

Dodger Stadium was dubbed by some the "Taj Majal of baseball," but critics pejoratively called the stadium the Taj O'Malley. One obvious Opening Day gaff was that the foul poles were installed completely in foul territory instead of lined up with the foul line (we're left to wonder why they don't call them fair poles if they're supposed to be in fair territory). For the first season, special dispensation from the league had to be granted for the unorthodox placement, until they could be moved by the next season.

Another early blunder: in a city where drinking water can be as precious as gold, no water fountains were installed at the park for fans that first season.

The Dodgers also shared their new digs with the expansion California Angels during the 1962–1965 seasons.

interior

Photo by Kevin O'Connell

THE ★ ULTIMATE ★ BASEBALL ★ ROAD ★ TRIP

Dodger Stadium was quietly called "Chavez Ravine" when the Angels were playing.

Despite the fact that they had to share their stadium with an expansion team, 1962 was a glorious year for the Dodgers, as they won 102 games and finished in a tie for the National League lead with their archrivals, the San Francisco Giants. On October 3, 1962, the two teams squared off in a one-game playoff at Dodger Stadium to decide who would represent the NL in the World Series. Unfortunately for the Dodgers, the Giants rallied with four runs in the ninth to post a 6–4 win, but the crowd of 45,693 gave the Dodgers a MLB record-setting attendance total of 2,755,184 for the year. Earlier in 1962, Jackie Robinson was inducted into the National Baseball Hall of Fame.

Dodger Stadium has always been a pitcher's park, and overpowering pitching has led the boys in blue to their success. In 1963, left-hander Sandy Koufax posted a 25–5 record alongside an ERA of 1.88 en route to winning the MVP, Cy Young, and MVP of the World Series after the Dodgers swept the Yankees in four straight games. In the final game the Dodgers managed only two hits, but Koufax pitched a complete game to beat the Yanks 2–1.

During the 1960s the Dodgers also had Don Drysdale and Johnny Podres in their rotation, as well as a fearless closer in Ron Perranoski. Koufax was the ace, however, and proved it in 1965 when the Dodgers captured their first Series as residents of Dodger Stadium. After a tough battle with the Minnesota Twins, the Dodgers prevailed in seven games, behind two complete game shutouts by Koufax. In Game 7 he tossed a masterful 2–0 gem.

Then almost mythically, after leading the NL in wins again the next season with twenty-seven Ws in 1966, Koufax, seemingly in the prime of his career, and with two World Series rings and MVPs to his credit, bowed out of baseball, exiting the game at the top of his form. His early retirement confounded many critics and fans at the time. For though he cited worsening arthritis and pain in his pitching elbow, he was still better than anyone else in the game. Five years after retiring, Koufax became the youngest man to be elected to the Hall of Fame, at the age of thirty-six in 1972.

The 1970s were also kind to the Blue Crew, as no team in the decade posted a divisional finish lower than third place. Though the Dodgers would lose in the World Series three times (to Oakland in '74, and to the Yankees in '77 and '78), those teams had some of the most memorable players to ever wear the Blue. Tommy Lasorda took over as manager in 1976, a post he would remain at as a fixture until moving up to the front office in 1997. Lasorda's lifetime record in twenty-one seasons as manager was 1,599 wins and 1,439 losses, for a .526 winning percentage. Outfielder Dusty Baker wore Dodger Blue in the 1970s and would later square off against 1980s Dodger catcher Mike Scioscia as opposing managers in the 2002 World Series that pitted two other California teams against each other.

Four dynamic infielders were the heart and soul of the next Dodgers' championship team. Consisting of Ron Cey at third-base, second bagger Davey Lopes, shortstop Bill Russell, and Steve Garvey at first, this infield stayed intact until 1981 when the team won the World Series. Fans responded well to these exciting players by showing up at Chavez Ravine in huge numbers, and Dodger Stadium became the first ballpark to surpass the three-million mark in attendance in 1978, then did it again in 1980.

While the infield was stellar, dominant pitching also played a hand in bringing a championship back to L.A. On Opening Day of the 1981 season the "Fernandomania" craze erupted across Dodgerland when Mexican rookie Fernando Valenzuela shut out the Astros

2–0. The twenty-year-old sensation pitched four shutouts in his first five starts that April. Not only did he start the season 5–0 with a 0.20 ERA, but he batted .438 in the month. Fernando's famous windup, where he would look to the heavens, perhaps for help from above from the angelic namesakes of the city, in addition to his sparkling smile and personality helped Fernandomania go nationwide. Valenzuela went on to capture not only Rookie of the Year honors, but also the Cy Young Award.

After the Dodgers dropped the first two games to the Yankees in the 1981 World Series, Valenzuela took the hill in Game 3. Though the rookie gave up nine hits and seven walks, he hung on to claim a 5–4 win, fueled by a three-run dinger by Cey in the first. The win gave the Dodgers the stopper that Lasorda was looking for, and the Blue Crew never looked back. Game 5 at Dodger Stadium would prove critical as the Series was deadlocked at two games apiece going in. The game was tied 1–1 heading into the bottom of the fourth when Yankee manager Bob Lemon decided to pinch-hit for his ace Tommy John (a former Dodger)—a decision that proved catastrophic. The Yankees failed to score in the inning, and John, who had been brilliant as the Game 2 winner, was suddenly on the bench. His replacement on the mound was George Frazier, and the Dodgers' Pedro Guerrero treated him the same way Muhammad Ali treated Joe Frazier, by clobbering him for five RBIs. The Dodgers went on to win the series four games to two, after having dropped the first two games. Coincidentally, this was the same trick the Yankees had pulled on the Dodgers the last time the two teams met in the World Series in 1978.

Valenzuela was still with the Dodgers in 1988 when they returned to the World Series, but by this time he was the "old shoe" of the rotation, something that every pitching staff needs. A young Orel Hershiser had assumed the mantle of the ace, and pitched fifty-nine scoreless innings during the regular season on his way to the Cy Young before being named MVP of the World Series. Tommy Lasorda dubbed him "the Bulldog" in an effort to make him appear more intimidating than his mild-mannered personality projected.

With Dodger history being so rich, the moment voted by L.A. fans as the greatest in Los Angeles Sports history came in Game 1 of the World Series, on October 15, 1988. Pinch-hitter Kirk Gibson hobbled up to the plate looking aged and injured and still somehow got enough meat on a Dennis Eckersley pitch to lift it into the Pavilion seats in right field, and propel the Dodgers over the Oakland A's. Gibson's only at-bat of the Series gave the Dodgers the beginning they needed and they won the Series in five games.

There is no more profound turning point in the history of baseball in New York than 1958, when the Brooklyn Dodgers, along with the New York Giants, decided to pull up stakes and head west. For the cities of Los Angeles and San Francisco it was a dream come true: two of the most successful and historic franchises in baseball were coming to play in their towns. And a fierce baseball rivalry continued further fueled by the Southern versus Northern California feud was already in place.

The Dodgers leaving Brooklyn completely crushed the city. Brooklynites have always had a proud, separate identity from other New Yorkers. And whether it was the fact that the move coincided with the economic downturn in the city at the time, or because the Dodgers were such a strong symbol of that separate and proud identity, two things were certain: the Dodgers were gone forever and Brooklyn would never be the same.

New York Mets fans, whose ranks were initially supposed to consist of ex-Dodgers and

Giants faithful, still to this day despise both these two teams for abandoning New York. It's odd because most living Mets fans saw neither the Dodgers nor Giants play in Brooklyn or Manhattan. Ah, well, baseball loyalties run very deep, especially in a town as rich in baseball history as New York.

Baseball had been played professionally in Brooklyn since 1849. The team that began playing in the early 1890s eventually emerged as the most prominent team in the area. The official name of the club was originally the "Brooklyn Baseball Club." But that name was lengthy, and didn't have much pizzazz. The club played under such nicknames as the Brooklyn Bridegrooms (because seven players got married at nearly the same time) as well as Hanlon's Superbas, Ward's Wonders, and Fout's Fillies, all after successful managers.

Though the original home of the ball club had been Washington Park, it was at Eastern Park where the name "Trolley Dodgers" came about, because fans had to cross over a maze of trolley lines to reach the field. Though the Brooklyn club continued to be called a variety of names, the Dodgers name slowly gained momentum and eventually won out.

A small wooden facility had been constructed at Washington Park and so the team returned in 1898. Washington Park, located at 3rd Avenue, between 1st and 3rd Streets in Red Hook, was built on the approximate location of George Washington's headquarters while the Continental Army fought the Battle of Long Island. The Dodgers won the National League title in 1899 and 1900 behind such stars as "Wee" Willie Keeler and "Brickyard" Kennedy.

In 1912 team owner Charles Ebbets started buying up property in the Flatbush area of Brooklyn in order to build his team a new ballpark. The area was known less than affectionately as "Pigtown" because swine roamed freely through the nearby dumps looking for food. It was a nicely poetic expression that symbolized the Brooklyn Dodgers who would eventually reside there. The Dodgers' reputation as the working man's team would remain with them as long as they stayed in Brooklyn.

Ebbets bought many parcels of property and eventually had to sell off half of his interest in the team to raise funds to build his new park. But it was worth it. Ebbets Field opened in 1913 and closed in 1947—only thirty-four short years—but no other ballpark has had as great an impact on our National Pastime. At least one aspect of the mythical ballpark has shown up in every new park built during the recent retro renaissance. Ebbets Field still floats ethereally in the minds of baseball fans, like the ancient walled city of Troy—a place where many great battles were fought, some won and some lost. A place that is no more.

The clearest image etched if the minds of folks who never attended a game at Ebbets Field is of the majestic front rotunda. Located at ·55 Sullivan Place, the rounded front entranceway featured grand arches and square windows and fit seamlessly into the landscape of Brooklyn, a borough with more than its share of churches. Inside, the rotunda was decorated in Italian marble, with a floor tiled with baseball stitching as decoration. Hanging from the twenty-seven-foot-high domed ceiling was a chandelier made of baseball globes and bat arms. Ball fans came to worship at Ebbets and plopped down their money at beautifully gilded ticket windows.

But though Ebbets Field had these high-class elements, what made it special was that it was bursting with the local personality of Brooklyn. Brooklynites were not Giants fans. They didn't socialize in the finer places that Manhattan had to offer. Brooklyn was working-class. Dodger fans drank in the beer halls and went to the game to blow off steam and root for "dem bums." They weren't the highfalutin fans of the pinstriped teams across the rivers. Ebbets Field reflected the fans' personality. Ebbets was a crazy place, where the feeling that just about anything was liable to happen was justified almost nightly. The right field wall was concaved, accounting for an estimated 289 different angles that sent shots bouncing off in thousands of different directions. To make matters more difficult for outfielders, a giant scoreboard jutted out of the stands at a forty-five-degree angle in center field.

The ballpark opened without a press box but one was added in 1929, hanging from the roof. Added in 1931 was a double-decked outfield grandstand, which effectively turned the ballpark from a pitcher's park into a hitter's park, enclosing all but the right field wall and increasing the seating capacity to thirty-two thousand. The roof above the upper deck actually hung over the field of play. But the ballpark's quirks were beloved at the time and made the park feel all the more homey to fans.

Ebbets Field was a magical place to watch a game, a cozy little ballpark where fans were right on top of the action. This closeness endeared the Dodgers to their fans, and made life miserable for opposing teams. One remarkable fan was Hilda Chester, who incessantly clanged her cowbell from the second deck of the left field bleachers, often to the dismay of even Dodger fans. "Shorty's Symphony Band" kept spirits lively with a cacophonous barrage of tunes, though many folks felt they couldn't find the tune they were playing to save their lives. And there were many other superfans who frequented Ebbets—home to the notoriously rowdiest fans in all of baseball.

The ballpark hosted four All-Star Games. The first televised game in baseball history was played at Ebbets on April 26, 1939, between the Dodgers and Cincinnati Reds. And the Dodgers and Reds played a nineteen-inning scoreless tie there on September 11, 1946.

During the 1940s and 1950s, baseball in New York blossomed into its halcyon years, as the Yankees seemed to be forever playing either the Dodgers or the Giants for the world championship. During the twenty-year span of the two decades, a New York team played in fourteen World Series, and in eight of those years both teams competing in the Series were from New York. During this time, the hapless Dodgers came into their own, advancing to the World Series seven times. But despite all their NL pennants, the Yankees were always at the World Series waiting for them, to snatch away the final glory.

In 1941 a dropped third strike by Dodgers catcher Mickey Owen would have ended Game 4, but set the stage for a Yankee comeback win. Had Owen held onto the ball the Dodgers would have evened the series at two games apiece, but instead the Yankees took a three-games-to-one lead. The pitcher of that dropped ball, Hugh Casey, admitted years later that he had thrown a spitball, taking some of the heat off of Owen.

Brooklyn owner Branch Rickey had the guts in 1947 to undo what never should have been done in the first place. He searched the country for a player—a very special player—who would have the physical skills, as well as the mental strength and fortitude of character to cross the hatred of the color barrier and integrate baseball for the first time since the unofficial owners agreement had barred African Americans from playing in the Major Leagues in 1898. The player he found was Jack Roosevelt Robinson.

Behind the clutch hitting of shortstop Pee Wee Reese, the power of Duke Snider, and the excellent all-around play of Robinson, "Dem Bums" from Brooklyn reached the World Series in 1947, 1949, 1952, and 1953, but lost to the Yankees in every one of those years.

The year 1952 ended particularly cruelly for Brooklyn as a quick second baseman named Billy Martin saved Game 7 of the World Series for the Yanks. Down 4–2 with two outs in the seventh and the bases loaded, Robinson hit a pop-up behind the mound. Reliever Bob Kuzuva and infielder Joe Collins couldn't locate the bloop as Dodgers runners came rushing around the bases. At the last minute Martin made a spectacular diving catch, just inches from the ground. Dodgers fans could do nothing but shout back their mantra "Wait till Next Year!" But even the most die-hard fans of the beloved losers must have started to suspect that "next year" might never come. For a city that seemed to have less and less going for it, the Dodgers and their losses became symptomatic of the city. The Dodgers were doomed, born losers. Even their name "Dodger" seemed a bit on the shady side.

But "next year" finally came for Brooklyn in 1955. Snider knocked a three-run shot into the second-level grandstands of center field to win Game 4 of the Series against the Yanks. Sandy Amoros caught a well-hit Yogi Berra drive to the left field corner in Game 7 to preserve a 2–0 lead. The losers from Brooklyn went on to beat the rival socialites from Manhattan. And people all over Brooklyn, the city that couldn't buy a break, celebrated wildly and drank themselves silly in the madness of the Flatbush night.

There is a famous photograph in which a bartender holds up a newspaper that reads: "WE WIN" in bold and brazen ink on the front page of the *Brooklyn Eagle*. But perhaps more importantly the toasting Dodgers fans all have glasses of beer raised in celebration. This photo symbolizes what it meant to a city of three million people, the fourth largest in America, for their bums, their lovable losers whose ballpark was built on a dump, to at last slay the mighty dragon and defeat the team that boasted all the talent that money could buy.

But even in victory, the Dodgers found a way to lose. When they failed to repeat as World Series champs, losing to the Yankees in seven games in 1956, the end was near. The long-standing Dodger mantra "Wait till Next Year," was changed by Brooklyn writer Roger Kahn to "Wait till Last Year." Brooklyn would forever look backward at their Dodgers. Khan's 1972 best-seller *Boys of Summer* is a classic text of the era, that chronicles the Brooklyn Dodger teams of the 1950s.

O'Malley, after failing in his attempts to obtain funding for a new ballpark from city officials, made arrangements to move the Dodgers out of Brooklyn. The move of the Braves to Milwaukee had preceded the Dodgers' migration west and had proved that it was financially lucrative to do so. O'Malley saw little chance of remaining competitive in Brooklyn without the new ballpark he deemed necessary to increase revenue for the team.

There were massive protests and scathing articles written. But the last game was played at Ebbets Field on September 24, 1957, witnessed by just 6,702 fans. So hurtful was the team's impending departure that the rowdiest and most loyal fans in baseball couldn't bear to show up. When asked to list the three most notorious villains of the twentieth century, Brooklynites chose Adolf Hitler, Joseph Stalin, and Walter O'Malley.

In moving to L.A., O'Malley transfigured that old Brooklyn soul from one of bums and perennial losers to clean-cut winning boys of summer. These new Dodgers of L.A. were no longer allowed to be called "Dem Bums" by the newspapers. That moniker died in Brooklyn alongside Ebbets Field. An all-American image in Dodger Blue was crafted, one more suitable to Los Angeles, and along with it, a tradition of winning World Series.

L.A.'s Memorial Coliseum, as horrible a spot to view a baseball game as ever was retrofitted,

TRIVIA TIMEOUT

People's Choice: Since Jackie Robinson was selected as the first Rookie of the Year in 1947, how many ROY awards have been won by Dodger's players? (Hint: the number is more than twice as many won by any other team.)

Golden Globe: Name the Cubs player who rescued the American Flag when a fan attempted to burn it in left field of Dodger Stadium.

Oscar: Name the three players who have hit the ball out of Dodger Stadium.

Look for the answers in the text.

was where the Dodgers awaited the building of their Elysian ballpark on the hill. The Dodgers played at the Coliseum from 1958 to 1962, and though it was fairly awful, it seated plenty. The farthest seats were more than seven hundred feet from home plate. In 1958 the L.A. Dodgers drew 1.85 million fans, some 600,000 more than the Brooklyn Dodgers had drawn the year before. The Coliseum seated well over 90,000 per game, as opposed to only 32,000 at Ebbets. The Coliseum also set World Series attendance records in 1959 when the Dodgers defeated the Chicago White Sox in six games. In the 1963 World Series the Dodgers swept the Yankees in four games. Clearly, the face-lift of the old Dodger Bums was complete.

Since claiming their fifth World Series title in 1988, the Los Angeles Dodgers have seen some of the greatest players of the game play at Dodger Stadium. Hideo Nomo, the first Japanese-born pitcher in the big leagues came to America first as a Dodger, then after leaving, returned to the team. Pitching phenom Ramon Martinez and perennial All-Star Mike Piazza also came up through the legendary Dodgers farm system.

Sellout Index: 10% of games sell out
Seating Capacity: 56,000
Ticket Office: (323) 224-1HIT
http://losangeles.dodgers.mlb.com

During its history, Dodger Stadium has hosted stadium acts ranging from the Beatles to U2. Pope John Paul II celebrated Mass there on September 16, 1987. The Placido Domingo, Luciano Pavarotti, and the third guy, uh, José Carerras, played a reunion show at Chavez Ravine titled "Encore—The Three Tenors."

Getting a Choice Seat

With some of the best sight lines in baseball and a stadium that is completely symmetrical in every way, it's not hard to figure out where the good seats are. But there are a few caveats at Dodger Stadium, so follow the guide below to maximize your ballpark visit.

The first point to remember is that nowhere in baseball is it more imperative to purchase a seat on the level in which you intend to sit. Ushers at Dodger Stadium are very kindly and polite, but they will only allow you to access the level of the stadium for which you have a ticket. Kevin tried his smooth-talking techniques on more than a few, but to these ushers it was like he was trying to talk his way into an exclusive Hollywood party. This means that unless you are skilled at the very dangerous practice of stadium level hopping (please do not try this) you'll do yourself a favor by purchasing a ticket for the tier in which you intend to sit. You can then perhaps do some seat hopping on that particular level.

Dodgers fans may be fashionably late, but they show up for the games whether the Dodgers win or lose. Finishing in third place is considered a poor year for the Boys in Blue, so they are usually at least competitive. This means that seat hopping in the early innings is likely to get you pinched. So wait until the relative safety of the fourth inning, unless traffic on the 101 is particularly bad.

Also beware of calling the ticket line by phone, as the ticket office charges a $2.25 per ticket "handling" charge.

Kevin: "That is tight!"

Josh: "Only in la-la land."

Club Seating

The seats in the Dugout Club, a section between the dugouts added to the ballpark in 2000, are undoubtedly better than their Stadium Club counterparts. Both have access to their own clubhouse, where if you can afford it you can be in the club, talk to other members of the club, and basically be in the club. Sounds like a *real good* time to us.

Field Level

Apparently you have to be dating a high-level Hollywood exec or your last name has to be Lasorda to sit in the Inner Field Box Seats (Field Aisles 1–41), because we couldn't even find pricing for them. When we asked about them we were taken to a special room and strip searched. Not really, but purchasing these seats is out of the question. Middle Field Box Seats (Field Aisles 42–49) are pricey, but excellent. Outer Field Boxes (Field Aisles 50–57) are less pricey (but still too much in our opinion) and less excellent. Much less excellent are Aisles

---

SEATING TIP

➡ NOTICE that there is an overlap between Inner Reserved and Outer Reserved Seats in Aisles 13–20. That is because these Aisles service both sections and price ranges. So beware: some Aisles only head up from the concourse toward the worse seats, while others go up toward the poorer seats, but also head down toward the better seats. Ask for seats in the lower rows of Aisles 23–24, 27–28, 31–32, 35–36, and 39–40, (as these rows also head upward) and your seats will be vastly improved within the same price range.

54–57 which all have foul pole obstructions to some degree. When you're paying this much for seats, foul poles should not block anything.

Loge Level

Inner Loge Box Seats (Loge Aisles 101–147) were also unavailable to us, unless we were willing to rent wheelchairs and angle for handicapped seating. While Josh toyed with the idea for a moment, we decided that it would be better not to spend the hefty sum of cash required. Middle Loge Box Seats (Loge Aisles 148–157) are worth the three dollars more than they charge for Outer Field Boxes. But the Outer Loge Box Seats (Loge Aisles 158–167) don't seem worth the price. If you can get into Aisles 158–159, then these seats are a better bargain than the Inner Reserved Seats, which are two more levels up. Aisles 164–167 have foul pole obstructions and should be avoided.

Reserved Level

The Inner Reserved Seats (Reserved Aisles 1–20) are also too pricey for how high up they are. Better to sit in a low row of the Top Deck and pay almost a third of this price. Outer Reserved Seats (Reserved Aisles 13–60) are probably the best seats for the money, if you can get them in Aisles 23–40. Inner Reserved Seats in Aisles lower than 20 share the middle concourse with Outer Reserved Seats that are above the concourse. These Outer Reserved seats are therefore that much worse, but they are also significantly cheaper seats, so it's a bit of a trade-off.

We don't recommend sitting in the Outer Reserved Seats, Aisles 41 and higher. You'll be much happier with seats in the Top Deck or the Pavilion. Any Aisle higher than 54 will have some type of foul pole obstruction.

Top Deck

In an odd, but wonderful pricing move, the

Dodgers offer Top Deck Seats (Aisles 1–14) at cheaper prices than are available on the lower level. These beauties are cheap and right behind the plate, a combination that we love. If you like sitting on top of the action, these seats are better than any of the Outer Reserved seats.

Pavilion (Pavilion Aisles 301–314)

The wavy topped roof that gives the stadium its distinctive look shades the upper sections of these seats. One enormous caveat about sitting in the bleachers: THEY DO NOT SELL BEER IN THE PAVILION. Yes, you read that correctly. And since there is no way to access the rest of the stadium, if you sit in the Pavilion you are essentially sitting in a "dry" section. So if you're interested in downing a few brews, head for the Top Deck.

Kevin: "That tip alone is worth the price of the book."

Josh: "Agreed."

Also important to know about the Pavilion seats: the orange seats up above the middle concourse are the same price as the blue seats down near the fence. So why not head down for the good seats? Often the ticket office will sell out the left field section before even opening up the right field Pavilion seats. So if all they have available are the top rows, we suggest waiting them out a few minutes until those crummy seats sell and getting into the newly opened section as soon as it opens.

Kevin: "But how will you know when right field has opened up?"

Josh: "Stand behind the ticket booth and listen in, or just keep pestering the ticket tellers."

The Black Market

Seeing as how the Dodgers keep such a tight watch on everything, there isn't much of a scalper scene around Chavez Ravine. Tickets to sold-out games can be found with ticket brokers, or as we like to call them "on-line scalpers."

Before/After the Game

The folks in Southern California sure know how to build parking lots. The twenty-one terraced levels surrounding the park are landscaped to perfection. The only problem is that tailgating is strictly prohibited. Since there is absolutely nothing else to do in these lots, we wonder if the Dodgers know what kind of opportunity they're wasting here. Think of the possibilities of inebriated entertainment: beer golf, downhill bowling, skateboarding. We also learned by observing a few college kids parked in the lot that there is a fine line between tailgating and "downing a 40" so quickly that no one will see you. Drinking in the parking lots is also illegal, so perhaps making this distinction isn't that important.

Traditionally the ballpark exterior is not its most attractive feature. But with all the money spent on landscaping, the Dodgers challenge conventional wisdom. Walking up the hills will bring you alongside all sorts of California foliage, flora, bushes, and desert trees. And the blue and teal exterior paint of the ballpark itself is very soothing.

Getting to Dodger Stadium

Freeways, freeways everywhere. This is Super-freewayland, so directions are difficult. But if you can find your way to the 101, take the Alvadaro Exit. Then turn right on Sunset and left onto Elysian Park, which spits you out into the parking lots.

From the 110, take the Dodger Stadium Exit; the off-ramp will shoot you right out into the parking lots.

From 5 north, exit at Stadium Way. Make a left onto Riverside Drive and then turn left again onto Stadium Way. Follow the blue baseball signs until you enter Dodger Stadium off of Academy Road. From 5 south simply take the Stadium Way Exit and turn left, then follow the blue signs and enter Dodger Stadium off Academy Road.

Parking

As you might expect, the parking section of the L.A. chapter will be quite extensive. The team lots are all marked by numbered baseballs, twenty-one in all, and are the only ones remotely close. They charge $8 for cars and motorcycles. If you intend on parking in the team lot, we suggest parking close to the "Think Blue" sign, near Gate C. The walk to the game will be a bit longer—much longer if you're not sitting in the outfield. But you'll thank us when it comes time to leave. For while all the other nearby lots feed into the same lane to exit, and thus are backed up for hours, people parking in these lots are treated to their own exit lane, exclusively marked by cones. You'll stroll past all the folks who left early and who are stuck in the chaos of cars, get into your own vehicle, and be back on the freeway in no time.

For the more daring, there are free parking spaces on Academy Street, just beyond the outermost lots. A word to the wise: park on the side of the street that faces downhill, otherwise you'll spend half your life trying to execute a three-point turn after the game.

Parking lots are available closer to downtown and go for as little as $4 for ball games. But the walk up the hill is a killer.

MASS TRANSIT OPTIONS

Ha, ha, ha, ha!!! This is L.A. And while they have recently built a subway, it runs nowhere near the ballpark, or the airport, or anywhere else that people might like to go. For folks who still prefer the bus, its best to contact Metro Bus via the Web at www.mta.net. For those lucky enough to be close to the train, find your way on the Metro Rail to the Union Station/Gateway Transit Center. Shuttle service runs from Union Station to Dodger Stadium Gate A every ten minutes from 5:30 P.M. to 8:00 P.M. and costs two dollars round-trip. Return buses begin running no later than the top of the eighth inning and the last bus leaves the stadium thirty minutes after the last out, or by 11:00 P.M. at the latest to make connections. Perhaps this is why folks are leaving the game so early—to catch the shuttle bus?

Outside Attractions

"THINK BLUE"

Reminiscent of the "Hollywood" sign and sitting atop a small hill just beyond the parking lots is a sign in Dodger Blue that reads only "Think Blue." Well, we thought "blue" for about as long as we could bear to, but being that we're not Dodgers fans, we didn't come up with much. Perhaps this is some new brand of philosophy, a particularly Dodger form of existentialist thought. Or it could be just a gimmick cooked up by Tommy Lasorda and the gang. We're not sure. But we do like the fact that the sign lights up at night.

FILL 'ER UP, AND COULD YOU CHECK MY BRAKE FLUID WHILE YOU'RE AT IT?

There is a gas station beyond the center field fence in the parking lot at Dodger Stadium. We are not kidding. Could something this perfect be made up? Now while we could make a cheap joke here about how the lines to get out of Dodger Stadium are so long that you will inevitably run out of gas and require a fill-up, we won't. Let's just call this a particularly California convenience, and leave it at that.

YOU CANNOT BE OVER "THIS" HIGH

Shorter fans (or Josh sitting on a footstool) can catch a view of a sellout game through small fences beyond the outfield walls. Only four times have these West Coast "knotholers" been lucky enough to chase balls hit completely out of the stadium and into the parking lot. Mark McGwire did it most recently in 1999. Before Big Mac a Mike Piazza shot left the yard in 1997. But before either of them Willie "Pops" Stargell sent two shots out, the first in 1969, the second in 1973.

Watering Holes and Outside Eats

With the maze of parking lots that cover Chavez Ravine, there is no place to have a pregame meal or drink in the area without getting back into your car. But of course this is L.A., and no one ever expects to go anywhere without a car, so it all has a strange sense of normalcy to it. And as L.A. is far too huge a city to try to list any number of cool places to go out, we're sticking to places close by the ballpark and places we like.

PINK'S HOT DOGS
(Corner of Melrose and La Brea)

Kevin's brother, Sean, who lives in L.A., took us to this place. Since 1939 Pink's has been dealing dogs and no visit to Hollywood would be complete without a stop. Options range in price from $1.50 to $6.00, and Pink's has found as many dog variations as anyplace we've visited. Sean had the Huell (Howser) dog, named after the unofficial mayor of Hollywood, that had two hot dogs stuffed into one bun. Kevin had the Brooklyn pastrami dog and it was delicious. Josh sampled the chili-cheese dog and was very pleased with his selection. Hoffy is the brand name for these dogs that are made specially for Pink's and they were some of the best dogs we ate on the entire road trip. The word is out on this place, so expect to stand in line for at least twenty minutes, regardless of time of day.

THE DRESDEN (1760 Vermont Avenue)

Remember that scene in the movie *Swingers* where Mikey, played by John Favreau, finally stops whining over his girlfriend back in New Jersey and goes out swing dancing, meets Heather Graham, and gets her phone number? That was shot at the Dresden, which has since become quite the hangout for hipsters and swingers in Silver Lake. This place is "happening" as crowds come to see Marty and Elaine, a Steve and Edie-style lounge act.

YE RUSTIC INN (1831 Hillhurst Avenue)

Near Silver Lake in Los Feliz, this small and dark quasi-sports joint caters to hipsters and locals. Waitresses heavily adorned with tattoos and piercings serve beer and mixed drinks. Like much of Silver Lake the gals want to look like Bettie Page and the guys are aiming for a Beck-like quality of cleanliness.

THE DRAWING ROOM (1800 Hillhurst Avenue)

The Los Feliz-Silver Lake area has become one of the coolest neighborhoods in town in recent years, and another of its many cool spots is the Drawing Room. This bar is cool in Kevin's sense of the word. In other words, it's a dive. When the Drawing Room opens at 6 A.M. there are folks waiting to get in.

THE RED LION TAVERN, GERMAN AND EUROPEAN KITCHEN (2366 Glendale Avenue)

German beers are on tap in the authentic outdoor beer garden on the second floor, and the waitresses bring them wearing the traditional German dirndl-serving outfits that look like the girl on the St. Pauli Girl beer label. So bring your lederhosen. Dogs, burgers, and fish and chips are on the menu, but traditionalists will go for the slightly pricier knockwurst, liverwurst, and bratwurst. Check out the wall of fame on the stairs, dedicated to famous Germans and German Americans.

BORN ON January 19, 1919, Jackie Robinson first put on a Dodgers uniform and stepped onto Ebbets Field on April 15, 1947—a moment in the history of baseball, the importance of which cannot be overstated. A brilliant second baseman for the Kansas City Monarchs as well as the Montreal Royals—a Dodgers minor league team—Robinson was hand-chosen by Branch Rickey in 1945 not because he was the best player from the Negro Leagues, but because Rickey was in his words, "looking for someone with the guts not to fight back."

Jackie Robinson had a history of exceptional success as an athlete. He was an All-American at UCLA, breaking school records in football, basketball, baseball, and track and field. He was the school's first four-letter man, and as such had achieved a certain degree of national fame. The fact that he was allowed to compete on the same field as white athletes in these other sports and that he excelled was a powerful argument for the integration of baseball.

Another important factor on the résumé of Jackie Robinson was the fact that he had been a solider in the U.S. Army from 1942 through 1944. Robinson had served his country during World War II, and was a decorated platoon leader. Also significant during his career in the military was an incident that was to set Robinson ever farther apart from the field in terms of character. He fought a court-martial leveled against him over an incident in which he refused to give up his seat on a bus. Jackie Robinson was not court-martialed, but rather discharged from the Army honorably after the trial. His strength of character had already been proven, as he had fought racial injustice and won a small victory.

But even Rickey—who expected Robinson to succeed—must have been impressed by the inner strength of character Robinson displayed on the baseball diamond. Robinson was called ugly names, was intentionally spiked by players, was ignored by teammates as if he weren't even there, and his own life and the lives of his family members were threatened constantly. The St. Louis Cardinals threatened to strike rather than play Robinson's Dodgers but on May 9, 1947, Ford Frick, the National League president stopped them, stating.

> If you do this, you will be suspended from the league. . . . I do not care if half the league strikes. . . . I don't care if it wrecks the National League for five years. This is the United States of America, and one citizen has as much right to play as another. The National League will go down the line with Robinson, whatever the consequence.

While many have stated that Rickey's interests in breaking the color barrier had financial undertones—the Dodgers instantly became black America's favorite team—the fact is that Rickey and Robinson needed one another to accomplish what they did. And though it may have been true that Robinson could not have accomplished all he did without Rickey and Frick, it is also true that these accomplishments would have not been possible for lesser men than Jackie Robinson. Imagine, being kicked and punched, and not taking any action to defend yourself, when you'd be very morally correct to do so. After all, which is easier? Giving in to your emotions, your natural feelings of rage and anger, or fighting anger and hatred with air of indifference? Robinson taught us all (again) that the strength needed not to fight, is far greater, surely.

After his career in baseball Jackie Robinson continued to fight injustice. He marched in Birmingham, Alabama, with the Reverend Dr. Martin Luther King, Jr. He testified before Congress on the unequal treatment of African Americans, and he worked for his people's causes in the political arena as well.

On October 23, 1972, Robinson died of a heart attack in Stamford, Connecticut.

People like Jackie Robinson make us all proud to be fans of the game of baseball. And perhaps the most laudable act of Commissioner Bud Selig was retiring Robinson's number 42 throughout all of baseball, never to be worn again.

BURRITO KING (Sunset Boulevard and Alvarado)

This is Mexican food the way we like it—very good, and very cheap. Sean said that there are plenty of Latino clubs along Sunset near the ballpark, but for most, "enter at your own risk."

OLVERA STREET

For many more great Mexican restaurants and Mexican culture, head down to Olvera Street, located in the pueblo at the heart of downtown. Olvera is a cobblestone street that boasts many places to eat, shop, and even listen to roaming mariachi bands. Try **La Luz Del Dia Mexican Restaurant**, or if you're like Kevin simply pick one at random.

THE TIKI TI (4427 Sunset Boulevard)

Also along Sunset, we recommend this spot for folks who intend to get the most drink for their dollar. These fishbowl drinks may cost $12 and up, but one'll do ya. The tacky tropical decor of this tiny joint is also noteworthy. Only open Wednesday through Sunday.

PHILIPPE'S FRENCH DIP SANDWICHES
(1001 N. Alameda Street)

For a taste of an old L.A. lunch counter, stop in at Philippe's. At this location since 1952, Philippe's has been in business since 1908. Offerings from behind the huge stainless steel warming counter include French dip to pork sandwiches, breakfast, pies, potato salad, and much more. Regular coffee is just nine cents. We hummed with delight over the French dip.

Near the front door an old wooden and glass drugstore counter contains candy and cigarettes for sale. The back room is dedicated to train memorabilia, and there's even a handful of early Dodgers photographs and signed baseballs displayed, with signatures rapidly fading.

But the main attractions at Philippe's are the lunch counter waitresses. With traditional uniforms and hair piled high, these women give the place its aura. The system of payment is unique, as the waitresses aren't allowed to actually touch the money. You place your bills down on a plate, then a nice lady hands the plate back to the cashier who makes your change, which is brought back to you on the same plate.

Kevin: "It's a little like the craps table in Vegas."

Josh: "I'm looking for cameras in the ceiling."

IT'S CHINATOWN, JAKE.

Ocean Seafood Restaurant (747 N. Broadway Street) is one place we can recommend in Chinatown, and **Yang Chow** (819 N. Broadway) is another. But there are literally hundreds of restaurants to explore in the area, if you're game. Old Chinatown is a great tourist spot where many movies have been shot.

Inside Dodger Stadium

At fifty-six thousand seats, this stadium is big, but does not suffer when compared to the smaller ballparks in the league. Even with the expansive foul territory, Dodger Stadium offers some of the best seats in the game. If you're looking for a ballpark filled with quirks, you should move on. Completely symmetrical in every way, Dodger Stadium has never been described as a quirky ballpark. It is too much like L.A., where looking good is everything. But there is plenty of charm to keep fans happy.

Ballpark Features

WAVY-TOPPED PAVILION ROOF

Perhaps the most distinctive feature of the ballpark is the roof that covers the Pavilion seats, slanted up and down in a wavelike design that looks like a row of cabana huts lined up. This architectural design element can be seen surrounding the upper deck of the park as well, though television cameras rarely show this.

WE'RE TRYING TO THINK BLUE

The rainbow-colored seats are original and run from yellow on the first level, orange on the second, blue on the fourth, and red in the upper. While they are beginning to show their age, we're not sure replacing them with all Dodgers Blue seats would be a good idea, considering nearly everything else inside the park is blue.

NUMBERS, NUMBERS, NUMBERS

Nearly hidden in the very blue outfield wall between the ads are the numbers most significant to Dodger history: 104 was the number of wins for the Dodgers in 1942 when they finished second to the Cardinals who won 106 games, and is the number of bases stolen by Maury Wills in 1962; 382 was the number of strikeouts Koufax had in 1965; 153 is the total RBI in 1962 by Tommy Davis; 6 is the number of Dodgers World Series titles; 233 is the number of Don Sutton's victories as a Dodger; 81 was the magical season of 1981 for Valenzuela and co.; 59 was the year the L.A. Dodgers first won the World Series as well as the consecutive innings pitched by Hershiser without giving up an earned run; 49 is the team record number of home runs hit by Shawn Green; and 52 is the record number of saves in a season by Eric Gagne in 2002.

The Dodgers also boast their share of retired numbers at Dodger Stadium: number 1, Pee Wee Reese; number 2, Tommy Lasorda; number 4, Duke Snider; number 19, Jim Gilliam; number 20, Don Sutton; number 24, Walter Alston; number 32, Sandy Koufax; number 39, Roy Campanella; number 42, Jackie Robinson; and number 53, Don Drysdale.

Josh: "What is the significance of the numbers 1, 71, 11, and 9?"

Kevin: "I'm no good with numbers."

Josh: "They're the numbers of today's umpires. Look up at the scoreboard where they're listed all game long."

One number not listed that should be is number 16. This is the number of Dodgers rookies who've earned the Rookie of the Year honor. From 1992 to1996 the Dodgers boasted a streak of five players in a row to win the award: Eric Karros, Mike Piazza, Raul Mondesi, Hideo Nomo, and Todd Hollandsworth. But the Dodgers also had another string of four ROYs in a row from 1979 to1982. They were Rick Sutcliffe, Steve Howe, Valenzuela, and Steve Sax, in that order.

DODGER STADIUM SUGGESTION BOX

OKAY, no ballpark is perfect. And any day at the ballpark is better than any day not at the ballpark. But here's where we do a little bit of complaining.

Why is the warning track still made of rubber and not dirt? We are aware that the ballpark was converted from turf to natural grass after the 1995 season, but why didn't they put in real dirt on the warning track to go with it? Perhaps it has to do with the complex underground hydrating system that was also installed with the grass to keep the ground appropriately wet, and the grass green and growing. But grass with a rubber warning track looks bush league. Plus there is no grass in the bull pens at all. Why not? This is a staple of ballparks of the era and should be remedied here.

The electronic scoreboards are another sore point with us. Though they are nicely shaped like an old TV, and of the period, they are that same color of orange that computer screens were in 1982. Computer manufacturers changed these because they caused eye irritation. The Dodgers also need to make the call across town to Hollywood to get its input on what should be done with that batter's eye. It's just a big black tarp that hangs in the outfield looking shabby. Plus the sound system ranks as the worst in the Majors, second only to Minneapolis. Call Hollywood and let those people show you how to razzle-dazzle the fans. Now we're not asking that the Dodgers sacrifice the classiness of their ballpark. We love that. But some of these things have to be fixed.

SO THERE ARE TOURS OF DODGER STADIUM?

Dodger Stadium tours are available on nongame days and by appointment only, and are $8 for adults, $4 for kids. The 1981 and 1988 World Series trophies are on the tour and are located in an area behind the dugout Club seats. So you can see them either by paying for those seats or going on the tour. The tour phone number is (323) 224-1HIT.

A VOICE TO REMEMBER

Vin Scully has been calling Dodgers games since they were still being played in Brooklyn. He joined the broadcasting booth alongside Red Barber and Connie Desmond in 1950 and he's been there ever since. Few broadcasters today are as synonymous with their team and their city as Scully is with the Dodgers and with Los Angeles. During his illustrious career Scully has called nearly every great moment for the L.A. Dodgers. One memorable moment occurred on April 25th during the bicentennial year of 1976, when two protesters were attempting to burn the American flag in left field. Chicago Cubs outfielder Rick Monday saved the flag from destruction, an event laden with symbolism.

Stadium Eats

Though Dodger Stadium offers some of the best seats in baseball, the same cannot be said for the food. It's very disappointing on the whole. Considering there are so many great places to eat in nearby Chinatown and in the Mexican portion of East L.A., we would have liked to have found some of these unique local franchises inside the park. Instead there are national burger chains and other fast-food offerings. And once again, Aramark got the concession deal here, and they've botched up another one.

NISSIN CUP OF NOODLES (Trademark Food)

Available with shrimp, these hot little cups of noodles would be a delicious snack if it weren't already eighty-five degrees out. Honestly, we searched the ballpark for something special and uniquely L.A. and found nothing. Perhaps in the Club level there is some delicious teriyaki chicken option, or freshly caught seafood, but we found nothing of the sort.

Though there was little food at Dodger Stadium that we loved, the cup of noodles did have two aspects that we did like very much: it was edible and it was cheap. There are plenty of offerings at Dodger Stadium that fulfill neither of these two requirements, and a few that are either one or the other.

DODGER DOG (Dog Rating)
The Fifteenth Best Hot Dog in the Majors

The Dodger Dog has received much press hailing it as the greatest dog experience in all of baseball, but we must disagree. The Farmer John-brand dog itself is longer than the bun (which is good) but is also on the thin and skimpy side. We like to call it the "Not too this, not too that," dog. Not too spicy, not too bland, not too salty, not bursting with flavor. It's the most average dog we every tasted, designed seemingly to offend no one. Therefore Kevin must rate it exactly in the middle, at fifteenth overall.

Josh: "You realize that dog number 15 is actually in the upper half, and that 15.5 would actually represent the midpoint, right?"

Kevin: "Yeah, I think *Star Trek* is about to come on the jumbotron, geek boy."

There was a controversy a few years back where Dodger fans—who rarely get worked up over anything—protested that their Dodger Dogs were no longer being grilled. The protests won out, and now all Dodger Dog stands advertise that the dogs are grilled. But beware. Most of the stands read "Dodger Dogs—Grilled." These were grilled at some point earlier in the day, then prewapped. Look for the stands that read "Grilled Dodger Dogs" and get one hot off the griddle for best results.

DODGER DAYS OF EBBETS FIELD PAST

THE CARNIVAL-LIKE atmosphere at Ebbets couldn't have been more different from the clean and pristine way that fans watch games at Dodger Stadium. Huge, colorful, and gaudy advertising signs hung wherever there was space to fill. Perhaps the most famous signs were those above and below the huge scoreboard. The upper sign was for Schaefer beer, where the "h" in Schaefer would glow in neon when there was a hit, and the first "e" would light up to indicate that the official scorer had ruled an error. Below the scoreboard was mounted a long low sign for a clothier named Abe Stark. "Hit sign, win suit," the famous marker read.

Josh: "Imagine that, a day when winning a suit would be a big deal for a player."

A singing newsboy patrolled the grandstands, selling papers and singing songs of Dodgers victories and woes. And for many years the hapless Dodgers provided much sad material for the young town crier. The Phillies defeated the Superbas 1–0 in the first game at Ebbets on April 9, 1913. Casey Stengel had recorded the first unofficial hit at Ebbets a few days earlier during an exhibition game. Stengel was traded to the Pirates in 1918, but later returned in 1918 to perform a gesture that would become a part of Ebbets Field folklore. Anticipating the raucous and crazed Dodger fans, Stengel came out to stand near the batter's box to boos and jeers. He calmly turned toward the stands, and tipped his hat to the crowd. When his hat came up, a bird flew out from under it, and away to the freedom of the Flatbush skies.

Though the Dodgers didn't win many games, there was plenty to keep folks entertained at Ebbets Field. The hated Giants, or "Gints" as they were called by Brooklynites, always played sellout games at Ebbets. On one occasion in 1924, tickets were so scarce that misguided fans used an old telephone pole as a battering ram to pound down the door of the banged-out park. Ebbets was also where yellow baseballs were introduced—and then quickly shelved—where a milkman threw batting practice, and where an umpire was once pummeled by an overexcited Dodgers fan after a questionable call.

BEST OF THE REST

Even though **Gordon Biersch's** garlic fries are a San Francisco thing and expensive, they are one of the most edible things at Dodger Stadium. **Krispy Kreme** is a chain, but the doughnuts are always good, and aren't any worse inside the ballpark than they are outside. The picante dog is a spiced up version of the bland Dodger Dog, and much tastier. Chips and salsa is difficult to screw up, so we can recommend that with confidence.

SAY "NO, THANKS," AND WALK AWAY

Undoubtedly the worst item on the menu is the Louisiana hot sausage, which tasted like an uncooked Jimmy Dean frozen sausage from the freezer aisle of the grocery store that had been left out to thaw. The bun was a soaking-wet mess and the peppers and onions had all the flavor boiled out of them.

Our **Wetzel's Pretzel** was old and stale, or new and fresh but just not very good. We couldn't be sure which, and certainly didn't want to try another one.

Camacho's Mexican Food looked promising to us at first. But the name scared us a tad, and the fact that of all the Latino people at the game, not one of them that we saw was eating the food. Our taste tests confirmed our fears.

Josh: "If you thought Hector "Macho" Camacho had a knockout punch, try eating a burrito at Camacho's then passing a standing eight count during the seventh-inning stretch."

STADIUM SUDS

The **Beers of the World** stand offers beers from across Europe at steeply inflated prices. Gordon Biersch is the California regional microbrew that is worth sampling.

Kevin: "Where's the Asahi Super Dry?"

Josh: "In Japan."

The Dodger Stadium Experience

The setting for baseball at Dodger Stadium is far superior to most other ballparks in the Majors. The view is unrivaled, both of the game and of the mountain backdrop. Weather is so rarely an issue at Dodger Stadium, it's almost a joke. The ballpark is clean, well maintained, and an excellent environment for families. The Dodgers have done a great job keeping advertisements from being too obtrusive, and they've essentially maintained the feel of the ballpark from the era in which it opened.

SPORTS IN THE CITY

JACKIE ROBINSON SIGHTS AND LOCALES

THOUGH BORN in Cairo, Georgia, in 1919, most of Jackie Robinson's young life was lived in and around Los Angeles. The baseball field on the UCLA campus was renamed for Robinson on February 7, 1981, three years before his induction into the UCLA sports hall of fame. Both are worthy of a visit. His boyhood home is located at 121 Pepper Street in Pasadena, California. Look for the marker placed in the sidewalk as a dedication. Unfortunately, you're on the wrong coast to visit Robinson's grave, which is at the Cypress Hills cemetery in Brooklyn, New York.

NO STANDING . . . NO SITTING . . . NO WALKING . . . NO TALKING

The ushers and food servers at Dodger Stadium are exceptionally polite, and very well dressed. But there are more dos and don'ts at Dodger Stadium than at any other ballpark in the country. These polite ushers will ask you to leave the area behind the last row of seats within seconds if you so much as slow down there to look at your ticket. It's as if they'd prefer you stand in the middle of the concourse and block traffic there. The mission of these friendly fascists seems to be whisking folks like sheep from their seats to the concession lines or bath-rooms, and then corralling them back again to their seats as quickly as possible before they start to cause trouble. Why would the Dodgers have such inane policies? They're not fan friendly, and they're an anomaly throughout all of baseball.

THE RETURN OF THE REAL BASEBALL ORGAN

Now this feature is a bit more like it. Nancy Bea is the Dodgers' organist and she fills the stadium with the classic sounds that your grandparents remember hearing at the ballpark in their childhood. It's a classy thing for the organization and a feature you just don't find at ballparks anymore. Newer parks seem to prefer hearing the opening riff to "Paranoid" by Black Sabbath four times a night, as players get their own theme music when they approach the plate. We prefer Nancy and her happy fingers.

RADAR GUN GUY (Superfan)

Mike Brito can always be found behind home plate clocking pitchers, and people speeding by on the 101 freeway as well. If Mike could only find a Dodger pitcher doing 101.

PEANUT GUY

Ultra-accurate peanut vendor Roger Owens had been patrolling Dodger Stadium for years, selling his nuts and giving away the entertainment side of the show for free.

Josh: "Is he any match for the peanut guy in Seattle?"

Kevin: "No."

INFO-TAINMENT

The Dodgers have teamed up with Hollywood to provide trivia questions that come off feeling like commercials for summer blockbusters. It's cheesy, but it's very L.A.

CENTURY BOULEVARD . . . WE LOVE IT! VICTORY BOULEVARD . . . WE LOVE IT!

When the Dodgers win, the meager sound systems plays "I Love L.A." by Randy Newman. Please do not confuse him with Gary Newman who sang the 1980s hit "Cars." Randy Newman is probably best known for his song "Short People," and for singing the theme songs that run during the opening credits of dozens of movies.

LOS ANGELES MEMORIAL COLISEUM
We received better access to this facility than we did to Dodger Stadium. The coliseum has been home to two Olympics and was the home of the first World Series victory in L.A. history. The familiar arched entryway is adorned with statues of buck-naked male and female athletes, as well as large bronze plaques commemorating the many great sporting events held there. Still, it was an ugly place for baseball.

BALLPLAYERS ON THE HOLLYWOOD WALK OF FAME
There are two former ballplayers who later went into acting and earned their own stars on the Hollywood Walk of Fame. Johnny Berardino hit .249 in eleven seasons with the Pirates, Indians, and Browns before turning his career aspirations toward Hollywood. His most memorable role was a thirty-three-year stint as Dr. Steve Hardy on *General Hospital*. Of course, when Johnny went Hollywood he changed his name slightly to John Beradino.

Another former Major League ballplayer on the Walk of Fame is Chuck Connors, star of the TV show *The Rifleman*. He batted .238 in a total of sixty-seven games, one for his hometown Brooklyn Dodgers in 1949, and sixty-six

World Series plaque

Photo by Kevin O'Connell

for the Cubs in 1951. Did the Rifleman have a rifle of an arm? We're guessing no, since he spent the majority of his time on the ball field playing first-base.

Of course cowboy star Gene Autry can also be found on the Walk of Fame. We're not sure if it's some kind of blasphemy to include Autry here, but we're sure the crosstown rival Angels love that we did. Autry owned the Angels for thirty-seven years.

Vin Scully also has his own star, as does Danny Kaye, a former owner of the Seattle Mariners.

SEATTLE,
WASHINGTON

680 miles to San Francisco
960 miles to Los Angeles
1,330 miles to Denver
1,385 miles to Minneapolis

SEATTLE MARINERS, SAFECO FIELD

Outdoor Baseball Returns to the Emerald City

GROWING UP in Western Washington, Kevin had no hometown hardball team to call his own. Then magically in 1977 his prayers were answered when Major League Baseball added Seattle and Toronto to the American League. Kevin, like all baseball fans in the Pacific Northwest, was elated. He found himself walking on clouds, smiling each time he sent the name of his new team rolling off his tongue, "the Seattle Mariners, the Seattle Mariners of the American League's Western Division, the Seattle Mariners of Major League Baseball." But there was a catch. The Mariners intended to play their home games at the Kingdome. Indoor baseball? To Kevin, that sounded like as much fun as kissing his sister.

Though the Mariners experienced a good number of lean years upon finally arriving, and though their ballpark sported artificial turf that looked about as real as the grass in the Brady Bunch's backyard, and a concrete roof instead of a blue sky, Kevin stuck by his hometown team. Like millions of other Seattleites, he never gave up hope that outdoor baseball would one day return to the Pacific Northwest, even as Mariners ownership threatened to move the team out of the city during the mid-1990s. Take courage Mariners fans. Seattle's once-troubled baseball waters are a thing of the past. Like the proverbial phoenix rising out of ashes and flame, Safeco Field has risen from the rubble that was the Kingdome, and appears to have permanently secured baseball's future in Seattle.

The Mariners' playoff run of 1995—now commonly referred to as "the season that saved baseball in Seattle," played a leading role in bringing about the current baseball renaissance in the city. Their inspired playoff run also did well by hardball fans all around the Majors who were frustrated by the strike-shortened seasons of 1994 and 1995.

In the afterglow of that magical year, plans were made to leave the Kingdome to football and build a new baseball park that would combine the charm of the classic older parks with all of the latest amenities. On all counts, "the Safe" delivers in spades. When Kevin first laid eyes on Safeco's green grass and rust-colored dirt, and looked up to see the Seattle skyline set against a perfect blue horizon, he wept with joy. Literally, he cried.

exterior

Photo by Kevin O'Connell

Making Safeco a reality was no small task given the area's economic climate in the mid-1990s. A bill to increase the sales tax by .01 percent was voted down by King County voters in September 1995. City and county officials recognized that the small margin of defeat of the proposition represented a good number of folks who would vote against them if the Mariners left town because a new ballpark could not be secured. So not long after, a financing package for Safeco Field was adopted that included hotel, rental car, and restaurant tax increases, ballpark admissions taxes, the selling of Mariner license plates, and scratch-ticket lottery games. One lottery game was called "My-Oh-My," named for a catchphrase of Dave Neihaus, the Mariners' colorful commentator. Later, the Safeco Insurance Company shelled out $40 million for the naming rights to the park.

More than thirty thousand fans cheered Ken Griffey, Jr. as he donned a pair of work gloves and partook in Safeco's ceremonial groundbreaking on March 8, 1997. From groundbreaking until the ballpark officially opened for play more than two years later, a webcam provided fans with continuous coverage of Safeco's construction site.

Safeco's most distinctive feature is undoubtedly its retractable roof. From the street behind Safeco, the roof of the building looks postindustrial. While from the street out front the Safe's brick facade provides a classic ballpark feel. But unlike the BOB in Arizona or SkyDome in Toronto, Safeco's roof *covers* but does not *enclose* the field, which allows wind to whip through, and preserves an open-air playing environment. The massive roof actually rests on tracks that are much higher than they need to be, giving the feeling that baseball is being played under an umbrella rather than indoors. Whether the roof is open or closed, baseball at Safeco always feels outside, which enhances the game-day experience over the Kingdome tremendously.

The roof's three independently moving panels span nine acres, weigh twenty-two million pounds, and contain enough steel to build a fifty-five-story skyscraper. The lid is capable of withstanding seven feet of snow and seventy-mile-per-hour winds. During Safeco's first few weeks, mechanical errors often caused the roof to open and close unexpectedly. The early kinks have since been ironed out. The roof's arching support trusses are "in play," provided the ball hits a truss in fair territory and also comes down in fair territory. We'll believe it when we see it, though.

If you think the roof is an engineering marvel, wait until you hear how the whiz kids of the West Coast have brought technology to their turf. The playing field is capable of absorbing twenty-five inches of rain in twenty-four hours, thanks to a layering of sand, pea gravel, and genetically engineered grass, combined with underground heating and drainage systems.

Josh: "Why bother? Safeco has a roof."

Kevin: "I guess management saw no harm in erring on the 'safe' side."

Unlike most parks, which open their gates for the first time on Opening Day, The Safe opened midway through the 1999 season on July 15, with a 3–2 Mariner interleague loss to the San Diego Padres. Once fully established in their new home, the Mariners captured consecutive American League West titles in 2000 and 2001 and tied the MLB record for the most wins in a season with a blistering 116 in 2001. Unfortunately though, the M's lost to the Yankees in the American League playoffs both years.

Though it didn't do much to enhance a ball game, the Kingdome had its share of memorable moments, not the least of which was its swan song. The Kingdome's demolition on March 26, 2000, was streamed live on the Internet, allowing millions worldwide to watch the implosion of the "Concrete Goiter," as it was not-so-affectionately called by some locals. The structure that was built to last a thousand years came down in just 16.8 seconds. Up until the time of its demolition, the Kingdome boasted the largest thin-shell concrete domed roof in the world. No ball ever hit the roof of the Kingdome, though players in batting practice constantly tried. On two occasions balls went up and never came down—in 1979 a ball hit by the Mariners' Ruppert Jones, and in 1983 a ball hit by Milwaukee's Ricky Nelson. Both got stuck in the sound system speakers and were ruled foul.

While the Jones and Nelson balls never fell back to earth, fifteen-pound tiles from the roof did in 1994, necessitating repairs that sent the M's on an extended road trip for the last month of the strike-shortened season.

Before achieving their first .500 season in 1991, the Mariners had posted a losing record in each of their first fourteen seasons. They were often considered a laughingstock around the league. During those lean years, the Mariners often resorted to gimmicks to boost attendance. In 1983 the USS Mariner set sail behind the left field fence, a gold-colored boat that would rise up and fire a cannon blast for Mariner wins and every time an M hit a home run. Meanwhile, the *Bullpen Tug* ferried relievers to the mound. Fence distances were measured in fathoms alongside the more traditional feet.

Josh: "I guess there is such a thing as extending a metaphor too far."

Another gimmick that was a fan favorite was the annual Buhner Buzz-cut Night, when the team would offer free admission to fans who shaved their heads to resemble Mariner right fielder/cult-hero Jay Buhner. Hundreds took part in the promotions every year.

A low-water mark for the Mariners came in the early 1990s when Dave Valle, a "defensive catcher" if ever there was one, was playing for the M's. Calling attention to Dave's futility at the plate, Swannies Bar offered well drinks at the daily price of the weak-hitting backstop's current batting average, before having to cancel the promotion when Dave's average dipped below .175. They simply couldn't afford to keep the promo going.

Kevin: "Buck seventy-five drafts . . . sign me up."

While baseball in Seattle during the 1970s and 1980s was an acquired taste to say the least, the region has a long tradition of hardball, though Seattle teams always seemed to be either coming or going. The city's earliest championship team was the Seattle Reds, who won the Pacific Northwest League in 1892. Unfortunately financial woes caused the PNL to fold soon thereafter.

Professional baseball returned to the region when D. E. Dugdale started up the Seattle Indians as part of the Northwestern League in 1896. The league included teams from regional cities such as Portland, Spokane, and Tacoma. By 1902 the Seattle and Portland teams had merged with teams from California to form the Pacific Coast League. For a brief while a second Seattle team, the Siwashes, were members of the PCL along with the Seattle Braves. But Seattle was too small a town to support two ball teams, and the Braves were forced to close up shop.

Great Seattle players showed a penchant for displaying their talents on the national stage. In 1903 Harry Lumley batted .387 and was sold to Brooklyn where he led the Majors in home runs and triples as a rookie in 1904. The next year Emil Frisk went to St. Louis to become a Brown. The Siwashes continued to play in the PCL, though losing their best players hurt attendance. They departed the league for the Class-B Northwestern League in 1907. Dugdale became the chief operator for the club, which played its home games at a ballpark named for him. Dugdale Park seated fifteen thousand and was located at the corner of McLennan and Rainier Streets.

The Siwashes made it back up into the PCL by 1919, though they were now called the Indians once again. They won the PCL title in 1924 but came upon hard times after that and dabbled in mediocrity. Dugdale Park burned down on July 5, 1932; the reason was never discovered. The Fourth of July fireworks had gone off without a hitch and were blameless.

By 1937 the team was sold to Emil Sick, owner of the Rainier Brewery. Sick renamed his team the Seattle Rainiers, and they were commonly called the Suds. Sick built a new ballpark in 1938 on the very site of old Dugdale Park and called it Sick's Stadium. The ballpark was very small, seating only twelve thousand fans, but featured a grassy knoll beyond the left field fence. The hill was dubbed "tightwad" hill because cheaper fans could watch the games while picnicking on the hill without paying a dime.

Josh: "That's where I'd be."

Rookie pitcher Fred Hutchinson won twenty-five games in 1938 for the Suds, before he was sold to the Detroit Tigers for cash and players. The Rainiers went on to win the PCL in 1940, 1941, and 1942, led by George Archie and Jo Jo White, players from that trade.

When the PCL changed from being an independent professional entity to being essentially a league of AAA affiliates for the Majors, Seattle Rainier attendance steadily declined. For more information on the Rainiers of the PCL, see the sidebar.

Big league ball returned to Seattle for one season only, when the expansion Seattle Pilots of the American League played their 1969 home games at Sick's Stadium. The Pilots were never really given the chance to succeed in Seattle. Sick's Stadium had been built in 1938 and was a cramped little ballpark for a Major League team to call home. Poor management and city officials who were inflexible caused the relationship to sour quickly.

Way back in 1969 Seattle fans well remember Mr. Allen H. Selig as the Milwaukee auto dealer who sneaked the Seattle Pilots out of town in the middle of the night to make them the Milwaukee Brewers. Not too many "Bud" fans in these parts. Maybe that's why the microbrews do so well. The Pilots only drew 678,000 fans, more than only Chicago and Cleveland in their sole season in Seattle. Their record was 64–98. The Brewers, in their first season in Milwaukee, only managed a record of 65–97, but their ballpark, County Stadium, helped increase attendance by a third.

There are, however, some interesting coincidences concerning the Seattle Pilots and the Seattle Mariners. For example, the starting pitcher in the Mariners' inaugural game in 1977 was Diego Segui, who also pitched for the Pilots. Another Pilot player, Lou Piniella, was the Pilots fourteenth pick in the expansion draft. Piniella was not that highly regarded by the Pilots and was traded to the Kansas City Royals, where he went on to become the Rookie of the Year. Later Piniella became the most successful manager in Mariners history, leading the M's to most of their winning seasons. Fans interested in learning more about the ill-fated Pilots should pick up a copy of pitcher Jim Bouton's classic book, *Ball Four*. Some say Bouton did a disservice to baseball with this book, but not us. We think it's hilarious.

Though the Kingdome was an inhospitable kingdom for Seattle baseball, there were many moments and memories that could only have occurred in that dark and ugly building. And sure the place could have used a bright coat of paint, but to Kevin, like other Mariners fans, those memories will always be beautiful.

The 1979 All-Star Game was hosted by Seattle, with Bruce Bochte the only Mariner on the roster. Gaylord Perry collected the three-hundredth win of his career at the Kingdome, as the Mariners beat the Yankees 7–3, on May 6, 1982. "Mr. Mariner" Alvin Davis won the Rookie of the Year honors in 1984. The second-place finisher was Mariners pitcher Mark Langston. And Harold Reynolds played outstanding second base for the M's from 1983 to 1992.

Then a nineteen-year-old phenom burst upon the Seattle baseball horizon named Ken Griffey, Jr. "The Kid" clobbered the first pitch he saw at the Kingdome, knocking it over the fence as he would go on to do more than any other player in team history. Griffey finished hitting dingers at the Kingdome when he belted number 377 on its closing day, June 27, 1999. Junior also played Gold Glove-caliber defense in center field, alongside his father Ken Griffey, Sr. who came out to play left field for the first time on August 31, 1990. The Griffeys became the first ever father-son duo to play on the same team. To further this great accomplishment, the Junior/Senior combination connected for back-to-back home runs at the Kingdome on September 14, 1990, against the Angels.

Edgar Martinez won his two batting titles in the Dome, hitting .343 in 1992 and .356 in 1995. Martinez was the first AL right-hander to win more than one batting title since 1942, when Joe DiMaggio accomplished the feat. Boston's Nomar Garciaparra has since joined the exclusive club.

The Mariners gave birth to the phrase "Refuse to Lose" in 1995 as they came from eleven games behind the falling Angels in August to tie for the AL West title, which resulted in a one-game playoff on October 2, 1995. The playoff game in Anaheim was winner-take-all, as a loss by either team would put it one-half game behind the New York Yankees in the wild card race. It was baseball's first one-game playoff in fifteen seasons, and was it a doozy.

Cy Young winner Randy Johnson came into the game as a relief pitcher for the Mariners and defeated the Angels' Mark Langston, the man the Mariners had traded to Montreal to obtain Johnson. With the Mariners leading 1–0 in the seventh and the bases loaded, Luis Sojo slapped a hit inside first-base that rolled along the tarp by the right field wall. A cruel bounce for the Angels and a throwing error by Langston allowed four runs to score on the play. There was no turning back for the Mariners. With destiny on their side, they prevailed 9–1.

The 1995 M's went on to sweep the Yankees at home in the dome, after losing the first two games in the Bronx. Griffey tied the postseason home run record with five—all in the first round. In the final game with the M's down 5–4 in the bottom of the eleventh inning, Edgar Martinez doubled down the first baseline to score two runs. The come-from-behind win was for many folks in Seattle the greatest moment in Mariners history.

And though they lost a tough-fought series against the Cleveland Indians for the American League Championship, fans stayed after the final game ended and gave the Mariners players a standing ovation—for nearly half an hour—for the great ride that was the 1995 season.

We don't know if it was fate or fortune, but Seattle voters were asked to decide on a ballot measure for building a new ballpark during the very same week that the Mariners were entering postseason play for the first time. There is little doubt that if the 1995 playoff run hadn't occurred, baseball in Seattle would have sailed away for greener pastures. That fortuitous season had been only Seattle's third with a winning record.

Since 1995 things have continued to roll the Mariners' way. Randy Johnson struck out nineteen hitters in a game not once, but twice in one season—1997. The next Seattle superstar to debut was Alex Rodriguez. A-Rod became the first shortstop to hit forty home runs and steal forty bases in 1998 and has gone on to be the highest-paid player is sports history, signing with the Texas Rangers.

With the Mariners' move to their new ballpark set firmly in motion by the exciting play of these superstars and others, the team then began to hemorrhage future Hall of Famers like they were going out of style. In four years the M's lost Johnson, Griffey, Rodriguez, and manager Piniella. While the losses should have been devastating, the M's have rebuilt their team with players whose egos don't get in the way. The entire team was worthy of mention, no one player more than another, as it broke records in 2001. Along with their Major League-leading 116 victories came a record twenty-nine road series won and Ichiro Suzuki's most hits by a rookie at 242. Other AL records broken during that year included most road wins (59), most at bats (692), and most singles (192) by a player (Ichiro), and most home runs by a second baseman (36, Bret Boone). Of course, this team shattered far too many franchise records to list.

The M's have rebuilt their team not around superstars, but around stingy defense, strong starting pitching, and a bull pen that's tougher than Chinese algebra.

The M's are currently owned by Hiroshi Yamauchi, a Japanese businessman who is also president of Nintendo. Though he's owned the team for more than ten years, Yamauchi has never seen a Mariners game in person. He was hoping to catch a game on March 25, 2003, when Seattle and Oakland were supposed to travel to Tokyo to kick off the big league season in Japan. But because of the outbreak of war with Iraq, MLB canceled the games. The Mariners are the Major League team of choice in Japan, among fans and migrating players alike.

These are good times for Mariners fans. The M's are experiencing great success, competing well, and selling tickets at Safeco by the score. All that is left for the Mariners is to fulfill the promise of the 1995 season and make it to their first World Series. And with a little luck, to win it for their fans.

TRIVIA TIMEOUT

Minnow: Which Mariner hit the first home run in Safeco Field history?
Trout: What song does the team play over the PA system when closing the retractable roof? (Hint: think German Opera.)
King Salmon: Name the Seattle baseball legend whose grandson was the first person to "round the bases" on Opening Day at Safeco?

Look for the answers in the text.

Getting a Choice Seat

Seattle has asserted itself as a bona fide big league town, selling out many games. Our guess is that empty seats will continue to be as scarce as bidders for Mark McGwire's seventieth home run ball in the years ahead. As is the case at the new parks, just about every one of the Safe's seats has a clear sight line and points toward home plate. That being said, some seats are much better than others.

Sellout Index: 60% of games sell out
Seating Capacity: 47,116
Ticket Office: (206) 622-HITS
www.mariners.mlb.com

Diamond Club (Sections 127–133)

The Diamond Club consists of the 370 box seats located directly behind home plate. Not only do these $100-plus seats provide their elite holders with Safeco's sweetest views but they also furnish free food and beverage refills all game long. Ticket holders are allowed access to both the Diamond Club Lounge and a special parking lot that comes complete with its own private entrance to the park. We call these the "screw-you" seats because if you have the money to afford them, you probably glide through life telling the rest of the world to screw. And you probably have no need for our book, with its cost-cutting and off-the-beaten-track ballpark tips, so we return the sentiment.

Lower Box (Sections 119–141)

If you can get your hands on seats in any of these sections and can afford them, do it! Without exception, they provide great views of the action. As an added attraction, the vendors are very attentive in the Lower Boxes. They're no fools; they know where the money's at.

Field Box (Sections 110–118, 142–150)

These begin where the infield dirt meets the outfield grass and extend to the foul poles on either side of the diamond. The first few sections (116–118, 142–144) are worth the price but beyond these, we recommend saving your money and sitting in the Lower Outfield Reserved.

The foul poles have been designed to run down the aisles, eliminating much of the blockage, but there are still some seats that do suffer infield obstructions. Section 150 is the one to avoid, but if you must sit there, try to get close to the Section 149 side for the better view.

On the right field side, avoid Section 110 if foul pole obstructions bother you. Section 109 provides cheaper seats without obstruction.

Lower Outfield Reserved (Sections 102–109, 151, 152)

We highly recommend Sections 105–109, which are in home run territory along the right field wall. If you're looking to snag a long ball or to be spotted on *SportsCenter* wearing your "I ♥ Ichiro" T-shirt, this is the place for you. Section 103 is an alcohol-free family section.

Sections 151 and 152 beside the bull pens in left field are also excellent, much better than Section 150, which is pricier. Sections 151 and 152 are also the same price as the View Boxes on the 300 Level and they're much better seats because they're down at field level.

AVAYA Terrace Club (Boxes 211–249)

These second-level boxes are pricey and exclusive. Beware of the infield Terrace boxes where high fly balls disappear because of the overhang of the View Level.

View Boxes/View Reserved (Sections 306–347)

At this altitude we don't see much reason to shell out the extra money for View Box seats, which are just a few feet closer to the action than the first row of the View Reserved. Of course, if you're left with a choice between the *first* row of the View Boxes and the very *last* row of the View Reserved, then that's a different story.

This upper deck is called the View level for a reason. Its exterior walkway extends from foul pole to foul pole, offering sweeping views of Puget Sound, the Olympic Mountains, and downtown Seattle. Above the highest seats are windowed panels that offer more view and also protect fans from the wind. Fans seated on the third-base side (Sections 337–347) are treated to a view of downtown and of the new football stadium, while on the first-base side (Sections 315–323) the Cascade Mountains in the east are the backdrop. But you came to see the ball game, right?

We advise staying away from Sections 306–314 in right field, as there is an underhang issue in these sections. You'll be much happier buying the cheaper bleacher seats in straightaway center. If the roof is open, Sections 306–310 face directly into sunlight for the first half of night games, or for the full game during afternoon games.

The best View seats are located in Sections 318–342, which provide a nice overview of the infield. The architects did an excellent job of protecting sight lines in these sections, and they are not significantly diminished as the row numbers increase. Beware of Section 342,

---

SEATING TIP

IF YOU don't like your seats, leave 'em. The Safe was constructed with the expectation that fans would do a fair amount of wandering. So take advantage. The entire second-level concourse is wide open on the inside, meaning you won't miss a single pitch while walking around or even while waiting in line for food. The bathrooms, however, are another story. This second level doubles as a standing-room area, so don't be afraid to stick around if you find a spot you like. The beer man will stop by shortly.

Another option is to hurry down to the first level when the park first opens so you can stake out a spot in the Center Field Terrace, which is available on a first-come, first-served basis. If you have bleacher seats, this is a chance to improve your view by a level or two, plus it's quite the popular singles hangout. It gets crowded as folks from the upper decks try to upgrade, but if you head right there when the gates open, you should be able to get a spot.

The Upper Terrace also offers first-come, first-served chairs and tables. From these seats you can look down into the bull pens or into the sod farm used to replenish the field. The Lower Terrace is usually reserved for private parties, so don't get any ideas. Scratch that. Work some magic and see if you can talk someone into offering an invite.

The **Bullpen Pub** is located, not surprisingly, next to the Mariner bull pen and under the park's main scoreboard. If you get to the park early, you can claim a stool facing the field and enjoy a ground-level view of the entire game while sitting at the bar sipping microbrews. Does life get any better than this? We're glad you asked, because it does. Along the left field wall of the pub are tiny portholes that allow fans to peek into the bull pen. Check it out, but don't linger—you don't want to lose your barstool!

---

as it is a "family" section. That means no beer allowed, not even for dad.

Sections 346–349 in the upper left field corner also suffer a bit of a loss of the left field corner, so avoid them if possible.

Left Field Bleachers (Sections 380–387)

The warning track is gone from view in these high bleacher seats, but that is all. All the grass is in full view, and there shouldn't be much missed from these sections. Be sure to sit in the lower rows of these sections, as the lighting supports block the views in the upper rows. These aren't bad for cheap seats, but we prefer the view from center field bleachers.

Center Field Bleachers (Sections 390–395)

If you're getting your tickets on game day, we highly recommend these. Despite their dirt-cheap price, they offer a surprisingly decent second-deck view of the action directly facing the plate. These seats are highly preferable to the 300 Level seats in the right field corner, and they're cheaper as well.

The Black Market

On game days, First Avenue South, Occidental Avenue, and Royal Brougham serve as scalper hotbeds. You'll find that ticket mongers increase in numbers as you approach the intersection of these streets. Follow Occidental and you'll know you've reached your destination when you see an ill-conceived statue of a baseball mitt with a hole in it. We're not kidding. As sad as this piece of art is, it's one of the most popular pregame meeting places, as well as "scalper central."

As you near the glove you'll encounter plenty of unabashed ticket hawkers. It's no problem approaching them, since selling tickets at face value is legal within the city limits. During our visit we also noticed plenty of deals going down above face value with no repercussions from local law enforcement. We also observed a regional peculiarity. Maybe it's a Northwest thing, or perhaps it's the general courtesy of folks who refuse to even jaywalk, but fans seeking tickets say nothing. They simply raised their arms extending fingers displaying the number of tickets they need. Then the scalpers approach them. Quietly and without much posturing, tickets and money change hands. Leave it to Seattle to find a civilized and courteous way to navigate the black market.

Buyer beware: Mariners tickets feature bar codes that are read by a machine at the ticket turnstile and thus, are never torn by an usher. So be certain of two things: (1) that you are not buying a ticket to a game that has already been played, and (2) that you are buying a full-length, bar-coded ticket.

Before/After the Game

The Safe was built in Seattle's SODO District. SODO used to stand for South of the Dome, but since the Kingdome was imploded the term SODO has come to mean South of Downtown. While the industrial SODO district has given rise to plenty of "SODO-Mojo" banners and a number of new loft-style warehouse spaces, it has performed rather poorly in the area of bar and restaurant development. We're hoping that the recent success of the M's and all of the fans coming into the area will trigger some dollar signs in the eyes of heads-up businessmen. How about a Wrigleyville-style row of watering holes along Occidental Avenue?

While there are a few spots worth ducking into in the immediate vicinity of the Safe, we strongly recommend schlepping six blocks to Pioneer Square where a host of old Kingdome favorites keep things lively.

Getting to Safeco

There are public parking lots both north and south of the park. These fill up early, are not cheap, and the streets around them are always clogged with traffic. We strongly recommend that you spare yourself the aggravation and take advantage of the Metro Bus System. But if driving into the city is your only option, be sure to stay away from the freeways, especially coming across Lake Washington from the east on either of the floating bridges—they're murder during game-day rush hours.

Here are a couple of tips to avoid the crowd in the immediate vicinity of the ballpark: park near the Seattle Center, then take the monorail to Westlake Center, about halfway to the ballpark. Sure it sounds a bit touristy, and there's still a healthy walk ahead of you, but how often do you get the chance to ride a monorail? You can also find a parking spot in Pioneer Square or the International District and plug the meter with enough quarters to last until 6:00 P.M.—after which time street spots are free—then walk or take the Metro Bus to the park. If your spot's within the ride-free zone you can take the bus at no charge to Jackson Street at the edge of Pioneer Square, then walk the last six blocks, or keep riding and pay from Jackson to Royal Brougham, which only costs a buck. The Metro has been voted one of the top bus services in the country. It's clean, comfortable, and efficient, but you're still stuck in rush-hour traffic, so allow extra time. For fare information visit http://transit.metrokc.gov.

If you're coming from the airport, take the No. 194 bus, which departs from the south end of the terminals on the arrivals level. This will take you right to the ballpark via a special street for buses only (4th Avenue). It's quite the handy way to get to the park if you can find someplace to ditch your luggage.

Outside Attractions

WE SCORE THIS ONE: E-5

Outside the left field entrance to the park, you'll find the aforementioned bronze baseball mitt where there should (and hopefully someday will) be a statue honoring the greatest designated hitter of all time, Edgar Martinez. With a career batting average in the .320s, an on-base percentage that exceeds .400, and more than twice as many career hits as strikeouts, this

guy deserves to be honored as the true "Ancient Mariner." Enough said.

Josh calls this "the Swiss Cheese Glove," while Kevin calls it "the Russ Davis Memorial." Davis, who hit the first home run in Safeco history, played third-base like he had a hole in his glove for the Mariners from 1996–1999. Now, we understand that good art is often nonrepresentational and that the hole is supposed to symbolize a ball. But come on! It's a hole and it's *inside* the mitt—a clear disconnect between art and subject. The glove was part of a $1.3 million investment by Seattle's Public Art Program to fill the park and surrounding area with works by prominent Northwest artists.

SNEAK A PEEK

As you walk along Royal Brougham you'll notice that you can see right into the park from street level. We peeked in on a rainy August day. The roof was closed tight while the grounds crew was busy at work inside hosing hundreds of gallons of water onto the field. Don't ask us why. We're just reporting what we saw.

Watering Holes and Outside Eats

PYRAMID BREWERY AND ALEHOUSE

(1201 First Avenue S)

The pub grub is expensive but the portions are large and the food is tasty. But at Pyramid, the food is secondary to darned good microbrews. We don't recommend microbrews in every city. In fact, most municipalities have yet to figure out the difference between the mash-tun and the mashed potatoes. But this is the Emerald City, so don't miss out on one of the region's crowning accomplishments. Here, you'll find many of the finest microbrews known to man. Going to Seattle and not trying the micros would be like going to Amsterdam and not sampling the . . . um . . . well never mind.

For beginners, we recommend Pyramid's Hefeweisen (German for "wheat beer") with a wedge of lemon. Whether your preference is light or dark, amber or ale, it's tough to go wrong in this mecca of microbreweries. Try a sampler, which provides a number of different beers in small glasses. The goal is to taste as many as you can and still be standing when the clock strikes midnight. So get into a West Coast groove, kick off your shoes (figuratively speaking), and let the good times roll.

BEER GARDENING

Germany may have invented the beer garden, but Seattle has perfected it. It seems you can't plan a public event of any kind in this town without applying for and receiving an outdoor drinking party permit. And Mariner Town, in this regard, doesn't disappoint. If you can't get a table at Pyramid, head for the spacious beer garden located in its parking lot.

Here's a primer on the beer garden scene: (1) there are fewer selections on tap; (2) the cups are plastic; (3) the girls think they're in college again and are much flirtier; (4) spilling on the ground, or on each other, is fair play; and oh yeah, (5) occasionally there's food. Think of beer gardening as tailgating without the hassle of parking the Winnebago, tapping the keg, and fumbling with the hibachi.

THE OUTBACK BEER-GARDEN
(Vacant Lot just south of Safeco)
Located across the street from the stadium's main entrance, the Outback Beer-Garden is a gravel lot that dispenses suds by the tanker-truck full. No kidding. It's nearly as good as a bar except when it rains—unlike the Safe, there's no retractable roof, only a tent.

IVAR'S ACRES OF CLAMS
(On the Waterfront at Pier 54)
Folks looking for a sit-down dinner with plenty of local flavor should visit Ivar's, which, although it is on the expensive side, offers great seafood. Salmon, local oysters and clams, and Alaskan king crab are favorites.

For the late-night crowd, the place to chow is **Ivar's Fish Bar**, which is far cheaper than Acres but just as good. A Seattle waterfront institution, the Fish Bar featuring deep-fried foods is open until 3:00 A.M. There's usually a line, but the salmon and chips are well worth the wait. So's the chowder.

F. X. MCRORY'S WHISKEY BAR AND CHOP HOUSE (419 Occidental Avenue S)
A favorite of Seattle sports fans, F.X. is a vintage Irish sports bar. Pacific oysters on the half-shell are a house favorite. Kevin devoured two dozen in twelve minutes while Josh didn't like the combination of gooey oysters and dark microbrew.

If old Kentucky moonshine is your thing, F.X. also boasts the largest selection of bourbon in the country. Daily specials are written on chalkboards along the wall. A few of our favorites are: Himan Walker's Ten High, Pappy VanWinkle, and Old Kentucky Senator.

Also featured at F.X. is the artwork of famous sports artist Leroy Neiman. Neiman's painting of the F. X. McRory's bar hangs on the wall as you head toward the restrooms. If you're not familiar with Mr. Neiman's paintings, check out *Playboy Magazine.*

SLUGGERS (539 Occidental Avenue S)
This fairly typical bar has undergone more name-changes and face-lifts in recent years than Ivana Trump. But we think the current incarnation is going to last a while. With lots of microbrews and Seattle sports memorabilia mounted on the walls, this would seem to be just what the fans ordered. Trivia buffs will enjoy playing the computerized nationwide satellite trivia game.

TRIANGLE PUB (533 1st Avenue S)
The beers are cheap at this historic Seattle pub, and hey, the building's shaped like a triangle. Peanuts are free and shells must be thrown on the floor. It's a house rule. We highly

WHILE THE move of the Brooklyn Dodgers to Los Angeles in 1958 broke the hearts of Brooklynites, it also spelled disaster for Western fans of the Pacific Coast League, including many Seattleites. The long-standing PCL contained such teams as the Seattle Rainiers, Spokane Indians, Vancouver Mounties, San Diego Padres, Salt Lake City Bees, Sacramento Solons, Portland Beavers, Oakland Oaks, Los Angeles Angels, Hollywood Stars, Hawaii Islanders, and San Francisco Seals.

In the 1950s, the PCL had hopes of joining the National and American Leagues as a legitimate third Major League. By 1952 the PCL was granted "Open Status" with Major League Baseball. No PCL team was affiliated in any way with any big league team, and players would have to clear waivers before they would enter. This was a critical step for the PCL's hopes to becoming a third Major League.

Though talent ran deep in the PCL, with the relocation of the Dodgers and Giants MLB demonstrated a clear preference to export its own Eastern teams to the West Coast. As a matter of survival, the Seattle Rainiers club signed an agreement to become part of the Cincinnati Reds organization. The Rainiers were then sold to the Boston Red Sox in 1961 and became their Triple-A club. When the Red Sox sold the Rainiers to the California Angels in 1965, the parent club demanded a name change, and the Seattle Rainiers, sadly, became the Seattle Angels.

Legendary Hall of Famer Rogers Hornsby managed the Rainiers to a PCL title in 1951 before being lured back to the Majors to manage the St. Louis Cardinals. Local baseball legend Fred "Hutch" Hutchinson returned to Seattle in 1955 after a 14-year career with the Detroit Tigers and managed the Rainiers to their final first place finish.

The first person to run around the bases on the day of Safeco's grand opening was Fred Hutchinson's five-year-old grandson, Willie. We like to think the open roof provided a clear view from above through which Hutch (who died of cancer in 1964) watched as the little tike touched all four.

The University of Washington's world-renowned cancer center is named after Fred Hutchinson.

---

recommend this pub for the off-the-beaten-path types. Arrive early though, because the joint is tiny. One other rule: no squares allowed.

PIONEER SQUARE NIGHTLIFE

One reason that the SODO district has been slow to develop its own Safeco scene, is that the pub scene in the Pioneer Square district has been the happening spot to go for many years. While the area can be a bit on the touristy side, there are plenty of places to get a cold beer, a great meal, and even play a hand of cards . . . for money. That's right, card rooms have been legal in Seattle since the days of the pioneers, so grab a space at a table if you're game and get in on some serious poker playing action. The **J & M Café & Card Room** located at 201 1st Avenue S is a popular spot, but like most places in Pioneer Square, the serious action is over well before game time, as these bars turn into frat parties in the late hours.

If you're the type who likes to shake your booty after a full day of baseball, we recommend getting in on the Pioneer Square joint-cover. Some thirteen bars have banded together to do something unusual: for a single cover charge patrons get a hand stamp that allows them to access any of the member clubs. It's a good deal and it's a hopping part of town seven nights a week. While just about all of these places are good, our favorites are **Larry's Blues Cafe**, **Doc Maynard's**, and the **Central Tavern**. In any of these establishments, you can find a map to, and list of, the other participating bars.

CENTRAL TAVERN (207 1st Avenue S)

Around since the Yukon gold rush days, the Central is Seattle's oldest saloon. A true Seattle must-taste is the alligator on a stick. Tastes like chicken to us. For grunge fans, seminal Seattle rock band Soundgarden was the house band here for years. Kevin saw them often back in his glory days.

NEW ORLEANS CAFÉ

Sample the gumbo or have a brew in this pub named for another great city. Cajun and Creole are the food specialties, while jazz, zydeco, and Dixieland are the musical selections.

SWANNIE'S SPORTS BAR AND RESTAURANT (222 S. Main Street)

Once the famed locale of well drinks that cost the same as Dave Valle's batting average, now Swannie's is a dive sports bar with cheap beer during the day and a comedy club at night.

MAC'S SMOKEHOUSE (1006 1st Avenue S)

This is the place to go if you like good old-fashioned barbecue. The brisket was a big winner with Josh. Though it used to be located closer to the park, Mac's is still only a short walk. Closed on Sundays. Even game Sundays.

SIZZLING SEATTLE SAUSAGE

Late-night carts cater to the postbar crowd in Pioneer Square. Josh wonders why they don't wheel their carts into SODO to pedal "the other white meat" to hungry baseball fans. Kevin has no answer, only a sad sigh and a microbrew to soothe Josh's hankering for encased pork.

KETTLE CORN

A local favorite, Kettle Corn is available at carts surrounding the park. This stuff is to popcorn what filet mignon is to steak. It's popped in huge copper kettles, then dusted with a delightful blend of sugar and salt. As you're walking past the peddlers say something like "Kettle Corn? We don't have that back home in Pigs Knuckle, Arkansas. Is it any good?" and they'll likely offer a free sample, betting that after one taste you'll be hooked.

SOUVENIR SHOP SUPREME

While the souvenir peddlers in the streets surrounding the ballpark carry the same merchandise available in most malls, **Ebbets Field Flannels**, located at 404 Occidental Avenue S is a must-visit for all true baseball fans. The store specializes in high quality woolen hats, jerseys, and jackets bearing the emblems of lost teams ranging from the Pacific Coast League to the Negro Leagues to the Caribbean Leagues, and dozens of other leagues as well. Whether you're a fan of the Xalapa Chileros of the Mexican League, Josh Gibson's mighty Homestead Grays, or the Seattle Rainiers, this store has something for you. The hats and flannel jerseys do not come cheap, but they are made to last.

A few years back the Ebbets Field Flannels company acquired longtime sporting goods manufacturer **Stall & Dean** of Massachusetts. Stall & Dean has been in business since the 1890s and manufactured some of the original baseball uniforms that the joint company now produces. Stall & Dean also brought to the merger a great variety of classic football, hockey, and basketball uniforms.

Inside the Park

Seattle is a city infamous for making ill-advised public works decisions, but they finally did something right with Safeco Field. Old-timers and baseball purists will thoroughly enjoy the Safeco atmosphere. And "newbies" will too. The purposely asymmetrical playing field features an unusual gap built into the 405-foot-deep left-center field. This is where late September home runs go to die in this notoriously pitcher-friendly yard.

Before he jumped town as a free agent, Alex Rodriguez asked the team to consider moving in the fences so he could pad his home run stats. "We like our park the way it is," the front office replied. So A-Rod departed, his Texas Rangers fated to finish last in the AL West in 2001, while the Mariners would post a league-leading team ERA of 3.54 en route to setting a new American League record for the most wins in a season. With their 116 wins the M's finished seventy games over .500. All this from a team that in the past went many a season without winning seventy games total.

The Roof . . . the Roof . . . the Roof Is on Fire

What can we say? The city built a retractable roof for baseball, even though studies indicated that an open-air stadium in Seattle would have fewer rainouts than Boston, New York, or Baltimore. Then the city turned around and built an open-air football stadium, even though it rains every day during the winter in Seattle. Go figure.

That said, the roof is an impressive monument to the age. Whether viewed from inside or out, the arching steel supports look like a postindustrial homage to labor. Notice that after the game is over, Wagner's "The Ride of the Valkyries" plays over the PA system as the roof closes. You know this tune. Think of a cowboy-hat-wearing Robert Duvall in the helicopter scene from *Apocalypse Now*. Ringing any bells? If not, maybe it's time to rent the movie.

If you're only in town for one game and the always iffy Northwest weather has you fretting, fear not. The game doesn't suffer much when the roof is closed because Safeco doesn't lock up airtight. Though a closed roof may give the illusion that baseball is being played under the "big top," it also preserves an outdoor atmosphere by leaving open the north and west sides of the park. So dress as you would for any other outdoor destination in Seattle—layers, but leave the umbrella at home.

Death, Taxes, and Ballpark Banter

"I heard it only costs $8 in electricity every time they close and open it," Josh said.

"Well," Kevin said, stroking his goatee, "If you factor in the extra two hundred million it cost to build it, then estimate an extremely generous twenty games per year when it actually needs to open and close, then factor that out over the average lifespan of a ballpark, say, thirty years . . ." Kevin looked skyward and slightly to his right, as if trying to perform the calculation in his head.

After a few minutes, Josh put him out of his misery. "That means it cost the taxpayers of the Northwest $333,333.33 every time it opens and closes for a game," Josh said, as always quite pleased to flaunt his mathematical wizardry.

"Seattle better have this ballpark more than thirty years," said Kevin.

Though the roof at Safeco opens and closes all year long, on game days and nongame days, this figure is clearly one to consider if city officials intend on building a new park in your hometown and are lobbying for a "much needed" roof. Remember it's baseball: sometimes it rains, and it's not the end of the world.

The Train

Fenway has its Green Monster, Wrigley its ivy-covered walls, Baltimore its B&O Warehouse. Safeco's trademark feature would have to be the procession of booming locomotives that rumble right through the bleachers in right field. This may sound like an exaggeration, but it isn't. The tracks of the Portland-Seattle Railroad line actually run directly beneath the ballpark's retracted roof on the inside of its huge supports.

Seattle fans love their trains and the way they boom like a clarion call signaling another late inning rally. But in the days leading up to the 2001 All-Star Game, baseball Commish Bud Selig lobbied to suspend all train traffic during the Midsummer Classic because he felt the noise would "detract from the game." Does this guy *get* baseball at all? That resonating train whistle is a distinctive reminder of Seattle's (and baseball's) working-class and pioneering heritage, and besides, it makes Safeco Field unique.

Iron Man

Speaking of the 2001 All-Star Game, Safeco provided a glorious stage for Cal Ripken's last Midsummer Classic hurrah. The venerable Oriole walked away with the game's MVP honors after blasting a dramatic home run that still gives us shivers when we watch the videotape. The Mariners installed a plaque in the Seattle bull pen to commemorate the spot where Cal's All-Star dinger landed.

I Didn't Realize They'd Actually Be *Pens*!

Aside from the Ripken plaque, Safeco's bull pens beyond the left field fence are highly distinctive in their own right. While close access to pitchers warming up is common at many older parks, Safeco takes the idea a step further. Fans can close in on relievers from almost every imaginable angle—at eye level on the first level, above from the second deck, through the portholes in the Bullpen Pub, or from the Center Field Terrace.

While we appreciated such rare access to the pop of a ninety-five-mile-per-hour fastball, we wondered if the fans might be a bit *too* close to the players here. Surely, we thought, relievers must resent being gawked at like zoo animals through the chain-link screen. That was our *initial* impression. But we have to admit the fans were exceptionally well behaved during the game we spent sitting along the visitor's pen. Here's our theory: the very proximity of players and fans is what keeps the drunken hecklers at bay. At other parks where fans aren't so close, they don't mind yelling "Hey, Rivera, you SUCK!" But at Safeco fans are close enough to see the effect of their words on the players' faces, so they don't get really nasty. That's our theory anyway.

Kids Clubhouse

Like many of the new parks, Safeco features a romper room for rambunctious kids and bored-silly parents. The KC is located toward the back of the center field plaza. It offers a playground, interactive baseball activities, a kiddy store, and more—or so we were told by a friendly mother of six we met while waiting in line for garlic fries. That's our story and we're sticking to it. Regardless of what the stadium police blotter says, Kevin did *not* get stuck on the slide, and Josh did not accidentally pop the bouncy-pen while trying to "get higher than he'd ever been before."

Home Plate Gate

By far the most impressive of the several entrances to the park, the Home Plate Gate is really something to see. The rounded rotunda design was directly influenced by the rotunda of Ebbets Field. Though Safeco's rotunda is unique, comparing the two side by side reveals the obvious influences of mythical Ebbets.

After passing through the gate and being handed back your electronically bar-coded ticket, you'll ride up an escalator, below a chandelier made of one thousand translucent glass baseball bats. This is one of the many pieces of art integrated into the Safe's design. You'll see another as you reach the main concourse. It's easy to be distracted by your first sweeping view of the field, but take a moment to look down. Tiled into the floor is the Nautical Compass Rose—the Mariner emblem—as well as the signature of each Mariner who played in the inaugural game at Safeco.

Mariner Hall of Fame

Located inside the park, the Mariner Hall of Fame opened its doors for the first time during the 2002 season. True to humble Mariners form, the MHOF announced just two charter inductees: Alvin Davis, the 1984 AL Rookie of the Year, and Dave Niehaus, the voice of the Mariners, who made famous such phrases as "My-oh-my, it's good-bye baseball!" and "Get out the mustard and the bread roll 'cause it's a Grand Salami!" Here's betting Edgar Martinez is a "MHOFer" before long. He's already a "bad" MHOFer in our book.

Stadium Eats

The delicious aroma of coffee wafts around the ballpark in combination with the seafood smells and the wonderful saltwater scent coming off Elliott Bay. The eating experience at Safeco will not disappoint. While there are foods to avoid, there is plenty of local fare to enjoy.

Another Safeco first, 411-ing yourself some eats. That's right, you can use your cell phone and/or wireless computer to have anything on the menu delivered right to your seat. And we thought the Internet was a waste of time. What will these Northwest computer geeks think of next?

IVAR'S FISH BAR (Trademark Food)

Local seafood establishment Ivar's features two stands inside the stadium and is not only a great trademark food of the ballpark, but also of Seattle. Give the deep-fried fish and chips a whirl for that "only-at-Safeco" dining experience. The fish is lightly fried to perfection and will warm your soul on those sea-breezy evenings of spring or fall. The homemade chowder and salmon sandwich are also exceptional. Deep-fried salmon and chips used to be our favorite, but they took it off the menu in the stadium stands. Hey, bring back the salmon.

THE SAFE PUP (Dog Rating)
The Fourth Best Hot Dog in the Majors

Safe Pup isn't this weenie's real name, but since Seattle has yet to come up with a creative dog moniker on its own, we took the liberty. Hebrew National got the concession deal on this one and as usual this brand doesn't disappoint. This is a meaty frank, rich in flavor. Plus it's kosher, and although we're not Jewish, its still for some reason oddly reassuring.

BEST OF THE REST

Many fans have been lauding Safeco's garlic fries as the ballpark's trademark food. We agree that chopped garlic and herbs unabashedly spread over crispy French fries makes for a delicious ball game treat. But the problem is, they've been serving garlic fries in San Francisco for years—first at Candlestick and now at PacBell Ballpark. Seattle ain't San Fran, nor is anywhere else for that matter. It has its own personality that should be reflected in its most cherished munchies.

With this in mind, Kevin chooses the Ichi-roll—named after 2001 AL Rookie of the Year and MVP Ichiro Suzuki—as his Best of the Rest selection. Available at **Sushi and Sake** in the **Bullpen Market** this is a sushi roll made of spicy tuna and rice, wrapped in delicious seaweed. It has become so popular at the ballpark in recent years that restaurants around town have started serving the Ichi-roll. Now to us, that is how ballpark food should be, leading the epicurean charge rather than lagging behind.

"What?" Kevin asked incredulously as Josh shied away from an Ichi-roll.

"Raw fish and weed don't do it for me," Josh hissed.

"Come on," Kevin goaded. "You've seen Ichiro playing right field Japanese style, and Kaz Sasaki's forkball from the land of the rising sun."

As Kevin dipped the roll into wasabi and soy then took a hellacious bite that made his nose run, Josh backed away from him like he was a leper on fire. "I will not be sampling that . . . that . . . that . . . that thing!" he cried. "Stop pointing it at me!"

"We need to experience each park's unique flavors, colors, smells, and noises, so you've gotta take a bite," Kevin said. "You owe it to our readers."

Josh considered this for a long time as Kevin continued to aim the fragrant end of his half-eaten Ichi-roll squarely at him. He looked at the sushi, then at his feet, then at the sushi again, then up at the roof. It seemed like he almost wanted to take a bite, but when it came down to it, he just couldn't shake his inhibitions. "Those garlic fries really filled me up," he said. "I'll try the Ichi-roll tomorrow."

When the next day came, Josh predictably forgot his vow and bought two **Kid Valley** burgers and a double order of garlic fries to fill up on.

Another favorite of Kevin's is the Daimajin roll, named after Mariner relief pitcher Kazuhiro Sasaki. This is made of scrumptious barbecued eel. No lie. "Daimajin," Sasaki's nickname in Japan, means "the big man who saves everyone."

Kid Valley burgers are pretty good. These are neither your standard issue ballpark burgers, nor are they the megachain fast-food variety either. This is more like a greasy delicious mom-and-pop-style burger, cooked fresh and topped with onions, lettuce, tomatoes, and cheese.

SAY "NO, THANKS," AND WALK AWAY

We give our most mediocre rating to the **Hit It Here Café**, which is located on the second deck. While ideas like this often seem great when stadiums are being designed, they usually turn out pretty average. This is no exception. The food is nothing special and it's hard to see the game from all but a few tables. Save your money and eat on one of the Terraces instead.

Also beware of **High Cheese Pizza**, available at several stadium locations. Pizza connoisseurs will rank this as purely fast-food pizza.

STADIUM SUDS: MICROBREW MANIA

As you are doubtlessly aware, indulging in a brew or two at the American ballpark has become so cost prohibitive that many fans are climbing back onto the wagon on game nights. At the Safe, you at least get a quality cup of brew for your hard-earned dollar. As previously mentioned, the microbrews of the Pacific Northwest are as big and bountiful as the great land itself. Sample them all if you have the stomach for it. But lightweights beware: these brews yield more bang for the buck, averaging an alcohol content of 5 to 8 percent compared to the 3.5 percent found in run-of-the-mill macros.

Our favorites at Safeco are Alaskan Amber, Mirror Pond, Widmere Hefeweisen (pronounce the Ws as Vs, lest ye sound like a tourist), Mac & Jack's African Amber, and of course, Red Hook. Be adventurous and cast aside the world of the ubiquitous macrobrew. This is the great Northwest. So buck up and try something new. You can go back to drinking watered-down swill when you get home.

The Safeco Experience

SODO-MOJO

You probably think Seattle fans sip their lattes with one eye on the game and the other on their dot-com stock prices. Or maybe you envision long-haired, flannel-clad computer hackers listening to blaring postgrunge music through wireless headphones at the park. You'll find a few of these types at Safeco, but mostly you'll find great baseball fans.

When the M's stopped trading away their best prospects and decided to put a quality product on the field, Seattle became one of the greatest baseball cities in America. Though most of the players who laid the groundwork have since left, the youngsters, remaining veterans, and fans built something special in this little city on Elliott Bay. SODO-Mojo is real, and so is the fans' "Two-outs-who-cares?" bravado. These folks believe their boys of summer can always win, all the while remaining polite and civilized.

An example of this civil behavior was told to us by Kevin's friend Jim Sander, who accompanied us to a game. As Jim tells the story, the M's were leading their divisional rivals, the Oakland A's, late in a game. David Justice was in right field when a few loud and drunken men began yelling "Hal-le Ber-ry! Hal-le Ber-ry!" in reference to the fact that Justice and the actress were once married. This offended one Seattle woman, who stood up and shouted back at the men, "Stop saying that! You could really hurt his feelings!" And that was it. The men shut up.

Though taunting a rival player occurs often, it rarely gets as vicious as it does in cities like New York and Boston. Seattle fans seem to prefer cheering on their favorite Mariners stars. While some might misread this as a lack of passion among Seattle fans, we don't see it that way. We see Seattle fans as folks who understand the power of positive thinking. And it's pretty tough to argue with the recent results.

When former coach Lou Pinella returned to Seattle as the manager of the Devil Rays, Seattle fans treated him to an extended standing ovation that brought a tear to the eye of the grizzled old skipper of the M's. It seems Seattle fans preferred to focus on the ten great years that Sweet Lou had given them, rather than the fact that he'd left.

LOUIE, LOUIE

During the seventh-inning stretch, after the obligatory singing of "Take Me Out to the Ball Game," Safeco fans can always plan on hearing "Louie, Louie," popularized by the 1960s Northwest rockers, The Kingsmen.

When the tune first became a national sensation, J. Edgar Hoover had a team of FBI special agents dedicate hundreds of taxpayer-financed hours trying to crack "the code" hidden within its cryptic lyrics. Why? We haven't a clue. Might as well ask why Hoover went parading around in ladies underwear. Makes you wonder, doesn't it?

In the 1970s "Louie, Louie" was featured in the Northwest film classic *Animal House*, which was filmed on the University of Oregon campus. In the 1980s a recurring ballot measure was voted on in the Washington State Legislature to make "Louie, Louie" the official state anthem. None of these measures passed, but the Mariners still play the song religiously.

THE ORIGINAL CRAZY PEANUT GUY

Rick Kaminsky has been tossing peanuts to Mariners fans since the Kingdome opened in 1977, and has made an art form out of his profession.

Picture yourself sitting in the sun on Safeco's first-base side. You feel a hankering for some hot roasted peanuts. You flag down a vendor with curly black hair tucked under his

SPORTS IN THE CITY

HAMMERS, POWER DRILLS, AND A WHOLE LOTTA HEARTACHE

WE DON'T necessarily recommend it, but fanatics might consider visiting the site of old Sick's Stadium, which was home to the American League's short-lived Seattle Pilots. The Pacific Coast League's Rainiers played at Sick's too, as did the West Coast Baseball Association's Seattle Steelheads, a Negro League team that like the Pilots played just one season (1946) in Seattle. It was a beautifully clunky little park that hosted outdoor baseball in Seattle for more than eighty years. But it was woefully small and inadequate for big league ball.

Those who embark upon this somber pilgrimage will find a large chain hardware store where Sick's Stadium once stood at 2700 Rainier Avenue S. It's enough to break your heart. But inside the store there is a glass display featuring Pilots and Rainiers memorabilia.

Tuba Guy Superfan

Photo by Kevin O'Connell

M's cap and a Harpo Marx-like grin on his face. He motions to throw you a bag over fifteen rows of people, and you literally leap out of your seat, having bitten for his fake. He fakes again, behind his back, then over his shoulder, then behind his back again, then between his legs, until you wonder if he's having some kind of a seizure. Then, before you know it, he's chucked a bag behind his back that's heading your way. As you watch it fly, wobbling and wavering above the innocent people seated below, you think, "Oh, the humanity," expecting the bag of hot salted nuts to bean some poor unsuspecting mother on the forehead. But

to your pleasant surprise the bag's flight is spot-on, and it hits you right in the hands. Just be warned: You will be booed lustily by the fans in your section if you don't catch Peanut Guy's throw.

Crazy Peanut Guy is an ace who rarely, if ever, misses. We love this guy's zest for life and for taking an otherwise ordinary job and turning it into a thing of ballpark beauty.

THE TUBA MAN (Superfan)

Edward Scott McMichael is the Tuba Man who makes appearances at all major sporting events in the greater Seattle area. You'll recognize him as the large hairy gent with a scraggly beard. He'll be decked out from head to toe in Seattle sports gear, and, oh, yeah, he'll be playing a tuba outside the ballpark!

Before he shows up, the Tuba Man "requires a ticket to the game, just like everyone else," he says. He might look a little odd, but the man is *one* with his oversized horn. He'll play any tune you like, though it may take a few bars before you recognize it down in the lower registers. Give him props for being a longtime Seattle sports fan, whether you request a song or find yourself stuck standing next to him in line when he's blowin' a rousing version of "Little Brown Jug."

BILL THE BEER MAN (Superfan Hall of Fame)

Bill the Beer Man used to be an actual beer man at the Kingdome who took breaks from peddling foam to lead the crowd in cheers. He quickly became a minor celebrity and quit sloshing suds to lead the crowd in cheers full-time for the M's, Seahawks, Sonics, and Huskies, but he has since retired. Oh, Billy, where did you go?

OAKLAND ATHLETICS,
NETWORK ASSOCIATES COLISEUM

Branded with the Emerald "A" in Oakland

**OAKLAND,
CALIFORNIA**

10 miles to San Francisco
331 miles to Los Angeles
641 miles to Phoenix
680 miles to Seattle

WITH AN EXTERIOR consisting of mounds of concrete and grassy slopes, Network Associates Coliseum makes an awkward first impression. And being plopped down into the middle of a sports complex amid parking lots and industrial warehouses does little to improve on that initial reaction. There is little of the awe that Yankee Stadium inspires, or the charm and intimacy of Wrigley Field. But a closer look reveals a place where many of the game's recent advances were born, and a fitting home to an enormously successful ball team that has been fighting for respect and survival since its very inception.

Completely round when it was originally built and with a field twenty-one feet below sea level, Network Associates has been a paradise for pitchers. The round shape of the seating bowl creates the largest foul territory in the majors. And the cool night air knocks down well-hit balls that would float right on out of a ballpark in a warmer climate. It's odd then that the Oakland A's best teams have traditionally been characterized as having rough-and-ready hitters. Perhaps that is because they reside in Oakland, a rough-and-ready town.

The city of Oakland is primarily populated by working-class people. While it is true that the dot-com boom of the 1990s gentrified sections of the East Bay, Oakland remains at its core a no-nonsense town. Network Associates Coliseum could not be a more perfect reflection of the city in which it resides. As you cross the walking bridge from the BART station and approach NAC, you look down on industrial storage areas filled with broken palettes, five-gallon buckets of paint, lumber, railroad tracks, and even a backwater slough. Though it may not be the most attractive ballpark entrance, it is perhaps the most honest. It's an area where working people ply their trade, and many critics say the same thing about Network Associates Coliseum. One thing is for certain, the Network Associates Coliseum is an ode to the strength and beauty that concrete can provide.

Built as a home for the Oakland Raiders of the NFL, as well as to potentially lure the A's away from Kansas City, Oakland-Alameda County Coliseum opened for football in 1966. The City of Oakland and the County of Alameda have remained joint owners of the facility to this day, through many thick and thin times for the franchises who have resided at the facility.

Charlie O. Finley had failed in a bid to move the Kansas City A's to Arlington, Texas, in 1962, and the team was not permitted by MLB to move to Oakland until 1968. Seattle was also considered by Finley as a possible location for his team, but Oakland was chosen primarily because the city already had the coliseum in place. The success of the Oakland Oaks fran-

chise of the Pacific Coast League was also a factor in Finley's decision.

Construction began on the coliseum in 1964 and was directed by the architectural firm of Skidmore, Owings & Merrill. The original cost of the facility was $25.5 million. The multiuse facility became part of the complex that would include the Sports Arena and Exhibition Hall. The city has brought two former Philadelphia teams to Oakland. In 1962 the National Basketball League Philadelphia Warriors were lured to the sports complex where they have remained as the Golden State Warriors.

The many great teams throughout the history of the Athletics in Oakland have always reflected the city's ethic of labor. Think of the "Moustache Gang" of the early 1970s that won three straight World Series, 1972–1974. The thought of these guys sipping tea and eating crumpets at a fine restaurant downtown is ridiculous. With a staff of strong arms like Jim

interior

Photo by Kevin O'Connell

"Catfish" Hunter, Vida Blue, and Rollie Fingers, and hitters such as Reggie Jackson, Sal Bando, and Joe Rudi, there was never a doubt that these guys played hard-nosed, working-class baseball like it was their job. Come to think of it, it was their job. And they attacked other teams the way a mechanic dismantles a manifold.

But fans in Oakland didn't come out to the ballpark too often during those early years. It took six seasons before the A's cracked the one million mark in attendance, and that was with Finley at the helm, one of the most promotion-happy owners in the big leagues. But Finley wasn't well loved by the Oakland community, especially after he sold off the "Swinging A's." Today, for some reason, the A's teams that won three straight World Series are rarely mentioned in discussions of greatest teams of all time.

But Oakland wasn't the only team suffering from low attendance. Baseball fan support was dipping everywhere in the 1970s, perhaps because the sentiment that baseball was too all-American was in vogue during the hippies' decade. Folks in the West were perhaps too busy protesting the war in Vietnam and the Watergate scandal to get on out to the ball game.

In the late 1970s the A's were again less than competitive as they finished in last place in 1977 and 1979, and next to last in 1978. The green and gold gang failed to win more than sixty-nine games in any of those three seasons. When the scoreboard went on the blink one day, the empty concrete coliseum took on the nickname "the Mausoleum."

Oakland's own Billy Martin took over the managerial reins in 1980 and brought to town a brand of baseball dubbed "Billy Ball" that would characterize the era. "Billy Ball" featured an NL-style of play with aggressive base stealing, the hit-and-run, and strong pitchers who would go all nine innings, all trademarks of Martin's pugilistic method. But the toll taken on pitchers throwing nine innings every five days had its downside, as numerous prospects with promising careers blew out their arms.

The return to glory for the A's was keyed by their strong farm system. The renaissance began in 1986 when Jose Canseco hit thirty-three home runs on the way to claiming AL Rookie of the Year honors. The next season, Mark McGwire kept the ROY in Oakland, bashing forty-nine home runs. In 1988 an A's player won the ROY for the third straight season when shortstop Walt Weiss took the award. McGwire and Canseco took on the nickname "the Bash Brothers," and along with teammate Rickey Henderson they carried forward the Oakland mold of working-class baseball heroes. These homegrown talents began the A's tradition of a strong farm system that continues to this day.

Innovation also played a large role in the A's return to success. Manager Tony LaRussa invented the modern "closer" in 1988 when he used Dennis Eckersley for the ninth inning and the ninth inning only of any game in which the A's had a close lead. Sure it's commonplace now, as nearly all bull pens have closers, setup men, seventh-inning pitchers, middle and long relievers, and left-handed specialists, but the experiment had never been attempted before LaRussa and Eckersley. And it has gone on to redefine the way managers use their bull pens.

National Football League owner Al Davis devastated the city when he moved the Raiders out of Oakland in 1981, heading for the supposed greener pastures of the Los Angeles Coliseum. The Raiders' twelve-year southern hiatus left an enormous hole in the hearts of Oakland fans, as the team had always been the top draw. In an effort to get their Raiders back, Oakland began a reconstruction process on the coliseum in the mid-1990s at Davis's request. The baseball-friendly outfield bleachers were removed and replaced with a massive four-tier concrete seating and luxury box structure that has come to be known derogatorily as "Mount Davis." A total of twenty-two thousand seats were added, most of which sit empty during baseball games. Also added during the renovation were two forty-thousand-square-foot clubhouses—the East and West clubs—125 luxury suites, a nine thousand-square-foot kitchen, and two new color video boards and two matrix scoreboards at the end zones. The price of the remodel was initially supposed to be $100 million, but some estimates have the total upward of $200 million.

Kevin: "They could have built a park like PNC on the bay for less money."

Josh: "Yeah, but don't forget, eight football games per year are *much more important* than eighty-one home baseball games."

Davis's bouncing of the Raiders back and forth between L.A. and Oakland and his threatening demands placed on the city of Oakland to expand the Coliseum have left voters and citizens gun shy when it comes to providing new funds for the A's. Folks just don't believe the local sports franchises will live up to their word, and it's easy to see why given their history with Davis. To say that Al Davis is the George Steinbrenner of the NFL may well be an insult to Mr. Steinbrenner.

In 1997 the coliseum was named UMAX Coliseum, after UMAX Technologies, a local division of a Taiwanese company, promised to pay $17 million over ten years. But a dispute arose between the parties, funds were never secured, and the original name was reinstituted in 1998. Network Associates, a networking technologies company from Santa Clara then agreed to pay $5.8 million to put its name on the coliseum for five years.

Josh: "What will it be called after that?"

Kevin: "Stay tuned."

What the new construction did, in essence, was transform the Oakland Coliseum from a relatively nice pitcher's paradise into a home-run-friendly stadium with more of a football feel than it previously had. Fans could once watch games for free from the concourse behind the field-level seats by peeking between slats in the wooden cyclone fence. Real bleacher seats were available to fans in left and right field. Behind them ran a concourse, complete with a grassy hill that collected long home runs, as well as flag poles and scoreboards that helped give the Coliseum its ballpark feel. There was also a view of the Oakland Hills. None of these aesthetically appealing elements remain at Network Associates Coliseum thanks to Mount Davis, or the Death Star, as our friend Matthew calls the megalithic structure. The price tag of Mount Davis also killed any chance that the A's would be able convince Oakland to build a new ballpark, which many feel they desperately need in order to survive as a franchise.

Though the A's organization has traveled across country in its history, casting off cities and ballparks the way most of us change batting gloves, it has managed a dead-heat tie with the St. Louis Cardinals (through 2003) for the second most successful franchise in history when it comes to World Series victories. The A's of Philadelphia collected nine American League pennants and won five World Series. The twelve years in Kansas City were not as productive, but since arriving in Oakland the A's have won four World Series in six trips to the big dance. That's fifteen trips to the Series and nine victories. The Cardinals have as many victories in two fewer attempts.

The Athletics organization began long ago when a tall and lanky Irishman named Cornelius McGillicuddy—aka Connie Mack—and his Philadelphia A's joined the American League in its inaugural season of 1901. When the A's won the American League and challenged the Senior Circuit for the World Series crown, another Irishman, John McGraw, the colorful manager of the National League's very established and successful New York Giants dismissed the American League A's, calling them white elephants. While McGraw's jab meant to imply that Mack should not be allowed to spend indiscriminately, the dual meaning of the metaphor is interesting. Calling something a "white elephant" is a way of saying that it is more trouble than it's worth, but it is also a fictitious animal, one that supposedly does not exist. Either way, Mack decided the team should wear the insult as a badge of honor and adopted a white elephant as the team's insignia. Posters and paraphernalia of the period bear the white elephant insignia with its raised trunk. Check the left sleeve of the current A's uniform, and you'll see the elephant to this day.

The A's won the American League in 1902, but the White Elephant moniker turned out to be correct in the second World Series ever played in 1905, as the A's fell to McGraw's Giants four games to one. Giants pitcher Christy Mathewson shut out the A's in Games 1, 3, and 5, allowing only fourteen hits in the three games. Mathewson and Joe McGinnity combined to pitch forty-four of the forty-five innings for the Giants in the Series.

But Connie Mack would not be denied, nor would his White Elephants. The man who managed the A's for fifty seasons (1901–50) countered by assembling his legendary $100,000 infield of 1909. Once again the term White Elephant applied.

Josh: "With the league minimum today set at $300,000, $100,000 would get you a third of a rookie third-baseman."

Kevin: "Would that equal a first-baseman?"

Made up of Stuffy McInnis (first base), Eddie Collins (second base), Jack Barry (shortstop), and Frank "Home Run" Baker (third base), the famed infield led the A's to World Series victories in 1910, 1911, and 1913—two over McGraw and the Giants. Baker earned his nickname "Home Run" by hitting an incredible (for the time) eleven dingers during the regular season in 1911, and two in the World Series. Remember, this was pre-Babe Ruth. Freak pitches like the spitball had not yet been declared illegal, and the ball had not yet been made lively.

It's been said of the thrifty Mack that he fielded two kinds of teams: either unbeatable or horrible. And after putting together the dynasty, he just as quickly sold the team off, perhaps because it was lucrative to do so, perhaps to challenge himself to build another team from the ground up. But the A's teams of the late 1910s and early 1920s wallowed in the cellar.

Then Mack did it again, putting together what many argue was the greatest team in history in 1929. Led by Jimmie Foxx, known as the right-handed Babe Ruth, the A's won the Series in '29, defeating the Cubs four games to one. The A's repeated in 1930, downing the Cardinals in six games. What was perhaps most impressive about this A's edition was how deftly it handled the Yankees: Ruth, Lou Gehrig, and all. While the 1931 team won 107 games, led by Foxx, Al Simmons, and Lefty Grove—who posted an incredible 31–4 record on the mound—this time the A's were downed in the World Series by the Cardinals.

The slide downhill after the A's glory days of the early 1930s was continuous as Mack again sold off his team. The players that he had developed went on to win pennants for teams in other cities, wearing other uniforms. The distinguished old man was getting old, and his teams suffered. In 1943 the Athletics lost twenty games in a row, tying the American League record set previously by the 1906 Red Sox. The record would stand until 1988, when the Baltimore Orioles lost their first twenty-one games.

The Philadelphia A's of this period played at Shibe Park, also known as Connie Mack Stadium. For more information on this classic ballpark, see the Philadelphia chapter. So influential was Mack during his time that an official Connie Mack Day was declared at Shibe Park by the city of Philadelphia and the state of Pennsylvania in 1941.

Connie Mack handed over the reins of control in 1950. The A's were sold to Arnold Johnson in 1954 and would reside in Kansas City by the 1955 season. Connie Mack was the very soul of the Philadelphia A's, and perhaps things had changed for Philadelphians with Mack no longer at the helm.

Finley, the team's second great owner, bought the A's while they were in KC, and tried to move them all over North America. But not before putting on a pretty good show in Kansas City. Stories about Finley and the A's during their years in Kansas City are included in the Kansas City chapter.

The KC A's acquired second baseman Billy Martin from the Yankees in 1957 after Martin was banned from the team by Casey Stengel over the infamous Copacabana incident. Martin played hard both on and off the field. He was out celebrating teammate Mickey Mantle's birthday at the Copacabana nightclub, when a fight broke out with a Bronx delicatessen owner. The deli owner wound up with a concussion and a broken jaw, and though Stengel had much affection for his second baseman, Martin shouldered the blame. Martin's career ended just four years later, but he returned to the A's in Oakland as a manager from 1980–1982.

In the A's first season in Oakland, Catfish Hunter hurled a perfect game against the Minnesota Twins on May 9, 1968. Not only was it the first perfect game in the American League in forty-six years, but Hunter drove in all three runs for the A's that day. (This was back before the DH.) Not a bad effort for the twenty-two year-old right-hander.

To complement the World Series win, Finley kept the ballpark atmosphere lively with promotions galore at the coliseum. To kick off the 1970 season, the A's introduced gold-colored bases for their home games. Oh, that incorrigible Charlie O. Needless to say, bases colored anything but white were banned soon thereafter by the Rules Committee.

World class sprinter Herb Washington served as Finley's "designated runner" during the 1974 and 1975 seasons. Washington played in 105 games without recording a single at-bat

TRIVIA TIMEOUT

Acorn: Which California Governor threw out the first pitch at Oakland Alameda Coliseum's inaugural season of 1968?

Sapling: Name the famous rap music star discovered by Charlie O. Finley dancing outside the coliseum for ticket money. (Hint: old school.)

Mighty Oak: Name the A's pitcher who appeared in all seven games of the 1973 World Series.

Look for the answers in the text.

or ever appearing in the field. On the base paths he stole thirty-one bases in forty-eight attempts, while scoring thirty-three runs. It seems that Finley was awaiting the coming of Rickey Henderson.

"Charlie O the Mule" made a reappearance at Oakland Coliseum, after first garnering fame in Kansas City. And Video Dot Racing, where dots race around a circle with ponglike technology was started at the coliseum by Finley.

Rickey Henderson burst onto the A's scene in 1979, stealing bases quicker than street toughs steal hubcaps. Rickey (we call Mr. Henderson "Rickey," not out of disrespect, but because that is what he calls himself, often referring to himself in the third person) went on to break the single-season stolen-base mark in 1982 when he swiped 130 bags. Then Rickey broke Ty Cobb's AL record, stealing his 893rd base in 1990, and Lou Brock's all-time record by stealing his 939th in 1991. Then Rickey broke the only steals record left to him, the world record of 1,065, held by Yutaka Fukumoto of Japan. And as of this writing Rickey Henderson is forty-four years old and still trying to find a place on a Major League roster and break his own records with every base he steals. There might be a base stealer on Mars who has more steals, but for our money Rickey is the greatest base stealer our universe has ever seen. Rickey also holds the record for most leadoff homeruns. Power and speed made an undoubted Hall of Famer out of Rickey.

After being downed by the Dodgers in the World Series of 1988, the Oakland A's, led by manager Tony LaRussa, returned to form by winning the "Bay Bridge" World Series of 1989. Game 3 at Candlestick Park will always be remembered as the game that was postponed by the earthquake that rocked the entire region. When the Series resumed twelve days later, the A's picked up where they left off, taking the final two games to complete the sweep. Dominating Dave Stewart was the MVP of the series, and was nearly flawless, pitching a five-hit shutout in Game 1, and a three-run, five hitter in Game 3. Stewart became the first pitcher in history to notch two wins in both the World Series and the ALCS.

It was as if that awful earthquake changed the world of baseball in the Bay area. While the A's could compete on a level playing field before that time, after the quake, the city of Oakland, one of the smallest markets in baseball with the tiniest of payrolls, began to catch up with the A's. Now whenever a young A's player performs well, it's inevitable that he outprices himself when free agency approaches, and the A's are forced to deal him to a team with deeper pock-

ets. No time was this more evident than with MVP first-baseman Jason Giambi, who wanted to remain with the A's, but demanded a no-trade clause, a financial deal the small-market team could not swing.

The Athletics' legendary farm system has continued to bring homegrown All-Star caliber talent to Network Associates Coliseum. General Manager Billy Beane is one of the best in the game at accomplishing great things with limited cash. Beane's economic baseball theories are detailed in the book *Moneyball: The Art of Winning an Unfair Game*, by Michael Lewis, and has kept the A's in the thick of the playoffs recently.

But the A's haven't won it all since 1989. And with fans still not attending in huge numbers—they didn't sell out their playoff games at the Coliseum in 2000, 2001, or 2002—the franchise's days in Oakland could be numbered. If the A's don't get more fans through the gates somehow, they'll have to hold bake sales to compete. Ownership feels a new ballpark would help the situation, but with attendance so low—even with the team's success—Oakland city officials are less than enthusiastic, especially after being burned so badly by the Raiders.

It's like Kevin's friend Tim says, "It's easy to be an A's fan, and it's difficult as well." When David takes on Goliath, everyone roots for the little guy, David. And that is just what the A's have become. A franchise-saving World Series might be won—one that would allow the owners to sell the team locally to someone with deep enough pockets to keep the team competitive during occasional lean years, and perhaps allow for the construction of a new ballpark. If not, then the nomadic A's may be looking for yet another city to call home.

Getting a Choice Seat

Getting into the coliseum is not the problem.

The stadium is big enough for you plus every other A's fan who decides to go to the game that day—unless of course it's a Yankee game, or a Giants interleague battle for cross-bay bragging rights. The problem on regular games comes in getting a seat that is close enough to the action so that you won't have to be pulling out the binoculars every few minutes.

The design of the seating bowl provides a very gradual incline much like Shibe Park/Connie Mack Stadium used to. And the bowl is round. This means that the seats behind the plate are very close, while as the circle extends outward, seats get farther away. This really only becomes a negative factor on the third level, as the designers have done well to hang the upper decks in toward the action. But that means there are overhang and under-hang issues to consider.

Plaza Club
(Sections 213–214)

These are your typical Club Level seats on the second tier of the ballpark with one tasty exception: Included with these seats is the Club Meal.

Josh: "Is that sort anything like a Happy Meal?"

Field Level (Sections 109–125, Sections 101–108 and 126–133)

The first twenty rows of Sections 109–125 are called MVP Infield Seats, and are the best seats your game-day dollar will buy. Network Associates Coliseum boasts some of the cheapest seats in the Majors, so take advantage. These seats are extremely reasonably priced compared with other ballparks.

Rows 21–38 in Sections 109–125 are also great seats and even cheaper, but we advise avoiding Rows 33 and higher as the overhang becomes a factor. While it's not the seating

SEATING TIP

ONE WAY for autograph hounds to maximize their experience at Network Associates, is to sit along the aisle in the first five rows of Section 115. Players walk right past on their way to the tunnel to get into the clubhouse. Sitting here will put you in close contact with the players, and many autographs were asked for and delivered as a result when we visited. Josh got Terrence Long and Chris Singleton to sign for him, two autographs he'll always treasure.

deck from above that is the problem, the supporting concrete structures detract from sight lines. There's more trouble in Sections 122–123 and 111–113 where camera platforms hang down from the second deck, further blocking views. Avoid all seats in these sections above Row 25.

Sections 101–102 have foul pole obstructions, but are otherwise good seats. Sections 131–132 have foul pole obstructions as well, and also sit behind the BBQ Terrace. So be prepared to view the game over the terrace umbrellas and through a screen of barbecue smoke. Or if you're like Josh, be prepared to walk out of the ballpark five pounds heavier than when you walked in.

Sections 101 and 133 are not only in the clear of all foul pole obstructions, but also along the terraced steps that give the ballpark its coliseum feel.

While the bleachers (Sections 134–150) are not the best bleacher seats that we've ever seen, and not nearly as good as those before Mount Davis was built, the most rabid A's fans in the entire coliseum sit in these sections, especially in left field. Drums beat and green and gold flags fly freely in Sections 134–139, some of the cheapest and most desired sections in the ballpark. (See the Superfans section

Sellout Index: 0% of games sell out
Seating Capacity: 43,662
Ticket Office: (510) 638-GOAS
http://oakland.athletics.mlb.com

below. Don't expect the best seats out here as the warning track is lost from view and many of the sections don't face the field directly. But no fans at the coliseum—perhaps even in baseball—are more committed, or having a better time. And that's what a day at the ballpark is all about.

Plaza Level Infield
(Sections 209–212 and 215–225)

The second deck is hung close to the action, but doesn't give that awkward feeling of being right on top of the action, looking down. As a result of the curve of the circle, the Plaza Level Infield seats are much closer to the action than other seats on the Plaza Level, and are well worth the extra money.

Plaza Level (Sections 200–208 and 226–234)

These are significantly worse seats than their infield counterparts, not only because of the shape of the coliseum, but also because the angle toward the action causes the support structures to get in the way and obstruct views, especially in the upper seats of the sections.

Plaza Bleachers (Sections 235–248)

These should really be avoided altogether. The under-hang from this section severely blocks much of the outfield below. These are seats for Mr. Davis and his football team, not for baseball.

Plaza Suites (Sections 67–96)

There is nothing in the world like expensive Suites way out in the outfield. What were they thinking when they built these? Oh, that's right. We know, they're football seats. So don't sit there.

Loge Level

Most of the Loge Level is occupied by the Loge Suites (Sections 7–60) which are unavailable.

But Sections 1–3 and 65–66 way out on both ends are available. The problem is that these seats are not very good for the money. It would be better by far to sit in the Upper Reserve Sections behind the plate. They are much cheaper seats, with better sight lines.

Upper Reserve (Sections 300–334)

We can highly recommend seats in Upper Reserve Sections 313–321. Again, the design of the rounded bowl structure and the hanging of the decks close make these sections some of the better upper level seats we've seen. Plus, they're priced right.

The other sections on the upper level (Sections 309–312 and 322–325) are fair. Seats beyond these in Sections 300–308 and 326–334 grow increasingly awful as you get closer to the foul poles. Sitting in the bleachers for the same price would be much preferable to these distant seats.

The Black Market

If you drive to Network Associates you may get the impression that the number of folks earning a living as scalpers in Oakland is a very small number. Arrival by BART makes the opposite impression. Scalpers line the walking bridge in increasing numbers as game time approaches. Remember: you can get good seats in the bleachers or in the upper deck for less than $10 at the ticket window, so don't overpay for anything else.

SEATING TIP

ONE-DOLLAR Wednesdays have become very popular at Network Associates. Yep. Only a buck for any seat in the Upper Level. Hot dogs are only a dollar as well. Sounds like a minor league ballpark promotion, doesn't it? Well, it's not. And on Wednesdays the upper deck is often filled to the brim, while seats on the lower levels are sparse.

Before/After the Game

Outside the sports complex lies a food and restaurant wasteland, a downtrodden strip of unappealing and run-down joints between the coliseum and the airport. Even the fast-food places are few and distant. It's simply not a destination in any way, as many of the folks hanging around are up to no good.

So what do folks do when there's no good places to go out near the ballpark? They tailgate, of course. The tailgating scene in the team lots is modest but is clearly the best option for folks who don't want to pay the extra money to eat and drink inside. These parking lots are a bit too vast for any real camaraderie between tailgating brethren, such as you'll find in Milwaukee. Plus this is Oakland, bub, not the Midwest. If you want free tailgating grub you'd better be a hilarious drunk decked out from head to toe in green and gold. Parking lots are patrolled by bicycle cops and the AAA, to assist with collisions between people and cars and cars and cars.

Too Legit to Quit

Hanging around outside Network Associates back in the 1970s was a kid from the neighborhood named Stanley Burrell. Young Stanley could be found on game days dancing for ticket money. Charlie O. Finley finally hired Burrell because of his obvious talent and his ability to entertain. Burrell worked in a variety of capacities for the team, starting out as a batboy and finally winding up as a vice president. Stanley Burrell is better known to the world as MC Hammer.

Getting to Network Associates Coliseum

After finding your way to I-880 from either direction, take the 66th Avenue Exit and follow the signs toward the team lots. The team lots lettered A–D are medium priced at $12, and

open two-and-a-half hours prior to game time. If you're planning on tailgating, this is clearly the way to go.

There are free parking spots available on the street between the BART station and the BART parking lots, as well as on the other side of the coliseum, beyond I-880. The rules with these spots are thus: the BART station spots get nabbed up quickly, so arrive early to park cheaply. The spots near I-880 are usually always available. Our friend Anne, an Oakland resident, tells us that the area can get pretty sketchy at night, so cheapskates beware.

Public Transportation is an excellent option in the Bay area. Take the Freemont/Richmond line of BART to the Coliseum-Airport Station, and walk across the bridge to Network Associates.

BART operates by selling travel cards out of kiosks. Just slide your card into the slot, and the turnstile will open. How much money you have left on your card is accessed at the turnstile on the end of your trip. The farther you travel, the more it costs. For travel information call BART at (510) 464-6000.

BART Traveling Tip: If you plan on returning home on BART, make sure you have at least enough money available on your card to get you back onto the train. If you wait until afterward the lines for the kiosks are horrendous. One way to avoid these lines is to add enough money onto your card before the game to get you to your destination. But what folks waiting in line don't seem to understand is that there are kiosks available before you exit the turnstiles at every station in the system. So if you don't have enough money on your card to get where you're going, don't wait in the long lines at the Coliseum station. Rather get on the train and add money to your card at the kiosk at your destination.

Outside Attractions

There couldn't be less to do outside of Network

Associates. No statues of Reggie Jackson, no tributes to the great teams during the A's glory years. There are a good deal of green and gold A's banners that decorate the exterior ramps of the Net. These banners can be changed out for silver and black when football season comes around.

The idea at Network Associates is to get fans inside and keep them happy. To this end, the A's accomplish their goals very well, as inside are some of the best foods and drinks in the Majors. But outside the coliseum there is absolutely nothing of interest. So either set up the hibachi and open the tailgate, or get yourself inside and partake in one of the most enthusiastic ball game experiences in the big leagues.

Watering Holes and Outside Eats

Oakland has great sports bars and plenty of places to get a good meal on the cheap. The problem is that none of them are anywhere near the coliseum. There's nothing even close. With that in mind we've selected a choice few of our favorites from the area. But you might as well get yourself a guide to the entire East Bay area, because there are simply too many places within an hour's drive to list here.

COLISEUM BURGER (7127 San Leandro Street)

Below the Coliseum/Airport BART station is this little burger joint that offers a burger special with jumbo fries and a drink for $3.89. If getting the most food for the price is your primary concern, this might be the place for you.

Josh: "At that price, I can't afford not to eat here."

JACK LONDON SQUARE

While most of the joints in this tourist trap on the water are far too trendy and expensive for our liking, **Heinold's First and Last Chance Saloon** (56 Jack London Square) is a noteworthy exception. Jack London actually drank and wrote in the saloon, and that gives it all the credibility it needs with us. Called "first and last chance" because the saloon was the closest to the ferry docks, passengers traveling in both directions would have either their first or last chance to have a drink here. London listened to tales of sailors who had traveled the world, and mentions Heinold's in many of his novels.

ROCK RIDGE/COLLEGE AVENUE AREA

Rock Ridge is a great area to head to if you're interested in hitting multiple pubs within a short walk of each other. College Avenue runs toward Berkeley and is loaded with coffeehouses, burrito shacks, restaurants, and all the various trendy stores that accompany such streets. **George and Walt's** (5445 College Avenue) is a dive bar that we liked favored by Raiders' fans, with cheap beer and stiff drinks. **Ben & Nick's** (5612 College Avenue) has a good burger, and if you wear the kitschy T-shirt from the bar and its sister joint, **Cato's Ale House** (3891 Piedmont Avenue), you can get a discount on drinks. Bright green **McNally's Irish Pub** (5352 College Avenue) boasts itself as the premier Irish Bar in the East Bay, and we cannot disagree. Also visit the **Public House**, historic building complete with the current local flavor of Oakland. Off the beaten path but worth the trip is **Kingfish** (5227 Claremont). Tickets from sporting events from all around the Bay area adorn the walls. Kevin could hardly resist a dive bar with live music and sports memorabilia that also serves a great pint of Guinness.

LOIS THE PIE QUEEN (851 60th Street)

This North Oakland establishment is famous not only for its many delicious pie selections, but also for its Reggie Jackson breakfast. Two fried pork chops, eggs, and grits kept "Mr. October" swinging all day long, and we bet you'll belt a few over the wall after eating here as well.

Inside the Coliseum

Like any other stadium its size, Network Associates Coliseum is rocking when full. When empty, it has all the charm and appeal of a concrete canyon. The city of Oakland loves a winner and hates a loser. So if the A's are in the thick of the AL West, expect fans to be crazier than nearly anywhere else. If not, enjoy the highly available seating and the few crazy diehards who have dedicated their lives—or at least their summers—to the A's.

While we've stated many times before that baseball suffers when a facility attempts to accommodate two sports, this is not the case at the coliseum. Though the dimensions are completely symmetrical, and Mount Davis is a huge intrusion into the baseball feel, the coliseum still feels more like a baseball field. A real dirt warning track and a grass field help give the coliseum a ballpark feel. Plus the traditional green wall with yellow foul poles and home run lines are a natural fit, giving the park an authentic look, as well as doubling as the team colors.

Ballpark Features

REACH OUT AND STEAL YOURSELF A HOME RUN

Fans who are unlucky enough to be sitting in the poor seats near the foul poles do have one recourse for revenge. They can lean out in front of those poles and catch fair home run balls. Just be careful; it is strictly prohibited. And Alameda County Jail is not the kind of place you'd want to spend the night (or so we've been told).

THE DEATH STAR

Our friend Matthew calls this outfield monstrosity "the Death Star," and it's clear that Mount Davis has messed up the baseball feel of this park for good. Where once there were real bleachers filled with rowdy fans, a walking terrace, and baseball pennants flying from flag poles, now stands nothing but concrete as far as the eye can see. All views of the Oakland Hills are blocked by this megalithic structure, designed to maximize football luxury box seats. It's as obnoxious as the man who ordered it built. For baseball, nearly all of the seats remain unsold. Even during the playoffs they can't sell them out. Mount Davis simply has too much outfield seating that's awful. Of the outfield sections that are supposed to be good, many of the bleacher sections don't even point towards the action, but rather toward where the fifty-yard line would be.

But the effect of the Death Star on the game of baseball has been great. While the coliseum, with all of its foul territory and cool evening winds was easily considered the best park for pitchers in the American League, now the massive concrete wall knocks down those evening breezes and allows fly balls to carry much farther.

To each side of the mountain tiered steps lead down to the field which not only give the stadium its coliseum feel, but now stand as a sad reminder of the single level of rounded outfield bleachers that once stood here, now crushed under the enormous weight of the massive Mount Davis.

NO BULL PENS?

Josh: "Hey, what gives? Why aren't there any bull pens?"

Kevin: "If you'll remember, there are no bull pens at Wrigley Field."

Josh: "Are you comparing Network Associates to Wrigley Field?"

Kevin: "I'm just saying."

The warm-up areas for pitchers run right next to the seats along the baselines, an added benefit for fans seated close by. And why not? There's enough foul territory here for three ballparks.

BASEBALL before 1974 was a very different ball game indeed, at least as far as the owners were concerned. Major League Baseball had the reserve clause in place, which bound players to their teams and gave them no say in where they could be traded. That is until former St. Louis Cardinals outfielder (and Oakland-raised) Curt Flood wrote a letter to baseball Commissioner Bowie Kuhn in 1969, objecting to a transaction. The trade would have sent Flood, along with catcher Tim McCarver, pitcher Joe Hoerner, and outfielder Byron Browne to Philadelphia, for first-baseman Dick Allen, infielder Cookie Rojas, and pitcher Jerry Johnson. Flood's refusal to report to Philadelphia resulted in a lawsuit against MLB, challenging the legality of the reserve clause.

Flood lost his lawsuit, which went to the Supreme Court, and was traded to the Phillies. The reserve clause survived, at least temporarily. Flood sat out the 1970 season, played a bit in 1971 with the Washington Senators, then retired after only a few games. He spent the 1978 season with the A's in the broadcasting booth.

The first free agent would come in Oakland in 1974, when an arbitrator ruled that a breach to Catfish Hunter's contract by Finley invalidated the entire contract, including the reserve clause. With his contract invalidated, Hunter could pursue a contract with any team that he chose. Free agency as we know it was born. George Steinbrenner bought the rights to Hunter, signing him to a deal worth $3.75 million. Steinbrenner and his investment partners had purchased the entire Yankees franchise for just $10 million.

After Hunter's deal, free agency has become the standard of the day. And though the reserve clause was unfair, we can't help but think that what has resulted from free agency—paying a journeyman left-hander $3 million a year to finish one game under .500—is not good for the game. In their quest to win, owners now compete with one another to pay even mediocre free agents ridiculous sums of money. Under other circumstances, the unbridled driving up of salaries wouldn't bother us at all. But these costs have been passed on to the consumers, the fans. In other words: us. We pay more because of free agency, and we don't like it.

Is it any surprise that not a single ballpark before free agency was named after a corporation, but since then, in order to remain competitive and keep up with sky-rocketing payrolls, teams have had to sell the naming rights of the game's most beloved parks? Is baseball better off or worse now that Comiskey Park has been renamed US Cellular Field? Can Fenway Park, Wrigley Field, and Dodger Stadium hold out much longer?

So as a matter of helping baseball to improve itself, we offer this simple solution: how about getting real and striking a compromise at the next bargaining session? Free agency has not had a completely positive impact on the game from the fans' perspective. Nor do we believe that going back to the rigid reserve clause is the answer either. Compromising on this issue will not be beneficial to players' bankbooks. But it will go a long way to repairing how fans feel about the players, owners, and the game of baseball itself. Remember, baseball is a game that we fans try our best to love. And it's easier to love the game when money, greed, and politics remain as far from the ball field as possible.

OAKLAND ATHLETICS HEROES REMEMBERED

The A's world championship banners fly proudly above the power alleys, near the 367-foot markers on both the left and right field sides.

Kevin: "What I wouldn't give for just one of those flying in Seattle."

Josh: "What I wouldn't give for one in the last eighty years flying in Boston."

Retired jerseys on the outfield wall honor only a scarce few of the A's greats. With all the great talent this team has produced, we couldn't help but wonder why so few. One retired jersey honors number 34, Roland "Rollie" Fingers, who was a four-time All-Star with the A's from 1973 to 1976, and the MVP of the 1974 World Series. James "Catfish" Hunter owned number 27 for the A's. Catfish began his

GAME TIME FOR BONZO

BACK WHEN the ballpark first opened (and it looked more like a ballpark) former U.S. President and Governor of California Ronald Reagan threw out the first pitch at Oakland Alameda Coliseum on April 17, 1968. The A's lost the game 4–1 to the Baltimore Orioles.

career with the Kansas City A's in 1965. Hunter posted 224 wins in his career, an ERA of 3.26, and was the Cy Young Award winner in 1974. That's it, two retired numbers in the team's history. The blue number 42 belongs to Jackie Robinson.

Down the right field line on the 300 Level concourse is the home of the Oakland Sports Hall of Fame. Immortalized in bronze are those great players who either played for Oakland teams or are native sons. Reggie Jackson, Billy Martin, Vada Pinson, Dick Bartell, Curt Flood, and Willie Stargell are remembered here.

Not mentioned in the A's Hall of Fame, though perhaps ought to be, Darold Knowles pitched in all seven games of the 1973 World Series for the A's.

Stadium Eats

While the exterior restaurant scene at this ballpark can only be rated poor at best, the food inside ranks among the best in the Majors. As diverse as the city itself, the ballpark munchies nearly all tasted good to us.

YOUR BLACK MUSLIM BAKERY
(Trademark Food)

All made to the exacting specification of the Muslim diet, this longtime ballpark and community favorite could only survive in an area such as Oakland.

Whether you prefer the barbecue bean, filet of fish, tofu, or vegetarian sandwich, none of these Muslim favorites will have you "eating the white man's pork," as Malcolm X was told to avoid. Piled high with lettuce, tomatoes, and pickles, and served on a sesame-seed bun, we like to think of these sandwiches as "big macs" for the Black Muslim community. Carrot and Bean Pies are as delicious as they are distinctive.

And while Kevin favored the vegetarian Black Muslim Bakery's filet of fish, Josh went to the other end of the spectrum toward **Saag's Specialty Sausages**. The grilled brats, Italians, linguesa, and Polish were above the standard sausage fair, and also must be included as a trademark food of this ballpark.

Kevin: "You realize linguesa is made with tongue, don't you."

Josh: "Yes, but it all comes together so nicely."

MILLER'S HOT DOG (Dog Rating)
The Best Hot Dog in the Majors

Thicker than nearly every other dog in the Majors and certainly juicier, these all-beef Miller dogs are grilled to perfection. The natural casing explodes in your mouth when you bite into them. Prepared the same way since 1910, they are available in four sizes: stadium, coliseum, jumbo, and super. Miller dogs are so good, they made us want to skip all of the other ballpark treats and have another dog. And if we didn't have to sample all the rest for the purposes of this book, that's exactly what we would have done.

BEST OF THE REST

Of the many other wonderful food choices at the Net, there are a few that stand out. **The Ribs 'N Things** stand, behind the BBQ Terrace in Section 132 offers just what the name says. Ribs, pulled pork, and all manner of scrumptious barbecue are available.

The Philly cheese steaks are no match for Geno's or Pat's, but are far superior to any other steaks we've tried outside Philly. If your craving is for the whiz, try this.

Another choice that might seem easy to pass over is the Chinese chicken salad from the **Deli** behind Section 115. Actually most of the offerings from the Deli are excellent, from the hot pastrami sandwich to the baked potato.

The garlic fries **are** awfully good as well, though Gordon Biersch has been using minced garlic these days instead of the fresh stuff they originally used. As our friend Anne says, "Beware of the garlic hangover."

SAY "NO, THANKS," AND WALK AWAY

Foods to avoid in this eater's paradise are the Mexican items—tacos, burritos, nachos—and the pizza. Like nearly all ballpark varieties of these foods: you can do much better outside the ballpark. Get a hot dog and save your appetite.

STADIUM SUDS

Gordon Biersch, Sierra Nevada, and Pyramid Ale top the microbrew options at the coliseum, and for our money Pyramid wins out. Heineken, Dos Equis, Corona, and Coors Light are also available for those who prefer a lighter beer on a hotter day.

For those folks who go by the adage "liquor is quicker," the mixed drinks served at the Net are stiff, and will treat you right.

THE FIELD—IRISH PUB

The very idea of an Irish Pub might be better suited at PacBell, as nearly all the Irish in the area settled across the Bay. Though not the authentic Irish pub experience offered at, say, the Plow and Stars in the city, we commend the A's for their attempts. And Jameson's tastes the same no matter where it's served. The Guinness came served in a plastic cup, and even so, it was not the worst pint Kevin has ever sampled. So we give our approval to the the Field.

Josh: "Long may the Guinness flow!"

Kevin: "Here's to Connie Mack! And Charlie O. Finley!"

Josh: "And Charlie O. the Mule!"

THE WEST IS THE BEST

The huge **East Club** buried inside of Mount Davis and the equally enormous **West Club** behind home plate on the 200 Level are open to plebeians such as ourselves during the game. Full meals are served at the tables, complete with white tablecloths and views of the action. And the bar is open as well. We were happy to see the A's open up an area such as this during the game to regular fans. Well done.

Josh: "I still would rather be down near the field."

Kevin: "Me too. Let's get outta here."

The Network Associates Coliseum Experience

Oakland is a city with an East Coast mentality stuck out in the West. It's a hard-nosed town that loves its sports teams, so expect a rabid fan base at the Net. So devoted are the A's fans when the team is doing well that it was difficult for us to decide on who were the superfans, and who were simply highly devoted fans.

SPORTS IN THE CITY

OAKLAND attracted its African American population during and after World War II because of the jobs available in the shipyards. And because baseball was king back in those days, the Oakland Public League became a hotbed of talent. Ballplayers who weren't born in Oakland but called it home form an impressive list, from Rickey Henderson, Joe Morgan, and Frank Robinson, to Curt Flood, Vada Pinson, and many others.

The decline of baseball in the inner city has given way to basketball being the king of the urban sports scene. Oakland has kept up this tradition, boasting such NBA greats as Bill Russell, Gary Payton, and Jason Kidd among the alumni of Oakland Public League ballers.

The wearing of the green and gold is carried to an extreme here, as you'll notice even the average fan with his hair dyed green, gold shirt, green shorts, and yellow socks. Any jersey with the right tint green and gold will do, regardless what the shirt says on it. Green Bay Packers and Seattle SuperSonics gear were popular choices alongside the traditional A's garb.

Oakland fans expect victory, and anything short will not suffice. They will boo even their best young players when perfection is not delivered. In fact we saw a kid with a mitt drop a batting-practice line drive that was hit pretty hotly to him in the corner below the foul pole. He was harassed unmercifully by two ushers for dropping the ball.

"You shoulda brung two mitts wit ya to make that play," one yelled down.

"Yeah," said the other, "My grandmuddah woulda had dat one."

Hammer Guys Superfans

Photo by Kevin O'Connell

THE A'S DRUM AND FLAG CORPS (Superfans)

The left field bleachers house the most famous A's superfans, though the Drum and Flag Corps can be seen and heard anywhere in the coliseum. An entire row of mad flag-waving fans hoist their green and gold banners into the air over the railing, blowing horns and chanting obscenities, while behind them sit the A's drummers, banging away at their broken down tom-toms with reckless abandon. They drum nothing special, a simple three-beat "Let's Go A's," and other such ballpark staples. But their enthusiasm and sheer volume are infectious.

So popular did the drummers get at one point, that the team gave them all season tickets and used them in a series of TV ads. During the 2001 playoffs, Little Napoléon, George Steinbrenner so feared that the drummers would affect his hitters that he attempted to have them removed. He said that since they didn't pay for their season tickets, that made them employees of the team. Though their season tickets may have been taken away because of this, the A's drummers remain, beating their skins and annoying Mr. Bonaparte. Though now they can only drum while the A's are hitting.

THE HAMMER GUYS (Superfans)

Nick Wong carries a cardboard hammer while his partner Austin Cross wields a cardboard mascot of the opposing team. Together they've hammered and danced their way onto ESPN's *SportsCenter*, and into the hearts of A's fans everywhere. While it appears that Wong's hammer is simply mauling Cross's mascot, the two fans point out that there is more to it than meets the eye. Apparently these two local kids are hip to the fact that "the hammer" is an old baseball term for a curve ball. Plus, "Hammer" used to rap outside the park.

THE A'S ANTIFAN (Superfan?)

The A's inspire much love from their many fans and superfans. They also inspire some hatred as well, at least in the mind of the A's Super-Antifan. This guy comes to nearly every A's home game wearing the cap of the opposing team.

Kevin: "Interleague play must be killing this guy."

The Super-Antifan spends all his time walking around the Net and rooting against the A's, cheering for whatever team they're playing against. Perhaps the only thing more bizarre than dedicating your life to the A's success, is dedicating your life to their destruction. While we admired the Antifan's dedication, to be honest, we were afraid to talk to him. File this one under the "Only in Oakland" bin.

WHAT IS THIS, A SOCCER MATCH?

There's more singing going on during an A's game at the Net than there is at a Manchester United match. When the A's drummers aren't leading the crowd in the traditional gutteral ballpark favorites, the song "Let's Go Oakland" takes over to get the A's rallies going. The nationwide ballpark phenomenon "YMCA," by the Village People began here when construction workers building Mount Davis started dressing like the Village People.

SOMETHING OLD, SOMETHING NEW

Real organ music is played for everyone's favorite seventh-inning-stretch tune, "Take Me Out to the Ball Game." It begins to give the coliseum the feel of an old-time ballpark. Of course, looking into the dugouts and seeing the advertising that is wallpapered all over the inside instantly dispels the old-time feel.

OAKLAND OAKS BALLPARK, EMERYVILLE, CALIFORNIA

The year 1948 was a magical season for the Oakland Oaks of the Pacific Coast League. Local hero Billy Martin was playing third-base, Casey Stengel was managing, and the long-suffering Oaks finally won the PCL pennant, after twenty-one seasons in the attempt. Stengel was awarded the key to the city.

Oaks Ballpark on San Pablo in Emeryville served as home to the Acorns for forty-two years, before being torn down in 1955 to make way for a cola bottling plant, which was later demolished to make way for a Pixar Animation Studio. There isn't much worth visiting at the address now, only fading memories of the old brick-and-stucco facility near the Key System trolley station.

SAN FRANCISCO,
CALIFORNIA

18 miles to Oakland
344 miles to Los Angeles
658 miles to Phoenix
679 miles to Seattle

SAN FRANCISCO GIANTS,
PACIFIC BELL PARK

The Miracle on Third Street

NO BALLPARK in the history of the grand old game has boasted better peripheral views than those offered at Pacific Bell Park in San Francisco. The ballpark is truly the culmination of Bay area fans' most fantastic and idyllic dreams. Built at the water's edge on glimmering San Francisco Bay, and part of the aging warehouse district called China Basin, "PacBell" fulfilled Giants fans' vision of a downtown ballpark on the bay. And better still, the new yard is shielded from the bitter evening winds that tormented the Giants and their fans when the team played at Candlestick Park.

PacBell was designed to fit on a relatively tiny thirteen-acre parcel of land. With the water of the bay just over the right field wall, this ballpark comes by its eccentric dimensions of a short right field porch (309 feet to the corner) very naturally. There are no quirks for quirks' sake at PacBell, as in so many other ballparks of the retro renaissance. Rather, this ball yard was designed—oddities and all—in the same manner as Fenway Park, the Polo Grounds, and all the clunky but endearing ballparks of old: by building it into the space that was available. And the result is a gem of a ball field, with distinctions and idiosyncrasies that are honest, unforced, and far more beautiful than had the quirks been added simply because of some regrettable notion conceived during the postdome and cookie-cutter eras: that they were missing.

Also as a result of the limited space, the upper-seating structure rises very steeply, getting in as many seats as reasonably possible. The structure extends down the right field line to the foul pole on the lowest level, but only three quarters of that distance in the upper deck, angling back obliquely to where it, too, meets the waters above McCovey Cove (so named after Hall of Famer and Giants fan favorite Willie McCovey). The entire seating structure on the left field side extends all the way down beyond the foul pole and across the outfield as one might expect. The overall impression is that the park would have been built symmetrically if that had been possible. But the quirks that the space limitations have created in the ballpark have given it its distinctive design and local flavor. And when Barry Bonds drops a crushing shot over that right field wall and it splashes down into the cove, who can argue that this park is something special, something unique, something so very San Franciscan?

The story of how the "Miracle on 3rd Street" came to be is as heartwarming to us as the Christmas tale *Miracle on 34th Street*. With the Giants faltering throughout the 1970s and 1980s, and playing their games in the cold and much-maligned Candlestick Park, there was often talk of moving the team to another city. Bob Lurie bought the team in 1976 to save it from moving to Toronto. During his ownership, Lurie would try countless times to get a ballpark built downtown, but there was little political will for such a project at the time. Finally in 1992 Lurie agreed to sell the Giants to a group of investors who would move the team to Tampa Bay, the supposed Holy Grail of baseball relocation destinations for decades. The transaction was nearly complete, but in an eleventh-hour deal a local investment group headed by grocery store magnate Peter MacGowan stole the team back home.

MacGowan and his partners managed to keep the Giants in San Francisco, at least temporarily, but knew that the long-term security of the franchise in the city rested on building a downtown ballpark. So they put forth to the voters "Proposition B," which would build a ballpark in the China Basin district of downtown San Francisco. The added feature was that the new park would be the first privately funded ballpark in baseball since the construction of Dodger Stadium in 1962.

Josh: "MacGowan must be your hero."

Kevin: "Who, Shane?

Josh: "No, Peter."

Kevin: "Oh yeah, because he's a true Giants fan and built a downtown ballpark without raising the taxes of the working-class folks?"

Josh: "That, and because he's Irish."

exterior view from McCovey Cove

Photo by Kevin O'Connell

Kevin: "Yeah, I'd have a pint of Guinness with the man."

Josh: "I'm sure he'll be honored to hear that."

Long-term sponsorship agreements were reached over the next several years with companies as varied as Anheuser-Busch, Visa, Old Navy, and many others to finance the ballpark. Naming rights were purchased by Pacific Bell Telephone Company for $50 million dollars over ten years. In addition to the numerous corporate sponsorship deals, fifteen thousand prime seats were sold on a lifetime basis for mucho dollars.

Kevin: "It's a good thing all these corporate sponsorships and seats sold to wealthy dot-commers occurred in the nineties. If it were today, PacBell may not have been built."

Josh: "Yeah, Enron was one of those sponsors. Enough said."

With the noted firm of HOK signed on as the architects, San Franciscans felt they were going to get something special in the design of PacBell. They had no idea how special. Ground was broken on December 11, 1997. In August of 1998 the official address of the ballpark changed from One Willie Mays Plaza, to 24 Willie Mays Plaza, in reference to the number that the "Say Hey Kid" wore his entire career with the Giants. By the time construction had finished, the ballpark had cost $318 million to build.

The first game at PacBell pitted the Giants against their archrivals, the Dodgers, on April 11, 2000; the Dodgers won 6–5. The teams combined for six home runs that day, a record for any ballpark inaugural. Another record, though rather dubious, came when the Giants lost their first six games at their new home. But fan support never faltered, as fans kept coming to see the superb new ballpark, that sold out every single game of the first season. More than 3.3 million fans visited PacBell in 2000,

and they were rewarded when the Giants captured the National League West title.

And though reviews of the beauty and setting of the new park were glowing, perhaps the most significant improvement of PacBell over Candlestick Park was the weather. PacBell, though located on the same bay as "the Stick," is punished by little of the latter ballpark's notoriously bitter evening winds. Prior to construction, an environment review process showed that if the ballpark was turned at a certain angle, the factor of the wind off the water would be lessened to a staggering degree. Plus the location of China Basin simply had milder weather than Candlestick Point.

These revelations have made all the difference in a city known for its summer chill. As Mark Twain once commented, "The coldest winter I ever spent, was a summer in San Francisco." Thankfully technology and environmental study have lessened the effects of the wind, cold, and fog that plagued Candlestick. After a San Francisco summer's day, it can still be awfully chilly standing on the exterior concourse of PacBell, but inside the ballpark a comfortable environment for baseball awaits.

Candlestick Park, built onto Candlestick Point in the southeastern section of the city, offered sweeping views of the San Francisco Bay, making the Stick as picturesque a setting for a ball game as anyplace in the big leagues. It was often warm and sunny when games began. But later in the day the wind, nicknamed "the hawk" by fans, would blow off the cold waters of the Pacific at an average speed of fifteen miles per hour, and would often gust to fifty miles per hour and higher. The wind would swirl around Bayview Hill and into the ballpark with alarming force, and it had an unpredictable effect on the flight of batted balls. To make matters worse, in the evening fog would roll in, San Fran's "natural air-conditioning," cutting down visibility and cooling things off even further. Temperatures would often drop twenty degrees in a few hours. Stories about the effects wind, cold, and fog on games at Candlestick are legendary.

The Stick was joked about, maligned, and clearly a disappointment from the beginning, though true Giants fans had a great love for the place. You could spot the diehards, bundled up in their scarves and winter coats on warm days. They knew what was coming—the Hawk, then the fog—and they would ridicule unsuspecting and underdressed visitors, especially from rival Los Angeles, who froze in the bone-chilling cold of August and September evenings. The cold was so bad that Giants management handed out "Croix de Candlestick" pins to all fans who braved the weather through extra-innings' night games.

When the ballpark was renovated in 1972 to make room for the National Football League 49ers, the open outfield was closed in with seats that many hoped would also block the wind. Some claim the effects of the wind were lessened a tad by the additional seating, while others felt that enclosing the ballpark simply caused the wind to swirl around in new directions. At any rate, the seating capacity was increased from 42,500 to 58,000. The natural grass that the ballpark opened with was replaced by artificial turf in 1971, but then returned in 1979. Heavy red clay was mixed in with the dirt to prevent the winds from turning the ballpark into a reenactment of the dust-bowl scenes of the *Grapes of Wrath*. Fences were tinkered with as well, brought in to give right-handers some help from the wind, but to little or no avail.

At the time of its design Candlestick Park was intended to be the finest baseball park in the country. It was the first ballpark to be built completely out of reinforced concrete, and thus had the best sight lines in baseball, as there were no steel pillars to obstruct views. Radiant heating was installed to keep the upper deck warm on cold San Francisco nights, but the hot-water pipes were buried too far into the concrete, and the system never worked. It was also the first Major League ballpark built in a nonurban area, a sign of things to come for many ballparks built afterward, as Americans were moving out of the cities and into the suburbs.

Candlestick Park hosted two All-Star Games and two World Series. The first Fall Classic was in 1962 when a McCovey line drive snagged by Yankees second baseman Bobby Richardson ended San Francisco's quest for a championship. But the structure really proved its mettle during the earthquake that rocked San Francisco during the Bay Bridge World Series of 1989. The A's held a 2–0 series lead heading into the start of Game 3, when at 5:00 P.M. on October 17, 1989, an earthquake measuring 7.1 on the Richter Scale walloped the region, collapsing the Embarcadero Freeway and causing millions of dollars of damage to homes, freeways, buildings, plus loss of life and bodily injury to many. Though Candlestick Park was packed with people, the concrete held, and not one person inside was injured. After brief repairs to the ballpark the Bay Bridge World Series continued, unfortunately for Giants fans, as their east Bay counterparts in the American League, the dreaded Oakland A's, swept the remaining games.

For all the abuse Candlestick Park has taken over the years, the ballpark performed well under duress. But the earthquake finally did in the structure. The toppling of the Embarcadero Freeway, though a tragedy, opened up the China Basin district of the city to development, with its new views of the Bay and newly created space on which PacBell Park could be built. However, this was the second earthquake to help the construction of the ballpark in this region. The famous earthquake of 1906 that destroyed much of the city caused much

interior

Photo by Kevin O'Connell

from the mound. Years of extra watering by the grounds crew near first-base created "Lake Maury," designed to slow down Dodgers base-stealer Maury Wills. Ah, we love a good rivalry, even if it was exported from the East Coast.

And though the San Francisco edition of the Giants franchise has never won a World Series, it has come close. After departing New York after the 1957 season, along with the rival Dodgers, the Giants played two seasons at Seals Stadium, awaiting the construction of their new baseball park by the bay. Seals Stadium, a single-decked intimate ballpark in the heart of the city, had been home to the two Pacific Coast Leagues teams, the Seals and the Missions. The Missions later left town to become the Hollywood Stars.

Three famous Seals were Joe DiMaggio, along with his brothers Dom and Vince. Joltin' Joe began his first extended hitting streak of sixty-one games as a rookie Seal in 1933, tallying five more games than his legendary Major League streak with the Yankees. The most popular Seals player would have to have been Lefty O'Doul, who also coached the team during the 1935–1951 seasons, when he would occasionally pinch-hit for the team.

With the Giants in town, however, the Seals were forced to find new digs, and the eventual collapse of the PCL's independence in 1958 caused great sadness among its many followers. Many great players of the Major Leagues were groomed in the PCL, including Ted Williams, Lefty Grove, the Yankee Clipper, and others.

The Giants organization goes back, of course, to New York, where the ball club won

more devastation. The resulting rubble that much of the city was reduced to was used as landfill in the Bay to create the area that became China Basin. So in essence it took two earthquakes to get this ballpark built in a part of the city where there was once only water.

Candlestick played host to more than its share of special moments. The Alou brothers, Felipe, Matty, and Jesus, made up the first all-brother outfield for the Giants in 1963. Willie Mays broke Mel Ott's National League home run record on May 4, 1966, when he smacked his 512th dinger. Back-to-back no-hitters were thrown at Candlestick Park on September 17 and 18, 1968, the first by Giants pitcher Gaylord Perry, the second by St. Louis Cardinals tosser Ray Washburn. Baseball's one-millionth run was scored at the Stick by Houston's Bob Watson, on May 4, 1975. And of course, the Beatles played their last concert (not including the jam session on the roof of Apple Records in London) at Candlestick Park on August 29, 1966.

No ticket was hotter than when the hated Dodgers came to town. These teams despised each other in New York and still do. Dodgers manager Tommy Lasorda would blow kisses at screaming and heckling fans on his way back championships and World Series for years, while the upstart Yankees of the Junior Circuit were mere fledglings. Such was their early dominance and impact on the game, that baseball teams from around the world—from as far away as Japan to as close to home as Central America—named themselves "Giants" to honor their heroes. The Negro Leagues had scores of teams named after the Giants, from Rube Foster's Chicago American Giants to the Brooklyn Royal Giants and the Cuban X-Giants to the Washington Elite Giants.

The New York Giants of the National League called the Polo Grounds home, a horseshoe-shaped but oddly attractive ballpark located just across the Harlem River from Yankee Stadium in the Coogan's Bluff area of Manhattan. Because of the long and narrow shape of the ballpark, along with the fact that it was named the Polo Grounds, a common assumption was that polo was once played on the site. But in actuality, the ballpark was built for baseball only. The narrowness of available space in Coogan's Hollow dictated the park's unusual shape.

Polo was played at the original Polo Grounds during the 1870s, the first home of the New York Gothams, who would later call themselves the Giants. But by 1883 baseball emerged victorious at this ballpark that was located at 110th Street and Sixth Avenue, at the northern end of Central Park. The Giants' first world championship came in 1888, when they defeated the St. Louis Browns of the American Association.

The Giants left the original Polo Grounds in 1889 for a parcel of land in the Southern half of Coogan's Hollow, where they built Manhattan Field at 155th Street and Eighth Avenue. This ballpark also became known as the Polo Grounds, the second incarnation of the name. The upstart Players Association had first dibs on the choice land in the northern half of the hollow, where it erected Brotherhood Park. Located at 157th Street and Eighth Avenue, Brotherhood's elongated shape was the result of needing to squeeze in between the second Polo Grounds and Coogan's Bluff, which arose next to it. Though the double-decked outfield bleachers had not yet been built, the trademark rounded double-deck grandstand behind home plate was in place from the beginning.

After only one season, the Players Association folded, and the Giants benefited by moving into the larger facility in 1891. Again they named their ballpark the Polo Grounds. The ballpark was open to the Harlem River, and many folks would stand or park their carriages beyond the outfield along the river to watch the game.

The Giants' second championship came in 1894, when they defeated the National League Baltimore Orioles (the American Association version of the team had met its end two years earlier). Christy Mathewson, the team's ace during the era, threw his first no-hitter on July 15, 1901. This new reign of Giants' dominance would be led by one of baseball greatest legends, iconoclastic manager John McGraw. In a move that today boggles the imagination, McGraw declined the opportunity to participate in the newly created World Series of 1904, citing the fact that the recently formed American League was only a "minor" league.

Kevin: "McGraw was right."

Josh: "Yeah, but the American League team from Boston won the first World Series ever played the year before in 1903."

McGraw lessened his stance by 1905 after a more appealing postseason rule plan was enacted and agreed to play the Philadelphia Athletics in the World Series, after once again dominating the National League regular season. Behind the arm of Mathewson, who threw three shutouts in the Series, the Giants added World Series champs to their already impressive list of accomplishments.

A play near the end of the 1908 season became one of the most famous in the history of baseball, known now only mythically as the "Merkle Boner."

Kevin: "This blunder made the ball going through Buckner's legs look like nothing."

Josh: "Ahhh, what do you know? Nothing, that's what."

Al Birdwell's single should have been the game winner for the Giants, as Harry McCormick scored from third. But Fred Merkle, who was standing on first at the time of the hit did not touch second-base—or so protested the Cubs to umpire Han O'Day. Cubs second-baseman Johnny Evers recovered the ball and stood on second while O'Day oversaw. Later that night, O'Day upheld the Cubs protest, and the NL president upheld O'Day's ruling and declared the game a tie. Since the two clubs had identical records, a one-game playoff took place on October 8, which the Cubs went on to win 4–2. The Cubbies also took the 1908 World Series, their most recent title to this day.

In 1911 tragedy struck the Polo Grounds as a fire destroyed the grandstands. The Giants shared the Yankees' Hilltop Park until June, before the Polo Grounds was deemed suitable for play again. Despite all the season's adversity, the Giants won the NL pennant, but lost in the World Series against the Philadelphia A's. The team John McGraw had callously dubbed "White Elephants" six years earlier had become the real deal. Who knew that one day these two rival ball clubs would one day be located only a few miles from one another, just across the San Francisco Bay?

A full renovation of the Polo Grounds was completed by the opening of the 1912 season, and this time the ballpark reflected the team's championship status. Decorated with Roman Coliseum frescoes on the facade, the new structure took on a regal look. The coats of arms of all the National League franchises

were displayed above the grandstand facade and gargoyles were perched on the roof, where flags and banners flapped in the wind. This was a home for champions, the New York Giants, one of the most successful franchises in baseball history up to this point.

This regal new Polo Grounds also became the home of the New York Yankees, as McGraw leased space to the Junior Circuit upstarts. While the younger franchise struggled to survive, the Giants struggled in their success, making it to three successive World Series (1911–1913) without garnering a title. It wouldn't be until 1921 that the Giants would reclaim the championship, defeating the Yankees in the very first Subway Series. It was the first time in World Series history that all seven games were played at the same ballpark. The next year the Giants repeated the accomplishment, downing the Yankees 4–0–1 in the 1922 Fall Classic. The 1922 World Series could not truly be called a sweep because Game 2 ended in a tie, called by the umpire because of darkness.

But the fortunes of the Giants had begun to change. The Yanks had begun to outdraw their landlords at the Polo Grounds, primarily due to an exiting young gate-attraction named Babe Ruth. McGraw's reaction to losing the attendance race in his own ballpark was to effectively evict the Yankees from the Polo Grounds. The Yanks responded by building a ballpark that suited their needs and those of their home-run-hitting phenomenon. The House That Ruth Built was no exaggeration.

The home-field advantage and the emergence of Ruth was too much for the Giants to overcome in 1923. Though they faced the Yankees in the World Series as two-time reigning champs, this time the Yanks were victorious, four games to two.

After evicting the Yankees the Polo Grounds was renovated once again, taking on the shape that most people associate it with. The double-decked grandstands were extended all the way down the lines. Only the outfield bleachers remained single-decked, divided by a sixty-foot-high building in center field that held team offices and clubhouses, and topped later by a Longines Clock and a flagpole.

But the Polo Grounds was awkward for baseball. The narrowness and length of the horseshoe made for very short porches in right and left, which highly favored pull hitters. A poke of 257 feet would clear the right field wall, or even a shorter shot could be hit up into the left field second deck, which hung in even closer to the plate. In left field the 279 feet to the fence tempted right-handers. Yet it took tremendous blasts to reach the fences in the power alleys, as right-center stood 449 feet away, and left-center 455 feet from home. In fact only four balls ever reached the center field bleachers at the Polo Grounds, the first hit by Luke Easter of the Homestead Grays in 1948, the second by Milwaukee's Joe Adcock, and the next two in 1962 by Milwaukee's Hank Aaron and Chicago's Lou Brock. No ball ever hit the clubhouse building in straightaway center.

An example of knowing your ballpark well and pitching accordingly came in the first game of the 1954 World Series, courtesy of the Giants' Don Liddle. Liddle threw a meatball across the center of the plate that was tattooed by Cleveland's Vic Wertz. The 460-foot shot would have been out of any ballpark today, but to Cleveland's dismay, a fantastic catch by center fielder Willie Mays turned the blast into a long out. Surely the expansive center field of the Polo Grounds was a perfect spot to display the talents of a fielder with Mays's speed and glove. In the 10th inning of the same game, Indians starter Bob Lemon allowed Dusty Rhodes to pull what should have been a routine fly ball into the upper-level seats for a game-winning home run. The tale of the tape: 261 feet. Pitch location was a key to the home-field advantage.

One hitter who took full advantage was Mel Ott, who hit 323 home runs at the Polo Grounds. Ott clubbed his first, 500th, and his final—511th—dinger at the old structure, during his twenty-two seasons in a Giants uniform.

Plenty of other quirks could be found at the Polo Grounds as well. The outfields were so crowned that managers in the dugout depths could only see the tops of their outfielders' heads. The bull pens were in fair territory in the power alleys. A five-foot statue was erected in center field of Captain Eddie Grant, who was killed in World War II. And fans atop Coogan's Bluff could watch ball games from the perch.

Bobby Thompson's famous "Shot Heard 'Round The World," was hit at the Polo Grounds, a moment that is considered one of the most exciting in baseball history. After

---

TRIVIA TIMEOUT

Toy Train: Name the four Giants players in baseball's 500 Home Run Club.
Trolley: Other than Barry Bonds, who was the only other Giants player to hit a ball into McCovey Cove through July of 2003? (Hint: he did it twice.)
Cable Car: How old was Lefty O'Doul when he got his final hit in the PCL?

Look for the answers in the text.

---

being thirteen-and-a-half games out of first place on August 11, the Giants went on a 16-game winning streak and wound up finishing the season tied for first with their archrivals, the Brooklyn Dodgers. In a one-game playoff the Dodgers carried a 4–1 lead into the bottom of the ninth. The Giants got one run across before Thompson came to the plate with one out and two men on base. Dodgers manager Charlie Dressen brought in Ralph Branca to face Thompson, who took a strike on the first pitch. Then a miracle happened.

We can still hear Russ Hodges with the call: "Branca throws . . . there's a long drive. It's going to be . . . I believe . . . ! The Giants win the pennant! The Giants win the pennant! The Giants win the pennant! The Giants win the pennant!" Though the Giants lost the World Series to the Yankees in six games, nothing could tarnish that comeback. For a superb rendering of the events of that game, read the first chapter of *Underworld* by Don Delillo.

New York National League fans (Mets, Dodgers, and Giants) are still bitter about the departure of the Giants and the Dodgers, even those who weren't born until after both teams had left. These types of feelings can only be handed down from father to son, mother to daughter, and are thus part of baseball's great tradition. The very same wrecking ball that brought down Ebbets Field leveled the Polo Grounds on April 10, 1964.

While the move to the Left Coast transformed the "bums" of Brooklyn into the cleanest-cut and winningest franchise of the latter half of the decade, the reverse is true of the Giants. They have nearly earned their reputation as the "Red Sox of the West Coast," and the 2002 World Series would prove this yet again. Leading the Angels three games to two, the Giants carried a five-run lead into the bottom of the seventh inning. It appeared as though the Giants were going to break their curse, defeat the Rally Monkey, and send Anaheim packing. But the bull pen crumbled, as did the lead, and eventually the series.

Getting a Choice Seat

Tickets at PacBell continue to be a hot commodity, as the Giants have been competitive every year since occupying their new park. The ballpark has reinvigorated the city's love affair with baseball, and the fans keep coming out to the ball game. Tickets are on the pricey side, but well worth the money.

Field Club (Sections 107–124)

We love these Club seats, mostly because Pac-Bell also offers far more desirable Premium Club seats. This further division of the good seats into more elite and premium-seating sections makes these lesser club folks feel second class.

Kevin: "Now you know how we feel!"

Josh: "Yeah, how do you like it? Suckers."

Lower Box Seats (Sections 101–135)

The grade of the lower bowl is fairly gradual and all seats angle toward the action. It's best to avoid all rows on the lower level numbered 37 and higher, as the overhang will affect views of fly balls. But the only seats that have perfect sight lines are in Sections 113–115. All others on the first level lose one of the outfield corners to a slight obstruction.

Sections 105–106, 125–126 and the middle rows of 107–124 make up the Premium Lower Boxes and go for a bit more. Sections 105–106 and 125–126 offer seats all the way down to the field and are the best for the buck in this price range.

Sections 101–104, the uppermost sections of 107–112 and 119–124, and Sections 127–135 make up the Lower Box Seats. Seats down near the field in Sections 127–135 are preferable to any upper seats in Sections 105–126. The vantage point is closer to the field, plus they are cheaper. Seats above Row 31 in Sections 123–125 and 107–108 are blocked by a photographer's perch that hangs down from the second level and blocks sight lines fairly

Sellout Index: 70% of games sell out
Seating Capacity: 40,800
Ticket Office: (510) 762-BALL
http://www.sanfrancisco.giants.mlb.com

severely. These seats cost far too much to be obstructed.

The uppermost seats in Sections 130–134 are called the Left Field Lower Boxes and are fairly poor. You can do better than these seats in the left field corner.

AAA Club Infield (Sections 202–234)

These second-level seats are for club-goers and their club-going friends. Joining this club is a bit like joining a cult, once you're in, you never want to come out. Come to think of it, first class on the plane is like that as well.

View Level (Sections 302–336)

Though the close seats on the first level give the park an intimate feeling, the seats on the View Level make the park seem huge. The best seats in all of these sections are the View Level Boxes, but we don't recommend spending the extra money. If you want better seats for less money, head for the bleachers. If you want to take in the sweeping views of the Bay, then perhaps the View Level seats are a good choice. But beware, this upper level is among the steepest in all of baseball, so if it's your turn to make the beer and dog runs, think about making two trips. Even a mild fear of heights is cause to sit elsewhere.

The first-base side in much preferable to the third-base side, because less of the corner is lost to view and the views are generally better. From the seats on the left field side the Bay Bridge and Treasure Island are in full view, while the right field side offers views of mostly industrial areas and parking lots.

The ballpark designers did a good job of protecting sight lines in the View Level, but by Section 326 the corner of the field is shaved off and it gets worse as the section numbers get higher. Section 332 feels very removed from the action, and we cannot recommend sitting anywhere past it. Sections 333–335 suffer a

SEATING TIP

➡ THE BLEACHER seats in left field (Sections 136–138) are far better for much less money than any Lower Box seats in the left field corner (Sections 132–135). Some seats in Sections 135 are obstructed by the foul pole while the bleachers are free from any such obstruction. The downside is that the bleachers have no seatbacks, but they're half the price and offer a better view, especially if you can get right along the left field wall.

We also feel it is far better to sit in the good seats of the outfield (see the section for caveats) rather than nearly anywhere on the View Level, except down the right field line.

severe loss of the corner and the left field wall, as well as foul pole obstruction. Section 336 is just plain terrible. These seats are bad enough that prices should be significantly lower.

Bleachers (Sections 136–144)

We love these bleacher sections and prefer them to the many more expensive seating options throughout the park. The low wall along the left field line blocks only the warning track, so most plays to the wall remain in view.

Bleacher seats to avoid, however, are the high seats too near the batter's eye. The seats right next to the batter's eye may not have views of the opposite infield, and should be removed. In Section 143 steer clear of Seats 1–10 in Row 33, and then angling down to Row 30, while in Section 142, avoid any seat numbered 25 and higher in Rows 30–33.

Arcade (Sections 145–152)

The Arcade-level seats are completely unique to PacBell Park. The sections are only two seats wide and run along the high oblique fence out in right field. The seats face the action, but the wall is angled, giving these sections a very distinctive feel. Section 149 has a few seats to avoid, as they have been poorly placed right behind the foul poles. Don't sit in Row 2 Seat 20, or Row 3 Seats 19–21.

The Black Market

Plenty of scalpers hawk their wares on nearly all the streets outside the ballpark. We even saw a few approaching the folks buying tickets in the day-of-game line, before ballpark officials shooed them away. But buying a scalped ticket at PacBell can be as cutthroat as a sellout game in the Bronx. For although the scalpers aren't as aggressive, they know they have a hot-ticket item and aren't going to let it go for cheap bucks. Any game that is even close to selling out leaves three options: (1) bite the bullet and

> **SEATING TIP**
>
> → ON A NICE DAY Section 302 offers one of the most spectacular 180-degree views in all of baseball. The game is in full view below, and from these seats it is easy to track the entire flight of any ball hit into McCovey Cove. The tops of the downtown buildings can also be seen, as well as the marina, the harbor, the Bay Bridge, Treasure Island, Oakland across the Bay, and the Lefty O'Doul Bridge. These are some of the coolest seats in baseball.

pay the scalper prices, (2) wait until after the game starts and watch the ticket prices come crashing down, or (3) visit the Double Play ticket window on King Street for season ticket holders who are not using their tickets. Get into line early enough and you'll only have to pay the team markup, which though steep, is significantly less than the scalpers charge.

Josh: "Sounds like legalized scalping to me."
Kevin: "Call it a transaction fee."

Before/After the Game

The two large clock towers that adorn the brick exterior of PacBell along King Street are the most prominent features of the ballpark's facade. The towers are capped by a pyramid-shaped roof and flagpoles, and stand outside the Willie Mays Plaza and near the Second Street Plaza entrance. Along with the smaller clock towers located at the Seals Plaza and Marina Gate entrance honoring the San Francisco Seals, and at the Lefty O'Doul Plaza and Bridge honoring the local son and baseball great, these featured architectural pieces tie the ballpark into the neighborhood along with its similarly sculpted King Street Railroad station a few blocks away.

Getting to PacBell Ballpark

There are far too many ways to get to PacBell for us to list them all. But here are the major routes. Coming from the west on I-80 or north on Highway 101, take the exits that are well marked and follow the signs to the ballpark. Otherwise aim your road-trip car for the corner of Third and King Streets, though the official address is 24 Willie Mays Plaza.

Don't even think about finding that elusive secret parking spot that time forgot. It doesn't exist. Of the seven parking places in San Francisco that are available, none of them are down by the ballpark. Rather, look for the $5 parking lots within the acceptable five-block radius. We found one at Fourth and Brannan. The team lots are located across the Lefty O'Doul Bridge and run upward of $20.

PacBell is also a very convenient ballpark for folks to reach via public transportation. The Embarcadero BART Station is a fifteen-minute walk to the ballpark, or you can get a transfer to the MUNI train that runs right out front and is only half-price if you're going to the game. MUNI trains can also get you to PacBell from all other points of service as well. Yet another train option is the CAL-TRAIN: the downtown station is a short three blocks away. For those still unsatisfied with the amount of public transportation, a Ferry services the ballpark from Oakland and other places, but the ferries are generally booze-cruises, rather than quick transportation for folks who'd like to get to the ballpark efficiently. If you bike to the ball game, just wheel around to the promenade and drop your two-wheeler off at the check stand and the folks inside will watch it for you for the entire game. Pretty nifty.

Outside Attractions

WILLIE MAYS STATUE AND PLAZA

The main entrance to PacBell is through Willie Mays Plaza, a cozy palm-tree-lined pregame meeting spot where folks ready themselves for the game.

The centerpiece of the plaza is a statue that honors the Say Hey Kid. Mays's swing is unmistakable for any other, and the sculpture captures perfectly the power that has just been uncorked. Mays's lower right leg drags behind parallel to the ground and on first glance it looks as if he is off-balance. But anyone who saw Mays's powerful swing knows that the struck ball has just been given a long ride. And the distant look in Mays's eyes give further indication that the ball is well on its way.

Mays hit the third most home runs in Major League history (the most in National League) playing half of his games at Candlestick, though fewer than a third (203) of his 660 dingers came at home. Had Mays played elsewhere, or been a left-hander where the wind gusts of Candlestick would have helped his totals rather than harmed them, many experts say his total home runs would have been closer to 800.

Josh: "I suppose you think Mays is the greatest player who ever lived."

Kevin: "Two words: the Catch."

Joining Mays in the 500 Home Run Club are fellow Giants Ott (511), McCovey (521), and

Willie Mays statue

Photo by Kevin O'Connell

Bonds (Kevin says destined for 756; Josh says "no way").

WALK THE WALK

Strolling the Promenade that runs behind Pac-Bell and along the marina constitutes a "must-do" for any first-time visitor to the ballpark. To truly appreciate the beauty of this setting, get to the ballpark early and watch folks in rafts and canoes battling for batting practice homers into the drink.

GLORIOUS HOLES

You can watch batting practice from out on the promenade as well, through screened-in viewing areas. These free viewing areas, reminiscent of the "knothole" of ballparks past, remain open all game long, and are the best free viewing locations in all of baseball. Courtesy dictates that if others are waiting to take

free seats

Photo by Kevin O'Connell

a peek, three innings is the maximum stay. During the 2002 World Series ticketless San Franciscans took full advantage, crowding the promenade for a chance to see the World Series for free.

WILLIE McCOVEY POINT AND STATUE

Cross over the Lefty O'Doul Bridge to get to McCovey Point. Honoring perhaps the most beloved Giants player of all, the great number 44, is a walkway featuring tiles that fans purchased to help fund the ballpark. Between each section of tiles appear plaques that make up the Giants History Walk, one for each season the team has played in San Francisco. The stats emblazoned in bronze record batting and pitcher leaders, Opening Day lineups, player rosters, as well as attendance figures.

At the end of the walkway, standing guard over the cove is a larger-than-life sculpture of "Stretch" himself, Willie McCovey. McCovey played baseball with dignity. His quiet manner and humble style of play earned him the admiration of the press, the fans, and fellow players. Today, the Giants' annual Willie Mac Award is the highest honor a Giants player can receive. Each recipient is honored with a bronze plaque,

inlaid in the stone plaza around the sculpture's feet.

Watering Holes and Outside Eats

China Basin has not only become hip because of the ballpark, it has also become a favorite living destination of dot-com millionaires who've bought condos in the former warehouse district. While many of these folks aren't interested in baseball, at least not to the degree that we are, restaurants and bars have been popping up in the area. A few blocks' walk will put you in range of many places to have a brew or get some grub, at greatly varying price ranges.

ACME CHOP HOUSE (24 Willie Mays Plaza)

Though technically inside the walls of PacBell, this restaurant is open to anyone, game day or otherwise. You can eat a meal and enter the ballpark through the Chop House if you have a ticket.

The upscale food at the Acme Chop House follows a "green" principle, which emphasizes healthy, natural, and locally raised produce and meats. The desserts are seasonal, only using fruits that are naturally available. The result is a wonderfully diverse and changing menu, where you can enjoy your meal without worrying that antibiotics and hormones will get between you and your health.

Having said all this, the Chop House in not an inexpensive place (health food never is). And if you're on a road trip with seventy-five friends, the Say Hey room might be for you. Then again, it might not. Hours of the Chop House vary, opening earlier on game days.

Kevin: "ACME once stood for American Companies Make Everything."

Josh: "You are a fountain of useless and unsubstantiated knowledge."

ZEKE'S SPORTS BAR
(Third Street and Brannan Street)

Though small, this traditional place gets packed near game time and is the most authentic sports bar in the area. Burgers and sandwiches are rather un-San Francisco; in other words they're not fancy and they are cheap. Entrées run $6 to $9. We sampled a local microbrew called Humback Wheat Ale, which was very refreshing.

RED'S JAVA HUT (Embarcadero Street at Bryant)

If you want to hang out with longshoremen and the occasional player getting a cup of joe, Red's is the spot. This long-standing dive on the pier is one of the few yet to cash in and sell out during the recent years' real estate boom in China Basin.

The special, a burger and a beer, is a solid choice for $5 for those who want to fill up before the game: a blue-collar burger, well done, topped with pickles, onions, and ketchup on a sourdough roll. Steer clear of the hot dog though.

Another place on Embarcadero is simply called **The Java House** and is not to be confused with Red's. The Java House special is a hot dog and a beer for $5, but we recommend walking the extra three blocks on down to Red's.

21ST AMENDMENT BREWERY, CAFÉ & BAR
(563 Second Street)

This joint jumps before the game, perhaps because of its beer, but more likely because it caters to the yuppie crowd. The sandwiches and pizza here are a tad fancier, with items like arugula, andouille sausage, and roast cumin-marinated pork as options. An impressive list of beer brewed on the premises includes Watermelon Wheat Summer Brew and Oyster Point Oyster Stout, made with real oyster shells.

HAPPY DONUTS
(Corner of Third Street and King)

Located directly across the street from the home plate entrance, Happy Donuts has been serving up the fried glazed dough since before the ballpark was here. Our friend Matthew goes here after every game, provided the Giants win and he's feeling happy.

MOMO'S AMERICAN BISTRO (760 Second Street)

With a menu on the pricier side, Momo's strength is its location and outdoor seating. Getting a table on the patio is key to enjoying the experience. The beer and drinks aren't cheap, but the people-watching is worthwhile. Entrées run from $15 to $30.

GORDON BIERSCH (2 Harrison Street)

Located on the Embarcadero along the waterfront this brewpub gone mini-chain is a great spot to get some authentic garlic fries before the game from the folks who invented them. The menu is vast and a tad on the pricey side, but the food is very good. The biers, uh, we mean beers on tap are Gordon Biersch's own, and range from Pilsner to Dunkels and every color and flavor in between. Look for unique seasonal beers. Our friend Kate recommends the delicious cocktails out on the patio.

KATE O'BRIEN'S (579 Howard Street)

This is a great spot to stop and have a few, and is especially convenient to those traveling on foot from the Embarcadero BART Station. A meal will run right around $10, be it fish-n-chips, pizza, or a burger. The beer and wine selection make the stop worthwhile.

SPENDY AND TRENDY

If your goal is to see and be seen, China Basin has become quite the scene in the past few years. One place worth checking out is **bacar** (448 Brannan Street). Notice the lower case "b" adding all sorts of cool points. Another oddly named and "way too cool for school" place is **Two B** (Second and Brannan). **Paragon** (701 Second Street) is another spiffy place where we didn't meet the dress code. The last joint we're going to mention, though these places are literally springing up by the dozen, is **The Slanted Door** (100 Brannan Street). Perennially voted one of the top restaurants in the city, it has moved temporarily from its original location on Valencia Street.

THE RAMP (855 China Basin Street)
For those Giants fans wanting to kick it, old style, the Ramp has been a Giants hangout since the team's days at the Stick. There's plenty of deck seating right on the water and the view is of a dilapidated pier, but still it's a cool place. With tropical drink specials and barbecue, the Ramp is half tiki lounge, half Margaritaville. You'll miss this bar if you're not looking for it. Cross the Lefty O'Doul Bridge, make a left onto 18th, and look for the sign at the intersection with Illinois.

SOUVENIRS IN MCDONALDS PARKING LOT
(Corner of Third & Townshend)
The souvenir dealer that regularly sets up in the parking lot of McDonalds offers great deals on official Giants gear, but he also has loads of more interesting stuff that you can't find in the team store.

Inside the Stadium

The view and the amenities aside, PacBell is a terrific place to see a game. But the bells and whistles are everywhere you look at this ballpark. From the authentic cable car near the Arcade seats in center field that dings its bell when a home run is hit, to the many advertisements that have been incorporated into the fabric of the ballpark, PacBell is designed to entertain. Most of these gizmos must be experienced in person or they lose some of their

effect. For example, anyone who's seen a televised game at PacBell knows that there is a giant mitt, fashioned after the old four-fingered-style mitts from the 1920s, in left-center field. But do those same TV viewers know that the mitt was created by scanning a 1927 mitt into a computer file—every bump and wrinkle—then rendering a computer router to be exactly thirty-six times the size of the original? PacBell is full of such surprises. Incidentally, for a player to hit this old-style mitt with a batted ball it would take a poke of well over five hundred feet. No one has hit this mouth-watering target yet.

Though this park is no Candlestick, the winds are still very much a factor. Winds off the Bay hold up fly balls that would float out of warmer, more humid ballparks. PacBell routinely yields the fewest home runs in the NL. This makes it a perfect park for pitchers who give up fly balls. It also makes Barry Bonds's record-breaking seventy-three home runs in 2001, and his many subsequent accomplishments, all the more impressive.

Ballpark Features

DROP ONE IN THE DRINK
Fenway has its Green Monster and PacBell has a variation of the old classic in Splash Landing. With arches built into the brick wall and an out-of-town scoreboard built into the arches, the right field wall is impressive enough. Home runs that clear the wall sail over standing-room fans, square pillars, and down into the waters of McCovey Cove. And as if this spectacle weren't enough, the pillars shoot mist explosions into the air to add to the celebration.

Though splash home runs are primarily a Bonds phenomenon (he's hit more than twenty-five), Felipe Crespo also dropped two in the drink, both in 2001.

BALLPARK DIRT QUIRKS
There are no bull pens at PacBell, simply warm-up mounds that run alongside fences. This we

did not find nearly as odd as the color of the warning track, which is dirt in the infield but rubberized in the outfield between the foul poles. Also odd to us is the fact that the dirt on the pitchers' mound is a decidedly lighter color than the traditional rust of the infield. Either that or they water it less, we couldn't tell.

AN OLD-TIME FEEL

PacBell has many features that fill our hearts with that traditional ballpark warm and fuzzy feel. One nice touch is the orange and black clock above the Jumbotron that simply reads "San Francisco Giants." Four pennants fly here as well, one for each year the San Francisco Giants have topped the National League. Also adding to the classic feel of the ballpark is the use of flags—flags go a long way in our book. Attached to the small roof, flags flap fiercely in the considerable wind, one for each team in the AL and the NL.

Josh: "They even remembered the Devil Rays. How considerate of them."

EVEN LARGER THAN THE OTHER GIANTS

Between the decks in the left field corner is a poor placement for the retired numbers, especially for a team that has a history as rich as the Giants. There are two "NYs" that have been retired, one for John McGraw and the other for

---

PITCH TO BARRY

A COUPLE OF interesting fan traditions were born during Barry Bonds's record-breaking season of 2001, and on into the World Series of 2002. Fans still bring their "Pitch to Barry" signs to the park to pay tribute to Bonds breaking Mark McGwire's single-season home run record and Babe Ruth's single-season walks record. Bonds walked an incredible 198 times in 2002, 68 of which were intentional, both records. Bonds drew 27 walks during the 2002 postseason to set a new record. During the World Series San Francisco fans responded by bringing rubber chickens to PacBell, and shaking them aggressively at Angels pitchers.

Though the chickens are still shaking in the stands as Bonds continues to draw walks, perhaps a greater tribute to Bonds's impact on the game is on the wall behind him in left field. The words "Bonds Squad" are nothing remarkable in themselves. Across the country players have special rooting sections. But the difference is "Bonds Squad" is painted on the wall, obviously approved by management. While some left fielders are left to wonder if they will be traded for a starting pitcher to help the team make a deep run in the playoffs, Barry Bonds has the assurance of his position from management painted right on the wall of his office, right behind him.

While it may be true that Bonds is tighter with Giants ownership than with many of his fellow players, his legacy has been much tarnished by the media that has labeled him "trouble" since his days playing in Pittsburgh. And what did he do to deserve his notorious reputation? Did Bonds throw a bat at another player he was trying to intimidate? No. Did Bonds give an interview with *Sports Illustrated* detailing his racist views to the nation? No. Did he drive one hundred miles-per-hour on the freeway with a loaded pistol on the seat beside him? No. What was Bonds's crime? As a young man, he didn't particularly like talking to the media and was famous for blowing off reporters. Big flippin' deal.

Let's face facts: love him or hate him, Barry Bonds is the greatest baseball player that many of us will ever see play this game in our entire lives. He is the only five-time MVP in history. While there are only three players who have hit three hundred or more home runs and stolen more than three hundred bases (Willie Mays, Bobby Bonds, and Andre Dawson), Barry Bonds has not only surpassed the astounding four-hundred–four-hundred mark, but eclipsed the five-hundred-stolen-base, six-hundred home run plateau. He may well break Hank Aaron's home run record, but it doesn't matter if he accomplishes this feat or not. Barry Bonds, son of Bobby Bonds, cousin of Reggie Jackson, and godson of Willie Mays, may be among baseball's royalty, but he is also a record-breaking machine, whose impact on the game can scarcely be measured, whether he talks to the media or not.

Christy Mathewson, both of whom played before players wore numbers. Number 3 belonged to Bill Terry, who hit .401 in 1930, marking the last time a National League player hit over .400. Number 4 was the number Mel Ott wore when he led the National League in home runs in six different seasons between 1932 and 1942. Number 11 was worn by Carl Hubbell, a nine-time All-Star who stitched together five straight twenty-win seasons from 1933 to 1937. Number 24, of course, belonged to Mays. Though his accomplishments are far too numerous to detail in total, Mays was an All-Star for twenty straight seasons, a Gold Glove Award winner for twelve straight seasons, a two-time MVP, third on the all-time home run list, and a man many consider to be the greatest player of all time. Number 27 belonged to Juan Marichal, the high-kicking nine-time All-Star who averaged twenty wins a season for ten years and posted a career ERA of 2.89. Number 30 was worn by Orlando Cepeda. Known as the "Baby Bull," Cepeda was a six-time All-Star who smacked 379 dingers and won the MVP award in 1967. Number 44 was worn by McCovey who tied Ted Williams with his 521 home runs and drove in 1,555 RBI.

ADVERTISEMENTS DISGUISED AS BALLPARK FEATURES . . . VERY CLEVER

A gasoline company has its advertising built into the wall in the left field corner. The rounded roofs of three cars actually form the wall down near the foul pole. Meanwhile, a cola company has a huge slide built into its signature bottle, located in the kids' plaza above the bleachers in left field, but large enough to be visible to everyone in the park.

Advertising in baseball parks has always been a part of the game. In the case of PacBell, we suppose this is the price we pay for a privately funded ballpark that did not increase the taxes of the citizenry. But the ads do little to enhance the charm of the ballpark.

KIDS AREA

Above the bleachers in left field resides the most expansive kiddie area in all of baseball. Whether little Giants prefer sliding down the slide that runs through the enormous neon cola bottle, pitching, or running the bases at the little tykes ballpark, this is the place for fans of any age who have an attention span that doesn't quite last the full nine innings.

STADIUM EATS

For a city that prides itself on having great food, San Francisco's ballpark offerings are surprisingly mediocre. San Franciscans even complain that the grub at PacBell is poor, but believe us, we've seen worse.

GARLIC FRIES (Trademark Food)

This delicacy, begun by **Gordon Biersch** back at Candlestick Park, has sprouted many imitators throughout America's ballpark landscape. While back in the day, you'd spend a few innings waiting for the servers to grind fresh garlic and Parmesan onto your fries, the process has become much more streamlined. Minced garlic is used now to speed things up, and as such, the garlic fries are not as good as they used to be. But still, they are pretty tasty. Just take our friend Anne's advice and beware of the "garlic hangover" that results from consuming too many of these.

HOT DOG (Dog Rating)

The Twenty-second Best Hot Dog in the Majors

With nothing snappy about it, the Giants Dog sagged in the bun and then on our taste buds. Though they advertise that these dogs are made in the Swiss tradition (we weren't even aware the Swiss made dogs) in Stockton, Calfornia, we can only recommend avoiding these sad dogs.

A much wiser dog option is available at stands named **Max Sternberg's Big City Reds**.

These are deliciously grilled all-beef dogs served in a variety of styles. Max's Big Reds would actually rate pretty high on our dog scale if they qualified for contention but they do not since they're not made for mass-stadium consumption. Once Max inks the deal, then we'll let him know where his dogs rank on the list. Until then, steer clear of the Chicago style, as they're just too sloppy, and choose one of the others. Kevin recommends the New York, piled high with sauerkraut and mustard.

BEST OF THE REST
While the stadium sausage is a pass, the **"Say Hey"** Sausages are quite a hit. Though the Italian was boiled rather than grilled, a big disappointment, the spicy **Louisiana Hot Link** was one of the better items in the park.

Another stand inside PacBell worth seeking out is run by two long-standing North Beach Italian restaurants, the **Stinking Rose** and the **Liguria Bakery**. From the Stinking Rose (325 Columbus Avenue) the 40-clove chicken sandwich was very tasty and a good bargain. Liguria (1700 Stockton Street) bakes fresh focaccia that is sure to be a favorite with vegetarians and kids.

Last but not least is the Cha-Cha Bowl, available from **Orlando Cepeda's BBQ** in the outfield. The Cha-Cha Bowl is filled to the brim with jerk chicken, rice, black beans, and a pineapple salsa. This is the one food item that the local press raves about. And on occasion Cepeda himself visits the stand.

SAY "NO, THANKS," AND WALK AWAY
From Orlando's BBQ comes our first item to avoid, the Baby Bull. This beef sandwich with barbecue sauce (applied afterward) and garlic-caramelized onions may sound good, but believe us, it's not. The meat is steamed and cut along the grain instead of against it. What does this mean to you? Two foot-long pieces of meat that are impossible to bite through that cause a sloppy mess on your pants with the onions and sauce. Our friend Paul described eating the Baby Bull as "exactly like eating a whole raw octopus."

The Macho Nachos should be avoided for their name alone. Available at the **Compadre** Mexican stands, these give Mexican food at PacBell the bad name it deserves. Save your appetite for Mexican until you get outside the ballpark.

The sausages available at the regular ballpark stands are pretty terrible. Or, they're great, if you like the spongy breakfast sausage at Denny's. We do not. These sausages were not grilled, and awful in every way. We kept passing our shared sandwich back and forth, each hoping the other one would finish it off. Better to head for the **"Say Hey"** Sausage stand and get one hot off the grill.

STADIUM SUDS
All of the usual beers are available, though like at most ballparks they have it strategically planned to only offer one beer at each station. We guess they don't want you to waste too much of their time deciding if you're getting Miller Light or Michelob.

Local microbrews available inside the ballpark include Lagunitas IPA, Red Tail Ale, Big Daddy Speakeasy IPA, and South Park Blonde, the latter from the 21st Amendment.

Hard liquor is cheaper than beer at PacBell and we recommend the Irish Coffee on cold summer days. It's good, warming, and liquoring.

Wine from the Coppola Winery can also be procured courtesy of the Stinking Rose of San Francisco's Italian North Beach neighborhood. Whether you prefer the Rosso California Red, or the Bianco California White, you might be interested to know that both wines are made by filmmaker and restaurateur Francis Ford Coppola. The wines themselves are decent, but we were expecting more from the man who made the *Godfather* movies.

THE PACIFIC COAST LEAGUE TRAIL

THE FIRST STOP for those folks interested in the PCL would have to be site of former **Seals Stadium**, located at the corner of 16th and Bryant Streets. While today it's nothing more than a Safeway Grocery Store (ironic, isn't it, that Giant majority owner Peter MacGowan also owns the Safeway chain?) it's rumored that ghosts of Seals Players walk the aisles at night. The light stanchions and some of the seating used at Seals Stadium are still in use today at Cheney Stadium, home of the **Tacoma Rainiers**, the Seattle Mariners' AAA affiliate and a member of the current PCL.

Stop number two on the PCL trail takes us to 333 Geary Street. This has been the location of **Lefty O'Doul's Restaurant** since 1958. While this Union Square haunt is a terrific sports bar, complete with a lunch counter as well as a Hoffbrau for the fans of the circular meats, there are also dozens of pictures on the walls of PCL players and Seals teams. Newspaper articles from the *San Francisco Chronicle* and other papers adorn the walls and tell the tales of great Seals moments, when the PCL was the king of West Coast baseball.

Francis Joseph "Lefty" O'Doul is something of a local baseball legend. Having pitched early in his career for the Seals, O'Doul left to play for the New York Giants from 1919 to 1923. O'Doul hit .398 in 1929 for the Philadelphia Phillies, enough to win the batting crown and lead the National League in on-base percentage. O'Doul also set the National League single-season record for hits that year at 254. That mark remains second on the all-time list, tied with Bill Terry. With a lifetime batting average of .349 in eleven seasons, Lefty made his mark on the big leagues, both beginning and finishing his career as a Giant.

When O'Doul returned to San Francisco to manage the Seals, he led them to PCL championships in 1931 and 1935. Lefty was the Seals manager who sent Joe DiMaggio up to the big leagues. And he was also known for putting himself into games as a relief pitcher and pinch-hitter. He collected his last hit at age fifty-nine while managing the Vancouver Mounties of the PCL. O'Doul went on to become a spokesman for the PCL, as well as an ambassador of the game of baseball in his many trips to Japan.

Kevin: "You gotta love the Irish."

Josh: "Lefty O'Doul was French."

Kevin: "But he wore a big green suit."

Josh: "That's just good marketing. He made the most of an Irish-sounding name."

The PacBell Experience

PacBell is a bit more rock 'n' roll than one might expect for a franchise this old and time-honored. No matter what happens, there seems to be a soundtrack provided. Conversely, the Giants still wear their old-school off-white flannel (-looking) uniforms without names across the back.

Giants fans are very into the game and knowledgeable. Perhaps this mix of old and new best describes a city such as San Francisco: with all of its history it remains on the cutting edge of music, fashion, food, architecture, and most other forms of culture.

We recommend dressing warmly for a game at PacBell, because it can be cold, especially in the summer. Though not as bone chilling as the Stick, we recommend dressing in layers. That way you can peel off coats, long-sleeve T-shirts, and such, when it gets too warm. The concourse behind home plate is enclosed, and for once we're happy about this fact. Any relief from the wind on the exterior concourse is welcome, as you're likely to be much too cold at PacBell, rather than too hot.

LUCILLE??? (MASCOT)

Honoring the San Francisco Seals of the Pacific Coast League is mascot Lou Seal. Clever name, but its technically short for Luigi Francisco Seal. Lou signed with the Giants in 1996, and has been performing better than average in the "mascot-acting-goofy" department ever since.

Though we love Lou, we can't help but wonder why "Crazy Crab" was deshelled as the Giants mascot. The crustacean that Giants fans loved to hate, Crazy Crab is perhaps our favorite mascot of all time. So despised was the pink Nerf crab that booing and heckling of Crazy became a sport. Crazy Crab eventually was limited to only appearing once a game, and he taunted the fans into hurling abuse at him—like they needed any encouragement. Though Crazy Crab was cracked and steamed long before Candlestick's demise, he was so unpopularly popular that he was brought out at the final game played at the Stick.

"I LEFT MY HEART . . ."
You know the rest . . . "In San Francisco." It's a classic popularized by Tony Bennett. And when the game at PacBell ends, win or lose, the Giants dim the lights and let Tony belt out this city's signature tune. Maybe the Giants should have hired Tony to write a few of their team songs.

FEELS LIKE A HITCHCOCK FILM
A ballpark built so close to the Bay has its disadvantage as well. It seems the sea gulls know just about how long ball games run, as hundreds gather as the game ends and circle overhead menacingly. Our game went into extra innings, so these vultures had to wait to dive down into the seats to get their nightly morsels of garlic fries and spilled barbecue sauce from Baby Bull sandwiches. So these winged stomachs lined up on the roof, perched, and awaited our departure.

Kevin: "I'm afraid of birds."

Josh: "You and Tippy Headroom."

THE JOE DIMAGGIO TRAIL
Another local boy that made good and left his heart in San Francisco was none other than the Yankee Clipper himself. Head to the historically Italian North Beach section of town and find the **North Beach Playground and Pool** (800 block of Columbus Street) to see where a youthful Joltin' Joe played his inner-city ball on pavement. Later in life DiMaggio would return often to the neighborhood in North Beach, hanging out at nearby Bimbos' nightclub (1025 Columbus Avenue). He even took Marilyn Monroe there on occasion.

For folks who can't get enough of Joe, he was born in Martinez, California, about an hour away by car depending on traffic. The **Martinez Museum** has a modest amount of DiMaggio-related items on display. Also on display at the **Martinez Marina Park** is the twenty-two-foot Chris-Craft sports boat, a gift from the Yankees. DiMaggio donated the boat, after he and Marilyn had made good use of it on the Bay.

APPENDIX: PLANNING YOUR TRIPS

ALL YOU NEED to begin charting your next baseball adventure is a copy of our book, a quality road atlas, a copy of the Major League schedule, and a general idea of how much vacation time you have coming to you from work. Oh, yeah, and having a few bucks in your pocket doesn't hurt either.

We thought we'd provide four examples of ways in which you might maximize your time on the road. We have provided one sample itinerary for the ballparks of the Northeast, one for the South, one for the Midwest, and one for the West. The shortest of these is the Northeast trip, which covers five Major League parks in just four days, while the longest is the West Coast trip, which covers eight Major League parks in seventeen days. To each of these trips we have tied a theme. The Northeast trip combines a focus on big eatin' with your ballpark tour. The South trip includes visits to baseball museums along the way. The Midwest trip includes stopovers at historic baseball diamonds. The West trip includes visits to Pacific Coast League ballparks along the way.

Remember that these themes are just examples of ways in which you might add a special wrinkle to your travels. And they are interchangeable. If you'd like to visit the minor league ballparks of the Northeast while traveling up or down the East Coast, or if you'd like to eat your way across the West, there's no reason why you shouldn't. We encourage you to chart your own adventures according to your own personal tastes and interests. Of course, you are free to follow in our footsteps exactly if you like. If this is the route you choose, we caution you not to make at least one of the mistakes that we did. It may sound tempting when you see the signs from the highway, but do try to avoid the Spam Museum.

Enjoy your travels. And please e-mail or write us with feedback and stories from the road.

The Babe Ruth Big Eaters' Tour

DAYS: FIVE

CITIES: FOUR

BALLPARKS: FIVE

Oriole Park at Camden Yards, *Baltimore, Maryland*

Citizens Bank Park, *Philadelphia, Pennsylvania*

Yankee Stadium, *New York, New York*

Shea Stadium, *New York, New York*

Fenway Park, *Boston, Massachusetts*

NO AMERICAN individual personified the indulgence and decadence of the Roaring Twenties with more gusto than Babe Ruth. And no American sports figure, past or since, defined his generation and reinvented his sport in quite the ways the Bambino did. Perhaps the only thing more famous than this icon's prodigious home run balls was his insatiable appetite—for food, drink, and women. This quick-hitting road trip through the Northeast corridor delivers plenty in the areas of food, drink, and Bambino-related attractions. As for women, well, that doesn't fall under our area of expertise.

The trip begins in Baltimore where the Babe was born, travels north through Philadelphia, then on to New York City where Ruth obliterated slugging record after slugging record. The tour finishes in Boston where the Babe both began and ended his Major League playing career.

Before Hitting the Road

Prior to this road trip we recommend reading Robert Creamer's *Babe: The Legend Comes to Life*, which does a superb job of demystifying the complex man who was George Herman Ruth. Another interesting book is John Robertson's *The Babe Chases 60: That Fabulous 1927 Season, Home Run by Home Run*, which provides a blow-by-blow account of Ruth's legendary record-shattering year. Finally, we recommend Dan Shaughnessey's *The Curse of the Bambino*, which details the fall from glory of the Red Sox and rise to prominence of the Yankees after Boston sold Ruth to its New York rival.

For preroad-trip viewing, we recommend *The Babe Ruth Story* (1948), which is widely considered the worst baseball movie ever made. For precisely that reason, you will enjoy it, especially after having read Creamer's biography of the Babe. This movie's hilarity begins with forty-two-year-old actor William Bendix playing the Babe as a teenager, then offers an outlandish account of the saintlike Babe's heroics. During the film, Ruth draws the wrath of his manager after missing a game to take an injured puppy to the hospital. Later he hits a home run that causes a crippled young boy to stand up out of his wheel chair in awe, even though doctors had told him he'd never walk again. The movie is chock-full of ridiculously sentimental moments. Trust us, this one's so bad, it's worth watching for a hoot, especially if you know a little beforehand about the Babe. The second film we recommend is *The Babe* (1991) starring John Goodman. The film succeeds by comparison in depicting Ruth as a human being, afflicted by human wants, needs, insecurities, and vulnerabilities. It also delves into Ruth's personal life, shedding light on the Babe's first marriage and his complex relationship with teammates.

The Road Trip

DAY ONE: BALTIMORE

In 1895 George Herman Ruth was born in Baltimore, two blocks from where Oriole Park at Camden Yards now resides. He spent much of his early childhood in the saloon on Emory

Street owned and run by his parents before being sent away to St. Mary's Industrial School for Boys on the outskirts of Baltimore in 1902. While the Babe grew up in this environment, his parents had seven other children, yet only one, a sister named Mary, survived infancy.

In February 1914, Jack Dunn, owner of the Baltimore Orioles, then a minor league team, assumed legal guardianship of Ruth in order to excise him from St. Mary's and sign him to a contract. But when the Orioles encountered financial difficulties, Dunn was forced to sell Ruth to the Boston Red Sox of the American League. Later that year, just ten months after leaving St. Mary's, Babe started his first Major League game as a pitcher for the Red Sox.

AFTERNOON: Visit **The Babe Ruth Birthplace and Museum** located just a few blocks from Camden Yards at 216 Emory Street in Baltimore's Inner Harbor. The museum is open from 10:00 A.M. until 7:00 P.M. on game days and admission is only $6. Favorite attractions include the 500 Home Run Exhibit which pays tribute to all of the Major Leaguers to hit five hundred career home runs, and the 714 Exhibit, which chronicles the Babe's career. For more information call (410) 727-1539 or visit www.baberuthmuseum.com.

GAME TIME: Enjoy a platter of Babe Ruth's Ribs available on **the Babe Ruth Plaza** located just inside the turnstiles. The plaza is a great place to snag a batting practice home run, especially toward the right field corner. Just bring a glove, because the competition is often fierce.

LATE NIGHT: While the crab-cake sandwiches inside the ballpark are very good, we recommend saving what's left of your appetite for later. After the game, visit **Bohager's Bar and Grill** at 515 South Eden Street, where the Boathouse Crab Deck serves up delicious Maryland blue crabs in heaping portions. Then head to the **Downtown Sports Exchange** at 200 West Pratt Street to catch the West Coast games and enjoy a nightcap.

DAY TWO: PHILADELPHIA

Wearing a Boston Braves uniform, the Babe played the very last game of his career at Philadelphia's Baker Bowl, longtime home of the Phillies, on May 30, 1935. But don't worry, that doesn't mean the Phillies' new ballpark has to be the last stop on your trip.

We recommend getting a good night's sleep after enjoying Baltimore's late-night scene and making your way into Philly by midafternoon. This will allow you to miss the morning rush hour on I-95 north. Baltimore and Philly are only one hundred miles apart so expect about a two-hour drive.

AFTERNOON: Ditch the road-trip car in a public parking lot and take a walk on famous South Street. If you're interested, check out the Liberty Bell Pavilion, Betsy Ross House, and Independence Hall, all of which are located on 5th and 6th Streets.

GAME TIME: Before the game begins, visit Allen's Alley inside the park, where plaques honor former Phillies and Athletics stars. Treat yourself to a snack—a Philly water ice from **Rita's** or a soft-pretzel—but stay away from the mediocre cheese steak inside the stadium. There will be time for steak later.

LATE NIGHT: Visit cheese-steak central. Philly invented the cheese steak so don't miss out on this tasty treat. After the bars close, head to the intersection of Passyunk Avenue and 9th Street where **Geno's Steaks** and **Pat's Steaks** sit on adjacent corners. Josh prefers a Pat's steak hoagie with provolone, while Kevin favors a Geno's sandwich topped with gooey orange Cheese Whiz. Either way you can't go wrong—well actually, you can. These joints aren't located in the city's best neighborhood so consider taking a cab across town and having the cabby wait for you while you get your steaks. Fainthearted types can visit **Jim's Steaks** on the corner of 4th Street and South Street where the steaks aren't quite as good but the environment is more tourist friendly.

DAY THREE: NEW YORK

The New York press loved the Babe's big appetite, larger-than-life persona, and gargantuan heart. This is where the Babe earned such monikers as "the Sultan of Swat," "the King of Swing," and "the Bambino," on the way to becoming the most recognized athlete on the planet. This is where he posed with a crown on his head for the famous *Life Magazine* cover, you've surely seen. This is where he allegedly once ate sixteen hot dogs prior to a game, then went out and homered in his first at-bat.

You'll want to arrive in the Big Apple early, and you'll want to bring your appetite. Philadelphia and New York City are about ninety miles apart, but driving into the city can be a nightmare. We recommend staying at a hotel in Jersey City or Newark and taking the Path Train into Manhattan and then the subway to the Bronx.

AFTERNOON: Stretch your stomach with an early lunch at **Mickey Mantle's Restaurant**, located at 42 Central Park South. The place is full of memorabilia and serves an impressive menu of upscale pub food.

After lunch stroll around Central Park, then hop on the 4 Express Train, which will take you into the Bronx. Upon descending the elevated-subway steps outside of Yankee Stadium, duck into **Billy's Sports Bar and Restaurant** on River Avenue to check out the mural of Babe Ruth.

Next, take **the Babe Ruth Tour**, a one-hour behind-the-scenes tour through Yankee Stadium, offered by the team Monday through Sunday at noon. The guided tour takes fans down onto the field, into the dugouts, and into the press box. The cost is $12 for adults, $6 for children fourteen and younger. For more information call (718) 579-4531.

After the tour either return to Billy's or bar-hop to one of the other South Bronx bars profiled in our Yankee Stadium chapter. Hungry yet? You'd better be. Before the game, treat yourself to some fried food at **U.S. Chicken** on Gerard Street.

GAME TIME: It is essential that you enter Yankee Stadium right when the gates open two hours prior to the first pitch. This will allow you adequate time to visit **Monument Park**, which remains open until forty minutes before the official start. Here you'll find the Bambino's retired number 3, his plaque, and most impressive of all, his monument. Have the camera ready and pose alongside the Babe!

During the game we recommend sampling a pastrami-on-rye sandwich from the **Kosher Deli** on the first level. Feeling bloated? We hope so. Remember, the Babe was a lanky lefty when he broke in with the Red Sox and by the time he left New York, well, he was rather chunky. So think like the Babe. Think big. And eat hardy.

LATE NIGHT: Take the 4 Train back into Manhattan and treat yourself at the tavern of your choice. The bars stay open until 4:00 A.M. and you're not driving very far tomorrow, so paint the city red.

DAY FOUR: NEW YORK

You've got another game to catch in New York, and you've got a few Babe Ruth attractions to catch. But let yourself sleep in a while if you need the rest.

AFTERNOON: Take a drive up Route 87 to nearby Hawthorne, New York, to visit **the Cemetery of the Gate of Heaven**. Here you'll find

Babe Ruth's grave site located in Section 25, Plot 1115, Grave 3.

Afterward, head back to the city and find your way to Times Square. Have lunch at the **ESPN Zone**. Check out the stairwell where a massive photo-mosaic of Babe Ruth resides, composed entirely of New York Yankees baseball cards.

GAME TIME: Take the 6 Train from Manhattan to Queens and catch a Mets game at Shea Stadium. Yes, the 6 is the subway line about which John Rocker made his infamous remarks. But John Rocker is an idiot. The 6 Train is just like every other New York subway line.

LATE NIGHT: Still tired from last night? If so, call it an early night and rest up for tomorrow. If not, the night is young, and this is the city that never sleeps.

DAY FIVE: BOSTON

Boston is where the Bambino's big league career began. After pitching the Red Sox to their last World Series title in 1918, winning two games, and posting a sparkling ERA of 1.06 in the October Classic, Ruth tried his hand at hitting the next season and bashed a league-record twenty-nine dingers in part-time action. After the season, the Sox sold him to the Yankees where he became a full-time outfielder, and the rest, as they say, is history. But it's a little-known fact that Ruth returned to Beantown in 1935 to finish his career with the National League's Boston Braves.

Two hundred and ten miles of highway lay between New York City and Boston. If you depart New York City by 8:00 A.M., you should arrive in Boston by 1:00 P.M., though often traffic and construction make for a longer ride.

AFTERNOON: Visit the **New England Sports Museum** located inside Boston's Fleet Center, home to the NHL's Bruins and NBA's Celtics. The Fleet Center is easily accessed by the subway's Green and Orange Lines, using the North Station stop, and is a short walk from Bowdoin Street at the end of the Blue Line. The museum is open from 11:00 A.M until 5:00 P.M and admission is $6. The NESM offers an extensive baseball exhibit, including plenty of Bambino memorabilia. For information call (617) 624-1234 or visit www.sportsmuseum.org.

For a late lunch, walk a few blocks into Boston's famous North End, an Italian restaurant-lover's paradise. The North End is a big neighborhood that makes New York's Little Italy look like nothing. We recommend **La Famiglia Georgio** on Salem Street for a delicious lunch. The portions are so huge you will shudder with disbelief. And the prices are fair. But in the North End, you really can go wrong only by paying too much.

After lunch, hop back on the Green Line, take it to the Kenmore Square stop and you'll be in the Fenway district. If the ballpark gates haven't opened yet, we recommend standing outside the Green Monster on festive **Lansdowne Street** to see if you can snag a batting practice homer. Or perhaps you'd prefer to sit down and have a pint of Bambino Ale at **Boston Beerworks**. Tip one back for the Babe!

GAME TIME: This is another one of those ballparks you want to enter early. Walk around during batting practice and soak up the history. Touch the Green Monster out in left field, walk down to field level in right field and try to imagine how the Babe must have felt ninety years ago taking the pitching mound in a brand new Fenway, less than a year removed from the orphanage at age nineteen. Though you might still be full from lunch, find room for a Fenway Frank.

LATE NIGHT: After the game, buy a sausage sandwich from one of the vendor carts outside the ballpark. Stand off to the side and savor it as the crowd marches past. You did it: five parks in five days!

The Dixieland Baseball Museum Tour

DAYS: NINE
CITIES: SEVEN
BALLPARKS: SEVEN

Pro Player Stadium, *Miami, Florida*
Tropicana Field, *St. Petersburg, Florida*
Turner Field, *Atlanta, Georgia*
Busch Stadium, *St. Louis, Missouri*
Kauffman Stadium, *Kansas City, Missouri*
The Ballpark at Arlington, *Arlington, Texas*
Minute Maid Field, *Houston, Texas*

MUSEUMS: SEVEN

Ted Williams Museum, *Hernando, Florida*
Braves Museum and Hall of Fame, *Atlanta, Georgia*
Ty Cobb Museum, *Royston, Georgia*
Cardinals Hall of Fame, *St. Louis, Missouri*
Negro Leagues Museum, *Kansas City, Missouri*
Jazz Hall of Fame, *Kansas City, Missouri*
Legends of the Game Museum, *Arlington, Texas*

AMERICA'S SOUTH houses a sampling of ballparks that represents the full spectrum of post-1960 ballpark construction trends. From a cookie-cutter to a dome to a retractable roof stadium to ballparks in the retro-classic style, the South truly has it all. Aside from offering baseball wanderers this diverse sampling of ball yards to visit, Dixieland also prides itself on its history and provides an assortment of opportunities for fans to brush up on their hardball knowledge through visits to baseball museums. So whether or not you've already made your first pilgrimage to the granddaddy of all baseball history halls in Cooperstown, New York, build a few extra days into your tour of the South and learn more about the game's early days as you simultaneously celebrate its present.

This is a great April trip for fans like Josh and Kevin who live in cold-weather climates.

Before Hitting the Road

In the month or so before this road trip head to your local video store and rent Ken Burns's epic documentary *Baseball* (1994). Or better yet, find the tapes at your local library where you'll be able to check them out free of charge. We known you've probably seen this film before, or at least parts of it. But even so, watching this nine-volume diary of the game's past—from start to finish—is a great way to spend a chilly week in February or a rainy week in March as you wait for the season to begin. We also recommend the *When It Was A Game* series, available from Warner Home Video. These tapes show well what the game of baseball used to be like.

The Road Trip

DAY ONE: MIAMI

There is plenty of baseball history in South Florida—much of it related to the Grapefruit League Spring Training Circuit. But there isn't much of a ballpark. There's a converted football stadium. But that's okay because the weather is nice and South Beach is hopping with coeds.

GAME TIME: Before the game, scope out the concourse outside Pro Player Stadium where a fourteen-foot-tall bronze statue of Mighty Casey stands. The Marlins don't have a multitude of baseball memories to celebrate, but then again, they do have a World Series title to their credit. With the installation of this Mudville piece the team has adopted a universal symbol of the game's drama, hope, and heartbreak.

DAY TWO: ST. PETERSBURG

Another day, another so-so ballpark. As far as domes go, Tampa Bay's Tropicana Field is one of the best. But it's still a dome.

AFTERNOON: Head down to the scenic

waterfront and check out venerable Al Lang Field, former Spring Training home of the New York Yankees and St. Louis Cardinals and current Grapefruit League home of the Devil Rays.

GAME-TIME: Pining for that old-time ballpark atmosphere? A well-done mural that covers much of the first and second levels of the concourses behind the stands will remind you of all you're missing at Tropicana Field. Take a long look, then head back out to watch the game, praying that no balls strike the catwalks while you're in town.

DAY THREE: ST. PETERSBURG TO ATLANTA

Most of this day will be spent driving from St. Pete to Hot-lanta. But a well-placed pit stop will keep your focus where it needs to be: on the game you love, the game that's led you on this crazy trip. Plan on spending at least an hour at Ted's place.

Ted Williams Museum, 2455 North Citrus Hills Boulevard, Hernando, Florida; (352) 527-6566: Pull into the lot and choose your parking spot wisely. Flagpoles—one in front of each spot—fly the team banners of each Major League team. The best spot in the lot, up front next to the handicapped spot, always belongs to the reigning World Series champs. The Red Sox team colors fly on a flagpole much higher than the rest.

Outside, pose with the sculpture of the Splendid Splinter, who sits on a park bench, as if waiting to dispense hitting tips. Inside, learn about Ted's childhood, military days, fishing exploits, and prolific baseball career. And see who Ted thought were the greatest hitters of their time, in the Ted Williams Hitter's Hall of Fame.

DAY FOUR: ATLANTA

Alas, a beautiful ballpark of the classical ilk in which to watch a game. Turner Field provides a great outdoor venue for hardball, especially in April and May before the Hot-lanta weather becomes too terribly oppressive.

Braves Museum and Hall of Fame: Arrive at the ballpark at least an hour early to visit the Braves Museum and Hall of Fame, which is accessible from outside the park as well as from within. Check out the old dugout benches and bat racks from Atlanta Fulton County Stadium and the old B&O Railroad car like the kind the players used to ride.

GAME TIME: On your way into the game walk through the Green Parking Lot where a large portion of the otherwise demolished Atlanta Fulton County Stadium wall still stands and where a smaller portion of the left field fence remains intact in tribute to Hank Aaron. This is where history happened: number 715. The ball cleared the wall and a new home run champion was crowned.

DAY FIVE: ATLANTA TO ST. LOUIS

Before heading west for St. Louis, drive a bit out of your way to the Ty Cobb Museum, located in Royston, northeast of Atlanta. Despite his reputation for being a real creep, Cobb was actually fairly generous to the people of his hometown. He funded construction of a hospital in his later years. Appropriately then, this small museum that pays tribute to his life is located inside the Joe A. Adams Professional Building of the Ty Cobb Healthcare System.

Ty Cobb Museum, 461 Cook Street, Royston, Georgia; (706) 245-1826: From Cobb's Shriners fez to his false teeth, this museum is filled with oddball remnants of his life as well as its fair share of baseball-related mementos.

Just a mile away on Highway 17 is the Rose Hill Cemetery where you will find Cobb's mausoleum, so be sure to pay a visit on your way out of town.

DAY SIX: ST. LOUIS

St. Louis is a great baseball town, and the Cardinals franchise is steeped in history. Yet for some reason—a marriage of convenience we suppose—the Cardinals Museum resides within the International Bowling Hall of Fame. But don't fret. The bowling exhibits are worth a few laughs, and the Red Bird wing is nicely done.

Cardinals Museum, 111 Stadium Plaza, St. Louis, Missouri; (314) 231-6340: Paying tribute to the many great players to have laced up spikes for the Cards and also to the oft-forgotten heroes of the St. Louis Browns, this museum contains World Series trophies, Gold Gloves, and MVP trophies won by Cardinals players. It also displays lockers from old Sportsman's Park, a series of pictures in sequence that show Ozzie Smith performing his trademark backflip, a car once owned by Mark McGwire, and a bench made entirely of baseball bats and balls. While Josh poured over each and every article in the museum, Kevin found that the bench was surprisingly comfortable.

GAME TIME: On your way into Busch Stadium, be sure to visit the Plaza of Champions near Gate 6. Here bronze statues honor great St. Louis players like Stan Musial, Dizzy Dean, and Satchel Paige, and nine Cardinals pennants fly in tribute to the team's nine championship seasons.

DAY SEVEN: KANSAS CITY

Out of the unconscionable exclusion of African Americans from the American and National Leagues grew a thriving culture of baseball in the Negro Leagues that—although separate from the Major Leagues—had an impact on the evolution of the game in a great many ways. The first night game in baseball history, for example, was a Negro League game.

Some may point—and perhaps rightly so—to the separation of black and white baseball players during this regrettable period in the country's history as contributing to the segregationist policies that caused so much damage to race relations. Others look back on the dismantling of the Negro Leagues with much sadness, as some of the teams were black owned, and all were sources of great pride in their communities. But it should not be forgotten that the eventual tearing down of the color barrier in baseball helped pave the way for other courageous Americans to right many of the other civil rights injustices that still plagued the country. The long overdue integration of baseball provided further proof of just how archaic and inane many of the country's other policies and mores were becoming.

Kansas City—home of Jackie Robinson's one-time team, the Kansas City Monarchs—is a fitting location for this museum.

Negro Leagues Museum, 1616 E. 18th Street, Kansas City, Missouri; (816) 221-1920: Plan on spending the better part of a morning or afternoon here, where the diamond kings of baseball's most shameful era are at last given their well-earned due. Learn more about figures like Josh Gibson and Rube Foster who didn't live long enough to play in the Major Leagues, and about other persevering souls like Jackie Robinson and Satchel Paige who did. Paige remains the oldest man to hurl in a big league game, his last appearance coming in 1965 at age fifty-nine.

Jazz Hall of Fame: Perhaps equally important to American culture is the music of jazz, the only purely American art form (other than baseball). And built into the same building as the Negro Leagues Museum is the museum that honors the great heroes of jazz. From Louis Armstrong to Ella Fitzgerald to Kansas City's own Charlie Parker, the Jazz Hall of Fame is a wonderfully interactive museum that allows you to experience the music of America in many different ways. The sense that this community of 18th and Vine Streets lived for jazz and baseball is evident in both these fine museums.

GAME-TIME: Inside Kauffman Stadium the Royals maintain a glass-enclosed display area that is called the team "Hall of Fame." The display features portraits of great players, coaches, and owners in team history, as well as the Royals' 1985 World Series trophy

DAY EIGHT: ARLINGTON

While the Texas Rangers may not yet have a championship season in their history to celebrate, they do have a beauty of a ballpark and the largest, most impressive collection of baseball memorabilia south of Cooperstown. More than just a Rangers museum, the three floor Legends of the Game Museum celebrates special players, ballparks, and moments in baseball's history in America. Many of the exhibits that appear here are on loan from the National Baseball Hall of Fame.

Legends of the Game: You know us, we're ballpark guys. So our favorite exhibits at Legends naturally are those that focus on the game's playing fields. One exhibit shows photos of the ballparks of the twentieth century, sorted by era. There's the classic ballpark group, the superstadiums, the cookie-cutters, the domes, the retro-classic ballparks and so on. We also liked the display of stadium seats and ticket turnstiles from many of the old-time parks.

GAME TIME: Like we said, the Rangers don't have too much history of their own. The lone statue inside the ballpark is of Nolan Ryan who won just fifty-one games while a member of the Rangers. But look at it this way: A-Rod's out there on the field making history in the present. Someday there will likely be a statue of the baby-faced shortstop out near the one of the grizzled Texas flame thrower and you'll be able to say you saw A-Rod in his prime.

DAY NINE: HOUSTON

Last stop, Houston. Road-weary and bloated with hot dogs and baseball history, you deserve a day to relax. And you can, because there's no baseball-related museum to visit in Houston. Perhaps take a drive over to the old Astrodome before the game and then treat yourself to some delicious Mexican food at **Irma's Southwest Grill**.

GAME TIME: On the way into Minute Maid Park, stop by the plaza on the Crawford Street side of the field. Here, larger-than-life statues of Jeff Bagwell and Craig Biggio play catch on a miniature baseball diamond. Inside the park, take a stroll along Home Run Alley, which runs behind the stands in left-center field. Here, bats and gloves of former Astros are on display.

Sit back and enjoy the game. Your trip is nearing its end. Hopefully you'll return home refreshed and ready to test your friends' and coworkers' baseball knowledge (and patience) with all of the hardball trivia you gathered while touring the baseball parks and museums of the South.

SAMPLE ITINERARY 3

The Ballparks, Ballparks, and More Ballparks Tour of the Midwest

DAYS: TEN
CITIES: SEVEN
BALLPARKS: EIGHTEEN (Eight current MLB parks)

PNC Park, *Pittsburgh, Pennsylvania*
Forbes Field site, *Pittsburgh, Pennsylvania*
Great American Ballpark, *Cincinnati, Ohio*
Crosley Field replica, *Blue Ash, Ohio*
Riverfront Stadium replica, *Blue Ash, Ohio*
Jacobs Field, *Cleveland, Ohio*
League Park site, *Cleveland, Ohio*
Wrigley Field, *Chicago, Illinois*
US Cellular Field, *Chicago, Illinois*
Comiskey Park, *Chicago, Illinois*
Comerica Park, *Detroit, Michigan*
Tiger Stadium, *Detroit, Michigan*
Miller Park, *Milwaukee, Wisconsin*

Helfaer Field, *Milwaukee, Wisconsin*
Field of Dreams, *Dyersville, Iowa*
Metrodome, *Minneapolis, Minnesota*
Metropolitan Stadium site, *Bloomington, Minnesota*
Midway Stadium, *St. Paul, Minnesota*

ASIDE FROM offering an assortment of top-notch baseball diamonds currently in use by MLB teams, the cities of the Midwest also house more than their fair share of old-time parks, novelty parks, and minor league parks. So build an extra day or two into your trip to accommodate some of the hardball pit stops just off the beaten track in the Heartland, and be sure to give Snoopy our regards when you pass through Minnesota.

Before Hitting the Road

Even though you've likely seen it before and even though you've probably soured on all-things-Costner by now, rent *Field of Dreams* from your local video store, pop some corn, and turn down the lights. Pay special attention to the field, the farmhouse, the ghost players, and even the background actors or "extras" on the periphery of the scenes. We'll explain why later. If time allows, you might also want to check out the book upon which the movie was based. W. P. Kinsella's *Shoeless Joe* is a quick and riveting read that contains a few twists and turns that aren't in the movie. We think you'll like it.

Next, rent *61** and *Major League*, paying special attention to the ballparks in which the two movies were filmed. See if you can guess which parks they actually used (hint: *61** was not filmed in Yankee Stadium and *Major League* was not filmed in Cleveland's Municipal Stadium).

Finally, warm up your throwing shoulder with a few games of long toss before you leave, and be sure to pack your mitt and a hardball along with your other road-trip necessities.

The Road Trip

DAY ONE: PITTSBURGH

No Major League town, Midwestern or otherwise, typifies quite so well as Pittsburgh the role that an intimate, charming, classical-era ballpark can play for a team and its fans. After enjoying the old-time flavor and feel of Forbes Field for more than sixty years (1909–1970), the Pirates and their fans suddenly found themselves in Three Rivers Stadium, a monolithic cookie-cutter, where they would remain for three decades. For a while the team maintained its winning ways in the new stadium, but eventually the Pirates sprang a leak and fans started abandoning ship. But now old-time hardball has returned to the 'Burgh in the form of a beautiful new ballpark that provides an up-close view of the ball game and striking views of the city and river beyond its outfield walls.

AFTERNOON: Visit the remains of Forbes Field located on the University of Pittsburgh campus. You'll find the outfield wall, covered in ivy, the flagpole that stood in the field of play, and even the original home plate under glass in the lobby of a nearby academic building.

GAME TIME: On your way to the game, linger for a moment or two as you walk across the Roberto Clemente Bridge and reflect upon how far Pittsburgh has come since its Three Rivers days. Be sure to get a ticket behind the plate or on the third-base side, preferably in the upper level (bet you never thought you'd hear us say that!) to allow for a view of the sun setting on the river and city beyond the outfield fences.

DAY TWO: CINCINNATI

Another day, another scenic retro ballpark located on the banks of a river. Ah, what a life! As was the case in Pittsburgh, Cincinnati once housed a regal old-time ball yard—Crosley Field—before building a cookie-cutter—Riverfront Stadium—and then finally building a retro park—Great American Ballpark. Notice a theme starting to develop on this trip? By the end of the day you should. You're sampling the three predominant ballpark types of the last century: old-time parks of the classical era, cookie-cutter/dome stadiums, and retro parks that mimic the classics.

AFTERNOON: While it's not possible to actually visit the recently imploded Riverfront Stadium, home to the Reds from 1971 to 2002, or the long-gone Crosley Field (1912–1970), there is hope yet for ye ballpark wanderers. On the ride from the 'Burgh to Cincy, make a pit stop in Blue Ash, Ohio, where you'll find adjacent replica ball fields that the Reds use for old-timers' games. One field mirrors the exact field dimensions of Riverfront Stadium, and the other, the dimensions of Crosley Field. A replica of the Crosley Field scoreboard stands in the new Crosley outfield, and there's even an outfield embankment like the one in the original park. Check out the multitude of plaques lining the dugouts that honor Reds greats, and then bust out your glove and take to the field of your choice for a game of catch.

GAME TIME: Same drill as Pittsburgh. Settle into a seat between the bases at Great American Ballpark and enjoy a game-long view of the river.

DAY THREE: CLEVELAND

Different town, same story. After enjoying countless games during baseball's early years in League Park (1891–1946), Cleveland built the monstrous and multipurpose Municipal Stadium (1932–1993) before unveiling in 1994 Jacobs Field, a baseball-only park that re-embraces the warm and cozy elements of the classical ballpark era.

AFTERNOON: Pay a visit to crumbling, but still-standing remnants of League Park. A youth field sits on the old grounds, but a great deal of the old park remains, more than any other old park we found. The actual ticket booths are intact as part of League Park Community Center, as is a very large part of the intricate facade along the left field wall. After snapping a few photos, whip out your glove, head on out to second base and make like Nap Lajoie!

GAME TIME: Pay a visit to the Bob Feller statue on the way into the Jake, grab a Panini sandwich, and enjoy the game.

DAY FOUR: DETROIT

When it comes to ballpark evolution, Detroit charted a different path than the first three cities on this trip. Motown wisely chose not to bite on the multipurpose movement that overtook much of the Midwest, opting instead to hold onto its old-time gem for as long as possible. Tiger Stadium (1912–1999) served the team well for the better part of a century before giving way to Comerica Park, which despite some imperfections provides a festive atmosphere for a ball game in an extremely open-air setting.

AFTERNOON: Take a drive past old Tiger Stadium, which stands today looking more or less the same as it did on the occasion of its final game in 1999. And if the streets of this down-on-its-luck neighborhood look quiet, maybe even get out of the car and walk the footprint of the city block that surrounds the park. Like a lot of the other old-time parks (Fenway, Wrigley) it may not look like too much from the outside, but spend a few minutes taking in the working-class aura of Tiger Stadium. After all, it won't be here forever. Eventually some developer will buy and destroy it making way for condos or a hotel or mall, hopefully signaling the dawn of a kinder time for this end of Tigertown. In the meantime, while it's true you can't get inside Tiger Stadium, you can rent the film *61**, which used the stadium as a dupe for Yankee Stadium in many scenes.

DAY FIVE: CHICAGO

On the North Side of the Windy City you'll find the best of the old-time ballparks personified in Wrigley Field, while on the South Side you'll find one of the least-inspired new parks in US Cellular Field, formerly known as Comiskey Park II. But what US Cellular lacks in intimacy is more than made up for by the friendly confines of Wrigley. Make no mistake about it, your three-games-in-two-days visit to Chicago will be a blast.

Ernie Banks was right on the money when he said, "It's a nice day, let's play two." You may not have the option of playing two, but you can certainly watch two games in one day if you arrange your visit to Chicago to occur at a time when the White Sox and Cubs schedules overlap.

GAME TIME: Welcome to Wrigleyville. Let the fun begin. Stop by the Billy Goat for a pregame burger with Cubs superfan Ronnie Woo Woo, throw down a few cans of Old Style at Murphy's Bleachers, then watch a game from the Wrigley Field bleachers. As far as ball game experiences go, this is second to none.

BETWEEN GAMES: Hop the "L" and head south. Your hardball dream day isn't nearly finished.

GAME TIME: Before entering US Cellular, check out the foul lines of old Comiskey, painted in white on the asphalt of the new stadium's parking lot. Then be sure to get a seat in the ballpark's lower level. If it's a hot and humid night, take a pregame stroll to the shower booth behind the bleachers on the left field concourse.

DAY SIX: CHICAGO

One game at Wrigley just wasn't enough for us. And here's betting it won't be for you either. You're in town and the sun's shining and the Cubbies are playing an afternoon game. So treat yourself.

MORNING: Bring your mitt and shag batting-practice home run balls with the crew of regulars who assemble each day on Waveland Avenue behind the left field bleachers.

GAME TIME: Same drill as yesterday.

DAY SEVEN: MILWAUKEE

The friendly folks in Brew City didn't have a Major League team back in the classical ballpark era. When the Braves came to town Milwaukee unveiled a multipurpose stadium in County Stadium (1953–2000), which later served as home to the Brewers. In 2001, the team unveiled a gigantic retractable dome stadium in Miller Park that provides a limited number of terrific lower-level seats and then quite a few Uecker seats.

AFTERNOON: Did somebody say "tailgate?" This is as good as it gets when it comes to pregame gorging. Arrive at the parking lot good and early and bring your appetite. Bratwurst and dilly beans are on the menu. After eating and drinking yourself silly, take a stroll across the parking lot to Helfaer Field, a Little League-sized park laid out at the approximate location of where County Stadium once stood. Play a game of catch on the field, then check out the plaques on the Helfaer concourse that provide historical information about old County Stadium. Remember the movie *Major League*? It was filmed at County Stadium, which played the part of Cleveland's Municipal Stadium.

GAME TIME: We can't stress enough the importance of getting a seat on the first or second level, preferably between the bases. The disparity between the good seats and bad seats is greater here than at almost any other park in the big leagues. With a good seat, you should have a great time at the ballpark.

DAY EIGHT: DYERSVILLE, IOWA/DRIVING DAY

You won't be seeing a game today, or maybe you will. On the ride from Milwaukee to Minneapolis, swing a few miles out of the way and head for Dyersville, to visit the *Field of Dreams* movie site. Toss a ball around the field, say hello to Don Lansing, who lives in the old white farmhouse from the movie and who appeared in several scenes as an extra. Then settle into the first-base bleachers. Watch the ghost players glide effortlessly toward the cornrows to make spectacular catches. Listen for the crack of the bat or the pop of the pitch hitting the catcher's glove. Watch those corn stalks rustle hypnotically in the breeze.

DAY NINE: MINNEAPOLIS

If you're interested in ballpark evolution, consider Minneapolis a must-visit on your tour of the Midwest. The Metrodome is the last dome of the multipurpose-stadium era still standing. We don't count SkyDome, since it came along much later and has a retractable roof. Enjoy the Metrodome for what it is—an aberration on the American ballpark landscape. The Metrodome opened in 1982, replacing Metropolitan Stadium, a converted minor league park that had housed the Twins for twenty years (1961–1981).

AFTERNOON: From the Field of Dreams to the Field of Screams. That's right, Metropolitan Stadium is now located inside the Mall of America's Camp Snoopy amusement park in Bloomington, Minnesota. The original home plate and a bleacher seat that Harmon Killebrew once hit with a mammoth home run are all that remain. The site is worth a visit though, if for no other reason than the joy of giving the life-sized Charles Schulz pup, Snoopy, a pat on the head after he leads you to home plate.

GAME TIME: You're in for a unique experience. From the super-bouncy turf to the baseball-colored roof, right field baggie and Jumbotron shenanigans, this is a field like none other in the modern game.

DAY TEN: ST. PAUL

After sleeping off your dome hangover, you owe it to yourself to see one more game in the great outdoors before returning home. We recommend a game at zany Midway Stadium, home to the St. Paul Saints of the independent Northern League.

AFTERNOON: Tailgating is quite popular among Saints fans, but arrive early as lot space is limited.

GAME TIME: Keep an eye out for actor Bill Murray, a part owner of the team who is occasionally on hand to coach third-base. Also be on the lookout for the potbellied pig that delivers game balls to the umpire, for the barber that cuts hair behind home plate, and for all kinds of other unexpected ballpark wonders. Have a few brats and a few brews; this is the minor leagues, they're cheap. And you earned them visiting eighteen ballparks in 10 days.

SAMPLE ITINERARY 4

West Coast Major/Minor Tour

DAYS: SEVENTEEN
CITIES: SEVENTEEN
BALLPARKS: SEVENTEEN (Eight MLB parks)
Coors Field, *Denver, Colorado*
Sky Sox Stadium, *Colorado Springs, Colorado*
Isotopes Stadium, *Albuquerque, New Mexico*
Tucson Electric Park, *Tucson, Arizona*
Bank One Ballpark, *Phoenix, Arizona*
Cashman Field, *Las Vegas, Nevada*
Petco Park, *San Diego, California*
Dodger Stadium, *Los Angeles, California*
Angel Stadium of Anaheim, *Anaheim, California*
Grizzlies Stadium, *Fresno, California*
PacBell Ballpark, *San Francisco, California*
Network Associates Coliseum, *Oakland, California*
Raley Field, *Sacramento, California*
PGE Park, *Portland, Oregon*

Cheney Stadium, *Tacoma, Washington*
Safeco Field, *Seattle, Washington*
TELUS Field, *Edmonton, Canada*

IF YOU'VE GOT a tank full of gas and the better part of a month to blow, this is the trip for you. Fans of minor league ball and students of the game's history will also dig this trip. To the uninformed observer, baseball may seem like a new phenomenon in many West Coast cities, but nothing could be further from the truth. The Pacific Coast League dates from 1903. That's right, it's nearly as old as the American League, and at one point—before the Giants and Dodgers jumped town for the West Coast—it was considered by many to be a third Major League. Ted Williams and Joe DiMaggio were well-known entities on the West Coast, starring in the PCL before becoming household names in the rest of the country. Today sixteen of the thirty big league teams have affiliates in the Triple-A PCL. The teams of the PCL play in some of the largest minor league parks going, with most holding a capacity of nearly ten thousand people. And they need all the seats they can squeeze in. The league drew almost seven million fans in 2002—a whopping total by minor league standards past or present.

Before Hitting the Road

We highly recommend Dick Dobbins' superbly researched book, *The Grand Minor League: An Oral History of the Old Pacific Coast League*.

The Road Trip

DAY ONE: DENVER
Baseball in the Mile High City. If you're sitting in the outfield, bring your fielders glove and your oxygen mask to Coors Field. Both may come in handy. Just be sure to avoid the Rocky Mountain Oysters.

DAY TWO: COLORADO SPRINGS
There isn't much of a drive between Denver and Colorado Springs, but the ride is nonetheless breathtaking here in Wile E. Coyote country. Be sure to visit Pike's Peak or one of the many other viewing areas. The Sky Sox play just sixty miles south of their parent club, the Rockies.

DAY THREE: ALBUQUERQUE
That's right, the Florida Marlins' PCL affiliate is named the Albuquerque Isotopes. *Simpsons* fans will be disappointed, however, to learn that the mascot is named Orbit and not Hungry, Hungry Homer.

Isotopes Stadium was renovated—basically rebuilt from the ground up—by HOK in 2003. The field of play features a grassy knoll beyond the outfield warning track that extends from right-center to left-center field. The hill tops out at 428 feet from the plate in both right and left but is only 400 feet in straightaway center.

DAY FOUR: TUCSON
Watch out for low-flying aircraft. The Tucson Sidewinders, snakelings of the Diamondbacks, play at Tucson Electric Park, located beside Davis Air Force Base. And fans are often treated to glimpses of stealth bombers landing and taking off.

DAY FIVE: PHOENIX
Still sunburned from yesterday's game? Don't despair. The BOB's got a roof and the folks in Arizona aren't afraid to use it. Buy some "frozen water" on the way into the park, then wait for the roof to open just before first pitch as is the local custom.

DAY SIX: LAS VEGAS
There isn't much else going on in this tiny desert town, so why not catch a game at Cashman Field? The ballpark is surrounded by palm and olive trees, while a desert mountain range

rises in the northeast. All right, we know you're not driving to Las Vegas to see the palm and olive trees. But Cashman Field really is a beauty.

DAY SEVEN: SAN DIEGO

Pay a visit to gorgeous new Petco Park. PETA says "no." Josh and Kevin say "yes." Who are you going to listen to? (Please note that no dogs or cats were harmed in the writing of this book.)

DAY EIGHT: LOS ANGELES

Dodger Stadium has seen more hardball history take place on its field than all of the other ballparks in the West combined. Think Blue!

DAY NINE: ANAHEIM

The Big A has improved by leaps and bounds since the football seats were carted away. Enjoy the view of the San Bernardino Mountains, smog permitting.

DAY TEN: FRESNO

We have a feeling you'll like Grizzlies Stadium, a downtown ballpark that opened in 2002 for the Triple-A affiliate of the San Francisco Giants.

DAY ELEVEN: SAN FRANCISCO

Here's hoping Barry puts one in the Bay while you're in town.

DAY TWELVE: OAKLAND

Be certain to make note of the announced attendance for your A's game at Network Associates Coliseum.

DAY THIRTEEN: SACRAMENTO

More than 820,000 fans turned out to cheer for the River Cats at Raley Field in 2002—good for the best attendance in the minors. The team's parent club, the A's, draws more than that, but not by much.

DAY FOURTEEN: PORTLAND

With a name like "Beavers," how can you root against the San Diego Padres' PCL affiliate?

DAY FIFTEEN: TACOMA

Tacoma is home to the Rainiers. No, it's not rainier in Tacoma than in the team's big league city Seattle. The Tacoma squad's name serves a dual purpose. First, the Rainier name honors the Seattle Rainiers, who played PCL baseball in the Emerald City long before the M's came to town, and who drew their name from owner Emil Sick's Rainier Beer. Second, the Rainier Brewery was named after Mount Rainier, which looms even larger in the city of Tacoma than it does in Seattle. Set in the Snake Lake area, Tacoma's Cheney Stadium dates from 1960.

DAY SIXTEEN: SEATTLE

Don't worry if it rains. The fans are all safe here.

DAY SEVENTEEN: EDMONTON, CANADA

Trappers versus Beavers must rank right up there with Stingers versus Sidewinders for best PCL animal rivalry. The Expos' PCL team plays its home games at TELUS Field in Edmonton's scenic river valley. Enjoy the game; a long and winding road trip is coming to an end.

SELECTED BIBLIOGRAPHY

Our task was made immeasurably more feasible thanks to the following books, magazines, newspapers, and Web sites that we used as reference sources:

Periodicals

Baseball Weekly/Sports Weekly, 1993–2003.
Sports Illustrated, 1988–2003.
The Boston Globe, 1925–2003.
The New York Times, 1979–2003.
The Sporting News, 2000–2003.
The San Diego Union, 2003.
USA Today, 1998–2003.

Books

Field of Schemes: How the Great Stadium Swindle Turns Public Money into Private Profit. Cagan, De Mause, eds. Monroe, ME: Common Courage Press, 1998.

Sotheby's: The Barry Halper Collection of Baseball Memorabilia, Japan: Barry Halper Enterprises, 1999.

The New York Yankees: New York Yankees—100 Years—The Official Retrospective, Ballantine Books, 2003.

The Stadium: Architecture of Mass Sport. Provoost, Michelle, ed. Netherlands: NAI Publishers, 2000.

The Ultimate Baseball Book. Okrent, Lewine, eds. Boston: Houghton Mifflin Company, 2000.

Total Baseball, 6th ed., New York: Total Sports, 1999.

Adair, Robert K. *The Physics of Baseball,* 3rd ed. New York: Harper Collins, 2002.

Adams, Bruce and Margaret Engel. *Fodor's Baseball Vacations: Great Family Trips to Minor League and Classic Major League Ballparks Across America.* 3rd ed. New York: Fodors Travel Publishing, 2002.

Ahuja, Jay. *Fields of Dreams.* New York: Citadel Press, 2001.

Angell, Roger. *The Summer Game.* New York: Viking Press, 1972.

Bouton, Jim. *Ball Four.* New York: Macmillan General Reference, 1990.

Bukowski, Douglas. *Baseball Palace of the World: The Last Year of Comiskey Park.* Chicago: Lyceum Books, 1992.

Cramer, Richard Ben. *Joe DiMaggio: The Hero's Life.* New York: Simon & Schuster, 2000.

Darnell, Tim. *The Crackers: Early Days of Atlanta Baseball,* Athens, Georgia: Hill Street Press, 1999.

Dobbins, Dick. *The Grand Minor League: An Oral History of the Old Pacific Coast League.* San Francisco: Woodford Publishing, 1999.

Goodwin, Doris Kearns. *Wait Till Next Year.* New York: Touchtone Books, 1998.

Halberstam, David. *Summer of '49*. New York: Avon Books, 1989.

James, Bill. *The New Bill James Historical Baseball Abstract*. New York: Free Press, 2001.

Kahn, Roger. *The Boys of Summer*. New York: HarperPerennial, 1998.

———. *The Era: 1947–1957, When the Yankees, the Giants, and the Dodgers Ruled the World*. Lincoln: University of Nebraska Press, 2002.

Leventhal, Josh. *Take Me Out to the Ballpark*. New York: Black Dog and Leventhal Publishers, Inc., 2000.

Lewis, Michael. *Moneyball: The Art of Winning an Unfair Game*. New York: W. W. Norton & Co., 2003.

Lyle, Sparky. *The Bronx Zoo*. New York: Crown Publishers, 1979.

Mandel, Mike. *SF Giants: An Oral History*. Santa Cruz, California: Mike Mandel, 1979.

Mock, Joe. *Joe Mock's Ballpark Guide*. Grand Slam Enterprises, 2001.

O'Neal, Bill. *The Pacific Coast League: 1903–1988*. Austin, Texas: Eakin Publications, 1990.

O'Neill, Buck. *I Was Right On Time*. New York: Simon & Schuster, 1996.

Peterson, Robert. *Only the Ball Was White: A History of Legendary Black Players and All-Black Teams*. New York: McGraw-Hill, 1984.

Riley, James A. *Biographic Encyclopedia of the Negro Baseball Leagues*. New York: Carroll and Graf Publishers, 2002.

Ritter, Lawrence. *The Glory of Their Times: The Story of the Early Days of Baseball by the Men Who Played It*. New York: Macmillan, 1966.

———. *Lost Ballparks: A Celebration Baseball's Legendary Fields*. New York: Penguin, 1994.

Ritter, Lawrence, and Donald Honig. *The 100 Greatest Baseball Players of All Time*. New York: Crown Publishers, Inc., 1981.

Rosen, Ira. *Blue Skies, Green Fields*. City: Clarkson N. Potter, 2001.

Shatzin, Mike, and Jim Charlton. *The Baseball Fan's Guide to Spring Training*. Reading, Massachusetts: Addison-Wesley Publishing Company, Inc., 1988.

Shaughnessy, Dan. *Curse of the Bambino,* Penguin USA Books, 2000.

Shaughnessy, Dan and Stan Grossfeld. *Spring Training: Baseball's Early Season*. Boston, Massachusetts: Houghton Mifflin Company, 2003.

Smith, Ron. *The Ballpark Book*. St. Louis: The Sporting News, 2000.

Stump, Al. *Cobb: A Biography*. Chapel Hill, North Carolina: Algonquin Books of Chapel Hill, 1994.

Sullivan, Neil J. *The Dodgers Move West*. New York: Oxford University Press, 1987.

Thornley, Stew. *Land of the Giants: New York's Polo Grounds*. Philadelphia: Temple University Press, 2000.

Veeck, Bill, with Ed Linn. *Veeck, as in Wreck*. New York: Putnam, 1962.

Von Goeben, Robert. *Ballparks*. New York: Metro Books, 2000.

Westcott, Rich. *Philadelphia's Old Ballparks*. Philadelphia: Temple University Press, 1996.

Wood, Bob. *Dodger Dogs to Fenway Franks*. New York: McGraw-Hill Publishing Co., 1988.

Web Sites

mlb.com
espn.com
thegrandstand.homestead.com
Planeta.com
all-baseball.com
ballparkwatch.com
baseballtour.com
ballparks.com
nationalpastime.com
baseballlibrary.com
baseball-almanac.com

Videos/DVDs

Burns, Ken. *Baseball: A Film By Ken Burns*. PBS Home Video, 1997.

When It Was a Game—Triple Play Collection. Warner Home Video, 2001.

ACKNOWLEDGMENTS

JOSH WOULD LIKE TO THANK his wife, Heather, for her patience and support; his father, Richard, for throwing countless "sponge balls" to him against the backyard chimney; his mother, Cathy, for instilling in him a passion for reading; and his brother, Jamie, for always being his first best reader.

Kevin would like to thank his wife, Meghan, in appreciation for everything she does, and for always believing in him; his brother, Sean, for all his research help and for helping him to build their first-baseball field together in the yard, despite living on a hill; his sister, Colleen, for being a big sister, a mother, a teacher, and a reader; his mother, Vickie, for her love of the Dodgers in the face of marrying into a family of Yankee fans; his father, Thomas, for crouching in the catcher's position three entire summers shagging misguided fastballs; and to Paul Schmitz for his friendship, encouragement, amazing memory, and his cross-referencing.

We extend special thanks to Pam Painter for believing in our project and helping us make our dream a reality. We also wish to thank Colleen Mohyde, our literary agent at the Doe Coover Agency, and George Donahue, our editor at Lyons.

For couches to sleep on and hot meals along the road, we wish to thank James McCarthy III, Chris Razoyk, Louis Galvan, Aaron and Debbie Fournier, Ed and Judy Gurrie, Kevin and Kristen Maguire, Joe and Jane Hernandez, Kevin Larsen, Rob Feaster, Rob and Maureen Vischer, Dave and Kate Hayden, Michael and Judy Coughlin, Heidi and Jason Torok, Clarissa Sansone, Brian Coughlin, Trish Brugger, Paul Iovino, Michael and Tuyet Rowe, John, Alexy, Kieran, and Patrick Coughlin, Krysia and Ricardo Vila-Roger, Curt and Janna Mitchke, John and Rosie Balding, Chris and Daisy Balding, Jeremy Davis, John and Tracy Lewis, Kathryn Halaiko, Aaron Kaufmann, and Anne Schmitz.

For help with content and for joining in on our little adventure we would like to thank Rich Hoffman, Kirk Hoffman, Chris Stagno, Matt Jordan, Leo Panetta, Mark Alberti, Michael Hernandez, Richie Platzman, Jon Gurrie, Jen Gurrie, Matthew Guilbeault, John Murphy, Rebecca Murphy, Douglas Hammer, Jim Kauss, Stuart Chapman, Randy Begoya, Doug Kierdorff, Jeff Schaffer, Sean and Chrissy Dooley, Mark "the Cruiser" Diver, Richard Cassinthatcher IV, Bob Boland, Lyle and Sarah Overbay, Tim and Kyle Malone, Matthew Schmitz, Jordan "the Assyrian" Parhad, James Sander, the Reverend Hubie Dolan, Tim Harrington, Paul Lukinich, Ken Betzler, Jay Knapp, and all the Gonzaga Gang.

We would also like to extend thanks to computer ace Joe Bird for setting up our Web site, to Butch Razoyk for computer equipment and encouragement, and to the multilinguistic, multitalented Chun-Mee Chaline for helping us compile a dictionary of French and Spanish baseball terms. Thanks also go out to the many Major League teams that provided us with complimentary seats and/or photographs of their ballpark.

ABOUT THE AUTHORS

Josh Pahigian swore off baseball for the first time at age twelve when the ball went through Buckner's legs. He rejoined Red Sox Nation the following March, when the Red Sox won their first Spring Training game. Josh has published short stories in a number of literary journals and has written for several newspapers. Currently he covers collegiate and high school sports for the *Portland Press Herald* in Portland, Maine, where he lives with his wife, Heather. He holds degrees from the College of the Holy Cross and Emerson College.

Kevin O'Connell was born into the baseball abyss that was the rain-soaked Pacific Northwest of the 1960s. He supported the San Francisco Giants as a youngster and then the hapless expansion Seattle Mariners. His conversion was finalized when Edgar Martinez arrived in Seattle. Kevin graduated from Gonzaga University and is an avid fan of college basketball as well as baseball. He holds a graduate degree from Emerson College. He and his wife now reside in Pittsburgh.

Both authors are interested in receiving reader feedback. Get in touch with them via email at pahigian35@yahoo.com or ktoconnell@hotmail.com.